A YEAR AMONGST

Edward Granville Browne was one Victorian travellers. This is his classic ac ... iate nineteenth-century Persia—between 1887- ... he indulged his inclinations to the full by thoroughly i ... ersing himself in the customs of the country. *A Year Amongst the Persians* was first published in 1893.

"Persian Browne" was born in Gloucestershire in 1862. He hated school and found the experience of learning Latin and Greek at Eton a torture. His great ambition was to serve as an officer in the Turkish army, to which end he learnt the language. But because of his father's opposition to this idea, he settled on a career in medicine and in 1879 went up to Cambridge, where he also started to learn Persian—soon becoming proficient. By the time he made his famous journey to Persia, he had qualified as a Doctor of Medicine and had been elected a Fellow of Pembroke College.

As well as being an outstanding and acclaimed scholar of the Islamic languages, Browne was also a kind man and a raconteur of especial wit and charm. He became a devoted husband after his marriage to Alice Blackburne-Daniell in 1906, and they enjoyed nineteen years together.

Edward Granville died in 1926, soon after the death of his wife. He had two sons: Michael and Patrick. Sir Patrick Browne lives in Cambridgeshire and has kindly contributed a foreword to this edition of *A Year Amongst the Persians.*

Also available in the Century Travellers series:

EOTHEN by A. W. Kinglake
SOUTHERN CROSS TO POLE STAR by A. F. Tschiffely
SOUTHERN GATES OF ARABIA by Freya Stark
THE VALLEYS OF THE ASSASSINS by Freya Stark
A TRAMP ABROAD by Mark Twain
HOLY RUSSIA by Fitzroy Maclean
A THOUSAND MILES UP THE NILE by Amelia B. Edwards
FORBIDDEN JOURNEY by Ella Maillart
FULL TILT by Dervla Murphy
A RIDE TO KHIVA by Fred Burnaby
GOLDEN CHERSONESE by Isabella Bird
THE TOMB OF TUTANKHAMEN by Howard Carter
VISITS TO MONASTERIES IN THE LEVANT by Robert Curzon
WHEN MEN AND MOUNTAINS MEET by John Keay
LORDS OF THE ATLAS by Gavin Maxwell
SOUTH by Ernest Shackleton
ONE MAN'S MEXICO by John Lincoln
OLD CALABRIA by Norman Douglas
ISABEL AND THE SEA by George Millar
A WINTER IN ARABIA by Freya Stark
SULTAN IN OMAN by James Morris
TRAVELLER'S PRELUDE by Freya Stark
BEYOND EUPHRATES by Freya Stark
WHERE THE INDUS IS YOUNG by Dervla Murphy
THE CRUISE OF THE NONA by Hilaire Belloc
GOOD MORNING AND GOOD NIGHT by The Ranee Margaret of Sarawak
IN MOROCCO by Edith Wharton
PERSEUS IN THE WIND by Freya Stark
A PERSON FROM ENGLAND by Fitzroy Maclean
THE STATION by Robert Byron
WANDERINGS IN SOUTH AMERICA by Charles Waterton
WILD WALES by George Borrow
IN ETHIOPIA WITH A MULE by Dervla Murphy
TRAVEL AND ADVENTURE IN SOUTH-EAST AFRICA by F. C. Selous
ALEXANDER'S PATH by Freya Stark
THE LEISURE OF AN EGYPTIAN OFFICIAL by Lord Edward Cecil
WHEN MISS EMMIE WAS IN RUSSIA by Harvey Pitcher

A YEAR AMONGST THE PERSIANS

IMPRESSIONS

AS TO THE LIFE, CHARACTER, & THOUGHT
OF
THE PEOPLE OF PERSIA

Received during Twelve Months' Residence in that Country in the Years
1887–1888

EDWARD GRANVILLE BROWNE

Introduction by Denis MacEoin

CENTURY PUBLISHING
LONDON

HIPPOCRENE BOOKS INC
NEW YORK

LESTER & ORPEN DENNYS DENEAU
MARKETING SERVICES LTD
TORONTO

First published by A & C Black Ltd in 1893

This edition published in 1984 by Century Publishing Co. Ltd
Portland House, 12–13 Greek Street, London W1V 5LE

Published in the United States of America by
Hippocrene Books Inc.
171 Madison Avenue
New York NY 10016
USA

Published in Canada by
Lester & Orpen Dennys Deneau Marketing Services Ltd
78 Sullivan Street, Toronto, Ontario, Canada

ISBN 0 7126 0453 7

Cover shows a detail of a carpet in the Victoria & Albert Museum, London

Reprinted in Great Britain by
Richard Clay (The Chaucer Press) Ltd,
Bungay, Suffolk

FOREWORD

Edward Granville Browne was a genius. And he showed again that it is impossible to foresee when or where Genius will appear. Before him, the family had mostly been soldiers or squires, mainly in Gloucestershire, where my father was born. His father was a distinguished engineer and industrialist, and was Chairman of the famous firm of Hawthorn, Leslie, who built ships and locomotives and marine engines on the Tyne. My father grew up in Newcastle, and always had a tenderness for Gloucestershire and Northumberland. The only precedent in the family history seems to be Granville Sharp, the 18th century crusader against the Slave Trade, who also learnt Hebrew in order to argue theological points with a rabbi.

My father tells in the first chapter of this book how he came to be interested in Oriental languages. This account also shows another of his most conspicuous characteristics—his passion for the under-dog.

After he came back from Persia, he spent the rest of his life in Cambridge. Until 1906 he lived in college in Pembroke. Those who knew him in those days describe his abundant hospitality, and his brilliant talk in his College rooms, which had once been occupied by the younger Pitt and by the poet Gray. In 1906 he married, most happily, and he and my mother went to live in a house called Firwood, on the Trumpington Road. There his tradition of hospitality and talk continued. No-one could understand how he found time for the immense amount of scholarly work he produced. He would entertain his guests until very late, and then settle down to work, sustained by strong tea and endless Turkish cigarettes.

His devotion to Persia and Persians, and theirs to him, continued all his life. Any Persian—and especially any political refugee—could be sure of an unlimited welcome at our house, and there were many of them. There were many other visitors too, scholars and men of affairs; in the years before 1914 my father was active in politics, mainly in the Persian Question, but also in others, for example Irish Home Rule.

The 1914 war filled him with horror, and I have been told that his feelings damaged his energy and brilliance to such an extent that he was only beginning to recover even several years after the war. He died in 1926, six months after my mother.

Of his scholastic achievements I am not competent to speak. But I suppose that his greatest achievement was his four volume *Literary History of Persia.* This has been reprinted by the Cambridge University Press more than once since his death, and is still in print. He always kept his interest in medicine, and I think that one of his honours which he prized most was his election as a Fellow of the Royal College of Physicians. He gave a series of lectures to the College on 'Arabian Medicine', a subject in which he was uniquely qualified.

Until a few years ago, he was still remembered and beloved in Persia. There used to be a street in Tehran named after him, and his statue there is said to have been the only statue of a European which was spared during the rule of Dr Mossadeg. I do not know whether he is still remembered now.

PATRICK BROWNE
Thriplow, Cambridgeshire
1984

INTRODUCTION

There could scarcely be a more appropriate time than the present for the appearance of a reprint of Edward Browne's classic account of travel in late nineteenth-century Iran. The country was "Persia" to the British then: an exotic staging-post on the overland route to India; a buffer between the expansionist Russian empire and the vital waters of the Gulf, its people the heirs of an ancient civilization that had freed the Jews from exile in Babylon, fought against the Greeks, and succumbed to Alexander. To more romantically-inclined Victorians, it was also the supreme example of the mysterious Islamic Orient, a land of turquoise domes, of delicate miniatures, and ornately-woven carpets, the home of poets like Hafez and Saadi. From the beginning of the century, the Land of the Great Sophy had worked its magic on more than one English writer, inspiring works as turgid as Moore's *Lallah Rookh*, as clever as Morier's *Hajji Baba*, and as languid as Fitzgerald's influential quatrain renderings of Omar Khayyam. What North Africa and the Levant were to Orientalist painting, Iran was to Orientalist literature.

The image of a world of roses and nightingales, coyly-veiled beauties and wine-imbibing poets proved hardy enough on the whole to withstand radical changes in the social conditions and political role of Iran until the Islamic Revolution of 1978 shattered it forever, and replaced it in our minds with new, grim images of black-robed mullas, midnight executions, and an unappeasable hunger for death embraced as martyrdom. We cannot, of course, blame Imam Khomeini and his followers for shattering our dreams of the Orient: they have their own dreams to cling to and make real if they can. The roses and maidens were, in any case, always more readily encountered in poems than in gardens. The stony-faced world of the Islamic Republic is not so much a new reality as the latest and most vivid expression of a host of ideals and images that have haunted the Iranian people through much of their recent history. The Iran that Edward Browne knew a century ago was also a place in which the Orientalist dream was often forced to evaporate in the face of a harsher and more brutal reality.

But Browne is not the antidote to whatever depression may have been provoked by dark images of the modern Iranian nightmare just because he tells us in passing that such images are not wholly new, or that life in Iran in his day could be equally nasty, brutish and short. If Browne saves us from despair, it is because he takes us gently away from the cruelty of princes or the zeal of prelates into another, more humane world from which the drama of obscurantism and venality appears a mere sideshow. And yet the benefit of reading Browne's narrative does not end in a brightening of our picture of Iran. Its pages are of equal value as an antidote to the surfeit of romantic yearnings that so plagued our grandparents and that still afflicts a fresh generation eager to find truth, wisdom, and salvation in the mysterious beckoning East. Though Browne's Iranian world is peopled by poets, mystics, philosophers, and sundry eccentrics, it is far from being a suitable setting for some Arabian Nights fantasy. Fitzgerald's Omar would have been as out of place there as Ayatollah Khalkhali. Morier's Hajji Baba alone might have felt at home.

What is, perhaps, more surprising is that Browne himself felt at home there. He was no mere observer, content to watch from the outside the people about whom he writes, like an anthropologist studying a tribe to which he can never feel he belongs. Browne does not observe, he participates. He never wholly casts aside his European sensibilities, he is often shocked or disgusted by what he encounters, but he is able to enter into the life of Persian society with a rare degree of empathy that time and again astonishes the reader with its strengths and subtleties. The title of his book is our first clue to the matters that lay at the heart of Browne's interest in Iran. Other travellers before and after him were passing through, leaving records of their adventures in specific geographical locations, describing the places and the sights they had seen, with or without accompanying illustrations. Browne also travelled from town to town, but the places he visited are incidental to his narrative and illustrations would have been irrelevant. His was less a journey through a country than a space of life spent among a people and their ideas.

This contrast between Browne and his contemporaries is most marked if we compare his book with another masterpiece about Iran that appeared one year before it, George Curzon's *Persia and the Persian Question.* Curzon, then MP for Southport and only ten years away from the Viceroyship of India, had spent six months travelling through Iran shortly after Browne's return to England, and a total of two years researching his book on the country. Like Browne's, Curzon's title tells us at once of the writer's preoccupations and perspectives, both of which are cogently summed up in the well-known words of the introduction:

> "Turkestan, Afghanistan, Transcaspia, Persia—to many these names breathe only a sense of utter remoteness or a memory of strange vicissitudes and of moribund romance. To me, I confess, they are the pieces of a chessboard upon which is being played out a game for the dominion of the world."

Persia and the Persia Question is a remarkable book, packed as it is with facts and figures gleaned at first and second hand, redolent of vast erudition and immense labour. Here, the reader may discover the names of the post-stations from Tabriz to Qazvin and the distances between them, or the total tonnage of petroleum exported from Batum in 1889, or the revenues of the Shrine of Reza in Mashhad, or the prices of bread, mutton, and chicken in the same city. Curzon was, in a sense, a one-man fact-finding expedition, and he carried out his task with a thoroughness that makes even his most energetic reader wilt at the thought of what another day's travel may bring.

By way of contrast, Browne is next to useless as a guide for the traveller or as a source of information for the merchant, the diplomat, or the statesman. His strengths lie in wholly different realms. And in the long run he tells us more of Iran and, above all, more of its people than any other traveller or long-term resident before or since. He does this, not by the lengthy exposition of external detail regarding customs, beliefs, or the routines of daily living, but by means of intimate impressionistic portraits of people with whom he became personally involved, whose lives and thoughts he shared to a greater or lesser degree. It is their thoughts, not their faces; their personal opinions, not their formal creeds that interest and beguile him, and these he reveals to us with remarkable accuracy and surprising depth. It is for this reason that Browne's book has outlived Curzon's. The latter is now chiefly of interest to historians of nineteenth-century Iran, but *A Year Amongst the Persians* introduces us to things that are perennial about the country, to aspects of the Persian mind and spirit that the perceptive traveller may encounter even today.

It is Browne's love for the Iranian people and his very real understanding of their inner being that make his book essential reading. It has become a commonplace of much recent writing, especially in the Muslim world, to condemn western scholars of the Orient as tools of the Imperialist purpose, as agents of the European subjugation of the East, reinforcing and protecting physical and economic conquest by means of an intellectual domination. "Orientalist" has become a pejorative term, almost a dirty word, and it seems that there is little to be gained by calling oneself instead an "Islamicist", "Middle East specialist", 'Iranologist", or whatever. When all is said and done, there is some truth in the modern critique of oriental studies. But if proof were needed that there is also much exaggeration and distortion in that critique,

Edward Browne alone would provide us with such proof. His devotion to Iran and its people was whole-hearted and genuine, so much so that he clashed on more than one occasion with the British government over what he held to be its self-serving policies in that region. Whereas Curzon's book on Persia was dedicated to "the officials, civil and military, in India whose hands uphold the noblest fabric yet reared by the genius of a conquering nation", Browne's later history of the Persian Revolution of 1905 to 1909 was offered "to all who by their thought, or word, or deed/Have aided Persia in her hour of need". The independence of Iran from external pressures and internal disunity remained for Browne a lifelong dream, and his unremitting and outspoken championship of that cause deserves to be remembered at a time when xenophobic accusations of British perfidy in Iran are, by their very stridency, drowning out all memory of men and women like Edward Browne.

There is probably no better way of explaining Browne's success in penetrating the mind and heart of Iran than to say simply that he had an inborn affinity for the Persian East. Like Robert Byron after him, he had the gift of empathizing with a culture and a people that presented their external features openly to the traveller, while guarding their true selves in an inner realm to which few could gain access. But where Byron could fall immediately in tune with the harmonies of a mosque or a landscape or a neglected monument, Browne remained ever oblivious of art and architecture and turned his attention instead to the cadences of a poem or the subtleties of a religious concept. Where the one went out of his way to visit the Qunbad-i Kabus because Diez's picture of it had, he writes, "decided me to come to Persia", the other undertook an exhausting journey to the former Babi stronghold of Shaykh Tabarsi in order to make a final pilgrimage before leaving the country forever.

It was, indeed as a pilgrim above all that Browne went to Iran. Edward Said has suggested that "from one end of the nineteenth century to the other . . . the Orient was a place of pilgrimage, and every major work belonging to a genuine if not always to an academic Orientalism took its form, style, and intention from the idea of pilgrimage there". That seems something of an overstatement—though we have seen the phenomenon repeated in our own day. Yet if any work were to be chosen to illustrate its basic truth, it would surely have to be the present narrative, for at the heart of it lie Browne's quest for the Babis, the members of a proscribed religion born in Iran less than fifty years previously, and his pilgrimages to places significant in the history of their faith.

Speaking of his first discovery of the Babis in the pages of Gobineau's famous work, *Religions et philosophies dans l'Asia Centrale*, Browne describes in vivid terms the radical change this brought about in him:

> "Count Gobineau's book . . . effected in a certain sense a complete revolution in my ideas and projects. I had long ardently desired to visit Persia and above all Shiraz, and this desire was now greatly intensified. But whereas I had previously wished to see Shiraz because it was the home of Hafiz and of Sa'di, I now wished to see it because it was the birthplace of Mirza 'Ali Muhammad the Bab. And, after Shiraz, not Tus and Nishapur, but Zanjan, Mazandaran, and Tabriz were the objects of my eager desire." (*A Traveller's Narrative* vol. I, p. xi)

How Browne found the Babis—most of whom had by that time adopted a modified form of the original movement in the shape of Baha'ism—and what experiences he had among them, the reader may discover for himself. Browne's descriptions of his meetings and conversations with the Babis, his initial excitement that gives way in the end to confusion and disappointment, and his unabated enthusiasm for probing the doctrines and history of the sect and for collecting its literature—these form, in a sense, the heart of the book: the pivot around which everything else revolves, the element above all others that sets it apart from almost any narrative of travel in the East.

Their richly-flavoured strangeness apart, however, these accounts have not become mere curiosities for the devotee of esoteric lore and the history of forgotten sects. They have their relevance even in the modern world. Much altered and bearing little resemblance to its Babi origins, the religion of the Baha'is remains active and expanding, not only in Iran, but also in India, Africa, South America and, on a small scale, here in Europe and in the United States. Browne's original perception that Babism might yet make its mark in the world did not go far astray. For that reason, his first-hand accounts of meetings with the Baha'is and their Azali rivals, including his later encounters with the heads of the two sects in Cyprus and Palestine and, more particularly, his later researches into early Babi history and doctrine, are all of abiding importance, not only to scholars working in that field, but also to anyone concerned with the origins and development of religion in the world today.

Babism was Browne's first great passion in scholarship, and his work on the subject was, as R. A. Nicholson later maintained, "the most original and valuable of all his contributions to our knowledge of Persia". But in the years that followed his return to England and the commencement of his illustrious academic career in the field of Iranian studies, he extended and deepened his enthusiasms to embrace the language, literature, history and contemporary politics of Iran to a degree unparalleled by any western scholar before or since. Yet it must remain a puzzle that Browne never again set foot in Iran nor, apart from his journey to Cyprus and Palestine in 1890, revisited the Islamic East. No explanation of this curious fact has ever, to my knowledge, been put forward, nor do I think any is likely to be. We know that he loved Cambridge and was profoundly contented in his rooms at Pembroke and later in his married home on Trumpington Road. Perhaps he felt that the pangs of separation would outweigh the benefits of travel. Perhaps he knew that his single year in Iran had given him sufficient experiences to draw on through a lifetime. But it matters very little in the end. From his library in Cambridge, he forged and strengthened his links with Iran by means of a vast and lively correspondence, through his numerous friendships with Iranians resident in England, and by his teaching, his writing, his advocacy of the cause of Persian independence, and, not least, the unbounded enthusiasm for all things Iranian that he communicated to those around him to the end of his life.

Edward Browne's dream of an independent Iran whose people had at last become the masters of their own destiny has found a strange and ironic fulfilment in the events of recent years. Were he alive today, however, I have little doubt that he himself would find no cause for rejoicing in the fundamentalism and frenzied violence that has accompanied the establishment of the Islamic Republic. He had no time for religious extremism and always abhorred the brutality, intolerance, and indifference to human suffering it so often provokes. More than most, he would have understood and sympathized with the rage and frustration of a people too long the victims of superpower rivalry without, and unenlightened despotism within, but I am sure he would have lamented the excesses that have been the price of an uncertain freedom. His book reappears, then, under a dark cloud. Our only consolation must be that its pages themselves do so much to dispel that darkness.

DENIS MACEOIN
The University
Newcastle Upon Tyne
1984

EXORDIUM

(DEDICATED TO THE PERSIAN READER ONLY)

In the name of God, the Merciful, the Forgiving

PRAISE be to GOD, the Maker of Land and Sea, the Lord of "'BE,' and it shall be":[1] *Who brought me forth from the place of my birth, obedient to His saying, "Journey through the Earth":*[2] *Who guarded me from the dangers of the way with the shield of "No fear shall be upon them and no dismay":*[3] *Who caused me to accomplish my quest and thereafter to return and rest, after I had beheld the wonders of the East and of the West!*

BUT AFTERWARDS. Thus saith the humblest and unworthiest of His servants, who least deserveth His Bounty, and most needeth His Clemency (may God forgive his failing and heal his ailing!): When from Kirmán and the confines of Bam I had returned again to the city on the Cam, and ceased for a while to wander, and began to muse and ponder on the lands where I had been and the marvels I had therein seen, and how in pursuit of knowledge I had forgone the calm seclusion of college, and through days warm and weary, and nights dark and dreary, now hungry and now athirst I had tasted of the best and of the worst, experiencing hot and cold, and holding converse with young and old, and had climbed the mountain and crossed the waste now slowly and now with haste, until I had made an end of toil, and set my foot upon my native soil; then, wishful to impart the gain which I had won with labour and harvested with pain (for "Travel is travail"[4] *say the sages), I resolved to write these pages, and, taking ink and pen, to impart to my fellow-men what I had witnessed and understood of things evil and good.*

Now seeing that to fail and fall is the fate of all, and to claim exemption from the lot of humanity a proof of pride and vanity, and somewhat of mercy our common need; therefore let such as read, and errors detect, either ignore and neglect, or correct and conceal them rather than revile and reveal them. For he is lenient who is wise, and from his brother's failings averts his eyes, being loth to hurt or harm, nay, meeting bane with balm. WA'S-SALÁM.

1 Ḳur'án, ii, 111; iii, 42, etc. 2 Ḳur'án, vi, 11; xxvii, 71, etc.
3 Ḳur'án, ii, 36, 59, 106, etc.
4 So Burton has well translated the Arabic proverb: "*Es-seferu ḳiṭ'atun mina's-saḳar.*" ("Travel is a portion of hell-fire.")

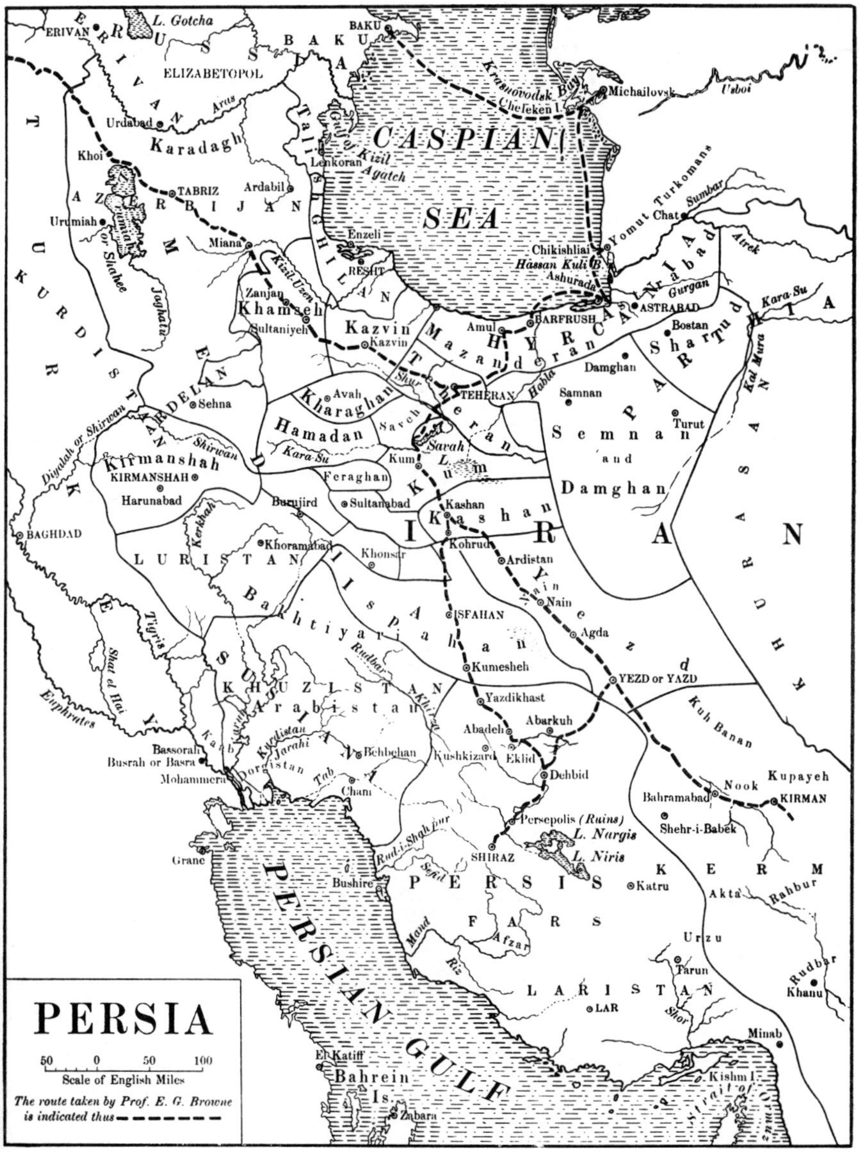
PERSIA
50 0 50 100
Scale of English Miles
The route taken by Prof. E. G. Browne is indicated thus
CASPIAN SEA
PERSIAN GULF
L. Gotcha
ERIVAN
BAKU
ELIZABETOPOL
Michailovsk
Uzboi
Krasnovodsk Bay
Cheleken I.
Aras
Urdabad
Karadagh
Khoi
TABRIZ
Ardabil
Lenkoran
Gulf of Kizil Agatch
Urumiah
Lake Urumiah or Shahee
Miana
Enzeli
RESHT
Kizil Uzen
Zanjan
Khamseh
Sultaniyeh
Joghatu
Kazvin
Amul
BARFRUSH
ASTRABAD
Gurgan
Atrek
Sumbar
Chat
Yomut Turkomans
Chikishliai
Hassan Kuli B.
Ashurada
Bostan
Kara Su
Kal Mura
Damghan
Samnan
Turut
Semnan and Damghan
Habla
TEHERAN
Shur
Sehna
Avah
Kharaghan
Saveh
Sarah
Hamadan
Kara Su
Kirmanshah
KIRMANSHAH
Harunabad
Diyalah or Shirwan
Shirwan
Kum
Feraghan
Burujird
Sultanabad
Kashan
Kohrud
Ardistan
Nain
Agda
BAGHDAD
Kerkhah
Khoramabad
Khonsar
LURISTAN
Bakhtiyari
ISFAHAN
Kumesheh
Rudbar
Tigris
Shat el Hai
Euphrates
KHUZISTAN
Arabistan
Yazdikhast
YEZD or YAZD
Kuh Banan
Abarkuh
Abadeh
Kushkizard
Eklid
Dehbid
Bassorah
Busrah or Basra
Mohammera
Kurdistan
Jarahi
Behbehan
Dorgistan
Tab
Cham
Nook
Kupayeh
Bahramabad
KIRMAN
Persepolis (Ruins)
Shehr-i-Babek
L. Nargis
L. Niris
SHIRAZ
Rud-i-Shahpur
Sefid
Granc
Bushire
PERSIS
Katru
KERMAN
Akta
Rahbur
FARS
Afzar
Mand
Urzu
Tarun
Riz
Rudbar
Khanu
LARISTAN
LAR
Shor
Minab
El Katiff
Bahrein Is.
Zabara
Kishm I.
Strait of Ormuz
HYRCANIA
Mazanderan
Teheran
Shahrud Astrabad
PARTHIA
KHURASAN
IRAN
Yezd
Ispahan
Kashan
Kum
KURDISTAN
AZERBIJAN
TURKEY
RUSSIA
ERIVAN
Talish
GHILAN
ARDELAN
SUSIANA

CONTENTS

CHAPTER I

INTRODUCTORY

"El-'ilmu 'ilmán: 'ilmu'l-adyán, wa 'ilmu'l-abdán."
"Science is twofold: Theology, and Medicine."

I HAVE so often been asked how I first came to occupy myself with the study of Eastern languages that I have decided to devote the opening chapter of this book to answering this question, and to describing as succinctly as possible the process by which, not without difficulty and occasional discouragement, I succeeded, ere ever I set foot in Persia, in obtaining a sufficient mastery over the Persian tongue to enable me to employ it with some facility as an instrument of conversation, and to explore with pleasure and profit the enchanted realms of its vast and varied literature. I have not arrived at this decision without some hesitation and misgiving, for I do not wish to obtrude myself unnecessarily on the attention of my readers, and one can hardly be autobiographical without running the risk of being egotistical. But then the same thing applies with equal force to all descriptions intended for publication of any part of one's personal experiences—such, for instance, as one's own travels. Believing that the observations, impressions, and experiences of my twelve months' sojourn in Persia during the years 1887–8 may be of interest to others besides myself, I have at length determined to publish them. It is too late now to turn squeamish about the use of the pronoun of the first person. I will be as sparing of its use as I can, but use it I must.

I might, indeed, have given to this book the form of a systematic treatise on Persia, a plan which for some time I did actually entertain; but against this plan three reasons finally decided me. *Firstly*, that my publishers expressed a preference for the narrative form, which, they believed, would render the book more readable. *Secondly*, that for the more ambitious project of writing a systematic treatise I did not feel myself prepared and could not prepare myself without the expenditure of time only to be obtained by the sacrifice of other work which seemed to me of greater importance. *Thirdly*, that the recent publication of the Hon. G. N. Curzon's encyclopædic work on Persia will for some time to come prevent any similar attempt on the part of anyone else who is not either remarkably rash or exceedingly well-informed. Moreover, the question "What first made you take up Persian?" when addressed to an Englishman who is neither engaged in, nor destined for, an Eastern career deserves an answer. In France, Germany, or Russia such a question would hardly be asked; but in England a knowledge of Eastern languages is no stepping-stone to diplomatic employment in Eastern countries; and though there exist in the Universities and the British Museum posts more desirable than this to the student of Oriental languages, such posts are few, and, when vacant, hotly competed for. In spite of every discouragement, there are, I rejoice to say, almost every year a few young Englishmen who, actuated solely by love of knowledge and desire to extend the frontiers of science in a domain which still contains vast tracts of unexplored country, devote themselves to this study. To them too often have I had to repeat the words of warning given to me by my honoured friend and teacher, the late Dr William Wright, an Arabic scholar whom not Cambridge or England only, but Europe, mourns with heart-felt sorrow and remembers with legitimate pride. It was in the year 1884, so far as I remember; I was leaving Cambridge with mingled feelings of sorrow and of hope: sorrow, because I was to bid farewell (for ever, as I then expected) to the University and the College to which I owe a debt of gratitude beyond the power of words to describe; hope, because the honours I had just gained in the Indian Languages Tripos made me sanguine of obtaining some employment which would enable me to pursue with advantage and success a study to which I was devotedly attached, and which even medicine (for which I was then destined), with all its charms and far-reaching interests, could not rival in my affections. This hope, in answer to an enquiry as to what I intended to do on leaving Cambridge, I one day confided to Dr Wright. No one, as I well knew, could better sympathise with it or gauge its chances of fulfilment, and from no one could I look for kinder, wiser, and more prudent counsel. And this was the advice he gave me—"If," said he, "you have private means which render you independent of a profession, then pursue your Oriental studies, and fear not that they will disappoint you, or fail to return you a rich reward of happiness and honour. But if you cannot afford to do this, and are obliged to consider how you may earn a livelihood, then devote yourself wholly to medicine, and abandon, save as a relaxation for your leisure moments, the pursuit of Oriental letters. The posts for which such knowledge will fit you are few, and, for the most part, poorly endowed, neither can you hope to obtain them till you have worked and waited for many years. And from the Government you must look for nothing, for it has long shown, and still continues to show, an increasing indisposition to offer the slightest encouragement to the study of Eastern languages."

A rare piece of good fortune has in my case falsified a prediction of which Dr Wright himself, though I knew it not till long afterwards, did all in his power to avert the accomplishment; but in general it still holds true, and I write these words, not for myself, but for those young English Orientalists whose disappointments, struggles, and unfulfilled, though legitimate, hopes I have so often been compelled to watch with keen but impotent sorrow and sympathy. Often I reflect with bitterness that England, though more directly interested in the East than any other European country save Russia, not only offers less encouragement to her sons to engage in the study of Oriental languages than any other great European nation, but can find no employment even for those few who, notwithstanding every discouragement, are impelled by their own inclination to this study, and who, by diligence, zeal, and natural aptitude, attain proficiency therein. How different is it in France! There, not to mention the more academic and purely scientific courses of lectures on Hebrew, Syriac, Arabic, Zend, Pahlavi, Persian, Sanskrit, and on Egyptian, Assyrian, and Semitic archæology and philology, delivered regularly by savants of European reputation at the Collège de France and the Sorbonne (all of which lectures are freely open to persons of either sex and any nationality), there is a special school of Oriental languages (now within a year or two of its centenary) where practical instruction of the best imaginable kind is given (also gratuitously) by European professors, assisted in most cases by native *répétiteurs*, in literary and colloquial Arabic, Persian, Turkish, Malay, Javanese, Armenian, Modern Greek, Chinese, Japanese, Annamite, Hindustání, Tamil, Russian, and Roumanian, as well as in the geography, history, and jurisprudence of the states of the extreme East. To these lectures (the best, I repeat, without fear of contradiction, which can be imagined) any student, French or foreign, is admitted free of charge. And any student who has followed them diligently for three years, and passed the periodical examinations to the satisfaction of his teachers, provided that he be a French subject, may confidently reckon on receiving sooner or later from the Government such employment as his tastes, training, and attainments have fitted him for. The manifold advantages of this admirable system, alike to the State and the individual, must be obvious to the most obtuse, and need no demonstration. All honour to France for the signal services which she has rendered to the cause of learning! May she long maintain that position of eminence in science which she has so nobly won, and which she so deservedly occupies! And to us English, too, may she become, in this respect at least, an exemplar and a pattern!

Now, having unburdened my mind on this matter, I will recount briefly how I came to devote myself to the study of Oriental languages. I was originally destined to become an engineer; and therefore, partly because—at any rate sixteen years ago—the teaching of the "modern side" was still in a most rudimentary state, partly because I most eagerly desired emancipation from a life entirely uncongenial to me, I left school at the age of fifteen and a half, with little knowledge and less love of Latin and Greek. I have since then learned better to appreciate the value of these languages, and to regret the slenderness of my classical attainments. Yet the method according to which they are generally taught in English public schools is so unattractive, and, in my opinion, so inefficient, that had I been subjected to it much longer I should probably have come to loathe all foreign languages, and to shudder at the very sight of a grammar. It is a good thing for the student of a language to study its grammar when he has learned to read and understand it, just as it is a good thing for an artist to study the anatomy of the human body when he has learned to sketch a figure or catch the expression of a face; but for one to seek to obtain mastery over a language by learning rules of accidence and syntax is as though he should regard the dissecting-room as the single and sufficient portal of entrance to the Academy. How little a knowledge of grammar has to do with facility in the use of language is shown by the fact that comparatively few have studied the grammar of that language over which they have the greatest mastery, while amongst all the Latin and Greek scholars in this country those who could make an extempore speech, dash off an impromptu note, or carry on a sustained conversation in either language, are in a small minority.

Then, amongst other evil things connected with it, is the magnificent contempt for all non-English systems of pronunciation which the ordinary public-school system of teaching Latin and Greek encourages. Granted that the pronunciation of Greek is very different in the Athens of to-day from what it was in the time of Plato or Euripides, and that Cicero would not understand, or would understand with difficulty, the Latin of the Vatican, does it follow that both languages should be pronounced exactly like English, of all spoken tongues the most anomalous in pronunciation? What should we think of a Chinaman who, because he was convinced that the pronunciation of English in the fourteenth century differed widely from that of the nineteenth, deliberately elected to read Chaucer with the accent and intonation of Chinese? If Latin and Greek alone were concerned it would not so much matter, but the influence of this doctrine of pan-Anglican pronunciation too often extends to French and German as well. The spirit engendered by it is finely displayed in these two sayings which I remember to have heard repeated—"Anyone can understand English if they choose, provided you talk loud enough." "Always mistrust an Englishman who talks French like a Frenchman."

Apart from the general failure to invest the books read with any human, historical, or literary interest, or to treat them as expressions of the thoughts, feelings, and aspirations of our fellow-creatures instead of as grammatical tread-mills, there is another reason why the public-school system of teaching languages commonly fails to impart much useful knowledge of them. When any intelligent being who is a free agent wishes to obtain an efficient knowledge of a foreign language as quickly as possible, how does he proceed? He begins with an easy text, and first obtains the general sense of each sentence and the meaning of each particular word from his teacher. In default of a teacher, he falls back on the best available substitute, namely, a good translation and a dictionary. Looking out words in a dictionary is, however, mere waste of time, if their meaning can be ascertained in any other way; so that he will use this means only when compelled to do so. Having ascertained the meaning of each word, he will note it down either in the margin of the book or elsewhere, so that he may not have to ask it or look it out again. Then he will read the passage which he has thus studied over and over again, if possible aloud, so that tongue, ear, and mind may be simultaneously familiarised with the new instrument of thought and communication of which he desires to possess himself, until he perfectly understands the meaning without mentally translating it into English, and until the foreign words, no longer strange, evoke in his mind, not their English equivalents, but the ideas which they connote. This is the proper way to learn a language, and it is opposed at almost every point to the public-school method, which regards the use of "cribs" as a deadly sin, and substitutes parsing and construing for reading and understanding.

Notwithstanding all this, I am well aware that the advocates of this method have in their armoury another and a more potent argument. "A boy does not go to school," they say, "to learn Latin and Greek, but to learn to confront disagreeable duties with equanimity, and to do what is distasteful to him with cheerfulness." To this I have nothing to say; it is unanswerable and final. If boys are sent to school to learn what the word disagreeable means, and to realise that the most tedious monotony is perfectly compatible with the most acute misery, and that the most assiduous labour, if it be not wisely directed, does not necessarily secure the attainment of the object ostensibly aimed at, then, indeed, does the public school offer the surest means of attaining this end. The most wretched day of my life, except the day when I left college, was the day I went to school. During the earlier portion of my school life I believe that I nearly fathomed the possibilities of human misery and despair. I learned then (what I am thankful to say I have unlearned since) to be a pessimist, a misanthrope, and a cynic; and I have learned since, what I did not understand then, that to know by rote a quantity of grammatical rules is in itself not much more useful than to know how often each letter of the alphabet occurs in *Paradise Lost*, or how many separate stones went to the building of the Great Pyramid[1].

It was the Turkish war with Russia in 1877–8 that first attracted my attention to the East, about which, till that time, I had known and cared nothing. To the young, war is always interesting, and I watched the progress of this struggle with eager attention. At first my proclivities were by no means for the Turks; but the losing side, more especially when it continues to struggle gallantly against defeat, always has a claim on our sympathy, and moreover the cant of the anti-Turkish party in England, and the wretched attempts to confound questions of abstract justice with party politics, disgusted me beyond measure. Ere the close of the war I would have died to save Turkey, and I mourned the fall of Plevna as though it had been a disaster inflicted on my own country. And so gradually pity turned to admiration, and admiration to enthusiasm, until the Turks became in my eyes veritable heroes, and the desire to identify myself with their cause, make my dwelling amongst them, and unite with them in the defence of their land, possessed me heart and soul. At the age of sixteen such enthusiasm more easily establishes itself in the heart, and, while it lasts (for it often fades as quickly as it bloomed), exercises a more absolute and uncontrolled sway over the mind than at a more advanced age. Even though it be transitory, its effects (as in my case) may be permanent.

So now my whole ambition came to be this: how I might become in time an officer in the Turkish army. And the plan

1 Many of my readers, even of those who may be inclined to agree with me as to the desirability of modifying the teaching of our public schools, will blame me for expressing myself so strongly. The value of a public-school education in the development of *character* cannot be denied, and in the teaching also great improvements have, I believe, been made within the last ten or fifteen years. But as far as my own experience goes, I do not feel that I have spoken at all too strongly.

which I proposed to myself was to enter first the English army, to remain there till I had learned my profession and attained the rank of captain, then to resign my commission and enter the service of the Ottoman Government, which, as I understood, gave a promotion of two grades. So wild a project will doubtless move many of my readers to mirth, and some to indignation, but, such as it was, it was for a time paramount in my mind, and its influence outlived it. Its accomplishment, however, evidently needed time; and, as my enthusiasm demanded some immediate object, I resolved at once to begin the study of the Turkish language.

Few of my readers, probably, have had occasion to embark on this study, or even to consider what steps they would take if a desire to do so suddenly came upon them. I may therefore here remark that for one not resident in the metropolis it is far from easy to discover anything about the Turkish language, and almost impossible to find a teacher. However, after much seeking and many enquiries, I succeeded in obtaining a copy of Barker's *Turkish Grammar*. Into this I plunged with enthusiasm. I learned Turkish verbs in the old school fashion, and blundered through the "Pleasantries of Khoja Naṣru'd-Dín Efendí"; but so ignorant was I, and so involved is the Ottoman construction, that it took me some time to discover that the language is written from right to left; while, true to the pan-Anglican system on which I have already animadverted, I read my Turkish as though it had been English, pronouncing, for example, the article *bir* and the substantive *ber* exactly the same, and as though both, instead of neither, rhymed with the English words *fir* and *fur*. And so I bungled on for a while, making slow but steady progress, and wasting much time, but with undiminished enthusiasm; for which I was presently rewarded by discovering a teacher. This was an Irish clergyman, who had, I believe, served as a private in the Crimean War, picked up some Turkish, attracted attention by his proficiency in a language of which very few Englishmen have any knowledge, and so gained employment as an interpreter. After the war he was ordained a clergyman of the Church of England, and remained for some years at Constantinople as a missionary. I do not know how his work prospered; but if he succeeded in winning from the Turks half the sympathy and love with which they inspired him, his success must have been great indeed. When I discovered him, he had a cure of souls in the Consett iron district, having been driven from his last parish by the resentment of his flock (Whigs, almost to a man), which he had incurred by venturing publicly to defend the Turks at a time when they were at the very nadir of unpopularity, and when the outcry about the "Bulgarian atrocities" was at its height. So the very religious and humane persons who composed his congregation announced to his vicar their intention of withdrawing their subscriptions and support from the church so long as the "Bashi-bozouk" (such, as he informed me, not without a certain pride, was the name they had given him) occupied its pulpit. So there was nothing for it but that he should go. Isolated in the uncongenial environment to which he was transferred, he was, I think, almost as eager to teach me Turkish as I was to learn it, and many a pleasant hour did I pass in his little parlour listening with inexhaustible delight to the anecdotes of his life in Constantinople which he loved to tell. Peace be to his memory! He died in Africa, once more engaged in mission work, not long after I went to Cambridge.

One of the incidental charms of Orientalism is the kindness and sympathy often shown by scholars of the greatest distinction and the highest attainments to the young beginner, even when he has no introduction save the pass-word of a common and much-loved pursuit. Of this I can recall many instances, but it is sufficient to mention the first in my experience. Expecting to be in, or within reach of, London for a time, I was anxious to improve the occasion by prosecuting my Turkish studies (for the "Bashi-bozouk" had recently left Consett for Hull), and to this end wished to find a proficient teacher. As I knew not how else to set about this, I finally, and somewhat audaciously, determined to write to the late Sir James (then Mr) Redhouse (whose name the study of his valuable writings on the Ottoman language had made familiar to me as that of a patron saint), asking for his advice and help. This letter I addressed to the care of his publishers; and in a few days I received, to my intense delight, a most kind reply, in which he, the first Turkish scholar in Europe probably, not only gave me all the information I required, but invited me to pay him a visit whenever I came to London, an invitation of which, as may be readily believed, I availed myself at the earliest possible opportunity. And so gradually I came to know others who were able and willing to help me in my studies, including several Turkish gentlemen attached to the Ottoman Embassy in London, from some of whom I received no little kindness.

But if my studies prospered, it was otherwise with the somewhat chimerical project in which they had originated. My father did not wish me to enter the army, but proposed medicine as an alternative to engineering. As the former profession seemed more compatible with my aspirations than the latter, I eagerly accepted his offer. A few days after this decision had been arrived at, he consulted an eminent physician, who was one of his oldest friends, as to my future education. "If you wanted to make your son a doctor," said my father, "where would you send him?" And the answer, given without a moment's hesitation, was, "To Cambridge."

So to Cambridge I went in October 1879, which date marks for me the beginning of a new and most happy era of life; for I suppose that a man who cannot be happy at the University must be incapable of happiness. Here my medical studies occupied, of course, the major part of my time and attention, and that right pleasantly; for, apart from their intrinsic interest, the teaching was masterly, and even subjects at first repellent can be made attractive when taught by a master possessed of grasp, eloquence, and enthusiasm, just as a teacher who lacks these qualities will make the most interesting subjects appear devoid of charm. Yet still I found time to devote to Eastern languages. Turkish, it is true, was not then to be had at Cambridge; but I had already discovered that for further progress in this some knowledge of Arabic and Persian was requisite; and to these I determined to turn my attention. During my first year I therefore began to study Arabic with the late Professor Palmer, whose extraordinary and varied abilities are too well known to need any celebration on my part. No man had a higher ideal of knowledge in the matter of languages, or more original (and, as I believe, sounder) views as to the method of learning them. These views I have already set forth substantially and summarily; and I will therefore say no more about them in this place, save that I absorbed them greedily, and derived from them no small advantage, learning by their application more of Arabic in one term than I had learned of Latin or Greek during five and a half years, and this notwithstanding the fact that I could devote to it only a small portion of my time.

I began Persian in the Long Vacation of 1880. Neither Professor Palmer nor Professor Cowell was resident in Cambridge at that time; but I obtained the assistance of an undergraduate of Indian nationality, who, though the son of Hindoo parents converted to Christianity, had an excellent knowledge not only of Persian and Sanskrit, but of Arabic. To this knowledge, which was my admiration and envy, he for his part seemed to attach little importance; all his pride was in playing the fiddle, on which, so far as I could judge, he was a very indifferent performer. But as it gave him pleasure to have a listener, a kind of tacit understanding grew up that when he had helped me for an hour to read the *Gulistán*, I in return should sit and listen for a while to his fiddling, which I did with such appearance of pleasure as I could command.

For two years after this—that is to say, till I took my degree—such work as I did in Persian and Arabic was done chiefly by myself, though I managed to run up to London for an afternoon once a fortnight or so for a Turkish lesson, till the Lent Term of 1881, when the paramount claims of that most exacting of taskmasters, the river, took from me for some weeks the right to call my afternoons my own. And when the Lent races were over, I had to think seriously about my approaching tripos; while a promise made to me by my father, that if I succeeded in passing both it and the examination for the second M.B. at the end of my third year (*i.e.* in June 1882), I should spend two months of the succeeding Long Vacation in Constantinople, determined me to exert all my efforts to win this dazzling bribe. This resolution cost me a good deal, but I was amply rewarded for my self-denial when, in July 1882, I at length beheld the minarets of Stamboul, and heard the *Mu'ezzin* call the true believers to prayer. I have heard people express themselves as disappointed with Constantinople. I suppose that, wherever one goes, one sees in great measure what one expects to see (because there is good and evil in all things, and the eye discerns but one when the mind is occupied by a preconceived idea); but I at least suffered no disenchantment, and returned to England with my enthusiasm for the East not merely undiminished, but, if possible, intensified.

The two succeeding years were years of undiluted pleasure, for I was still at Cambridge, and was now able to devote my whole time to the study of Oriental languages. As I intended to become a candidate for the Indian Languages Tripos in 1884, I was obliged to begin the study of Hindustání, a language from which I never could succeed in deriving much pleasure. During this period I became acquainted with a very learned but very eccentric old Persian, Mírzá Muḥammad Báḳir, of Bawánát in Fárs, surnamed Ibráhím Ján Mu'aṭṭar. Having wandered through half the world, learned (and learned well) half a dozen languages, and been successively a Shí'ite Muḥammadan, a dervish, a Christian, an atheist, and a Jew, he had finished by elaborating a religious system of his own, which he called "Islamo-Christianity," to the celebration (I can hardly say the elucidation) of which in English tracts and Persian poems, composed in the most bizarre style, he devoted the greater part of his time, talents, and money. He was in every way a most remarkable man, and one whom it was impossible not to respect and like, in spite of his appalling loquacity, his unreason, his disputatiousness, his utter impracticability. I never saw anyone who lived so entirely in a fantastic ideal world of his own creation. He was totally indifferent to his own temporal interests; cared nothing for money, personal comfort, or the favour of the powerful; and often alienated his acquaintances by violent attacks on their most cherished beliefs, and drove away his friends by the ceaseless torrent of his eloquence. He lived in a squalid little room in Limehouse, surrounded by piles of dusty books, mostly theological treatises in Persian and Arabic, with a sprinkling of Hebrew and English volumes, amongst which last Carlyle's *Sartor Resartus* and *Heroes and Hero-Worship* occupied the place of honour. Of these, however, he made but little use, for he generally wrote when alone, and talked when he could get anyone to listen to him. I tried to persuade him to read with me those portions of the *Masnaví* and the *Díván of Háfiẓ* set for my examination, and offered to remunerate him for his trouble; but this plan failed on its first trial. We had not read for twenty minutes when he suddenly pushed away the *Háfiẓ*, dragged out from a drawer in the rickety little table a pile of manuscript, and said, "I like my own poetry better than this, and if you want me to teach you Persian you must learn it as I please. I don't want your money, but I do want you to understand my thoughts about religion. You can understand Háfiz by yourself, but you cannot understand my poetry unless I explain it to you." This was certainly true: allusions to grotesque visions in which figured grass-eating lions, bears, yellow demons, Gog and Magog, "Crusaders," and Hebrew and Arab patriarchs, saints, and warriors, were jumbled up with current politics, personal reminiscences, Rabbinic legends, mystical rhapsodies, denunciations, prophecies, old Persian mythology, Old Testament theology, and Ḳur'ánic exegesis in a manner truly bewildering, the whole being clothed in a Persian so quaint, so obscure, and so replete with rare, dialectical, and foreign words, that many verses were incomprehensible even to educated Persians, to whom, for the most part, the "Little Sun of London" (*Shumeysa-i-Landaniyya*—so he called the longest of his published poems) was a source of terror. One of my Persian friends (for I made acquaintance about this time with several young Persians who were studying in London) would never consent to visit me until he had received an assurance that the poet-prophet-philosopher of Bawánát would be out of the way. I, however, by dint of long listening and much patience, not without some weariness, learned from him much that was of value to me besides the correct Persian pronunciation. For I had originally acquired from my Indian friend the erroneous and unlovely pronunciation current in India, which I now abandoned with all possible speed, believing the "French of Paris" to be preferable to the "French of Stratford atte Bowe."

Towards the end of 1884 Mírzá Báḳir left London for the East with his surviving children, a daughter of about eighteen and a son of about ten years of age, both of whom had been brought up away from him in the Christian religion, and neither of whom knew any language but English. The girl's failing health (for she was threatened with consumption) was the cause of his departure. I had just left Cambridge, and entered at St Bartholomew's Hospital, where I found my time and energies fully occupied with my new work. Tired as I often was, however, when I got away from the wards, I had to make almost daily pilgrimages to Limehouse, where I often remained till nearly midnight; for Mírzá Báḳir refused to leave London till I had finished reading a versified commentary on the Ḳur'án on which he had been engaged for some time, and of which he wished to bestow the manuscript on me as a keepsake. "My daughter will die," said he, "as the doctors tell me, unless she leaves for Beyrout in a short time, and it is you who prevent me from taking her there; for I will not leave London until you have understood my book." Argument was useless with such a visionary; so, willing or no, I had to spend every available hour in the little room at Limehouse, ever on the watch to check the interminable digressions to which the reading of the poem continually gave rise. At last it was finished, and the very next day, if I remember rightly, Mírzá Báḳir started with his children for the East. I never saw him again, though I continued to correspond with him so long as he was at Beyrout, whence, I think, he was finally expelled by the Ottoman Government as a firebrand menacing the peace of the community. He then went with his son to Persia (his daughter had died previously at Beyrout), whence news of his death reached me a year or two ago.

And now for three years (1884–7) it was only an occasional leisure hour that I could snatch from my medical studies for a chat with my Persian friends (who, though they knew English well for the most part, were kind enough to talk for my benefit their own language), or for quiet communing in the cool vaulted reading-room of the British Museum with my favourite Ṣúfí writers, whose mystical idealism, which had long since cast its spell over my mind, now supplied me with a powerful antidote against the pessimistic tendencies evoked by the daily contemplation of misery and pain. This period was far from being an unhappy one, for my work, if hard, was full of interest; and if in the hospital I saw much that was sad, much that made me wonder at man's clinging to life (since to the vast majority life seemed but a succession of pains, struggles, and sorrows), on the other hand I saw much to strengthen my faith in the goodness and nobility of human nature. Never before or since have I realised so clearly the immortality, greatness, and virtue of the spirit of man, or the misery of its earthly environment: it seemed to me like a prince in rags, ignorant alike of his birth and his rights, but to whom is reserved a glorious heritage. No wonder, then, that the Pantheistic idealism of the *Maṣnaví* took hold of me, or that such words as these of Háfiz thrilled me to the very soul:

> "*Turá ẓi kungara-i-'arsh mí-ẓanand ṣafír:*
> *Na-dánamat ki dar ín khákdán ché uftádast.*"

> "They are calling to thee from the pinnacles of the throne of God:
> I know not what hath befallen thee in this dust-heap" (the world).

Even my medical studies, strange as it may appear, favoured the development of this habit of mind; for physiology, when it does not encourage materialism, encourages mysticism; and nothing so much tends to shake one's faith in the reality of the objective world as the examination of certain of the subjective phenomena of mental and nervous disorders.

But now this period, too, was drawing to a close, and my dreams of visiting Persia, even when their accomplishment seemed most unlikely, were rapidly approaching fulfilment. The hopes with which I had left Cambridge had been damped by repeated disappointments. I had thought that the knowledge I had acquired of Persian, Turkish, and Arabic might enable me to find employment in the Consular Service, but had learned from curt official letters, referring me to printed official regulations, that this was not so, that these languages were not recognised as subjects of examination, and that not they, but German, Greek, Spanish, and Italian were the qualifications by which one might hope to become a consul in Western Asia. The words of Dr Wright's warning came back to me, and I acknowledged their justice. To my professional studies, I felt, and not to my linguistic attainments, must I look to earn my livelihood.

I had passed my final examinations at the College of Surgeons, the College of Physicians, and the University of Cambridge, received from the two former, with a sense of exultation which I well remember, the diplomas authorising me to practise, and was beginning to consider what my next step should be, when the luck of which I had despaired came to me at last. Returning to my rooms on the evening of 30th May 1887, I found a telegram lying on the table. I opened it with indifference, which changed, in the moment I grasped its purport, to ecstatic joy. I had that day been elected a Fellow of my College.

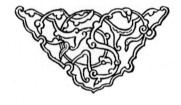

CHAPTER II

FROM ENGLAND TO THE PERSIAN FRONTIER

"*Fa má adrí, idhá yammamtu arḍan*
Urídu'l-khayra, ayyuhumá yalíní:
A'al-khayru'lladhí ana abtaghíhí,
Ami'sh-sharru'lladhí huwa yabtaghíní."

"And I know not, when bound for the land of my quest, if my portion shall be
The good which I hope for and seek, or the evil that seeketh for me."

(*Al-Muthaḳḳibu'l-'Abdí.*)

SO at last I was really to go to Persia. About that there could be no question. For I had long determined to go if I got the chance; and now, not only had the opportunity come, but, in view of the probability that the University would soon require a resident teacher of Persian, I was urged by my friends at Cambridge to spend the first year of my fellowship in the way which would best qualify me for this post. Yet, as the time for my departure approached, a strange shrinking from this journey which I had so much desired—a shrinking to which I look back with shame and wonder, and for which I can in no wise account—took possession of me. It arose partly, I suppose, from the sudden reaction which unexpected good fortune will at times produce; partly, if not from ill health, at least from that lowering of the vitality which results from hard work and lack of exercise and fresh air; partly also from the worry inseparable from the preparations for a long journey into regions little known. But, whatever its cause, it did much to mar my happiness at a time when I had no excuse for being otherwise than happy. At length, however, it came to an end. Bewildered by conflicting counsels as to the equipment which I should need and the route which I had best take, I at last settled the matter by booking my passage from Marseilles to Batoum at the London office of the Messageries Maritimes, and by adding to the two small portmanteaus into which I had compressed so much clothing as appeared absolutely indispensable nothing but a Wolseley valise, a saddle and bridle, a pith hat (which was broken to pieces long before the summer came round), a small medicine-chest, a few surgical instruments, a revolver, a box of a hundred cartridges, a few books, a passport with the Russian and Turkish *visas*, and a money-belt containing about £200 in gold, paper, and circular notes. At the last moment I was joined by an old college friend, H——, who, having just completed a term of office at the hospital, was desirous to travel, and whose proposal to join me I welcomed. He was my companion as far as Ṭeherán, where, as I desired to tarry for a while, and he to proceed, we were obliged to separate.

We had booked our passage, as I have said, to Batoum, intending to take the train thence to Baku, and so by the Caspian to Resht in Persia. For this route, unquestionably the shortest and easiest, I had from the first felt little liking, my own wish being to enter Persia through Turkey, either by way of Damascus and Baghdád, or of Trebizonde and Erzeroum. I had suffered myself to be persuaded against my inclinations, which, I think, where no question of principle is involved, is always a mistake, for the longer and harder way of one's own choosing is preferable to the shorter and easier way chosen by another. And so, as soon as I was withdrawn from the influences which had temporarily overcome my own judgment and inclination, I began to repent of having adopted an uncongenial plan, and to consider whether even now, at this eleventh hour, it was not possible to change. The sight of the Turkish shore and the sound of the Turkish tongue (for we stayed two days at Constantinople, whence to Trebizonde the deck of the steamer was crowded with Turks and Persians, with whom I spent the greater part of each day in conversing) swept away my last scruples as to the wisdom of thus reversing at the outset a decision which had been fully discussed. I consulted with H——, who raised no objection; and we decided on reaching Trebizonde (where the steamer anchored on 4th October) to enquire at the British Consulate as to the safety and practicability of the old caravan road leading thence into Central Asia, and, if the report were favourable, to adopt that route.

There was a heavy swell in the open roadstead, and the wind, which rolled back the rain-clouds on the green, thickly-wooded hills, seemed to be rising, as we clambered into one of the clumsy boats which hovered round the steamer to go ashore. Nor had the gruff old captain's answer to my enquiry as to how long the steamer would lie there tended to reassure me. "If the wind gets up much more," he had said, "I may start at any time." "And if we are on shore," I demanded, "how shall we know that you are starting?" "*Vous me verrez partir, voilà tout,*" he replied, and, with a shrug of his shoulders, walked off to his cabin. So I was somewhat uneasy in my mind lest, while we were conducting our enquiries on shore, the steamer might put out to sea, bearing with it all our worldly goods. This disquieting reflection was dispelled by the shock of the boat striking against the little wooden jetty. We stepped out, and found ourselves confronted by one of the Turkish police, who demanded our passports. These had not been presented, as theoretically they should have been, at Constantinople for a fresh *visa*, and I feared we might consequently have some trouble in landing. However, I assumed an air of confident alacrity, produced the passports, and pointed to the seal of the Turkish Consulate given in London. As the *visa*—"*bon pour se rendre à Constantinople*"—to which this was attached was in French, the officer was not much the wiser, and, after scrutinising the passports (which he held upside down) with a critical air, he returned them and stood aside to let us pass.

And this is typical of Turkey, where the laws, though theoretically stringent, are not practically troublesome; in which point it has the advantage over Russia.

Guided by a boy belonging to our boat, we ascended through narrow, tortuous streets to the British Consulate, where, though unprovided with recommendations, we received from the Consul, Mr Longworth, that courteous and kindly welcome which, to their honour be it said, Englishmen (and, indeed, other Europeans, as well as Americans) resident in the Turkish and Persian dominions seldom fail to give the traveller. In reply to our enquiries, he told us that the road to the Persian frontier was perfectly safe, and that we should have no difficulty in hiring horses or mules to convey us to Erzeroum, whence we could easily engage others for the journey to Tabríz. He also kindly offered to send his dragoman, an Armenian gentleman, named Hekimian, to assist us in clearing our baggage at the custom-house. So we returned to the steamer to bring it ashore. As we pushed our way through the deck-passengers to the side of the ship, some of my Persian acquaintances called out to me to tell them why I was disembarking and whither I was going, and, on learning my intention of taking the old caravan road through Erzeroum, they cried, "O dear soul, it will take you three months to get to Ṭeherán thus, if indeed you get there at all! Why have you thus made your road difficult?" But the step was taken now, and I paid no heed to their words.

The custom-house, thanks to the ægis of the British Consulate, dealt very gently with us. We were even asked, if I remember right, which of our packages we should prefer to have opened. H——'s Wolseley valise was selected; but we forgot that his rifle had been rolled up in it. The Turkish excisemen stroked their chins a little at this sight (for fire-arms are contraband), but said nothing. When this form of examination was over we thanked the *mudír*, or superintendent, for his courtesy, gave a few small coins to his subordinates, and, with the help of two or three sturdy porters, transported our luggage to the one hotel which Trebizonde possesses. It is called the "Hôtel d'Italie," and, though unpretentious, is clean and comfortable. During the three days we spent there we had no cause to complain either of being underfed or overcharged.

Next morning our preparations began in earnest. Hekimian was of inestimable service, arranging everything and accompanying us everywhere. The Russian paper-money with which we had provided ourselves for the earlier part of the journey was soon converted into Turkish gold; tinned provisions and a few simple cooking utensils and other necessaries were bought in the bazaars; and arrangements were concluded with two sturdy muleteers for the journey to Erzeroum. They on their part agreed to provide us with five horses for ourselves and our baggage, to convey us to Erzeroum in six or seven days, and to do what lay in their power to render the journey pleasant; while we on our part covenanted to pay them 6¼ Turkish pounds (£3 down, and the remainder at Erzeroum), to which we promised to add a trifle if they gave us satisfaction.

There remained a more important matter, the choice of a servant to accompany us on the journey. Two candidates presented themselves: an honest-looking old Turkish *Ḳavvás* of the Consulate, and a shifty Armenian, who, on the strength of his alleged skill in cookery, demanded exorbitantly high wages. We chose the Turk, agreeing to pay him one Turkish pound a week, to guarantee this payment for six months, and to defray his expenses back to Trebizonde from any point at which we might finally leave him. It was a rash agreement, and might have caused us more trouble than it actually did, but there seemed to be no better alternative, seeing that a servant was an absolute necessity. The old Turk's real name was 'Omar; but, having regard to the detestation in which this name is held in Persia (for he whom Sunnite Muḥammadans account the second Caliph, or successor of the Prophet, is regarded by the sect of the Shí'a as the worst of evil-doers and usurpers)[1], it was decided that he should henceforth bear the more auspicious name of 'Alí, the darling hero of the Persian Shí'ites. As for our old servant's character, viewed in the light of subsequent experience, I do him but justice when I express my conviction that a more honest, straightforward, faithful, loyal soul could not easily be found anywhere. But, on the other hand, he was rather fidgety; rather obstinate; too old to travel in a strange country, adapt himself to new surroundings, and learn a new language; and too simple to cope with the astute and wily Persians, whom, moreover, religious and national prejudices caused him ever to regard with unconquerable aversion.

This business concluded, we had still to get our passports for the interior. Hekimian accompanied us to the Government offices, where, while a courteous old Turk entertained me with coffee and conversation, a shrewd-looking subordinate noted down the details of our personal appearance in the spaces reserved for that purpose on the passport. I was amused on receiving the document to find my religion described as "English" and my moustache as "fresh" (*ter*), but not altogether pleased at the entries in the "head" and "chin" columns, which respectively were "*tōp*" (bullet-shaped) and "*deyirmen*" (round). Before leaving the Government-house we paid our respects to Surúrí Efendí, the governor of Trebizonde, one of the judges who tried and condemned the wise and patriotic Midḥat Páshá. He was a fine-looking old man, and withal courteous; but he is reputed to be corrupt and bigoted.

In the evening at the hotel we made the acquaintance of a Belgian mining-engineer, who had lived for some time in Persia. The account which he gave of that country and its inhabitants

1 The repetition of the following curse on the three first Caliphs of the Sunnís is accounted by Persian Shí'ites as a pious exercise of singular virtue: "*O God, curse 'Omar: then Abú Bekr and 'Omar: then 'Othmán and 'Omar: then 'Omar: then 'Omar!*"

was far from encouraging. "I have travelled in many lands," he said, "and have discovered some good qualities in every people, with the exception of the Persians, in whom I have failed to find a single admirable characteristic. Their very language bears witness against them and exposes the sordidness of their minds. When they wish to thank you they say, '*Luṭf-i-shumá ziyád*,' 'May your kindness be increased,' that is, 'May you give me something more'; and when they desire to support an assertion with an oath they say '*Bi-ján-i-'azíz-i-khudat*,' 'By thy precious life,' or '*Bi-marg-i-shumá*,' 'By your death,' that is, 'May *you* die if I speak untruly.'[1] And they would be as indifferent to your death as to the truth of their own assertions."

Although we were ready to start on the following day, we were prevented from doing so by a steady downpour of rain. Having completed all our arrangements, we paid a visit to the Persian Consulate in company with Mr Longworth. In answer to our enquiry as to whether our passports required his *visa*, the Persian Consul signified that this was essential, and, for the sum of one *mejídiyyé* apiece, endorsed each of them with a lengthy inscription so tastefully executed that it seemed a pity that, during the whole period of our sojourn in Persia, no one asked to see them. Though perfectly useless and unnecessary, the *visa*, as a specimen of calligraphy, was cheap at the price.

Next day (Friday, 7th October) the rain had ceased, and at an early hour we were plunged in the confusion without which, as it would seem, not even the smallest caravan can start. The muleteers, who had been urging us to hasten our preparations, disappeared so soon as everything was ready. When they had been found and brought back, it was discovered that no bridle had been provided for H——'s horse; for, though both of us had

1 Apart from the doubtful justice of judging a people by the idioms of their language, it may be pointed out that, with regard to the two last expressions, they are based on the idea that to swear by one's own life or death would be to swear by a thing of little value compared to the life or death of a friend.

brought saddles from England, he had thought that it would be better to use a native bridle. Eventually one was procured, and, about 9 a.m., we emerged from the little crowd which had been watching our proceedings with a keen interest, and rode out of the town. Our course lay for a little while along the coast, until we reached the mouth of the valley of Khosh Oghlán, which we entered, turning to the south. The beauty of the day, which the late rains had rendered pleasantly cool, combined with the novelty of the scene and the picturesque appearance of the people whom we met on the road, raised our spirits, and completely removed certain misgivings as to the wisdom of choosing this route which, when it was too late to draw back, had taken possession of my mind. The horses which we rode were good, and, leaving the muleteers and baggage behind, we pushed on until, at 2.30 p.m., we reached the pretty little village of Jevizlik, the first halting-place out of Trebizonde. Here we should have halted for the night; but, since the muleteers had not informed us of their plans, and it was still early, we determined to proceed to Khamsé-Kyüy, and accordingly continued our course up the beautiful wooded valley towards the pass of Zighána-dágh, which gleamed before us white with newly fallen snow. During the latter part of the day we fell in with a wild-looking horseman, who informed me that he, like all the inhabitants of Khamsé-Kyüy, was a Christian.

It was quite dark before we reached Khamsé-Kyüy, and it took us some little time to find a *khán* at which to rest for the night. The muleteers and baggage were far behind, and at first it seemed probable that we should have to postpone our supper till their arrival, or else do without it altogether. However, 'Alí presently succeeded in obtaining some bread, and also a few eggs, which he fried in oil, so that, with the whisky in our flasks, we fared better than might have been expected.

At about 9 p.m. the muleteers arrived and demanded to see me at once. They were very tired, and very angry because we had not waited for them at Jevizlik. I did not at first easily understand the cause of their indignation (for this was my first experience of this kind of travelling, and my ideas about the capacity of horses were rather vague) till it was explained to me that at the present rate of proceeding both men and animals would be wearied out long before we reached Erzeroum. "O my soul!" said the elder muleteer in conclusion, more in sorrow than in anger, "a fine novice art thou if thou thinkest that these horses can go so swiftly from morning till evening without rest or food. Henceforth let us proceed in company at a slower pace, by which means we shall all, please God, reach Erzeroum with safety and comfort in seven days, even as was agreed between us." Not much pleased at thus being admonished, but compelled to admit the justice of the muleteer's remarks, I betook myself to the Wolseley valise which I had, after much deliberation, selected as the form of bed most suitable for the journey. Excellent as this contrivance is, and invaluable as it proved to be, my first night in it was anything but comfortable. As I intended to stuff with straw the space left for that purpose beneath the lining, I had neglected to bring a mattress. Straw, however, was not forthcoming, and I was therefore painfully conscious of every irregularity in the ill-paved floor; while the fleas which infest most Turkish *khāns* did not fail on this occasion to welcome the advent of the stranger. In spite of these discomforts and the novelty of my surroundings I soon fell fast asleep.

Looking back at those first days of my journey in the light of fuller experience, I marvel at the discomforts which we readily endured, and even courted by our ignorance and lack of foresight.

Bewildered by conflicting counsels as to equipment, I had finally resolved to take only what appeared absolutely essential, and to reduce our baggage to the smallest possible compass. Prepared by what I had read in books of Eastern travel to endure discomforts far exceeding any which I was actually called upon to experience, I had yet to learn how comfortably one may travel even in countries where the railroad and the hotel are unknown. Yet I do not regret this experience, which at least taught me how few are the necessaries of life, and how needless are many of those things which we are accustomed to regard as such. Indeed, I am by no means certain that the absence of many luxuries which we commonly regard as indispensable to our happiness is not fully compensated for by the freedom from care and hurry, the continual variety of scenery and costume, and the sense of health produced by exposure to the open air, which, taken together, constitute the irresistible charm of Eastern travel.

On the following morning we were up betimes, and after a steep ascent of an hour or so reached the summit of the pass of Zighána-dágh, which was thinly covered with a dazzling garment of snow. Here we passed a little *khán*, which would have been our second resting-place had we halted at Jevizlik on the preceding day instead of pushing on to Khamsé-Kyüy. As it was, however, we passed it without stopping, and commenced the descent to the village of Zighána-Kyüy, where we halted for an hour to rest and refresh ourselves and the horses. Excellent fruit and coffee were obtainable here; and as we had yielded to the muleteers' request that we should not separate ourselves from the baggage, we had our own provisions as well, and altogether fared much better than on the previous day.

After the completion of our meal we proceeded on our journey, and towards evening reached the pretty little hamlet of Kyüpri-báshí situated on a river called, from the town of Ardessa through which it flows, Ardessa-irmághi, in which we enjoyed the luxury of a bathe. The inhabitants of this delightful spot were few in number, peaceable in appearance, and totally devoid of that inquisitiveness about strangers which is so characteristic of the Persians. Although it can hardly be the case that many Europeans pass through their village, they scarcely looked at us, and asked but few questions as to our business, nationality, or destination. This lack of curiosity, which, so far as my experience goes, usually characterises the Turkish peasant, extends to all his surroundings. Enquiries as to the name of a wayside flower, or the fate of a traveller whose last resting-place was marked by a mound of earth at the roadside, were alike met with a half-scornful, half-amused "*kim bilir?*" ("who knows?"), indicative of surprise on the part of the person addressed at being questioned on a matter in which, as it did not concern himself, he felt no interest. In Persia, more especially in Southern Persia, it is quite otherwise; and, whether right or wrong, an ingenious answer is usually forthcoming to the traveller's enquiries.

Our third day's march took us first through the town of Ardessa, and then through the village of Demirjí-súyú, on emerging from which we were confronted and stopped by two most evil-looking individuals armed to the teeth with pistols and daggers. My first idea was that they were robbers; but, on riding forward to ascertain their business, I discovered that they were excisemen of a kind called *díghtabán*, whose business it is to watch for and seize tobacco which does not bear the stamp of the Ottoman Régie. It appeared that some one, either from malice or a misdirected sense of humour, had laid information against us, alleging that we had in our possession a quantity of such tobacco. A violent altercation took place between the excisemen and our servant 'Alí, whose pockets they insisted on searching, and whose tobacco-pouch was torn in two in the struggle. Meanwhile the muleteers continued to manifest the most ostentatious eagerness to unload our baggage and submit it to examination, until finally, by protestations and remonstrances, we prevailed on the custom-house officers to let us pass. The cause of the muleteers' unnecessary eagerness to open our baggage now became apparent. Sidling up to my horse, one of these honest fellows triumphantly showed me a great bag of smuggled tobacco which he had secreted in his pocket. I asked him what he would have done if it had been detected, whereat he tapped the stock of a pistol which was thrust into his belt with a sinister and suggestive smile. Although I could not help being amused at his cool impudence, I was far from being reassured by the warlike propensities which this gesture revealed.

Continuing on our way, and still keeping near the river, we passed one or two old castles, situated on rocky heights, which, we were informed, had been built by the Genoese. Towards noon we entered the valley of Gyumish-Kháné, so-called from the silver mines which occur in the neighbourhood. This valley is walled in by steep and rocky cliffs, and is barren and arid, except near the river, which is surrounded by beautiful orchards. Indeed the pears and apples of Gyumish-Kháné are celebrated throughout the district. We passed several prosperous-looking villages, at one of which we halted for lunch. Here for the first time I tasted *petmez*, a kind of treacle or syrup made from fruit. In Persia this is known as *dúsháb* or *shíré*; it is not unpalatable, and we used occasionally to eat it with boiled rice as a substitute for pudding. Here also we fell in with a respectable-looking Armenian going on foot to Erzeroum. Anyone worse equipped for a journey of 150 miles on foot I never saw. He wore a black frock-coat and a fez; his feet were shod with slippers down at the heels; and to protect himself from the heat of the sun he carried a large white umbrella. He looked so hot and tired and dusty that I was moved to compassion, and asked him whether he would not like to ride my horse for a while. This offer he gladly accepted, whereupon I dismounted and walked for a few miles, until he announced that he was sufficiently rested and would proceed on foot. He was so grateful for this indulgence that he bore us company as far as Erzeroum, and would readily have followed us farther had we encouraged him to do so. Every day H—— and myself allowed him to ride for some distance on our horses, and the poor man's journey was, I trust, thereby rendered less fatiguing to him.

During the latter part of the day our course lay through a most gloomy and desolate valley, walled in with red rocks and utterly devoid of trees or verdure. Emerging from this, and passing another fine old castle situated on a lofty and precipitous crag, we arrived about 5 p.m. at the little hamlet of Tekké, where we halted for the night. It is rather a miserable place, containing several *khán*s swarming with Persian camel-drivers, but very few private houses. A shallow river which runs near it again enabled us to enjoy the luxury of a bathe.

Our fourth day's march was very dreary, lying for the most part through gloomy ravines walled in with reddish rocks, like that which we had traversed at the end of the previous day's journey. In addition to the depressing character of the scene, there was a report that robbers were lurking in the neighbourhood, and we were consequently joined by several pedestrians, all armed to the teeth, who sought safety in numbers. Shortly after noon we halted at a small roadside inn, where we obtained some cheese, and a not very savoury compound called *kawúrma*, which consists of small square lumps of mutton imbedded in fat. At 3 p.m. we reached the solitary *khán* of Ḳádarak, which was to be our halting-place for the night. A few *zabṭiyyés* were lounging about outside, waiting for the post, which was expected to pass shortly. As it was still early, I went out into the balcony to write my diary and contemplate the somewhat cheerless view; but I was soon interrupted by our Armenian fellow-traveller, who came to tell me that the *zabṭiyyés* outside were watching my proceedings with no favourable eye, and suspected that I was drawing maps of the country. He therefore advised me either to stop writing or to retire indoors, lest my diary should be seized and destroyed. Whether the Armenian spoke the truth, or whether he was merely indulging that propensity to revile the ruling race for which the Christian subjects of the Porte are conspicuous, I had no means of deciding, so I thought it best to follow his advice and retire from the balcony till I had completed my writing.

Our fifth day's march led us through the interesting old

Armenian village of Varzahán. Just before reaching this we passed several horsemen, who were engaged in wild and apparently purposeless evolutions, accompanied with much firing of guns. It appeared that these had come out to welcome the *Ḳá'im-maḳám* of Diyádín, who had been dismissed from office, and was returning to his native town of Gyumish-Kháné; and we had scarcely passed them when he appeared in sight, met, and passed us. I wished to examine the curious old churches which still bear witness that Varzahán, notwithstanding its present decayed condition, must formerly have been a place of some importance. Our Armenian fellow-traveller offered to conduct me, and I was glad to avail myself of his guidance. After I had examined the strange construction of the churches, the Armenian inscriptions cut here and there on their walls, and the tombstones which surrounded them (amongst which were several carved in the form of a sheep), my companion suggested that we should try to obtain some refreshment. Although I was anxious to overtake our caravan, I yielded to his importunity, and followed him into a large and dimly-lighted room, to which we only obtained admission after prolonged knocking. The door was at length opened by an old man, with whom my companion conversed for a while in Armenian, after he had bidden me to be seated. Presently several other men, all armed to the teeth, entered the room, and seated themselves by the door. A considerable time elapsed, and still no signs of food appeared. The annoyance which I felt at this useless delay gradually gave way to a vague feeling of alarm. This was heightened by the fact that I was unable to comprehend the drift of the conversation, which was still carried on in Armenian. I began to wonder whether I had been enticed into a trap where I could be robbed at leisure, and to speculate on the chances of escape or resistance, in case such an attempt should be made. I could not but feel that these were slender, for I had no weapon except a small pocket revolver; five or six armed men sat by the heavy wooden door, which had been closed, and, for anything that I knew, bolted; and even should I succeed in effecting an exit, I knew that our caravan must have proceeded a considerable distance. My apprehensions were, however, relieved by the appearance of a bowl of *yoghúrt* (curds) and a quantity of the insipid wafer-like bread called *lawásh*. Having eaten, we rose to go; and when my companion, whom I had suspected of harbouring such sinister designs against my property and perhaps my life, refused to let me pay for our refreshment, I was filled with shame at my unwarranted suspicions. On emerging once more into the road I found the faithful 'Alí patiently awaiting me. Perhaps he too had been doubtful of the honesty of the Armenian villagers. At any rate he had refused to proceed without me.

About 2 p.m. we arrived at the town of Baiburt, and found that H—— and the muleteers had already taken up their quarters at a clean and well-built *khán* owned by one Khalíl Efendí. We at once proceeded to explore the town, which lies at the foot of a hill surmounted by an old fortress. Being too lazy to climb this hill, we contented ourselves with strolling through the bazaars which form so important a feature of every Eastern town, and afford so sure an index of the degree of prosperity which it enjoys. We were accompanied by the indefatigable Armenian, who, thinking to give me pleasure, exerted himself to collect a crowd of Persians (mostly natives of Khúy and Tabríz), whom he incited to converse with me. A throng of idlers soon gathered round us to gaze and gape at our unfamiliar aspect and dress, which some, bolder or less polite than the rest, stretched out their hands to finger and feel. Anxious to escape, I took refuge in a barber's shop and demanded a shave, but the crowd again assembled outside the open window, and continued to watch the proceeding with sustained interest. Meanwhile 'Alí had not been idle, and on our return to the *khán* we enjoyed better fare, as well as better quarters, than had fallen to our lot since we left Trebizonde.

Our sixth day's march commenced soon after daybreak. The early morning was chilly, but later on the sun shone forth in a cloudless sky, and the day grew hot. The first part of our way lay near the river which flows through Baiburt, and the scenery was a great improvement on anything that we had seen since leaving Gyumish-Kháné. We halted for our midday rest and refreshment by a clump of willow trees in a pleasant grassy meadow by the river. On resuming our march we entered a narrow defile leading into the mountains of Kōpdágh. A gradual ascent brought us to the summit of the pass, just below which, on the farther side, we came to our halting-place, Páshá-punárí. The view of the surrounding mountains standing out against the clear evening sky was very beautiful, and the little *ḳhán* at which we alighted was worthy of its delightful situation. We were lodged in a sort of barn, in which was stored a quantity of hay. How fragrant and soft it seemed! I still think of that night's sleep as one of the soundest and sweetest in my experience.

Early on the morning of the seventh day we resumed our march along a circuitous road, which, after winding downwards amongst grassy hills, followed the course of a river surrounded by stunted trees. We saw numerous large birds of the falcon kind, called by the Turks *doghán*. One of these H—— brought down with his rifle while it was hovering in the air, to the great delight of the muleteers. At a village called Ásh-Ḳalʿa we purchased honey, bread, and grapes, which we consumed while halting for the midday rest by an old bridge. Continuing on our way by the river, we were presently joined by a turbaned and genial Turk, who was travelling on horseback from Gyumish-Kháné to Erzeroum. I was pleased to hear him use in the course of conversation certain words which I had hitherto only met with in the writings of the old poet Fuẓúlí of Baghdad, and which I had regarded as archaic and obsolete. The road gradually became more frequented than it had been since leaving Baiburt, and we passed numerous travellers and peasants. Many of the latter drove bullock-carts, of which the ungreased axles sent forth the most excruciating sound. The sun had set before we reached our halting-place, Yeni-Khán, and so full was it that we had some difficulty in securing a room to ourselves.

The eighth day of our march, which was to conclude the first portion of our journey, saw us in the saddle betimes. After riding for four hours through a scorched-up plain, we arrived about 10.30 a.m. at the large village of Ílija, so named from its hot springs, over which a bath has been erected. From this point the gardens and minarets of Erzeroum were plainly visible, and accordingly we pushed on without halting. Fully three hours elapsed, however, ere we had traversed the weary stretch of white dusty road which still separated us from our goal; and the sun was well past the meridian when we finally entered the gate of the city, and threaded our way through the massive fortifications by which it is surrounded.

Erzeroum has one hotel, which stands midway in the scale of development between the Hôtel d'Italie at Trebizonde and an average caravansaray. Were these two towns connected by a railroad, so as to bring them within a day's journey of one another, this institution might perhaps form a happy transition between the West and the East. As things are at present, it is too much like a caravansaray to be comfortable, and too much like a casino to be quiet.

On alighting at this delectable house of entertainment, we were met by a young Armenian representing the bank on which our cheque was drawn, who informed us in very fair French that his name was Missak Vanétzian, and that his principal, Simon Dermounukian, had been apprised of our coming by letter from Trebizonde, and instructed to give us such help as we might need. After a brief conversation in the balcony of a coffee-room thronged with Turkish officers and enlivened by the strains of a semi-Oriental band, he departed, inviting us to visit his chief so soon as we were at leisure.

We now requested an attendant to show us our room, and were forthwith conducted to a large, dingy, uncarpeted apartment on the first floor, lighted by several windows looking out upon the street, and containing for its sole furniture a divan covered with faded chintz, which ran the whole length of one side, and a washing-stand placed in a curtained recess on the other. It was already occupied by a Turkish *mudír*, bound for the frontier fortress of Báyezíd, whom the landlord was trying to dislodge so that we might take possession. This he very naturally resented; but when I apologised, and offered to withdraw, he was at once mollified, declared that there was plenty of room for all of us, and politely retired, leaving us to perform our ablutions in private.

Just as we were ready to go out, an officer of the Turkish police called to inspect our passports, so, while H—— went to visit Mr Devey, the acting British Consul, I remained to entertain the visitor with coffee and cigarettes—an attention which he seemed to appreciate, for he readily gave the required *visa*, and then sat conversing with me till H—— returned from the consulate. We next paid a visit to our banker, Simon Dermounukian, called by the Turks "Símún Ághá," a fine-looking old man, who only spoke Turkish and Armenian, and whose appearance would have led one to suppose that the former rather than the latter was his native tongue. After the ordinary interchange of civilities, we drew a cheque for three or four pounds, and returned to the hotel to settle with the muleteers. On the way to Erzeroum these had frequently expressed a wish to go with us as far as Ṭeherán; but since their arrival they had been so alarmed by fabulous accounts of the dangers of travelling in Persia, the inhospitality of the country, and the malignant disposition of the people, that they made no further allusion to this plan, and on receiving the money due to them, together with a small gratuity, took leave of us with expressions of gratitude and esteem.

After a thoroughly Turkish dinner, I again proposed to go out, but the *mudír* told me that this was impossible, as the streets were not lighted, and no one was allowed to walk abroad after nightfall without a lantern. He offered, however, to introduce me to some acquaintances of his who occupied an adjoining room. One of these was a Turk who spoke Persian with a fluency and correctness rarely attained by his countrymen; the other was a Christian of Cæsarea. Both were men of intelligence, and their conversation interested me so much that it was late before I retired to rest on the chintz-covered divan, which I would gladly have exchanged for the fragrant hay of Páshá-punárí.

Next day our troubles began. The news that two Englishmen were about to start for Persia had got abroad, and crowds of muleteers—Persians, Turks, and Armenians—came to offer their services for the journey. The scene of turmoil which our room presented during the whole morning baffles description, while our ears were deafened with the clamour of voices. It was like the noisiest bazaar imaginable, with this difference, that whereas one can escape from the din of a bazaar when it becomes insupportable, this turmoil followed us wherever we went. An Armenian called Vartán demanded the exorbitant sum of £5 T. per horse to Tabríz. A Persian offered to convey us thither in a mighty waggon which he possessed, wherein, he declared, we should perform the journey with inconceivable ease. This statement, which I was from the first but little disposed to credit, was subsequently denied in the most categorical manner by our friend the *mudír*, who assured me that he had once essayed to travel in such a vehicle, but had been so roughly jolted during the first stage that he had sworn never again to set foot in it, and had completed his journey on horseback. Any lingering regrets which we might have entertained at having renounced the prospect of "inconceivable ease" held out to us by the owner of the waggon were entirely dispelled some days later by the sight of a similar vehicle hopelessly stuck, and abandoned by its possessor, in the middle of a river which we had to ford.

At length, partly because no better offer seemed forthcoming, partly from a desire to have done with the matter and enjoy a little peace and quietude for the remainder of our stay in Erzeroum, we accepted the terms proposed by a Persian muleteer called Farach, who promised to supply us with five horses to Tabríz at £2 T. and 2 *mejídiyyés* a head; to convey us thither in twelve days; and to allow us the right of stopping for two days on the road at whatever place we might choose.

I now flattered myself that I should be allowed a little peace, but I found that I had reckoned without my host. No sooner had I satisfied myself as to the efficiency of Farach's animals, agreed to the terms proposed by him, and accepted the *peh* (a pledge of money, which it is customary for the muleteer to place in the hands of his client as a guarantee that he will hold to the bargain, and be prepared to start on the appointed day), than our ears were assailed on all sides with aspersions on the honesty and respectability of the successful candidate. Farach, so I was assured, was a native of the village of Seyván, near Khúy, and the Seyvánlís were, as was well known, the wickedest, most faithless, and most dishonest people in Persia. In this assertion all the muleteers present agreed, the only difference being that while the Persians rested content with the reprobation of the Seyvánlís, the non-Persians further emphasised it by adding that the Persians were the wickedest, most faithless, and most dishonest people in the world.

At first I paid no attention to these statements, but my suspicions were in some degree aroused by Farach's disinclination to go before the Persian Consul, and by the doubts expressed by Vanétzian and Símún Ágha as to his honesty and trustworthiness. With Vanétzian I was somewhat annoyed, because he, being present when I engaged Farach, had withheld his advice till it was too late to be useful. I therefore told him that he should either have spoken sooner or not at all, to which he replied that it was still possible to rescind the bargain. Farach was accordingly summoned and requested to take back his pledge. This, however, he resolutely declined to do, and I could not help admitting that he was in the right.

Finally Vanétzian desisted from his attempts to annul the contract, and indeed retracted to some extent the objections which he had raised against it. What motive impelled him to this change of front I cannot say, and I am unwilling to credit an assertion made to me by Farach a few days later, to the effect that the Armenian's sole object in these manœuvres was to extort a bribe from the poor muleteer, and that having obtained this he was content to withdraw all opposition.

Although these annoyances, combined with a temporary indisposition (due, probably, to the badness of the water-supply), somewhat marred the pleasure of our stay in Erzeroum, the kindness shown us by Mr Devey, the British Consul, and Mr Chambers, an American missionary, and his wife, rendered it much more agreeable than it would otherwise have been. Before leaving we paid a visit to the Persian Consul, who received us very courteously, and gave us a letter to Páshá Khán of Ávajiḳ, the Persian Warden of the Marches, from whom, he added, we should receive an escort to conduct us to Khúy, should this be necessary. Beyond Khúy the country was perfectly safe, and no such protection would be required.

The consul next enquired whether we were travelling with our own horses or with hired animals, and, on learning that the latter was the case, insisted on summoning the muleteer to "admonish" him. Knowing that Farach was unwilling to appear before the consul, I ventured to deprecate this proceeding, and made as though I had forgotten the muleteer's name. The consul, however, insisted, and at once despatched some of his servants to make enquiries. These returned in a surprisingly short space of time, bringing with them the muleteer, whose appearance indicated the utmost disquietude. After demanding his name and that of his native place, the consul asked him whether it was true that he had promised to convey us to Tabríz in twelve days, and whether, if so, he had any intention of keeping this promise. To these questions the muleteer replied in a voice trembling with fear, that "perhaps, *In-sha'lláh*, he would do so." This statement was received by the consul with derision. "You lie, Mr Perhaps," cried he; "you eat dirt, Mr *In-sha'lláh*; hence, rascal, and be assured that if I hear any complaints about you, you shall give a full account of your conduct to me on your return to Erzeroum!" Whether in consequence of this "admonition," or whether, as I believe, because the muleteer was really an honest fellow, we certainly had no cause for complaint, and, indeed, were glad to re-engage Farach at Tabríz for the journey to Ṭeherán.

On Monday, 17th October, we quitted Erzeroum. In consequence of the difficulty of getting fairly under way, to which I have already alluded, it is usual to make the first stage a very short one. Indeed, it is often merely what the Persians call "*Naḳl-i-maḳán*" (change of place), a breaking up of one's quarters, a bidding farewell to one's friends, and a shaking one's self free from the innumerable delays which continue to arise so long as one is still within the walls of an Eastern town. We therefore did not expect to get farther than Ḥasan-Ḳal'a, which is about three hours' ride from Erzeroum. Before we had finished our leave-taking and settled the hotel bill (which only reached the modest sum of 108 piastres—about £1 sterling—for the two of us and 'Alí for three days) the rest of the caravan had disappeared, and it was only on emerging from the town that I was able to take note of those who composed it. There were, besides the muleteers, our friend the *mudír* and his companions and servants, who were bound for Báyezíd; a Turkish *ẓabṭiyyé*, who was to escort us as far as Ḥasan-Ḳal'a; and three Persians proceeding to Tabríz. Of these last, one was a decrepit old man;

the other two were his sons. In spite of the somewhat ludicrous appearance given to the old man by a long white beard of which the lower half was dyed red with henna, the cause which had led him to undertake so long a journey in spite of his advanced age commanded respect and sympathy. His two sons had gone to Trebizonde for purposes of trade, and had there settled; and although he had written to them repeatedly entreating them to return to Tabríz, they had declined to comply with his wishes, until eventually he had determined to go himself, and, if possible, persuade them to return home with him. In this attempt he had met with the success which he so well deserved.

As we advanced towards the low pass of Devé-boyún (the Camel's Neck), over which our road lay, I was much impressed with the mighty redoubts which crown the heights to the north-east and east of Erzeroum, many of which have, I believe, been erected since the Russian war. Beyond these, and such instruction and amusement as I could derive from our travelling companions, there was little to break the monotony of the road till we arrived at our halting-place about 3 p.m. As the *khán* was full, we were obliged to be content with quarters even less luxurious; and even there the *mudír*, with prudent forethought, secured the best room for himself and his companions.

Ḥasan-Ḳal'a is, like Ílija, which is about equidistant from Erzeroum on the other side, remarkable for its natural hot-springs, over which a bath has been erected. The *mudír* was anxious to visit these springs, and invited us to accompany him. To this I agreed, but H——, not feeling well, preferred to remain quiet. The bath consists of a circular basin, twenty-five or thirty feet in diameter, surrounded with masonry and roofed in by a dome. In the summit of the dome was a large aperture through which we could see the stars shining. The water, which is almost as hot as one can bear with comfort, bubbles up from the centre of the basin, and is everywhere out of one's depth. After a most refreshing bathe, we returned to our quarters.

Next day we started about 6 a.m., and were presently joined by a Turkish *muftí* proceeding to Báyezíd, with whom I conversed for some time in Persian, which he spoke very incorrectly and with great effort. He was, however, an amusing companion, and his conversation beguiled the time pleasantly enough till we halted about midday at a large squalid Armenian village called Kúmásúr. Our Turkish fellow-travellers occupied the *musáfir-ōda*, or guest-room, and intimated to us that they wished to be left undisturbed for their midday devotions, so we were compelled to be content with a stable. As the rest of the caravan had not yet come up, we had nothing for lunch but a few biscuits and a little brandy and water, which we fortunately had with us. Several of the Armenian villagers came to see us. They were apathetic and dull, presenting a sad contrast to the Armenians of the towns. They talked much of their grievances, especially of the rapacity of the *multeẓim*, or tax-gatherer, of the district, who had, as they declared, mortally wounded one of the villagers a few days previously, because he had brought eight piastres short of the sum due from him. They said that the heaviest tax was on cereals, amounting to 1 in 8 of their total value, and that for the privilege of collecting this the tax-gatherer paid a certain fixed sum to the Government and made what profit he could.

Quitting this unhappy spot as soon as the rest of our caravan appeared, we again joined the *mudír's* party, which had been further reinforced by a *cháwúsh* (sergeant) and two *ẓabṭiyyés*, one of whom kept breaking out into snatches of song in the shrillest voice I ever heard. For some time we succeeded in keeping up with these, who were advancing at a pace impossible for the baggage animals, but presently our horses began to flag, and we were finally left behind, in some doubt as to the road which we should follow. Shortly after this, my horse, in going down a hill to a river, fell violently and threw me on my face. I picked myself up and remounted, but having proceeded some distance, discovered that my watch was gone, having probably been torn out of my pocket when I fell. We rode back and sought diligently for it, but without success; and while we were still so occupied, Farach the muleteer came up with 'Alí. These joined us in the fruitless attempt to find the lost watch, the former attributing my misfortune to the inconsiderate haste of the *mudír*, the latter attempting to console me with the philosophical reflection that some evil had evidently been destined to befall me, and that the loss of the watch had probably averted a more serious catastrophe. At length the near approach of the sun to the horizon warned us that we must tarry no longer; and though we made as much haste as possible, it was dark before we reached the village of Deli Bábá.

Here we obtained lodgings in a large stable, at one side of which was a wooden platform, raised some two feet above the ground and covered with a felt carpet. On this our host spread cushions and pillows, but the hopes of a comfortable night's rest which these preparations raised in our minds were not destined to be fulfilled, for the stable was full of fowls, and the fowls swarmed with fleas. There were also several buffaloes in the stable, and these apparently were endowed with carnivorous instincts, for during the night they ate up some cold meat which was to have served us for breakfast. At this place I tasted buffalo's milk for the first time. It is very rich, but has a peculiar flavour, which is, to my mind, very disagreeable.

On starting the next day, we found that the *mudír*, who had obtained quarters elsewhere in the village, had already set out; neither did we again overtake him. Soon after leaving our halting-place we entered a magnificent defile leading into the mountains and surrounded by precipitous crags. On the summit of one of these crags which lay to our left was a ruined castle, said to have been formerly a stronghold of the celebrated bandit-minstrel, Kurroghlu. The face of the rock showed numerous cave-like apertures, apparently enlarged, if not made, by the hand of man, and possibly communicating with the interior of the castle.

About noon we reached a Kurdish village, situated amidst grassy uplands at the summit of the pass, and here we halted for a rest. Most of the male inhabitants were out on the hills looking after their flocks, but the women gathered round us staring, laughing, and chattering Kurdish. Some few of them knew a little Turkish, and asked us if we had any *munjas* to give them. This word, which I did not understand, appeared to denote some kind of ornament.

On quitting this village our way led us through fertile uplands covered thinly with low shrubs, on which hundreds of draught camels were feeding. The bales of merchandise, unladen from their backs, were piled up in hollow squares, in and around which the Persian camel-drivers were resting till such time as the setting of the sun (for camels rarely travel by day) should give the signal for departure.

A little farther on we passed one of the battlefields of the Russian war, and were shown an earthwork close to the road, where we were told that Fáriḳ Páshá had been killed. Soon after this, on rounding a corner, the mighty snow crowned cone of Mount Ararat burst upon our view across a wide hill-girt plain, into which we now began to descend. During this descent we came upon a party of Kurdish mountebanks, surrounded by a crowd of peasants. In the midst of the group a little girl, in a bright red dress, was performing a dance on stilts, to the sound of wild music, produced by a drum and a flute. It was a pretty sight, and one which I would fain have watched for a time; but the muleteers were anxious to reach the end of our day's journey, and indeed it was already dusk when we arrived at the village of Zeyti-Kyán. The inhabitants of this place were, as we entered it, engaged in a violent altercation, the cause of which I did not ascertain; while a few Turkish *ẓabṭiyyés* were making strenuous efforts to disperse them, in which they eventually succeeded. It was only after 'Alí had been to half the houses in the village that he succeeded in obtaining a lodging for us in the house of a poor Armenian family, who were content to share with us their only room. As usual, no sort of privacy was possible, numbers of people coming in to stare at us, question us, and watch us eat.

Next day's march was both short and uninteresting. At 2 p.m. we reached the large squalid village of Ḳará Kilísá. As the day was still young, and the place far from attractive, we were anxious to proceed farther, but this the muleteers declined to do, answering, after the manner of their class, that they had agreed to take us to Tabríz in twelve days from Erzeroum, and that this they would do; but that for the rest we must allow them to arrange the stages as they thought fit. Farach concluded the argument by making me a propitiatory gift of a melon, which he had just received from a fellow-countryman whom he had met on the road; and, half amused, half annoyed, I was obliged to acquiesce in his arrangement.

We obtained wretched quarters in the house of a very ill-favoured and inquisitive Armenian, and, after allaying our ill-humour with tea, strolled through the village to see the *yuz-báshí*, or captain of the police, about securing a *ẓabṭiyyé* as an escort for the morrow. From him we learned that our friend the *mudír* had not forgotten us, for on his way through the village that morning he had left instructions that we were to be provided with a *ẓabṭiyyé*, should we require one. The dustiness of the streets, combined with the inquisitiveness of the inhabitants, soon drove us back to our lodging, where a night disturbed by innumerable fleas concluded a miserable day.

In spite of our desire to quit so unattractive a spot, we did not start till 7.45 a.m. (a much later hour than usual), partly because we knew that the stage before us was a short one, and had no reason to anticipate better quarters at the end of it than those we were leaving; partly because 'Alí's whip had disappeared, and could not be found till our host was informed that no money would be paid him until it was forthcoming; whereupon it was speedily produced. We were accompanied by a fine old Armenian *ẓabṭiyyé*, who presented a thoroughly soldierly, as well as a very picturesque, appearance. The scenery through which we passed reminded me more of England or Scotland than anything which I had seen since leaving home. Close to the road ran a beautiful clear river, rippling down over its stony bed to join the Western Euphrates. On either side of this lay undulating grassy hills, beyond which appeared in the distance more lofty mountains. The warm, cloudy day, too, and the thin mists which lay on the hills, favoured the fancy that we were back once more in our native land.

About 1 p.m. we reached our halting-place, Táshlí-Cháy, and found lodgings in a gloomy hovel, which served the double purpose of a resting-place for guests and a stable for buffaloes. The people, however, were better than the place. Our host was an old Persian with henna-dyed beard and nails, who manifested his good feeling towards us by plunging his hand, with an introductory "*Bismi'lláh*," into the dish of poached eggs which was set before us for luncheon. His son, a bright handsome lad of sixteen or seventeen, made every effort to enliven us, and, on my enquiring whether there were any fish in the river, offered to conduct us thither, and show us not only where they were, but how to catch them. Having collected several other youths, he commenced operations by constructing a dam of stones and turf half across the river, at a point where it was divided into two branches by a bed of shingle. The effect of this was to direct the bulk of the water into the left-hand channel, while the depth of that which remained in the right-hand channel (at the lower end of which a boy was stationed to beat the water with a stick, and so prevent the imprisoned fish from effecting their escape) sunk to a few inches. Having completed these preparations, the operators entered the water with sticks in their hands, struck at the fish as they darted past, thereby killing or stunning them, and then picked them up and tossed them on to the bank. One lad had a sort of gaff wherewith he hooked the fish very dexterously. In less than an hour we had nearly fifty fish, several of which must have weighed $2\frac{1}{2}$ or 3 lbs. Some of these we ate for supper; others we gave to the muleteers and to our fellow-travellers. They were not unpalatable, and made a pleasing change from the fowls and eggs of which our fare had so long consisted.

Although our lodging was not much superior, in point of cleanliness and comfort, to that of the preceding night, it was with something like regret that I bade farewell to the kindly folk of Táshlí-Cháy. Farach had started on in front with the baggage, leaving his brother Feyẓu'lláh, of whom we had hitherto seen but little, to bear us company. This Feyẓu'lláh was a smooth-faced, narrow-eyed, smug-looking, sturdy rascal, whose face wore a perpetual and intolerable grin, and whose head was concealed rather than crowned by the large, low, conical, long-haired *pápáḵ* which constitutes the usual head-dress of the peasants inhabiting that region which lies just beyond the Turco-Persian frontier. We were also accompanied by a Turkish *ẓabṭiyyé*, who proved to be unusually intelligent; for when we were come opposite to the village of Uch-Kilísá, which lies on the farther side of the river, he told us that there was an old Armenian church there which was worth looking at, and that we should by no means neglect to pay our respects to an aged Armenian ecclesiastic, entitled by him the "*Muraḵhḵhaṣ Efendí*," who, as he assured us, enjoyed such influence in the neighbourhood that, were he to give the command, a hundred men would escort us to Tabríz.

We therefore turned aside from our course (to the infinite disgust of Feyẓu'lláh, whose only desire was to reach the end of the stage as soon as possible), and first proceeded to the church. This was a fine old building, but it had suffered at the hands of the Kurds during the Russian war, and the beautiful designs and paintings with which it had before that time been adorned had for the most part been destroyed by fire. Leaving the church, we passed the house and mill of the "*Muraḳhḳhaṣ Efendí*," who, on hearing of our approach, came out to meet us, and begged us to enter his house and partake of some refreshment. The opposition offered by Feyẓu'lláh to any further delay compelled us to decline his hospitality; yet would he scarcely take nay for an answer, saying that he was ashamed to let strangers pass by without alighting at his house. Finally, seeing that we were firm in our resolve, he bade us farewell with the words, "I pray Almighty God that He will bring you in safety to Tabríz."

It was with a sense of comfort and encouragement that we parted from the venerable and reverend old man; but this feeling was presently changed to one of indignation against Feyẓu'lláh, who had urged the length of the stage as a reason for hastening on, when, not much after 1.30 p.m., we arrived at the wretched town of Diyádín, where we were to sleep for the last time on Turkish territory. A more desolate spot I do not think I have ever seen; the dirty, dusty town, which scarcely contains two respectable houses, stands in a barren, treeless waste, and is half encompassed by a vast crescent-shaped chasm with precipitous sides. Heaps of refuse lie about in all directions, both before the doors of the miserable hovels which compose the town, and amongst the graves of the extensive and neglected cemetery which surrounds it. Of the two respectable houses which I have noticed, one belongs to the governor, the other is the post-office. To the latter we paid a visit, and conversed for a while with the postmaster and telegraph-clerk (for both functions were united in one individual), who was a Turk of Adrianople. He complained bitterly of the dullness of Diyádín, where he had been for two years, and to which a marriage contracted with a Kurdish girl had failed to reconcile him. On returning to our lodging we found that the aperture in the roof which did duty for window and chimney alike admitted so much wind and dust that we were compelled to cover it with sacking; while to add to our miseries we discovered that all our candles were used up. Having eaten our supper by the dim light of a little earthenware lamp, we had therefore no resource but to seek forgetfulness of our discomforts in sleep.

Next morning (23rd October), the seventh day of our departure from Erzeroum, we were in the saddle by 6 a.m. My spirits were high, for I knew that before sunset we should enter the land which I had so long and so eagerly desired to behold. The *ẓabṭiyyé* who accompanied us (remarkable for an enormous hooked nose) took pains to impress upon us the necessity of keeping well together, as there was some danger of robbers. Presently, on rounding a corner, a glorious view burst upon us. Ararat (which had been hidden from us by lower hills since we first saw it from the heights above Zeyti-Kyán) lay far to the left, its snowy summit veiled in clouds, which, however, left unconcealed the lower peak of little Ararat. Before us, at the end of the valley, perched midway up the face of a steep, rocky mountain, lay the town and fortress of Báyezíd, which keeps solitary watch over the north-east frontier of the Turkish Empire. This we did but see afar off, for, while two or three hours' march still separated us from it, we turned sharply to the right into the valley leading to Ḳizil-Dízé, the last village on Turkish soil. At this point we left the telegraph wires, which had, since our departure from Trebizonde, kept us company and indicated the course of our road.

Soon after mid-day we reached Ḳizil-Dízé, and, leaving our baggage in the custom-house, betook ourselves for rest and refreshment to a large and commodious *khán*. The custom-house officials gave us no trouble; but as soon as we were again on the road Farach informed us, with many lamentations, that they had exacted from him a sum of forty-five piastres, alleging, as a pretext for this extortion, that whereas he had brought seven horses with him on his last journey into Turkey, he was returning with only five; that they suspected him of having sold the two missing horses in Turkish territory; and that they should therefore exact from him the duty payable on animals imported into the country for purposes of commerce. It was in vain that Farach protested that the two horses in question had died on the road, for they demanded documentary proof of this assertion, which he was unable to produce. And, indeed, to me it seemed an absurd thing to expect a certificate of death for an animal which had perished in the mountains of Asia Minor.

The hook-nosed veteran who had accompanied us from Diyádín had yielded place to a fresh *ẓabṭiyyé*, who rode silently before us for two hours, during which we continued to ascend gradually through wild but monotonous hills, till, on reaching a slight eminence over which the road passed, he reined in his horse, and, turning in his saddle, said, "Farther I cannot go with you, for this is our frontier, and yonder before you lies the Persian land."

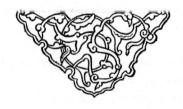

CHAPTER III

FROM THE PERSIAN FRONTIER TO TABRÍZ

"*Ché khush báshad ki ba'd az intizárí*
Bi-ummídí rasad ummídvárí!"

"How good it is when one with waiting tired
Obtaineth that which he hath long desired!"

(*Sa'dí.*)

"*Kunj-i-'uzlat, ki tilismát-i-'ajá'ib dárad,*
Fat-h-i-án dar nazar-i-himmat-i-darvíshán-ast."

"The talisman of magic might, hid in some ruin's lonely site,
Emerges from its ancient night at the mild glance of dervishes."

(*Háfiz*, rendered by Herman Bicknell.)

THERE is always a pleasant sense of excitement and expectation in entering for the first time a foreign country. Especially is this the case when to visit that country has long been the object of one's ambition. Yet that which most sharply marks such a transition, and most forcibly reminds the traveller that he is amongst another race—I mean a change of language—is not observable by one who enters Persia from the north-west; for the inhabitants of the province of Ádharbáyján, which forms this portion of the Persian Empire, uniformly employ a dialect of Turkish, which, though differing widely from the speech of the Ottoman Turks, is not so far removed from it as to render either language unintelligible to those who speak the other. If, amongst the better classes in the towns of Ádharbáyján, and here and there in the villages, the Persian language is understood or spoken, it is as a foreign tongue acquired by study or travel; while the narrow, affected enunciation of the vowels, so different from the bold, broad pronunciation of Persia proper, and the introduction of the Y-sound after K and G, at once serve to mark the province to which the speaker belongs. It is not till Ḳazvín is reached, and only four or five stages separate the traveller from Ṭeherán, that the Persian distinctly predominates over the Turkish language; while even four stages south of the capital, as far as the sacred city of Ḳum, the latter is still generally understood.

The country immediately beyond the frontier was as desolate and devoid of cultivation as that which we had just quitted, and it was not until we reached the Persian frontier-village of Ávajiḳ that we had any opportunity of observing that change of costume which constitutes the other great sign of entry amongst a new race. Indeed the approach of night, which overtook us ere we reached our destination, prevented us even then from getting more than a very partial idea of the differences which distinguish a Persian from a Turkish village. So far as we could see, however, the change was distinctly for the better; the square houses, built of unbaked clay, were clean and commodious, while a goodly array of poplar trees gave to the place an appearance of verdure which contrasted pleasantly with our too vivid recollections of the hideous waste of Diyádín.

Immediately on our arrival we sent our letter of introduction, which had been given to us by the Persian Consul at Erzeroum, to Páshá Khán, the *sar-ḥadd-dár*, or Warden of the Marches, intending to pay our respects to him in the morning before our departure. While we were eating our supper, however, a message came from him to say that he would, if we pleased, receive us at once, as he was in the habit of rising late. As this invitation was practically equivalent to a command, we hastened, in spite of our weariness and disinclination to move, to respond to it, and were presently ushered by our host, who was one of the great man's retainers, into the presence of Páshá Khán, having previously removed our boots on an intimation from the *farráshes* who stood at the door of the presence-chamber. We were invited to seat ourselves on the floor opposite the frontier-chief, who sat in a corner of the room, on the side next the door, reclining on cushions. On one side of him was seated his *vazír*, on the other a grim-looking secretary, whose face was adorned with a pair of fierce moustaches, and whose hand still held the letter of introduction which he had been reading to Páshá Khán. The Warden of the Marches conversed with me for a short time, in a somewhat fitful manner, in Persian, enquiring particularly about the terms on which England stood with Russia. Seeing, however, that he was disinclined to prolong the interview, and that he appeared moody and preoccupied (a fact due, as we subsequently learned, to a quarrel which had arisen between him and his brother), we were preparing to take our leave when several servants entered bearing trays of *piláw* and *sherbet*, of which, though we had already supped, we were compelled by politeness to partake. The *sherbet* was excellent, as was also the *piláw* (consisting of pieces of lamb's flesh buried in rice), which we had to eat, awkwardly enough, with our hands. This accomplishment, which, in spite of assiduous efforts, I never succeeded in thoroughly acquiring, is far from being so easy as might at first sight appear. The rice is pressed by the four fingers into a wedge-shaped bolus, which is then thrust into the mouth by an upward motion of the terminal joint of the thumb, placed behind it. Any grains of rice which remain clinging to the fingers must then be collected by a semi-circular sweep of the thumb into another smaller bolus, which is eaten before a fresh handful of rice is taken up. It is wonderful what dexterity the Persians acquire in this method of eating, which is indeed far more cleanly and convenient than might be supposed. To the foreigner, however, it is hardly less difficult of acquisition than the Persian manner of sitting on the heels; and if, on this our first attempt, we did not meet with the ridicule of our entertainers, it was rather from their politeness than from any dexterity on our part. On the conclusion of the meal we took our leave, Páshá Khán ordering our host in his capacity of *farrásh* to accompany us on our journey as far as Ḳará Ayné. For this we were very grateful, not so much because we hoped for any advantage from our escort, as because we had feared that it might be larger; for a large escort naturally involves considerable expense.

Next day (24th October) we started a little before 8 a.m., and we were now able to contrast the appearance of the numerous villages through which we passed with those on the Turkish side of the frontier. The comparison was certainly very much to the advantage of Persia. The houses, surrounded by gardens of poplars, were neater, cleaner, and better built than is usual in Turkey; while nearly every village contained at least one house of considerable size. The change in the costume of the people was equally striking: the fez had entirely disappeared, and its place was taken either by the thickly-lined, close-fitting skull-cap of cloth trimmed with black wool, which is called "*shiḳárí*," or by the hideous long-haired *pápáḳ* of black or brown colour which I have already noticed as constituting the head-dress of our muleteers.

Before we had gone very far we were overtaken by two more of Páshá Khán's mounted irregulars, who appeared desirous of attaching themselves to us as an additional escort, in spite of our unwillingness to accept their services. About 2 p.m. we reached the village of Ḳará Ayné, which was to be our halting-place for the night. Hearing that there was a bazaar, I was minded to visit it, but found it to be a single shop kept by a leper, whose stock-in-trade appeared to consist chiefly of small tawdry mirrors and very rank tobacco.

On the following day we were joined by two more armed horsemen, making five in all, so that our cavalcade now presented a most imposing appearance, and there seemed to be every chance that, at this rate of proceeding, we should accumulate a small army before reaching Tabríz. In order, as I believe, to sustain our flagging faith in their utility, and to convince us of the danger of the road, an alarm of robbers was started by our escort as we were traversing a narrow defile.

Assuring us that only three days ago three men had been robbed and murdered in this very spot, they galloped wildly ahead, now cautiously ascending and peeping over the summit of a hillock, now madly descending it at break-neck speed, and scouring across the country. In the caravan all were huddled together in a compact mass; and, in spite of our scepticism, 'Alí insisted on the rifle being got ready for action, while he continued to brandish an old sword (which he had bought at Erzeroum) in the most truculent manner. Notwithstanding all these preparations, no robbers appeared; and, after we had been sufficiently entertained by the evolutions of our escort, we were permitted to lapse once more into tranquillity. Early in the afternoon, after fording a river (the eminently picturesque bridge being broken down), and passing a pretty hamlet situated by the side of a stream, we arrived at the village of Zoráwa, where we halted for the night. Here we obtained very fair quarters in the house of a fine-looking old man, with some knowledge of Persian. Four or five of the inhabitants came in to stare at us and smoke their *ḳalyáns* ("hubble-bubbles"), with intermittent attempts to mend a broken door. 'Alí struck up a great friendship with our host, and, inspired by this, and the reflection that on the morrow we should reach a town of some importance, made him a present of all that remained of our tea.

Next day (26th October) we found to our delight that our escort was reduced to two, who still continued their attempts to scare us with alarms of robbers. Whether the road was indeed dangerous I do not know, but it was certainly amazingly bad. About mid-day, on emerging from a very fine gorge, we saw at our feet a wide and cultivated plain, surrounded almost entirely by mountains, except to the right, in the direction of Urumiyyé. In this plain lay the beautiful little city of Khúy, and, somewhat nearer to us, the suburb of Píré—both surrounded by a mass of gardens. The latter we reached in about an hour, and here we rested for a while. Thence onwards to the very walls of

Khúy (appropriately styled "*Dáru'ṣ-ṣafá*," "the Abode of Delight") our way lay through pleasant gardens of poplars, willows, and fruit-trees, and fields planted with cotton. At 3.30 p.m. we entered the town, and put up at a clean and well-constructed caravansaray.

While the baggage was being unloaded, I perceived that we were undergoing an attentive scrutiny on the part of a magnificent-looking dervish, who wore on his head a green turban, of which one end depended over his shoulder, and carried in his hand a shining battle-axe. Presently he began to address enquiries to 'Alí, and, on learning from him that I spoke Persian, approached me and entered into conversation. He proved to be a native of Kirmán, Mír Jalálu'd-Dín by name; and his extraordinary fertility of imagination, which often carried him far beyond the bounds, not only of the probable, but of the possible, rendered him a very amusing companion, if not a very reliable informant. He at once constituted himself our guide, philosopher, and friend, and hardly quitted us during the three days which we spent at Khúy, declaring that he perceived us to be excellent fellows, worthy of his society and conversation. He assured us that he had travelled much, and had thrice visited London, once in company with the Sháh; that he had instructed members of the Russian royal family in Persian; and that besides this, his native tongue, he was conversant with no less than ten languages, including Kurdish, Russian, and the dialect of Sístán on the eastern frontier of Persia. Having given us these details about himself, he began to question us as to our destination, and, on learning that we were bound for Tabríz, told us that we must on no account omit to visit the towns of Salmás, Khusravábád, and Dilmaghán, more especially the last, in which, as he declared, there were no less than a thousand English residents, who, through converse with dervishes and Ṣúfís, had become enlightened and philosophical. While we were engaged in conversation, a man entered the room to enquire our names and whence we came, the object for which this information was sought being, as Mír Jalálu'd-Dín informed us with perfect gravity, that it might be inserted in the newspapers of Tabríz! His imagination being now temporarily exhausted, our worthy friend bade us good-night; and, promising to be with us betimes in the morning, and to show us something of the town, left us to repose.

Our first business on awaking in the morning was to make enquiries as to the possibility of obtaining a bath in the adjacent *ḥammám*, and this indulgence was without difficulty accorded to us. On our return we found our friend the dervish awaiting our arrival. He at once launched out into a disquisition on things pertaining to his order. The true *'árif* or adept, he informed us, was distinguished by four external signs: the *tabar*, or axe, which serves to protect him during his wanderings in the desert from ferocious beasts; the *ḳeshḳúl*, or gourd slung on chains, in which he receives alms; the *táj*, or felt cap embroidered with texts, which crowns his head; and the *gísú*, or long locks, which fall over his shoulders. He then showed me some pills, compounded, as he assured me, after a prescription of the sage Loḳmán, of a substance called *barsh*, and known by the name of *ḥabb-i-nisháṭ*, or "pills of gladness." One of these he offered me to eat, assuring me that it would not fail to produce a most delightful sense of exhilaration and ecstasy; but, although I complied with his invitation, I failed to observe any such effect.

About 11 a.m. we accompanied him for a stroll through the town. He first took us to a neighbouring caravansaray and introduced us to a Syrian Christian of Urumiyyé, named Simon Abraham, who practised the trade of a photographer, and spoke English (which he had learned from the missionaries settled at that place) very well. He, in his turn, introduced us to another Syrian Christian, called Dr Samuel, who kept a dispensary at the opposite side of the caravansaray, and who likewise possessed a good knowledge of English. Both received us very cordially, and did much to render pleasant our sojourn at Khúy.

In the afternoon we were taken by the indefatigable Mír Jalálu'd-Dín to visit a *tekyé*, or retreat for dervishes, situated near the walls of the town. The dervishes, who were a most heterogeneous crew, including, besides Persians, Kurds and negroes, received us very hospitably, and gave us tea. On our return to the caravansaray, our companion introduced us to a *rammál*, or geomancer, who occupied a room adjacent to ours. This votary of the occult sciences, Mírzá Taḳí by name, was a native of Kirmánsháh. So far as I could see, he never quitted his cell, dividing his time between opium-smoking, tea-drinking, and casting the four dice-like brass cubes pivoted together whereby he essayed to unravel the mysteries of the future. After offering us a share of his tea, he proceeded to cast his dice and tell me my fortune, scribbling on a piece of paper the while, somewhat as follows:—"*Three*, *two*, *one*, *two*" (counting the numbers uppermost on the dice), "Praise be to Alláh! thou wert born under a lucky star. *One*, *one*, *three*, *four*; thy journey will be a long one, and seven months at least will elapse ere thou shalt see again thy native land. *Two*, *two*, *four*, *two*; I take refuge with Alláh, the Supreme, the Mighty! What is it that I see? Thou shalt without doubt incur a great danger on the road, and indeed it seemeth to me that one will attempt thy life before thou reachest Tabríz. *Four*, *three*, *one*, *four*; thou hast already lost, or wilt shortly lose, two things of value——" (I immediately thought of my watch, and then recollected that I had informed Mír Jalálu'd-Dín of its loss). "*Four*, *four*, *two*, *one*; our refuge is in God! A violent storm will overtake thee on thy voyage homewards, but from this thou wilt, *In-sha'lláh*, escape, by means of a talisman which I will prepare for thee. *Three*, *one*, *one*, *three*; on thy return home thou wilt marry and have four sons and three daughters. *Four*, *two*, *three*, *one*; thou hast, alas! several powerful enemies, and an evil influence threatens thy star; but shouldst thou escape these (as, please God, thou wilt do, by the help of a charm which I will presently write for thee), thou wilt without doubt gain the favour of thy Queen, and attain unto great prosperity—*In-sha'lláh!* Thy fortune," he continued, sweeping up the implements of his craft, "is, praise be to Alláh, far from bad; a proof of which is that thou hast fallen in with one truly skilled in the occult sciences, and endowed with all kinds of knowledge, who is able not only to warn thee of the misfortunes which threaten thee, but also to provide thee with the means of averting, or at least of mitigating, the same. The talismans which thou needest now are as follows:—One to protect thee from the attempt on thy life which will be made before thou reachest Tabríz; one to ensure thy safety in the storm which will assail thee on thy homeward voyage; one——"

"Honoured sir!" I interrupted at this point, "before giving you the trouble of writing so many charms, I would fain have some further proof of the efficacy of your science. I do not, indeed, like many of my countrymen, deny its existence, but of its truth I would desire a proof which you can easily afford me. To describe the events of the past is without doubt less difficult than to predict those of the future. Tell me, then, the name of my birthplace, the number of my brothers and sisters, and the adventures which have already befallen me. Then, indeed, shall I know for certain that you are a skilful magician, and that the science which you practise is not (as some of my unbelieving countrymen assert) a vain and useless thing."

Reasonable as this request appeared to me to be, it did not seem to meet with the approbation of the geomancer, who appeared suddenly to lose interest in the conversation, seeing which we withdrew to our own room, where we subsequently received a visit from our Syrian friends.

Next morning, before I was dressed, Mír Jalálu'd-Dín appeared with two small manuscripts, both of which, he said, belonged to a poor Ṣúfí, who was willing to sell them for a small sum only because he was stricken down by a mortal disease. One of these manuscripts contained, besides the well-known philosophical poem of Sheykh Maḥmúd Shabistarí known as the *Gulshan-i-Ráz* or "Rose Garden of Mystery," a treatise on the mystical science of managing the breath, from which he read me several long extracts. The other consisted of a few scattered pages from a work on medicine, which, he gravely informed me, had been written *by the hand of Galen himself*, and discovered by himself and a comrade amongst the ruins of *one of the pyramids destroyed by the English!* Not wishing to hurt the feelings of my ingenious friend by giving expression to my doubts, and thinking that some compensation was due to him for the trouble which he had been at to entertain us, I agreed to purchase these manuscripts for the moderate sum which he named.

We next visited the dispensary of Dr Samuel, whither H—— had already preceded us. Here for the first time I was able to appreciate the difficulties incidental to the practice of medicine amongst a people whose curiosity prompts them to hover round the physician long after their own cases have been dealt with, and who are only too eager to throw out hints on diagnosis and treatment whenever they get the opportunity. Our visit to the dispensary was so far unfortunate that, on returning to our caravansaray towards evening, after a stroll in the bazaar and a chat with the postmaster, I found a crowd of people assembled outside, who, on beholding me, cried out, "He comes! the Firangí *ḥakím* has arrived," and thronged after me into the square. This assembly consisted of several sick people, accompanied by a number of their friends and relatives, who, hearing that we had some knowledge of medicine, were anxious to consult us. On enquiry I learned that they had previously been attending Dr Samuel, from whom they had obtained medicine, of which they had only made a very brief trial. I therefore told them that they had better give his treatment a fair chance before deserting it for some new remedy, especially as I was convinced, both by conversation with the Syrian doctor, and by observation of his practice, that he was at least as competent as myself to advise them.

It was with much regret that on the following morning (29th October) we prepared to quit Khúy. For some time I despaired of ever getting off. Inside the room, where we were vainly attempting to pack our things, were our Syrian friends, together with Mír Jalálu'd-Dín, who had come to bid us farewell. Outside were crowds of sick people come for advice and treatment, irregular soldiers anxious to be engaged as an escort, and idle spectators; while above all was visible the ugly grinning face of Feyẓu'lláh, the muleteer, trying to hasten our departure with cries of "*Gidakh!*" which, in the Turkish dialect of Ádharbáyján, signifies "Let us go." At length, about 11 a.m., our preparations were completed, and we were on the point of starting, when Mír Jalálu'd-Dín (who had disappeared for a while previously) approached me to bid me farewell and to give me two more proofs of his good will. The first of these was a letter of introduction to a brother dervish at Tabríz, who, he assured me, would very probably consent to accompany me on my travels, and would perhaps even return with me to my native country. Unfortunately, I was unable to put this statement to the test, and the letter was never used. The second was a small white circular object, looking like an unperforated and much-worn shirt button, which he said was a talisman, sufficient, in all probability, to protect me against the danger of being robbed or murdered which had been predicted by the opium-smoking geomancer. As a further precaution, however, he added that I should do well, in the event of robbers making their appearance, to dismount from my horse, take a handful of dust from the road, blow on it, and scatter it around me, at the same time uttering the "*Bismi'lláh*," when the robbers would infallibly disperse. He then asked me to give him a *nadhr*, or offering of money, for the dervishes, who would exert their influence to protect me from harm, and, having received this, he finally bade me farewell.

Quitting the town by a gate opposite to that by which we had entered it, we passed through a long avenue of poplars, and shortly afterwards reached a point where the road bifurcated, one branch running southwards in the direction of Urumiyyé, and the other, which we pursued, eastwards towards the hills which we must cross to reach Tabríz. Near the summit of one of these hills was a small *imámzádé*, or shrine, which, as Farach informed us, was reputed most efficacious in curing persons afflicted with hydrophobia, or bitten by a serpent. After a short stage of four hours we reached a little village called Seyyid Táju'd-Dín, where we halted for the night.

Next day we continued to ascend for about two hours, until we reached the top of the pass. From this we had a magnificent view of the great salt lake of Urumiyyé, glittering in the sun, and studded with numerous rocky islands, which, as an effect of the mirage, appeared deeply indented at the base. Descending by the dry bed of a river which did duty for a road, we soon entered the plain which skirts the lake on this its northern side. Here we fell in with a wandering snake-charmer, who, after exhibiting to us the immunity with which he handled his snakes, pressed us to buy pieces of dirty bread, which he assured us would prove an infallible remedy for snake-bites. This, however, I declined to do, for I thought myself sufficiently provided with talismans for the present.

Before 2 p.m. we reached our halting-place, Tásuch, a large but uninteresting village distant about a mile from the shore of the lake. Nothing worthy of note befell us here, except the loss of a purse of money, which event our friend the geomancer, had he known of it, might perhaps have claimed as the fulfilment of a part of his prediction.

The following day's march took us to Dízé-Khalíl, a good-sized village with a fair bazaar, situated amidst gardens of poplars near the north-east corner of the lake. Here we obtained good quarters, where our host brought us, together with a present of flowers, an old copy of the *Pilgrim's Progress* left behind by some previous traveller.

Next day, Tuesday, 1st November, after a tedious march of nearly ten hours, broken by a short halt about 2 p.m. at a disconsolate village called Miyán, we reached Tabríz, the capital of the province of Ádharbáyján, the residence of the *Valí-'ahd*, or Crown Prince, and one of the largest, if not the largest, of the cities of Persia. Although we were provided with letters of introduction to Mr Abbott, the British Consul, it was too late to think of presenting them that evening, and accordingly, after threading our way for nearly an hour through the vast suburbs which surround the city, we were glad to alight at the first respectable caravansaray which we came to.

On the following morning we repaired to the British Consulate, and were very kindly received by Mr Abbott and his wife, who invited us to be their guests during our sojourn in Tabríz. We gladly accepted this invitation, for we had not seen a European since leaving Erzeroum, and had not slept in a proper bed since we quitted the Hôtel d'Italie at Trebizonde.

We remained at Tabríz four days. During this time we became acquainted with Mr Whipple, one of the American missionaries, who kindly undertook to pilot us through the interminable labyrinth of bazaars (perhaps the most extensive in Persia), and the Turkish Consul, Behjet Bey, who, in addition to an excellent knowledge of Persian, possessed the best temper, the keenest sense of humour, the cheeriest laugh, and the most voracious appetite that I have ever seen in one of his nation.

Although Tabríz is so important a town, it offers few attractions to the sight-seer beyond the bazaars, the "Blue Mosque" (*Masjid-i-Kabúd*), and the citadel (*Arg*), of which the two last are said to date from the time of Hárúnu'r-Rashíd.

Both of these monuments of antiquity we visited on the second day after our arrival. The Blue Mosque is now little more than a ruin, but the handsome tiles and inscriptions which still adorn its walls bear witness to its ancient splendour. The citadel (also said to have been originally a mosque) consists of a square enclosure with a single entrance, opposite to which rises a lofty, massive rectangular tower, accessible by means of a staircase in the left lateral wall of the quadrangle. The opposite side of the quadrangle is formed by a large *anbár*, or magazine, now used as a storehouse for arms and ammunition.

The view from the summit of the citadel is very extensive, and enabled me in some degree to realise the magnitude of the city, which lay below us like a map. From this height, in former days, criminals were sometimes hurled into the ditch below. On one occasion, we were informed, a woman condemned to suffer death in this manner was so buoyed up by the air inflating her loose garments that she reached the ground uninjured. Whether this story is true or false I cannot say, neither did I pay much attention to its recital, my thoughts being occupied with the tragic death of the young prophet of Shíráz, Mírzá 'Alí Muḥammad, better known as the Báb, which took place on 9th July 1850, at or near this spot. As I shall have to say a good deal about the Bábí religion in subsequent chapters, it may not be altogether out of place to give here a brief account of the life and death of its founder, although the history of these is well known, and has been repeatedly set forth[1].

Mírzá 'Alí Muḥammad was born at Shíráz on 9th October 1820. His father, Seyyid Muḥammad Riẓá, a cloth-merchant in that town, died while he was still of tender age, leaving him to the care of his uncle Ḥájí Seyyid 'Alí. At the age of seventeen he was sent to the port of Bushire on the Persian Gulf, where, while engaged in transacting the business with which he had been entrusted, he rendered himself conspicuous not less by the

1 See Gobineau's *Religions et Philosophies dans l'Asie Centrale*; Mírzá Kazem-Beg's articles on *Bab et les Babys* in the *Journal Asiatique* for 1866; several articles by myself in the *Journal of the Royal Asiatic Society* for 1889 and 1892; the *Traveller's Narrative, written to illustrate the Episode of the Báb*, edited, translated, and annotated by me for the Syndics of the Cambridge University Press (1891); and my translation of the *New History of Mírzá 'Alí Muḥammad the Báb* (1893).

austerity of his morals than by the sweetness and amiability of his disposition. Addicted from an early age to religious meditation, he was soon impelled to abandon commercial pursuits and to undertake a pilgrimage to Mecca and the shrines of the Imáms (so dear to every pious Persian) at Nejef and Kerbelá. Here he became the pupil of Ḥájí Seyyid Káẓim of Resht, a theologian who, notwithstanding the enmity and opposition of the orthodox Shí'ite clergy, had already begun to exert a considerable influence on Persian thought, and to gather round him a numerous band of ardent disciples. Mírzá 'Alí Muḥammad, in spite of his youth and retiring disposition, soon attracted the attention of this teacher, who did not fail to be struck by the sweet and thoughtful countenance of the young Shírází. Nor was Seyyid Káẓim the only one who yielded to a charm which few could wholly resist. Many other learned and devout men began to look with respect and affection on one whose humility only served to throw his other virtues into bolder relief. Thus were sown the seeds of that devotion which was destined ere long to write the testimony of its sincerity in letters of blood throughout the length and breadth of the Persian land, and which was to prove once more to the world that all the torments which the tyrant can devise or the torturer execute are impotent to subdue the courage born of faith and enthusiasm.

It is unnecessary for me to describe in detail the process whereby there grew up in the mind of Mírzá 'Alí Muḥammad a conviction that he was destined to become the reformer and saviour of his nation. Suffice it to say, that, after a prolonged inward struggle, on 23rd May 1844 he proclaimed himself to the world as the *Báb* or Gate whereby men might win to the sacred mysteries and spiritual truths of which he had become the recipient.

Before long he had gathered round himself a number of disciples. Amongst these were many of the most distinguished pupils of Seyyid Káẓim, whose recent death had left them temporarily without a recognised head. They eagerly adopted the doctrines of their former fellow-student, and began to preach them openly wherever they went, so that in a short time the fame of Mírzá 'Alí Muḥammad was noised abroad throughout the whole of Persia, and everywhere men began to say that the Imám Mahdí had come at last for the deliverance of the nations and the establishment of universal justice and peace.

At first but little attention was paid to the new sect by the government or clergy, but towards the end of the summer of 1845 they began to be alarmed at its rapid spread, and took measures to check its progress. The Báb, who had just returned from Mecca to Bushire, was brought to Shíráz and placed in confinement. His followers were prohibited from discussing his doctrines in public, and some of the more active were beaten, mutilated, and expelled from the town. In the early summer of 1846, however, a plague broke out in Shíráz, and, during the general consternation caused by this, the Báb effected his escape, and made his way to Iṣfahán, where he was well received by Minúchihr Khán, governor of that city, who afforded him protection and hospitality for nearly a year.

Early in 1847 Minúchihr Khán died, and his successor, anxious to curry favour with the Government, sent the Báb, under the care of an escort of armed horsemen, to the capital. So serious were the apprehensions already entertained by the Government of a popular demonstration in the prisoner's favour, that his guards had received instructions to avoid entering the towns by which they must needs pass. At Káshán, however, a respectable merchant named Mírzá Jání[1], who subsequently suffered

1 Mírzá Jání's chief claim to distinction is as the historian of the movement for which he gave his life. His history, of primary importance for the study of Bábíism, contains a vast number of curious particulars, doctrinal and biographical, which have been omitted (not unintentionally) by later Bábí writers. It is, however, extremely rare. So far as I know, only two manuscripts of it exist, and one of these contains only a third part of the work. Both these manuscripts belonged formerly to the Comte de Gobineau, and both are now in the Bibliothèque Nationale at Paris. See my translation of the *New History*, Introduction, and Appendix ii.

martyrdom for his faith, prevailed on them by means of a bribe to allow their prisoner to tarry with him two days. At the village of Khánliḳ, also near Ṭeherán, a number of believers came out to meet the Báb. Amongst these was Mírzá Ḥuseyn 'Alí of Núr in Mázandarán, who, at a later date, under the title of *Behá'u'lláh* ("the Splendour of God"), was recognised by the great majority of the Bábís as their spiritual chief, and who, till his death on 16th May 1892, resided at Acre in Syria, surrounded by a band of faithful followers, and visited yearly by numbers of pilgrims.

The king, Muḥammad Sháh, and his chief minister, Ḥájí Mírzá Āghásí, dreading the effect likely to be produced in the capital by the presence of the Báb, determined to send him to the fortress of Mákú on the north-west frontier of Persia, without allowing him to enter Ṭeherán. Thither he was accordingly conveyed; but at Zanján and Mílán he received a popular ovation, and even at Mákú it was found impossible to prevent him from receiving occasional letters and visits from his adherents. Nor did the plan of transferring him to the sterner custody of Yaḥyá Khán, governor of the castle of Chihríḳ, near Urumiyyé, meet with much better success in this respect.

Meantime, while the Báb was occupying the weary days of his imprisonment in compiling and arranging the books destined to serve as a guide to his followers after the fate which he had but too much cause to apprehend should have removed him from their midst, his emissaries were actively engaged in propagating his doctrines. Fiery enthusiasm on the part of these was met by fierce opposition from the orthodox party, headed by the clergy, and it needed only the confusion and disorder introduced into all departments of the empire by the death of Muḥammad Sháh (5th October 1848) to bring the two factions into armed collision. The strife, once kindled, rapidly assumed the most alarming proportions, and the reign of the new king, Náṣiru'd-Dín Sháh, was inaugurated by formidable insurrections of the Bábís at Yezd, Níríz, Zanján, and in Mázandarán. Of the two latter risings I shall have to say something when I come to speak of the places at which they occurred. For the present it is sufficient to state that, after the rising in Mázandarán had been suppressed with great difficulty and the sacrifice of many lives, a revolt, which threatened to defy the united efforts of the whole Persian army, broke out at Zanján. Thereupon, by the advice of Mírzá Taḳí Khán (at that time prime minister to the young king), an attempt was made to strike terror into the hearts of the insurgents, and to fill their minds with despair, by the public execution of the Báb, who, though innocent of any direct share in the plans or councils of the rebels, was regarded as the source from which they drew the enthusiasm which inspired them with a resolution so obstinate and a courage so invincible.

Accordingly, orders were despatched to Tabríz to bring the Báb thither from his prison-house, and, after the form of a trial, to put him to death. After enduring all manner of insults at the hands of the Government authorities, the clergy, and the rabble of the city, through the streets of which he was dragged for many hours, he was finally brought to the place of execution, near the citadel, a little before sundown. An immense crowd, drawn thither some by sympathy, others by a vindictive desire to witness the death of one whom they regarded as an arch-heretic, but actuated for the most part, probably, by mere curiosity, was here assembled. Many of those who composed it were at least half-convinced of the divine mission of the Báb; others, who had come with feelings of animosity or indifference, were moved to compassion by the sight of the youthful victim, who continued to manifest the same dignity and fortitude which had characterised him during the whole period of his imprisonment.

The Báb was not to suffer alone. The sentence which had been pronounced against him included also two of his disciples. One of these, Áḳá Seyyid Ḥuseyn of Yezd, who had been his companion and amanuensis during the whole period of his captivity, either actuated by a momentary but uncontrollable fear of death, or, as the Bábís assert with more probability, obediently to orders received from his Master, bidding him escape at all hazards and convey to the faithful the sacred writings of which he was the depository, declared himself willing to renounce the creed for which he had already sacrificed so much, and the Master to whom he had hitherto so faithfully adhered. His recantation was accepted and his life spared, but his death was only deferred for two years. In September 1852 he met the fate which he no longer affected to fear amongst the martyrs of Ṭeherán.

The other disciple was a young merchant of Tabríz, named Ákạá Muḥammad 'Alí. Although every effort was made to induce him to follow the example of his comrade, and though his wife and little children were brought before him, entreating him with tears to save his life, he stood firm in his faith, and only requested that at the moment of death he might still be allowed to fix his gaze on his Master. Finding all efforts to alter his decision unavailing, the executioners proceeded to suspend him alongside of his Master at the distance of a few feet from the ground by means of cords passed under the arms. As he hung thus he was heard to address the Báb in these words: "Master! art thou satisfied with me?" Then the file of soldiers drawn up before the prisoners received the command to fire, and for a moment the smoke of the volley concealed the sufferers from view. When it rolled away, a cry of mingled exultation and terror arose from the spectators, for, while the bleeding corpse of the disciple hung suspended in the air pierced with bullets, the Báb had disappeared from sight! It seemed, indeed, that his life had been preserved by a miracle, for, of the storm of bullets which had been aimed at him, not one had touched him; nay, instead of death they had brought him deliverance by cutting the ropes which bound him, so that he fell to the ground unhurt.

For a moment even the executioners were overwhelmed with amazement, which rapidly gave place to alarm as they reflected what effect this marvellous deliverance was likely to have on the inconstant and impressionable multitude. These apprehensions, however, were of short duration. One of the soldiers espied the Báb hiding in a guardroom which opened on to the stone platform over which he had been suspended. He was seized, dragged forth, and again suspended; a new firing-party was ordered to advance (for the men who had composed the first refused to act again); and before the spectators had recovered from their first astonishment, or the Bábís had had time to attempt a rescue, the body of the young prophet of Shíráz was riddled with bullets.

The two corpses were dragged through the streets and bazaars, and cast out beyond the city gates to be devoured by dogs and jackals. From this last indignity, however, they were saved by the devotion of Suleymán Khán and a few other believers, who, whether by force, bribes, or the influence of powerful friends, succeeded in obtaining possession of them. They were wrapped in white silk, placed in one coffin, and sent to Ṭeherán, where, by order of Mírzá Yaḥyá *Ṣubḥ-i-Ezel* ("the Morning of Eternity," who, though but twenty years of age, had been chosen to succeed the Báb), they were deposited in a little shrine called *Imám-zádé-i-Ma'ṣúm*, which stands by the Hamadán road not far from Ribáṭ Karím. Here they remained undisturbed for seventeen or eighteen years, till the schism originated by Behá deprived his half-brother Ezel of the supremacy in the Bábí Church which he had hitherto enjoyed, when they were removed by the Behá'ís, to whom alone is now known the last resting-place of the glorious martyrs of Tabríz.

CHAPTER IV

FROM TABRÍZ TO ṬEHERÁN

"We have a horrour for uncouth monsters; but, upon experience, all these bugs grow familiar and easy to us."—(*L'Estrange.*)

ON Monday, 7th November, bidding farewell to our kind host, we quitted Tabríz as we had entered it, with Farach's animals, which we had decided to re-engage at sixty-five *ḳráns* a head (nearly £2 sterling) for our journey to the capital. Contrary to the general rule, we managed to begin our journey with a good long stage of eight *farsaḳhs*[1]. We passed nothing of interest except a large sheet of water, lying to the north of the road, on which were multitudes of water-fowl; and, as we had made a late start, it was more than an hour after sundown when we reached Ḥájí-Áḳá, where we halted for the night.

Next day we were joined on the road by a horseman of respectable appearance, who accompanied us on our journey as far as Miyáné. His name, as I discovered, was Mírzá Háshim, and his conversation did much to beguile the tediousness of the way. Approaching the subject with some diffidence, I asked him to tell me what he knew about the Bábí insurrection at Zanján. He answered that he could not tell me much about it, except that the insurgents, whose numbers hardly exceeded 300 fighting

1 The *farsakh*, *farsang*, or parasang is a somewhat variable measure of length averaging about 3¾ miles. As Dr Wills has remarked (*Land of the Lion and the Sun*), it varies with the nature of the ground, being longer when the road is good, and shorter when it is bad. This leads me to believe that it is intended to indicate the distance which can be traversed in an hour by a good horse going at walking pace. It is, however, considerably longer than the Turkish "hour" (*sá'at*), which is only 3 miles. A caravan rarely covers a *farsakh* in an hour.

men, held at bay an army of nearly 10,000 men for nine months. He added that he had himself known one of them who had succeeded in effecting his escape after the sack of the town, and who used to boast that he had with his own hand slain 1000 of the royal troops!

In the course of the morning we passed a fine-looking though somewhat ruined building, situated on the left side of the road opposite to the village of Tikmé-Tásh, which our companion informed us was a palace built for the Sháh nearly forty years before, on the occasion of his visiting this part of his dominions. Since then it has remained unused, and has been allowed to fall into disrepair. Another neglected palace of this sort exists farther east, at Sulṭániyyé.

Farther on we passed two fine old caravansarays, constructed with the care and solidity which characterise all the work done in the glorious days of the Ṣafaví kings. These, however, we passed without halting, and pushed on to Ḳará Chiman, a picturesquely situated village, lying somewhat to the south of the main road in a little valley through which runs a river bordered with groves of poplar trees. Here we obtained very good quarters in a clean, well-constructed *bálá-khána* (upper room), commanding a fine view of the valley, river, and village.

Next morning (9th November) we passed, soon after starting, two large villages, situated at some distance from the road, the one to the north, the other to the south. The former is called Báshsiz, the latter Bulghawár. Beyond these there was little worthy of note in the parched-up undulating country through which our road lay, until, about 3 p.m., we reached our halting-place, Súmá, where we obtained good quarters at the house of one Mashhadí Ḥasan. In the evening we received a visit from our travelling companion, Mírzá Háshim; and as our next stage would bring us to Miyáné, which enjoys so evil a reputation by reason of the poisonous bugs which infest it, we asked him whether it was true, as is currently reported, that the bite of these animals proves fatal to a stranger. After assuring us that this was sometimes the case, he informed us that the so-called "Miyáné bug," or "*mala*," was not altogether confined to that town, but that it also occurred in Súmá, the village wherein we then were. The villagers, he added, have the following curious story about its origin:—

Once upon a time a native of Súmá went to the neighbouring village of Hashtarúd, where he became involved in a quarrel with the inhabitants, which culminated in his being murdered by them. From the body of the murdered man emerged a number of these *malas*, which established themselves in the village of Súmá. Whenever a native of Hashtarúd arrives there, they remember the blood-feud which exists, and avenge the death of their "ancestor" by inflicting a fatal bite upon the descendant of his murderers. To all others, however, their bite, though painful, is comparatively harmless.

Mírzá Háshim then told us of the severity of the winters at Ardabíl, and showed us a woollen cap with coverings for the ears, admirably adapted for a protection against severe cold. Having informed me that he had refused to sell it for fifteen *ḳráns* (rather less than ten shillings), he offered to make me a present of it. Of course I politely declined his offer, telling him that I could not consent to deprive him of so valuable a possession; for I had no need of the cap, and did not think it worth the sum he had mentioned.

Europeans travelling in Persia have sometimes complained of what they regard as the meanness of the Persians in offering presents in return for which they expect money. It appears to me that this complaint arises from a failure to understand the fact that such an offer from a man of distinctly lower rank than oneself is merely tantamount to a declaration that he is willing to sell or exchange the article in question. When he offers to give it as a present, he merely uses the same figure of speech as did Ephron the Hittite in negotiating the sale of the cave of

Machpelah with Abraham. All peoples make use, to a greater or less extent, of similar euphemisms, and we have no more right to blame a poor Persian for offering us a "present," in return for which he expects to receive equivalent value, than to censure as sordid the desire expressed by a cabman to be "remembered" by us.

As I have touched on this subject, I may as well say something about presents in general. There are not fewer than eight words more or less commonly used in Persian in this sense. Of these, three, viz. *armaghán*, *rah-ávard*, and *sawghát*, signify any object which one brings back from a journey to give to one's friends at home. *Yádigár* is a keepsake, to remind the owner of the absent friend by whom it was given. *Hadiyyé* is a general term for any sort of present. There remain the terms *ta'áruf*, *písh-kesh*, and *in'ám*, each of which requires a somewhat fuller explanation.

The first of these signifies a present given to some one of about the same social rank as the donor. In such cases no return is usually expected, at any rate in money. Sometimes, however, the term is used by one who, while desirous of receiving the monetary equivalent of that which he offers, does not wish to admit his social inferiority to the person to whom the "present" is offered by using the term *písh-kesh*.

When, however, a peasant, servant, muleteer, gardener, or the like, offers a present of flowers, fruits, or fowls to the traveller, he calls it a *písh-kesh* (offering), and for such he generally expects at least the proper value in money of the article so offered. When the "present" is something to which a definite monetary value can be assigned (*e.g.* an article of food), this is only right and proper. To expect a poor villager to supply travellers gratis with the necessaries of life, which he can often ill spare, and to blame him for desiring to receive the value of the same, is surely the height of absurdity. With presents of flowers the case is somewhat different. It often happens that the traveller, on visiting a garden, for instance, is confronted on his exit by a row of gardeners, each of whom offers him a bunch of flowers. He is then placed in rather a dilemma, for, on the one hand, he feels some delicacy in refusing what may, after all, be a gift prompted solely by courtesy and kindness; while, on the other hand, he may not care to pay several *ḳráns* for that which is of no use to him. Even in this case I think that Europeans are partly to blame for a custom which has, in some of the more frequented parts of Persia, become an intolerable nuisance. My reason for believing that what sometimes amounts to little less than a system of extortion (theoretically capable of unlimited expansion so long as there is a handful of flowers in the village and a peasant to bring and offer the same) originally grew out of a graceful and courteous custom of welcoming a stranger by presenting him with a nosegay, is that in parts of Persia less frequently visited by Europeans, such as the neighbourhood of Yezd and Kirmán, I have often been given a handful of roses or other flowers by a passing peasant, who continued on his way after the accomplishment of this little act of courtesy without once pausing or looking back in expectation of receiving a reward.

As regards the last kind of present, the *in'ám*, or gratuity, it is, as its name implies, one bestowed by a superior on an inferior, and is almost always given in the form of money. The term is applied not only to the presents of money spoken of above, but to the gratuities given to villagers in whose houses one puts up for the night, keepers of caravansarays and post-houses at which one alights, *shágird-chápárs* who accompany one on each stage in posting to show the way and bring back the horses, servants in houses at which one stays, and, in short, anyone of humble rank who renders one a service. To determine the amount which ought to be given in any particular case is sometimes rather a difficult matter for the traveller.

A reliable native servant is of great use in this matter; and should the traveller possess such, he will do well to follow his advice until he is able to judge for himself. The most costly *in'áms*, and those which one is most inclined to grudge, are such as must occasionally be given to the *farráshes* of a governor or other great man, who are sent to bear a present from their master, or to meet the traveller and form his escort. To these I shall have occasion to allude again.

I must now return from this digression to our march of 10th November. The day was cloudy and overcast, and soon after we had started a gentle rain began to fall. We crossed the river Ḳizil Uzan in several places, and for a considerable distance wended our way along its broad gravelly bed. Traversing the crest of a hill soon after mid-day, we came in full view of the little town of Miyáné, which looked very pretty with its blue domes and background of poplars and willows. We had no sooner reached the outskirts of the town than we were met by a number of the inhabitants, each eager to induce us to take up our quarters at his house, the advantages of which he loudly proclaimed. No sooner had we alighted at one place to examine the quarters offered, than all the competitors of its owner cried out with one accord that if we put up there we should assuredly suffer from the bite of the poisonous bugs with which, they averred, the house in question swarmed. We accordingly moved on to another house, where the same scene was repeated, each man representing his own house as the one place in the town free from this pest, and everyone except the owner uniting in the condemnation of any quarters which we seemed likely to select. Finally, in despair we selected the first clean-looking room which presented itself, and occupied it, regardless of the warnings of the disappointed competitors, who at length departed, assuring us that we had pitched on one of the very worst houses in the whole town.

Soon after our arrival we took a walk through the town, and visited the tolerably good bazaars (in which we purchased some dried figs, and a fruit called *ídar*, or, in Turkish, *ḳhunnáb*, somewhat resembling a small date, with a very large stone), and the *imámzádé*, of which the blue dome is the most conspicuous feature of Miyáné. Here, as it was Thursday evening (*shab-i-jum'a*, the eve of Friday), many people were assembled to witness a *ta'ziya*, or representation of the sufferings of the Imáms Ḥasan and Ḥuseyn. In the enclosure surrounding the building was seated a half-naked man, who held in his hand a scourge armed with iron thongs, wherewith he occasionally struck himself on the shoulders and back. All those who entered this enclosure, from which we were excluded, kissed the chains which hung in festoons across the gate.

On returning to our quarters we found a man who had brought his horse to consult us about its eye, which had received a slight injury. After advising him as to its treatment, we entered into conversation with him. He warned us that in spite of the apparent cleanliness of our lodging, he knew for certain that there were bugs in it; but on questioning him further, it appeared that his only reason for saying so was that he had seen one three years ago. Nevertheless, he advised us to take two precautions, which he assured us would protect us from injury: firstly, to keep a candle burning all night; secondly, to take a small quantity of the spirit called *'araḳ* just before going to bed. We neglected the first of these measures, but not the second; and whether owing to this, or to the absence of the *malas*, we slept untroubled by the noxious insects which have given to Miyáné so evil a reputation.

Our road next day led us towards the imposing-looking mass of the Ḳaflán-Kúh. A tortuous path brought us to the summit of the pass, whence we again descended to the river, which we crossed by a fine bridge. On the other side of this bridge we were met by a man who besought us to help him in recovering his horse from the soldiers at an adjacent guard-house, who had, as he alleged, forcibly and wrongfully taken it from him. We accordingly went with him to the guard-house, and endeavoured to ascertain the truth of the matter, and, if possible, effect a satisfactory settlement. In answer to our enquiries, the soldiers informed us that they had reason to suspect that the horse had been stolen, as it was too valuable an animal to be the lawful property of the man in whose possession they had found it. They added that if he desired to recover it, he must go to Miyáné and obtain a paper from some respectable citizen to certify that the horse really belonged to him, when it would be restored to him. With this explanation and promise we were compelled to be satisfied, and proceeded on our way till we reached another pass. On crossing this, we entered on an immense flat table-land, the surface of which was thrown into conical mounds resembling gigantic ant-hills, and thinly covered with mountain plants, which perfumed the air with their fragrance. The ground was riddled with the holes of what appeared to be a kind of jerboa. These little animals were very fearless, and allowed us to approach quite close to them before they retreated into their burrows.

About 4 p.m. we reached the compact and almost treeless village of Sarcham, where we halted for the night. Just before reaching it we came up with one of those "caravans of the dead," so graphically described by Vámbéry. The coffins (which differ in some degree from those used in Europe, the upper end being flat instead of convex, and furnished with two short handles, like a wheelbarrow) were sewn up in sacking, to which was affixed a paper label bearing the name of the deceased. Each animal in this dismal caravan was laden with two or three coffins, on the top of which was mounted, in some cases, a man or woman, related probably to one of the deceased, whose bodies were on their way to their last resting-place in the sacred precincts of Ḳum.

We had no difficulty in getting lodgings at Sarcham, for the place contains an extraordinary number of caravansarays, considering its small size, and the inhabitants vied with each other in offering hospitality.

Next day (Saturday, 12th November) we started early, being

given to understand that a long stage lay before us. All day we followed the course of the river, which is a tributary of the Ḳizil Uzan, though here it seems to be known by the name of the Zanján-áb. Dense fogs obscured the sun in the earlier part of the day, but these rolled away as the heat increased, leaving a cloudless sky. The air was perfumed with the scent of the plant which we had observed on the preceding day. On our march we passed three immense caravans, consisting respectively of 102, 72, and 39 camels, bearing merchandise to Tabríz. There is to my mind an indescribable dignity about the camel, who seems to eye one scornfully with half-turned head as he passes majestically on his way; and the sight of a string of these animals was one of which I never grew weary. On the road we saw a serpent, as well as numbers of lizards, and a small tortoise, which our muleteers called *sparghá*, a word which I have never heard elsewhere, and which seems to be purely local.

About 3 p.m. we reached the village of Níkh-beg, where we halted. It is a squalid-looking place, devoid of trees, and only remarkable for a very fine old caravansaray of the Ṣafaví period, which bears an inscription over the gateway to the effect that it was repaired by order of Sháh Ṣafí, who alighted here on his return from the successful siege of the fortress of Erivan. While copying this inscription, we were surprised and pleased to perceive the approach of Mr Whipple, the American missionary, who was posting from Tabríz to Hamadán to visit his fellow-workers there.

Our next stage brought us to the considerable town of Zanján, so celebrated for its obstinate defence by the Bábís against the royal troops in the year 1850. It lies in a plain surrounded by hills, and is situated near, but not on, the river called Zanján-áb, which is at this point surrounded by gardens. The town has never recovered from the effects of the siege, for, besides the injury which it sustained from the cannonade to which it was exposed for several months, a considerable portion was burnt by the besieged on one occasion, when they were hard pressed by the enemy, to create a diversion. We entered the town by the western gate, passing on our left an extensive cemetery, of which two blue-domed *imámzádés* constitute the most conspicuous feature.

We alighted at a caravansaray near the bazaar, which we visited shortly after our arrival. It is not very extensive, being limited to one long street running east and west more than half through the town (which is much longer in this direction than from north to south). The great drawback to Zanján is the enormous number of beggars who throng its streets and importune the traveller for alms with cries of "*Alláh neját versin! Alláh neját versin!*" ("May God give you salvation!"). In this respect it is unrivalled, so far as I have seen, by any town in Persia, with the exception of Kirmán; and even there, though the poverty of the mendicant classes is probably greater, their importunity is far less.

In the evening we received a visit from a very rascally-looking Ṭeheráni with a frightful squint, who enquired if we had any *'araḳ*, and, on learning that we had, requested permission to introduce some companions of his who were waiting outside. These presently appeared, and, having done full justice to the *'araḳ*, which they finished off, suggested that we might perhaps like to hear a song. Without waiting for an answer, one of them broke forth into the most discordant strains, shouting the end of each verse which struck him as peculiarly touching into the ear of the man who sat next him, who received it with a drunken simper and a languid "*Bali*" ("Yes"), as though it had been a question addressed to him. When this entertainment had come to an end, the eyes of our visitors fell on my pocket-flask, which they began to admire, saying, "This bottle is very good, and admirably adapted for the pocket...but we have already given enough trouble." As I affected not to understand the purport of their remarks, they presently departed, to our great satisfaction.

From the difficulty which the squint-eyed man seemed to experience in getting his feet into his shoes, I fancied that our '*araḳ* was not the first which he had tasted that night.

We remained at Zanján during the next day, for I was anxious to examine the town and its walls, with a view to obtaining a clearer idea of the history of the siege, and the causes which had enabled the Bábí insurgents to keep the royal troops at bay so long. Sir Henry Bethune, quoted by Watson in his *History of Persia under the Kájár Dynasty*, says that in his opinion the place ought to have been subdued by a regular army in a few days, and, so far as I can judge, it possesses no natural advantages as a stronghold. It is true that it is surrounded by a wall (now destroyed in some places), but though this averages twenty or twenty-five feet in height, it is built of no stronger material than unbaked clay. The desperate resistance offered by the Bábís must therefore be attributed less to the strength of the position which they occupied than to the extraordinary valour with which they defended themselves. Even the women took part in the defence, and I subsequently heard it stated on good authority that, like the Carthaginian women of old, they cut off their long hair and bound it round the crazy guns to afford them the necessary support. The fiercest fighting was on the north and north-west sides of the town, by the cemetery and Tabríz gate. Unfortunately there was no one from whom I could obtain detailed information about the siege. This I regretted the more because I was convinced that, could I have found them, there must have been many persons resident in Zanján who had witnessed it, or even taken part in it. I had, however, at that time no clue to guide me to those who would probably have preserved the most circumstantial details about it, viz. the Bábís. There was therefore nothing to induce me to prolong my stay, and accordingly, after one day's halt, we left Zanján on 15th November for Sulṭániyyé.

The road from Zanján to Sulṭániyyé runs through a perfectly flat stony plain bounded by low hills to the north and the south, and is devoid of interest. Nearly three hours before reaching the latter place we could plainly see the great green dome of the mosque for which it is so celebrated. From a distance this appeared to form part of a mass of buildings, which, on nearer approach, proved to be a large palace constructed in the modern style, and situated some way to the north-west of the mosque.

We paid a visit to the mosque immediately on our arrival, and were shown over it by an old Seyyid who spoke Persian. It is built in the shape of an octagon, and is surmounted by the large green dome which forms so conspicuous a feature of the landscape. From one side of the octagon (that farthest from the road) is thrown out a rectangular annexe containing the *miḥráb*. The main entrance is on the east side. The interior of the building is lined with most exquisite tile-work, and beautiful inscriptions in Arabic. In some places, where these tiles have been destroyed or removed, an older, deeper layer of still finer pattern is visible. As the mosque is no longer used, the European traveller meets with none of the difficulties which usually form an insuperable obstacle to visiting similar buildings in Persia. The village of Sulṭániyyé must formerly have been a flourishing place, but it now consists of only a few hovels, which form a sad contrast to the ancient splendour of the mosque.

As to the date when the mosque was built, our guide was unable to inform us, but he said that it had been repaired and beautified by Sháh Khudá-bandé, concerning whom he repeated some lines of doggerel, which we had already heard from the muleteer, and which ran as follows:—

"*Ey Sháh Khudá-bandé,*
Ẓulm kunandé,
Íkí ṭá'úḳ bir kandé!"

"O Sháh Khudá-bandé, practiser of tyranny, two fowls to one village!"

The last line of this is Turkish: what event it alludes to, or what its real purport is, I was unable to ascertain. Our guide informed us that some time ago a European engineer had spent a week at this place, making elaborate plans and drawings of the mosque. Having completed our inspection, we offered a small sum of money to the old Seyyid who had accompanied us; but he bade us give whatever we wished to his son, a little boy, who had also followed us. I accordingly gave him two *ḳráns*, which appeared to me a sufficient recompense for the amount of trouble we had given, but the Seyyid seemed to be of a different opinion, remarking that it was "a very trivial sum for people of distinction." I asked him what reason he had for supposing that we were "people of distinction," to which he only replied that we were "*mukhtár*"—free to do as we pleased.

Besides the mosque and the palace, there are several little *imámzádés* at Sulṭániyyé, and I was anxious to remain another day to examine these. Farach, however, appeared to divine my intention and took pains to frustrate it, for he avoided me all the evening, instead of coming in after supper, as he usually did, to discuss the events of the day, and sent off all the baggage early in the morning, so that we had no course open to us but to proceed. After another uneventful stage, we reached our next halting-place of Khurram-dére—a pretty village situated on a river, surrounded by poplars and willows—about 4.30 p.m. Here, as usual, we were very hospitably received by the villagers, two of whom came out some distance to meet us and conduct us to their house, where we were lodged in a very good upper room, thickly carpeted, and furnished with eight large windows provided with shutters.

Next day we started early, the muleteers pretending that they would try to reach Ḳazvín that evening, which, as I believe, they had from the first no intention of doing. Our road ran towards the north-east in the direction of a low range of hills. On reaching the highest point of the ridge we could see before us the mighty range of the Elburz mountains, which separates Persian 'Iráḳ from the humid, richly-wooded provinces bordering on the Caspian Sea. Between us and these mountains lay a wide, flat, stony plain, in which the position of Ḳazvín was clearly indicated by the thin pall of blue smoke which hung over it. Towards this plain our road now began to descend, and in a few minutes we arrived at the village of Kirishkín, where the muleteers announced their intention of halting for the night—a decision from which it was impossible to move them, and to which I was in great measure reconciled by the kindly welcome given to us by the inhabitants. Here, indeed, a marked change was observable in the people, who appeared much brighter, more intelligent, and more amiable than the natives of Adharbáyján. The latter, with their scowling faces and furtive gray eyes, are not popular amongst the Persians, whose opinion about the inhabitants of their metropolis, Tabríz, is expressed in the following rhyme:—

"*Zi Tabrízí bi-juz ḥízí na-biní:*
Hamán bihtar ki Tabrízí na-biní."

"From a Tabrízí thou wilt see naught but rascality:
Even this is best, that thou shouldst not see a Tabrízí."

The change in the appearance of the people is accompanied by a change in language, for this was the first place we came to at which the Persian tongue appeared to preponderate over the Turkish.

At this village we obtained the most sumptuous quarters in a large room, twenty-five feet long by fifteen wide, thickly spread with carpets. A few works of Persian poetry, placed in niches in the wall, showed that our entertainers united a taste for literature with a love of comfort. In the course of the evening we received a visit from our host and his sons. One of the latter—the one to whom the books chiefly belonged—was a bright intelligent youth who discussed the merits of various Persian and Turkish poets with great zest. I was much amused at one remark which he made. Speaking of the recently-concluded *ta'ziyas* (dramatic representations of various moving episodes in the lives of the Prophet and his successors), and especially of the scene wherein the "Firangí ambassador" at the court of Damascus, moved by the misfortunes and patience of the captive believers, embraces Islám, and is put to death by the cruel tyrant Yezíd, he said, "How I wish you had come here a little earlier, for then we could have borrowed your hats and clothes for the Firangís, and indeed you might have even taught us some words of your language to put in the mouths of the actors who personated them. As it was, not knowing anything of the tongue of the Firangís, we had to make the actors who represented them talk Turkish, which seemed to us the nearest approach possible to Firangí speech."

Next day we reached Ḳazvín after a short stage, during which we descended into the plain of which I have already spoken. Here we intended to halt for a day to see the town, which is of considerable size and contains many fine buildings. Amongst these is a *mihmán-kháné*, or guest-house, which is one of a series constructed between Enzelí and Ṭeherán, and thence as far south as Ḳum. At this, however, we did not put up, as I was anxious to cling for a few days longer to the more Oriental abodes to which I had become not only accustomed, but attached, and which I foresaw would have to be abandoned on reaching Ṭeherán in favour of more civilised modes of existence. Unfortunately, our muleteers, either through indifference or ignorance, took us to a very poor caravansaray, far inferior in comfort to the quarters which we had enjoyed since leaving Zanján, where we had suffered in a similar way. Indeed it is usually the case that the traveller (unless provided with introductions) fares less well in the towns than in the villages.

We spent most of the following day in wandering through the bazaars and examining the appearance of the town and its inhabitants. The bazaars were much like those which we had already seen at Khúy, Tabríz, and Zanján; but as regards the people, the advantage was decidedly in favour of the Ḳazvínís, who are more pleasing in countenance, more gentle in manners, and rather darker in complexion than the Ádharbáyjánís. Persian is spoken by them universally, but almost all understand Turkish as well.

The road from Resht to Ṭeherán, which is the route usually taken by those entering Persia from Europe, passes through Ḳazvín. This road we now joined, and by it we proceeded to the capital, accomplishing the journey thither in three days. As it is probably the best known and the least interesting of all the roads in Persia, I will not describe it in detail, and will only notice certain points which appear worthy of mention.

First of all the *mihmán-khánés*, or guest-houses, of which I have already spoken, merit a few words. They were built, I believe, by order of Náṣiru'd-Dín Sháh on his return from his first visit to Europe. They are intended to afford the traveller by the ordinary route to the capital greater comfort and better accommodation than are obtainable in caravansarays, and to fulfil in some degree the functions of a hotel. I cannot say that I was at all favourably impressed by these institutions, at the first of which, called Ḳishlákh, we arrived on the evening of the day of our departure from Ḳazvín (20th November). It is true that they are well built, and stand in gardens pleasantly surrounded by trees; that the rooms are furnished with European beds, chairs, and tables; and that cooked food can be obtained from the attendants. But these advantages are, to my mind, far more than counterbalanced by the exorbitance of the charges and the insolence of the servants, which contrasted painfully with the ready hospitality, genial courtesy, and slight demands of the villagers in whose humble but cleanly homes we had hitherto generally found a resting-place at the end of our day's journey.

The *mihmán-khánė́*, in short, has all the worst defects of a European hotel without its luxury. Let me briefly describe our experiences at one—that of Ḳishlákh—as a specimen which will serve for all. On our first arrival we are discourteously told that there is no room. Remonstrances and requests are alike useless, so we prepare to move on and try to find a village where we can halt for the night, which is now rapidly advancing. We have hardly started, after a considerable delay to allow of the baggage-animals coming up, when a man runs after us and informs us that there *is* room. No explanation or apology is offered for the previous statement, but, as no other habitation is in sight, we decide to turn back. On dismounting, we are conducted to a room littered up, rather than furnished, with several beds, a number of cane-bottomed chairs, and a table or two. The windows are furnished with tawdry curtains; the walls are bedecked with tinselled mirrors and gaudy pictures; while on the washing-stand a single ragged tooth-brush is ostentatiously displayed by the side of a clothes-brush, which would seem to be intended to serve as a hair-brush as well.

While contemplating this chaos of luxury, and meditating somewhat sadly on the unhappy effect produced in Eastern lands by the adoption of Western customs, I became aware of a stir outside, and, rushing out, was just in time to see the *Imám-Jum'a*, or chief ecclesiastic, of Tabríz drive up in a carriage followed by a number of attendants in other vehicles. By the side of the road lay the bleeding carcase of a sheep, whose throat had just been cut to do honour to the approaching dignitary. This not very graceful custom is common in Persia, and Mr Abbott, the British Consul at Tabríz, informed me that he had great difficulty in preventing its performance whenever he returned to Persia after an absence in Europe.

Before we retired for the night—not on the unattractive-looking beds, but, as usual, on our Wolseley valises—we received another proof of the advance of European ideas in the neighbourhood of the capital in the form of a *bill* (a thing which we had not seen since we left Erzeroum), in which two *ḳráns* were charged for "service," which charge the bearer of the document was careful to inform us was not intended to prevent us from bestowing on him a further gratuity. The total amount of the bill was eight *ḳráns*—not much, indeed, but about double the sum which we had usually expended for a night's lodging hitherto—and we were requested to settle it the same evening—a request which showed that a becoming suspicion of one's fellow-creatures was amongst the European "improvements" introduced by the *mihmán-khánés*.

The muleteers, who had been compelled to pay an exorbitant price for food for their animals, were not less disgusted than ourselves, and declared that they would henceforth avoid *mihmán-khánés* entirely. Next day, accordingly, passing two of these, we made a long stage, and halted about nightfall at a walled village called Ḳal'a-i-Imám-Jum'a, where we were assured by Farach that we should find "everything that our hearts desired." Unless he fancied that our hearts would desire nothing but melon-peel, which was scattered freely about the floor of the little cell where we took up our quarters, Farach's promise must have been dictated less by a strict regard for truth than by a fear of being compelled by us to halt at a *mihmán-khánė*. However, we eventually succeeded in obtaining some bread from a kindly Persian who had become cognisant of our need, and with this, and the last remains of the preserved meats bought at Trebizonde, we managed to appease our hunger, consoling ourselves with the thought that this would be our last night in the wilderness for the present, and that on the morrow we should be amongst the fleshpots of Ṭeherán.

Next morning we were astir early, for the excitement of being so near the Persian capital made sloth impossible. Yet to me at least this excitement was not free from a certain tinge of sorrow at the thought that I must soon bid farewell to the faithful Farach, whom, notwithstanding his occasional obstinacy and intractability, I had learned to like. Moreover, difficult as may be the transition from European to Asiatic life, the return is scarcely easier. I sighed inwardly at the thought of exchanging the free, unconstrained, open-air existence of the caravan for the restraints of society and the trammels of town life; and it was only when I reflected on the old friends I should see again, and the new friends I hoped to make, that I felt quite reconciled to the change before me.

This day's march was the most interesting since leaving Ḳazvín. To the north, on our left hand, towered the long range of the Elburz mountains, much loftier and bolder in outline here than at their western extremity; nor had we proceeded far when there burst suddenly on our view the majestic snow-capped cone of Mount Demávend, where, as ancient legend runs, the tyrant-parricide, Ẓaḥḥáḳ, lies bound in chains. At the base of this giant wall are gentler slopes, covered with villages which serve as a summer retreat to the more opulent when the heat of the capital has become intolerable. Near the road for some distance runs the river Karach, bright and rippling; while, to the south of this, numerous little villages set with poplars diversify the monotony of the gray stony plain. Once or twice we passed bands of soldiers returning from their military service to their homes in Ádharbáyján, and then a mighty caravan of 111 camels wending its slow course westwards. Then, all at once, our eyes were dazzled by flashes of light reflected from an object far away towards the south, which shone like gold in the sun. This I at first imagined must be the situation of the capital, but I was mistaken; it was the dome of the holy shrine of Sháh 'Abdu'l-'Aẓím, situated five or six miles south of Ṭeherán, which, lying as it does somewhat in a hollow, is not clearly seen until it is almost reached. At length, however, at a little roadside tea-house, where we halted for refreshment, we came in sight of it.

Many such tea-houses formerly existed in the capital, but most of them were closed some time ago by order of the Sháh. The reason commonly alleged for this proceeding is that they were supposed to encourage extravagance and idleness, or, as I have also heard said, evils of a more serious kind. Outside the town, however, some of them are still permitted to continue their trade and provide the "*bonâ fide* traveller" with refreshment, which, needless to say, does not include wine or spirits.

At length, about sunset, we entered the city by the *Derwázé-i-Naw* (New Gate), and here we were accosted by one Yúsuf 'Alí, who, though he wore the Persian dress, was, as he proudly informed us, a British subject of Indian nationality. We asked him what accommodation was to be found in Ṭeherán. He replied that there were two hotels, one kept by a family called Prevost, of French or Swiss extraction, the other by a man called Albert, and advised us to go to the latter, because it was cheaper. As, however, we purposed making a sojourn of some length in the capital, and the comfort of our abode was therefore a matter of more importance than when we were halting only for a night or two, we determined to inspect both places on the following day, and in the meantime, as it was now late, to take up temporary quarters at a caravansaray situated not far from the gate whereby we had entered.

CHAPTER V

ṬEHERÁN

"There was a most ingenious Architect, who had contrived a new Method for building Houses, by beginning at the Roof, and working downwards to the Foundation, which he justified to me, by the like Practice of those two prudent Insects, the Bee and the Spider."—(*Swift.*)

HITHERTO I have, in describing my travels, followed pretty closely the journals which I kept during their continuance, only amplifying such things as appeared unfamiliar or interesting, and suppressing or abridging entries which I deemed to be of consequence to no one but myself. Now, however, a different plan becomes necessary; for since I continued at the Persian capital for about ten weeks, and since many days passed uneventfully, either in study or in conversation with friends and acquaintances, a full record of this period would necessarily be both prolix and unprofitable. I shall therefore include in this chapter all that I have to say about the people, topography, institutions, public buildings, gardens, squares, palaces, mosques, and educational establishments of Ṭeherán, to which I shall add a short notice on the royal family, a description of some entertainments to which I was admitted as a guest, and a few anecdotes illustrative of the Persian genius and character.

Now, my stay at Ṭeherán was divided into two periods, differing somewhat in character. During the first, which began on the second day after our arrival (24th November), and ended with the departure of my companion H—— on 29th December, we lodged at Prevost's Hotel, and were for the most part occupied with sight-seeing and social distractions, from both of which we derived much profit and pleasure. But when we had become thus generally conversant with the life of the capital, H——, who had no special interest in the language, literature, or science of the Persians, and whose time was, moreover, limited, desired to continue his journey to the Persian Gulf; while I, finding at Ṭeherán facilities for the prosecution of my studies which I was unwilling to let slip, wished to remain there. So, finding our objects incompatible, we were compelled to separate. He left Ṭeherán for the south on 29th December, taking with him our Turkish servant 'Alí, who was unwilling to remain in Persia longer than he could help, since he found the people and the climate equally uncongenial. These, then, journeyed gradually southwards, halting for a while at the chief towns through which they passed, until about the beginning of April they reached Bushire, and thence took ship homewards.

Soon after their departure, about the beginning of the new year (1888), I was invited by my friend the Nawwáb Mírzá Ḥasan 'Alí Khán, a Persian nobleman whose acquaintance I had made in London, to take up my abode with him in a house which he had rented near the English Embassy. Of this kind offer I very gratefully availed myself, and continued for the remainder of my stay in Ṭeherán (*i.e.* till 7th February 1888) an inmate of his house, to my great pleasure and advantage. For my whole desire was, as my host well knew, to obtain as full an insight as possible into Persian life; and though he was thoroughly conversant with the English language, yet, out of regard for me, he rarely talked with me save in Persian, except that in the evening he would sometimes ask me to read with him a chapter of Carlyle's *Heroes and Hero-Worship*, which work, by reason of the favourable opinion of the Prophet Muḥammad entertained by the author, is very highly esteemed by Muḥammadans acquainted with English. Moreover most of my host's visitors and all his servants were Persian, and spoke, for the most part, only Persian (though his younger brother, an officer in the Persian army, and two of his nephews, whom I had known in London, had been educated partly in England and spoke English extremely well), so that I was not only able but forced to make much progress in speaking and understanding. And during all this time I was able to benefit by the teaching of a very able scholar, Mírzá Asadu'lláh of Sabzawár, a pupil of the late Ḥájí Mullá Hádí of Sabzawár, the greatest philosopher whom Persia has produced during the nineteenth century. Thus was I enabled to obtain some insight into the philosophical doctrines current in Persia, of which I shall say something in the next chapter.

The European colony in Ṭeherán is considerable, and the society which it affords equally remarkable for distinction and hospitality. It comprises the *corps diplomatique* attached to the different embassies (and almost every European nation of note is represented, as well as the United States of America); the staff of the Indo-European Telegraph; the American missionaries; several merchants and men of business; and a few Europeans employed in the Persian service. From many of these I received much hospitality and kindness, which I shall not soon forget, and on which I would gladly dwell did I feel justified in so doing. But my business at present is not to attempt an inadequate discharge of personal obligations (a discharge, moreover, which would probably be unacceptable to those to whom I am so indebted), but to depict with such fidelity as I may the life, character, and customs of the Persians. Of the European colony, then, I will say no more than this, that it is associated in my mind with every feeling of gratitude and every pleasant remembrance which kindness and hospitality received in a strange land can evoke in the heart or impress on the mind of the recipient.

Ṭeherán, as everyone knows, was not always the capital of Persia. In the most ancient days the province of Fárs, or Persia proper, and at a later time Iṣfahán, generally enjoyed this dignity. At other times, when, on the decay of some great dynasty, the empire was split up into numerous fragments, princes of different dynasties often reigned over one or two provinces, fixing the seat of government at the most important town in their dominions. Under the Ṣafaví kings, when the ancient greatness of Persia enjoyed a temporary revival, it was Iṣfahán which was graced by their splendid court. About a century ago, when the great struggle between the Zend dynasty and the family of the Ḳájárs was in progress, the former, represented by the noble and generous Karím Khán, had its capital at Shíráz, while the latter, personified by that atrocious and bloodthirsty tyrant Áḳá Muḥammad Khán, fixed their headquarters at Ṭeherán. On the final victory of the latter, the northern city, situated as it is near the lands from which sprung the originally Turkish tribe of the Ḳájárs, was definitely raised to the rank of capital, and has enjoyed this dignity ever since, while each of the three kings who succeeded the founder of the dynasty further exerted himself to enlarge and beautify the city.

Ṭeherán, as it is at present, is a large town lying in a slight hollow, just sufficient to prevent its being seen from any distance on the plain; roughly speaking circular in shape; and entirely surrounded by walls of unbaked clay, and for the most part by a ditch as well. Access is given to the interior by twelve gates, which are as follows:—

Between the north and the east—

1. The *Derwázé-i-Behjetábád*,
2. The *Derwázé-i-Dawlat*,
3. The *Derwázé-i-Shimrán*,

leading to the gardens, palaces, and villages situated to the north of the city on the slopes of Elburz.

Between the east and south—

4. The *Derwázé-i-Dawshán-tepé*, leading to the Sháh's hunting-palace of Dawshán-tepé ("Hare-hill").
5. The *Derwázé-i-Dúláb* ("the Mill Gate").
6. The *Derwázé-i-Mashhad* ("the Mashhad Gate").

Between the south and west—

7. The *Derwázé-i-Sháh-'Abdu'l-'Azím* (through which passes the great caravan road to the south).
8. The *Derwázé-i-Ghár* ("the Cave Gate").
9. The *Derwázé-i-Naw* ("the New Gate").

Between the west and north—

10. The *Derwázé-i-Gumruk* ("the Custom-house Gate").
11. The *Derwázé-i-Ḳazvín* ("the Ḳazvín Gate").
12. The *Derwázé-i-Asp-daváni* ("the Race-course Gate").

To the north of the city are numerous gardens; some, like Behjetábád and Yúsufábád, situated within a short walk of the walls; some in the villages of Shimrán, like Ḳulahak and Tajrísh, which serve as summer retreats to the Europeans and rich Persians, distant five or six miles from the town; and others yet more distant, on the slopes of Elburz. Some of the gardens belonging to the royal family are very beautifully laid out, as, for example, the garden called *Kámrániyyé*, which is the property of the Sháh's third son, the Ná'ibu's-Salṭana. The Persians take the greatest delight in their gardens, and show more pride in exhibiting them to the stranger than in pointing out to him their finest buildings. Yet to one accustomed to the gardens of the West they appear, as a rule, nothing very wonderful. They generally consist of a square enclosure surrounded by a mud wall, planted with rows of poplar trees in long straight avenues, and intersected with little streams of water. The total absence of grass seems their greatest defect in the eyes of a European, but apart from this they do not, as a rule, contain a great variety of flowers, and, except in the spring, present a very bare appearance. But in the eyes of the Persian, accustomed to the naked stony plains which constitute so large a portion of his country, they appear as veritable gardens of Eden, and he will never be happier than when seated under the shade of a poplar by the side of the stream, sipping his tea and smoking his *ḳalyán*. What I have said applies to the great majority of gardens in Persia, but not to all; for some of those in Shíráz are very beautiful, and, except for the lack of the well-trimmed lawns which we regard as so indispensable to the perfect beauty of a garden, might well defy all competition.

Many of the gardens near Ṭeherán are cultivated by "Guebres," the remnant of the ancient faith of Zoroaster. The headquarters of Zoroastrianism in Persia are at Yezd and Kirmán, in and about which cities there may be in all some 7000 or 8000 adherents of the old creed. In other towns they are met with but sparingly, and are not distinguished by the dull yellow dress and loosely-wound yellow turban which they are compelled to wear in the two cities above-mentioned. As I shall speak of this interesting people at some length when I come to describe my stay amongst them in the only two places in Persia where they still exist in any numbers, I will not at present dwell on their characteristics further than to allude briefly to their *dakhmé*, or "tower of silence," situated two or three miles south of Ṭeherán, on one of the rocky spurs of the jagged mountain called Kúh-i-Bíbí Shahr-bánú.

Bíbí Shahr-bánú was the daughter of the unfortunate Yezdigird III, whose sad fate it was to see the mighty empire of the Sásánians and the ancient religion of Zoroaster fall in one common ruin before the savage onslaught of the hitherto despised Arabs, ere he himself, a hunted fugitive, perished by the hand of a treacherous miller in whose house he had taken refuge. The daughter subsequently married Ḥuseyn, the son of 'Alí, thus uniting the royal blood of the house of Sásán with the holy race of the Imáms and the kindred of the Arabian prophet. To this union is perhaps to be attributed in some degree the enthusiasm with which the Persians, bereft of their old religion, espoused the cause of 'Alí and his successors (or in other words the Shí'ite faction of the Muḥammadans) against the usurpations of those whom the Sunnís dignify with the title of *Khalífa*, or vicegerent of the Prophet. After the calamities suffered by the family of 'Alí at the hands of their ruthless foes, Bíbí Shahr-bánú is said to have fled to Persia, and to have found a refuge from her oppressors in the mountain just to the south of Ṭeherán which still bears her name. It is said that the place where she hid is still marked by a shrine which has the miraculous property of being inaccessible to men, though women may visit it unimpeded. Where this shrine is I do not know, neither did I make any attempt to test the truth of the legend.

The Guebres' *dakhmé* is situated midway up a sharp ridge which descends from the summit of this mountain on the northern side, and is a conspicuous object from a distance. It consists of a circular tower of clay or unbaked brick, of the grayish colour common to all buildings in Persia. The wall, which is provided with no door or gate, is about forty-five feet high on the outside; inside (as we could see by ascending the spur on which it stands to a point which overlooks it) its height, owing to the raised floor, is probably not more than ten feet. The floor of the tower consists of a level surface broken at regular intervals by rectangular pits. Whenever a Zoroastrian dies, his body is conveyed hither, and deposited by two of his co-religionists (set apart for this duty) inside the *dakhmé* and over one of these pits. The carrion birds which hover round this dreary spot soon swoop down, tear it in pieces, and devour its flesh, till nothing is left but the disarticulated bones, which fall into the pit below. Little, therefore, remains to tell of those who have been laid in this charnel-house; and from the ridge above, where I could see almost the whole of the interior, I counted not more than two skulls and a few long bones. Of course the total number of Zoroastrians in Ṭeherán is very small, and the deaths do not probably exceed two or three a year, which may to some extent explain the paucity of remains in the *dakhmé*. Yezd and Kirmán have each two *dakhmés*, similarly constructed, and situated in like manner on the spurs of mountains at a distance of several miles from the city. These five *dakhmés* constitute, so far as I know, the total number now in use in Persia. This method of disposing of the dead often strikes Europeans as very disgusting, and, indeed, it would clearly be inapplicable to a thickly-populated, flat country with a humid atmosphere. In Persia, however, where the air is so clear, the sun so strong, the population so sparse, and mountains so numerous, I can well imagine that no inconvenience was caused by its adoption, even in the days when the whole population was Zoroastrian.

Near the mouth of the valley which lies to the north of the Kúh-i-Bíbí Shahr-bánú, and on the opposite side to the *dakhmé*, is a tablet cut in the rock (in rough imitation of the ancient monuments about Persepolis), bearing the figure of a king, and an inscription in modern Persian. Though of such recent date, it possesses none of the clearness still discernible in its Sásánian prototypes, and the writing on it is already almost illegible.

Below this, at the end of the valley, are to be seen the remains of gigantic mud walls, which are said to have formed a portion of the ancient city of Rey (Rhages), though by some this is supposed to have lain farther from Ṭeherán towards the east, near the present village of Varámín. Rather nearer to the Sháh 'Abdu'l-'Aẓím road (which crosses the mouth of the valley at right angles) are two high brick towers, one of which is called the Tower of Ṭoghrul.

Of the little town of Sháh 'Abdu'l-'Aẓím itself, which is chiefly notable for its very fine mosque and its very detestable population (the place being what is called "*bast*," that is, a sanctuary or city of refuge, where all criminals are safe from pursuit), I shall have something to say in another chapter. It was to this place that the railway of which such great things were expected, and which it was hoped might be extended farther south—perhaps even to the Persian Gulf—was laid from Ṭeherán. When I returned there in the autumn of 1888 on my way home, this railway was open, and was running some eight or ten trains a day each way. Its prosperity, alas! was short-lived: before the end of the year it was torn up and completely wrecked by a mob, exasperated at the accidental death of a man who had tried to leap from the train while it was in motion.

That the friends of this man, whose death was brought about solely by his own folly and rashness, acted unreasonably in revenging themselves on the railway I do not for a moment wish to deny. That the deep-seated prejudice against this and other European innovations which found its manifestation in this act is equally unreasonable, I am not, however, disposed to admit. I think that the jealousy with which the Persian people are prone to regard these railways, tramways, monopolies, concessions, and companies, of which so much has been heard lately, is both natural and reasonable. These things, so far as they are sources of wealth at all, are so, not to the Persian people, but to the Sháh and his ministers on the one hand, and to the European promoters of the schemes on the other. People who reason about them in Europe too often suppose that the interests of the Sháh and of his subjects are identical, when they are in fact generally diametrically opposed; and that the Sháh is an enlightened monarch, eager for the welfare and progress of a stubborn and refractory people who delight in thwarting his benevolent schemes, when in reality he is a selfish despot, devoid of public spirit, careful only of his own personal comfort and advantage, and most averse to the introduction of liberal ideas amongst a people whose natural quickness, intelligence, and aptitude to learn cause him nothing but anxiety. He does everything in his power to prevent the diffusion of those ideas which conduce to true progress, and his supposed admiration for civilisation amounts to little more than the languid amusement which he derives from the contemplation and possession of mechanical playthings and ingenious toys.

I can only pause to notice one other object of interest outside the city walls, to wit, the pleasantly-situated palace of Dawshán-tepé (which means in Turkish "Hare-hill"), where the Sháh often goes to pursue the chase, to which he is passionately devoted. This palace, of dazzling whiteness, stands on an eminence to the north-east of the town, and forms a very conspicuous feature in the landscape. Besides the palace on the hill, there is another in a garden on its southern side, attached to which is a small menagerie belonging to the Sháh. This collection of animals is not very extensive, but includes fine specimens of the Persian lion (*shír*)[1], whose most famous haunt is in the forests of Dasht-i-Arjín, between Shíráz and Bushire, as well as a few tigers (*babr*), leopards (*palang*), and baboons (*shangál*).

Having spoken of what is without the city, I must now say something about the chief monuments contained within its walls. These are very few, and, for the most part, of little interest. Ṭeherán is an essentially modern town, and as such lacks the charm which invests Iṣfahán, Shíráz, Yezd, and other Persian cities of more respectable antiquity. In the eyes of its own inhabitants, however, it appears the *ne plus ultra* of splendour. It has two European hotels; it is intersected, especially in the northern quarter, by several wide, straight thoroughfares, some of which are even lighted by gas, and one of which certain Europeans and their Persian imitators are pleased to designate the "Boulevard des Ambassadeurs." There are also several large squares, some of which are embellished with tanks and fountains worthy of a sincere admiration. In addition to all this the bazaars (situated in the southern quarter) are extensive and flourishing; the situation of the town, in full view of the snow-capped mountains of Elburz, is unquestionably fine; and the air is clear and exhilarating. In a word, it is a pleasant place to stay in, rather than an interesting place to see. Nevertheless, some of my readers may desire to obtain a clearer notion of what is, after all, the present capital of Persia. Let me ask them, then, to accompany me in imagination for a stroll through the northern quarter of the city, in which are situated most of the parks, palaces, and public buildings, all the embassies except the Russian, and the residences of almost all the Europeans and many of the more opulent and influential Persians.

1 I mention this chiefly because this word, mispronounced *shēr* (like English "share"), is applied in India to the tiger, which animal is properly termed *babr* in Persian, as stated in the text.

We will begin our walk at the northern end of the *Khiyábán-i-'Alá'u'd-Dawla* ("Boulevard des Ambassadeurs"), a fine broad, straight avenue, running almost due north and south. Entering this from the north through the waste land which intervenes (or did intervene in 1887) between it and the Behjetábád and Dawlat Gates, we first pass, on the right-hand side, the fine garden and buildings of the English Embassy. Lower down on the same side are the German and American Legations. Near the latter, a street running westwards leads to the church, schools, and residences of the American missionaries. On the left (east) side of the avenue the finest building is the Turkish Embassy, remarkable for a magnificent gate adorned with an inscription in letters of gold. On the same side are the French and Italian Legations, and a little lower down the office of the Indo-European Telegraph. Beyond this are a few European shops, as well as the two hotels already mentioned; opposite these are several more shops, one of which belongs to a photographer—a Russian, I believe—who sells excellent photographs at the very cheap price of four *túmáns* (about twenty-four shillings) a hundred. Below this point, as well as in some places above it, the sides of the avenue are formed by colonnades of brick, within which are situated a few small Persian shops, dealing chiefly in groceries. Passing under an archway guarded by sentries, we enter the north-west corner of the *Meydán-i-Topkháné*, or Artillery Square. This is of great size, and is surrounded by barracks, the white walls of which are profusely decorated with rude representations of the national symbol, the lion and the sun.

From this square emerge five great streets or avenues; one, sometimes called the "Rue de Gaz," on the east side; two on the south; and two (one of which we have already traversed) on the north. Leaving the three which belong to the eastern portion of the square for future consideration, we continue in a direct southward line across the western end, and enter another avenue, which leads us past some of the Persian Government

Offices (the road opposite to which is, during a considerable part of the day, blocked by carriages and horses) into a very pretty square, well paved and girt with trees, called the *Meydán-i-Arg* ("Citadel Square"). The central portion of this is occupied by a large basin of water of octagonal shape, surrounded by gas lamps. At its southern end is a raised stone platform, on which stands a large gun mounted on wheels. This gun is remarkable, in common with Sháh 'Abdu'l-'Aẓím, the royal stables, and sundry other places, as affording sanctuary to those who are pursued by the law. It has, indeed, the disadvantage of being a very small "city of refuge," and one which would not long be tenable; nevertheless, for the time being, the fugitive is safe in its shadow.

Quitting the *Meydán-i-Arg*, and traversing a short bazaar containing a few small shops, we come out into another broad street, which at this point runs at right angles to our path, but which, if we turned to the left and followed its course eastwards, would be found to bend gradually into a northerly direction, and would conduct us back to the *Meydán-i-Topkháné*. By this road we propose to return; but before doing so, let us take a glance at the intricate mazes of the bazaar. To do this, we cross the road and enter a square known as the *Sabzé-Meydán*, or "Herb Market." In its centre is the usual tank of water, and it is surrounded by the shops of watchmakers, tobacconists, and other tradesmen, mostly of Armenian nationality. We cross towards its southern side, and enter the hatmakers' bazaar (*Kúché-i-kuláh-dúzán*), where any variety of Persian head-dress may be purchased, from the light cloth hat affected by the Armenians and Europeanised (*firangí-ma'áb*) Persians, costing only three or four *ḳráns* (about two shillings), to the genuine lambskin *kuláh*, costing thirty, forty, or even fifty *ḳráns*.

Having passed the hatmakers, we come to the shoemakers, and, if we continue our way perseveringly towards the south, we shall eventually arrive at the gate of Sháh 'Abdu'l-'Aẓím, unless, as may easily happen, we lose our bearings hopelessly in the labyrinthine mazes which we must traverse, distracted either by a string of majestic camels, past which we contrive to edge ourselves, or by a glittering array of antique gems, seals, and turquoises, exposed in a case at our very elbow.

As, however, we have already visited the *dakhmé* in the Mountain of Bíbí Shahr-bánú and the ruins of Rey, and as we shall pass through Sháh 'Abdu'l-'Azím on our journey southwards, it is unnecessary to explore the bazaar any farther at present. Bazaars, after all, are much alike, not only in Persia, but throughout the Muḥammadan world; there are the same more or less tortuous vaulted colonnades, thronged with horses, camels, and men; the same cool recesses, in which are successively exhibited every kind of merchandise; the same subdued murmur and aroma of spices, which form a *tout ensemble* so irresistibly attractive, so continually fresh, yet so absolutely similar, whether seen in Constantinople or Kirmán, Ṭeherán or Tabríz.

Instead of pursuing our way farther, therefore, we strike to the left from the shoemakers' bazaar, and, without even pausing to examine the array of saddles, bridles, whips, saddle-bags, leather water-bags, and other travellers' requisites exhibited to our gaze, make for the *Bázár-i-dunbál-i-khandak* ("Market behind the moat"), and, following this for a while, soon emerge once more into the broad open street which we crossed at a point farther west to reach the *Sabzé-Meydán*. At the point where we have now entered it, it has already begun to assume a northerly direction to reach the *Meydán-i-Topkháné*, towards which we again bend our steps. On our left we pass the very modern-looking palace called *Shamsu'l-'Imára* ("the Sun of Architecture"), with its lofty tower, and come to the *Dáru'l-Funún*, or university. Here English, French, Russian, Medicine (both ancient and modern), Mathematics, and other useful accomplishments are taught on European methods. The students vary in age from mere boys to youths of eighteen or nineteen, and are distinguished by a military-looking uniform. They not only receive their education free, but are allowed one meal a day and two suits of clothes a year at the public expense, besides being rewarded, in case of satisfactory progress and good conduct, by a very liberal distribution of prizes at the end of the session. Arabic, Theology, and Metaphysic do not enter into the curriculum, but are relegated to the ancient *madrasas* attached to some of the mosques and endowed by pious bequests. The best *madrasas*, however, must be sought for, not in Ṭeherán, but in Iṣfahán, the former capital.

Just above the *Dáru'l-Funún* is another fine building, intended, I believe, to serve as a Central Telegraph Office which shall combine the hitherto separated European and Persian branches. Not far above this we re-enter the *Meydán-i-Topkháné*, this time at the south-east corner. To our right the "Rue de Gaz" emerges from the square, and runs eastwards. In it dwells a Turkish haircutter of well-deserved fame, but beyond this it possesses few features of interest, and we may therefore pass it by, and cross to the north-east corner of the square, whence we enter another avenue similar to and parallel with the *Khiyábán-i-'Alá'u'd-Dawla* in which we commenced our walk. This avenue is bounded on the right by a fine garden, the *Bágh-i-Lálé-zár* ("Garden of the Tulip-bed"), which belonged, I believe, to the talented Riẓa-Ḳulí Khán, generally known as the *Lálá-báshí*, or chief tutor of the Sháh, whose numerous works, varied in matter but uniform in merit, are alone sufficient to prove that Persian literary ability has not, as some would pretend, ceased to exist. Little else besides this claims our attention here, and if we pursue our way up this avenue we shall finally reach a point where it is crossed by another broad road running at right angles to it. This latter, if we follow it to the left, will bring us out where we started from, in front of the English Embassy.

Although the walk just described has led us through most of the principal streets and squares, and past a number of the chief buildings and palaces, a few objects of interest which lie apart from the route traversed deserve a brief notice.

First amongst these I will mention—because it can be disposed of in a very few words—another large square, called *Meydán-i-Mashk* ("Drill Square"), which lies to the north-west of the *Meydán-i-Topkháné*. Though somewhat smaller than the latter, it is very spacious, and serves admirably the purpose to which, as its name implies, it is appropriated—that of a *place d'armes*, or exercising-ground for the troops.

Next to this, the palace called *Nigáristán* ("Picture Gallery"), which was the favourite residence of the second king of the Ḳájár dynasty, Fatḥ-'Alí Sháh, deserves mention. It is situated at no great distance from the English Embassy, and derives its name from the numerous highly-finished paintings with which the walls of some of its chambers are decorated. In the largest room I counted no less than 118 full-length portraits, which included not only Fatḥ-'Alí Sháh and his numerous sons and ministers, but also the staffs of the French and English Embassies (headed respectively by General Gardanne and Sir John Malcolm) then resident at the Persian Court, the names of all these being indicated in Persian characters. The portraits, which seem to have been carefully and accurately executed, were completed in the year A.H. 1228 (A.D. 1812–13) by one 'Abdu'lláh, as is witnessed by an inscription placed under them. The only other noticeable feature of the *Nigáristán* is a beautiful marble bath, furnished with a long smooth *glissoire*, called by the Persians *sursurak* ("the slide"), which descends from above to the very edge of the bath. Down this slope the numerous ladies of Fatḥ-'Alí Sháh's harem used to slide into the arms of their lord, who was waiting below to receive them.

It remains to say a few words about the mosques, which are of less interest than those of almost any other Muḥammadan city of equal size. One of the finest is quite recent, and was, indeed, still in process of construction when I visited it. It was commenced by the late *Sipáhsálár*, whose career is generally reported to have been brought to an abrupt close by a cup of "Ḳájár coffee," while he was in retirement and disgrace at Mashhad. The construction of the mosque, rudely interrupted by this sad event, was subsequently resumed by his brother, the *Mushíru'd-Dawla*, whom I had the honour of visiting. He received me with the easy courtesy characteristic of the Persian nobleman; questioned me as to my studies, the books I had read, and the towns I proposed to visit on leaving Ṭeherán; and, after allowing me to inspect the various rooms (some furnished in Persian and others in European style) in his large and beautiful house, kindly sent a servant with me to show me the mosque, which I might otherwise have had difficulty in seeing. The fine large court of the mosque, in the centre of which is a tank of water, is surrounded by lofty buildings, devoted partly to educational, partly to religious purposes. On the walls of these is inscribed on tiles the *waḳf-námé*, or detail of the endowment, in which is set forth the number of professors and students of theology and the kindred sciences who are to be maintained within the walls of the college. Of the former there were to be four, and of the latter, I think, 150.

It is generally very difficult to visit the interior of mosques in Persia; for in this respect the Shí'ite Muḥammadans are much more strict than the Sunnís, and a non-Muslim can, as a rule, only enter them in disguise. I once resorted to this expedient to obtain a glimpse of another mosque in Ṭeherán, the *Masjid-i-Sháh*, which I visited with two of my Persian friends. Although we only remained in it for a very short time, we did not wholly escape the critical gaze of sundry *mullás* who kept hovering round us, and I was not sorry to emerge once more into the bazaar; for the consequences of discovery would have been, to say the least of it, disagreeable. From the little I have seen of the interiors of Persian mosques, I should say that they were decidedly less beautiful than those of Constantinople or Cairo.

I have already had occasion to speak of the *Dáru'l-Funún*, or university, and I mentioned the fact that it included a school of medicine. Through the kindness of Dr Tholozan, the Sháh's physician, I was enabled to be present at one of the meetings of the *Majlis-i-Ṣiḥḥat* ("Congress of Health," or Medical Council), held once a week within its walls. The assembly was presided over by the learned *Mukḥbiru'd-Dawla*, the Minister of Education, and there were present at it sixteen of the chief physicians of the capital, including the professors of medicine (both the followers of Galen and Avicenna, and those of the modern school). The discussion was conducted for the most part in Persian, Dr Tholozan and myself being the only Europeans present; but occasionally a few remarks were made in French, with which several of those present were conversant. After a little desultory conversation, a great deal of excellent tea, flavoured with orange-juice, and the inevitable *ḳalyán*, or water-pipe, the proceedings commenced with a report on the death-rate of Ṭeherán, and the chief causes of mortality. This was followed by a clear and scientific account of a case of acute ophthalmia successfully treated by inoculation, the merits of which plan of treatment were then compared with the results obtained by the use of jequirity, called in Persian *chashm-i-ḳhurús*, and in Arabic *'aynu'd-diḳ*, both of which terms signify "cock's eye." Reports were then read on the death-rates and causes of mortality at some of the chief provincial towns. According to these, Kirmánsháh suffered chiefly from ague, dysentery, and small-pox, while in Iṣfahán, Kirmán, and Sháhrúd, typhus, or typhoid, joined its ravages to those of the above-mentioned diseases. My faith in these reports was, however, somewhat shaken when I subsequently learned that they were in great measure derived from information supplied by those whose business it is to wash the corpses of the dead. Some account was next given of a fatal hæmorrhagic disease which had lately decimated the Yomut Turkmáns. As these wild nomads appeared to entertain an unconquerable aversion to medical men, no scientific investigation of this outbreak had been possible. Finally, a large stone, extracted by lithotomy, was exhibited by a Persian surgeon; and after a little general conversation the meeting finally broke up about 5 p.m. I was very favourably impressed with the proceedings, which were, from first to last, characterised by order, courtesy, and scientific method; and from the enlightened efforts of this centre of medical knowledge I confidently anticipate considerable sanitary and hygienic reforms in Persia. Already in the capital these efforts have produced a marked effect, and there, as well as to a lesser extent in the provinces, the old Galenic system has begun to give place to the modern theory and practice of medicine.

Having now spoken of the topography, buildings, and institutions of the capital, it behoves me to say something about its social aspects. I begin naturally with the royal family.

Of Náṣiru'd-Dín Sháh, the reigning king, I have already said something. His appearance has been rendered so familiar in Europe by his three visits to the West, that of it I need hardly speak. He has had a long reign, if not a very glorious one, for he was crowned at Ṭeherán on 20th October 1848, and there seems every likelihood that he will live to celebrate his jubilee. He came to the throne very young, being not much more than seventeen or eighteen years of age. Before that time he had resided at Tabríz as governor of the province of Ádharbáyján, an office always conferred by Ḳájár sovereigns on the Crown Prince. The Ḳájárs, as I have already said, are of Turkish origin, and the language of Ádharbáyján is also a dialect of Turkish; whence it came about that Náṣiru'd-Dín Sháh, on his accession, could scarcely express himself at all in Persian—a fact to which Dr Polak, about that time his court physician, bears testimony. Even now, though he habitually speaks and writes Persian, and has even composed and published some poems in that language, he prefers, I believe, to make use of Turkish in conversation with such of his intimates as understand it.

I wish to insist on the fact that the reigning dynasty of the Ḳájárs are essentially of Turkish race, because it is often overlooked, and because it is of some political importance. When the Sháh was in England, for instance, certain journals were pleased to speak of him as a "descendant of Cyrus," which is about as reasonable as if one should describe our own Prince of Wales as a descendant of King Arthur. The whole history of Persia, from the legendary wars between the Kiyánian kings and Afrásiyáb down to the present day, is the story of a struggle between the Turkish races whose primitive home is in the region east of the Caspian Sea and north of Khurásán on the one hand, and the southern Persians, of almost pure Aryan race, on the other. The distinction is well marked even now, and the old antipathy still exists, finding expression in verses such as those quoted above at p. 84, and in anecdotes illustrative of Turkish stupidity and dullness of wit, of which I shall have occasion to give one in a subsequent chapter. Ethnologically, therefore, there is a marked distinction between the people of the north and the people of the south—a distinction which may be most readily apprehended by comparing the sullen, moody, dull-witted, fanatical, violent inhabitants of Ádharbáyján with the bright, versatile, clever, sceptical, rather timid townsfolk of Kirmán. In Fárs, also, good types of the Aryan Persian are met with, but there is a large admixture of Turkish tribesmen, like the Ḳáshḳá'ís, who have migrated and settled there. Indeed this intermixture has now extended very far, but in general the terms "northern" and "southern" may, with reservation, be taken as representing a real and significant difference of type in the inhabitants of Persia. Since the downfall of the Caliphate and the lapse of the Arabian supremacy, the Turkish has generally been the dominant race; for in the physical world it is commonly physical force which wins the day, and dull, dogged courage bears down versatile and subtle wit. Thus it happens that to-day the Ḳájárs rule over the kinsmen of Cyrus and Shápúr, as ruled in earlier days the

Ghaznavids and the Seljúḳs. But there is no love lost between the two races, as anyone will admit who has taken the trouble to find out what the southern peasant thinks of the northern court, or how the Ḳájárs regard the cradle of Persia's ancient greatness.

Of the Sháh's character I do not propose to add much to what I have said already, for, in the first place, I am conscious of a prejudice against him in my mind arising from the ineffaceable remembrance of his horrid cruelties towards the Bábís; and, in the second place, I enjoyed no unusual facilities for forming a weighty judgment. I have heard him described by a high English official, who had good opportunities of arriving at a just opinion, as a liberal-minded and enlightened monarch, full of manliness, energy, and sound sense, who, in a most difficult situation, had displayed much tact and wisdom. It must also be admitted that, apart from the severities practised against the Bábís (which, with alternate remissions and exacerbations, have continued from the beginning of his reign down to the present time), his rule has been, on the whole, mild, and comparatively free from the cruelties which mar nearly every page of Persian history. During the latter part of his reign, especially, executions and cruel punishments, formerly of almost daily occurrence, have become very rare; but this is partly to be attributed to the fear of European public opinion, and desire to be thought well of at Western courts and in Western lands, which exercise so strong an influence over his mind.

For most of the more recent Bábí persecutions the Sháh was not directly responsible. It was his eldest son, the Ẓillu's-Sulṭán, who put to death the two "Martyrs of Iṣfahán" in 1879, and Mírzá Ashraf of Ábádé in 1888; and it was in his jurisdiction (though during his absence) that the persecutions of Sih-dih and Najaf-ábád occurred in the summer of 1889[1]; while the cruel

[1] See *Journal of the Royal Asiatic Society* for 1889, pp. 998–9; and vol. ii of my *Traveller's Narrative*, pp. 400–412.

murder of seven innocent Bábís at Yezd in May 1890 lies at the door of Prince Jalálu'd-Dawla, son of the Ẓillu's-Sulṭán, and grandson of the Sháh. The last Bábí put to death actually by the Sháh's order was, I think, the young messenger, Mírzá Badí', who brought from Acre, and delivered into the king's own hands at Ṭeherán, the remarkable apology for the Bábí faith addressed to him by Behá'u'lláh[1]. This was in July 1869.

In extenuation of the earlier and more wholesale persecutions, it has been urged that the Bábís were in rebellion against the Crown, and that the most horrible of them, that of September 1852, was provoked by the attempt made by three Bábís on the Sháh's life. But this attempt itself (apart from the fact that, so far as can be ascertained, it was utterly unauthorised on the part of the Bábí leaders) was caused by the desperation to which the Bábís had been driven by a long series of cruelties, and especially by the execution of their Founder in 1850[2]. Amongst the victims, also, were several persons who, inasmuch as they had been in captivity for many months, were manifestly innocent of complicity in the plot, notably the beautiful Ḳurratu'l-'Ayn, whose heroic fortitude under the most cruel tortures excited the admiration and wonder of Dr Polak[3], the only European, probably, who witnessed her death.

These executions were not merely criminal, but foolish. The barbarity of the persecutors defeated its own ends, and, instead of inspiring terror, gave the martyrs an opportunity of exhibiting a heroic fortitude which has done more than any propaganda, however skilful, could have done to ensure the triumph of the cause for which they died. Often have I heard Persians who did not themselves belong to the proscribed sect tell with admiration how Suleymán Khán, his body pierced with well-

1 A translation of this is given in my *Traveller's Narrative*, vol. ii, pp. 108–151, and 390–400.

2 See p. 68 *supra*.

3 See Polak's *Persien*, vol. i, p. 353.

nigh a score of wounds, in each of which was inserted a lighted candle, went to the place of execution singing with exultation:

> "*Yak dast jám-i-bádé, va yak dast zulf-i-yár—*
> *Raḳṣí chunín meyáné-i-meydánam árzúst!*"

> "In one hand the wine-cup, in the other the tresses of the Friend—
> Such a dance do I desire in the midst of the market-place!"

The impression produced by such exhibitions of courage and endurance was profound and lasting; nay, the faith which inspired the martyrs was often contagious, as the following incident shows. A certain Yezdí rough, noted for his wild and disorderly life, went to see the execution of some Bábís, perhaps to scoff at them. But when he saw with what calmness and steadfastness they met torture and death, his feelings underwent so great a revulsion that he rushed forward crying, "Kill me too! I also am a Bábí!" And thus he continued to cry till he too was made a partaker in the doom he had come out only to gaze upon.

During my stay in Ṭeherán I saw the Sháh several times, but only once sufficiently near to see his features clearly. This was on the occasion of his visiting the new telegraph office on his way to the University, where he was to preside over the distribution of prizes. Through the kindness of Major Wells, then superintendent of the Indo-European Telegraph in Persia, H—— and myself were enabled to stand in the porch of the building while the Sháh entered, surrounded by his ministers. We afterwards followed him to the University and witnessed the distribution of prizes, which was on the most liberal scale, most of the students, so far as I could see, receiving either medals, or sums of money averaging three or four *túmáns* (about £1). The Sháh sat in a room opening out into the quadrangle, where the secretaries of state (*mustawfís*), professors, and students were ranged in order. Around him stood the princes of the royal family, including his third son, the *Ná'ibu's-Salṭana*, and the ministers of state. The only person allowed to sit beside him was his little favourite, "*Maníjak*," who accompanied him on his last journey to Europe.

The Sháh's extraordinary fondness for this child (for he did not, at the time I saw him, appear to be more than eleven or twelve years old) was as annoying to the Persian aristocracy as it was astonishing to the people of Europe. It galled the spirit of the proud nobles of Persia to watch the daily-increasing influence of this little wizened, sallow-faced Kurdish lad, who was neither nobly born, nor of comely countenance, nor of pleasant manners and amiable disposition; to see honours and favours lavished upon him and his ignoble kinsmen; to be compelled to do him reverence and bespeak his good offices. All this now is a thing of the past. Within the last year or so Ghulám 'Alí Khán, the Kurd, better known as "*Maníjak*" (which, in the Kurdish tongue, signifies a sparrow), and somewhile dignified by the title of *'Azízu's-Sulṭán* ("the Darling of the King"), fell from favour, and was hurled from the pinnacle of power down to his original obscurity. The cause of his fall was, I believe, that one day, while he was playing with a pistol, the weapon exploded and narrowly missed the Sháh. This was too much, and "*Maníjak*" and his favoured kinsmen were shorn of their titles and honours, and packed off to their humble home in Kurdistán. Perhaps it was, after all, as well for them; for "the Darling of the King" was far from being the "Darling of the Court." Sooner or later his fall was bound to come, and had it been later it might have been yet more grievous.

The Sháh has five sons. Two of these, the *Sáláru'l-Mulk* and the *Ruknu'l-Mulk*, were, at the time of which I write, mere children. They were described as beautiful and attractive boys, but neglected by their father in favour of *Maníjak*. The third son is entitled *Ná'ibu's-Salṭana*. He resided in Ṭeherán, and to him was entrusted the government of the city and the supreme military command.

The two elder sons were born of different mothers, and as the mother of the *Valí-'ahd* was a princess, he, and not his elder brother, was chosen as the successor to the throne. That the *Ẓillu's-Sulṭán* inwardly chafed at being thus deprived of his birth-right is hardly to be doubted, though he was in the meanwhile compensated for this in some measure by being made governor of the greater part of Southern Persia, including the three important cities of Shíráz, Yezd, and Iṣfahán, at the last of which he resided in almost regal state. Here he collected together a considerable body of well-drilled troops, who were said to be more efficient and soldierly than any of the regiments in Ṭeherán. Besides these he had acquired a number of guns, and his magazines were well provided with arms and ammunition. In view of these preparations, and the energy and decision of character discernible in this prince, it was thought possible that, in the event of his father's death, he might dispute the crown with his younger and gentler brother, the *Valí-'ahd*, in which case it appeared not improbable that he might prove victorious, or at least succeed in maintaining his supremacy over Southern Persia.

All such speculations, however, were cast to the winds by an utterly unforeseen event which occurred towards the end of February 1888, while I was at Iṣfahán. In the beginning of that month both the *Ẓillu's-Sulṭán* and the *Valí-'ahd* had come to Ṭeherán, the former from Iṣfahán, the latter from Tabríz, to pay a visit to their father. A decoration was to be presented to the former by the English Government for the protection and favour which he had extended to English trade and enterprise, towards which he had ever shown himself well disposed. Suddenly, without any warning, came the news that he had been deprived of all his governments, with the exception of the city of Iṣfahán; that he and some of his ministers who had accompanied him to the capital were kept to all intents and purposes prisoners within its walls; that his deputy-governors at Yezd, Shíráz, and other towns were recalled; and that his army was disbanded, his artillery removed to Ṭeherán, and his power effectually shattered. On first hearing from the Sháh that of all the fair regions over which he had held sway, Iṣfahán only was left to him, he is reported to have said in the bitterness of his heart, "You had better take that from me too"; to which the Sháh replied, "I will do so, and will give it to your son" (Prince Jalálu'd-Dawla, then governor for his father at Shíráz). This threat was, however, not carried out, and the *Ẓillu's-Sulṭán* was left in possession of the former capital as a remnant of his once wide dominions.

Passing from the Sháh and his sons, we must now turn our attention to one or two other members of the royal family. Foremost amongst these is (or rather *was*, for he died in 1888, while I was still in Persia) the Sháh's aged uncle, Ferhád Mírzá, *Mu'tamadu'd-Dawla*, with whom, through the kindness of Dr Torrence of the American Missionary Establishment, and by means of his interest with Prince Iḥtishámu'd-Dawla (the son of Ferhád Mírzá, and, since the downfall of the *Ẓillu's-Sulṭán*, governor of Shíráz and the province of Fárs), I obtained the honour of an interview. We found him seated, amidst a pile of cushions, in his *andarún*, or inner apartments, surrounded by well-stocked shelves of books. He received us with that inimitable courtesy whereby Persians of the highest rank know so well how to set the visitor completely at his ease, and at the same time to impress him with the deepest respect for their nobility. I was greatly struck by his venerable appearance and dignified mien, as well as by the indomitable energy and keen intelligence expressed by the flashing eye and mobile features, which neither old age nor bodily infirmity was able to rob of their animation. He talked much of a book called *Niṣáb*, written by himself to facilitate the acquisition of the English language (with which he had some acquaintance) by his countrymen. Of this work he subsequently presented me with a copy, which I value highly as a souvenir of its illustrious author. It is arranged on the same plan as the

Arabic *Niṣábs*[1] so popular in Persia—that is to say, it consists of a sort of rhymed vocabulary, in which the English words (represented in the text in Persian characters, and repeated in English characters at the head of the page) are explained successively by the corresponding Persian word. The following lines, taken from the commencement of the work, and here represented in English characters, will serve as a specimen of the whole:—

> "*Dar mah-i-Dey jám-i-mey dih, ey nigár-i-máhrú,*
> *Kaz shamím-i-án dimágh-i-'akl gardad mushk-bú.*
> 'Hid' *sar-ast, ú* 'nōz' *bíní,* 'lip' *lab-ast, ú* 'áy' *chu chashm;*
> 'Túth' *dindán,* 'fút' *pá, ú* 'hand' *dast, ú* 'feys' *rú.*
> *Gúsh ú gardan* 'í'r' *ú* 'nik'; 'chík' *chihré,* 'tang' *ámad zabán;*
> *Náf* 'ní'vil' *dán, ú pistán-rá* 'buzam'; *khwán* 'hí'ar' *mú.*"

> "In the month of Dey[2] give the cup of wine, O moon-faced beauty,
> So that by its fragrance the palate of the intellect may become perfumed as with musk.
> Head is *sar*, and nose *bíní*, lip is *lab*, and eye like *chashm*;
> Tooth *dindán*, foot *pá*, and hand *dast*, and face *rú*.
> *Gúsh* and *gardan* ear and neck; cheek *chihré*, tongue becomes *zabán*;
> Recognise *náf* as navel, and *pistán* as bosom; call hair *mú*."

I doubt greatly whether such a method of learning a language would commend itself to a European student, but with the Persians, endowed as they are with a great facility for learning by heart, it is a very favourite one.

Prince Ferhád Mírzá professed a great kindliness for the English nation as well as for their language; nor, if the following narrative be true, is this to be wondered at, since his life was once saved by Sir Taylor Thomson when endangered by the anger of his nephew, the Sháh. Fleeing from the messengers of the king's wrath, he took refuge in the English Embassy, and threw himself on the protection of his friend the Ambassador, who promised to give him shelter so long as it should be necessary. Soon the

1 The best known of these is the *Niṣábu'ṣ-Ṣibyán* of Abú Naṣr Faráhí, who flourished in the beginning of the seventh century of the *hijra* (thirteenth of our era).

2 The tenth month of the old Persian solar year, corresponding to December—January.

royal *farráshes* arrived, and demanded his surrender, which demand was unhesitatingly refused. They then threatened to break in by force and seize their prisoner, whereupon Sir Taylor Thomson drew a line across the path and declared that he would shoot the first man who attempted to cross it. Thereupon they thought it best to retire, and Ferhád Mírzá remained for a while the guest of the British Embassy, during which time Sir Taylor Thomson never suffered him to partake of a dish without first tasting it himself, for it was feared that, violence having failed, poison might, perhaps, be employed. Ultimately the Sháh's anger subsided, and his uncle was able again to emerge from his place of refuge.

Before the close of our audience, Ferhád Mírzá asked me how long I intended to stop in Ṭeherán, and whither I proposed to go on leaving it. I replied that my intention was to proceed to Shíráz as soon as the spring set in, since that it was the *Dáru'l-'Ilm* ("Abode of Knowledge"), and I thought that I might better pursue my studies there. "That," replied Ferhád Mírzá, "is quite a mistake: 500 years ago Shíráz was the *Dáru'l-'Ilm*, but now that has passed, and it can only be called the *Dáru'l-Fisḳ*" ("Abode of Vice").

Ferhád Mírzá had little reason to like Shíráz, nor had Shíráz much better reason to like Ferhád Mírzá. He was twice governor of that town and the province of Fárs, of which it is the capital, and was so unpopular during his administration that when he was recalled the populace did not seek to hide their delight, and even pursued him with jeers and derisive remarks. Ferhád Mírzá swore that the Shírázís should pay for their temporary triumph right dearly, and he kept his word. After a lapse of time he was again appointed governor of the city that had insulted him, and his rule, never of the gentlest, became sterner than ever. During his four years of office (ending about 1880) he is said to have caused no less than 700 hands to be cut off for various offences. In one case a man came and complained that he had lost an ass, which was subsequently found amongst the animals belonging to a lad in the neighbourhood. The latter was seized and brought before Ferhád Mírzá, who, as soon as the ass had been identified by the plaintiff, ordered the hand of the defendant to be cut off without further delay, giving no ear to the protestations of the poor boy that the animal had of its own accord entered his herd, and that he had not, till the accusation of theft was preferred against him, been able to discover its owner. Besides these minor punishments, many robbers and others suffered death; not a few were walled up alive in pillars of mortar, there to perish miserably. The remains of these living tombs may still be seen just outside the *Derwázé-i-Ḳaṣṣáb-khḥáné* ("Slaughter-house gate") at Shíráz, while another series lines the road as it enters the little town of Ábádé, situated near the northern limit of the province of Fárs. On another occasion a certain Sheykh Madhkúr, who had revolted in the *garmsír*, or hot region bordering on the Persian Gulf, and had struck coins in his own name, was captured and brought to Shíráz, together with two of his followers, one of whom was his chief executioner. Ferhád Mírzá first compelled the Sheykh to eat one of his own coins, and then caused him and his followers to be strangled and suspended from a lofty gibbet as a warning to the disaffected. Notwithstanding his severity, Ferhád Mírzá enjoyed a great reputation for piety, and had accomplished the pilgrimage to Mecca. His son, as I have said, was, early in 1888, appointed Governor of Shíráz, where the reputation of his father caused his advent to be looked forward to with some apprehension.

The only other member of the Persian royal family whom I met was one of the brothers of the Sháh, entitled *'Izzu'd-Dawla*, who, if less important a personage than Ferhád Mírzá, was by no means less courteous. He asked many questions about recent inventions in Europe, manifesting an especial interest, so far as I remember, in patent medicines and dynamite.

Having now completed all that I have to say about the reigning dynasty, I will speak shortly of Persian dinner-parties at Ṭeherán.

As these are seen in a more truly national form in the provinces, where chairs, tables, knives, and forks have not yet obtruded themselves to such an extent as in the semi-Europeanised capital, I shall leave much that I have to say on this subject for subsequent pages. Most of the Persians with whom I was intimate at Ṭeherán had adopted European habits to a considerable extent; and during my residence there I was only on two occasions present at a really national entertainment.

The order of procedure is always much the same. The guests arrive about sundown, and are ushered into what corresponds to the drawing-room, where they are received by their host and his male relations (for women are, of course, excluded). *Ḳalyáns* (water-pipes) and wine, or undiluted spirits (the latter being preferred), are offered them, and they continue to smoke and drink intermittently during the whole of the evening. Dishes of "*ájíl*" (pistachio nuts and the like) are handed round or placed near the guests; and from time to time a spit of *ḳebábs* (pieces of broiled meat) enveloped in a folded sheet of the flat bread called *nán-i-sangaḳ*[1], is brought in. These things bring out the flavour of the wine, and serve to stimulate, and at the same time appease, the appetite of the guests, for the actual supper is not served till the time for breaking up the assembly has almost arrived, which is rarely much before midnight.

As a rule, music is provided for the entertainment of the guests. The musicians are usually three in number: one plays a stringed instrument (the *si-tár*); one a drum (*dunbaḳ*), consisting of an earthenware framework, shaped something like a huge egg-cup, and covered with parchment at one end only; the third sings to the accompaniment of his fellow-performers. Sometimes

1 *Sangak* ("pebble") is the diminutive of *sang* ("a stone"). This bread is called "pebble-bread" because the bottom of the oven in which it is baked is formed by a sloping bank of pebbles, on which the flat cakes of dough are thrown. It is very pleasant to the taste, and the only objection to it is that sometimes a stray pebble gets incorporated in its substance, to the manifest peril of the teeth of the consumer.

dancing-boys are also present, who excite the admiration and applause of the spectators by their elaborate posturing, which is usually more remarkable for acrobatic skill than for grace, at any rate according to our ideas. These, however, are more often seen in Shíráz than at Ṭeherán. Occasionally the singer is a boy; and, if his voice be sweet and his appearance comely, he will be greeted with rapturous applause. At one entertainment to which I had been invited, the guests were so moved by the performance of the boy-singer that they all joined hands and danced round him in a circle, chanting in a kind of monotonous chorus, "*Báraka'lláh, Kúchulú! Báraka'lláh, Kúchulú!*" ("God bless thee, little one! God bless thee, little one!"), till sheer exhaustion compelled them to stop.

When the host thinks that the entertainment has lasted long enough, he gives the signal for supper, which is served either in the same or in another room. A cloth is laid on the floor, round which are arranged the long flat cakes of "pebble-bread" which do double duty as food and plates. The meats, consisting for the most part of *piláws* and *chiláws*[1] of different sorts, are placed in the centre, together with bowls of sherbet, each of which is supplied with a delicately-carved wooden spoon, with deep boat-shaped bowl, whereof the sides slope down to form a sort of keel at the bottom. The guests squat down on their knees and heels round the cloth, the host placing him whom he desires most to honour on his right side at the upper end of the room (*i.e.* opposite the door). At the lower end the musicians and minstrels take their places, and all, without further delay, commence an attack on the viands. The consumption of food progresses rapidly, with but little conversation, for it is not usual

1 The basis of both *piláws* and *chiláws* is boiled rice flavoured with different meats; the difference between them is, that in the former the mixture is effected by the cook, in the latter by the guest, who takes with the plain rice whatever delicacy most tempts his palate. There are many varieties of *piláw*, two of the nicest of which, in my opinion, are *orange-piláw* and what is called *bábúné-piláw*.

in Persia to linger over meals, or to prolong them by talk, which is better conducted while the mouth is not otherwise employed. If the host wishes to pay special honour to a guest, he picks out and places in his mouth some particularly delicate morsel. In about a quarter of an hour from the commencement of the banquet most of the guests have finished and washed their hands by pouring water over them from a metal ewer into a plate of the same material, brought round by the servants for that purpose. They then rinse out their mouths, roll down their sleeves again, partake of a final pipe, and, unless they mean to stay for the night, depart homewards, either on foot or on horseback, preceded by a servant bearing a lantern.

Such is the usual course of a Persian dinner-party; and the mid-day meal (*nahár*), to which guests are sometimes invited, differs from it only in this, that it is shorter and less boisterous. Although I have described the general features of such an entertainment in some detail, I fear that I have failed to convey any idea of the charm which it really possesses. This charm results partly from the lack of constraint and the freedom of the guests; partly from the cordial welcome which a Persian host so well knows how to give; partly from the exhilarating influence of the wine and music (which, though so different from that to which we are accustomed, produces, in such as are susceptible to its influence, an indescribable sense of subdued ecstasy); but more than all from the vigour, variety, and brilliancy of the conversation. There is no doubt that satiety produces somnolence and apathy, as is so often seen at English dinner-parties. Hence the Persians wisely defer the meal till the very end of the evening, when sleep is to be sought. During the earlier stages of the entertainment their minds are stimulated by wine, music, and mirth, without being dulled by the heaviness resulting from repletion. This, no doubt, is one reason why the conversation is, as a rule, so brilliant; but beyond this the quick, versatile, subtle mind of the Persian, stored, as it usually is, with anecdotes, historical, literary, and incidental, and freed for the time being from the restraint which custom ordinarily imposes on it, flashes forth on these occasions in coruscations of wit and humour, interspersed with pungent criticisms and philosophical reflections which display a wonderful insight. Hence it is that one rarely fails to enjoy thoroughly an evening spent at a Persian banquet, and that the five or six hours during which it lasts hardly ever hang heavily on one's hands.

The Persians have only two full meals in the day—*nahár*, which one may call indifferently either breakfast or lunch, since on the one hand it is the first meal of the day, and on the other it is not taken till a little before noon; and *shám*, or supper, which, as I have already stated, is eaten the last thing before retiring for the night. Besides these two meals, tea is taken on rising in the morning, and again in the afternoon.

The usual way in which a Persian of the upper classes spends his day is, then, somewhat as follows: He rises early, often before sunrise (which, indeed, he must do, if devotionally inclined, for the morning prayer), and, after drinking a glass or two of tea (without milk, of course) and smoking a *ḳalyán*, sets about the business of the day, whatever it may be. About noon, or a little earlier, he has his breakfast (*nahár*), which differs little from supper as regards its material. After this, especially if the season be summer, he usually lies down and sleeps till about 3 p.m. From this time till sunset is the period for paying calls, so he either goes out to visit a friend, or else stays at home to receive visitors. In either case, tea and *ḳalyáns* constitute a prominent feature in the afternoon's employment. Casual visitors do not, as a rule, remain long after sunset, and on their departure, unless an invitation to supper has been given or received, the evening is quietly passed at home till the time for supper and bed arrives. In the case of government employés, as well as shopkeepers, tradesmen, and others, whose hours of work are longer, a considerable portion of the afternoon may have to be spent in business, but in any case this rarely lasts after 4 or 5 p.m. Calls may also be paid in the early morning, before the day's work commences. The true Persian life is, however, as I have before remarked, much better seen in the provinces than in the capital, where European influences have already wrought a great change in national customs. Further remarks on it will therefore find a fitter place in a subsequent chapter.

I must now return to my life in the Nawwáb's house, and the society which I there met. Amongst the visitors were a certain number of Afghans who had formed the suite of Ayyúb Khán before his attempted escape, and who were now to be transferred to Ráwal Pindí in India, by way of Baghdád. The arrangements for their journey were entrusted mainly to my host, and, for a time, few days passed without his receiving visits from some of them. On these occasions I used often to remain in the room during the conversation, half of which, although it was conducted in Persian, was nearly unintelligible to me; for the Afghans speak in a manner and with an accent quite peculiar to themselves. These Afghans, who wore coloured turbans wound round a conical cap, after the Indian fashion, were troublesome and cantankerous fellows, seeming never to be satisfied, and always wanting something more—a larger allowance of money, more horses, or more sumptuous litters for the journey. As a rule, too, their expressions betokened cruelty and deceit, though some of them were fine-looking men, especially an old *mullá* called Ḳáẓí 'Abdu's-Salám, who had held an important position under the late Amír, Shír 'Alí.

For the most part, however, the visitors were Persians, and of these a large proportion were natives of Shíráz, to whose eulogies of their beloved city (for all Shírázís are intensely patriotic) I used to listen with unwearying delight. They would praise the beautiful gardens, the far-famed stream of Ruknábád, the soft, sweet speech of the south, and the joyousness of the people; but when I exclaimed that Shíráz must be a very paradise, they would shake their heads sadly and say, "the place, indeed, has no fault—*valí ṣáḥibí na-dárad*—but it has no master," thinking, perhaps, of the happy time when the virtuous and noble Karím Khán the Zend held his court there, and rejoiced in his palace, when he heard the sounds of merriment from the town, that his people should be free from care and sadness.

One constant visitor was the Nawwáb's brother-in-law, Áḳá Muḥammad Ḥasan Khán of the Ḳáshḳá'í tribe which dwells in the neighbourhood of Shíráz. When he had ceased for a while the disquisitions on philosophy which were his favourite theme, and had temporarily exhausted the praises of "the Master," as he called his teacher in the science, Mírzá Abu'l-Ḥasan-i-Jilvé, he, too, used to revert to the inexhaustible subject of the beauties of his native land. "You must on no account postpone your visit to Shíráz later than the Nawrúz" (the Persian New Year's Day, which corresponds with the vernal equinox), he would say, "for then, indeed, there is no place on the face of the earth so beautiful. You know what the Sheykh (*i.e.* Sa'dí) says—

'*Khushá tafarruj-i-Nawrúz, kháṣṣé dar Shíráz,*
Ki bar kanad dil-i-mard-i-musáfir az waṭanash.'

'Pleasant is the New Year's outing, especially in Shíráz,
Which turns aside the heart of the traveller from his native land.'"

In the evening, when I was alone with the Nawwáb, or his brother 'Ísá Khán, a colonel in the Persian army, or my old friends, his nephews, the talk would turn on religion, philosophy, or literature. Sometimes they would entertain me with anecdotes of celebrated men and accounts of curious superstitions and customs; sometimes the Nawwáb would play on the *si-tár*, on which he was a proficient; while sometimes they would explain to me the intricacies of the Muḥammadan prayers and ablutions, and the points wherein the Shí'ites differ from the Sunnís, both in practice and belief. They did not fail on these occasions to point out the meaning which underlies many of the ordinances of Islám. "The fast of Ramaẓán," they said, "appears to you a most grievous burden for a prophet and legislator to lay upon his followers, but in truth in this is its very value, for, as it is enjoined on all alike, the rich are made to realise what hunger and thirst, which they would otherwise never experience, really are. Thus they are enabled to understand the condition of those who are always exposed to these trials, and brought to sympathise with them and to strive to ameliorate their lot more than they would otherwise do. So, too, with our prayers, and the ablutions by which they must be preceded. It is true that there is no special virtue in praying and washing oneself five times a day; but it is evident that one who is enjoined to remember his Creator thus often, and to keep his body pure and clean, will always have these objects in view, and will never through negligence fall into forgetfulness of God and disregard of personal cleanliness. Moreover, we are forbidden to pray in any place which has been forcibly taken from its owner, or in which he does not give us permission to perform our devotions. This continually serves to remind us to be just and courteous in all our dealings, that our prayers may be acceptable to God."

Sometimes the conversation was of a lighter character, and turned on the sayings of witty and learned men, their ready replies, and pungent sarcasms. Of these anecdotes I will give a few specimens.

Sheykh Sa'dí was unrivalled in ready wit and quickness of repartee, yet even he once met with his match. It happened in this wise. The young prince of Shíráz, who was remarkable for his beauty, went one day, accompanied by his retinue, to visit a mosque which was being built by his orders, and which is still standing. As he passed by a workman who was digging, a piece of mud flew up from the spade and touched his cheek. Sa'dí, who was walking near him, saw this, and immediately exclaimed, making use of a quotation from the Ḳur'án, "*Yá laytaní ḳuntu turábá!*" ("O would that I were earth!"[1]). The prince, hearing

1 Ḳur'án, ch. lxxviii, v. 41.

Sa'dí speak, but failing to catch his remark, asked, "What does the Sheykh say?" Another learned man who was present instantly interposed: "May I be thy sacrifice! it was naught but a quotation from the Holy Book—'*fa-ḳála'l-ḳáfiru, "Yá laytanı ḳuntu turábá!*"'" ("and the infidel said, 'O would that I were earth!'") Sa'dí had made use of the quotation, forgetting for the moment in whose mouth the words were placed. His rival had not forgotten, and, while appearing merely to justify Sa'dí, succeeded in applying to him the opprobrious term of *ḳáfir* (infidel).

'Obeyd-i-Zákání was another celebrated poet, chiefly noted for the scathing satires which flowed from his pen. Even when he was on his death-bed his grim humour did not desert him. Summoning successively to his side his two sons and his daughter, he informed them, with every precaution to ensure secrecy, that he had left behind for them a treasure, which they must seek for, on a particular hour of a certain day after his death and burial, in a place which he indicated. "Be sure," he added in conclusion, "that you go thither at that hour and at no other, and above all keep what I have said secret from my other children." Shortly after this the poet breathed his last, and when his body had been consigned to the grave, and the day appointed for the search had come, each of his three children repaired secretly to the spot indicated. Great was the surprise of each to find that the others were also present, and evidently bent on the same quest. Explanations of a not very satisfactory character ensued, and they then proceeded to dig for the treasure. Sure enough they soon came on a large parcel, which they eagerly extracted from its place of concealment, and began to unfold. On removing the outer covering they found a layer of straw, evidently designed to protect the valuable and perhaps fragile contents. Inside this was another smaller box, on opening which a quantity of cotton-wool appeared. An eager examination of this brought to light nothing but a small slip of paper on which something was written. Disappointed in their search, but still hoping that this document might prove of value, either by guiding them to the real treasure, or in some other way, they hastily bore it to the light, and read these words—

"*Khudáy dánad, ú man dánam, ú tú ham dání*
Ki yak fulús na-dárad 'Obeyd-i-Zákání!"

"God knows, and I know, and thou too knowest,
That 'Obeyd-i-Zákání does not possess a single copper!"

Whether the children were able to appreciate this final display of humour on the part of their father is not narrated by the historian.

Satire, though, for obvious reasons, cultivated to a much smaller extent than panegyric, did not by any means cease with the death of 'Obeyd-i-Zákání, which occurred about the year A.D. 1370. The following, composed on the incapable and crotchety Ḥájí Mírzá Āḳásí, prime minister of Muḥammad Sháh, may serve as an example:—

"*Na-g'zásht dar mulk-i-Sháh Ḥájí dirамí;*
Kard kharj-i-ḳanát ú túp har bísh ú kamí;
Na mazra'-i-dúst-rá az án ḳanát namí,
Na kháyé-i-dushman-rá az án túp ghamí."

"The Ḥájí did not leave a single *dirham* in the domains of the king;
Everything, small or great, he expended on *ḳanáts* and guns—
Ḳanáts which conveyed no water to the fields of his friends,
And guns which inflicted no injury on his enemies." [1]

The wasteful and useless extravagance of Ḥájí Mírzá Āḳásí here held up to ridicule was unfortunately far from being his greatest or most pernicious error. It was he who ceded to the

1 A *ḳanát* is an underground channel for bringing water from those places where its presence has been detected by the water-finder (*muḳanní-báshí*) to towns or villages where it is needed. The horizontal shaft is made by first sinking vertical ones and connecting these with one another by tunnelling. The cost of these *ḳanáts* (which abound in most parts of Persia) is very great. They are generally made by a rich man at his own risk and expense, according to the advice of the *muḳanní-báshí*. The water is then sold to those who use it. The object of this satire was celebrated for his passion for trying to invent new guns, and making *ḳanáts* which proved worthless. (See Gobineau, *Religions et Philosophies dans l'Asie Centrale*, p. 163.) The last line, containing, as it does, a crude but forcible Persian idiom, I merely paraphrase.

Russians the sole right of navigating the Caspian Sea, remarking, with a chuckle at his own wit, "*Má murghábí nístím ḳi áb-i-shúr lázim dáshté báshím*," "We are not waterfowl that we should stand in need of salt water," to which he presently added the following sage reflection:—"*Baráyi mushtí áb-i-shúr na-mí-shavad ḳám-i-shírín-i-dúst-rá talḳh namúd*" ("It wouldn't do to embitter the sweet palate of a friend for the sake of a handful of salt water").

Readiness is a *sine quâ non* in a Persian poet. He must be able to improvise at a moment's notice. One day Fatḥ-'Alí Sháh was riding through the bazaars surrounded by his courtiers when he happened to notice amongst the apprentices in a coppersmith's shop a very beautiful boy, whose fair face was begrimed with coal dust.

"*Bi-gird-i-'áriz-i-mis-gar nishaste gard-i-zughál*"

("Around the cheeks of the coppersmith has settled the dust of the coal"), said the king, improvising a hemistich; "now, Sir Laureate" (turning to his court-poet), "cap me that if you can!"

"*Ṣadá-yi mis bi-falak mí-ravad ki máh giriftast*"

("The clang of the copper goes up to heaven because the moon is eclipsed"), rejoined the Laureate, without a moment's hesitation. To appreciate the appositeness of this verse the reader must know that a beautiful face is constantly compared by the Persians to the moon, and that when there is an eclipse of the moon it is customary in Persia to beat copper vessels to frighten away the dragon which is vulgarly supposed to have "eaten" it. This rhetorical figure (called "*ḥusn-i-ta'líl*"), whereby an observed effect is explained by a fanciful cause, is a great favourite with the Persian poets. Here is another instance of a more exaggerated type, in a verse addressed by the poet Rásikh to his sweetheart—

"*Ḥusn-i-mah-rá bá tú sanjídam bi-mízán-i-ḳiyás:*
Pallé-i-mah bar falak shud, ú tú mándí bar zamín!"

"I weighed thy beauty against that of the moon in the balance of my judgment:
The scale containing the moon flew up to heaven, and thou wert left on the earth!"

Could a neater compliment, or one more exaggerated, be imagined?

It is the fashion with some scholars to talk as if literary and poetical talent were a thing of the past in Persia. No mistake could possibly be greater. Everyone is aware of that form of hallucination whereby the Past is glorified at the expense of the Present; that illusion which is typified both in the case of individuals and nations in the phrase, "the happy days of childhood." Men not only forget the defects and disagreeables of the past, and remember only its glories, but they are very apt to weigh several centuries of the Past against a few decades of the Present. "Where," the enthusiastic admirer of older Persian literature exclaims, "are the Rúdagís, the Firdawsís, the Niẓámís, the 'Omar Khayyáms, the Anvarís, the Sa'dís, the Ḥáfiẓes, the Jámís, of the glorious Past? Where are such mighty singers to be found now?" Leaving aside the fact that these immortal bards ranged over a period of five centuries, and that when, at certain periods, the munificent patronage of some prince collected together a number of contemporary poets (as at the so-called "Round Table" of Sulṭán Maḥmúd of Ghazní), posterity (perhaps wisely) often neglected to preserve the works of more than one or two of them, it may confidently be asserted that the nineteenth century has produced a group of most distinguished poets, whose works will undoubtedly, when duly transfigured by the touch of antiquity, go to make up "portions and parcels" of the "glorious Past." Of modern Persian poets the greatest is perhaps Ḳá'ání, who died about A.D. 1854. In panegyric and satire alike he is unrivalled; and he has a wealth of metaphor, a flow of language, and a sweetness of utterance scarcely to be found in any other poet. Although he lacks the mystic sublimity of Jámí, the divine despair of 'Omar Khayyám, and the majestic grandeur of Firdawsí, he manifests at times a humour rarely met with in the older poets. One poem of his, describing a dialogue between an old man and a child, both of whom stammer, is very humorous. The child, on being first addressed by the old man, thinks that his manner of speech is being imitated and ridiculed, and is very angry; but, on being assured and finally convinced that his interlocutor is really afflicted in the same way, he is appeased, and concludes with the words—

"*Ma-ma-man ham gu-gu-gung-am ma-ma-mithl-i-tu-tu-tú,*
Tu-tu-tú ham gu-gu-gungí ma-ma-mithl-i-ma-ma-man."

"I also am a stammerer like unto thee;
Thou also art a stammerer like unto me."

The best poets at present living are Mírzá-yi-Farhang[1] and Mírzá-yi-Yezdání, both of whom I met at Shíráz. They are the only two surviving brothers of Mírzá Dávarí, also a poet of great merit; their father, whose *nom de guerre* was Wiṣál, was widely famed for his poetic talent; and their sons already manifest unmistakable signs of genius.

The conversation of my kind friends, who desired that I might become acquainted with everything calculated to illustrate Persian life, did not, however, confine itself only to the masterpieces of national poetry. Nursery rhymes and schoolboy doggerel also came in for a share of attention. As a specimen of these I may quote the following:—

"'*Tabbat yadá Abí La'—*'
Ákhúnd bi-kesh tavíla;
Káhash bi-dih bi-míré',
Javash bi-dih na-míré'."

Which may be paraphrased thus:—

"'*Abú Lahab's pride shall fall*'—[2]
Put the master in the stall;
He will die, if chaff you give,
Give him oats and he will live."

1 Mírzá-yi-Farhang, I regret to say, is no longer alive. The news of his death reached me a few months ago. [This was written between 1890 and 1893.]

2 The first line is a mutilated fragment of the first verse of the 111th *súra* of the Ḳur'án—"*Tabbat yadá Abí Lahab^{in} wa tabb,*" "The hands of Abú Lahab shall perish and he shall perish." This chapter, being one of the shorter ones at the end of the Ḳur'án, is amongst the earliest learnt by Persian children.

I have already alluded to practical jokes, and described one perpetrated by a wit of the fourteenth century. Let me add another of the present day, which, if rougher than that of 'Obeyd-i-Zákání, was at least intended to convey a salutary lesson to the person on whom it was practised. Amongst the dependents of the governor of a certain town was a man who was possessed by the desire to discover some means of rendering himself invisible. At length he had the good fortune (as he thought) to meet with a dervish who agreed, for a certain sum of money, to supply him with some pills which would produce the desired effect. Filled with delight at the success which appeared at length to have crowned his efforts, the would-be dabbler in the occult sciences did not fail to boast openly before his comrades, and even before the governor, that on a certain day he would visit them unseen and prove the efficacy of his new acquisition. On the appointed day, having taken one or two of the magical pills, he accordingly came to the governor's palace, filled with delightful anticipations of triumph on his own part and envious astonishment on the part of his friends. Now the governor was determined, if possible, to cure him of his taste for the black art, and had therefore given orders to the sentries, servants, and other attendants, as well as to his own associates, that when the would-be magician arrived they were all to behave as though they were unable to see him. Accordingly, when he reached the gate of the palace, he was delighted to observe that the sentries omitted to give him the customary salute. Proceeding farther, he became more and more certain that the dervish's pills had produced the promised effect. No one looked at him; no one saluted him; no one showed any consciousness of his presence. At length he entered the room where the governor was sitting with his associates. Finding that these too appeared insensible to his presence, he determined to give them a proof that he had really been amongst them in invisible form—a fact which they might otherwise refuse to credit. A *ḳalyán*, or water-pipe, was standing in the middle of the room, the charcoal in it still glowing. The pseudo-magician applied his lips to the mouth-piece and began to smoke. Those present at once broke out into expressions of astonishment. "Wonderful!" they exclaimed, "look at that *ḳalyán!* Though no one is near it, it is just as if some one were smoking it: nay, one can even hear the gurgle of the water in the bowl." Enchanted with the sensation he had caused, the "invisible" one became bolder. Some lighted candles were in the room; one of these he blew out. Again exclamations of surprise arose from the company. "Marvellous!" they cried, "there is no wind, yet suddenly that candle has been blown out; what can possibly be the meaning of this?" The candle was again lighted, and again promptly blown out. In the midst of fresh expressions of surprise, the governor suddenly exclaimed, "I have it! I know what has happened! So-and-so has no doubt eaten one of his magical pills, and is even now present amongst us, though we cannot see him; well, we will see if he is intangible as well as invisible. Ho, there! *bacha-há!*[1] Bring the sticks, quick! Lay about you in all directions; perhaps you will be able to teach our invisible friend better manners." The *farráshes* hastened to rain down a shower of blows on the unfortunate intruder, who cried out loudly for mercy. "But where are you?" demanded the governor. "Cease to be invisible, and show yourself, that we may see you." "O master," cried the poor crestfallen magician, "if I be really invisible, how happens it that all the blows of the *farráshes* reach me with such effect? I begin to think that I have been deceived by that rascally dervish, and that I am not invisible at all." On this, amidst the mirth of all present, the sufferer was allowed to depart, with a recommendation that in future he should avoid the occult sciences; an injunction which one may reasonably hope he did not soon forget.

1 *Bacha-há* means "boys," "children"; but the term is also commonly employed in summoning servants, in this case the *farráshes*, whose duty it is to administer corporal punishment.

CHAPTER VI

MYSTICISM, METAPHYSIC, AND MAGIC

"*Guftagú-yi kufr u dín ákhir bi-yak já mí-kashad:*
Khwáb yak khwáb-ast, ammá mukhtalif ta'bír-há."

"Free-thought and faith—the upshot's one; they wrangle o'er a name:
Interpretations differ, but the dream is still the same."

(*Ṣá'ib.*)

"*Hích kas 'ukda'í az kár-i-jihán báz na-kard:*
Har ki ámad girihí chand bar ín tár fuzúd."

"No one yet hath unravelled a knot from the skein of the universe,
And each who came and essayed the same but made the tangle worse."

THE most striking feature of the Persians as a nation is their passion for metaphysical speculation. This passion, so far from being confined to the learned classes, permeates all ranks, and manifests itself in the shopkeeper and the muleteer, as well as in the scholar and the man of letters. Not to give some account of this aspect of Persian life would, then, be a grave omission, calculated to prevent the reader from obtaining a just impression of the national character.

That dogmatic theology is unfavourable to speculation is obvious, and as few theological systems are more dogmatic and uncompromising than that of Islám, it might be expected that Persia, being one of the strongholds of the Muḥammadan faith, would afford at best a sterile soil for the growth of other systems. Such, however, is far from being the case. Persia is, and always has been, a very hot-bed of systems, from the time of Manes and Mazdak in the old Sásánian days, down to the present age, which has brought into being the Bábís and the Sheykhís.

When, in the seventh century, the warlike followers of the

Arabian prophet swept across Írán, overwhelming, in their tumultuous onslaught, an ancient dynasty and a venerable religion, a change, apparently almost unparalleled in history, was in the course of a few years brought over the land. Where for centuries the ancient hymns of the Avesta had been chanted, and the sacred fire had burned, the cry of the *mu'ezzin* summoning the faithful to prayer rang out from minarets reared on the ruins of the temples of Ahura Mazda. The priests of Zoroaster fell by the sword; the ancient books perished in the flames; and soon none were left to represent a once mighty faith but a handful of exiles flying towards the shores of India, and a despised and persecuted remnant in solitary Yezd and remote Kirmán. Truly it seemed that a whole nation had been transformed, and that henceforth the Aryan Persian must not only bear the yoke of the Semitic "lizard-eater" whom he had formerly so despised, but must further adopt his creed, and almost, indeed, his language.

Yet, after all, the change was but skin-deep, and soon a host of heterodox sects born on Persian soil—Shí'ites, Ṣúfís, Ismá'ílís, philosophers—arose to vindicate the claim of Aryan thought to be free, and to transform the religion forced on the nation by Arab steel into something which, though still wearing a semblance of Islám, had a significance widely different from that which one may fairly suppose was intended by the Arabian prophet.

There is, indeed, another view possible—that of M. Gobineau, whose deep insight into Persian character entitles his opinion to careful consideration—viz., that from the very beginning there were latent in the Muḥammadan religion the germs of the most thorough-going pantheism, and that Muḥammad himself did but revive and formulate somewhat differently the ancient beliefs of Mesopotamia[1]. Whether this be true or not (and the point is one

1 See Gobineau's *Religions et Philosophies dans l'Asie Centrale*, especially chapter iii, "La Foi des Arabes."

which, in my opinion, cannot be regarded as altogether settled until the history of Ṣúfíism *amongst those of Arab race* shall have been more carefully studied), there is no doubt that certain passages in the Ḳur'án are susceptible to a certain degree of mystical interpretation. Take, for instance, the 17th verse of the 8th chapter, where God reminds Muḥammad that the victory of Bedr was only in appearance won by the valour of the Muslims: —"*Fa lam taḳtulúhum, wa láḳinna'lláha ḳatalahum; wa má rameyta idh rameyta, wa láḳinna'lláha ramá,*"—"And thou didst not slay them, but God slew them; and thou didst not shoot when thou didst shoot, but God shot." Although there is no need to explain this otherwise than as an assurance that God supported the faithful in their battles, either by natural or (as the commentators assert) by supernatural means, and although it lends itself far less readily than many texts in the New and even in the Old Testament to mystical interpretation, it nevertheless serves the Persian Ṣúfís as a foundation-stone for their pantheistic doctrines. "The Prophet," they say, "did not kill when men fell by his hand. He did not throw when he cast the handful of stones which brought confusion into the ranks of the heathen. He was in both cases but a mirror wherein was manifested the might of God. God alone was the Real Agent, as He is in all the actions which we, in our spiritual blindness, attribute to men. God alone IS, and we are but the waves which stir for a moment on the surface of the Ocean of Being, even as it runs in the tradition, '*God was, and there was naught but HE, and it is now even as it was then.*' Shall we say that God's creation is co-existent with Him? Then are we Manichæans and dualists, nay, polytheists; for we associate the creature with the Creator. Can we say that the sum of Being was increased at the time when the Phenomenal World first appeared? Assuredly not; for that would be to regard the Being of God as a thing finite and conditioned, because capable of enlargement and expansion. What then can we say, except that even as God (who alone is endowed with real existence) was in the Beginning and will be in the End (if, indeed, one may speak of 'Beginning' and 'End' where Eternity is concerned, and where Time, the element of this illusory dream which we call 'Life,' has no place) alone in His Infinite Splendour, so also, even now, He alone IS, and all else is but as a vision which disturbs the night, a cloud which dims the Sun, or a ripple on the bosom of the Ocean?"

In such wise does the Ṣúfí of Persia read the Ḳur'án and expound its doctrine. Those who are familiar with the different developments of Mysticism will not need to be reminded that there is hardly any soil, be it ever so barren, where it will not strike root; hardly any creed, however stern, however formal, round which it will not twine itself. It is, indeed, the eternal cry of the human soul for rest; the insatiable longing of a being wherein infinite ideals are fettered and cramped by a miserable actuality; and so long as man is less than an angel and more than a beast, this cry will not for a moment fail to make itself heard. Wonderfully uniform, too, is its tenor: in all ages, in all countries, in all creeds, whether it come from the Brahmin sage, the Greek philosopher, the Persian poet, or the Christian quietist, it is in essence an enunciation more or less clear, more or less eloquent, of the aspiration of the soul to cease altogether from self, and to be at one with God. As such it must awaken in all who are sensible of this need an echo of sympathy; and therefore I feel that no apology is required for adding a few words more on the ideas which underlie all that is finest and most beautiful in Persian poetry and Persian thought.

To the metaphysical conception of God as Pure Being, and the ethical conception of God as the Eternally Holy, the Ṣúfí superadds another conception, which may be regarded as the keynote of all Mysticism. To him, above all else, God is the Eternally Beautiful—"*Jánán-i-Ḥaḳíḳí*," the "True Beloved." Before time was, He existed in His Infinite Purity, unrevealed and unmanifest. Why was this state changed? Why was the troubled phantasm of the Contingent World evoked from the silent depths of the Non-Existent? Let me answer in the words of Jámí, who, perhaps, of all the mystic poets of Persia best knew how to combine depth of thought with sweetness and clearness of utterance. Poor as is my rendering of his sublime song, it may still suffice to give some idea of the original. The passage is from his *Yúsuf ú Zuleykhá*[1], and runs as follows:—

"In solitude, where Being signless dwelt,
And all the Universe still dormant lay
Concealed in selflessness, One Being was
Exempt from 'I-' or 'Thou-' ness, and apart
From all duality; Beauty Supreme,
Unmanifest, except unto Itself
By Its own light, yet fraught with power to charm
The souls of all; concealed in the Unseen,
An Essence pure, unstained by aught of ill.
No mirror to reflect Its loveliness,
Nor comb to touch Its locks; the morning breeze
Ne'er stirred Its tresses; no collyrium
Lent lustre to Its eyes: no rosy cheeks
O'ershadowed by dark curls like hyacinth,
Nor peach-like down were there; no dusky mole
Adorned Its face; no eye had yet beheld
Its image. To Itself It sang of love
In wordless measures. By Itself It cast
The die of love.
But Beauty cannot brook
Concealment and the veil, nor patient rest
Unseen and unadmired: 'twill burst all bonds,
And from Its prison-casement to the world
Reveal Itself. See where the tulip grows
In upland meadows, how in balmy spring
It decks itself; and how amidst its thorns
The wild rose rends its garment, and reveals
Its loveliness. Thou, too, when some rare thought,
Or beauteous image, or deep mystery
Flashes across thy soul, canst not endure
To let it pass, but hold'st it, that perchance
In speech or writing thou may'st send it forth
To charm the world.

1 The passage in question is the 11th section of the poem. It will be found on pp. 11–12 of the Lucknow edition, and on pp. 16–17 of Rosenzweig's edition.

Wherever Beauty dwells
Such is its nature, and its heritage
From Everlasting Beauty, which emerged
From realms of purity to shine upon
The worlds, and all the souls which dwell therein.
One gleam fell from It on the Universe,
And on the angels, and this single ray
Dazzled the angels, till their senses whirled
Like the revolving sky. In divers forms
Each mirror showed It forth, and everywhere
Its praise was chanted in new harmonies.
. . . . . .

Each speck of matter did He constitute
A mirror, causing each one to reflect
The beauty of His visage. From the rose
Flashed forth His beauty, and the nightingale
Beholding it, loved madly. From that Light
The candle drew the lustre which beguiles
The moth to immolation. On the sun
His Beauty shone, and straightway from the wave
The lotus reared its head. Each shining lock
Of Leylá's hair attracted Majnún's heart
Because some ray divine reflected shone
In her fair face. 'Twas He to Shírín's lips
Who lent that sweetness which had power to steal
The heart from Parvíz, and from Ferhád life.

His Beauty everywhere doth show itself,
And through the forms of earthly beauties shines
Obscured as through a veil. He did reveal
His face through Joseph's coat, and so destroyed
Zuleykhá's peace. Where'er thou seest a veil,
Beneath that veil He hides. Whatever heart
Doth yield to love, He charms it. In His love
The heart hath life. Longing for Him, the soul
Hath victory. That heart which seems to love
The fair ones of this world, loves Him alone.

Beware! say not, 'He is All-Beautiful,
And we His lovers.' Thou art but the glass,
And He the Face[1] confronting it, which casts
Its image on the mirror. He alone
Is manifest, and thou in truth art hid.

1 So it is written in the Ḳur'án, "*Kullu shey'*[in] *hálik*[un] *illá wajhu-hu,*" "All things shall perish save His Face" (Ḳur'án, xxviii, 88).

Pure Love, like Beauty, coming but from Him,
Reveals itself in thee. If steadfastly
Thou canst regard, thou wilt at length perceive
He is the mirror also—He alike
The Treasure and the Casket. 'I,' and 'Thou'
Have here no place, and are but phantasies
Vain and unreal. Silence! for this tale
Is endless, and no eloquence hath power
To speak of Him. 'Tis best for us to love,
And suffer silently, being as naught."

But is this the sum of the Ṣúfí's philosophy? Is he to rest content with earthly love, because he knows that the lover's homage is in truth rendered, not to the shrine at which he offers his devotion, but to the Divine Glory—the Shekinah—which inhabits and irradiates it? Not so. Let us listen once more to the utterance of Jámí—

"Be thou the thrall of love; make this thine object;
For this one thing seemeth to wise men worthy.
Be thou love's thrall, that thou may'st win thy freedom,
Bear on thy breast its brand, that thou may'st blithe be.
Love's wine will warm thee, and will steal thy senses;
All else is soulless stupor and self-seeking.
Remembrances of love refresh the lover,
Whose voice when lauding love e'er waxeth loudest.
But that he drained a draught from this deep goblet,
In the wide worlds not one would wot of Majnún.
Thousands of wise and well-learned men have wended
Through life, who, since for love they had no liking,
Have left nor name, nor note, nor sign, nor story,
Nor tale for future time, nor fame for fortune.
Sweet songsters 'midst the birds are found in plenty,
But, when love's lore is taught by the love-learned,
Of moth and nightingale they most make mention.
Though in this world a hundred tasks thou tryest,
'Tis love alone which from thyself will save thee.
Even from earthly love thy face avert not,
Since to the Real it may serve to raise thee.
Ere A, B, C are rightly apprehended,
How canst thou con the pages of thy Ḳur'án?
A sage (so heard I), unto whom a student
Came craving counsel on the course before him,
Said, 'If thy steps be strangers to love's pathways,
Depart, learn love, and then return before me!

For, shouldst thou fear to drink wine from Form's flagon,
Thou canst not drain the draught of the Ideal.
But yet beware! Be not by Form belated;
Strive rather with all speed the bridge to traverse.
If to the bourn thou fain wouldst bear thy baggage
Upon the bridge let not thy footsteps linger.'"[1]

The renunciation of self is the great lesson to be learned, and its first steps may be learned from a merely human love. But what is called love is often selfish; rarely absolutely unselfish. The test of unselfish love is this, that we should be ready and willing to sacrifice our own desires, happiness, even life itself, to render the beloved happy, even though we know that our sacrifice will never be understood or appreciated, and that we shall therefore not be rewarded for it by an increase of love or gratitude.

Such is the true love which leads us up to God. We love our fellow-creatures because there is in them something of the Divine, some dim reflection of the True Beloved, reminding our souls of their origin, home, and destination. From the love of the reflection we pass to the love of the Light which casts it; and, loving the Light, we at length become one with It, losing the false self and gaining the True, therein attaining at length to happiness and rest, and becoming one with all that we have loved—the Essence of that which constitutes the beauty alike of a noble action, a beautiful thought, or a lovely face.

Such in outline is the Ṣúfí philosophy. Beautiful as it is, and worthy as it is of deeper study, I have said as much about it as my space allows, and must pass on to speak of other matters.

Mysticism is in its nature somewhat vague and difficult to formulate, varying in character between an emotional philosophy and a devotional religion. On one side of it stands metaphysic, and on the other theology. Of Muḥammadan theology I do not

1 These two translations are reprinted, almost without alteration, from my article on "Ṣúfiism" in *Religious Systems of the World* (Swan Sonnenschein and Co.), where I first published them.

propose to speak, save incidentally, as occasion arises; neither is this the place to treat systematically of the various schools of philosophy which have sprung up in Persia. Of the earlier ones, indeed, one may say generally that they are adaptations of either Aristotle or Plato, and that they may most fitly be described as the scholasticism of Islám. Of two of the later philosophers, however—Mullá Ṣadrá of Shíráz, and Ḥájí Mullá Hádí of Sabzawár—I shall say a few words, inasmuch as they mark a new development in Persian thought, while at the same time they are less known in Europe than the Avicennas, the Ghazzálís, and the Fárábís of earlier days.

Mullá Ṣadru'd-Dín Muḥammad ibn Ibráhím ibn Yaḥyá, commonly known as Mullá Ṣadrá, flourished in the latter half of the seventeenth century. He was the son of a rich merchant of Shíráz, who had grown old without being blessed with a son. Being very desirous of leaving an heir to inherit his wealth, he made a vow that if God would grant him this wish he would give the sum of one *túmán* (about 6*s.*) a day to the poor for the rest of his life. Soon afterwards Mullá Ṣadrá was born, and the father faithfully accomplished his vow till his death. When this occurred, Mullá Ṣadrá, who had already manifested an unusual aptitude for learning and a special taste for philosophy, decided, after consulting with his mother, to bestow the greater portion of the wealth which he had inherited on the poor, and to go to Iṣfahán to prosecute his studies.

It was the time when the Ṣafaví kings ruled over Persia, with their capital at Iṣfahán, and the colleges of that city were famed throughout the East. Mullá Ṣadrá enquired on his arrival there who were the most celebrated teachers of philosophy, and was informed that they were three in number, Mír Abú'l-Ḳásim Fandaraskí, Mír Muḥammad Báḳir, better known as Mír Dámád, and Sheykh Behá'u'd-Dín 'Ámilí. He first presented himself before Mír Dámád, and asked for advice as to his studies. The latter replied, "If you want inward meaning only, go to Mír

Fandaraskí; if you want mere outward form, go to Sheykh Behá; but if you desire to combine both, then come to me." Mullá Ṣadrá accordingly attended the lectures of Mír Dámád regularly, but did not fail to profit as far as possible by the teaching of the other professors.

At length it happened that Mír Dámád desired to undertake the pilgrimage to Mecca. He therefore bade each of his pupils compose during his absence a treatise on some branch of philosophy, which should be submitted to him on his return, in order that he might judge of the progress they had made. Acting on this injunction, Mullá Ṣadrá wrote his first great work, the *Shawáhid-i-Rubúbiyyé* ("Evidences of Divinity"), which he presented to his teacher on his return from the pilgrimage.

Some time afterwards, when Mullá Ṣadrá was walking beside Mír Dámád, the latter said to him, "*Ṣadrá ján! Kitáb-i-merá az meyán burdí!*" ("O my dear Ṣadrá, thou hast taken my work out of the midst"—meaning that he had superseded it by the work which he had just composed). This generous recognition of his merit by his teacher was the beginning of a wide celebrity which has gone on increasing till this day. Yet this celebrity brought him into some danger from the fanatical *mullás*, who did not fail to detect in his works the savour of heterodoxy. It was during his residence at Ḳum especially that his life was jeopardised by the indignation of these zealots, but on many occasions he was subjected to annoyances and persecutions. He lived at a time when the clerical power was paramount, and philosophy in disrepute. Had he lived later, he might have been the recipient of favours from the great, and have enjoyed tranquillity, and perhaps even opulence: as it was, his was the glory of once more bringing back philosophy to the land whence it had been almost banished.

Mullá Ṣadrá gained numerous disciples (some of whom, such as Mullá Muḥsin-i-Feyẓ, attained to great fame), and left behind him a multitude of books, mostly in Arabic, of which the

Shawáhid-i-Rubúbiyyé already mentioned, and a more systematic and voluminous work called the *Asfár-i-arba'a* ("Four treatises"), enjoy the greatest reputation. The three points claimed as original in Mullá Ṣadrá's teaching[1] are as follows:—

(1) His axiom "*Basíṭu'l-ḥaḳíḳat ḳullu'l-ashyá wa leysa bi-shey'in minhá*"—"The element of Real Being is all things, yet is none of them."

(2) His doctrine that true cognition of any object only becomes possible by the identification of the knower with the known.

(3) His assertion that the Imagination is independent of the physical organism, and belongs in its nature to the world of the soul: hence that not only in young children, but even in animals, it persists as a spiritual entity after death. In this point he differed from his predecessors, who held that it was only with the development of the Rational Soul that immortality became possible.

I must now pass on to Ḥájí Mullá Hádí of Sabzawár, the greatest Persian philosopher of the nineteenth century. He was the son of Ḥájí Mahdí, and was born in the year A.H. 1212 (A.D. 1797–8). He began his studies when only seven years old, under the tuition of Ḥájí Mullá Ḥuseyn of Sabzawár, and at the early age of twelve composed a small treatise. Anxious to pursue his studies in theology and jurisprudence, he visited Mashhad in company with his teacher, and remained there for five years, living in the most frugal manner (not from necessity, for he was far from poor, but from choice), and continuing his studies with unremitting ardour. When in his seventeenth year he heard of the fame of Mullá 'Alí Núrí, who was then teaching in Iṣfahán, he was very anxious to proceed thither at once, but was for several years prevented from so doing by the opposition of his

1 A further account of Mullá Ṣadrá, differing in some points from that which is here given, will be found in Gobineau's *Religions et Philosophies dans l'Asie Centrale*, pp. 80–90.

friends. Ultimately, however, he was enabled to gratify his wishes, and to take up his residence at Iṣfahán, where he diligently attended the lectures of Mullá 'Alí Núrí. He appears, however, to have received more advantage from the help of one of Mullá 'Alí's pupils, named Mullá Ismá'íl, "the One-eyed." In Iṣfahán he remained for seven years, devoting himself with such avidity to the study of philosophy that he rarely slept for much more than four hours out of the twenty-four. To combat slothfulness he was in the habit of reposing on a cloak spread on the bare brick floor of the little room which he occupied in the college, with nothing but a stone for his pillow.

The simplicity and indeed austerity of his life was far from being his chief or only merit. Being possessed of private means greatly in excess of what his simple requirements demanded, he used to take pains to discover which of the students stood most in need of pecuniary help, and would then secretly place sums of money varying from one to five or even ten *túmáns* (six shillings to three pounds) in their rooms during their absence, without leaving any clue which could lead to the identification of the donor. In this manner he is said to have expended no less than 100,000 *túmáns* (about £30,000), while he was in Iṣfahán, leaving himself only so much as he deemed necessary for his own maintenance.

Having completed his studies at Iṣfahán, he made a pilgrimage to Mecca, whence he returned by way of Kirmán. There he remained for a while and married a wife, whom he took back to his native town of Sabzawár. Soon after his return he paid another visit to Mashhad, and remained there ten months, giving lectures on philosophy, but soon returned thence to settle in Sabzawár, whither his increasing renown began to draw students from all parts of Persia. During the day he used to give two lectures, each of two hours' duration, on Metaphysics, taking as his text either some of the writings of Mullá Ṣadrá, or his own notes. The rest of his time was spent for the most part in study and devotion. In person he was tall of stature, thin, and of slender frame; his complexion was dark, his face pleasing to look upon, his speech eloquent and flowing, his manner gentle, unobtrusive, and even humble. His abstemiousness was such that he would never eat more than the limited number of mouthfuls which he deemed necessary, neither would he accept the invitations which he often received from the great. He was always ready to help the widow, the orphan, and the stranger, and ever exemplified in his demeanour the apophthegm of Bú 'Alí Síná (Avicenna): "*Al-'árifu hashsh*^{un}, *bashsh*^{un}, *bassám*^{un}*; wa ḳeyfa lá, wa huwa farḥán*^{u} *bi'l-ḥaḳḳi wa bi-ḳulli shey?*" ("The gnostic is gentle, courteous, smiling; and how should it be otherwise, since he rejoices in God and in all things?") The complete course of instruction in philosophy which he gave lasted seven years, at the end of which period those students who had followed it diligently were replaced by others. Many, of course, were unable to complete their education; but, on the whole, nearly a thousand satisfactorily accomplished it. Till within three days of his death Ḥájí Mullá Hádí never disappointed his eager audience of a single lecture, and he was actually engaged in teaching when struck down by the disease which terminated his life. The eager throng of students surrounded him in a circle, while he was speaking of the Essence and Attributes of God, when suddenly he was overcome by faintness, and laid down the book which he held in his hand, saying, "I have so often repeated the word '*Hú*,' '*Hú*'" ("HE," *i.e.* God; in which sense only the Arabic pronoun is used by the Persians) "that it has become fixed in my head, and my head, following my tongue, seems to keep crying '*Hú*,' '*Hú*.'" Having uttered these words, he laid down his head and fainted, and two days later he peacefully passed away in the year A.H. 1295 (A.D. 1878), sincerely mourned by those to whom he had been endeared alike by his learning and his benevolence. He was buried, according to instructions contained in his will, outside the Mashhad gate of Sabzawár.

A handsome tomb has been raised over his grave by orders of the Grand Vizier, and the spot is regarded as one of great sanctity, and is visited by numerous pilgrims[1].

So died, after a noble and useful life, the Sage of Sabzawár. His major works amount to about seventeen in number, including an elementary treatise on philosophy, written in Persian, in an easy style, at the request of the Sháh, and entitled *Asráru'l-Ḥikam* ("Secrets of Philosophy"). He was a poet as well as a metaphysician, and has left behind him a Díván in Persian, as well as two long and highly esteemed versified treatises in Arabic, one on logic, the other on metaphysic. He had three sons, of whom the eldest (who was also by far the most capable) survived him only two years; the other two are still [1893] living at Sabzawár, and one at least of them still teaches in the college on which his father's talents shed so great a lustre.

The pupils of the Sage of Sabzawár entertained for him an unbounded love and veneration. They even believe him to have been endowed with the power of working miracles (*kerámát*), though he himself never allowed this statement to be made before him. My teacher, Mírzá Asadu'lláh, informed me, however, that the following was a well-known fact. Ḥájí Mullá Hádí's son-in-law had a daughter who had been paralysed for years. One night, a year after the Ḥájí's death, she saw him in a dream, and he said to her, "Arise, my daughter, and walk." The excessive joy which she experienced at seeing him and hearing these words caused her to wake up. She immediately roused her sister, who was sleeping beside her, and told her what she had dreamed. The latter said, "You had better get up and try if you can walk; perhaps there is more in the dream than a mere fancy." After a little persuasion the girl got up, and found

1 All these details I obtained from my teacher, Mírzá Asadu'lláh of Sabzawár, who compiled the original memoir, not only from his own recollections of his venerated master in philosophy, but from information supplied by one of Mullá Hádí's sons. It is chiefly by reason of the good authority on which they rest that I have decided to give them almost in full.

to her delight that she really was able to walk quite well. Next day she went to the Ḥájí's tomb to return thanks, accompanied by a great crowd of people, to whom her former affliction was as well-known as her present recovery was obvious.

Another event, less marvellous, however, than the above, was related to me as follows. When a detachment of the army was passing through Sabzawár, a soldier, who had been given a requisition for corn for the horses drawn on a certain *mullá*, brought the document to Ḥájí Mullá Hádí and asked him in whose name it was drawn, as he himself was unable to read. The Ḥájí looked at it, and, knowing that the *mullá* who was therein commanded to supply the corn was in impoverished circumstances, and could ill support the loss, replied, "I must supply you with what you require; go to the storehouse and take it." Accordingly the soldier carried off as much corn as he needed, and gave it to the horses. In the morning, however, on entering the stable, the soldiers found that the corn was untouched. Enquiries were made whence it came, and on its being discovered that it was the property of the Ḥájí, it was returned to him. This story soon gained currency and credence amongst officers and men alike, and added not a little to the Ḥájí's reputation, notwithstanding that he himself continued to make light of it, and even to deny it.

It may not be amiss to give some details as to the course of study which those who desired to attend the Ḥájí's lectures were expected to have already pursued, and the subjects in which they had to produce evidence of proficiency before they were received as his pupils. These preliminary studies were as follows:—

I. Grammar, Rhetoric, etc. (*Edebiyyé*), also called "Preliminaries" (*Muḳaddamát*).—Under this head is included a competent knowledge of Arabic and its grammar, with ability to read such works as *Jámí's* commentary, *Suyúṭí*, and the *Muṭawwal.*

II. Logic (*Manṭiḳ*), as contained in such treatises as the *Kubrá*, the *Shamsiyyé*, and the *Sharḥ-i-Maṭáli'*.

III. Mathematics (including Euclid and Astronomy), which is studied *pari-passu* with Logic.

IV. Elements of Jurisprudence (*Fiḳh*).

V. Scholastic Theology (*'Ilm-i-Kelám*), as set forth in the following works:—

1. The *Hidáyé* of Meybudí, a concise but knotty compendium of the elements of this science in Arabic.
2. The *Tajríd* of Náṣíru'd-Dín of Ṭús, with the commentary of Mullá 'Alí Ḳúshjí.
3. The *Shawáriḳ* of Mullá 'Abdu'r-Razzáḳ Láhijí, the son-in-law of Mullá Ṣadrá.

Those students who were able to show that they had acquired a satisfactory knowledge of these subjects were allowed to enroll themselves as the pupils of Ḥájí Mullá Hádí, and to commence their study of Metaphysic proper (*Ḥikmat-i-Iláhí*), as set forth in his works and in those of Mullá Ṣadrá.

I trust that I have succeeded in making it sufficiently clear that the study of Persian philosophy is not a thing to be lightly undertaken, and that proficiency in it can only be the result of diligent application, combined with good natural capacity. It is not a thing to play with in a dilettante manner, but is properly regarded by its votaries as the highest intellectual training, and the crown and summit of all knowledge. It was not long ere I discovered this fact; and as it was clearly impossible for me to go through a tenth part of the proper curriculum, while at the same time I was deeply desirous of becoming, in some measure at least, acquainted with the most recent developments of Persian thought, I was fain to request my teacher, Mírzá Asadu'lláh, to take compassion on my infirmities, and to instruct me as far as possible, and in as simple a manner as possible, concerning the essential practical conclusions of the doctrines of which he was the exponent. This he kindly exerted himself to do; and though any attempt at a systematic enunciation of Ḥájí Mullá Hádí's philosophy, even were I capable of undertaking it, would be out of place here, I think that it may not be uninteresting if I notice briefly some of its more remarkable features—not as derived from his writings, but as orally expounded to me, with explanations and illustrations, by his pupil and disciple.

As in the Ṣúfí doctrine, Being is conceived of as one: "*Al-vujúdu ḥaḳíḳat^{un} váḥidat^{un} basíṭat^{un} va lahu marátib^{u} mutafáḍila*":—"Being is a single simple Reality, and it has degrees differing in excellence." Poetically, this idea is expressed in the following quatrain:—

"*Majmú'a-i-kawn-rá bi-ḳánún-i-sabaḳ*
Kardím taṣaffuḥ varaḳ^{an} ba'da varaḳ:
Ḥaḳḳá ki na-khwándím ú na-dídím dar-ú
Juz Dhát-i-Ḥaḳḳ, u ṣifát-i-dhátiyyé-i-Ḥaḳḳ."

"Like a lesson-book, the compendium of the Universe
We turned over, leaf after leaf:
In truth we read and saw therein naught
Save the Essence of God, and the Essential Attributes of God."

The whole Universe, then, is to be regarded as the unfolding, manifestation, or projection of God. It is the mirror wherein He sees Himself; the arena wherein His various Attributes display their nature. It is subsequent to Him not in sequence of *time* (for time is merely the medium which encloses the phenomenal world, and which is, indeed, dependent on this for its very existence), but in sequence of *causation*; just as the light given off by a luminous body is subsequent to the luminosity of that body *in causation* (inasmuch as the latter is the source and origin of the former, and that whereon it depends and whereby it subsists), but not subsequent to it in *time* (because it is impossible to conceive of any time in the existence of an essentially luminous body antecedent to the emission of light therefrom). This amounts to saying that the Universe is co-eternal with God, but not co-equal, because it is merely an Emanation dependent on Him, while He has no need of it.

Just as the light proceeding from a luminous body becomes weaker and more diffuse as it recedes from its source, so the Emanations of Being become less real, or, in other words, more gross and material, as they become farther removed from their focus and origin. This gradual descent or recession from the Primal Being, which is called the *Ḳaws-i-Nuzúl* ("Arc of Descent"), has in reality infinite grades, but a certain definite number (seven) is usually recognised.

Man finds himself in the lowest of these grades—the Material World; but of that world he is the highest development, for he contains in himself the potentiality of re-ascent, by steps corresponding to those in the "Arc of Descent," to God, his Origin and his Home. To discover how this return may be effected, how the various stages of the *Ḳaws-i-Ṣu'úd* ("Arc of Ascent") may be traversed, is the object of philosophy.

"The soul of man is corporeal in origin, but spiritual in continuance" ("*An-nafsu fi'l-ḥudúthi jismániyya, wa fi'l-baḳá'i teḳúnu rúḥániyya*"). Born of matter, it is yet capable of a spiritual development which will lead it back to God, and enable it, during the span of a mortal life, to accomplish the ascent from matter to spirit, from the periphery to the centre. In the "Arc of Ascent" also are numerous grades; but here again, as in the "Arc of Descent," seven are usually recognised. It may be well at this point to set down in a tabular form these grades as they exist both in the Macrocosm, or Arc of Descent, and in the Microcosm, or Arc of Ascent, which is man:—

I. ARC OF ASCENT. SEVEN PRINCIPLES IN MAN (*Laṭá'if-i-sab'a*).	II. ARC OF DESCENT. SERIES OF EMANATIONS.
1. The most subtle principle (*Akhfa*).	1. Exploration of the World of Divinity (*Seyr dar 'álam-i-Láhút*)[1].
2. The subtle principle (*Khafá*).	2. The World of Divinity (*'Álam-i-Láhút*)[1].
3. The secret (*Sirr*).	3. The World of the Intelligences (*'Álam-i-Jabarút*).
4. The heart (*Ḳalb*).	4. The World of the Angels (*'Álam-i-Malakút*).
5. The spirit (*Rúḥ*).	5. The World of Ideas (*'Álam-i-Ma'ná*).
6. The soul (*Nafs*).	6. The World of Form (*'Álam-i-Ṣúrat*).
7. The nature (*Ṭab'*).	7. The Material World (*'Álam-i-Ṭabí'at*).

[1] I do not think that these first two should stand thus, for at most they only

A few words of explanation are necessary concerning the above scheme. Each stage in either column corresponds with that which is placed opposite to it. Thus, for instance, the mere matter which in the earliest stage of man's development constitutes his totality corresponds to the material world to which it belongs. In the material world the "Arc of Descent" has reached its lowest point; in man, the highest product of the material world, the ascent is begun. When the human embryo begins to take form it rises to the World of Soul, thus summing up in itself two grades of the Arcs. It may never ascend higher than this point; for, of course, when the upward evolution of man is spoken of, it is not implied that this is effected by all, or even by the majority of men. These "seven principles" do not represent necessarily co-existing components or elements, but successive grades of development, at any one of which, after the first, the process of growth may be arrested. The race exists for its highest development; humanity for the production of the Perfect Man (*Insán-i-Kámil*), who, summing up as he does all the grades of ascent from matter—the lowest point of the series of emanations—to God, is described as the Microcosm, the compendium of all the planes of Existence (*ḥaẕrat-i-jámi'*), or sometimes as the "sixth plane" (*ḥaẕrat-i-sádisa*), because he includes and summarises all the five spiritual planes.

It has been said that some men never rise beyond the second grade—the World of Soul or Form. These are such as occupy themselves entirely during their lives with sensual pursuits—

mark two different phases in the experience of the soul—an attaining unto the World of Divinity, and a journeying therein. My impression is that they should be replaced thus:—1. The World of Divinity (*i.e.* the Divine Essence, '*Álam-i-Láhút*); 2. The World of the Attributes ('*Álam-i-Ráḥút*). This corresponds to the views given in the commentaries on the *Fuṣúṣ* of Sheykh Muḥyi'd-Dín ibnu'l-'Arabí and other similar works, where the "Five Planes" (*Ḥaẕrat-i-khams*), which coincide with the first five grades given here (*i.e.* those which belong to the Spiritual World), are discussed. I have not, however, considered myself justified in making any alteration in Mírzá Asadu-'lláh's scheme.

eating, drinking, and the like. Previously to Mullá Ṣadrá it was generally held by philosophers that these perished entirely after death, inasmuch as they had not developed any really spiritual principle. Mullá Ṣadrá, however, took great pains to prove that even in these cases where the "Rational Soul" (*Nafs-i-náṭiḳa*) had not been developed during life, there did exist a spiritual part which survived death and resisted disintegration. This spiritual part he called "Imaginations" (*Khiyálát*).

Yet even in this low state of development, where no effort has been made to reach the plane of the reason, a man may lead an innocent and virtuous life. What will then be the condition after death of that portion of him which survives the body? It cannot re-enter the material world, for that would amount to Metempsychosis, which, so far as I have been able to ascertain, is uncompromisingly denied by all Persian philosophers. Neither can it ascend higher in the spiritual scale, for the period during which progress was possible is past. Moreover, it derives no pleasure from spiritual or intellectual experiences, and would not be happy in one of the higher worlds, even could it attain thereto. It desires material surroundings, and yet cannot return to the material world. It therefore does what seems to it the next best thing: it creates for itself subjective pseudo-material surroundings, and in this dream-dwelling it makes its eternal home. If it has acted rightly in the world according to its lights, it is happy; if wrongly, then miserable. The happiness or misery of its hereafter depends on its merit, but in either case it is purely subjective and absolutely stationary. There is for it neither advance nor return: it can neither ascend higher, nor re-enter the material world either by Transmigration or Resurrection, both of which the philosophers deny.

What has been said above applies, with slight modifications, to all the other grades, at any rate the lower ones. If a man has during his life in the world attained to the grade of the spirit (the third grade in order of ascent) and acquired rational or intellectual faculties, he may still have used these well or ill. In either case he enters after death into the World of Ideas, where he is happy or miserable according to his deserts. But, so far as I could learn, anyone who has during his life developed any of the four highest principles passes after death into a condition of happiness and blessedness, since mere intellect without virtue will not enable him to pass beyond the third grade, or World of the Spirit. According to the degree of development which he has reached, he enters the World of the Angels, the World of the Intelligences, or the World of Divinity itself.

From what has been said it will be clear that a bodily resurrection and a material hereafter are both categorically denied by the philosophers. Nevertheless, states of subjective happiness or misery, practically constituting a heaven or hell, exist. These, as has been explained, are of different grades in both cases. Thus there is a "Paradise of Actions" (*Jannatu'l-Af'ál*), where the soul is surrounded by an ideal world of beautiful forms; a "Paradise of Attributes" (*Jannatu'ṣ-Ṣifát*); and a "Paradise of the Essence" (*Jannatu'dh-Dhát*), which is the highest of all, for there the soul enjoys the contemplation of the Divine Perfections, which hold it in an eternal rapture, and cause it to forget and cease to desire all those objects which constitute the pleasure of the denizens of the lower paradises. It is, indeed, unconscious of aught but God, and is annihilated or absorbed in Him.

The lower subjective worlds, where the less fully developed soul suffers or rejoices, are often spoken of collectively as the *'Álam-i-Mithál* ("World of Similitudes"), or the *'Álam-i-Barzakh* ("World of the Barrier," or "Border-world"). The first term is applied to it because each of its denizens takes a form corresponding to his attributes. In this sense 'Omar Khayyám has said[1]—

> "*Rúzí ki jezá-yi-har ṣifat khwáhad búd*
> *Ḳadr-i-tú bi-ḳadr-i-ma'rifat khwáhad búd;*

1 Ed. Whinfield, London, 1883, p. 155, No. 228.

Dar ḥusn-i-ṣifat kúsh, ki dar rúz-i-jezá
Ḥashr-i-tú bi-ṣúrat-i-ṣifat khwáhad búd."

"On that day when all qualities shall receive their recompense
Thy worth shall be in proportion to thy wisdom.
Strive after good qualities, for in the Day of Recompense
Thy resurrection shall be in the *form of the attribute*."

Thus a greedy gluttonous man takes the form of a pig, and it is in this sense only that metempsychosis (*tanásukh*) is held by the Persian philosophers. On this point my teacher was perfectly clear and definite. It is not uncommon for Ṣúfís to describe a man by the form with which they profess to identify him in the "World of Similitudes." Thus I have heard a Ṣúfí say to his antagonist, "I see you in the World of Similitudes as an old toothless fox, desirous of preying upon others, but unable to do so." I once said to Mírzá Asadu'lláh that, if I rightly understood his views, hell was nothing else than an eternal nightmare: whereat he smiled, and said that I had rightly apprehended his meaning.

Although a soul cannot rise higher than that world to which it has assimilated itself during life, it may be delayed by lower affinities in the "World of the Barrier" on its way thither. All bad habits, even when insufficient to present a permanent obstacle to spiritual progress, tend to cause such delay, and to retard the upward ascent of the soul. From this it will be seen that the denizens of the "World of the Barrier" are of three classes, two of these being permanent, and abiding for ever in the state of subjective happiness or misery which they have merited, and the third consisting of souls temporarily delayed there to undergo a species of probation before passing to the worlds above.

On one occasion I put the following question to Mírzá Asadu-'lláh:—"Two persons, *A* and *B*, have been friends during their lifetime. The former has so lived as to merit happiness hereafter; the latter, misery. Both die and enter the 'World of the Barrier,' there receiving forms appropriate to their attributes; the one, moreover, is happy, the other wretched. Will not *A* have cognisance of *B*'s miserable condition, and will not this knowledge tend to mar his felicity?"

To this question my teacher replied as follows:—"*A*'s world is altogether apart from *B*'s, and the two are entirely out of contact. In *A*'s world are present all things that he desires to have in such form as he pleases, for his world is the creation of his Imaginative Faculty freed from the restraints of matter and the outward senses, and endowed with full power to see what it conceives. Therefore if *A* desires the presence of *B* as he knew him formerly, *B* will be present with him in that form under which he was so known, and not in the repulsive form which he has now assumed. There is no more difficulty in this than in a person dreaming in ordinary sleep that he sees one of his friends in a state of happiness when at that very time his friend is in great pain or trouble."

Such, in outline, are the more remarkable features of this philosophy as expounded to me by Mírzá Asadu'lláh. That it differs considerably from the ideas formed by most European scholars of the philosophy current in Persia, as represented in the books, I am well aware. I can only suppose that Gobineau is right as to the extent to which the system of "*ketmán*" (concealment of opinions) prevails in Persia—a view which my own experience strongly tends to confirm. He says, for example, in speaking of Mullá Ṣadrá (*Religions et Philosophies dans l'Asie Centrale*, p. 88), in whose footsteps Ḥájí Mullá Hádí for the most part followed:—

"Le soin qu'il prenait de déguiser ses discours, il était nécessaire qu'il le prît surtout de déguiser ses livres; c'est ce qu'il a fait, et à les lire on se ferait l'idée la plus imparfaite de son enseignement. Je dis à les lire sans un maître qui possède la tradition. Autrement on y pénètre sans peine." Such a system of concealment may seem strange to those accustomed to the liberty of thought enjoyed in Europe, but it is rendered necessary in the

East by the power and intolerance of the clergy. Many a philosopher like Sheykh Shihábu'd-Dín Suhravardí, many a Ṣúfí like Manṣúr-i-Ḥalláj, has paid with his life for too free and open an expression of his opinions.

For the rest, many of the ideas here enunciated bear an extraordinary similarity to those set forth by Mr Sinnett in his work entitled *Esoteric Buddhism*. Great exception has been taken to this work, and especially it has been asserted that the ideas unfolded in it are totally foreign to Buddhism of any sort. Of this I am not in a position to judge: very possibly it is true, though even then the ideas in question may still be of Indian origin. But whatever the explanation be, no one, I feel sure, can compare the chapters in Mr Sinnett's book, entitled respectively, "The Constitution of Man," "Devachan," and "Kama Loca," with what I have written of Ḥájí Mullá Hádí's views on the Nature of Man and his Hereafter, without being much struck by the resemblance.

Certain other points merit a brief notice. The physical sciences as known to Persian philosophy are those of the ancients. Their chemistry regards earth, air, fire, and water as the four elements: their astronomy is simply the Ptolemaic system. Furthermore they regard the Universe as finite, and adduce many proofs, some rather ingenious, others weak enough, against the contrary hypothesis. Of these I will give one only as a specimen.

"Let us suppose," they say, "that the Universe is infinite. Then from the centre of the earth draw two straight lines, diverging from one another at an angle of 60°, to the circumference, and produce them thence to infinity. Join their terminal points by another straight line, thus forming the base of the triangle. Now, since the two sides of the triangle are equal (for both were drawn from one point to infinity), therefore the angles at the base are equal; and since the angle at the apex is 60°, therefore each of the remaining angles is 60°, and the triangle is equilateral. Therefore, since the sides are infinite in length, the base is also infinite in length. But the base is a straight line joining two points (viz. the terminal points of the sides); that is to say, it is limited in both directions. Therefore it is not infinite in length, neither are the sides infinite in length, and a straight line cannot be drawn to infinity. Therefore the Universe is finite. Q.E.D."

This theorem scarcely needs comment. It, along with the endless discussions of a similar nature on the "Indivisible Atom" (*Jawhar-i-fard*) and the like, is an inheritance from the scholastic theology (*'Ilm-i-Kelám*), the physics of which have been retained by all Persian metaphysicians up to the present day.

A few words may be said about the psychology of the system in question. Five psychic faculties (corresponding to the five senses) are supposed to exist. These, with their cerebral seats, are as follows:—

FORE-BRAIN	1. The compound perception (*Ḥiss-i-mushtaraké*), which has the double function of receiving and apprehending impressions from without. It is compared to a two-faced mirror, because on the one hand it "reflects" the outward world as presented to it by the senses, and on the other, during sleep, it gives form to the ideas arising in the *Mutaṣarrifa*, which will be mentioned directly. 2. The Imagination (*Khiyál*), which is the storehouse of forms.
MID-BRAIN	3. The Controlling or Co-ordinating Faculty (*Mutaṣarrifa*), which combines and elaborates the emotions or ideas stored in the *Váhimé*, and the images stored in the Imagination. It is therefore sometimes called the "keeper of the two treasuries." 4. The Emotional Faculty (*Váhimé*), which is the seat of love, hate, fear, and the like.
HIND-BRAIN	5. The Memory (*Ḥáfiẓa*), which is the storehouse of ideas.

All these faculties are partial percipients (*Mudriḳát-i-juẓ'iyyé*), and are the servants of the Reason (*'Aḳl-i-ḳullí-i-insání*, or *Nafs-i-náṭiḳa*), which is the General Percipient (*Mudriḳ-i-ḳullí*). Of these faculties the Imagination would appear to be regarded as the highest, since, as we have seen, in those cases in which the Reason or Rational Soul (*Nafs-i-náṭiḳa*) is not developed, it constitutes that portion of the individual which survives death and resists disintegration. Indeed these five faculties are better regarded as different stages in the development of the Reason. Nothing below the plane of the Imagination, however, survives death: *e.g.* in the lowest animals, whose culminating faculty is a sense of touch (like worms), death brings about complete disintegration.

Finally, a few words may be added concerning the view taken of the occult sciences. I was naturally desirous to learn to what extent they were recognised as true, and accordingly questioned Mírzá Asadu'lláh on the matter. His reply (which fairly represents the opinion of most thoughtful Persians of the old school) was briefly to this effect:—As regards Geomancy (*'Ilm-i-raml*) and Astrology (*'Ilm-i-nujúm*) he had no doubt of their truth, of which he had had positive proof. At the same time, of the number of those who professed to understand them the majority were impostors and charlatans. Their acquisition was very laborious, and required many years' patient study, and those who had acquired them and knew their value were, as a rule, very slow to exhibit or make a parade of their knowledge. As regards the interpretation of dreams, he said that these were of three kinds, of which only the last admits of interpretation. These three classes are as follows:—

I.—Dreams due to disordered Health.—

Due to predominance of—
1. *Blood.* Red things, such as fire, etc., are seen.
2. *Bile.* Yellow things, such as the sun, gold, etc., are seen.
3. *Phlegm.* White things, such as water, snow, etc., are seen.
4. *Melancholy.* Black things, such as ink, etc., are seen.

II.—Dreams arising from Impressions produced during Waking Hours.

III.—Dreams not arising from the External or Internal Causes above enumerated.—These are reflections obtained during sleep from the World of Similitudes (*'Álam-i-Mithál*). In some rare cases they indicate events as they actually will occur. Generally, however, they show them forth in a symbolical manner, and require interpretation. Just as every man has his appropriate "form" in the World of Similitudes, so also has everything else. *Knowledge*, for instance, is symbolised by *milk*; an *enemy* by a *wolf*, etc.

I discussed the occult sciences with several of my friends, to discover as far as possible the prevailing opinion about them. One of them made use of the following argument to prove their existence:—"God," he said, "has no *bukhl* (stinginess, avarice): it is impossible for Him to withhold from anyone a thing for which he strives with sufficient earnestness. Just as, if a man devotes all his energies to the pursuit of spiritual knowledge, he attains to it, so, if he chooses to make occult sciences and magical powers the object of his aspirations, they will assuredly not be withheld from him."

Another of my intimate friends gave me the following account of an attempt at conjuration (*iḥẓár-i-jinn*) at which he had himself assisted:—"My uncle, Mírzá ——," he said, "whose house you may perhaps see when you visit Shíráz, was a great believer in the occult sciences, in the pursuit of which, indeed, he dissipated a considerable fortune, being always surrounded by a host of magicians, geomancers, astrologers, and the like. On one occasion something of value had disappeared, and it was believed to have been stolen. It was therefore determined to make an attempt to discover the thief by resorting to a conjuration, which was undertaken by a certain Seyyid of Shíráz, skilled in these matters. Now you must know that the operator cannot himself see the forms of the *jinnís* whom he evokes: he needs for this purpose the assistance of a young child. I, being then quite a child, was selected as his assistant. The magician began by drawing a talismanic figure in ink on the palm of my hand, over which he subsequently rubbed a mixture of ink and oil, so that it was no longer visible. He then commenced his incantations; and before long I, gazing steadily, as I had been instructed to do, into the palm of my hand, saw, reflected in it as it were, a tiny figure which I recognised as myself. I informed the magician of this, and he commanded me to address it in a peremptory manner and bid it summon the 'King of the *jinnís*' (*Maliku'l-jinn*). I did so, and immediately a second figure appeared in the ink-mirror. Then I was frightened, and began to cry, and hastily rubbed the ink off my hand. Thereupon another boy was brought, and the same process was repeated till the 'King of the *jinnís*' appeared. 'Tell him to summon his *vazír*,' said the magician. The boy did so, and the *vazír* also appeared in the ink-mirror. A number of other *jinnís* were similarly called up, one by one, and when they were all present they were ordered to be seated. Then the magician took a number of slips of paper, wrote on each of them the name of one of those resident in the house, and placed them under his foot. He then drew out one without looking at it, and called out to the boy, 'Who is here?' The boy immediately read off the name in question in the ink-mirror. The same process was repeated till the name of one of the servants in the house was reached. 'Well,' said the magician, 'why do you not tell me what you see in the mirror?' 'I see nothing,' answered the boy. 'Look again,' said the magician; 'gaze more fixedly on the mirror.' After a little while the boy said, 'I see no name, but only the words *Bismi'lláhi'r-Raḥmáni'r-Raḥím*' ('In the name of God, the Merciful, the Clement'). 'This,' said the magician, 'which I hold in my hand is the name of the thief.' The man in question was summoned and interrogated, and finally confessed that he had stolen the missing article, which he was compelled to restore."

In this connection it may not be out of place to give the experiences of another experimenter in the occult sciences, who, although at the time sufficiently alarmed by the results he obtained, subsequently became convinced that they were merely due to an excited imagination. My informant in this case was a philosopher of Iṣfahán, entitled *Amínu'sh-Sharí'at*, who came to Ṭeherán in the company of his friend and patron, the *Banánu'l-*

Mulk, one of the chief ministers of the *Zillu's-Sultán*. I saw him on several occasions, and had long discussions with him on religion and philosophy. He spoke somewhat bitterly of the vanity of all systems. "I have tried most of them," he said. "I have been in turn Musulmán, Ṣúfí, Sheykhí, and even Bábí. At one time of my life I devoted myself to the occult sciences, and made an attempt to obtain control over the *jinnís* (*Taskhír-i-jinn*), with what results I will tell you. You must know, in the first place, that the *modus operandi* is as follows:—The seeker after this power chooses some solitary and dismal spot, such as the Hazár-Déré at Iṣfahán (the place selected by me). There he must remain for forty days, which period of retirement we call *chillé*. He spends the greater part of this time in incantations in the Arabic language, which he recites within the area of the *mandal*, or geometrical figure, which he must describe in a certain way on the ground. Besides this, he must eat very little food, and diminish the amount daily. If he has faithfully observed all these details, on the twenty-first day a lion will appear, and will enter the magic circle. The operator must not allow himself to be terrified by this apparition, and, above all, must on no account quit the *mandal*, else he will lose the results of all his pains. If he resists the lion, other terrible forms will come to him on subsequent days—tigers, dragons, and the like—which he must similarly withstand. If he holds his ground till the fortieth day, he has attained his object, and the *jinnís*, having been unable to get the mastery over him, will have to become his servants and obey all his behests. Well, I faithfully observed all the necessary conditions, and on the twenty-first day, sure enough, a lion appeared and entered the circle. I was horribly frightened, but all the same I stood my ground, although I came near to fainting with terror. Next day a tiger came, and still I succeeded in resisting the impulse which urged me to flee. But when, on the following day, a most hideous and frightful dragon appeared, I could no longer control my terror, and rushed from the circle, renouncing all further attempts at obtaining the mastery over the *jinnís*. When some time had elapsed after this, and I had pursued my studies in philosophy further, I came to the conclusion that I had been the victim of hallucinations excited by expectation, solitude, hunger, and long vigils; and, with a view to testing the truth of this hypothesis, I again repeated the same process which I had before practised, this time in a spirit of philosophical incredulity. My expectations were justified; I saw absolutely nothing. And there is another fact which proves to my mind that the phantoms I saw on the first occasion had no existence outside my own brain. I had never seen a real lion then, and my ideas about the appearance of that animal were entirely derived from the pictures which may be seen over the doors of baths in this country. Now, the lion which I saw in the magic circle was exactly like the latter in form and colouring, and therefore, as I need hardly say, differed considerably in aspect from a real lion."

In Ṭeherán I saw another philosopher of some reputation, Mírzá Abú'l-Ḥasan-i-Jilvé. The last of these names is the *takhalluṣ* or *nom de guerre* under which he writes poetry—for he is a poet as well as a metaphysician. Unfortunately I did not have the advantage of any prolonged conversation with him, and even such as I had chiefly consisted in answering his questions on the different phases of European thought. He was greatly interested in what I told him about the Theosophists and Vegetarians, and was anxious to know whether the Plymouth Brethren were believers in the transmigration of souls!

Although, as will have already appeared, I acquired a considerable amount of information about certain phases of Persian thought during my sojourn in Ṭeherán, there was one which, notwithstanding my most strenuous efforts and diligent enquiries, had hitherto eluded all my attempts to approach it. This one was Bábíism, of the history of which I have already had occasion to speak more than once, and to which I shall have to refer repeatedly in the course of subsequent chapters. Although I exerted to the utmost all the skill, all the tact, and all the caution which I had at my command, I was completely foiled in my attempts to communicate with the proscribed sect. I heard something about them, it is true, and what I heard served only to increase my desire to know more. I was told tales of their unflinching courage under torture, of their unshakable faith, of their marvellous skill in argument. "I once met one of them," said a man of great learning to me, "as I was returning from Kerbelá, and he succeeded in drawing me into a discussion on religious matters. So completely was I worsted by him at every turn, so thorough was his knowledge of the Ḳur'án and Traditions, and so ingenious was the use he made of this knowledge, that I was finally compelled to effect my escape from his irresistible logic by declaring myself to be *lá-madhhab* (a free-thinker); whereupon he left me, saying that with such he had nothing to do."

But whether my friends could not give me the knowledge I sought for, or whether they did not choose to do so, I was unable during my stay in Ṭeherán to become acquainted with any members of the sect in question. Some, indeed, of those with whom I was acquainted at that time were, as I subsequently discovered, actually Bábís; yet these, although at times they asked me about the course of my studies, commended my devotion to philosophy, and even tantalised me with vague promises of introductions to mysterious friends, who were, as they would imply, endowed with true wisdom (*ma'rifat*), would say nothing definite, and appeared afraid to speak more openly. After arousing my curiosity to the highest pitch, and making me fancy that I was on the threshold of some discovery, they would suddenly leave me with an expression of regret that opportunities for prolonged and confidential conversation were so rare.

I tried to obtain information from an American missionary, with similar lack of success. He admitted that he had foregathered with Bábís, but added that he did not encourage them to come and discuss their ideas, which he regarded as mischievous and fanciful. I asked how he succeeded in recognising them, since I had sought eagerly for them and had failed to find them. He replied that there was not much difficulty in identifying them by their conversation, as they always spoke on religious topics whenever an opportunity presented itself, and dwelt especially on the need of a fuller revelation, caused by the progress of the human race. Beyond this I could learn nothing from him. Once, indeed, I thought that I had succeeded in meeting with one of the sect in the person of an old Shírází merchant, who, to my astonishment, launched forth before several other Persians who were present on the excellences of the new religion. He declared that of their sacred books those written in Arabic were more eloquent than the Ḳur'án, and those composed in Persian superior in style to the writings of Sa'dí. He spoke of an Arabic book of theirs, of which a copy, written in gold, and worth at least 500 *túmáns* (£150), existed in Ṭeherán. This, he added, he might perhaps some day take me to see. All the time he was talking he kept looking at me in a peculiar way as though to watch the effect produced by his words. I met him once again when no one else was present, and easily induced him to resume the topic. He spoke of the numerous signs and wonders which had heralded the birth of Mírzá 'Alí Muḥammad, the Báb; of the wonderful quickness of apprehension manifested by him when still but a child; and of the strange puzzling questions he used sometimes to put to his teachers. Thus, on one occasion when he was receiving instruction in Arabic grammar, he suddenly demanded, "'*Huwa' ḳist?*" ("Who is 'HE'?"). My informant further declared that the Franco-German war and other events had been foretold by the Báb's successor[1] some time before they actually occurred.

1 *i.e.*, Mírzá Ḥuseyn 'Alí *Behá'u'lláh*, now deceased, who was regarded by most of the Bábís as "He whom God shall manifest." See my first paper on "The Bábís of Persia," in the *Journal of the Royal Asiatic Society* for July 1889, p. 492, and pp. 348–9 *infra*.

On another occasion, in my eagerness to acquire knowledge on this matter, I committed a great indiscretion, and, I fear, caused considerable pain to my teacher, Mírzá Asadu'lláh. I had been informed that he had some time previously been arrested as a Bábí, and though he was released almost immediately on the representations of the English Embassy, it was hinted to me that possibly this powerful protection, rather than any clear proof of his orthodoxy, was the cause of his liberation. I therefore determined to sound him on the matter, and, unable to control my impatience and await a favourable opportunity, I approached the subject as cautiously as I could the very next time that I saw him. Alluding to a previous discussion on the finality attributed by Muḥammadans to the revelation of their prophet, I said that I had recently heard that there existed in Persia a number of people who denied this, and alleged that a subsequent revelation had been accorded to mankind even within the lifetime of many still living. Mírzá Asadu'lláh listened to what I said with a gradually increasing expression of dismay, which warned me that I was treading on dangerous ground, and made me begin to regret that I had been so precipitate. When I had finished, he continued silent for a few minutes, and then spoke as follows:—

"I have no knowledge of these people, although you have perhaps been informed of the circumstances which give me good cause to remember their name. As you have probably heard some account of these, I may as well tell you the true version. Two or three years ago I was arrested in the village of Ḳulahak (which, as you know, serves the English residents for a summer retreat) by an officer in command of a party of soldiers sent to seize another person suspected of being a Bábí. They had been unable to find him, and were returning disappointed from their quest when they espied me. 'Seize him!' said the officer; 'that he is devoted to philosophy every one knows, and a philosopher is not far removed from a Bábí.' Accordingly I was arrested, and the books I was carrying, as well as a sum of money which

I had on me, were taken from me by the officer in command. I was brought before the *Ná'ibu's-Salṭana* and accused of being a Bábí. Many learned and pious men, including several *mullás*, hearing of my arrest, and knowing the utter falsity of the charge, appeared spontaneously to give evidence in my favour, and I was eventually released. But the money and the books taken from me I never recovered; and then the shame of it, the shame of it! But though, as you see, I have suffered much by reason of these people of whom you spoke just now, I have never met with them or had any dealings with them, save on one occasion. I was once returning from Sabzawár through Mázandarán, and at each of the more important towns on my way I halted for a few days to visit those interested in philosophy. Many of them were very anxious to learn about the doctrines of my master, Ḥájí Mullá Hádí, and I was, as a rule, well received and kindly entertained. One day—it was at Sárí—I was surrounded by a number of students who had come to question me on the views of my master, when a man present produced a book from which he read some extracts. This book, he said, was called '*Ḥaḳíḳat-i-Basíṭa*,' and, as this was a term used by Ḥájí Mullá Hádí, I thought it bore some reference to the philosophy I was expounding. I accordingly stretched out my hand to take the book, but the man drew it back out of my reach. Though I was displeased at his behaviour, I endeavoured to conceal my annoyance, and allowed him to continue to read. Presently he came to the term '*marátib-i-aḥadiyyat*' ('degrees of the Primal Unity'). Here I interrupted him. 'I do not know who the author of the work you hold in your hand may be,' I said, 'but it is clear to me that he does not understand what he is talking about. To speak of the *degrees* of Primal Unity, which is Pure and Undifferentiated Being, is sheer nonsense.' Some discussion ensued, and eventually I was permitted to look at the book. Then I saw that it was very beautifully written and adorned with gold, and it flashed upon me that what I held in my hand was one of the sacred books of the Bábís, and that those amongst whom I stood belonged to this redoubtable sect. That is the only time I ever came across them, and that is all that I know about them."

And that was all—or nearly all—that I knew about them for the first four months I spent in Persia. How I came across them at last will be set forth in another chapter.

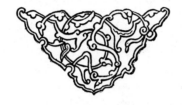

CHAPTER VII

FROM ṬEHERÁN TO IṢFAHÁN

"CHR.—'But what have you seen?' said Christian.

"MEN.—'Seen! Why, the Valley itself, which is as dark as pitch; we also saw there the Hobgoblins, Satyrs, and Dragons of the Pit: we heard also in that Valley a continual Howling and Yelling, as of a People under unutterable misery, who there sat bound in affliction and Irons; and over that Valley hang the discouraging clouds of Confusion; Death also doth always spread his wings over it: in a word it is every whit dreadful, being utterly without Order.'"—(BUNYAN'S *Pilgrim's Progress.*)

ALTHOUGH, owing to the kindness of my friends, life in the capital was pleasant enough to make me in no hurry to leave it, nevertheless the praises of beautiful Shíráz and the descriptions of venerable Persepolis which I so often heard were not without their effect. I began to grow restless, and to suffer a kind of dread lest, if I tarried much longer, some unforeseen event might occur to cut short my travels and to prevent me from reaching what was really the goal of my journey. After all, Persis (*Fárs*) is really Persia, and Shíráz is the capital thereof; to visit Persia and not to reach Fárs is only a degree better than staying at home. Therefore, when one morning the Nawwáb came into my room to inform me that he had received instructions to proceed to Mashhad in the course of a week or two, and asked me what I would do, I replied without hesitation that I would start for the South. As he expected to leave Ṭeherán about 10th February, I determined to arrange my departure for the 7th, which, being my birthday, seemed to me an auspicious day for resuming my travels.

'Alí the Turk having gone South with H——, I was for a time left without a servant. Soon after I had become the guest of the

Nawwáb, however, he advised me to obtain one, and promised to help me in finding some one who would suit me. I was anxious to have a genuine Persian of the South this time, and finally succeeded in engaging a man who appeared in every respect to satisfy my requirements. He was a fine-looking young fellow, of rather distinguished appearance, and a native of Shíráz. He made no boast of any special accomplishments, and was satisfied to receive the very moderate sum of three *túmáns* a month while in Ṭeherán, where he had a house and a wife; he proved, however, to be an excellent cook, and an admirable servant in every respect, though inclined at times to manifest a spirit of independence.

Ḥájí Ṣafar—for that was his name—received the announcement that I should start for the South in a few days with evident satisfaction. A Persian servant has everything to gain when his master undertakes a journey. In the first place his wages are raised fifty per cent. to supply him with money for his expenses on the road (*jíré*). In the second place he receives, before starting, an additional sum of money (generally equivalent to a month's wages) to provide himself with requisites for the road, this allowance being known as *púl-i-chekmé va shalwár* ("boots and breeches money"). In the third place he has more chance of making himself indispensable to his master, and so obtaining increased wages. Last of all, there is probably hardly a Persian to be found who does not enjoy travelling for its own sake, though in this particular case the charm of novelty was lacking, for Ḥájí Ṣafar had visited not only Mecca and Kerbelá, but nearly all the more important towns in Persia as well.

Four or five days before the date fixed for my departure, he brought me a formidable list of necessaries for the road—cooking-pots, with all the appliances for making *piláw*; saddle-bags, sponges, cloths, towels, whips, cups, glasses, spits, brooms, tongs, and a host of other articles, many of which seemed to me unnecessary, besides quantities of rice, onions, potatoes, tea, sugar, candles, matches, honey, cheese, charcoal, butter, and other groceries. I struck out a few of what I regarded as the most useless articles, for it appeared to me that with such stores we might be going to Khiva, whereas we should actually arrive at the considerable town of Ḳum three or four days after leaving Ṭeherán. On the whole, however, I let him have his own way, in consequence of which I enjoyed a degree of comfort in my future journeyings hitherto quite unknown to me, whilst the addition to my expenses was comparatively slight.

Then began the period of activity and bustle which inevitably precedes a journey, even on the smallest scale, in the East. Every day I was down in the bazaars with Ḥájí Ṣafar, buying cooking utensils, choosing tobaccos, and examining the merits of saddle-bags, till I was perfectly weary of the bargaining, the delays, and the endless scrutiny of goods which had to be gone through before the outfit was complete. Indeed at last I nearly despaired of being ready in time to start on the appointed day, and resigned the management into Ḥájí Ṣafar's hands almost entirely, only requesting him not to invest in any perfectly useless chattels or provisions.

Another and a yet more important matter still remained, to wit, the discovery of a muleteer possessed of a small number of reasonably good animals, prepared to start on the day I had fixed, and willing to make the stages as I wished. This matter I regarded as too important to be arranged by deputy, for, when one is travelling by oneself, the pleasantness of the journey greatly depends on having a cheerful, communicative, and good-natured muleteer. Such an one will beguile the way with an endless series of anecdotes, will communicate to the traveller the weird folk-lore of the desert, will point out a hundred objects of interest which would otherwise be passed unnoticed, and will manage to arrange the stages so as to enable him to see to the best advantage anything worth seeing. A cross-grained, surly fellow, on the other hand, will cast a continual gloom over the caravan, and will throw difficulties in the way of every deviation from the accustomed routine.

Here I must speak a few words in favour of the much-maligned *chárvádár*. As far as my experience goes, he is, as a rule, one of the best fellows living. During the period which elapses between the conclusion of the agreement and the actual start, he is, indeed, troublesome and vexatious beyond measure. He will invent endless excuses for making extra charges; he will put forward a dozen reasons against starting on the proposed day, or following the proposed route, or halting at the places where one desires to halt. On the day of departure he will rouse one at a preternaturally early hour, alleging that the stage is a long one, that it is eight good *farsakhs* at least, that it is dangerous to be on the road after dark, and the like. Then, just as you are nearly ready, he will disappear to procure some hitherto forgotten necessary for the journey, or to say farewell to his wife, or to fetch one of those scraps of sacking or ropes which supply him with an unfailing excuse for absenting himself. Finally, you will not get off till the sun is well past the meridian, and may think yourself fortunate if you accomplish a stage of ten miles.

But when once he is fairly started he becomes a different man. With the dust of the city he shakes off the exasperating manner which has hitherto made him so objectionable. He sniffs the pure exhilarating air of the desert, he strides forward manfully on the broad interminable road (which is, indeed, for the most part but the track worn by countless generations of travellers), he beguiles the tediousness of the march with songs and stories, interrupted by occasional shouts of encouragement or warning to his animals. His life is a hard one, and he has to put up with many disagreeables; so that he might be pardoned even if he lost his temper oftener than he usually does.

For some time my efforts to discover a suitable muleteer were fruitless. I needed only three animals, and I did not wish to attach myself to a large caravan, foreseeing that it would lead to difficulties in case I desired to halt on the way or deviate from the regular track. A very satisfactory arrangement concluded with two young natives of Ḳum, who had exactly the number of animals I required, was broken off by their father, who wished to make me hire his beasts by the day instead of for the whole distance to Iṣfahán. To this I refused to agree, fearing that he might protract the journey unduly, and the contract was therefore annulled. At length, however, two days before I had intended to start, a muleteer who appeared in every way suitable presented himself. He was a native of the hamlet of Gez, near Iṣfahán, Raḥím by name; a clumsy-looking, weather-beaten young man, the excessive plainness of whose broad, smooth face was redeemed by an almost perpetual smile. The bargain was concluded in a few minutes. He engaged to provide me with three good animals, to convey me to Iṣfahán in twelve or thirteen days and to allow me a halt of one day each at Ḳum and Káshán, for the sum of ten *túmáns* (nearly £3).

All was now ready for the journey, and there only remained the always somewhat depressing business of leave-taking, which fully occupied my last hours in Ṭeherán. Finally the day of departure came, but (as indeed invariably happens) endless delays arose before I actually got off, so that it was determined that we should that day proceed no farther than Sháh 'Abdu'l-'Aẓím (situated some five or six miles to the south of the metropolis), whence we could make a fair start on the morrow. One of my friends, a nephew of my kind host the Nawwáb, announced his intention of accompanying me thus far. This ceremony of setting the traveller on his way is called *badraḳa*, while the converse—that of going out to meet one arriving from a journey—is called *istiḳbál*. Of these two, the former is more an act of friendship and less a formality than the latter.

Persian servants having often been described as the most sordid and rapacious of mankind, I feel that, as a mere act of justice, I must not omit to mention the disinterested and generous conduct exhibited by those of the Nawwáb's household. The system of "tips" being extremely prevalent in Persia, and conducted generally on a larger scale than in Europe, I had, of course, prepared a sum of money to distribute amongst the retainers of my host. Seizing a favourable opportunity, I entered the room where they were assembled, and offered the present to the major-domo, Muḥammad Riẓá Khán. To my surprise, he refused it unhesitatingly, without so much as looking at it. When I remonstrated, thinking that he only needed a little persuasion, he replied, "The master told us when you came here that you were to be treated in every way as one of the family: we should not expect or desire a present from one of the family; therefore we do not expect or desire it from you. You have been welcome, and we are glad to have done what we could to make you comfortable, but we desire nothing from you unless it be kindly remembrance." In this declaration he persisted, and the others spoke to the same effect. Finally, I was compelled to accept their refusal as definite, and left them with a sense of admiration at their immovable determination to observe to the full their master's wishes.

At length all was ready. The baggage-mules had started; the last cup of tea had been drunk, and the last *ḳalyán* smoked; and the horses stood waiting at the gate, while Ḥájí Ṣafar, armed with a most formidable whip, and arrayed in a pair of enormous top-boots, strutted about the courtyard looking eminently business-like, and evidently in the best of spirits. As I was just about to take my last farewells, I observed the servants engaged in making preparations of which the object was to me totally mysterious and inexplicable. A large metal tray was brought, on which were placed the following incongruous objects:—A mirror, a bowl of water with some narcissi floating in it, a plate of flour, and a dish of sweetmeats, of the kind called *shaḳar-panír* ("sugar-cheese"). A copy of the Ḳur'án was next produced, and I was instructed to kiss it first, and then to dip my hand in the water and the flour, to rub it over the face of the old servant who had brought the tray, pass under the Ḳur'án, which was held aloft for that purpose, and mount my horse without once turning or looking back. All these instructions I faithfully observed amidst general mirth, and as I mounted amidst many good wishes for my journey I heard the splash of the water as it was thrown after me. What the origin of this curious ceremony may be I do not know, neither did I see it practised on any other occasion.

Our progress not being hampered by the presence of the baggage, we advanced rapidly, and before 4 p.m. rode through the gate of the city of refuge, Sháh 'Abdu'l-'Aẓím. I have already stated that the holy shrine for which this place is famous protects all outlaws who succeed in reaching its vicinity. In a word, the whole town is what is called "*bast*" ("sanctuary"). There are, however, different degrees of *bast*, the area of protection being smaller and more circumscribed in proportion as the crime of the refugee is greater. Murderers, for instance, cannot go outside the courtyard of the mosque without running the risk of being arrested; debtors, on the other hand, are safe anywhere within the walls. It may be imagined that the populace of such a place is scarcely the most respectable, and of their churlishness I had convincing proof. I was naturally anxious to get a glimpse of the mosque, the great golden dome of which forms so conspicuous an object to the eyes of the traveller approaching Ṭeherán from the west; and accordingly, as soon as we had secured our horses in the caravansaray (for the rest of the caravan had not yet arrived), I suggested to my companion that we should direct our steps thither. Of course I had no intention of attempting to enter it, which I knew would not be permitted; but I thought no objection would be made to my viewing it from the outside. However, we had hardly reached the entrance of the bazaar when we were stopped and turned back. Discouraged, but not despairing, we succeeded in making our way by a devious and unfrequented route to the very gate of the mosque. I had, however, hardly begun to admire it when forth from some hidden recess came two most ill-looking custodians, who approached us in a threatening manner, bidding us begone.

My companion remonstrated with these churlish fellows, saying that as far as he was concerned he was a good Musulmán, and had as much right in the mosque as they had. "No good Musulmán would bring a Firangí infidel to gaze upon the sacred building," they replied; "we regard you as no whit better than him. Hence! begone!" As there was nothing to be gained by stopping (and, indeed, a fair prospect of being roughly handled if we remained to argue the matter), we prudently withdrew. I was much mortified at this occurrence, not only on my own account, but also because the good-nature of my companion had exposed him likewise to insult. I feel bound to state, however, that this was almost the only occasion on which I met with discourtesy of this sort during the whole time I spent in Persia.

On returning to the caravansaray we found that Ḥájí Ṣafar and the muleteers had arrived, the former being accompanied by a relative who had come to see him so far on his journey, and at the same time to accomplish a visit to the shrine from the precincts of which we had just been so ignominiously expelled. As it was now getting late, and as most of the gates of Ṭeherán are closed soon after sunset, my friend bade me farewell, and cantered off homewards, leaving me with a sense of loneliness which I had not experienced for some time. The excitement of feeling that I was once more on the road with my face fairly turned towards the glorious South soon, however, came to my relief, and indeed I had enough to occupy me in attempting to introduce some order into my utterly confused accounts. Before long Ḥájí Ṣafar, who had been busy ever since his arrival with culinary operations, brought in a supper which augured well for the comfort of the journey, so far as food was concerned.

I had finished supper, and was ruminating over tea and tobacco, when he re-entered, accompanied by his relative, who solemnly placed his hand in mine and swore allegiance to me, not only on his behalf, but for the whole family, assuring me in a long and eloquent harangue that he (the speaker) would answer for Ḥájí Ṣafar's loyalty and devotion, and asking me in return to treat him kindly and not "make his heart narrow." Having received my assurances that I would do my best to make things agreeable, they retired, and I forthwith betook myself to rest in preparation for the early start which we proposed to make on the morrow.

Next day we were astir early, for there was no temptation to linger in a spot from the inhabitants of which I had met with nothing but incivility; and, moreover, I was anxious to form a better idea of the muleteers who were to be my companions for the next fortnight. However, I saw but little of them that day, as they lagged behind soon after starting, and passed me while I was having lunch. The road, except for several large parties of travellers whom we met, presented few points of interest; nevertheless, a curious history is attached to it, which, as it forms a significant commentary on what one may call the "Board of Public Works" in Persia, I here reproduce[1].

On leaving Sháh 'Abdu'l-'Aẓím the road runs for a mile or so as straight as an arrow towards the south. A little before it reaches a range of low hills which lie at right angles to its course it bifurcates. One division goes straight on and crosses the hills above-mentioned to the caravansaray of Kinár-i-gird; the other bends sharply to the west for about three-quarters of a mile, thus turning the edge of the hills, and then resumes its southward course. Of these two roads, the first is the good old direct caravan-route, described by Vámbéry, which leads to Ḳum by way of Kinár-i-gird, Ḥawẓ-i-Sulṭán, and Pul-i-Dallák; the second is the new "improved" road made some years ago by order of the *Amínu's-Sulṭán*, the history of which is as follows:—

1 It is given in Curzon's *Persia*, vol. ii, pp. 2–6, but I have nevertheless decided to let it remain here, as I wrote it before the publication of that work.

When the rage for superseding the venerable and commodious caravansaray by the new-fangled and extortionate *mihmán-khání* was at its height, and when the road between Ṭeherán and Ḳazvín had been adorned with a sufficient number of these evidences of civilisation, the attention of the *Amínu's-Sulṭán* and other philanthropists was turned to the deplorable and unregenerate state of the great southern road. It was decided that, at least so far as Ḳum, its defects should be remedied forthwith, and that the caravansarays of Kinár-i-gird, Ḥawẓ-i-Sulṭán, and Pul-i-Dallák, which had for generations afforded shelter to the traveller, should be replaced by something more in accordance with modern Europeanised taste. Negotiations were accordingly opened by the *Amínu's-Sulṭán* with the owners of the caravansarays in question, with a view to effecting a purchase of the land and "goodwill." Judge of the feelings of this enlightened and patriotic statesman when the owner of the caravansaray at Ḥawẓ-i-Sulṭán refused—yes, positively refused—to sell his heritage. Perhaps he was an old-fashioned individual, with a distaste for innovations; perhaps he merely thought that his caravansaray brought him in a better income than he was likely to get even by a judicious investment of the money now offered for it. Be this as it may, he simply declined the offer made to him by the *Amínu's-Sulṭán*, and said that he preferred to retain in his own possession the property he had inherited from his father.

What was to be done? Clearly it was intolerable that the march of civilisation should be checked by this benighted old conservative. In the rough days of yore it might have been possible to behead or poison him, or at least to confiscate his property, but such an idea could not for a moment be seriously entertained by a humane and enlightened minister of the fourteenth century of the *hijra*; no, annoying and troublesome as it was, there was nothing for it but to leave the old road *in statu quo*, and make a new one. This was accordingly done at considerable expense, the new road being carried in a bold curve to the west, and garnished at suitable intervals with fancifully constructed *mihmán-khánés*, situated amidst little groves of trees, supplied with runnels of sweet, pure water from the hills, and furnished with tables, chairs, and beds in unstinted profusion. But alas for the obstinacy of the majority of men, and their deplorable disinclination to be turned aside from their ancient habits! The muleteers for the most part declined to make use of the new road, and continued to follow their accustomed course, alleging as their reason for so doing that it was a good many *farsakhs* shorter than the other, and that they preferred the caravansarays to the new *mihmán-khánés*, which were not only in no wise better adapted to their requirements than their old halting-places, but were very much more expensive. Briefly, they objected to "go farther and fare worse."

There seemed to be every prospect of the new road being a complete failure, and of the benevolent intentions of the *Amínu's-Sulṭán* being totally frustrated by this unlooked-for lack of appreciation on the part of the travelling public, when suddenly the mind of the perplexed philanthropist was illuminated by a brilliant idea. Though it would not be quite constitutional to forcibly overthrow the caravansarays on the old road, it was evidently within the rights of a paternal government to utilise the resources of nature as a means of compelling the refractory "sons of the road" to do what was best for them. Luckily, these means were not far to seek. Near the old road, between Ḥawẓ-i-Sulṭán and Pul-i-Dallák, ran a river, and this river was prevented from overflowing the low flat plain which it traversed, ere losing itself in the sands of the Dasht-i-Kavír, by dykes solidly constructed and carefully kept in repair. If these were removed there was every reason to hope that the old road would be flooded and rendered impracticable. The experiment was tried, and succeeded perfectly. Not only the road, but an area of many square miles round about it, was completely and permanently submerged, and a fine lake—almost a sea—was added to the realms of the Sháh. It is, indeed, useless for navigation, devoid of fish (so far as I could learn), and (being impregnated with salt) incapable of supporting vegetable life; but it is eminently picturesque, with its vast blue surface glittering in the sun, and throwing into bolder relief the white, salt-strewn expanse of the terrible desert beyond. It also constitutes a permanent monument of the triumph of science over obstinacy and prejudice.

The *Amínu's-Sulṭán* might now fairly consider that his triumph was complete: suddenly, however, a new difficulty arose. The management of the posts was in the hands of another minister called the *Amínu'd-Dawla*, and he, like the muleteers, considered the charges which it was proposed to make for the use of the new (now the only) road excessive. As, however, there appeared to be no course open to him but to submit to them (since the posts must be maintained, and the old road was irrecoverably submerged), the *Amínu's-Sulṭán* determined to withstand all demands for a reduction. But the *Amínu'd-Dawla* was also a minister of some ingenuity, and, having the example of his colleague fresh in his mind, he determined not to be outdone. He therefore made yet another road, which took a yet wider sweep towards the west, and, transferring the post-houses to that, bade defiance to his rival.

Thus it has come to pass that in place of the old straight road to Ḳum there is now a caravan-road longer by some fourteen miles, and a post-road longer by nearly twenty miles[1]. The last, indeed, on leaving Ṭeherán, follows the Hamadán road for about a stage and a half, diverging from it some distance to the south-west of Ribáṭ-Karím, the first post-house, and curving back towards the east by way of Pík and Kúshk-i-Bahrám to join the *Amínu's-Sulṭán's* road near the *mihmán-kháné* of Sháshgird, about ten *farsakhs* from Ḳum.

1 Dr Wills (*Land of the Lion and the Sun*) gives the distance from Ṭeherán to Ḳum by the old road as twenty-four *farsakhs*. The present post-road is reckoned and charged as twenty-eight *farsakhs*, but they appear to me to be very long ones.

On the second day after leaving Ṭeherán (9th February), soon after quitting the *mihmán-kháné* of Ḥasanábád, we entered the dismal region called by the Persians *Malaku'l-Mawt Déré* (the "Valley of the Angel of Death"). Around this spot cluster most thickly the weird tales of the desert, to which I have already alluded. Indeed its only rival in this sinister celebrity is the *Hazár déré* ("Thousand valleys"), which lies just to the south of Iṣfahán. Anxious to become further acquainted with the folk-lore of the country, I succeeded in engaging the muleteer in conversation on this topic. The substance of what I learned was as follows:—

There are several species of supernatural monsters which haunt the gloomy defiles of the Valley of the Angel of Death. Of these the *ghúls* and *'ifríts* are alike the commonest and the most malignant. The former usually endeavour to entice the traveller away from the caravan to his destruction by assuming the form or voice of a friend or relative. Crying out piteously for help, and entreating the unwary traveller to come to their assistance, they induce him to follow them to some lonely spot, where, suddenly assuming the hideous form proper to them, they rend him in pieces and devour him.

Another monster is the *nasnás*, which appears in the form of an infirm and aged man. It is generally found sitting by the side of a river, and bewailing its inability to cross. When it sees the wayfarer approaching, it earnestly entreats him to carry it across the water to the other side. If he consents, it seats itself on his shoulders, and, when he reaches the middle of the river, winds its long supple legs round his throat till he falls insensible in the water and perishes.

Besides these, there is the *pá-lís* ("Foot-licker"), which only attacks those who are overtaken by sleep in the desert. It kills its victim, as its name implies, by licking the soles of his feet till it has drained away his life-blood. It was on one occasion circumvented by two muleteers of Iṣfahán, who, being benighted in the desert, lay down feet to feet, covering their bodies with cloaks. Presently the *pá-lís* arrived, and began to walk round the sleepers to discover their feet, but on either side it found a head. At last it gave up the search in despair, exclaiming as it made off:

"*Gashté-am hazár ú sí ú si deré,*
Ammá na-didé-am mard-i-du seré."

"I have wandered through a thousand and thirty and three valleys,
But never yet saw a two-headed man!"

Another superstition (not, however, connected with the desert), of which I heard at Ṭeherán, may be mentioned in this connection. A form of cursing used by women to each other is "*Ál-at bi-zanad!*" ("May the *Ál* strike thee!"). The belief concerning the *Ál* is that it attacks women who have recently been confined, and tries to tear out and devour their livers. To avert this calamity various precautions are taken; swords and other weapons are placed under the woman's pillow, and she is not allowed to sleep for several hours after the child is born, being watched over by her friends, and roused by cries of "*Yá Maryam!*" ("O Mary!") whenever she appears to be dozing off. It is worthy of note that the *Ál*, as well as its congeners, is supposed to have flaxen hair.

The scenery through which we passed on leaving the Malaku'l-Mawt Déré was savage and sublime. All around were wild, rugged hills, which assumed the strangest and most fantastic shapes, and desert sparsely sown with camel-thorn. As we reached the highest point of the road, rain began to fall sharply, and it was so cold that I was glad to muffle myself up in ulster and rug. Now for the first time the great salt-lake made by the *Amínu's-Sulṭán* came in view. It is of vast extent, and the muleteers informed me that its greatest width was not less than six *farsakhs* (about twenty-two miles). Beyond it stretches the weird expanse of the Dasht-i-Kavír, which extends hence even to the eastern frontier of Persia—a boundless waste of sand, here and there glimmering white with incrustations of salt, and broken in places by chains of black savage-looking mountains. The desolate grandeur of this landscape defies description, and surpasses anything which I have ever seen.

The *mihmán-khání* of 'Alí-ábad, which we reached an hour or so before sunset, presents no features worthy of remark except this, that in the room allotted to me I found three books, which proved on examination to be a copy of the Ḳur'án, a book of Arabic prayers, and a visitors' book! It was evident that here, at least, the prototype was afforded by the Bible and prayer-book which are usually to be found in every bedroom of an English hotel, and the visitors' book which lies on the hall-table. I examined this visitors' book with some curiosity. It was filled with long rhapsodies on the *Amínu's-Sulṭán* penned by various travellers, all complimentary, as I need hardly say. "How enlightened and patriotic a minister! How kind of him to make this nice new road, and to provide it with these admirable guest-houses, which, indeed, might fairly be considered to rival, if not to excel, the best hotels of Firangistán!" I could not forbear smiling as I read these effusions, which were so at variance with the views expressed in the most forcible language by the muleteers, who had continued at intervals throughout the day to inveigh against the new road, the *mihmán-khánés*, and their owner alike.

The next day brought us to Ḳum, after a long, quick march of nearly ten hours. The muleteers were suddenly seized with one of those fits of energetic activity to which even the most lethargic Persians are occasionally subject, so that when, early in the afternoon, we reached the *mihmán-khání* of Sháshgird (or *Manẓariyyé*—the "Place of Outlook"—as it is more pretentiously styled), and Ḥájí Ṣafar proposed to halt for the night, they insisted on pushing on to the holy city, which they declared they could reach before sundown. A lively altercation ensued, which concluded with a bet of five *ḳráns* offered by Ḥájí Ṣafar, and taken by the muleteers, that we should not reach the town before sunset. The effect of this stimulus was magical. Never before or since did I see muleteers attain such a degree of speed. With eyes continually directed towards the declining sun, they ran along at a steady trot, occasionally shouting to their animals, and declaring that they would fare sumptuously that night off the delicacies of Ḳum with the money they would earn by their efforts. The road seemed interminable, even after the golden dome of the mosque of *Ḥaẓrat-i-Ma'ṣúma* ("Her Holiness the Immaculate") rose up before us across the salt swamps, and as the sun sank lower and lower towards the horizon the efforts of the muleteers were redoubled, till, just as the rim of the luminary sank from sight behind the western hills, we crossed the long, graceful bridge which spans a river-bed almost dry except in spring, and, passing beneath the blue-tiled gate, rode into the holy city.

I have already had occasion to allude to the Indo-European Telegraph, and to mention the great kindness which I met with from Major Wells (in whose hands the control thereof was placed), and from all other members of the staff with whom I came in contact. This kindness did not cease with my departure from Ṭeherán. A message was sent down the line to all the telegraph stations (which are situated every three or four stages all the way from Ṭeherán to Bushire) to inform the residents at these (most of whom are English) of my advent, and to ask them to extend to me their hospitality. Although I felt some hesitation at first in thus quartering myself without an invitation on strangers who might not wish to be troubled with a guest, I was assured that I need have no apprehensions on that score, and that I should be certain to meet with a hospitable welcome. This, indeed, proved to be the case to a degree beyond my expectations; at all the telegraph offices I was received with a cordial friendliness and geniality which made me at once feel at home, and I gladly take this opportunity of expressing the deep sense of gratitude which I feel for kindnesses the memory of which will always form one of my pleasantest recollections of the pleasant year I spent in Persia.

The first of these telegraph stations is at Ḳum, and thither I at once made my way through the spice-laden twilight of the bazaars. On arriving, I was cordially welcomed by Mr Lyne and his wife, and was soon comfortably ensconced in an easy-chair before a bright fire, provided with those two great dispellers of weariness, tea and tobacco. My host, who had resided for a long while at Ḳum, entirely surrounded by Persians, was a fine Persian and Arabic scholar, and possessed a goodly collection of books, which he kindly permitted me to examine. They were for the most part formidable-looking treatises on Muḥammadan theology and jurisprudence, and had evidently been well read; indeed, Mr Lyne's fame as a "*mullá*" is great, not only in Ḳum, but throughout Persia, and I heard his erudition warmly praised even at distant Kirmán.

Perhaps it was owing to this that I met with such courtesy and good nature from the people of Ḳum, of whom I had heard the worst possible accounts. My treatment at Sháh 'Abdu'l-'Aẓím had not given me a favourable idea of the character of holy cities and sanctuaries, and this prejudice was supported in this particular case by the well-known stricture of some Persian satirist on the towns of Ḳum and Káshán:

"*Sag-i-Káshí bih az akábir-i-Ḳum,*
Bá-vujúdí ki sag bih az Káshíst."

"A dog of Káshán is better than the nobles of Ḳum,
Although a dog is better than a native of Káshán."

Whether the inhabitants of Ḳum have been grossly maligned, or whether their respect for my host (for, so far as my experience goes, there is no country where knowledge commands such universal respect as in Persia) procured for me an unusual degree of courtesy, I know not; at any rate, when we went out next day to see the town, we were allowed, without the slightest opposition, to stand outside the gate of the mosque and look at it to our heart's content; several people, indeed, came up to us and entered into friendly conversation. Further than this, I was allowed to inspect the manufacture of several of the chief products of the city, the most important of which is the beautiful blue pottery which is now so celebrated. This, indeed, is the great feature of Ḳum, which might almost be described as the "Blue City"; nowhere have I witnessed a greater profusion of blue domes and tiles. Many small articles are made of this ware, such as salt-cellars, lamps, pitchers, pipe-bowls, beads, and button-like amulets of divers forms and sizes, which are much used for necklaces for children, and for affixing to the foreheads of horses, mules, and the like, as a protection against the evil eye. Of all of these I purchased a large selection, the total cost of which did not exceed a few shillings, for they are ridiculously cheap.

Besides the mosque and the potteries, I paid a visit to a castor-oil mill worked by a camel, and ascended an old minaret, furnished with a double spiral staircase in a sad state of dilapidation. From this I obtained a fine view of the city and its surroundings. It has five gates, and is surrounded by a wall, but this is now broken down in many places, and the whole of the southern quarter of the town is in a very ruined condition. Altogether, I enjoyed my short stay in Ḳum very much, and was as sorry to leave it as I was pleased to find how much better its inhabitants are than they are generally represented to be. Their appearance is as pleasant as their manner, and I was greatly struck with the high average of good looks which they enjoy, many of the children especially being very pretty. Though the people are regarded as very fanatical, their faces certainly belie this opinion, for it seemed to me that the majority of them wore a singularly gentle and benign expression.

I could not, however, protract my stay at Ḳum without subjecting my plans to considerable alteration; and accordingly, on the second day after my arrival (12th February) I again set out on my southward journey. As I was in no hurry to bid a final farewell to my kind host and hostess, the muleteers had been gone for more than half an hour before I finally quitted the telegraph-office; but about this I did not greatly concern myself, making no doubt that we should overtake them before we had gone far. In this, however, I was mistaken; for when we halted for lunch, no sign of them had appeared. Supposing, however, that Ḥájí Ṣafar, who had travelled over the road before, knew the way, I thought little of the matter till the gathering shades of dusk recalled me from reveries on the future to thoughts of the present, and I began to reflect that it was a very odd thing that a stage of only four *farsakhs* had taken so long a time to accomplish, and that even now no signs of our destination were in view. Accordingly I pulled up, and proceeded to cross-examine Ḥájí Ṣafar, with the somewhat discouraging result that his ignorance of our whereabouts proved to be equal to my own. It now occurred to me that I had heard that the caravansaray of Pasangán was situated close under the hills to the west, while we were well out in the plain; and I therefore proposed that we should turn our course in that direction, especially as I fancied I could descry, in spite of the gathering gloom, a group of buildings under the hills. Ḥájí Ṣafar, on the other hand, was for proceeding, assuring me that he saw smoke in front, which no doubt marked the position of our halting-place. While we were engaged in this discussion, I discerned in the distance the figure of a man running towards us, shouting and gesticulating wildly. On its closer approach I recognised in it the muleteer Raḥím. We accordingly turned our horses towards him and presently met him; whereupon, so soon as he had in some measure recovered his breath, he proceeded to upbraid Ḥájí Ṣafar roundly. "A wonderful fellow art thou," he exclaimed (on receiving some excuse about "the smoke ahead looking like the *manzil*"); "do you know where that smoke comes from? It comes from an encampment of those rascally Sháh-sevans, who, had you fallen into their midst, would as like as not have robbed you of every single thing you have with you, including my animals. If you don't know the road, keep with us who do; and if you thought you were going to discover a new way to Yezd across the desert, I tell you you can't; only camels go across there; and if you had escaped the Sháh-sevans (curses on the graves of their fathers!), it is as like as not that you would have just gone down bodily into the salt-swamps, and never have been seen or heard of again, as has happened to plenty of people who knew more about the desert than you." So he ran on, while we both felt very much ashamed of ourselves, till we finally reached Pasangán, and took up our quarters at the post-house, which looked more comfortable than the caravansaray.

Next day was beautifully fine and warm, almost like a bright June day in England. Our way still lay just beneath the hills to the west, and the road continued quite flat, for we were still skirting the edge of the great salt-strewn Dasht-i-Kavír. About mid-day we halted before the caravansaray of Shúráb for lunch: here there is some verdure, and a little stream, but the water of this is, as the name of the place implies, brackish. Soon after leaving this we met two men with great blue turbans, carelessly and loosely wound. These Ḥájí Ṣafar at once identified as Yezdís. "You can always tell a Yezdí wherever you see him," he explained, "and, indeed, whenever you hear him. As you may like to hear their sweet speech, I will pass the time of day with them, and ask them whence they hail and whither they are bound." So saying, he entered into a brief conversation with them, and for the first time I heard the broad, drawling, singsong speech of Yezd, which once heard can never be mistaken.

We reached the caravansaray of Sinsin quite early in the afternoon, the stage being six light *farsakhs*, and the road good and level. This caravansaray is one of those fine, spacious, solidly constructed buildings which can be referred, almost at a glance, to the time of the Ṣafaví kings, and which the tradition of muleteers, recognising, as a rule, only two great periods in history—that of Ferídún, and that of Sháh 'Abbás the Great—unhesitatingly attributes to the latter. The building, although it appeared totally neglected, even the doors being torn away from their hinges, is magnificently constructed, and I wandered with delight through its long, vaulted, dimly-lit stables, its deserted staircase, and untenanted rooms. The roof, however, solidly built of brickwork, and measuring no less than ninety paces from corner to corner of the square, was the great attraction, commanding as it did an extensive view of the flat plain around, the expanse of which was hardly broken by anything except the little group of houses which constitute the village, and a great caravan of camels from Yezd, kneeling down in rows to receive their evening meal from the hands of their drivers.

While I was on the roof I was joined by a muleteer called Khudá-bakhsh, whom I had not noticed at the beginning of the journey, but who had cast up within the last day or two as a recognised member of our little caravan, in that mysterious and unaccountable way peculiar to his class. He entered into conversation with me, anxiously enquired whether I was not an agent of my government sent out to examine the state of the country, and refused to credit my assurances to the contrary. He then asked me many questions about America ("*Yangí-dunyá*"—not, as might at first sight appear, a mere corruption of the term commonly applied by us to its inhabitants, but a genuine Turkish compound, meaning "the New World"), and received my statement that its people were of the same race as myself, and had emigrated there from my own country, with manifest incredulity.

Next day brought us to another considerable town—Káshán—after an uneventful march of about seven hours, broken by a halt for lunch at a village called Naṣrábád, at which I was supplied with one of the excellent melons grown in the neighbourhood. On leaving this place we fell in with two Kirmánís—an old man and his son—who were travelling back from Hamadán, where they had gone with a load of shawls, which had been satisfactorily disposed of. They were intelligent and communicative, and supplied me with a good deal of information about the roads between Shíráz and Kirmán, concerning which I was anxious for detailed knowledge.

About 3.30 p.m. we reached Káshán, but did not enter the town, alighting at the telegraph-office, which is situated just outside the gate. Here I was kindly welcomed by Mr Aganor, an Armenian, who spoke English perfectly. Though it was not late, I did not go into the town that day, as we received a visit from the chief of the custom-house, Mírzá Ḥuseyn Khán, who was very pleasant and amusing. Besides this, a man came with some manuscripts which he was anxious to sell, but there were none of any value. In the evening I had some conversation with my host about the Bábís, whom he asserted to be very numerous at Yezd and Ábádé. At the former place, he assured me, the new religion was making great progress even amongst the Zoroastrians.

Next morning we went for a walk in the town. Almost every town in Persia is celebrated for something, and Káshán is said to have three specialities: first, its brass-work; second, its scorpions (which, unlike the bugs of Miyáné, are said never to attack strangers, but only the natives of the town); and third, the extreme timorousness of its inhabitants. Concerning the latter, it is currently asserted that there formerly existed a Káshán regiment, but that, in consideration of the cowardice of its men, and their obvious inefficiency, it was disbanded, and those composing it were told to return to their homes. On the following day a deputation of the men waited on the Sháh, asserting that they were afraid of being attacked on the road, and begging for an escort. "We are a hundred poor fellows all alone," they said; "send some horsemen with us to protect us!"

The scorpions I did not see, as it was winter; and of the alleged cowardice of the inhabitants I had, of course, no means of judging; but with the brass-bazaar I was greatly impressed, though my ears were almost deafened by the noise. Besides brass-work, fine silk fabrics are manufactured in large quantity at Káshán, though not so extensively as at Yezd. The road to this latter city quits the Iṣfahán and Shíráz route at this point, so that Káshán forms the junction of the two great southern roads which terminate respectively at Bandar-i-'Abbás and Bushire on the Persian Gulf.

In the afternoon Mírzá Ḥuseyn Khán, the chief of the customs, came again. He had his little child of seventeen months old (to which he seemed devotedly attached) brought for me to look at, as it was suffering from eczema, and he wished for advice as to the treatment which should be adopted. Later in the evening, after the child had gone home, he returned with his secretary, Mírzá 'Abdu'lláh, and stayed to supper. We had a most delightful evening, the Khán being one of the most admirable conversationalists I ever met. Some of his stories I will here set down, though it is impossible for me to convey an idea of the vividness of description, wealth of illustration, and inimitable mimicry, which, in his mouth, gave them so great a charm.

"What sort of a supper are you going to give us, Aganor Ṣáḥib?" he began; "Persian or Firangí? O, half one and half the other: very good, that is best; for this Ṣáḥib is evidently anxious to learn all he can about us Persians, so that he would have been disappointed if you hadn't given him some of our foods; while at the same time, being fresh from Firangistán, he might perhaps not have been able to eat some of the things which we like. How do you like our Persian food so far?" he continued, turning to me; "for my part, I doubt if you have anything half so nice as our *piláws* and *chiláws* in your country. Then there is *mást-khiyár* (curds and cucumbers); have you tasted that yet? No? Well, then, you have a pleasure to come; only after eating it you must not drink water to quench the slight thirst which it produces, or else you will suffer for it, like Mánakjí

Ṣáḥib, the chief of the Guebres, who is now residing at Ṭeherán to look after the interests of his people.

"How did he suffer for eating *mást-khiyár*? Well, I will tell you. You must know, then, that when he was appointed by the Parsees at Bombay to come and live in Persia and take care of the Guebres, and try to influence the Sháh in their favour, he knew nothing about Persia or the Persians; for, though of course the Parsees are really Persians by descent, they have now become more like Firangís. Well, Mánakjí Ṣáḥib set sail for Persia, and on board the vessel (being anxious to remedy this lack of knowledge on his part) he made friends with a Persian merchant of Iṣfahán, who was returning to his country. In the course of the voyage the ship touched at some port, the name of which I have forgotten, and, as it was to remain there all day, the Iṣfahání suggested to Mánakjí Ṣáḥib that they should go on shore and see the town, to which proposition the latter very readily agreed. Accordingly, they landed, and, since the town was situated at a considerable distance from the harbour, hired donkeys to convey them thither. Now the day was very hot, and as the sun got higher, Mánakjí Ṣáḥib found the heat unbearable; so, espying a village near at hand, he suggested to his companion that they should rest there under some old ruins, which stood a little apart, until the sun had begun to decline and the heat was less oppressive. To this his companion agreed, and further suggested that he should go to the village and see if he could find something to eat, while Mánakjí rested amongst the ruins. So they arranged with the muleteer to halt for an hour or two, and the Iṣfahání went off to look for food. Presently he returned with a number of young cucumbers and a quantity of *mást* (curds), with which he proceeded to concoct a bowl of *mást-khiyár*.

"Now Mánakjí (like you) had never seen this compound, and (being a man of a suspicious disposition) he began to fancy that his companion wanted to poison him in this lonely spot, and take his money. So when the *mást-khiyár* was ready, he refused to partake of it, to the great surprise of his companion. 'Why, just now you said you were so hungry,' said the latter; 'how is it that you now declare you have no appetite?' 'I found a piece of bread in my pocket,' said Mánakjí, 'and ate it while you were away in the village, and now my hunger is completely gone.' The more his companion pressed him to eat, the more suspicious he grew, and the more determined in his refusal. 'Very well,' said the Iṣfahání at last, 'since you won't join me, I must eat it by myself,' and this he proceeded to do, consuming the *mást-khiyár* with great relish and evident enjoyment. Now when Mánakjí saw this, he was sorry that he had refused to partake of the food. 'It is quite clear,' said he to himself, 'that it is not poisoned, or else my companion would not eat it; while at the same time, from the relish with which he does so, it is evident that, strange as the mixture looks, it must be very nice.' At last, when his companion had eaten about half, he could stand it no longer. 'Do you know,' he said, 'that my appetite has unaccountably come back at seeing you eat? If you will allow me, I think I will change my mind and join you after all.' His companion was rather surprised at this sudden change, but at once handed over the remainder of the food to Mánakjí, who, after tasting it and finding it very palatable, devoured it all.

"Now certain rules must be observed in eating some of our Persian foods, and in the case of *mást-khiyár* these are two in number. The first rule, as I have told you, is that you must not drink anything with it or after it; for, if you do, not only will your thirst be increased, but the food will swell up in your stomach and make you think you are going to die of suffocation. The second rule is that you must lie down and go to sleep directly you have eaten it. Now Mánakjí Ṣáḥib was ignorant of these rules, and so, when his companion lay down and went to sleep, he, feeling somewhat thirsty, took a draught of water, and then lay down to rest. But, so far from being able to rest, he found himself attacked by a strange feeling of oppression, and his thirst soon returned twofold. So he got up and took another drink of water, and then lay down again, but now his state was really pitiable: he could hardly breathe, his stomach swelled up in a most alarming manner, and he was tormented by thirst. Then his suspicions returned with redoubled force, and he thought to himself, 'There is no doubt that my companion really has poisoned me, and has himself taken some antidote to prevent the poison from affecting him. Alas! alas! I shall certainly die in this horrible, lonely spot, and no one will know what has become of me!'

"While he was rolling about in agony, tormented by these alarming thoughts, he suddenly became aware of a strange-looking winged animal sitting on a wall close to him, and apparently gloating over his sufferings. It was nodding its head at him in a derisive manner, and, to his excited imagination, it seemed to be saying, as plain as words could be, '*Aḥwál-i-shumá ché-ṭawr-ast? Aḥwál-i-shumá ché-ṭawr-ast?*' ('How are you? How are you?'). Now the animal was nothing more than one of those little owls which are so common in ruined places, but Mánakjí didn't know this, never having seen an owl before, and thought it must certainly be the Angel of Death come to fetch his soul. So he lay there gazing at it in horror, till at last he could bear it no longer, and determined to wake his companion; 'for,' thought he, 'even though he has poisoned me, he is after all a human being, and his companionship will at least enable me better to bear the presence of this horrible apparition.' So he stretched out his foot, and gave his companion a gentle kick. Finding that did not rouse him, he repeated it with greater force, and his companion woke up. 'Well,' said he, 'what is the matter?' Mánakjí pointed to the bird, which still sat there on the wall, nodding its head, and apparently filled with diabolical enjoyment at the sufferer's misery. 'Do you see that?' he enquired. 'See it? Of course I see it,' replied his companion, 'What of it?' Then some inkling of the nature of Mánakjí's terrors and suspicions came into his mind, and he determined to frighten him a little more, just to punish him. 'Doesn't it appear to you to be saying something?' said Mánakjí; 'I can almost fancy that I hear the very words it utters.' 'Saying something!' answered the Iṣfahání, 'Of course it is: but surely you know what it is, and what it is saying?' 'Indeed I do not,' said Mánakjí, 'for I have never before seen anything like it; and as to what it is saying, it appears to me to be enquiring after my health, which, for the rest, is sufficiently bad.' 'So it would seem,' said the other; 'but do you really mean to tell me that you don't know what it is? Well, I will tell you: it is the spirit of the accursed 'Omar, who usurped the Caliphate, and whose generals overran Persia. Since his death he has been permitted to assume this form, and in it to wander about the world. Now he has come to you, and is saying, "I, in my lifetime, took so much trouble to overthrow the worship of Fire, and do you dare come back to Persia to attempt its restoration?"'

"On hearing this Mánakjí was more frightened than ever; but at last his friend took pity on him, and picking up a stone threw it at the bird, which instantly flew away. 'I was only joking,' he said; 'it is nothing but an owl.' So Mánakjí's fears were dispelled, and he soon recovered from the *mást-khiyár*; but though he subsequently found out the proper way of eating it, I am not sure that he ever had the courage to try it again."

We laughed a good deal at this story, and I remarked that it was an extraordinary thing that Mánakjí Ṣáḥib should have been so frightened at an owl.

"Well," he said, "it is. But then in the desert, and in solitary, gloomy places, things will frighten you that you would laugh at in the city. I don't believe in all these stories about *ghúls* and '*ifríts* which the *chárvádárs* tell; but at the same time I would rather listen to them here than out there in the *kavír*. It is a terrible place that *kavír*! All sand and salt and solitude, and tracks not more than two feet wide on which you can walk with safety.

Deviate from them only a hand's breadth, and down you go into the salt-swamps, camel, man, baggage, and everything else, and there is an end of you. Many a brave fellow has died thus.

"Have I seen anything of the *ḳavír*? No, nor do I wish to do so; hearing about it is quite sufficient for me. I was once lost in the salt-mountains near Semnán when a boy, having run away from my father, who had done something to offend me. I only remained amongst them one night, and, beyond the bitter brininess of the bright-looking streams at which I strove to quench my thirst, and the horror of the place and its loneliness, there was nothing half so bad as the *ḳavír*, yet I wouldn't go through the experience again on any account. You have probably heard plenty of stories about the desert from your *chárvádárs* on the road; nevertheless, as you seem to like hearing them, I will tell you one which may be new to you."

We begged him to give us the story, and he proceeded as follows:—"A poor man was once travelling along on foot and alone in the desert when he espied coming towards him a most terrible-looking dervish. You have very likely seen some of those wandering, wild-looking dervishes who go about all over the country armed with axes or clubs, and fear neither wild beast nor man, nor the most horrible solitudes. Well, this dervish was one of that class, only much more ferocious-looking and wild than any you ever saw; and he was moreover armed with an enormous and ponderous club, which he kept swinging to and fro in a manner little calculated to reassure our traveller. The latter, indeed, liked the appearance of the dervish so little that he determined to climb up a tree, which fortunately stood close by, and wait till the fellow had passed.

"The dervish, however, instead of passing by, seated himself on the ground under the tree. Of course the poor traveller was horribly frightened, not knowing how long the dervish might choose to stop there, and fearing, moreover, that his place of retreat might have been observed. He therefore continued to watch the dervish anxiously, and presently saw him pull out of his pocket five little clay figures, which he placed in a row in front of him. Having arranged them to his satisfaction, he addressed the first of them, which he called 'Omar, as follows:—

"'O 'Omar! I have thee now, thou usurper of the Caliphate! Thou shalt forthwith answer to me for thy crimes, and receive the just punishment of thy wickedness. Yet will I deal fairly with thee, and give thee a chance of escape. It may be that there were mitigating circumstances in the case which should not be overlooked: inform me, therefore, if it be so, and I promise thee I will not be unmerciful.... What! thou answerest nothing at all? Then it is evident thou can'st think of no excuse for thy disgraceful conduct, and I will forthwith slay thee.' Saying this, the dervish raised his mighty club over his head, and, bringing it down with a crash on the little image, flattened it level with the ground.

"He next addressed himself to the second image thus: 'O Abú Bekr! Thou also wert guilty in this matter, since thou didst first occupy the place which by right belonged to 'Alí. Nevertheless thou art an old man, and it may be that thou wert but a tool in the hands of that ungodly 'Omar, whom I have just now destroyed. If it be so, tell me, that I may deal mercifully with thee. ...What! thou too art silent! Beware, or I will crush thee even as I crushed thine abettor in this offence....Thou still refusest to answer? Then thy blood be on thine own head!' Another blow with the club, and the second figure had followed the first.

"The dervish now turned to the third figure: 'O Murtaẓá 'Alí,' he exclaimed, 'tell me, I pray thee, now that these wretches who deprived thee of thy rights have met with their deserts, how it was that thou, the chosen successor of the Prophet, didst allow thyself to be so set aside. After all, thou didst in a manner acquiesce in their usurpation, and I desire to know why thou didst so, and why thou didst not withstand them even to the death. Tell me this, therefore, I pray thee, that my difficulties may be solved....What! thou also art silent? Nay, but thou shalt speak, or I will deal with thee as with the others....Still thou answerest nothing? Then perish!' Down came the club a third time, while the poor man in the tree was almost beside himself with horror at this impiety.

"This horror was further increased when the dervish, turning to the fourth clay figure, addressed it as follows:—'O Muḥammad! O Prophet of God! Since thou didst enjoy Divine Inspiration, thou didst without doubt know what would occur after thy death. How, then, didst thou take no precautions to guard against it? Without doubt, in this, too, there is some hidden wisdom which I would fain understand, therefore I beseech thee to tell me of it....Thou answerest not a word? Nay, but thou shalt answer, else even thy sacred mission shall in nowise protect thee from my just wrath....Still thou maintainest silence? Beware, for I am in earnest, and will not be trifled with. ...Thou continuest to defy me? Then perish with the rest!' Another heavy blow with the club, and the figure of the Prophet disappeared into the ground, while the poor man in the tree was half-paralysed with dread, and watched with fascinated horror to see what the dervish would do next.

"Only one clay figure now remained, and to this the dervish addressed himself. 'O Alláh!' he said, 'Thou who hadst knowledge of all the troubles which would befall the family of him whom Thou didst ordain to be the successor of Thy Prophet, tell me, I pray Thee, what divine mystery was concealed under that which baffles our weak comprehension!...Wilt Thou not hear my prayer?...Art Thou also silent?...Nay, Thou shalt answer me or——'

"'Wretch!' suddenly exclaimed the man in the tree, his terror of the dervish for the moment mastered by his indignation, 'Art thou not satisfied with having destroyed the Prophet of God, and 'Alí, his holy successor? Wilt thou also slay the Creator? Beware! Hold thy hand, or verily the heavens will fall and crush thee!'

"On hearing this voice, apparently from the clouds, the dervish was so terrified that he uttered one loud cry, dropped his uplifted club, and fell back dead. The man in the tree now descended, and cautiously approached the body of the dervish. Being finally assured that he was really dead, he proceeded to remove his cloak, which he was surprised to find of enormous weight, so that he began to think there must be something concealed in the lining. This proved to be the case, for, as he cut it open, a hidden hoard of gold pieces poured forth on to the ground. These the poor traveller proceeded to pick up and transfer to his pockets. When he had completed this task, he raised his face to heaven and said, 'O Alláh! Just now I saved Thy life by a timely interference, and for this Thou hast now rewarded me with this store of gold, for which I heartily thank Thee.'"

"What a very foolish man the traveller must have been," we remarked when the story was concluded; "he certainly met with better fortune than he deserved. Of course the dervish was nothing better than a madman."

"Yes," answered the Khán, "and of the two a fool is the worse, especially as a friend, a truth which is exemplified in the story of the Gardener, the Bear, and the Snake, which well illustrates the proverb that 'A wise enemy is better than a foolish friend.' If you do not know the story I will tell it you, for it is quite short.

"Once upon a time there was a gardener, into whose garden a bear used often to come to eat the fruit. Now, seeing that the bear was very strong and formidable, the gardener deemed it better to be on good terms with it, thinking that it might prove a useful ally. So he encouraged it to come whenever it liked, and gave it as much fruit as it could eat, for which kindness the bear was very grateful.

"Now, there was also a snake which lived in a hole in the garden wall. One day, when the snake was basking in the sun half asleep, the gardener saw it and struck at it with a spade which he had in his hand. The blow wounded the snake and caused it a great deal of pain, but did not kill it, and it succeeded in dragging itself back into its hole. From this time forth it was filled with a desire for revenge, and a determination to watch the gardener's movements carefully, so that, if ever it saw him asleep, it might inflict on him a mortal wound.

"Now, the gardener knew that the snake had escaped, and was well aware that he had made a deadly enemy of it, so he was afraid to go to sleep within its reach unprotected. He communicated his apprehensions to his friend the bear, which, eager to give some proof of its gratitude, readily offered to watch over him while he slept. The gardener gladly accepted this offer, and lay down to sleep; while the snake, concealed in its hole, continued its watch, hoping for an opportunity of gratifying its revenge.

"Now, the day was hot, and the flies were very troublesome, for they kept buzzing round the gardener's face, and even settling upon it. This boldness on their part annoyed the bear very much, especially when he found that he could only disperse them for a moment by a wave of his paw, and that they returned immediately to the spot from which they had been driven.

"At last the bear could stand it no longer, and determined to have done with the flies once and for all. Looking round he espied a large flat stone which lay near. 'Ah, now, I have you,' he thought, as he picked up the stone and waited for the flies to settle again on the gardener's face; 'I'll teach you to molest my friend's slumbers, you miserable creatures!' Then, the flies having settled, *thud!* down came the stone with a mighty crash on—the gardener's head, which was crushed in like an egg-shell, while the flies flew merrily away to torment some new victim, and the snake crept back into its hole with great contentment, muttering to itself the proverb in question, 'A wise enemy is better than a foolish friend.'"

And now, just outside the walls surrounding the telegraph-office, rose a prolonged and dismal howl, followed by another and yet another; while from the city, like an answer, came back the barking of the dogs. "Are those jackals howling outside?" I asked, "and do they come so close to the town?" "Yes," answered the Khán, "they always do so, and the dogs always answer them thus. Do you know why? Once upon a time the jackals used to live in the towns, just as the dogs do now, while the latter dwelt outside in the desert. Now, the dogs thought it would be much nicer to be in the town, where they would be sheltered from the inclemency of the weather, and would have plenty to eat instead of often having to go without food for a long time. So they sent one of their number to the jackals with the following message: 'Some amongst us,' they said, 'are ill, and our physicians say that what they need is change of air, and that they ought, if possible, to spend three days in the town. Now, it is clearly impossible for us dogs and you jackals to be in one place at the same time, so we would ask you to change places with us for three days only, and to let us take up our quarters in the city, while you retire into the desert, the air of which will doubtless prove very beneficial to you also.'

"To this proposition the jackals agreed, and during the following night the exchange was effected. In the morning, when the people of the city woke up, they found a dog wherever there had been a jackal on the previous night. On the third night the jackals, being quite tired of the desert, came back to the gates of the town, filled with pleasant anticipations of resuming their luxurious city life. But the dogs, being very comfortable in their new quarters, were in no hurry to quit them. So, after waiting some time, the jackals called out to the dogs, '*Ná-ḵhush-i-shumá ḵhúb shudé-é-é-é?*' ('Are your sick ones well yet?'), ending up with a whine rising and falling in cadence, just such as you heard a minute ago, and (as Mírzá 'Abdu'lláh, who is a native of Iṣfahán, will tell you) just such as you may hear any day in the mouth of an Iṣfahání or a Yezdí. But the dogs, who are

Turks and speak Turkish, only answered '*Yokh! Yokh!*' ('No! no!') and so the poor jackals had to go back into the desert. And ever since then they come back at night and hail the dogs with the same question, as you heard them do just now; and the dogs always give the same reply, for they have no wish to go back to the desert. And that is why the jackals come and howl round the town after dusk, and why the dogs always answer them."

At this point our host interrupted the conversation to tell us that supper was ready. "Supper!" exclaimed the Khán, who had already commenced another story, "Supper, indeed! Am I to have my stories cut short and spoiled by supper? No, I shall not go on with what I was saying, even though you do beg my pardon; but I will forgive you, provided always that you ask an 'English pardon' and not a 'Persian pardon.'"

"What do you mean by a 'Persian pardon'?" I asked; "please explain the expression."

"No, I shall keep my word and tell you no more stories to-night," answered the Khán. "I have told you plenty already, and you will probably forget them all, and me too. Now you will remember me much better as having refused to satisfy your curiosity on this one point, and whenever you hear the expression '*Párdum-i-Írání*' (so he pronounced it) you will think of Mírzá Ḥuseyn Khán of Káshán."

After supper we had some songs accompanied on the *si-tár*, all present, except myself, being something of musicians, and thus the evening passed pleasantly, till the guests announced that they must depart, and I was astonished to find that it was close on midnight, and high time to retire for the night.

Next day (16th February) our road continued to skirt the plain for some twelve or fifteen miles, and then turned to the right into the mountains. We at first ascended along a river-bed, down which trickled a comparatively small quantity of water. I was surprised to see that a number of dams had been constructed to divert the water from its channel and make it flow over portions of the bank, whence it returned charged with mud. On asking the reason of this strange procedure, I was informed that it was done to *prevent the water evaporating*, as muddy water evaporates less readily than that which is clear!

On ascending somewhat higher, we came to a place where there was a smooth, rather deep, oblong depression in the face of the rock. Inside this, as well as on the ground beneath, were heaps of small stones and pebbles; while in every cranny and chink of the cliff around and below this spot were planted little bits of stick decorated with rags of divers colours placed there by pious passers-by. As we came up to this place, Khudá-bakhsh, the muleteer, who was a few paces in front, sprang up towards the depression, shouting "*Yá 'Alí!*" and drew his hand down it, thus affording an indication of the manner in which the wonderful smoothness of its walls had been produced. He then informed us that the depression in question was the mark left by the hoof of 'Alí's steed, Duldul, and that there were only two or three more such in the whole of Persia. Near the village of Gez, he added, there was the mark of 'Alí's hand in the rock. Ḥájí Ṣafar, on learning these facts, added his quota of pebbles to those already collected on the slope.

Proceeding onwards through very fine scenery, we suddenly came upon a mighty wall of rock wherewith the channel of the stream was barred, and beyond this a vast sheet of water formed by the damming-up of the water-course. This splendid, half-natural reservoir, which serves to keep the city of Káshán well supplied with water during the hot, dry summer, was constructed, like so many other useful and beneficial public works, during the period of prosperity which Persia enjoyed under the Ṣafaví kings, and is known as the *Band-i-Ḳohrúd*. Winding round the right side of this great lake, we presently began to see around us abundant signs of cultivation—plantations of trees, orchards, and fields laid out in curious steps for purposes of irrigation, and already green with sprouting corn. Soon we entered tortuous lanes, enclosed by stout walls of stone, and overshadowed by trees, and, after traversing these for some distance, we arrived at the village of Javínán, the strange-looking inhabitants of which came out to see us pass. The women for the most part wore green shawls and did not cover their faces. As we passed we could hear them conversing in the curious dialect, incomprehensible to the ordinary Persian, of which I shall have to speak directly.

About a mile farther on we came to the village of Ḳohrúd, where, the *chápár-ḳháné* (post-house) being occupied, we found quarters at the house of a Seyyid, who appeared to be one of the chief men of the village. I had already heard from General Houtum-Schindler, who possesses probably more knowledge about the geography, ethnology, and local dialects of Persia than any man living, of the curious dialect spoken in and around Ḳohrúd and Naṭanz, and, anxious to acquire further information about it, I mentioned the matter to my host, who at once volunteered to bring in two or three of the people of the place to converse with me. Accordingly, as soon as I had had tea, a man and his son came in, and, bowing ceremoniously, took their seats by the door.

I first asked them as to the distribution of their dialect, and the extent of the area over which it was spoken. They replied that it was spoken with slight variations in about a dozen or fifteen villages round about, extending on the one hand to the little town of Naṭanz, in the valley to the east, and on the other to the mountain-village of Ḳamsar. Of its age, history, and relations they knew nothing definite, merely characterising it as "*Furs-i-ḳadím*" ("Ancient Persian"). From what I subsequently learned, I infer that it forms one branch of a dialect or language spoken with greater or less variations over a large portion of Persia. With the dialect of Naṭanz it seems almost identical, so far as I can judge from a comparison of the specimen of that vernacular (consisting of some thirty words) given by

Polak[1] with my own collection of Ḳohrúd words. With the so-called *Darí* language of the Zoroastrians of Yezd and Kirmán it has also close affinities[2], and it would also seem to be near akin to the dialect spoken about Sívand, three stages north of Shíráz. The relations of these dialects to one another, and to the languages of ancient Persia, have not yet been fully worked out, though excellent monographs on several of them exist, and the quatrains of the celebrated Bábá Ṭáhir, "the Lur," have been published with translation and notes by M. Clément Huart[3]. It would be out of place here to discuss the philological bearings of this question, and I will merely observe that the wide distribution of these kindred dialects, and the universal tradition of their age, alike point to something more than a merely local origin.

I now for the first time realised the difficulty of obtaining precise information from uneducated people with regard to their language. In particular, it was most difficult to get them to give me the different parts of the verbs. I would ask, for example, "How would you say, 'I am ill'?" They gave me a sentence which I wrote down. Then I asked, "Now, what is 'thou art ill'?" They repeated the same sentence. "That can't be right," I said; "they can't both be the same." "Yes, that is right," they answered; "if we want to say 'thou art ill' we say just what we have told you." "Well, but suppose you were ill yourself what would you say?" "Oh, then we should say so-and-so." This readiness in misapprehending one's meaning and reversing what

1 *Persien, Das Land und seine Bewohner*, von Dr Jakob Eduard Polak, Leipzig, 1865, vol. i, p. 265.

2 On this dialect, see *Zeitschrift der Deutschen Morgenländischen Gesellschaft*, vol. xxxv, pp. 327–414, *Ueber die Mundart von Jezd*, by Ferdinand Justi; and *ibid.* vol. xxxvi, pp. 54–88, *Die Parsen in Persien, ihre Sprache und einige ihrer Gebräuche*, by General A. Houtum-Schindler. See also *Journal Asiatique*, 1888, viii série, 11, where M. Clément Huart protests against the application of the term *Darí* to this dialect, which he includes along with Kurdish, Mázandaráni, the patois of Semnán, etc., under the general appellation of '*Pehlevi Musulman*,' or '*Modern Medic*.' Cf. p. 426, *infra*.

3 *Journal Asiatique*, 1885, viii série, 6, pp. 502–545.

one had said gave rise to one class of difficulties. Another class arose from the extreme simplicity of the people. For instance, after asking them the words for a number of common objects in their language, I asked, "And what do you call 'city'?" "Káshán," they replied. "Nonsense!" I said, "Káshán is the name of a particular city: what do you call cities in general?" "No," they said, "it is quite right: in Persian you say '*shahr mí-ravam*,' 'I am going to the city': we say '*Káshán mí-ravam*': it is all the same." It was useless to argue, or to point out that there were many other cities in the world besides Káshán: to these simple-minded folk Káshán remained "the city" *par excellence*, and they could not see what one wanted with any other. Finally I had to give up the struggle in despair, and to this day I do not know whether the Ḳohrúdí dialect possesses a general term for "city" or not.

I here append a list of the words and expressions which I took down during the short opportunity I had for studying the Ḳohrúd dialect, as I am not aware that anything has been published on that particular branch of what M. Huart calls "Pehlevi Musulman." For the sake of comparison, I place in parallel columns the equivalents in the Naṭanz dialect given by Polak, and those of the so-called Darí of Yezd given by General Schindler and Justi. The transcription of these latter I have only altered so far as appeared necessary to convey the proper pronunciation to the English reader, *e.g.* in substituting the English *y* for the German *j*[1].

English	Persian	Ḳohrúdí	Naṭanzí	Darí of Yezd
Father	*Pidar* *Bábá*	*Bábá*	..	*Per*, *Pedar* (S.) *Báb*, *Bábú* (J.), *Bâwg* (S.)
Mother	*Mádar*	*Múné*	*Múné* (P.)	*Már*, *Má*, *Mer* (S.) *Memu* (J.)

1 In this table the second column contains the Persian words; the third their equivalents in the Ḳohrúd dialect as taken down by myself; the fourth the Naṭanz equivalents given by Polak (*loc. cit.*), which are marked (P.); and the fifth and last the equivalents in the Darí of Yezd, as given by Schindler (S.) and Justi (J.) respectively.

English	Persian	Ḳohrúdí	Naṭanzí	Darí of Yezd
Brother	*Birádar* *Dádar* (old)	*Dádú*	..	*Berár* (S.) *Dúhar* (J.)
Son	*Pisar* *Púr* (old)	*Púrá*	*Púrá* (P.)	*Púr* (J.) *Porer* (S.)
Daughter	*Dukhtar*	*Dútá*	*Dútá* (P.)	*Duteh* (J.) *Dut*, *Duter*, *Doter* (S.)
Child	*Bacha*	*Vacha*	..	*Vacha* (S. and J.)
Woman	*Zan*	*Yaná*	*Yená* (P.)	*Yen*, *Yenúk* (S.)
House	*Kháné* *Kedé*	*Kiyá*	*Ki'è* (P.)	*Kedeh*, *Kedah* (S.) *Khada* (J.)
Door	*Dar*	*Bar*	..	*Bar* (S. and J.)
Wood	*Chúb*	*Chúgá*	..	*Chú* (S.)
Tree	*Dirakht* *Bun* (gen. in comp.)	*Baná*	*Bená* (P.)	*Dirakht* (J. and S.)
Water	*Áb*	*Ô*	*Au* (P.)	*Vúv*(Berésine, quoted by J.)[1] *Vô* (Yezd), *Ô* (Kirmán) (S.)
Fire	*Átash*	*Atash*	..	*Tash* (J. and S.)
Apple	*Síb*	*So*	..	*Súv* (J.)
Garden	(*Raz* = vine)	*Raz*	*Raz*	[*Raz* = vine (S.)]
Night	*Shab*	*Shüyé*	..	*Shô* (J. and S.)
Bird	..	*Kárgé*	*Kærge* (P.)	
Dog	*Sag*	*Ispá*[2]	..	*Sabah* (S. *Sevá* (J.)
Cat	*Gurba*	*Máljí*	*Múljin* (P.)	*Malí* (S.)
Snow	*Barf*	*Váfrá*	..	*Vabr*(Berésine, quoted by J.)
To-day	*Imrúz*	*Iru*	..	*Emru* (J.)
Yesterday	*Dí-rúz*	*Izzé*	..	*Heze* (S.)
To-morrow	*Ferdá*	*Hiyá*	..	*Ardah* (S.)
Begone!	*Bi-raw* *Bi-shaw*	*Báshé*	*Bashé*	*Ve-sho* (S.)

From this sample of the Ḳohrúd dialect it will be seen that the following are some of its chief peculiarities, so far as generalisations can be drawn from so small a vocabulary:—

(1) Preservation of archaic forms; *e.g. púr*, *ispá*, *váfrá* (Zend, *vafra*), etc.

(2) Change of *B* into *V*; *e.g. vacha* (Pers. *bacha*), *valg* (Pers. *barg*, leaf); but this change does not go so far as in some other dialects, *B* for instance being preserved in the prefix to the imperative, as in *Báshé* (Pers. *bi-shaw*, Yezdí, *ve-sho*). The change of *Shab* (Pers.) into *Shaw* or *Shô* (Yezdí) and *Shüyé* (Ḳohrúdí); of *Síb* (Pers.) into *Súv* (Yezdí) and *So* (Ḳohrúdí); and of *Áb*

1 Berésine, *Recherches sur les dialectes persanes*, Kazan, 1853.

2 Zend, *çpan* (see Darmesteter, *Études Iraniennes*, Paris, 1883, vol. i, p. 13).

(Pers.) into Ô (Ḳohrúdí and Kirmání) and *vô* (Yezdí), is doubtless to be accounted for in this way.

(3) R standing *before* a consonant in a Persian word often stands *after* it in the Ḳohrúd dialect; *e.g. váfrá* (Pers. *barf*); sometimes its place is taken by L; *e.g. valg* (Pers. *barg*).

(4) *G* is sometimes replaced by *V*; *e.g. várg* (Pers. *gurg*, wolf).

(5) *P* is sometimes replaced by *F*; *e.g. asf* (Pers. *asp*, horse).

(6) *Kh* sometimes drops out when it is followed by another consonant; *e.g. bá-süt* (Pers. *súkhté*, burnt)[1].

A few short sentences may be given in conclusion, without comment or comparison. I come—*Átún*. He is coming to-day—*Írú átí*. We are coming—*Hamá átimá*. You are coming to-night—*Ishá átimá*. They are coming—*Átanda*. Come, let us go into the country!—*Bürya, báshima ṣaḥrá!* Bring some oil here—*Rúghan urgé bürya*. Take this and give it him—*Urgí bú'í de*. Take the donkey, go and load it with earth, and come here—*Khar urgí, báshé khák bár kí bürya*. Throw down the blanket here and sit down—*Pá bé galím ur bunú, dúmé húchin*. Sit here—*Hákum unchís*. I sat—*Hochistum*. He sat—*Hochish*. He came here—*Bamé andé*. I have not gone there—*Nígé náshtima*. It was day—*Rú wá bú*. My brother is ill—*Dúdún ná-sáz-á*. Is your brother better?—*Aḥwál-i-dúdú bihtar-á?* It is seven farsakhs from here to Káshán—*Andé tá Káshán haft farsangá*. How far is it from here to there?—*Andé tá nígé chan farsang-á?* What is your name?—*Ismat ché-chígá?* What does he say?—*Ají chí?* When do you go? *Ké ashima?* Whose is this house?—*Nú kiyá án-i-ki-á?* Where do you belong to?—*Tú ki gá ègí?* Whence comest thou?—*Írú kí godáté?* I come from Ḳamsar—*Ḳamsar d'átún*. How many days is it since you left?—*Chand rúg-á báshté'í?* It is ten days since I left—*Dah rúg-á báshtá'ún*. This wood is burned—*Na chúgá básút*. The fire has gone out—*Atash bá-mar*. 'Abdu'lláh is dead—'*Abdu'lláh bá mardá*. Take the pillow and come and put it under

1 Cf. M. Huart's article on the Quatrains of Bábá Ṭáhir, *Journal Asiatique*, 1885, viii série, 6, pp. 508–9. In these quatrains *súté* stands for *súkhté*; *sátan* for *sákhtan*, etc., almost uniformly.

my head—*Bálish úrgí bürya, zír-i-saram nú.* Why art thou such an ass?—*Chirá nandagar khari?* It has laid eggs—*Tukhm yú dádá.*

At last I asked my informants (whose number had been greatly increased by additions from without) what they said in their language for *pidar-súkhté* ("burnt-father," the commonest term of abuse in Persian). "*Bábá-bá-süt,*" they cried unanimously, and with much relish; "but we have many other bad names besides that, like *bábá bá-mar*, 'dead father,' and ——"; here they poured forth a torrent of Ḳohrúdí objurgations, which would probably have made me shudder if I had understood them. As it was, confusion being prevalent, and supper ready, Ḥájí Ṣafar turned them all out of the room.

That night snow fell heavily, and I was surprised to see that the Ḳohrúdís appeared to feel the cold (though they were well wrapped up) much more than any of us did. In the morning there was a layer of snow on the ground nearly six inches deep, and much more than this in the hollows. Luckily there had been but little wind, else it might have gone hard with us. As it was, we had difficulty enough. We were delayed in starting by the purchase of a quantity of *juzghand* (a kind of sweetmeat made with sugar and walnuts), in which, as it was a peculiar product of the place, Ḥájí Ṣafar advised me to invest. Then various people had to be rewarded for services rendered, amongst these my instructors of the previous night. The people were a grasping and discontented lot, and after I had given the man who had come to teach me the elements of Ḳohrúdí a present for himself and his son, the latter came and declared that he had not got his share, and that his father denied my having given him anything.

At last we got off, accompanied by another larger caravan which had arrived before us on the preceding evening. The path being completely concealed, one of the muleteers walked in front, sounding the depth of the snow with his staff. At first we got on at a fair pace, but as we advanced and continued to ascend it got worse and worse. Once or twice we strayed from the road, and had to retrace our steps. The last part of the climb which brought us to the summit of the pass was terrible work. The muleteers lost the road entirely, and, after blundering about for a while, decided to follow the course of the telegraph poles, so far as this was possible. In so doing, notwithstanding the sounding of the snow, we kept getting into drifts; many of the baggage-mules fell down and could not regain their feet till they had been unloaded; and every time this happened the whole caravan was brought to a standstill till the load had been replaced, the muleteers uttering loud shouts of "*Yá Alláh! Yá 'Alí!*" and the women in the *ḳajávés* (a sort of panniers) sending forth piteous cries whenever the animals which bore them stumbled or seemed about to fall. Altogether, it was a scene of the utmost confusion, though not lacking in animation; but the cold was too intense to allow me to take much interest in it.

After we had surmounted the pass, things went somewhat better; but we had been so much delayed during the ascent that it was nearly 6 p.m., and getting dusk, before we reached the rather bleak-looking village of Soh. Here also there is a telegraph-office, whither I directed my steps. Mr M'Gowen, who was in charge of the office, was out when I arrived, but I was kindly received by his wife, an Armenian lady, and his little boy. The latter appeared to me a very clever child: he spoke not only English, Persian, and Armenian with great fluency, but also the dialect of Soh, which is closely allied to, if not identical with, the Ḳohrúd vernacular. His father soon came in, accompanied by two Armenian travellers, one of whom was Darcham Bey, who is well known over the greater part of Persia for the assiduity with which he searches out and buys up walnut-trees. I often heard discussions amongst the Persians as to what use these were put to, and why anyone found it worth while to give such large sums of money for them. The general belief was that they were cut into thin slices and subjected to some process which made "pictures come out in the wood"—these pictures being, in the opinion of many, representations of events that had occurred under the tree which had supplied the wood.

I had a good deal of conversation with Darcham Bey, though much less than I might have done had I been less overcome with somnolence induced by exposure to the cold. He had travelled over a great part of Persia, especially Luristán, which he most earnestly counselled me to avoid. "The only people that I have seen worse than the Lurs," he said, "are the Ḳáshḳá'ís, for though the former will usually rob you if they can, and would not hesitate to murder you if you refused to give up your possessions to them, the latter, not content with this, will murder you even if you make no resistance, alleging that the world is well quit of one who is such a coward that he will not fight for his own."

Next day's march was singularly dull and uneventful, as well as bitterly cold. I had expected a descent on this side of the pass corresponding to the rapid ascent from Káshán to Ḳohrúd, but I was mistaken: it even seemed to me that the difference in altitude between the summit of the pass and Soh was at any rate not much greater than between the former and Ḳohrúd, while from Soh to our next halting-place, Múrchékhár, the road was, to all intents and purposes, level. At the latter place we arrived about 5 p.m. It is an unattractive village of no great size. Finding the caravansaray in bad repair, I put up at the post-house, where I could find little to amuse me but two hungry-looking cats, which came and shared my supper, at first with some diffidence, but finally with complete assurance. They were ungrateful beasts, however, for they not only left me abruptly as soon as supper was over, but paid a predatory visit to my stores during the night, and ate a considerable portion of what was intended to serve me for breakfast on the morrow.

The following day's march was a good deal more interesting. Soon after starting we saw three gazelles (*áhú*) grazing not more than 100 yards off the road. The wind being towards us from them, they allowed us to approach within a very short distance of them, so that, though I had no gun, I was almost tempted to take a shot at them with my revolver.

A little farther on, at a point where the road, rising in a gentle incline, passed between two low hills before taking a bend towards the east and descending into the great plain in which lies the once magnificent city of Iṣfahán, we came to the ruins of a little village, amidst which stood a splendid, though somewhat dismantled, caravansaray of the Ṣafaví era. Concerning this, one of the muleteers told me a strange story, which, for the credit of the Ḳájár dynasty, I hope was a fiction. "The Sháh," he said, "was once passing this spot when his courtiers called his attention to the architectural beauty and incomparable solidity of this building. 'In the whole of Persia,' they said, 'no caravansaray equal to this is to be found, neither can anyone at the present day build the like of it.' 'What!' exclaimed the Sháh, 'are none of the caravansarays which I have caused to be built as fine? That shall be so no longer. Destroy this building which makes men think lightly of the edifices which I have reared.'" This command, if ever given, was carried out somewhat tenderly, for the destruction is limited to the porches, mouldings, turrets, and other less essential portions of the structure. But, indeed, to destroy the buildings reared by the Ṣafaví kings would be no easy task, and could hardly be accomplished without gunpowder.

A little way beyond this we reached another ruined village, where we halted for lunch. We were now in the Iṣfahán plain, and could even discern the position of the city by the thin pall of blue smoke which hung over it, and was thrown into relief by the dark mountains beyond. To our left (east) was visible the edge of the Dasht-i-Kavír, which we had not seen since entering the Ḳohrúd Pass. Its flat, glittering expanse was broken here and there by low ranges of black mountains thrown up from the plain into sharp rocky ridges. To the right (west) were more hills, amongst which lies the village of Najaf-ábád, one of the strongholds of the Bábís.

Resuming our march after a short halt, we passed several flourishing villages on either side (amongst them, and some distance to the east of the road, Gurgáb, which is so celebrated for its melons), and, about 4 p.m., reached our halting-place, Gez. I think we might without much difficulty have pushed on to Iṣfahán, which was now clearly visible at a distance of about ten miles ahead of us, but the muleteers were natives of Gez, and naturally desired to avail themselves of the opportunity now afforded them for visiting their families. Personally, I should have preferred making an attempt to reach the city that night, for Gez is by no means an attractive spot, and I could find no better occupation than to watch a row of about a dozen camels kneeling down in the caravansaray to receive their evening meal, consisting of balls of dough (*nawálé*), from the hands of their drivers. Later on, Khudá-bakhsh, the second muleteer, brought me a present (*píshkesh*) of a great bowl of *mást* (curds), and two chickens.

Next day (20th February) we got off about 8.30. Khudá-bakhsh, having received his present (*in'ám*), testified his gratitude by accompanying us as far as the outskirts of the village, when I bade him farewell and dismissed him; Raḥím, assisted by a younger brother called Mahdí-Ḳulí, whom he had brought with him from the village, undertaking to convey us to Iṣfahán. I had, while at Ṭeherán, received a most kindly-worded invitation from Dr Hoernle, of the English Church Mission, to take up my abode with him at the Mission-House during my stay in the city; and as that was situated in the Armenian quarter of Julfá, beyond the river Záyanda-Rúd (Zindé-Rúd of Ḥáfiẓ), the muleteers wished to proceed thither direct without entering the city; alleging that the transit through the bazaars would be fraught with innumerable delays. As, however, I was desirous of obtaining some idea of the general aspect of the city as soon as possible, I requested them to do exactly the contrary to what they proposed, viz. to convey me to my destination through as large a portion of the bazaars as could conveniently be traversed. This they finally consented to do.

During a portion of our way to the city we enjoyed the company of a *muḳanní-báshí*, or professional maker of *ḳanáts*—those subterranean aqueducts of which I have already spoken—with whom I conversed for a time on the subject of his profession, since I was very desirous to learn how it was possible for men possessed of but few instruments, and those of the rudest kind, to sink their shafts with such precision. I cannot say, however, that my ideas on the subject were rendered much clearer by his explanations.

As we drew nearer to the city, its numerous domes, minarets, and pigeon-towers (*ḳaftar-ḳháné*) began to be clearly discernible, and on all sides signs of cultivation increased. We passed through many poppy-fields, where numbers of labourers were engaged in weeding. The plants were, of course, quite small at this season, for they are not ready to yield the opium till about a month after the Nawrúz (*i.e.* about the end of April). When this season arrives the poppy-capsules are gashed or scored by means of an instrument composed of several sharp blades laid parallel. This is done early in the morning, and in the afternoon the juice, which has exuded and dried, is scraped off. The crude opium (*tiryáḳ-i-ḳhám*) thus obtained is subsequently kneaded up, purified, dried, and finally made into cylindrical rolls about $\frac{1}{2}$ inch or $\frac{1}{3}$ inch in diameter.

At length we entered the city by the gate called Derwázé-i-Chárchú, and were soon threading our way through the bazaars, which struck me as very fine; for not only are they lofty and spacious, but the goods exposed for sale in the shops are for the most part of excellent quality. The people are of a different type to the Ṭeheránís; they are not as a rule very dark in complexion, and have strongly-marked features, marred not infrequently by a rather forbidding expression, though the average of good looks is certainly fairly high. The character which they bear amongst other Persians is not altogether enviable, avarice and niggardliness being accounted their chief characteristics. Thus it is commonly said of anyone who is very careful of his expenditure that he is "as mean as the merchants of Iṣfahán, who put their cheese in a bottle, and rub their bread on the outside to give it a flavour."[1] Another illustration of this alleged stinginess is afforded by the story of an Iṣfahání merchant, who one day caught his apprentice eating his lunch of dry bread and gazing wistfully at the bottle containing the precious cheese; whereupon he proceeded to scold the unfortunate youth roundly for his greediness, asking him if he "couldn't eat plain bread for one day?" Nor have the poets failed to display their ill-nature towards the poor Iṣfahánís, as the following lines testify:—

" *Iṣfahán jannatíst pur ni'mat;*
Iṣfahání dar-ú namí-báyad."

"Iṣfahán is a paradise full of luxuries;
There ought (however) to be no Iṣfahánís in it."

At last we emerged from the bazaars into the fine spacious square called *Meydán-i-Sháh*. On our right hand as we entered it was the '*Álí Ḳápí* ("Supreme Gate"), which is the palace of the Ẓillu's-Sulṭán, the Prince-Governor of Iṣfahán, of whom I have already spoken. In front of us, at the other end of the square, was the magnificent mosque called *Masjid-i-Sháh*, surmounted by a mighty dome. Quitting the Meydán at the angle between these residences of ecclesiastical and temporal power, and traversing several tortuous streets, we entered the fine spacious avenue called *Chahár Bágh*, which is wide, straight, well-paved, surrounded by noble buildings, planted with rows of lofty plane-trees, and supplied with several handsome fountains. This avenue must

1 See Haggard and Le Strange's *Vazír of Lankurán*, translation of Act I, p. 48, and note on the same, pp. 91, 92.

have been the pride of Iṣfahán in the good old days of the Ṣafavís, and is still calculated to awaken a feeling of deep admiration in the mind of the traveller; but it has suffered considerably in later days, not only by the state of dilapidation into which many of the buildings situated on its course have been allowed to fall, but also by the loss of many noble plane-trees which were cut down by the Ẓillu's-Sulṭán, and sent to Ṭeherán to afford material for a palace which he was building there.

On reaching the end of the Chahár Bágh we came in sight of the river Záyanda-Rúd, which separates the city of Iṣfahán from the Christian suburb of Julfá. This river, though it serves only to convert into a swamp (the Gávkháné Marsh) a large area of the desert to the east, is at Iṣfahán as fine a stream as one could wish to see. It is spanned by three bridges, of which the lowest is called *Pul-i-Ḥasanábád*, the middle one *Pul-i-sí-ú-sih chashmé* ("the bridge of thirty-three arches"), and the upper one *Pul-i-Márún*, all of them solidly and handsomely built. We crossed the river by the middle bridge, obtaining while doing so a good view of the wide but now half-empty channel, the pebbly sides of which were spread with fabrics of some kind, which had just been dyed, and were now drying in the sun. The effect produced by the variegated colours of these, seen at a little distance, was as though the banks of the river were covered with flower-beds. On the other side of the stream was another avenue closely resembling the Chahár Bágh, through which we had already passed, and running in the same line as this and the bridge, viz. towards the south. This, however, we did not follow, but turned sharply towards the right, and soon entered Julfá, which is not situated exactly opposite to Iṣfahán, but somewhat higher up the river. It is a large suburb, divided into a number of different quarters, communicating with one another by means of gates, and traversed by narrow, tortuous lanes planted with trees; in many cases a stream of water runs down the middle of the road dividing it in two. After passing through a number of these lanes we finally reached the Mission-House, where I was met and cordially welcomed by Dr Hoernle, who, though I had never seen him before, received me with a genial greeting which at once made me feel at home. Dr Bruce, who had kindly written to him about me, was still absent in Europe, so that all the work of the mission had now devolved on him, and this, in itself no small labour, was materially increased by the medical aid which was continually required of him; for Dr Hoernle was the only qualified practitioner in Iṣfahán. Nevertheless, he found time in the afternoon to take me to call on most of the European merchants resident in Julfá, and the cordial welcome which I received from these was alone necessary to complete the favourable impression produced on me by Iṣfahán.

CHAPTER VIII

IṢFAHÁN

> *"Ṣafáhán ma'ni-yi-lafẓ-i-jihán-ast;*
> *Jihán lafẓ-ast, u ma'ní Iṣfahán-ast."*
>
> "Iṣfahán is the idea connoted by the word 'world';
> 'World' is the word, and Iṣfahán is the meaning."
>
> *"Jihán-rá agar Iṣfahání na-búd,*
> *Jihán-áfarín-rá jihání na-búd."*
>
> "If the world had no Iṣfahán,
> The World-Creator would have no world."
>
> *"Man ṭalaba shey'^{an}, wa jadda, wajada."*
>
> "Whosoever seeketh a thing, and is strenuous in search, findeth it."

JULFÁ is, as I have said, situated at some distance from Iṣfahán, and to walk from the Mission-House to the bazaars requires the best part of an hour. Hence it happened that, although I remained a fortnight in this place, I did not visit the city more than five or six times, and then chiefly for business in the bazaars or caravansarays. Four or five days after my arrival, however, I accompanied Mr Aghanor, the British agent, into the town, and he kindly devoted several hours to showing me some of its more interesting features. Some of these I have already noticed, and it only remains to say a few words about the rest.

The first public building which we visited was the *Madrasa*, or College, built by Sulṭán Ḥuseyn, in whose unfortunate reign (A.D. 1694–1722) the glory of the Ṣafaví dynasty, and with it the glory of Iṣfahán, was brought to a disastrous end by the Afghan invasion. The *Madrasa* is built in the form of a hollow square, and contains about 120 rooms for students and teachers, but of these two-thirds are untenanted. In the centre of the spacious courtyard is a large tank of water, pleasantly overshadowed by plane-trees. The entrance to the college is through a corridor, now used as a small bazaar, furnished on the side towards the road with massive gates overlaid with exquisite brasswork, and adorned with Arabic inscriptions in the centre and Persian on the margin. The walls of the corridor are also ornamented with tiles bearing inscriptions.

Leaving this, we proceeded to the *Chahil sutún* ("forty columns"), so-called because of a double row of plane-trees standing by the side of a stream which traverses the garden. The trees in question are only twenty in number, their reflections in the limpid water beneath constituting the other twenty "columns." At the farther end of this garden is the beautiful little palace called *Hasht Bihisht* ("Eight Paradises"). This had belonged to the Ẓillu's-Sulṭán's minister, *Ṣárimu'd-Dawla*, whose life had recently been brought to an abrupt close by an obscure and rapidly fatal disease which defied the skill of the physicians. Such was the official report received from the capital, where his decease had occurred: popular rumour, however, ascribed his death to a cup of "Ḳajár coffee," which had disagreed with the unfortunate nobleman. The walls of this palace are beautifully decorated, and adorned with six fine paintings representing scenes of battle or revelry. Concerning the latter, an old Seyyid, who was present, remarked with indignation that they were productions of a later age, since such scenes of dissipation never disgraced the court of the pious Ṣafavís. Of the three battle scenes, one represented the rout of the Uzbegs by the Persian army; another, an engagement between the Persians and the Ottoman Turks under Selím I; and the third, one of the wars of Nádir Sháh with the Indians. Besides these, and the two banquet scenes which had roused the indignation of the Seyyid, there was a picture representing Sháh Ṭahmásp I receiving the fugitive emperor of Hindústán, Humáyún.

Signs of the prevailing vandalism were apparent alike in the palace and the garden. In the former, the beautiful mural decorations (except the pictures) were being covered with hideous brick-red paint. In the latter, the plane-trees were falling beneath the axes of a party of woodcutters. A remonstrance addressed to the latter merely elicited the thoroughly Persian reply, "*Dígar...ḥukm-ast*" ("Well...it is ordered"). They seemed sorry to be engaged in destroying the relics of the glorious past, but—"*dígar*"—what else could they do? They could no more refuse to carry out the Prince's wishes than they could venture to criticise his decision.

In another room in a building at the other end of the garden were two portraits of a former governor of Iṣfahán, Minúchihr Khán, the Georgian eunuch, who died in A.D. 1847. He is described by Gobineau as a man "redouté et redoutable par ses talents et un peu aussi par sa cruauté," and was so powerful that it is related that on one occasion the king, Muḥammad Sháh, summoned him to Ṭeherán and said to him, "I have heard that you are like a king at Iṣfahán," to which the wily old minister promptly replied, "Yes, your Majesty, that is true, and you must have such kings as your governors, in order that you may enjoy the title of '*Sháhinsháh*' ('King of kings')."

We passed through a portion of the palace and paid a visit to the *Ruknu'l-Mulk*, who was acting as deputy-governor during the absence of the Ẓillu's-Sulṭán. He was a fine-looking Shírází, and received us with great urbanity, bidding us be seated, and ordering tea and *ḳalyáns* to be brought to us. At his side sat the *Munajjim-báshí*, or Chief Astrologer. We presently asked if there was any news from the capital, whereupon he informed us, without any outward sign of the emotion which so startling an event must have produced in him, that a telegram had just arrived announcing that the Prince-Governor, the Ẓillu's-Sulṭán, had "resigned" all his extensive governments in Southern Persia, retaining nothing but the city of Iṣfahán. From what I have already said in a previous chapter, it will be sufficiently evident that the term "resignation" was a euphemism.

I took several walks round the environs of Julfá, and one of the first places which I visited was the Armenian cemetery. Here, after some search, I found the grave of the Swiss watchmaker who was put to death by the Muḥammadan clergy two centuries ago, for having, in self-defence, killed a Musulmán. He was a great favourite with the king, who exerted himself to save his life, but the only condition on which this was possible was that he should consent to embrace Islám, which he refused to do. The heavy oblong stone which marks the spot where his body rests bears the simple inscription "CY GIT RODOLFE." Round about this are the graves of a number of European merchants, for the most part Dutch or Swiss, who had been attracted to the then famous capital of the Ṣafavís during the latter part of the seventeenth and earlier part of the eighteenth century. Of the few English tombstones which I discovered, one bore the following curious inscription:—

MEMENTO MORI

HIC IACET INSIGNIS DOCTOR R. EDVARDVS PAGETT ANG.
S. TRINITATIS COLLEGII APVD CANTABRIGIAM SOCIVS
THEOLOGVS ET MATHEMATICVS LVSTRABAT ORBEM TER
VT DIVINA COGNOSCERET ET MVNDANA
SED MVNDVM VERE REPVTANS VT PVNCTVM
EXTENDEBAT LINEAS VLTRA TEMPVS
VT PVLCRVM EX ETERNITATE CIRCVLVM FORMARET
TANDEM QVINQVAGENARIVS VLTIMO PVNCTO VITAM CLAVSIT
IN PATRIAM PER TERRAM REDEVNTEM SISTEBAT MORS
OBIIT ENIM SPAHANI DIE 21 IANV. A. 1702 SEC^{DVM} STYL. VET.
ABI VIATOR ET AB INSIGNI DOCTORE
DISCE IN TEMPORE ETERNITATEM.

I also ascended two of the mountains which lie beyond the cemetery to the south of Julfá. One of these, situated just to the west of the Shíráz road, is called *Kúh-i-Ṣúfí*. On the northern face of this is a ruined building, whence I obtained a fine view of Iṣfahán, the size of which now became apparent, though the miles of ruins which surround it show how much larger it was in former days. The whole of that portion of the plain in which the city lies was spread like a map at my feet. To the east was the ill-famed Hazár Deré, the fabled abode of *ghúls* and *'ifríts*, a waste of conical hillocks; and near that side of it which bordered on the Shíráz road could be seen the single tree which marks the site of the "Farewell Fountain" (*Chashmé-i-Khudá-ḥáfiẓ*), the spot to which the traveller journeying towards the south is usually accompanied by his friends. Right across the plain from west to east meandered the Záyanda-Rúd, spanned by its three bridges, and girt with gardens. On the farther side of this rose the domes and minarets of Iṣfahán; opposite the city, and on the south side of the river, lay the great Musulmán cemetery, called *Takht-i-Fúlád*; while on the same side of the river, but farther to the west, stretched the Christian suburb of Julfá.

The other mountain which I ascended is called the *Takht-i-Rustam*, and forms the extreme western limit of the range which terminates to the east in the Kúh-i-Ṣúfí above described. This mountain is crowned by a great crest of overhanging rocks, along the base of which I had to creep before I could ascend to the summit, where stands a small building of brick in a very dilapidated condition. From this point I could see far away to the west, in the direction of Chár Maḥáll and the Bakhtiyárí country, and a wild, forbidding landscape it was, hemmed in by black lowering mountains. Straight below me, on the farther side of the road leading to Chár Maḥáll, was a remarkable mass of rock, which, seen from certain points of view, looks like a gigantic lion. It is often called "the Sphinx" by Europeans. Beyond this were gardens and walled villages on either side of the river, and beyond these a background of mountains, in the bosom of which lies the village of Najaf-ábád, one of the Bábí strongholds. The exquisite clearness and purity of the atmosphere in Persia, enabling one as it does to see for an almost unlimited distance, lends an indescribable charm to views such as the one which now lay before me, and I long gazed with admiration on the panorama to the westward. But when I glanced down into the dark valley to the south of the ridge on which I now stood, towards which the mountain fell away so rapidly that it seemed as if one might cast a stone into it without effort, a feeling akin to terror at its savage loneliness and utter isolation overcame me, and I was glad to commence the descent with all speed, lest some uncontrollable impulse should prompt me to cast myself down into this gloomy ravine.

Another day I paid a visit to the celebrated, but somewhat disappointing, "shaking minarets" (*mináré-i-junbán*) situated to the west of Julfá, which were duly rocked to and fro for my entertainment. Beyond these is a curiously-shaped hill called the *Átash-gáh*, on which, as its name implies, there is said to exist a ruined Fire-temple. To this, however, I had not time to extend my excursion.

Thus passed the time I spent at the ancient capital, partly in walks and sight-seeing, partly in the genial society of Dr Hoernle and the other European residents. In the late afternoon we often played tennis, there being two very fairly good grounds in Julfá. Of Persian society I saw but little, and indeed for the first week I hardly had occasion to talk Persian at all except to the Mírzá employed by the Mission—a man of considerable erudition, not devoid of a certain degree of scepticism in religious matters. I several times questioned him about the Bábís, and begged him to put me in communication with them, or at least to obtain for me some of their books. Whether he could or would have done so I know not, for an occurrence which took place about a week after my arrival rendered me independent of such help, brought me into immediate contact with the proscribed sect which had hitherto eluded all my search, and gave an entirely new turn to the remainder of my sojourn in Persia. The event which thus unexpectedly enabled me to gratify to the full a curiosity which difficulties and disappointments had but served to increase, was as follows.

One afternoon, rather more than a week after my arrival, and the day after the ascent of the Takht-i-Rustam above described, I was sitting lazily in the sitting-room which overlooked the courtyard, wondering when I should again start on my travels, and turning over in my mind the respective advantages of Shíráz and Yezd, when two *dallāls* (brokers, or vendors of curiosities), armed with the usual collection of carpets, brasswork, trinkets, and old coins, made their appearance. Rather from lack of anything else to do than because I had any wish to invest in curiosities which were as certain to be dear as they were likely to be spurious, I stepped out into the porch to inspect the strange medley of objects which they proceeded to extract from their capacious bags and to display before me. None of them, however, particularly took my fancy, and I accordingly refused to treat the prices which they named as serious statements, and offered only such sums as appeared to me obviously below their real value, hoping thereby to cause the *dallāls*, of whose company I was now tired, to withdraw in disgust. The *dallāls* did not fail to discern my object, and the elder one—an old man with henna-dyed beard—ventured a remonstrance. "Ṣáḥib," he said, "we have come a long way to show you our goods, and you have taken up a great deal of our time. You will not be dealing fairly with us if you send us away without buying anything." I was about to remind him that I had not asked him to come, and had only consented to examine his wares at his own request, and on the distinct understanding that by so doing I was not in any way binding myself to become a purchaser, when the younger *dallāl* stepped up on to the platform where I was standing, put his mouth close to my ear, and whispered, "*You are afraid we shall cheat you. I am not a Musulmán that I should desire to cheat you:* I AM A BÁBÍ."

To this day I am at a loss to account for the motives which prompted this extraordinary frankness. Perhaps some rumour had reached the man (for rumours in Persia get about in the most unaccountable manner) that I was anxious to make acquaintance with the sect to which he belonged; perhaps he imagined that all Christians were better disposed towards the Bábís than towards the Muḥammadans; perhaps the admission was merely a random shot, prompted by the consideration that at least it was unlikely to expose him to any risk. Be this as it may, the effect produced on me by these words was magical. Here at last was the long desired opportunity for which I had waited and watched for four months. All my apathy was in a moment changed into the most eager interest, and my only fear now was that the *dalláls* would take me at my word and go.

"You are a Bábí!" I said, as soon as my astonishment allowed me to speak. "Why, I have been looking for Bábís ever since I set foot in Persia. What need to talk about these wares, about which I care but little? Get me your books if you can; that is what I want—your books, your books!"

"Ṣáḥib," he said, "I will do what is possible to gratify your wishes: indeed I can promise you at least one or two books which will tell you about our beliefs. But how is it that you are so desirous of these? Where did you hear about us, if, as you say, you never yet met with one of our religion?"

"I heard about you," I replied, "long before I came to Persia, or even thought that I should ever do so. A learned Frenchman who was living in Ṭeherán soon after the Báb began to preach his doctrines, who witnessed some of the terrible persecutions to which his followers were exposed, and who was filled with wonder and admiration at their fortitude and disregard of death, wrote the history of all these things in his own language when he returned to Europe. This history I have read, and this wonder and admiration I share, so that I desire to know more of what you believe. Hitherto I have sought in vain, and met with nothing but disappointment. Now, please God, by means of your help I shall attain my object."

"So the news of the 'Manifestation' has reached Firangistán!" he exclaimed. "That is indeed well! Surely I will do all in my power to assist you in your search for knowledge of this matter. Nay, if you would desire to converse with one of us who is learned and pious and has suffered much for the cause, I will arrange that you shall meet him. He is our chief here, and once a fortnight he visits the house of each one of us who have believed, to assure himself that our households are maintained in a becoming manner, and to give us instruction and encouragement. I am but a poor ignorant *dallál*, but he will tell you all that you desire to know." Our whispered colloquy was now brought to an end, as the elder *dallál* began to manifest unmistakable signs of impatience. Hastily selecting a few small articles, I presented him with a sum of money sufficient to compensate him for his trouble and restore his good temper, and took leave of him and his comrade, entreating the latter by no means to fail in bringing me the books, which he promised to do, if possible, on the morrow.

Next day, at about the same hour, my anxiety was brought to an end by the reappearance of the Bábí *dallál*, who signified, in answer to my look of enquiry, that he had brought the books. I immediately conducted him to my room, but for some time I had to restrain my impatience owing to the presence of Ḥájí Ṣafar, who seemed possessed by a desire to inspect the wares brought by my new friend, which was as unaccountable as it was exasperating. I was afraid to tell him to go, lest I should still further arouse that curiosity which I had learned to regard as the dominant characteristic of Persians in general and Persian servants in particular, so I had to wait patiently till he chose to retire.

No sooner was he out of the room than the Bábí produced the books, telling me that he expected his companion momentarily, and that as the latter was a Musulmán we should do well to make the best use of the time at our disposal, since his arrival would put an end to conversation on religious topics.

The books in question were two in number: one was a manuscript copy of the *Íḳán* ("Assurance"), which my companion declared to be an incontrovertible proof of the new faith, and by far the most important work to prepare me for a full comprehension of the Bábí doctrines; the other was a small tract, written, as I afterwards learned, by 'Abbás Efendí (the son of Behá'u'lláh, who is the present chief of the Bábís and resides at Acre in Syria[1]) at the request of 'Alí Shevket Páshá in explanation of the tradition "*I was a Hidden Treasure, and I desired to be known; therefore I created creation that I might be known*"; which tradition, stated to have been revealed to David, constitutes one of the corner-stones of Ṣúfí mysticism.

The purchase of these books was soon effected, for I was prepared to give a much higher price than was actually demanded. Specimens of calligraphy were next produced, some of which were the work of one of Behá's sons, others of the renowned *Mushkín-Ḳalam*, who was one of the Bábís exiled to Cyprus in A.D. 1868 by the Turkish Government[2], and who was, as I

1 He died since these words were written, on 16th May 1892, and was succeeded by one of his sons entitled *Ghuṣn-i-A'ẓam* ("The Most Mighty Branch"). See *Journal of the Royal Asiatic Society* for 1892, pp. 706–10.

2 I cannot here repeat all that I have written elsewhere on the history, especially the later history, of the Bábís. Those who desire full information on the subject I must refer to my papers in the *Journal of the Royal Asiatic Society* (July and October 1889; April, July, and October 1892), and to my translations of the *Traveller's Narrative* (Cambridge, 1891), and the *New History* (Cambridge, 1893). For the benefit of the general reader, I give the following brief epitome, which will suffice to render intelligible what is said in this book about the sect. The Báb, before his death (9th July 1850), had nominated as his successor a youth nineteen years of age named Mírzá Yaḥyá, and entitled *Ṣubḥ-i-Ezel* ("The Dawn of Eternity"), who belonged to a noble family of Núr in Mázandarán. His succession was practically undisputed; and till 1866 he was recognised by all the Bábís, including his half-brother Mírzá Ḥuseyn 'Alí, entitled *Behá'u'lláh* ("The Splendour of God"), who was about thirteen years senior to him, as the Head of the Bábí Church. In 1852, in consequence of the violent persecution of the Bábís which followed the attempt on the Sháh's life, the headquarters of the sect were transferred to Baghdád. There the Bábí chiefs remained till 1862 or 1863, when, at the request of the Persian Government, they were transferred by the

gathered, related in some way to my friend the *dallál*. *Mushkín-Ḳalam's* skill in calligraphy is a matter of notoriety amongst the Bábís, and his writing is, indeed, very beautiful. Especially curious were some of his productions, in which the writing was so arranged as to take the form of a bird (*Khaṭṭ-i-murghí*). The *dallál* informed me that these would be eagerly sought after by Persians of all classes, were it not that they all bore, as the signature of the penman, the following verse:

"*Dar diyár-i-khaṭṭ shah-i-ṣáḥib-'alam,*
Bandé-i-Báb-i-Behá, Mushkín-Ḳalam."

"In the domain of writing a king of note,
The servant of Báb-i-Behá, *Mushkín-Ḳalam*."

As it was, the sale of these works of art was limited entirely to the Bábí community.

When the inspection of these treasures was completed, I asked the *dallál* whether he knew where the two Seyyids who suffered martyrdom for the Bábí faith about the year 1879 were buried.

"Yes," he replied, "I know the spot well, and will take you there if you wish it; but surely, Ṣáḥib, you who are so eager to obtain our books, who desire to visit the graves of our martyrs,

Turkish authorities to Constantinople (where they remained four months), and thence to Adrianople. While they were at Adrianople, *Behá'u'lláh* announced himself to be "*Him whom God shall manifest*," that Great Deliverer and Fulfiller of the New Dispensation, whose advent the Báb had announced. Most of the Bábís admitted his claim, and became Behá'ís; some few adhered to *Ṣubḥ-i-Ezel*, who vigorously contested it, and were henceforth known as Ezelís. Disputes and quarrels ensued, and finally, in the summer of 1868, the rivals were separated by the Turkish Government. *Ṣubḥ-i-Ezel*, with his family and a few of *Behá'u'lláh's* followers, including *Mushkín-Ḳalam*, was sent to Famagusta, in Cyprus, where he still (1893) resides, being now a pensioner of the English Government. *Behá'u'lláh*, with his family, a number of his followers, and six or seven of the followers of *Ṣubḥ-i-Ezel*, was sent to Acre, on the Syrian coast. This is still the headquarters of the Behá'ís (who constitute the vast majority of Bábís at the present day), but *Behá'u'lláh* himself, as stated in a previous note, died on 16th May 1892. After the occupation of Cyprus by the English, the surviving exiles there interned were given permission to depart if they so pleased. Of this permission *Mushkín-Ḳalam* availed himself. He left Cyprus in September 1886 for Acre where I met him in April 1890.

must be prompted by some motive beyond mere curiosity. You have been to Acre, you have been honoured by beholding the Blessed Countenance, you are yourself a Bábí. Say, is it not so? There is no need to conceal anything from me."

"My friend," I answered, "I am neither a Bábí, nor have I been to Acre; yet I confess that I am actuated by something more than mere curiosity. I cannot but feel that a religion which has produced examples of such heroic courage and fortitude as yours, merits a careful examination, since that must needs contain noble thoughts which can prompt to noble deeds. In visiting the graves of your martyrs I would fain pay a tribute of respect to those who gave up wealth, ease, and consideration, nay, even life itself, for the faith which they held dearer than all else."

At this point our conversation was interrupted by the entrance of the other *dallál* with a collection of pictures, articles of brass-work, and other curiosities, from which I proceeded to make a selection. It was proposed by myself, and readily agreed to by the *dalláls*, that there should be no bargaining: they would state the price which they had actually paid for each of the articles in question, and I, if it appeared to me reasonable, would give it, together with a small percentage for their profit. In consequence of this, the transaction was one of the shortest and pleasantest I had ever effected in the East, where bartering and haggling about prices is usually inevitable; and, so far as I could judge, I obtained the full value of my money.

Just as they were leaving, the Bábí found an opportunity of whispering in my ear, "Do not forget next Saturday. I will make arrangements for someone to meet you at a given spot in the town; if I cannot find anyone else, I will come myself. Whoever your conductor may be, you will recognise him by a sign, and will follow him: he will bring you safely to my house, and there you will meet our chief. I will see you again before then, and inform you of the spot determined on. May God be your keeper!"

Saturday came at last, and at an early hour my friend the *dallál* appeared. After a brief consultation we agreed on one of the principal caravansarays in the city as the best rendezvous. I was to be in waiting there shortly after mid-day, and either my friend or his associate would come to meet me.

At the appointed time I was in readiness at the spot designated, and I had not waited long before the elder *dallál* appeared, caught my attention, signed to me to follow him, and plunged once more into a labyrinth of the bazaars. Once assured that I was following him, he hardly looked back, till, after half an hour's rapid walking, we reached the house of the Bábí, who welcomed me at the door, led me into the sitting-room, and, in the intervals of preparing tea for me and the distinguished guest he was still expecting, pointed out to me a number of his treasures. These included a photograph of the above-mentioned *Mushkín-Ḳalam* and his two sons, and another photograph of the graves of the "Martyrs of Iṣfahán," which he assured me had been taken by a European resident who was greatly attached to the murdered men.

After a short while there came a knock at the outer door; my host hastened out and immediately returned, ushering in the Bábí missionary, to whom he presented me. He was a grave, earnest-looking man of about forty-five years of age, as I should guess; and as he sat opposite to me sipping his tea, I had plenty of time to observe his countenance attentively, and to note the combination of decision, energy, and thoughtfulness which it expressed. His manners were pleasing, and his speech, when he spoke, persuasive. Altogether he was a man whom one would not readily forget, even after a single interview, and on whose memory one dwells with pleasure.

The elder *dallál*, who had absented himself for a short time, soon returned, and with him another Bábí, a tile-maker by trade. The presence of the former put some restraint on the conversation, so that I was unable to ask many questions. I learned, however, that he whom I now beheld was one of the chief missionaries of the new faith, for which he had suffered stripes, imprisonment, and exile more than once. I begged him to tell me what it was that had made him ready to suffer these things so readily. "You must go to Acre," he replied, "to understand that."

"Have you been to Acre?" I said, "and if so, what did you see there?"

"I have been there often," he answered, "and what I saw was a man perfect in humanity."

More than this he would not say. "You are leaving Iṣfahán, as I understand, in a few days," he remarked, "and opportunity is lacking to explain to you what you desire to know. I will, however, write to the 'Friends' at Shíráz, and Ábádé also if you wish, requesting them to expect your arrival, and to afford you all facilities for discussing these matters. Should you intend to visit other towns at a subsequent date, they will furnish you with all necessary recommendations and instructions. The 'Friends' are everywhere, and though hitherto you have sought for them without success, and only at last chanced on them by what would seem a mere accident, now that you have the clue you will meet them wherever you go. Write down these two names (here he gave me the names and addresses of two of his co-religionists at Ábádé and Shíráz respectively), and when you arrive enquire for them. Before your arrival they will be duly informed of your coming, and of your reason for desiring to converse with them. Now farewell, and may God direct you unto the truth."

"Áḳá," said the *dallál*, "the Ṣáḥib desires to visit the graves of the 'King of Martyrs,' and the 'Beloved of Martyrs,' and I have promised to take him there. Will you not also accompany us, that we may beguile the way with profitable conversation?"

"It is well that he should visit these graves," answered the other, "and we thank him for the good-will towards us which his desire to do so implies. Nevertheless, I will not come, for

I am perhaps too well known of men, and it is not wise to incur needless risk. Farewell!"

Soon after the departure of the chief, I also, finding it later than I had supposed, rose to go. The tile-maker volunteered to guide me back to the caravansaray. There was but little opportunity for conversation on the way thither, nor would it have been safe to talk of those matters which occupied our minds in the open street. "You see, Ṣáḥib," whispered my companion, "what our condition is. We are like hunted animals or beasts of prey, which men slay without compunction; and this because we have believed in God and his Manifestation."

On arriving at the caravansaray whence I had started, I bade farewell to my guide, and betook myself to the office of Messrs Ziegler's agents to conclude the arrangements for my journey to Shíráz. A muleteer was found, a native of the village of Khuraskán, called 'Abdu'r-Raḥím, who agreed to furnish me with three animals at the rate of three *túmáns* (rather less than £1) a head, to convey me to Shíráz in fourteen marches, and to halt for one day at any place on the road which I might choose. Half the money was at once paid down, and, the bargain being satisfactorily concluded, I walked home to Julfá with Messrs Ziegler's agent, who had kindly assisted me in making these arrangements.

Next day, early in the afternoon, my friend the *dallál* came to conduct me to the tombs of the martyrs. After a walk of more than an hour in a blazing sun, we arrived at the vast cemetery called *Takht-i-Fúlád* ("the Throne of Steel"). Threading our way through the wilderness of tombstones, my companion presently espied, and summoned to us, a poor grave-digger, also belonging to the persecuted sect, who accompanied us to a spot marked by two small mounds of stones and pebbles. Here we halted, and the *dallál*, turning to me, said, "These are the graves of the martyrs. No stone marks the spot, because the Musulmáns destroyed those which we placed here, and, indeed, it is perhaps as well that they have almost forgotten the resting-places of those they slew, lest, in their fanaticism, they should yet further desecrate them. And now we will sit down for a while in this place, and I will tell you how the death of these men was brought about. But first it is well that our friend should read the prayer appointed for the visitation of this holy spot."

The other thereupon produced a little book from under his cloak, and proceeded to read a prayer, partly in Arabic, partly in Persian. When this was concluded, we seated ourselves by the graves, and the *dallál* commenced his narrative.

"This," said he, pointing to the mound nearest to us, "is the tomb of Ḥájí Mírzá Ḥasan, whom we call *Sulṭánu'sh-Shuhadá*, 'the King of Martyrs,' and that yonder is the resting-place of his elder brother, Ḥájí Mírzá Ḥuseyn, called *Maḥbúbu'sh-Shuhadá*, 'the Beloved of Martyrs.' They were Seyyids by birth, and merchants by profession; yet neither their descent from the Prophet, nor their rare integrity in business transactions and liberality to the poor, which were universally acknowledged, served to protect them from the wicked schemes of their enemies. Amongst their debtors was a certain Sheykh Báḳir, a *mullá* of this city, who owed them a sum of about ten thousand *túmáns* (£3000). Now Sheykh Báḳir knew that they were of the number of the 'Friends,' and he thought that he might make use of this knowledge to compass their death, and so escape the payment of the debt. So he went to the *Imám-Jum'a* of Iṣfahán, who was the chief of the clergy, and said to him, 'These men are Bábís, and as such they are, according to the law of Islám, worthy of death, since they do not believe that Muḥammad, the Apostle of God, is the last of the Prophets, but hold that Mírzá 'Alí Muḥammad of Shíráz received a new revelation whereby the Ḳur'án is abrogated. To my knowledge, also, they are very wealthy, and if they be slain for their apostasy from Islám, their wealth will be ours.' The *Imám-Jum'a* was easily persuaded to become a party to this design, and these two wicked men accordingly went to the

Ẓillu's-Sulṭán, the Prince-Governor, and laid the matter before him. He was by no means averse to a scheme which seemed fraught with profit to himself, but nevertheless hesitated to decree the death of those whose descent from the Prophet, apart from their blameless lives, appeared to entitle them to respect and consideration. At length he answered thus: 'I cannot myself command their execution, since they have committed no crime against the state. If, however, you, in the name of the sacred law of Islám, condemn them to death, I shall, of course, not interfere with the execution of the sentence.'

"Sheykh Báḳir and the *Imám-Jum'a* therefore withdrew, and summoned seventeen other *mullás*; and these, after a brief deliberation, unanimously signed the death-warrant of the two Seyyids, who were forthwith arrested and cast into prison. When this transpired there was great consternation and distress amongst all classes, including the European residents, to whom the uprightness and virtue of the doomed men were well known. Application for the remission of the sentence was made by telegraph to Ṭeherán, and the request was supported by one of the European Ambassadors resident there. The Sháh consented to grant a reprieve, and telegraphed to the Ẓillu's-Sulṭán to that effect, but too late to stop the execution of the sentence. The two Seyyids, having refused to purchase life by apostasy[1], had their throats cut; cords were then attached to their feet, and their bodies were dragged through the streets and bazaars to the gate

1 The account actually given me by the *dallál* on this occasion begins here. What precedes was told me subsequently at Shíráz by another of the Bábí missionaries, who added other particulars, amongst which was a statement, which one cannot but hope may be untrue, that the telegram containing the reprieve actually reached the Ẓillu's-Sulṭán before the execution had taken place; that he divined its contents, laid it aside unopened till news reached him that the Seyyids had been put to death, and then sent an answer to Ṭeherán expressing regret that the sentence had been carried out before the remand came. I have thought it better to put the whole story in outline in the mouth of the *dallál*, reserving a few incidents which I subsequently learned for narration in their proper place.

of the city, where they were cast under an old mud wall, which was then overthrown upon them.

"When it was night an old servant of the martyred men, who had marked the spot where their bodies were cast, came thither, and extricated them from the *débris* of the ruined wall, the fall of which had scarcely injured them. He tenderly washed away the blood and dust which covered them with water from the Záyanda-Rúd, and then bore them to the cemetery, where he buried them in two freshly-made graves.

"In the morning the soldiers and servants of the Prince discovered the removal of the bodies. Suspicion fell on the faithful old servant, but he refused to reveal anything under the cross-examination to which he was subjected, so that eventually they were compelled to let him go, and the bodies of the martyrs were left in peace. But we cannot mark the spot where they are buried with a stone, for when one was put up, the Musulmáns, whose malignity towards us is unbounded, and who know very well that we pay visits to these graves in secret, overthrew it. Our friend here" (pointing to his companion) "was brought to believe by means of these martyrs. Was it not so?"

"Yes," answered the other, "some time after their death I saw in a dream vast crowds of people visiting a certain spot in the cemetery. I asked in my dream, 'Whose are these graves?' An answer came, 'Those of the "King of Martyrs" and the "Beloved of Martyrs."' Then I believed in that faith for which they had witnessed with their blood, seeing that it was accepted of God; and since then I visit them continually, and strive to keep them neat and orderly, and preserve the spot from oblivion by renewing the border of bricks and the heap of stones which is all that marks it."

"He is a good man," rejoined the *dallál*, "and formerly those of the 'Friends' who came to visit the graves used to rest for a while in the little house which he has near here, and partake of tea and *ḳalyáns*. The Musulmáns, however, found this out, made a raid on his house, abused and threatened him, and, before they departed, destroyed his tea-things and pipes. He is very poor," he added in a whisper, "give him a *ḳrán* for his trouble; it is an action which has merit."

I accordingly gave a small present to our guide, who departed with expressions of gratitude. After sitting a little while longer we too rose to go, and, taking a last look at the graves, from each of which I carried away a small stone as a memento, we once more turned our faces towards the city. On our way towards the gate of the cemetery we again passed the poor grave-digger with his little boy, and he again greeted me with expressions of thankfulness and good wishes for my journey.

I was much touched by the kindliness of these poor people, and communicated something of my thoughts to my companion.

"Yes," he answered, "we are much nearer to you in sympathy than the Muḥammadans. To them you are unclean and accursed: if they associate with you it is only by overcoming their religious prejudices. But we are taught to regard all good men as clean and pure, whatever their religion. With you Christians especially we have sympathy. Has it not struck you how similar were the life and death of our Founder (whom, indeed, we believe to have been Christ Himself returned to earth) to those of the Founder of your faith? Both were wise, even in their childhood, beyond the comprehension of those around them; both were pure and blameless in their lives; and both at last were done to death by a fanatical priesthood and a government alarmed at the love and devotion which they inspired in their disciples[1]. But besides this the ordinances enjoined upon us are in many respects like those which you follow. We are recommended to take to our-

1 The Bábís for the most part, unlike the Muḥammadans, believe that Christ was actually crucified by the Jews, and not, as the latter assert, taken up into heaven miraculously, while another, resembling Him in appearance, was crucified in His stead. But few of the Muḥammadans are conversant with the Gospels, while the reverse holds good of the Bábís, many of whom take pleasure in reading the accounts of the life and death of Jesus Christ.

selves only one wife, to treat our families with tenderness and gentleness, and, while paying the utmost attention to personal cleanliness, to disregard the ceremonials of purification and the minute details concerning legal impurity, of which the Musulmáns make so much. Further, we believe that women ought to be allowed to mix more freely with men, and should not be compelled to wear the veil. At present, fear of the Muḥammadans compels us to act as they do in these matters, and the same consideration affects many other ordinances which are not obligatory on us when their observance would involve danger. Thus our fast is not in Ramaẓán, but during the nineteen days preceding the *Nawrúz* ('New Year's Day'[1]); we are now in this period, but I am not observing the fast, because to do so would expose me to danger, and we are forbidden to incur needless risk. Our salutation, too, is different from that of the Muḥammadans; when we meet, we greet one another with the words '*Alláhu abhá*' ('God is most bright'). Of course we only use this form of greeting when none but 'Friends' are present."

"Can you recognise one another in any special way?" I asked.

"I think we can do so by the light of affection," answered my companion, "and in support of this I will tell you a curious thing which I myself observed. My little boy, who is not ten years old, greeted Mírzá Ḥasan 'Alí, whom you met in my house yesterday, with the words '*Alláhu abhá*' the very first time he saw him, while I have never known him use this form of salutation to a Muḥammadan."

"Your doctrines and practices," I observed, "certainly seem to me very much better than those of the Musulmáns, so far as I have understood them at present."

"Their doctrines," he rejoined, "are as untenable as their actions are corrupt. They have lost the very spirit of religion,

1 *I.e.* the old Persian New Year's Day, which falls about 21st March, at the vernal equinox.

while degrading symbols into superstitions. See, for example, what they say concerning the signs of the Imám Mahdí's coming. They expect Antichrist to come riding on an ass, the distance between the ears of which shall be a mile, while at each stride it shall advance a parasang. They further assert that each of the hairs on its body shall emit the sweetest melodies, which will charm all who allow themselves to listen into following Antichrist. Some of the *mullás* believe that this ass, the existence of which it is impossible to credit, if one reflects for a moment on the absurdity of the characteristics attributed to it, is concealed in *Yangí-dunyá* ('the New World,' *i.e.* America), which they say is 'opposite' to Iṣfahán, and that in the fullness of time it will appear out of a well in this neighbourhood. The absence of these impossible and imaginary signs was the excuse whereby they justified their disbelief in His Highness the Point (*i.e.* the Báb), and refused to see in him the Promised Deliverer whom they professed to be expecting. But we, who understand all these signs in a metaphorical sense, see very well that they have been already fulfilled. For what is Antichrist but a type of those who oppose the truth and slay the holy ones of God? What is the ass of Antichrist, striding across the earth, and seducing all those who will give ear to the sweet strains proceeding from it, but these same foolish *mullás* who support the temporal powers in attempting to crush the Truth, and please the natural inclinations and lusts of men by their false teachings. 'The possessions of the infidel are lawful unto you,' they proclaim. How easy a doctrine to receive, and how profitable! This is but one instance of these 'sweet strains' to which all whose eyes are not opened to the Truth of God, and whose hearts are not filled by the Voice of His Spirit, lend their ears so readily. In a similar manner do we understand all the symbols which they have degraded into actual external objects. Thus the *Bridge of Ṣiráṭ*, over which all must pass to enter Paradise, which is 'finer than a hair and sharper than a sword,' what is it but faith in the

Manifestation of God, which is so difficult to the hard of heart, the worldly, and the proud?"

Conversing thus, we arrived at the side of the river, just where it is spanned by the bridge called Pul-i-Khájú, a much finer structure than even the bridge of thirty-three arches which I had admired so much on my entry into Julfá. My companion suggested that we should sit here awhile on the lower terrace (for the bridge is built on two levels) and smoke a *ḳalyán*, and to this I readily consented.

After admiring the massive piers and solid masonry of the bridge, and the wide sweep here made by the Záyanda-Rúd, we resumed our way along the southern bank in the direction of Julfá. On our way we visited the deserted palace called *Haft-dast* ("Seven Hands"). Here was visible the same neglected splendour and ruined magnificence which was discernible elsewhere. One building, the *Namaḳ-dán* ("Salt-cellar"), had just been pulled down by one of the ministers of the Ẓillu's-Sulṭán to afford material for a house which he was building for himself. Another, called *Á'íné-ḳháné* ("the Chamber of Mirrors"), was nearly stripped of the ornaments which gave it its name, the remainder being for the most part broken and cracked. Everywhere it was the same—crumbling walls, heaps of rubbish, and marred works of art, still beautiful in spite of injuries, due as much to wanton mischief as to mere neglect. Would that some portion of that money which is spent in building new palaces in the capital, and constructing *mihmán-ḳhánés* neither beautiful nor pleasant, were devoted to the preservation of the glorious relics of a past age! That, however, is as a rule the last thing an Oriental monarch cares about. To construct edifices which may perpetuate his own name is of far more importance in his eyes than to protect from injury those built by his predecessors, which, indeed, he is perhaps not sorry to see crumbling away like the dynasties which reared them. And so it goes on—king succeeding king, dynasty overthrowing dynasty, ruin added to ruin; and through it all the mighty spirit of the people "dreaming the dream of the soul's disentanglement," while the stony-eyed lions of Persepolis look forth in their endless watch over a nation which slumbers, but is not dead.

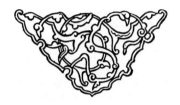

CHAPTER IX

FROM IṢFAHÁN TO SHÍRÁZ

"*Wa jalá's-suyúlu 'ani't-ṭulúli, ka'annahá*
Zuburᵘⁿ, tujiddu mutúna-há aḳlámu-há.
Fa-waḳaftu as'alu-há: fa-keyfa sú'álu-ná
Ṣummᵃⁿ khawálida, má yabínu kalámu-há?"

"And the torrents have laid bare its traces, as though
'Twere a book of which a pen renews the characters.
And I stood questioning them: but how can we question
Dumb rocks, whose speech is not clear?"—(*Mo'allaḳa of Lebíd.*)

"*Shíráz, u áb-i-Rukná, va án bád-i-khush-nasím;*
'Ayb-ash ma-kun, ki khál-i-rukh-i-haft kishvar-ast!"

"Shíráz, and the stream of Ruknábád, and that fragrant breeze—
Disparage it not, for it is the beauty-spot of the seven regions!"
(*Ḥáfiẓ.*)

"*Chún mí-guẓarí bi-khák-i-Shíráẓ*
Gú man bi-fulán ẓamín asír-am!"

"When thou passest by the earth of Shíráz
Say I am a captive in such-and-such a land!"

ONCE again the vicissitudes and charms of the road are before me, but in this case a new and potent factor, hitherto absent, comes in to counteract the regret which one must always feel in quitting a place where one has been kindly received and hospitably entertained, and where one has made friends, most of whom one will in all probability never meet again. This potent incentive to delay my departure no longer is the thought that when I quit Iṣfahán, less than a week will see me in the classical province of Fárs, less than a fortnight will bring me to the glories of Persepolis, and that after that two short days will unfold before my longing eyes the shrines and gardens of "the pure earth of Shíráz," which has been throughout the goal of my pilgrimage.

Of course the first day's march was no exception to the general rule I have already laid down. I was aroused before 8 a.m., and informed that the muleteers were ready to start, and desired to do so at once, as they proposed to "break a stage," as the expression goes—that is, to push on a distance of eight or nine parasangs to Mayár, the second halting-place out of Iṣfahán to the south. I accordingly dressed hurriedly, and finished packing, full of anxiety to secure so desirable a consummation as the shortening of the less interesting part of the journey by a whole day. When I descended, I found that the muleteer had gone off again to fetch the inevitable sacking and ropes which are always wanted, and apparently always forgotten. I was compelled, therefore, to abandon all hopes of getting further than Marg, some three parasangs distant from Julfá, and to resign myself to an idle morning. It was not till after lunch that all was ready for the start, and, bidding farewell to my kind host, Dr Hoernle, I mounted the sorry steed assigned to me, and, with my mind filled with delightful anticipations, turned my face in the direction of Shíráz. Karapit, the head servant of the Mission, accompanied me on my way as far as the "Farewell Fountain" (rendered conspicuous by the solitary tree which stands beside it), and even for some distance beyond it, till the post-house of Marg appeared in the distance. Then he turned back, wishing us a good journey; and a monotonous ride of an hour or so brought us to our halting-place (which the muleteers, for some reason, had changed from Marg to a village somewhat farther on, called Ḳal'a-i-Shúr) while it was still early in the afternoon. We put up at a dilapidated caravansaray, where nothing occurred to vary the monotony, except the arrival, some time after sunset, of a party of Jewish minstrels and dancing-boys, who were, like ourselves, bound for Shíráz.

Next day we left the plain, and entered the rugged defile

known as the Urchiní Pass, the somewhat monotonous grandeur of which was enlivened by numbers of pilgrims bound for Kerbelá, by way of Iṣfahán and Kirmánsháh, whom Ḥájí Ṣafar did not fail to greet with a salutation of "*Ziyáratat ḳabúl!*" ("May your pilgrimage be accepted!"). Here I may remark that the greetings used on the road differ from those employed elsewhere, and each one has its appropriate answer. The commonest of them are, "*Furṣat báshad!*" ("May it be an opportunity!"), to which the answer is, "*Khudá bi-shumá furṣat dihad!*" ("May God give you opportunity!"); and "*Oghúr báshad!*" ("May it be luck!"), the reply to which is, "*Oghúr-i-shumá bi-ḳhayr bád!*" ("May your luck be good!").

It was not yet 3 p.m. when we reached Mayár, and halted at an old caravansaray, the construction of which was, as usual, attributed to Sháh 'Abbás. There was nothing to do but to while away the time as well as might be by lounging about, looking at the few travellers who had taken up their quarters at this disconsolate spot, and superintending the culinary operations of Ḥájí Ṣafar.

The next day's march was almost precisely similar to that of the previous day—a gray, stony, glaring plain (thinly covered with camel-thorn and swarming with lizards), on either side of which were bare black hills of rugged outline. Soon after 2 p.m. we came in sight of the blue dome of an *Imámzádé*, situated in the precincts of the considerable town of Ḳumishah. As it was a Thursday (*Shab-i-Jum'a*, Friday Eve), which is the great day for performing minor pilgrimages and visiting the graves of deceased friends, we met streams of the inhabitants coming forth from the town bent on such pious errands. Taking them all round, I think they were the most ill-favoured, dour-looking people I ever saw in Persia. Generally, however forbidding the appearance of the men may be (of the women one cannot judge, since they keep their faces veiled), the children at least are pretty and attractive. But in all these files of people whom we met I hardly saw a single face which was otherwise than sour and forbidding.

Before 3 p.m. I reached the telegraph station, and was welcomed by Mr Gifford, the resident telegraphist, and his wife. The son of the Governor of Ḳumishah, Mírzá Áḳá by name, was there, and later he was joined by his father, Mírzá Mahdí Khán, who had come to try and extract some information about the political outlook in Iṣfahán. It appeared that an unfortunate man from Ízidkhwást had arrived in Ḳumishah on that or the preceding day, bringing the news of the Ẓillu's-Sulṭán's dismissal. This news was naturally very unwelcome to the Governor—so unwelcome that he not only declined to believe it, but ordered the man who brought it to be bastinadoed. Although this had the effect of checking further speculation and gossip, the Governor was unable to overcome a certain feeling of uneasiness as to his future tenure of office, and hence these visits to the telegraph-office.

Next morning the muleteer came to see me early, and offered to push on to Amín-ábád that day and to Shulghistán in Fárs on the morrow. I found, however, that this procedure would involve passing some distance to the east of the curious village of Ízidkhwást or Yezdikhwást, which I was anxious to see. I therefore decided to go no farther than Maḳṣúd Beg, and as this was only four parasangs distant, I gladly accepted the invitation of my kind host to stay to lunch and start after mid-day. The march was absolutely without interest, and the village of Maḳṣúd Beg, where we arrived about 4.30 p.m., was a most desolate-looking spot. Here we found the Jewish minstrels who had overtaken us at Marg entertaining the muleteers and villagers with a concert in the caravansaray. The music appeared to me very pleasing. This, and the exhilarating thought that on the morrow I should bid farewell to 'Iráḳ, and enter the classical province of Fárs, the cradle of Persian greatness, enabled me to bear with equanimity the dullness of the dilapidated caravansaray. I was further regaled with a dissertation by Ḥájí Ṣafar on the virtues of the wood-louse. This animal, he informed me, only appears for a short period before the *Nawrúz*. At that great festival people take it in their hands along with gold coins, "for luck." It bears different names in the north and south: in Ṭeherán it is called *khar-i-khákí* ("Earth-ass"), while in Shíráz it enjoys the more pretentious title of *kharak-i-khudá'í* ("Divine little donkey").

On the following morning (10th March) we got off about 7.45 a.m. The scenery was similar to that of the preceding two days—a stony valley, bounded by parallel chains of hills. As we advanced, the hills to the east became lower and lower, finally being reduced to broken fin-like ridges, situated one behind another, while beyond these, bordering the western edge of the plain, high snow mountains began to come into view, which the muleteer informed me belonged to the province of Luristán. About 11.15 a.m. we halted for lunch at Amín-ábád, the last village in 'Irák. From this point we could clearly see before us a small conical hill, beyond which lay the hamlet of Yezdikhwást, which I was so anxious to see. I had read many accounts of this natural fastness, perched on a precipitous rock, and accordingly, as we drew near the conical hill (which is called *Telé-piláw*, I suppose from its resemblance in shape to the pile of rice which constitutes this dish), I strained my eyes eagerly to catch a glimpse of its eyry-like abodes.

My first impressions were a mixture of disappointment and surprise. On passing the hill I could plainly discern the green dome of a little *Imámzádé* surrounded by a straggling cemetery: beyond this, apparently on the same level, and situated on the flat plain which we were traversing, appeared the village of Yezdikhwást. Where was its boasted inaccessibility, and the sheer precipices which, as all travellers asserted, rendered it one of the most marvellous natural fastnesses to be found in the world? No amount of exaggeration, I thought, could account for such a description of the place I saw before me, which apparently did not enjoy even the most trifling elevation above the surrounding plain. While I was reflecting thus, and wondering if the muleteers had, for some object of their own, deceived me, we passed through the cemetery, and all at once came upon one of the most remarkable sights I ever saw.

Right across our path lay a mighty chasm, looking like the dry bed of some giant river of the past. In the middle of this stood what I can only describe as a long narrow island, with precipitous sides, the summit of which was crowned with tier upon tier of gray, flat-roofed dwellings, which even hung over the edge of the cliff, supported by beams and rafters. These, projecting outwards in all directions, gave to the place the appearance of some strange collection of birds' nests rather than of human habitations. At the upper (*i.e.* the western) end this island was almost joined to the northern edge of the chasm, the comparatively shallow depression which separated them being spanned by a drawbridge, by raising which all access to the town can be cut off. At all other points a sheer precipice, increasing in height towards the east, protects it from all possibility of invasion.

At Yezdikhwást the road to Shíráz bifurcates. What is called the *sar-ḥadd*, or summer road, bears to the south-west into the mountains; while the *garmsír*, or winter road, crosses the chasm or valley below Yezdikhwást, and trends towards the south-east. As it was still early in the year, and the snow was not yet gone from the uplands traversed by the former, we had determined on following the latter, which course had this additional advantage, that it would lead us past Persepolis.

The inhabitants of Yezdikhwást do not apparently care to have strangers dwelling in their cliff-girt abode; at any rate, the caravansaray and post-house are both situated at the bottom of the chasm, across the little river (Áb-i-Marván) which flows through it, and to the south-east of the crag on which the village stands. On coming in sight of the brink of the chasm we therefore made a detour to the right (west) which brought us to the point where the drawbridge is placed, whence a path leads down the side of the gully to the caravansaray, where we arrived in about a quarter of an hour. It is a very fine edifice, built, as an inscription over the gateway testifies, by "the most potent king and most generous prince, the diffuser of the faith of the pure Imáms,...the dog of the threshold of 'Alí the son of Abú-Ṭálib,...'Abbás the Ṣafaví, may God perpetuate his kingdom and rule!" The inscription is very beautifully executed, but unfortunately it has been greatly injured, many of the tiles having been removed, and others broken. I asked the villagers why they did not take better care of a building of which they ought to feel proud. They replied that it was not their fault: thirteen or fourteen years ago a "Firangí" came by, and, wishing to possess some of the tiles, offered one of the men at the post-house two or three *túmáns* if he would remove some of them. The temptation was too strong for the latter, and accordingly he went the same night with a hammer and chisel to carry out the traveller's wishes. Of course he broke at least as many tiles as he removed, and a noble monument of the past was irreparably injured to gratify a traveller's passing whim.

I was anxious to see the interior of the village, and accordingly asked some of the inhabitants who came to stare at me whether they could take me over it. They readily agreed to do so, and after tea I sallied forth with my guides, crossed the fields, already green with sprouting wheat, and, skirting the southern face of this natural citadel, reached the drawbridge at the western end. Passing over this, we entered a dark passage, which, with occasional outlets into comparatively open spaces, traverses, or rather tunnels through, the whole village from west to east. This is the only street, for the rock is narrow, though long, and there is not room in most places for more than two houses side by side. My guides informed me that their town, of which they seemed proud in no small degree, was very old—300 years older than Iṣfahán—and, in proof of their assertion, they pointed to a stone in the gateway on which they said I should find the date. As a matter of fact, the only date I could see was (A.H.) 1218 (about A.D. 1803), but there appeared to be other more or less obliterated characters which the gloom pervading even the entrance of this dim passage would not suffer me to decipher.

As we advanced, the street, at first open above, became entirely covered over by houses, and the darkness was such that we could not see a yard ahead, and were only saved from continual collisions with other passengers by the cries of "*Yá Alláh*" uttered by my companions to give warning of our approach.

The houses are for the most part three or four stories high, and are entered by stairs communicating directly with the street. On the outer side they are furnished with platforms or balconies, one above the other, which overhang the cliff in a most perilous manner. On to some of these my guides took me that I might admire the view, but my enjoyment of this was somewhat marred by the sense of insecurity with which the very frail appearance of the platforms inspired me. "I should have thought," said I to my guides, "that these platforms would have been very dangerous to your children, for I observe that they are provided with no rail to prevent anyone from falling over." "They are dangerous," was the quite unconcerned reply; "hardly a year passes without two or three falling over and being killed." "I wonder the houses themselves don't fall," I remarked after a brief interval, during which the palpable weakness of the flimsy structure had become more than ever manifest to me. "They do," replied the unmoved villagers; "look there." I turned my eyes in the direction indicated, and saw a dismal wreck hanging over the edge of the cliff. Feeling my curiosity quite satisfied, I suggested that we should continue our tour of inspection, whereupon they took me into one of the houses, which appeared to be the chief shop of the place, and set before me an array of nuts and fruits, a few of which I felt compelled to eat as a matter of courtesy, while the villagers watched me with grave and polite attention.

We next visited the mosque, which seemed ancient, though I could find no date graven on its walls—nothing but the usual summary of Shí'ite faith: "*There is no God but God: Muḥammad is the Apostle of God: 'Alí is the Friend of God.*" Though more solid in structure than the other buildings, it is very simply adorned, for it contains nothing but a *minbar*, or pulpit, looking more like a step-ladder than anything else. This, and the arch of the *miḥráb* by which it stood, were the sole features whereby one could divine that the place was not intended for a barn or a granary.

On leaving the mosque we visited the one other shop which this primitive place contains, where I was politely compelled to accept of a quantity of that gruesome sweetmeat known as *shaḳḳar-panír* ("sugar-cheese"). Then we quitted the village by the same way whereby we had entered it (for indeed there is no other), and returned to the caravansaray. Though I retired to bed early, I lay awake for some time watching the lights which twinkled from the airy dwellings of Yezdikhwást and gave to the shadowy outline of the great rock somewhat the appearance of a gigantic vessel lying at anchor in a river.

Next day we ascended the southern side of the gully by a road running eastwards, until we again reached the summit of the plateau. Here I halted for a few moments to gaze once more on the picturesque scene, and then we struck off towards the south, still bearing somewhat to the east. On the road we met many peasants and some few travellers; they nearly all carried arms, and were as a rule darker in complexion and fiercer in aspect than the inhabitants of 'Iráḳ. About 2.30 p.m. we arrived at Shulghistán, a small picturesque village, rendered conspicuous by a green-domed *Imámzádé*, close to which is situated the dilapidated caravansaray. Since the latter appeared incapable of furnishing comfortable quarters, we betook ourselves to the *chápár-khâné* (post-house) opposite, where I was provided with a very comfortable room. The postmaster (*ná'ib-chápár*) was extremely courteous and attentive, and sat conversing with me for some time. From him I learned that the news of the Ẓillu's-Sulṭán's fall, and the consequent dismissal of all his deputy-governors, had created great excitement throughout Fárs, and especially at Shíráz, where the Ṣáḥib-Díván, in whom the administration of the province had hitherto been virtually vested, was greatly disliked. His dismissal was the signal for universal rejoicing, and it was said that Riẓá Khán, the chief of one of the Arab tribes settled in the neighbourhood of Shíráz, was encamped near the Tomb of Cyrus at Murgháb, waiting for the arrival of the ex-governor, against whom he was breathing threats of vengeance. The postmaster thought, however, that the tidings of the advance of the new governor, Prince Iḥtishámu'd-Dawla, who had already reached, or nearly reached, Iṣfahán, would prevent him from proceeding to extremities.

Later on another man came in, whose one sole topic of conversation was dervishes, for whom he professed the most unbounded regard. His enthusiasm had apparently been aroused by the recent visit of some celebrated saint from Kirmán. I ventured to ask him if there were any Bábís in Shulghistán, at the very idea of which he expressed the utmost horror, adding with pride, "We would at once slay anyone whom we suspected of belonging to that sect, for here, thank God, we are all followers of Murtaẓá 'Alí."

His attitude towards the Bábís did not encourage me to make further enquiries in this direction, and I therefore allowed him to ramble on about his dervishes, Imáms, and miracles. He informed me, amongst numerous other stories of equal probability, that there was a mountain two parasangs to the east of Yezdikhwást called Sháh Ḳannáb. There, he said, the two sons of

"Ḥaẓrat-i-'Abbás" took refuge in bygone days from the "army of the infidels." The mountain opened to receive them, and they passed within it; the infidels followed after them, but no sooner had they entered than the rocks closed up behind them, and shut them in.

"That was very wonderful," I said, "but tell me what became of them, for I should have thought that it would have been better if the mountain had closed before the 'army of the infidels' could follow the two saints. As it was, it seems to me that they were all shut up together."

"Yes," replied the narrator, "but, you see, the infidels were all turned into stone at once. You might see them still if you knew the way which leads to that wondrous cavern—men, horses, camels, camel-drivers, children at their lessons, still holding in their hands the books they were reading—all turned to stone! It is a wonderful thing!"

"So I should think," I answered, wondering inwardly whether armies of infidels usually carried a host of school-children about with them when they went in pursuit of fugitive saints; "but you haven't told me what happened to the Imáms who were so miraculously preserved. Did they make their escape after this signal mark of Divine Displeasure had been accomplished?"

"No, they did not," rejoined my informant; "they dwell there still, and by their holy influence many wonderful miracles are wrought, some of which I will tell you. There is a shrine with two minarets on the mountain, and these minarets every year recede farther and farther apart, a fact well known to all in this neighbourhood. Furthermore, whoever goes there, and prays, and then fixes his thoughts on anything which he desires to possess—gold, silver, or precious stones—can take it from the rock to his heart's content."

"And pray," I asked, "can one find one's way to this marvellous mountain?"

"No, you cannot," retorted the other; "I could take you

there if I chose, but I will not do so. —— Ṣáḥib, who was formerly *telegráfchí* at Ábádé, offered me money if I would show him the way, but I refused, for it is not lawful to reveal to unbelievers these holy spots."

"That is a pity," I said; "and I venture to suggest that you act unwisely in thus hindering them from witnessing miracles whereby they might perhaps be brought to embrace Islám. It is precisely for unbelievers that miracles are intended."

"Well," replied my informant, "there is perhaps reason in what you say. But it is not necessary to go there to witness proofs of the power possessed by the blessed Imáms. Of this we had a signal proof during last Muḥarram. A *pázan* (ibex or mountain-goat) came at that time to the *Imámzádé* across the road, and took up its abode there for six months. Finally it died, and is buried under a tree in the courtyard. We had no doubt but that it was sent thither by the command of the blessed Imáms to strengthen the faith of all of us who witnessed it."

Altogether, I spent a very amusing evening with my talkative friend, who, delighted to find an appreciative listener, remained while I ate my supper, and did not finally leave till it was time to retire for the night.

Next day was bright and windy. The scenery through which we passed was of the usual type—a stony plain full of camel-thorn (now putting forth beautiful crimson blossoms from its apparently sapless branches) between parallel ranges of barren hills. The ground swarmed with lizards of two distinct types, the ordinary brown lizard and the *Buz-majjé*. This latter is an animal which, as I subsequently learned, sometimes attains a length of three or four feet, but the length of most of those which I saw did not exceed as many inches. They have big clumsy heads furnished with spines, and long tails constricted at the point where they join the body, which they have a habit of jerking up into an erect position. They are very nimble in their movements, and when frightened dart away like a dusky shadow for a few feet, and again come to a standstill. Ḥájí Ṣafar began to tell me a long rambling story about the creation of the *Buz-majjé*, whereby he sought to account for its harmlessness. He related this story in the dreamy, visionary manner which occasionally came over him, and in the soft lisping accents of the South. I was not paying much attention to his narrative, the upshot of which appeared to be that the animals after their creation all came into the presence of their Creator and sought permission to be allowed to injure man, their master and tyrant, at some appointed time. All received this permission, except the *Buz-majjé*, which came late, and so was forced to be content with a harmlessness far removed from its malicious desires.

My attention revived, however, when he began to talk about Shíráz. "In eleven days more, Ṣáḥib, you will see Shíráz: perhaps in ten, if you do not stop at *Takht-i-Jamshíd* (Persepolis). You will then enter it on the *Nawrúz*: all the people—men, women, and children—will be out in the gardens and fields; many of them in the *Tang-i-Alláhu-Akbar*, through which you will catch your first glimpse of the city. All will be dressed in new clothes, as smart as they can make themselves, enjoying the beautiful green fields, singing, smoking *kalyáns*, and drinking tea. There is no other city like Shíráz: all about it the earth is green with grass; even the roofs of the bazaars are covered with herbage. It is the Green City of Solomon (*shahr-i-sabz-i-Suleymán*). And the people are so quick and clever and generous. Not like those miserable, miserly Iṣfahánís, nor yet like those stupid, thick-headed Khurásánís. Have I ever told you the verses made by the Iṣfahání, the Shírází, and the Khurásání, Ṣáḥib?"

"No," I answered; "I should like to hear them very much."

"Once upon a time," he resumed, "an Iṣfahání, a Shírází, and Khurásání were travelling together. Now, one night they succeeded in getting a dish of *piláw*, and the Iṣfahání, being a witty fellow, as well as stingy (like all his rascally countrymen), suggested that no one should be allowed to have a share of the *piláw* unless he could make a verse about his native country. To this they agreed, and the Iṣfahání began—

'*Az Ṣafahán meyve-i-haft-rang mí-áyad birún.*'
('From Iṣfahán fruits of seven colours come forth.')

The Shírází, without a moment's hesitation—for all Shírázís have a natural gift for versifying—went on—

'*Áb-i-Ruknábád-i-má az sang mí-áyad birún.*'
('Our stream of Ruknábád comes forth from the rock.')

It was now the Khurásání's turn, but he, poor fellow, being very stupid and slow, after the manner of his countrymen, could not think of a rhyme for a long time, and was in great fear that he would lose his *piláw* after all, when suddenly an inspiration came to him, and he concluded the stanza thus:—

'*Az Khurásán miṣl-i-man aldang mí-áyad birún.*'
('Out of Khurásán come forth blackguards like me.')

Aldang, you know, is the Khurásání word for a *lúṭí*, a rough, or street vagabond."

About 2 p.m. we arrived at the little town of Ábádé, another stronghold of the Bábís. It will be remembered that the Bábí missionary at Iṣfahán, on bidding me farewell, had promised to write to one of his co-religionists here, as well as at Shíráz, to be on the look-out for me. I therefore hoped that I might have an opportunity of holding further conversation with the members of the proscribed sect, but in this hope I was disappointed, for the shortness of my stay in the town, and the hospitality of Sergeant Glover of the telegraph station, did not give me leisure to seek out the person indicated to me. I was very favourably impressed with Ábádé in every way, and the approach to it, through lanes surrounded by orchards and gardens, the trees of which were already bursting into blossom and filling the air with their fragrance, was very beautiful.

At the telegraph station I was cordially received by Sergeant Glover and his eldest son, a bright, clever boy of about fifteen, who had an excellent knowledge of Persian. I was most hospitably entertained, and after dinner we sat up late discussing Persian folk-lore, concerning which my host was a perfect mine of information. He told me of a place called the *Parí-hol*, or fairy hole, near Soh; of marvellous wells and caves in the mountains; and of a hill where an old fire-worshipper was said to have taken refuge from his persecutors, who marked the spot with a pile of stones, meaning to return next day and renew their search. During the night, however, by the Divine Power, the whole hill was covered with similar heaps of stones, which utterly baffled the search of the persecutors. These heaps are said still to be visible.

Next day a short march of about three hours brought us to the post-house of Surmé. On arriving there, I was surprised to see a European traveller standing at the door, who greeted me in English. He proved to be one of the telegraph staff at Shíráz travelling up to Iṣfahán and Ṭeherán, and kindly offered me a share of the *bála-kháné* (upper-room), which was the only respectable apartment in the post-house. Even that was horribly cold and draughty, for a violent wind was still blowing. Notwithstanding this, we spent a very pleasant evening together, and, by combining our resources, managed to produce a very respectable supper.

Next day, after a leisurely breakfast, we parted on our respective roads. The wind had dropped, the sky was cloudless, and the sun very powerful. We could see the road stretching away straight before us for three parasangs or so, when it took a sudden turn to the left round an angle of the mountains. As we advanced—very slowly, owing to the sorry condition of our beasts—the plain gradually narrowed, and became broken by great crests of rock rising abruptly out of the ground. The mountains on the right (west) grew gradually higher and higher, and their summits were now crowned with snow. On reaching the angle of the road above-mentioned we halted by some rocks for lunch. The spot was not devoid of beauty, which was enhanced by the numerous pink and crimson blossoms of the camel-thorn (*sháh-pasand*), which grew in profusion round about.

On leaving this place we began to ascend, and continued to do so till, about 4 p.m., we reached the disconsolate stone caravansaray of Khán-i-Khurré, which stands quite alone and apart from other habitations. It was crowded with people of all sorts: Bakhtiyárís, and other tribesmen on their migrations towards their summer quarters; people who had come out from Shíráz and elsewhere to meet the new Governor and do him honour; and a certain small contingent of ordinary travellers. I might have had some difficulty in obtaining quarters if my acquaintance of the previous day had not informed me that there was a special room in the caravansaray, set apart for members of the telegraph staff, which I might have by applying to the caravansaray-keeper for the key. I did so, and thus obtained a warm, snug room, where I might otherwise have been compelled to put up with the most miserable quarters. Though the caravansaray was in the most ruined and filthy condition, the ground being strewn with dead camels and horses in various stages of decay, the scene was not lacking in interest owing to the strange costumes and stranger appearance of the tribesmen. The women do not cover their faces, and many of them are endowed with a certain wild beauty.

After tea I had a visit from the postmaster (*na'ib-chápár*), who came to consult me about some disorder of the chest from which he was suffering. He soon, however, forgot the object which had brought him, and wandered off into a variety of topics, which he illustrated with a surprising number of quotations from the poets; and it was only when he rose to depart that he again recurred to his ailments. His dreamy abstracted manner had already led me to suspect that he was a votary of opium and other narcotics, and in reply to a question to this effect he answered that he did occasionally indulge in a pipe of *tiryáḳ* when depressed in spirits.

"Perhaps you take *ḥashísh* now and then for a change?" I asked.

"Well," he replied, "I don't deny that I do now and then."

"Of course you smoke the *ḳalyán* too?"

"Yes," he said, "what else is there to do in this desolate spot where there is no society except these tribesmen?"

"Well," I said, "I wish very much that I could do anything for you, but the state of the case is this: the essential principle of treating diseases is to remove their cause, and unless this can be done it is very little use to give medicines. Now, smoking *ḳalyáns* in excess disorders the chest, and I understand that you do smoke them very often. Whether the opium and *ḥashísh* which you also take are answerable for the evil in any degree I can't say, but at any rate it is scarcely likely that they do you any good. Just now you quoted this couplet from Ḥáfiẓ—

> '*Dihḳán-i-sál-khurdé ché khush guft bá pisar,*
> "*K'ey núr-i-chashm-i-man, bi-juz az kishte na-d'raví!*"'

> 'How well said the aged farmer to his son,
> "O Light of my eyes, thou shalt not reap save that which thou hast sown!"'

Now people who 'sow' *ḳalyáns* (opium) and *ḥashísh* necessarily 'reap' bad chests; and I am afraid that, unless you can manage to give them up, or at any rate confine your indulgence in them to moderate limits, your chest will not get any better. Do you think you can do this?"

"You are right," he replied (convinced, I feel sure, more by the quotation from Ḥáfiẓ than by anything else), "and I will try to follow your advice." So saying, he departed and left me alone.

Next day we started early, as the muleteers were anxious to "break" a stage—that is, to go three stages in two days; so that our halting-place for the night was not to be Dihbíd, where there is a telegraph station, but Khán-i-Kirgán, situated some two hours' march beyond it. Our road continued to ascend almost till we reached Dihbíd, and once or twice we enjoyed a fine view to the east across the Plain of Abarḳúh to the great range of mountains beyond which lies the city of Yezd. We were joined for some distance by a dark, stalwart man, who turned out to be a *ḳáṣid* (courier) carrying letters from Ábádé to Bawánát. He was conversationally inclined, and told me tales of encounters with wolves and other wild animals which abound in these mountains, but the dialect which he spoke was difficult to comprehend, and prevented me from profiting by his anecdotes as fully as I might otherwise have done. Suddenly we came to a road crossing ours at right angles, and thereupon our companion took a long draught from our water-bottle, and, without a word of farewell, disappeared in a valley leading down into the Plain of Abarḳúh.

After his departure Ḥájí Ṣafar entertained me with a long disquisition on *ḳáṣids* and their marvellous powers of endurance. He assured me that one had walked from Ṭeherán to Shíráz in five days, while another had gone from Bushire to Shíráz in two days. He added that the latter had come near forfeiting his life for his prowess, because Prince Ferhád Mírzá, then Governor of Fárs, hearing of his exploit, had said, "Such a man had best be put to death forthwith, for one who can go on foot from here to Bushire in two days might commit murder or highway robbery, and be in another province before his crime was even discovered." I am fain to believe that this was only a grim jest on the part of Ferhád Mírzá; at any rate the sentence, as I was informed, was not carried out.

The wind, which had been gradually increasing in strength since the morning, began now to cause us much annoyance, and indeed Dihbíd, as I subsequently learnt by experience, is one of the windiest places in Persia. Ḥájí Ṣafar, however, declared that in this respect it was far behind Dámghán, on the Mashhad road. "This is but a place which the wind visits at times," he remarked, "but it lives there: its abode is in a well, and anyone can arouse it at any time by throwing dirt or stones into the well, when it rushes out in anger."

Our road was redeemed from dreariness by the variety of beautiful flowers with which the advancing spring had bedecked the upland meadows. I noticed particularly the wild hyacinth (*sunbul-i-biyábání*), and the sight of its long narrow dark green leaves enabled me better to understand the appositeness of the comparison between it and the "tresses of the beloved" so often made by the Persian poets.

It was nearly 1.30 p.m. when we reached Dihbíd, a small village consisting of about fifteen or twenty cabins, a very dilapidated caravansaray, a post-house, and the telegraph-office. To the latter I at once made my way, and was welcomed very cordially by Mr and Mrs Blake. They expressed great regret on learning that I could not stop with them for the night, and repeatedly pressed me to do so with a hospitality so evidently genuine that I would gladly have altered my plans and relinquished the idea of "breaking a stage" had that been possible; but the muleteer had gone on with the baggage, and I was therefore compelled to adhere to my original intention, contenting myself with a halt of three or four hours for rest and refreshment.

It was beginning to grow dusk when I again set out, and the gathering shades of evening warned me that I must bestir myself, especially as the muleteer was no longer with us to direct our course. Mr Blake kindly volunteered to ride some distance with me to put me in the right way, and this offer I was glad to accept. Crossing the little river just beyond the village we saw a flight of about a dozen storks, and farther on four gazelles. Half a mile or more to the west of the road stood an old withered tree close to a ruined caravansaray, and this spot, as Mr Blake informed me, was reputed to be haunted by a "white lady," but with the details of this superstition he was unable to acquaint me.

When we had ridden a *farsakh*, my host bade me farewell and turned back, whereupon we quickened our pace so as to make the best use of what daylight still remained. Long before we reached our halting-place, however, it was quite dark, and we were left to pick our dubious way by the light of the stars and a crescent moon; so that it was more by good luck than good management (for the road had here dwindled to the merest track) that we were finally apprised by the barking of dogs of the proximity of human habitations. In five minutes more we crossed a bridge and found ourselves at the solitary caravansaray of Khán-i-Kirgán.

As it was quite dark, and I was, moreover, very cold and tired, I had no opportunity of making any observations on the nature of the place or its inhabitants that night, but on the following morning I discovered that here also were domiciled multitudes of tribesmen on their way to their summer quarters. On the road, which wound through beautiful grassy valleys bedecked with sweet spring flowers, we met many more, all bound for the highland pastures which we were leaving behind us, and a pretty sight it was to see them pass; stalwart, hardy-looking men, with dark, weather-beaten faces; lithe, graceful boys clothed in skins; and tall, active women with resolute faces, not devoid of a comeliness which no veil concealed. They were accompanied by droves of donkeys bearing their effects, and flocks of sheep and goats, which paused here and there to nibble the fresh grass.

Early in the afternoon we descended into the valley of Murgháb, and, passing the hamlet of that name (a well-built and thriving-looking village, pleasantly situated by a beautiful clear streamlet) halted at Dih-i-Naw, some three miles farther on. The feeling of regret at not having sought for a lodging at the former, which the first sight of the somewhat squalid appearance of the latter caused me, was at once removed when I learned that the group of ancient ruins generally identified with the site of the city of Pasargadæ on European maps, and known to the Persians as *Takht-i-Suleymán* ("the Throne of Solomon") and *Masjid-i-*

Mádar-i-Suleymán ("the Mosque of the Mother of Solomon"), was situated within a few minutes' walk of the village. As it was not much past four o'clock in the afternoon, I determined at once to visit them, and thus to obtain a general idea of their appearance and arrangement, reserving a closer inspection of them for the morning. They have been so often and so well described that I shall confine myself to a brief account of their more salient features.

Leaving Dih-i-Naw on the south, or Shíráz, side, the first object of interest reached is the *Takht-i-Suleymán*. This, consisting of a large platform faced with masonry, projects from the face of a hill situated a little to the left (east) of the high road, not five minutes' walk from the village. Its frontage must be about 150 feet, and here the conscientious thoroughness and solidity of the masonry is most easily appreciated. I noticed the holes for the iron clamps (which have themselves been removed) noticed by Sir R. Ker Porter, and also the peculiar marks on most of the stones which he, if I remember rightly, was inclined to regard as characters of some ancient language. The villager who accompanied me declared that they were marks placed by each mason on the stone at which he had worked, in order that the amount of his work and the wages due to him might be proved; and I have no doubt that such is their nature. At any rate, they in no wise resemble the characters of any known alphabet.

From the platform of the *Takht-i-Suleymán* the whole plain of Pasargadæ is clearly visible. The Shíráz road takes a bold sweep towards the west ere it quits the plain and enters the grand defile through which flows the river Pulvár, and all the ruins except the Tomb of Cyrus (or *Masjid-i-Mádar-i-Suleymán*, as the Persians call it) are situated within a short distance of it and of one another, on the left hand of the southward-bound traveller. The Tomb of Cyrus lies about half a mile beyond them, on the opposite side of the road: it is encircled by a little village, and is regarded by the Persians as a place of considerable sanctity.

The first building to which I came on descending from the *Takht-i-Suleymán* is that called by Ker Porter *Átash-kedé* ("the Fire-Temple"). My guide, however, gave it the name of *Zindán-khané* ("the Prison-house"). It is situated close to the road, which it faces, and is very solid and massive in structure, but bears no inscriptions or carvings. The western end of the building only is standing; it is about thirty feet high, and contains sixteen courses of stones, and a window, below which is a buttress.

The next object which presents itself is a solitary square pillar of white stone in twelve courses, bearing a cuneiform inscription of four lines, of which the second is separated from the third, and the third from the fourth, by a blank space. I could not learn that it had any popular name.

A short distance beyond this lies the main group of ruins, called *Nakkára-khané-i-Suleymán* ("the Music-hall of Solomon"). Amongst these the most conspicuous object is a very tall slender column about sixty feet high, white in colour, and circular in shape, composed of four stones placed one on the other, the length of each one diminishing from below upwards. This column is quite plain, and bears no inscription. There are two or three other pillar-like structures, which appear to have formed the corners of the ruined edifice. At the back of each I noticed the hollowing-out of the stone noticed by Ker Porter. One of them bears on its north face a cuneiform inscription similar to that already noticed on the first column, but containing four or five different characters. On the western side of this group of ruins (*i.e.* on the side facing the road) are the remains of two doorways, each about five feet in width. The stones forming the sides of these are blackish in colour and susceptible of a high degree of polish. They are broken off within two feet of the ground, and on their inner surfaces are carved two pairs of feet, both turned towards the entrance. Of these, the outer pair are human feet, the inner pair feet like those of a bird: both are beautifully executed. A fragment of a similar doorway also exists on the south side, and this is adorned with two pairs of human feet. A little beyond this is a portion of wall standing, some of the stones of which bear marks similar to those observable on the *Takht-i-Suleymán*.

A little distance to the east of this group of ruins, *i.e.* farther from the road, stands a solitary column, on the west side of which is carved in bas-relief the beautiful winged figure described and depicted by Ker Porter and others. I was still absorbed in delighted contemplation of this, when my guide, impatient at the long delay, called attention to the approach of evening, and urged me to return, declaring that it was unsafe to be out in the plain after dusk, and reminding me that I could complete my examination of the ruins next day. With regret I acceded to his request, and reluctantly retraced my steps. On the way back my companion talked freely of the state of the country and the dismissal of the old *Ṣáḥib-Díván* from the government of Fárs, at which he expressed unbounded delight. I asked if the *Ṣáḥib-Díván* had been a cruel governor that he had so aroused the hatred of the people. To this question my guide replied in the negative, alleging his incapacity and lack of integrity as the reason why he was so much disliked. "He has made everything dear," he concluded, "and we enjoy no sort of protection from the rapacity of the wandering tribes, who carry off our cattle and flocks without the least fear of reprisals. Riẓá Khán, his old enemy, is now encamped between Seydún and Sívand with all his tribe, and has sworn to slay him if he can waylay him on his journey north; in which attempt I, for my part, wish him all success. He has already begun stripping and plundering all the followers and retainers of the ex-governor on whom he can lay his hands, including forty of Zeynu'l-'Ábidín's men who were sent out to catch him or drive him away, and who came back to Shíráz crestfallen and discomfited, with nothing but their shirts. As for the new governor, the Iḥtishámu'd-Dawla, if he is like his father, Prince Ferhád Mírzá, he will keep things in better order. Indeed, already the marauders have desisted from their raids, and our flocks and cattle are once more safe." So my companion ran on; and I was surprised to see that his fear was not so much that the new governor might be too harsh, as that he might not govern the province with a sufficiently firm hand.

Next day on quitting Dih-i-Naw I again visited the ruins above described, and, after reluctantly tearing myself away from them, proceeded to explore the Tomb of Cyrus. This, as I have already mentioned, is called by the Persians "the Mosque of the Mother of Solomon," and is regarded as a holy place, so that I had some fear lest they should prevent me from entering it. This fear fortunately proved to be groundless; indeed, one of the inhabitants of the adjacent village volunteered to accompany me as a guide, though such assistance was quite unnecessary.

The Tomb of Cyrus, being built of white stone, forms a most conspicuous landmark in the plain of Pasargadæ. It consists of a rectangular roofed chamber of extraordinary solidity, situated on a square platform approached on all sides by steep and lofty steps, up which one must climb, rather than walk, to reach the low entrance. The building bears no inscriptions in cuneiform or Pahlaví characters, but numerous Musulmán visitors have engraved their names on its walls and steps. I had hitherto imagined that the passion for leaving such memorials of one's visit was peculiar to the West, and reached its highest development with the English and Americans; but not only the ruins of Pasargadæ and Persepolis, but every post-house and caravansaray in Persia, bear witness to the fact that this habit is hardly less rife amongst the Persians. De Sacy was, I think, the first to direct attention to these interesting relics of former travellers. In the presence of the ancient cuneiform characters, which carry us back to the time of the Achæmenian kings, one is tempted to overlook them, though not a few of them date back to the earlier Muḥammadan period. The longest of these inscriptions is situated on the wall to the right of one entering the mausoleum. This wall is adorned with a rude *miḥráb* (probably made by those who first conceived the idea of sanctifying the burial-place of the ancient fire-worshipping monarch by connecting it with the name of Solomon), on the lower portion of which is cut the word *Alláh.* This is surrounded by a long rectangular border raised into a subsidiary rectangle on the upper side to embrace the *miḥráb*, the whole length of which is occupied by a much-worn Arabic inscription, only legible in parts, beginning: "*In the Name of God the Merciful, the Clement. Verily we have opened unto thee a perspicuous victory....*" At the left-hand lower corner of this border, close to the ground, is a Neo-Persian inscription in Arabic characters of an archaic type. Across the end of the chamber opposite to the door was hung a string, on which were suspended ribbons, pieces of cloth, beads, pipe-bowls, and other votive offerings brought by pious visitors to the shrine; and in the corner lay a copy of the *Ḳur'án.*

Leaving the mausoleum, I turned to descend, examining the steps and the inscriptions cut on them on my way. Some of the stones bore mason's marks similar to those referred to in speaking of the *Takht-i-Suleymán.* Besides these there were a great many Neo-Persian inscriptions, mostly undated, or of comparatively recent date, some almost illegible, others as clear as though cut yesterday.

Around the base of the steps is a small burial-ground strewn with fragments of other buildings which have perished. At its entrance are two long stones, propped one against the other in the shape of an inverted V, which form a sort of gate to the enclosure. Each of these is engraved on its inner surface with a line of Arabic in a fine bold character. The space left between the two stones is very narrow, and their surfaces are worn as smooth as glass by the passage of generations of pilgrims and visitors. These stones are supposed to be endowed with healing virtues, and my guide informed me that anyone bitten by a mad dog can be cured by crawling through the narrow interstice which separates them. To the faith of the people in this theory, if not to its truth, the high degree of polish on the inner surfaces of the stones in question bore witness.

Turning at length with much reluctance from this interesting spot, I again mounted and rode forward, and, in a few minutes, quitted the plain and entered the splendid rocky defile through which the river Pulvár flows down towards Shíráz. This defile, with occasional widenings into fertile grassy valleys, continues to within two stages of Shíráz. There, a little beyond the post-house of Púzé, its rocky walls fall sharply away to the east and west as it enters the great plain of Marv-Dasht. At that point its width is three or four miles; in the rocks to the right are the tombs called by the Persians Naḳsh-i-Rustam; on the left, opposite to these, are the sculptures of Naḳsh-i-Rajab, the ruins of Iṣṭakhr, and just round the angle formed by the Kúh-i-Raḥmat ("Mountain of Mercy") the stupendous remains of Persepolis, of which I shall shortly have to speak.

This defile of the Pulvár offers some of the finest and most picturesque views in Persia: the rugged cliffs which hem it in on either side; the rushing river meandering through fertile meadows under the willows which fringe its banks; the fragrant shrubs and delicate flowers which, at this season, perfume the air and delight the eye; the gaily-plumaged hoopoes—the birds of Solomon—which dart through the clear sunny air; but most of all, perhaps, the memories of the glorious Past which every footstep awakens, all combined to render this one of the most delightful parts of my journey.

Soon after turning into the defile we ascended the rocks to the right for some distance, and entered the *Sang-bur* ("Rock-cutting"), a passage two or three hundred yards in length, just wide enough to admit a man and horse, hewn out of the mountain side. While marvelling at this enduring triumph of the engineering skill of ancient Persia, a vision arose in my mind's eye of gorgeously apparelled horsemen spurring in hot haste with messages to or from the "Great King" through the Rock-cutting. I pictured to myself the white temples and lofty halls of Pasargadæ first bursting on their sight, and sighed inwardly as I thought of that departed splendour, and of the fickleness of fortune, which has taken away the very tomb of Cyrus from him to bestow it upon Solomon.

Soon after leaving the *Sang-bur* I was startled—almost frightened—by the sudden apparition of four or five armed men, who sprang out from behind a rock and barred my progress. The reports which I had heard of the disturbed state of Fárs, the turbulence of its inhabitants, and the deeds of Riẓá Khán flashed through my mind; and I was in full expectation of a summons to surrender my money or my life, when I was reassured by a humble request on the part of the spokesman of the party that I would be kind enough to "remember the poor *tufankchí*" who watched over the safety of the roads. I was so relieved that I readily gave him what he desired; and it was not till I had passed on, and these guardians of the peace had once more hidden themselves in their ambush, that I was struck by the ludicrous nature of the proceeding. Imagine policemen or sentinels in England hiding behind rocks and leaping out on the passing traveller to ask him for a "present" in recognition of their vigilance!

About mid-day I halted in a pleasant meadow by the river for lunch. The infinitely-varied shades of green and red exhibited by the willows, just bursting into foliage, the emerald hue of the grass, and the pleasant murmur of the rushing river flowing past me, rendered the spot charming beyond all description. Ḥájí Ṣafar, whose spirits appeared to rise higher and higher as he drew nearer to Shíráz (for, whatever he may say, in his heart of hearts every Shírází thinks his own native city incomparable and peerless), was in high good humour—a fact which always disclosed itself by his giving me a better meal than usual—and on this occasion he went so far as to kindle a fire and make some tea, which he brought me triumphantly when I had finished eating.

Reluctantly quitting this delightful spot, we again continued on our way through scenery as varied as it was grand, and presently passed through one of the wide cliff-girt valleys into which the Pulvár defile here and there expands. Here the rich pastures were dotted with groups of black tents belonging to the wandering tribes (*ílyát*) moving northward into the mountains, while their flocks of sheep and goats, tended by dark-eyed graceful shepherd boys, moved hither and thither over the plain. Leaving this happy valley we entered another defile, which brought us, a little before 6 p.m., to the village of Sívand, in which is situated the last telegraph station before Shíráz. Here I was received with the utmost kindness by Mr and Mrs Whittingback, whose little boy had ridden out to meet me some while before, for I was expected earlier.

Next morning I did not start till about ten o'clock, being unwilling to leave the hospitable roof of my kind entertainers. The post-road to Shíráz continues on the left bank of the river, but as I wished to visit the inscriptions on the rocks above Ḥájí-ábád, which lies on the opposite side, we forded the stream, and followed the western bend of the valley, thus shortening our day's march by nearly a parasang. Soon after mid-day the village of Ḥájí-ábád came in sight, and, as I was uncertain as to the exact position of the inscriptions, I began carefully to scrutinise the rocky cliffs to the right, in the hopes of discerning some trace of them. Presently I detected a small squarish hole hewn in the face of the rocks some distance up the side of one of the mountains (which at this point receded considerably from the road), and at once proceeded to scramble up to it. As usual, the clearness of the atmosphere led me to underrate the distance, and it was only after a long and hot climb that I finally reached the spot, where, to my disappointment, no inscription was visible —nothing but the shallow excavation, which in the distance looked like the mouth of a tunnel. For what purpose and by whom it was made I do not know, but I saw several similar excavations in the neighbourhood. Disappointed in my search, I again descended to the foot of the mountains, and continued my way along their base, eagerly scanning the rugged cliffs above me. I was much afraid that after all I might fail in discovering the object of my search, so numerous were the clefts, valleys, and ravines by which the mountains were indented and intersected at this point. Presently, however, I came to the opening of a wider valley, running straight up into the hills, where it divided into two small glens, which ascended to the right and left, to lose themselves in the mountain above. In the mouth of this valley were pitched two or three tents, near which a tribesman was watching his grazing flock. Accosting him, I enquired whether he knew where the writing on the rocks was to be found.

"Do you mean the *writing* or the *sculptures*?" he demanded.

"The writing," I answered; "I know that the sculptures are lower down the valley."

"And what do you want with the writing?" asked the shepherd, suspiciously. "Can you read it?"

"No," I replied, "unfortunately I cannot; nevertheless I have heard that there are writings from the ancient time somewhere in these rocks, and I am desirous of seeing them."

"You *can* read them, I know very well," said he, "and you hope to find treasures there; many Firangís come here seeking for treasures. However, if you must know, they are up there," and he pointed up the valley. I wished to ask him in which bifurcation of the valley they were, but he had returned to his sheep, evidently disinclined to give me any further information.

There was nothing for it but to explore both of the gullies in question, and I began with the one to the right. It led me up into the heart of the mountain, and, after scrambling up amongst huge rugged boulders, I finally found myself at the mouth of a most gloomy-looking cavern, which appeared to run straight into the hillside. From the rocks above and around the water dripped with a sullen plash; a few bones scattered on the ground irresistibly suggested the thought that I was in close proximity to the lair of some wild beast, and caused me instinctively to feel in my pocket for my revolver; while the silence and loneliness of the spot, whence I could not even see the road, being hemmed in on all sides by beetling rocks, made me in no wise sorry to retrace my steps as soon as I was well assured that the object of my search was not to be found here.

I now proceeded to explore the other ravine, which, if less gloomy, was hardly less imposing than that which I had just quitted. As I ascended, its sides grew steeper and steeper, until, approaching one another more and more closely, they terminated in sheer precipices. At this point several huge boulders lay at their feet, seeming to bar all further progress, and I was beginning to doubt the advisability of trying to proceed farther, when, raising my eyes to the rocks on the right, I espied, some distance up, a long depression, looking dark in the sunshine, on the wall of which I thought I could discern a prepared tablet of cruciform shape. Hastily ascending to this, I perceived with joy that my conjecture was right. On the rock forming the back of this hollow was a prepared surface, shaped roughly like a cross with very thick limbs, along the transverse length of which were four tablets hewn in the mountain face. Of these tablets the two situated to the left were bare, having apparently never received the inscriptions for which they were destined; but each of the other two bore an inscription of some length in Pahlaví characters. The inscriptions in question have been fully treated of by Haug in his admirable *Essay on the Pahlaví Language*, and it is therefore unnecessary for me to say more of them in this place than that one of them is in Sásánian, and the other in Chaldæo-Pahlaví; that both belong to the reign of Shápúr I, the son of Ardashír Bábakán, the founder of the dynasty; and that consequently they date from the third century of the Christian era.

Having satisfied my curiosity, I returned to Ḥájí Ṣafar, who was awaiting me with the horses in the road, and we proceeded in a straight line towards the village of Zangavar (situated on the same side of the river as Ḥájí-ábád, nearer the end of the valley), where I proposed to halt for the following day, as it forms the best starting-point for visiting Persepolis and the rock-sepulchres of Naḳsh-i-Rustam. Our progress was, however, soon checked by innumerable streams and ditches, and we were compelled to return to the road skirting the base of the mountains on the western side of the valley. Annoying as this delay at first appeared, it was in truth a most fortunate occurrence, for, while looking about for signs of a path which would lead us more directly to our goal, I suddenly caught sight of a large cruciform excavation on the face of the rock, which I at once recognised, from the descriptions I had read and the sketches I had seen, as one of the tombs of Naḳsh-i-Rustam, on which I had thus unexpectedly chanced. Ḥájí Ṣafar seemed scarcely so well pleased as I was, for he well knew that this discovery would involve a further delay, and, as the day had now turned cold and windy, he would doubtless fain have reached the halting-place as soon as possible. Since an hour or two of daylight still remained, however, it was obviously out of the question to waste it; and as I knew that the morrow would be all too short fully to explore the wonders of Persepolis, I was anxious to get a clear impression of the monuments which so thickly beset this angle of the valley.

Accordingly I spent about an hour in examining and taking notes of these—a delightful hour, which passed only too quickly. The monuments in question are well-known to all travellers and antiquarians, and have been fully described in many books, so I shall content myself with merely enumerating them.

They are as follows:—

(i) Four rock-sepulchres dating from Achæmenian times. Externally, these present the appearance of crosses cut in the rock, with limbs equal in length and about half as wide as they are long. The aperture affording access to the inner gallery (which corresponds to the horizontal limbs of the cross in length, height, and position) is near the centre. Of the interior I shall have to speak shortly. Two pillars carved out of the rock stand on either side of this aperture, which is forty or fifty feet above the ground. The upper limb of the cross is adorned with sculptured symbols, amongst which a fire-altar surmounted by a crescent moon, a priest engaged in devotional exercises, and, over all, the winged figure girt with the symbol of infinity, which forms so constant a feature in the Achæmenian tombs, are most conspicuous.

(ii) Six tablets bearing inscriptions and bas-reliefs of Sásánian workmanship. Close to the first of these (proceeding from the north southwards) is a modern Persian inscription [1], bearing the date A.H. 1127 (A.D. 1715), which is already almost as much defaced as the Sásánian inscriptions by the side of which it stands, and far more so than the exquisite cuneiform of the Achæmenians. Of the six Sásánian tablets, most of which are commemorative of victories over the Romans, and one or two of which bear long Pahlaví inscriptions, the *first* is adjacent to the Neo-Persian inscription noticed above, and stands about half-way between the first and second rock-tombs, but close to the

1 This is not the only place where the kings of modern Persia have adopted this time-honoured means of perpetuating their fame. A similar tablet, bearing a bas-relief of the king on horseback spearing a lion, as well as a Neo-Persian inscription (also barely legible), may be seen in the rocks to the north of what is generally regarded as the site of Rey, near Ṭeherán. I believe that it was cut by order of Fatḥ-'Alí Sháh. Another and a much better tablet, containing, besides a Persian inscription, bas-relief portraits of Náṣiru'd-Dín Sháh (by whose command it was cut) surrounded by his ministers, forms a conspicuous object on the rocks above the admirably-constructed new road leading through Mázandarán from the capital to Ámul, about two stages south of the latter town. This will be further noticed in its proper place.

ground; the *second* is placed under the second rock-tomb; the *third* between the second and third rock-tombs; the *fourth* under the fourth rock-tomb; and the *fifth* and *sixth*, one above the other, just before the angle formed by the falling away of the cliffs to the west where the valley enters the plain of Marv-Dasht.

(iii) Opposite the last rock-tomb, on the other side of the road (which runs close to the face of the cliff), is a square building of very solid construction, bearing some resemblance to the Tomb of Cyrus. This can be entered by climbing without much difficulty. It is called by the villagers *Ka'ba-i-Zarátusht* ("the Caaba of Zoroaster").

(iv) On a summit of the rocks which form the angle of the valley is a cylindrical pillar about five feet high, sunk in a socket cut to receive it. This is called *Dasta-i-Píré-Zan* ("the Old Woman's Pestle").

(v) Beyond the angle formed by the junction of the Pulvár valley with the Marv-Dasht, and consequently concealed from the sight of one standing in the former, are two altars, each about four and a half feet high, hewn out of the solid rock. These are well described and figured by Ker Porter.

The above list comprises all the remains included by the Persians under the name "Naḳsh-i-Rustam," and, with the exception of a brief description of the interior of one of the rock-tombs which I shall shortly attempt, I shall say no more about them, since they have been exhaustively described by many writers far more competent in this matter than myself.

While engaged in examining the Naḳsh-i-Rustam, we were joined by a villager who had been collecting a plant called *ḳangar* in the mountains. Some of this he gave to Ḥájí Ṣafar, who cooked it for my supper. It is by no means unsavoury, and resembles celery more than anything else I can think of. This villager proved to be a native of Zangavar, the village whither we were bound; and on learning that I proposed to spend the morrow there, so as to explore the antiquities in the neighbourhood, he offered to obtain the help of one or two other men who, by means of a rope, would haul me up to the platform of the rock-tombs, so as to enable me to examine its interior.

As the gathering dusk warned me that I must postpone further explorations till the morrow, I regretfully turned my back on the Naḳsh-i-Rustam, and, after a ride of fifteen or twenty minutes, reached the large straggling village of Zangavar. Here I was informed that the *Kedkhudá* (chief man of the village), apprised by the muleteer of my arrival, had assigned quarters to me in the *takyé* consecrated to the Muḥarram passion-plays. Proceeding thither, I found a clean and comfortable room set apart for me, in which I had hardly installed myself when the *Kedkhudá* in person, accompanied by one or two friends, came to pay his respects. He was a nice old man, very courteous and kindly in his manners, and we had a long conversation, of which the antiquities in the neighbourhood formed the principal topic. He told me that a little while ago two Frenchmen (working for M. Dieulafoy) had been engaged for some time in making plans and taking photographs of Persepolis and the Naḳsh-i-Rustam, in front of which they had erected a sort of scaffold (*manjaníḳ*) the better to reach its upper part. They had lodged in this village; but, the *Kedkhudá* complained, had been very unsociable and reticent, refusing to allow the people to watch their work or see their photographs and sketches.

This subject exhausted, the *Kedkhudá* began to question me concerning our religion, and to ask me whether I had heard of the European doctor who had recently embraced the Muḥammadan faith at Shíráz. I answered that I had read about his conversion in a Persian newspaper which I had seen at Iṣfahán, and that I was very desirous of conversing with him, so that I might learn the reasons which had led him to abandon his own creed in favour of Islám.

"Perhaps you, too," said the *Kedkhudá*, "will, by the grace of God, be brought to believe in the religion of our Prophet. You have come to see our country from afar; do not, like the majority of the Firangís, occupy yourself with nothing but dumb stones, vessels of brass, tiles, and fabrics; contemplate the world of ideas rather than the world of form, and seek for Truth rather than for curiosities. Why should you not even pay a visit to the most holy tombs of our Imáms at Kerbelá and Nejef? There you might see the miracles whereby they prove to all that they still live and rule."

"Gladly would I do as you advise," I replied, "and I trust that I am not so bigoted as to refuse fairly to consider whatever proofs can be adduced in favour of your religion. Unfortunately, however, your countrymen and co-religionists, so far from offering any facilities to 'unbelievers' for witnessing the miracles whereby, as you say, the Imáms continue to manifest their power and presence to the world, would drive me from their shrines like a dog if I attempted to approach them, even as they did at the shrine of Sháh 'Abdu'l-'Aẓím. Surely they act most unwisely in this matter; for if, as you say, miracles are there wrought, they must be intended not so much for those who believe as for those who doubt, and who might be convinced thereby."

"You are perhaps right," said the *Kedkhudá*, after a moment's reflection, "yet still I would urge you to make the attempt, even if you must disguise yourself as a Persian to do so. It would be a pity that you should come here at so much trouble and expense, and should take back nothing with you but a collection of those curiosities and antiquities with which your people seem for the most part to be so strangely infatuated." So saying, the *Kedkhudá* took his departure and left me to myself.

Although I was up in good time next day, all eagerness to make the best use of an opportunity which I should in all probability never again enjoy, I was delayed in starting for some time by a crowd of people who, hearing that I possessed some medical knowledge, desired to consult me about their various disorders; and it was not till nine o'clock that I finally left the village, accompanied by the villager whom I had met on the previous day, two younger men provided with ropes, and a little boy who enlivened the way with his childish prattle. Arrived opposite the Naḳsh-i-Rustam, my guides advanced to the second rock-tomb, which is somewhat nearer the ground than the others, and more readily accessible. One of them climbed up the rocks with marvellous agility to the narrow platform which crosses the entrance. He then let down the rope, by the aid of which the others followed him. The rope was again lowered, I bound it firmly round my waist, and, not without sundry bumps and abrasions, was hauled up to where they stood.

Entering the tomb by the low doorway opening on to this ledge or platform, I found myself in a long gallery corresponding to the transverse limb of the cross carved on the face of the rock. This gallery was twenty-seven paces in length from end to end, three paces in width, and perhaps twenty feet in height. On the side opposite to the entrance, four rectangular recesses are hewn out of the rock, the width of each being about four and a half paces. The floors of these are not level with the ground, but raised some three feet above it. Out of each of these floors are hewn three parallel tombs or sarcophagi, their greatest length being parallel to the gallery, and consequently transverse to the recess in which they lie. These sarcophagi were, of course, empty (except for some *débris* of stones and rubbish), and their coverings had been destroyed or removed.

On completing my examination of the tomb and descending to the ground, I found a small knot of people collected. These asked me whether I could read the inscriptions, and would hardly believe my assertion that I was unable to do so, asking me if I were not a "*mullá*." Indeed, one or two appeared to imagine that they were written in my own language, or in one of the languages of Firangistán.

We now struck across the valley towards Persepolis—"*Taḳht--Jamshíd*" ("the Throne of Jamshíd"), as it is called by the

Persians—fording the river Pulvár, and passing a square stone platform on its further side, called "*Taḳht-i-Tá'ús*" ("the Peacock Throne"). Following the eastern side of the valley for a short distance, we presently turned the corner formed by its junction with the great plain of Marv-Dasht, and all at once there burst on my wondering gaze the stupendous ruins of Persepolis.

Of the ruins of Pasargadæ, the Tomb of Cyrus, and the rock-sepulchres of Naḳsh-i-Rustam I have attempted to set down some description, however meagre. In the case of Persepolis it would be vain to make this attempt, since the three or four hours during which I wandered through its deserted halls, trod its silent stairs, and gazed in admiration, such as I have seldom before experienced, on the endless succession of lofty columns, giant statues, and delicate traceries (whose beauty long ages, kinder than the besotted Macedonian who first stretched forth his impious hand against them, have scarcely marred), were hardly sufficient to enable me to do more than wonder and admire. To study Persepolis would require months; to describe it, volumes. It has already been studied and described by others far more competent than myself. All that I shall do, then, is to notice certain minor details which happened to strike me.

On the stones of Persepolis, as on the monuments which I have already noticed, a host of travellers of many ages and many nations have carved their names, their sentiments, and their reflections, by the side of the ancient cuneiform inscriptions. Only, by as much as Persepolis exceeds all the other ruins in extent and splendour, by so much do these memorials exceed all the rest in number and interest. The two great stone lions which guard the entrance of the eastern hall, and the adjacent walls, seem to have been the favourite spots. Amongst the European names recorded here, those of Malcolm and his suite, carved in large bold Roman characters, are most conspicuous; while, amidst the remainder, cut or written in every possible fashion, the names of not a few distinguished travellers are to be found. The sense of admiration and awe with which the place inspired me made me feel that to follow their example would be almost a profanation, and I turned to examine the similar memorials left by Musulmán visitors.

Many of these consisted, like their European congeners, of mere names and dates, and to these I paid but little attention. Here and there, however, a few lines of poetry, or a reflection on the transitoriness of earthly glory in Arabic or Persian, showed me that the same feeling of mixed awe and sadness with which the place inspired me had affected others. Some of these inscriptions were not devoid of grace and beauty, and I could not help thinking that, if one must leave a token of one's visit to such a spot, these records of the solemn feelings evoked thereby were more seemly and more congruous than aught else. As a specimen of their tenour I append translations of two, both in Arabic: one in prose, one in verse.

The first was written in A.H. 1206 (A.D. 1791–2) by a son of Sháh-Rukh Mírzá, and runs as follows:—

"*Where are the proud monarchs of yore? They multiplied treasures which endured not, neither did they endure.*"

The second consists of four lines of poetry, attributed by the carver to 'Alí, the successor of the Prophet:—

"*Where are the kings who exercised dominion*
Until the cup-bearer of Death gave them to drink of his cup?
How many cities which have been built betwixt the horizons
Lay ruined in the evening, while their dwellers were in the abode of death?"

This was cut by 'Alí ibn Sulṭán Khalíd ibn Sulṭán Khusraw.

In one of the windows a stone was pointed out to me, so highly polished that I could clearly see therein my reflection as in a mirror. Here and there excavations have laid bare long-buried chambers. Some of these excavations were undertaken by the command of Ferhád Mírzá, the Sháh's uncle—less, I fear, from a disinterested love of antiquarian research than from a hope of finding treasure, which, according to the universal belief of the Persians (based, perhaps, on traditions embodied in Firdawsí's *Book of Kings*), is concealed in the neighbourhood. My guides assured me that a large "brick" or ingot of solid gold had actually been discovered, and that it had been sent to Ṭeherán, where it was preserved in the treasury of the Sháh. They also pointed out to me the spot where Ferhád Mírzá had caused some delinquent to be hanged over the parapet of the great terrace.

It was sad to note how in many places the faces of such bas-reliefs and figures as could be reached from the ground had been wilfully defaced by fanaticism or ignorance, while many of the animals carved on the walls and staircases had been made the targets of marksmen, as witnessed by the numerous bullet-marks which they bore. But in all cases, so far as I saw, the winged genius girt with the girdle typifying infinity, which, looking forth from almost every column and cornice, seemed to watch still over the cradle of Persia's greatness, had escaped uninjured.

On reaching the edge of the platform next the mountain from the face of which it is built out, two sepulchres on the hillside above attracted my attention, and I was making towards them when I suddenly espied two figures approaching me. The pith hat worn by one stamped him at once as a European, and I, thinking that it must be my friend and late fellow-traveller, H——, hastened forward to meet him. A nearer approach, however, showed that I was mistaken. The wearer of the pith hat proved to be an English officer who had been staying for some days in Shíráz on his homeward road from India. He was now bound for Ṭeherán, and thence for England by way of Russia. From him I learned that H—— had posted up to Persepolis and back to Shíráz a day or two before, and that he had probably already set out for Bushire. After a short conversation we separated, and I proceeded to examine the tombs above mentioned, which, in general plan, closely resemble the sepulchres of Naḳsh-i-Rustam, with this important difference, that being situated on a sloping hillside, instead of on the face of a cliff, they are entered without difficulty, the inner floor being level with the ground outside. Besides this, they only contain two sarcophagi apiece, and a single recess, which is vaulted instead of being rectangular.

Short as the time had seemed to me, symptoms of impatience began to manifest themselves in my guides. Although it was not yet four o'clock, they declared that the lateness of the hour made it advisable to withdraw from this solitary spot, lest robbers, tempted from their hiding-places in the mountains by the approach of night, should waylay us. Without attaching much credence to their representations I was forced to yield to them, and, with many a backward glance of regret, to turn my back on Persepolis. On the way back to the village I lingered for a while to examine the Sásánian bas-reliefs of Naḳsh-i-Rajab, which are situated in a little hollow on the mountain side just behind the post-house of Púzé, and attempted to transcribe the Greek inscription of Shápúr I, which afforded the key whereby the mysteries of the anomalous and ambiguous Pahlaví tongue were first unlocked.

Next morning I quitted Zangavar, and again turned my face southwards. Our departure was greatly delayed by a crowd of sick people seeking medical advice, and, even when we at length escaped from these, an unwise attempt to take a short cut towards the main road resulted in a further loss of time. All the morning our course lay across the flat marshy plain of Marv-Dasht—a vast amphitheatre, surrounded by mountains of which some of those to the west assume the wildest shapes. Amongst these one, on which the ruins of an ancient fortress are said still to exist, is conspicuous for its precipitous and apparently inaccessible summit. The day was cold and cloudy with some rain, a state of things which rendered travelling over the naturally moist and marshy plain rather unpleasant. I was surprised, at this distance from the sea, to observe a number of gulls. They are called by the Persians *Murgh-i-Nawrúzí* ("New Year's Bird"), so that their appearance (which is, perhaps, limited to this season) was very appropriate; for we were now within a day of that most ancient and most popular festival, the feast of the New Year (*'Íd-i-Nawrúz*), whereby the Persians have, from time immemorial, celebrated the advent of spring.

About mid-day we reached the end of the plain and entered another valley, in which we presently came to a great sheet of water, stretching away to the east towards the *Band-i-Amír*[1]. This is traversed by a stone causeway, and swarms with a variety of waterfowl. Leaving this behind, and bending somewhat to the left towards the mountains which form the eastern limit of the valley, we reached Zargán, our last stage before Shíráz, about dusk.

During the morning we had passed eight or ten horsemen, whose arrogant bearing and unprovoked incivility proclaimed them servants of the ex-governor; and while passing the sheet of water above mentioned we had heard numerous shots in the surrounding hills and on the borders of the lake, which testified to the presence of a party of sportsmen. Rumour had, moreover, apprised us of the fact that Prince Jalálu'd-Dawla (the son of the fallen Prince Ẓillu's-Sulṭán, and the nominal governor of Shíráz), as well as the aged Ṣáḥib-Díván, the virtual governor, had quitted the city, in which they had no excuse for remaining longer, and were on their way northwards to the capital with a large company of followers and retainers. On reaching Zargán it was, therefore, with more annoyance than surprise that I found the whole town filled with the soldiers and servants of the young prince and his minister. Enquiries for lodgings were everywhere met with the same reply, that there was not a room to be had for love or money in the place; and it was only after

1 The "Bendemeer's stream" of the poet Moore. Its name signifies "the Amír's Dyke."

a protracted search through every part of the town that I was fortunate enough to secure a lodging for the night in a small room which served during the day as a weaver's shop. While the implements of the owner's craft were being removed, I was scrutinised with sullen curiosity by a small knot of villagers, over whose spirits the presence of the soldiers appeared to have cast a gloom which rendered them silent and abstracted.

And here at Zargán I was like to have suffered yet graver trouble, and came near perishing, as Ḥájí Ṣafar poetically observed, "like a moth consumed in the candle of Shíráz," ere ever I set eyes on that beautiful and classical city. For while, according to my wont, I lay smoking and reading in my camp-bed before composing myself to sleep, slumber overtook me unawares, and I lost all consciousness of my surroundings till I suddenly awoke with a sense of suffocation and contact with something hot. A moment's examination showed me that the quilt on which I lay was smouldering and aglow with sparks. I immediately sprang up and dragged it on to the ground, when I found the mischief to be much more extensive than I had imagined, at least a third of its lower fold being in a state of ignition. Having neither water nor light at my disposal, I was compelled to awaken Ḥájí Ṣafar, who was sleeping outside on the ground; and our united efforts soon succeeded in extinguishing the flames, but not till the greater part of the quilt had been consumed. Neither was this the only mischief done, for my coat and waistcoat had both suffered in greater or less degree, while the smoke and steam produced by the conflagration and its extinction filled the room, and rendered the atmosphere well nigh unbearable. I was thankful enough, however, to have escaped so lightly from the effects of my own carelessness, and, leaving the door open, and rolling myself up as best I could in the remnants of my bedding, was soon asleep again. Ḥájí Ṣafar, who, though at times self-willed and refractory, was never wanting in time of need, insisted, in spite of my remonstrances, in covering me with his cloak, which he could ill spare (the night being chilly), so that I enjoyed a greater measure of comfort than I deserved.

When I awoke in the morning all recollections of the disaster of the previous night were obliterated by the joyous thought that before the sun was down I should set foot in that city which, for seven years, it had been the chief ambition of my life to behold. Leaving Zargán, we had first to strike out into the plain to join the main road (remarkable for its excessive stoniness), which, crossing over a low pass, brought us to a building called *Báj-gáh* ("the Toll-House"), where customs' dues were formerly levied. I was surprised at the number of travellers whom we met—more, I think, than on any previous day's march since we quitted Trebizonde. Many of these were servants or messengers of the old or the new administration, but at all times the traffic between Zargán and Shíráz seems to be considerable. Beyond this there was little to attract my interest till, about 1.30, on surmounting another pass, Ḥájí Ṣafar cried out "*Ruknábád! Ruknábád!*" and, with a thrill of pleasure, I found myself at the source of that stream, so dear to every Shírází, of which Ḥáfiẓ declared, in perhaps the best known of his poems, that Paradise itself could not boast the like.

But for the rich associations which the sight of it evoked in my mind, I might perhaps have experienced that sense of disappointment with which Vámbéry declares he was affected by the first view of this classic stream. As it was, I saw nothing but the limpid water rushing from its rocky source; heard nothing but its melodious ripple; thought nothing but those thoughts which rise in the mind of one who first stands in the favourite haunt of an immortal bard who immortalises all that he touches. One often hears the expression, "I had heard so much of such-and-such a thing that when I saw it I was quite disappointed." This may happen in the case of objects admired or loved only for themselves, but not of those endeared by their associations. One does not love Ḥáfiẓ because he wrote of

Ruknábád: one loves Ruknábád because it was written of by Ḥáfiẓ.

In this pleasant spot I tarried for about an hour, eating my lunch under the shadow of one of the trees which stand by the edge of the stream. Again setting out, we came in about an hour to a building called *Khil'at-púshí*, where, as its name implies, governors of Shíráz, honoured by receiving such a distinction from the Sháh, come out to meet the bearers of the royal favours, and are invested with the robe of honour. Shortly after passing this spot we perceived a horseman advancing towards us, who proved to be the chief servant of my host, the Nawwáb Mírzá Ḥaydar 'Alí Khán. After presenting the Nawwáb's compliments and regrets that he had been unable himself to come out to welcome me by reason of the multitudinous social duties incidental to the *Nawrúz*, the servant turned his horse's head and led the way towards the city. We were, I gathered, quite close to it now, and I was so full of expectancy that I had but little inclination to talk. Suddenly we turned a corner, and in that moment—a moment of which the recollection will never fade from my mind—there burst upon my delighted gaze a view the like of which (in its way) I never saw.

We were now at that point, known to all students of Ḥáfiẓ, called *Tang-i-Alláhu Akbar*, because whoever first beholds Shíráz hence is constrained by the exceeding beauty of the sight to cry out in admiration "*Alláhu Akbar*"—"God is most great!" At our very feet, in a grassy, fertile plain girt with purple hills (on the loftier summits of which the snow still lingered), and half concealed amidst gardens of dark stately cypresses, wherein the rose and the judas-tree in luxuriant abundance struggled with a host of other flowers for the mastery of colour, sweet and beautiful in its garb of spring verdure which clothed the very roofs of the bazaars, studded with many a slender minaret, and many a turquoise-hued dome, lay the home of Persian culture, the mother of Persian genius, the sanctuary of poetry and philosophy, Shíráz. Riveted on this, and this alone, with an awe such as that wherewith the pilgrim approaches the shrine, with a delight such as that wherewith the exile again beholds his native land, my eyes scarcely marked the remoter beauties of the scene—the glittering azure of Lake Mahálú to the east, the interminable gardens of Masjid-Bardí to the west. Words cannot describe the rapture which overcame me as, after many a weary march, I gazed at length on the reality of that whereof I had so long dreamed, and found the reality not merely equal to, but far surpassing, the ideal which I had conceived. It is seldom enough in one's life that this occurs. When it does, one's innermost being is stirred with an emotion which baffles description, and which the most eloquent words can but dimly shadow forth.

From the Tang-i-Alláhu Akbar the road runs broad and straight to the gate of the city, to reach which a wide and well-built bridge spanning a river-bed (which, even in spring, contains comparatively little water except after heavy showers, and which in summer must be almost dry) is crossed. Descending this road, which at this festal season was enlivened by hundreds of pleasure-seekers, who, dressed in their best, had come out from the city to enjoy the fragrance of the air and the beauty of the fields, we first passed under the arch, in a chamber over which is preserved the great "Ḳur'án of 17 maunds" (*Ḳur'án-i-hafdah maní*), whereof it is fabled that a single leaf, if removed, would weigh as much as the whole volume. Lower down, just to the right of the road, Muṣallá, another favourite haunt of Ḥáfiẓ, was pointed out to me. The building which at present stands there is quite modern, and the "rose-walks," on which Ḥáfiẓ dwells so lovingly, have disappeared. To the left of the road were the gardens of *Ján-numá*, *Dil-gushá*, *Chahil-tan* and *Haft-tan*; beyond these were visible the cypresses which overshadow the grave of Ḥáfiẓ; while farther still the tomb of Sa'dí could just be discerned. To the right lay a multitude of other gardens of less note; everywhere the fresh grass clothed the plain with a robe of verdure such as is seen but rarely in Persia; while the soft spring air was laden with the perfume of a thousand flowers. I ceased to wonder at the rapturous enthusiasm wherewith the Shírází speaks of his native city, or to regard as an exaggeration far removed from the truth that verse of Sa'dí's which I have already quoted:—

"*Khushá tafarruj-i-Nawrúz, kháṣṣé dar Shíráz,*
Ki bar kanad dil-i-mard-i-musáfir az waṭanash."

"Pleasant is the New Year's outing, especially in Shíráz,
Which turns aside the heart of the wanderer from his native land."

Nay, in these "meadows set with slender galingale," in this "land where all things always seemed the same," I felt constrained to "fold my wings, and cease from wanderings"; almost as though a voice from the unseen had whispered them, there sounded in my ears the lines—

"Our island home
Is far beyond the wave; we will no longer roam."

A little before reaching the bridge which leads to the Iṣfahán gate, we turned to the right, and continued outside the city wall till we came to the "Gate of the King's Garden" (*Derwázé-i-Bágh-i-Sháh*), by which we entered. A short ride through the narrow, tortuous streets brought us at length to the house of my host, the Nawwáb. Dismounting at the gate, I was ushered into a large and handsome courtyard paved with stones and traversed by a little stream of clear water which flowed from a large square tank at the upper end. On either side of this stood a row of stately sycamores, interspersed with orange-trees, while a mass of beautiful flowers tastefully grouped lent brightness to the view and fragrance to the air.

As I stood here the Nawwáb himself came out to welcome me with that easy courtesy and unaffected hospitality wherein the Persians excel all other nations. Taking me by the hand, he led me into a room opening into the courtyard, where, as is customary at the New Year, and for the twelve days which succeed it (during which all work is laid aside, and paying and receiving congratulatory visits is the sole business of all), a multitudinous array of all manner of sweetmeats was laid out. The *samávar* (urn) hissing in a corner gave promise of the welcome tea, which did not delay to make its appearance. After I had partaken of two or three cups of this, and answered the usual questions concerning the friends I had left at Ṭeherán, the journey, and my health, the Nawwáb rose and conducted me to the rooms which, at the special request of his elder brother, the Nawwáb Mírzá Ḥasan 'Alí Khán (in whose house at Ṭeherán I had spent so pleasant and profitable a month), had been set apart for me. Pleasant and commodious as they were, and luxurious as they seemed after the hardships of the road, their chief charm in my eyes was that they had given shelter to poets whose names form the brightest ornament of modern Persian literature—poets amongst whom in sweetness, melody, wealth of metaphor, and purity of diction, the brilliant genius of Ḳá'ání stands unrivalled and unsurpassed.

CHAPTER X

SHÍRÁZ

"Dil mi-barand Ḳazvínián, shakar-laband Tabrízián,
Khúband Iṣfahánián, man banda-am Shíráz-rá."

"The Ḳazvínís steal our hearts, the Tabrízís have lips like sugar,
Beautiful are the Iṣfahánís, but I am the slave of Shíráz."

"Khushá Shíráz u vaz'-i-bí-miṣál-ash!
Khudávandá, nigah dár az zawál-ash!"

"Sweet is Shíráz and its incomparable site!
O God, preserve it from decline!"—(Ḥáfiẓ.)

TO the three weeks which I spent in Shíráz I look back with unmixed pleasure. The associations connected with it are familiar to every student of Persian; its natural beauties I have already feebly attempted to depict; its inhabitants are, amongst all the Persians, the most subtle, the most ingenious, the most vivacious, even as their speech is to this day the purest and most melodious.

For seeing all that was most worth seeing, mixing in the society of the town, and forming an estimate of its life and thought, I enjoyed rare facilities. Living as I did in the heart of the city, in the house of one universally respected, not merely as the representative of an ancient and noble family, but as a gentleman whose genial manners, enlightened views, and liberal patronage of talent, rendered him peculiarly fitted for the responsible post which he occupied of Agent to the British Government, I was enabled to move freely in circles to which I might otherwise have failed to gain access. For acquiring fluency in the Persian language also I had continual opportunities. My host, it is true, possessed some knowledge of English, but preferred to employ his own language in conversation; a preference which, it is needless to say, I was far from regretting; while few of the visitors, and none of the servants, with whom I came into daily contact, spoke anything but Persian.

Although the visitors who came to the house were numerous, there was, except my host (with whom, when no other engagement prevented it, I took my meals), but one constant guest at table. This was the Nawwáb's uncle, "*Ḥájí Dá'í*" ("Uncle Ḥájí"), as he was usually called for the sake of brevity, who had come from Fasá (where he habitually resided) to Shíráz on a New Year's visit. For him I conceived, after a while, a great liking and admiration, though at first unable to penetrate his unusual taciturnity. Except in this respect, he was a thorough Persian of the old school, in dress as in everything else, and I was never tired of admiring the scrupulous neatness of his appearance, or the beautiful brocade lining revealed by the backward turn of the cuffs of his *ḳabá*. As I have already said, he was sparing of words, but when he spoke it was to the point; while the interesting details concerning the country east of Shíráz which at times he would give me were enhanced by a peculiar piquancy of idiom and expressiveness of gesture which I have never seen equalled. Thus, for example, in speaking of the length of a stage between two places near Ḳum he remarked, "They call it seven *farsakhs*, but such a seven *farsakhs* as would burn the father of nine *farsakhs*" ("*hamchunín haf' farsakhí ki pidar-i-nuh farsakh-rá bi-súzánad*"); in answering my question as to whether the water in Lake Níríz was fresh or salt, he said, "So salt that I take refuge with God!" ("*chunán talkh ki penáh bar Khudá!*"); neither shall I ever forget the tone of the "*Estaghfiru'lláh!*" ("I ask pardon of God!") with which, in true Persian fashion, he would answer any question which he wished emphatically to negative.

Besides Ḥájí Dá'í there was but one of the Nawwáb's relatives resident in the house whom I often saw (for from the society of his sisters and other female relations I was naturally excluded). This was the son of my friend Áḳá Muḥammad Ḥasan Khán Ḳáshḳá'í, who, when he bade me farewell at Ṭeherán, had specially commended his boy to my notice. The latter, who was also the Nawwáb's nephew, came to pay me a visit a day or two after my arrival. He was a bright handsome lad of about twelve or thirteen years of age, and, though rather shy at first, soon became very friendly, and would eagerly listen to anything which I told him about my native land or my travels.

Of the Nawwáb's numerous servants one or two deserve some brief mention. Of these the chief was he who had come out to meet me on my first arrival, and who was indeed rather a steward than a servant. He had a brother, Shukru'lláh by name, who played with exquisite skill on the rebeck (*si-tár*), to the accompaniment of which he would also sing in a sweet melodious voice. The poor fellow was blind, and I shall never forget the pathos of his tones when, as I was seated one evening with the Nawwáb and a chance guest by the side of the stream in the courtyard under the moonlit plane-trees, he heard the former address me in an interval of the music as "*Ḥaḳím Ṣáḥib*," and eagerly exclaimed, "*Ḥaḳím!* did you say *ḥaḳím*, Master? Is our guest a physician? Can he not perhaps cure my blindness and enable me once more to behold the light?" And when the Nawwáb answered gently, "No, my poor fellow, he is a metaphysician (*ḥaḳím-i-iláhí*) rather than a physician (*ḥaḳím-i-ṭabí'í*); he can do nothing for you," it went to my heart to see the momentary expression of anxious hope which had crossed the face of the blind minstrel pass, through a quiver of disappointment, into the look of patient sadness which his countenance habitually wore.

Of all the servants, however, he with whom I had most to do, and indeed the only one with whom I habitually conversed much, was a black called *Elmás* ("Diamond"). He had been in the family, to which he was deeply attached, for many years, and had, I suppose, been born in Persia or brought thither when a child; at any rate he spoke Persian with no foreign accent which I could detect. To him was entrusted the duty of attending on me; he used to bring me my tea in the morning, announce meals or visitors, and often, when I was alone, would stop and talk for an hour at a time. A pious Musulmán, and extremely attentive to all the duties of his religion, he yet seemed quite free from that fanaticism and distrust of those belonging to other creeds with which piety is sometimes associated. Often he would talk to me of his master and his master's friends; of the noble families of Shíráz, its poets, its learned men, and its governors, especially Ferhád Mírzá, concerning whom he related many strange things; how he had hanged Sheykh Madhkúr on a lofty gibbet, after making him eat one of the coins he had struck in his own name; how he had put down Muḥammad Ṭáhir Gilladárí, who, from the fastness near Dárábjird where he dwelt, sallied forth to plunder caravans till none dared pass that way; how he had bricked-up alive a multitude of less notable outlaws by the side of the highways which had witnessed their depredations; and how, never forgetting the slight put upon him by the people of Shíráz when he was recalled from his first administration, he ever cherished towards the city and its inhabitants an unconquerable aversion.

Thoroughly imbued with the superstitions of the country, Elmás would sometimes talk of Jinnís, Ghúls, 'Ifríts, and other sprites and hobgoblins which are said to infest its desert places. One day, soon after my arrival, while crossing the courtyard with the Nawwáb on my way to lunch, I saw a strange sight. Lying on his back on the ground, with outstretched arms, legs raised in the air, and soles upturned to heaven as though to receive an invisible bastinado, was a man of the lower classes whom I did not recognise as one whom I had previously seen about the house. How he came there I know not, nor what ailed him; and when I asked my host he merely shook his head silently. As we continued to watch him, he suddenly gave a deep groan, and rolled over on his side with legs still flexed; whereupon Elmás, who had been standing quietly by, an unmoved spectator of the scene, approached him, and began to adopt the necessary measures for his revival. In the evening when Elmás came to my room I questioned him as to this strange occurrence.

"It was the Jinnís," he answered; "this man had doubtless offended them, and therefore do they torment him thus."

"In what way do men offend the Jinnís?" I asked.

"In many ways," replied Elmás, "as, for instance, by throwing a stone without first giving them warning by exclaiming '*Bismi-'lláhi'r-Raḥmáni'r-Raḥím*' ('in the name of God the Merciful, the Clement'). In such cases the stone may strike an invisible Jinní and blind him or otherwise cause him injury; such injury the Jinnís never forgive, but continue at intervals to inflict chastisement on the offender, even as you saw to-day."

I then proceeded to tell Elmás the stories I had heard from the muleteers in the Valley of the Angel of Death about the various hobgoblins whose favourite haunt it is supposed to be. With most of these he acquiesced, but of the Nasnás he gave a somewhat different account.

"It does not injure people"; he said, "it is of a playful disposition, and contents itself with frightening. For instance, a man was riding between Shíráz and Bushire when he saw what he took to be a lamb by the roadside. He picked it up and placed it in front of him across his saddlebow. After he had gone some distance, he chanced to glance down on it, and saw with terror and amazement that it had grown and grown in length till its head and tail trailed on the ground on either side of the horse: whereat, being greatly alarmed, he cast the thing from him and galloped off as hard as he could. These are the sort of pranks the Nasnás delights to play; but, so far as I have heard, it never inflicts more serious injury."

One morning, a day or two after my arrival, Elmás announced to me that Mírzá Farhang, with his brother Mírzá Yezdání (both poets of note, and sons of the celebrated poet Wiṣál), were below and desired to see me. Anxious to make the acquaintance of two of the most talented men in Shíráz, from a perusal of whose poetry (which, though perhaps scarcely equal to that of their elder brother, Mírzá Dávarí, now deceased, is extremely fine) I had already derived much pleasure, I hastened down to greet my illustrious visitors. Mírzá Yezdání was accompanied by his son, and the son of another of his brothers (also deceased), who wrote under the name of Himmat. My conversation was entirely with the elder poets, chiefly with Mírzá Farhang; for however talented a son may be, and however honoured, it is contrary to Persian custom and etiquette for him to speak much in the presence of his father. I was greatly impressed with the appearance and manners of my talented visitors, especially with those of Mírzá Farhang, to whose conversation an unusual breadth of knowledge and quickness of apprehension, combined with a soft voice and gentle unassuming manner, lent an irresistible charm. Poetry and philosophy naturally formed the chief topics of discussion; concerning the philosophy of the Hindús, and the method employed in deciphering the cuneiform inscriptions, Mírzá Farhang manifested a special interest. The time passed all too quickly, and I was equally surprised and sorry when the visitors, declaring that they had already outstayed the ordinary limits of a morning call, rose to go.

To the European doctor who had embraced Islám I have already alluded. I was naturally anxious to see him, and learn what causes had induced him to take this step. This at first appeared to be more difficult than I had supposed, for he seemed to dislike meeting other Europeans, though whether this arose from fear of being made the object of reproaches, or from a feigned fanaticism, I could not learn. At length, after several disappointments, business brought him to the Nawwáb's house, and he sent up a message by Ḥájí Ṣafar that he would be glad to pay me a visit if I was disengaged. I at once sent word that I should be pleased to see him if he would come up, and in a few minutes he entered the room. The Persian dress which he had adopted did not appear to sit easily on him, and harmonised ill with his personal appearance, which was anything but Oriental; neither did he seem to have become accustomed to his new part, for, on entering the room, he removed his lamb-skin hat, revealing hair cut in the Persian fashion, the natural reddish hue of which had been heightened rather than concealed by the henna with which it had been dyed. Thinking it unwise to question him at once on the causes which had led him to change his creed, I asked him concerning his adventures and travels. He informed me in reply that, having completed his medical studies at one of the large London hospitals, he had taken a post as surgeon on board an emigrant ship, in which capacity he had visited America, China, India, and Australia. After many wanderings and adventures, including a quarrel in the gold-fields wherein he had received a shot in the arm (the scar of which he showed me), he had finally arrived at Jedda. While he was residing there (according to his account) a message came that the Sheríf of Mecca had been wounded with a knife in the abdomen, and desired the services of a European surgeon, if such were obtainable. Accordingly he proceeded thither, and treated the wound of his distinguished patient so successfully that in a short time it was cured, and the Sheríf, moved by gratitude to his preserver, not only allowed him to remain at Mecca during the Pilgrimage, but also permitted him to visit Medina. The ceremonies of the Ḥajj, especially the "stoning the devil" at 'Arafát, and the sacrifice of sheep at Miná, he described in detail; of the latter he spoke with mingled disgust and amazement, declaring that the ground was literally covered with innumerable carcases of slaughtered animals, which were, for the most part, left to rot and poison the atmosphere with their noisome stench. From

Mecca he had returned to Jedda, and thence by Bushire to Shíráz, where he had resided three or four months as a medical practitioner.

"I am tired of this place now," he said in conclusion, "and as I have seen everything worth seeing in the city, including Sháh Chirágh and the other mosques (to which, I suppose, you have not been able to gain access), I intend to move on somewhere else. Where are you going when you leave?"

"Yezd and Kirmán," I answered, wondering inwardly if he would propose to accompany me, a plan to which, for several reasons, I should have refused to consent; "and you?"

"I think that will be about my line of country," he replied. "I want to get to Mashhad, whence I shall return home, for I am tired of wanderings and adventures, and would like to see my old mother again, who must be wondering at my long absence, if, indeed, she be not anxious on my account."

At this moment a young friend of mine, with whom I had first become acquainted some years before in Europe, and whom I shall henceforth designate as Mírzá 'Alí, entered the room, accompanied by an aged Seyyid. As I knew the latter to be not only a follower but a relation of the Báb, and as the renegade doctor was accompanied by an individual professedly devoted to the Ṣúfí philosophy and styling himself *Murshid* (spiritual director), who was bitterly opposed to the new religion, I became very uneasy lest some collision should occur between my visitors. Such ill-timed encounters fill us with anxiety even in England, where self-restraint and avoidance of dangerous topics are inculcated on all: in Persia, where religious questions form one of the most usual subjects of conversation, where religious feeling is so strong, the passion for discussion so great, and caution so scanty, they become positively dreadful, and I would almost as lief carry a lighted brand through a powder magazine as assist again at some of those terrible *réunions* at which (especially in Kirmán) it was my fate—I can hardly say my privilege—to be present.

On this occasion, however, my worst apprehensions were not destined to be fulfilled, though the direction given to the conversation by Mírzá 'Alí kept them fully alive till the doctor and his companion departed, leaving the field to the Bábís. It was, of course, necessary that I should introduce my Muḥammadan compatriot to the newcomers; I hesitated whether to style him by the name which he had adopted on changing his creed, or by that which he had previously borne. Eventually I chose the latter course.

"May I introduce to you Dr ——," I said, "if, as it appears, you have not already made his acquaintance?"

"If I have not met him I have heard about him," answered Mírzá 'Alí; then, turning to the renegade, "What evil did you see in your own religion," said he, "or what good in Islám, that you have abandoned that for this? You, who appear to me to speak Persian but indifferently, do you know enough Arabic to understand the Ḳur'án?"

The object of this somewhat scornful address replied that he had read a translation of the sacred book.

"Translation!" exclaimed Mírzá 'Alí with ill-concealed contempt, "and pray what particular passage or doctrine so commended itself to you that you became convinced of the divine origin of Islám? For of course you had some strong reason for casting aside the faith in which you were born."

The other muttered something about "liking the whole thing," "being a Voltairian who regarded Christian and Muḥammadan as one and the same," and "doing at Rome as Rome does,"—to all of which his interrogator vouchsafed no reply but a short laugh and a silence more chilling than words. The situation was painful and constrained in the extreme, and I was sincerely thankful when it was brought to an end by the departure of the discomfited doctor and his ally *Murshid*.

The latter was present at another similarly ill-assorted gathering which chanced in the same room a few days later. On that occasion he was accompanied by another friend, whom he introduced as a profound philosopher, but whom the Bábís described subsequently as a notorious atheist (*lá-madhhab*). They had hardly entered when they were followed by two of my Bábí friends, one of whom was a zealous propagandist and missionary of the sect, the friend, fellow-worker, and companion in numerous hardships of him whom I had met in the house of the *dallál* at Iṣfahán. Though he was only a temporary resident at Shíráz, which he has since quitted, I do not consider it advisable to mention his real name, and (since I shall have occasion to allude to him repeatedly) shall henceforth designate him as Ḥájí Mírzá Ḥasan. His companion was a young Seyyid, well known as a zealous partisan of the new religion. Although, fortunately, no overt passage of arms took place (the Bábís, as before, being soon left in complete possession of the field), *Murshid's* suspicions were aroused by meeting notorious Bábís in my room on each of the two occasions on which he had visited me. A few days before I left Shíráz I was informed by a young Armenian gentleman with whom I was pretty intimate that *Murshid*, who was assisting him in his studies, had sent me a special message warning me against Ḥájí Mírzá Ḥasan, and assuring me that I should do well to be more careful in choosing my associates, as a report (probably originated by himself) had got about Shíráz that I had become, or was on the point of becoming, a Bábí. To this caution it is almost needless to say that I paid no attention, being amused rather than disquieted by this absurd rumour; indeed, I confess that I considered myself honoured rather than insulted by being identified with a body which can boast of a past so heroic.

This was not the first warning which *Murshid* had given me on this point. The occasion of his first attempt to alienate me from his enemy, Ḥájí Mírzá Ḥasan, affords an example of that extraordinary readiness in divining one's train of thought frequently possessed by the Persians, concerning which Vámbéry says that it often caused him the most lively disquietude when, in dervish habit, he was pursuing his adventurous journey to Turkistán. To explain how the occasion in question arose, it is necessary to make a digression, and go back to the circumstances which first made me acquainted with *Murshid.*

My young Armenian friend (who, though born in Persia, had received an English education in Bombay, and spoke my native language at least as fluently as his own) was extremely kind in taking me to see whatever was of interest in the neighbourhood. Indeed, but for his good-nature my stay at Shíráz would have been much less entertaining and profitable than it actually was, and many places of interest to which he guided me would have remained unvisited. One day he asked me if I should like to accompany him on a visit to some distinguished Persian friends of his.

"I came to know them through my Mírzá (*Murshid*)," said he, "and as I must go and see them to offer them my congratulations for the New Year, I thought you might like to accompany me. They are of royal blood, being descended from the *Farmán-farmá*, who was the eldest son of Fatḥ 'Alí Sháh, and a man of great consequence and some literary attainments[1]. If you care to come, I am sure that they will be pleased to see you."

Of course I readily agreed to the proposition, being always eager to enlarge my knowledge of Persian society. Accordingly, in the afternoon I accompanied my Armenian friend to the house of his aristocratic acquaintances, who received us very

1 He wrote several works, including the *Shíráz-námé* ("Book of Shíráz"), *Kitáb-i-Dilgushá* ("Book of Dilgushá," or "Book expanding the Heart") and *Safínatu'n-Naját* ("Ark of Salvation"), ruled Shíráz and the province of Fárs for nearly forty years, and adorned the former with the garden called *Bágh-i-Naw.* His daughter was the mother of the late Nawwáb Muḥammad-Ḳulí Khán, whose sons my new acquaintances were. These details were given me by *Murshid*, who professed himself devoted to the family, at whose house he was a constant guest.

hospitably, and urged us to partake of the tea, *ḳalyáns*, sweetmeats, and other delicacies which, conformably to Persian custom at this festal season, were set before us in unstinted profusion. I was surprised to see amongst these a dish of dried prawns, which, I was informed, are brought from the Persian Gulf. They are called in Persian *meygú*, and are esteemed a luxury, though, in my opinion, undeservedly.

The Princes were very curious to know what had brought me to Persia, how I liked Shíráz, and how I was in the habit of travelling. They affected great surprise on learning that I had no horse of my own, and had only hired three animals from a *chárvádár*. I met their expressed astonishment and implied contempt not by an argument (which I knew would be useless), but by an apologue.

"I have read in some book," I remarked, "that the great philosopher Diogenes used continually to decry the luxury which he saw around him, declaring that for him three things sufficed as furniture and clothing: the cloak wherewith he covered his nakedness, the staff wherewith he supported his steps, and the cup wherewith he quenched his thirst. Now one day, as he was drawing near to a stream to drink, he saw a child bending down over it, and raising the water to its lips by means of its hands, which it had placed together to form a cup. When Diogenes saw this, he threw away the cup which he carried, and cried out, 'Alas! alas! for years I have been inveighing against unnecessary luxury, and all the while I carried with me an encumbrance of which this child has taught me the uselessness!' The moral of this is obvious, to wit, that what is really indispensable to us is but little."

"*Wah! wah!*" replied my hosts, "that is indeed *tajarrud*" (freedom from worldly ties): "we have only the name; you have the reality."

Harmony being thus happily restored, I was taken to see a room, the walls of which were adorned with family portraits and paintings illustrative of scripture history. The portraits, of which my friends seemed justly proud, included one of Fatḥ 'Alí Sháh, very finely executed; one of the grandfather of my hosts; and one of their uncle. The scripture subjects were four: Moses and the Burning Bush; Abraham offering up Ishmael (according to the version of this event given in the Ḳur'án); Joseph taking leave of Jacob; and Christ with the Virgin Mary. While examining these works of art (which, indeed, well deserved attentive consideration) sundry little giggles of laughter and whisperings, proceeding from behind a carved wooden screen occupying the upper portion of the wall on one side of the room, caused me to glance in that direction, where several pairs of bright eyes, just visible through the interstices of the woodwork, left no doubt in my mind that the ladies of the harem were making merry at my expense.

Before I left, my hosts exacted from me a promise that I would accompany them, on a day subsequently to be fixed, to an old ruin called *Ḳaṣr-i-Abú-Na r*, situated some miles to the east of Shíráz, which they declared to be equal in age to Persepolis. The day fixed for this excursion was that succeeding the morning which had witnessed the encounter between *Murshid* and the Bábís, in my room. The time was afternoon. The party consisted of *Murshid*, my Armenian friend, and myself, together with our hosts, the princes, and one or two servants.

We left Shíráz by the gate of the slaughter-house (*Derwáẓé-i-ḳaṣṣáb-ḳháné*), somewhat appropriately so named, as it seemed to me; for just outside it, on either side of the road, was a double series of pillars of mortar, ten or twelve in number, each of which had formed the living tomb of an outlaw. There they stood, more or less disintegrated and destroyed, exposing here and there a whitened bone, to bear grim testimony to the rigour of the redoubtable Ferhád Mírzá.

Turning my back on these dismal relics, as well as on the tomb of Sheykh Rúz-bihán, a saint of some repute, I rode slowly forward with *Murshid.* A pause occurring in the course of conversation, I said, more for the sake of making a remark than anything else:

"I heard rather a curious expression the other day."

"Did you?" replied *Murshid*, "what was it?"

Now the expression in question was "ass's head" (in Arabic, *ra'su'l-ḥimár*; in Persian, *sar-i-khar*), which signifies one whose presence in an assembly prevents free and unrestrained conversation. Though I had indeed heard it from the Bábís, and though it most happily described the position of *Murshid* in my room on the previous day, it had not been applied to him, though a train of thought, of which I was myself unconscious, undoubtedly prompted me to make this unhappy and very *mal-à-propos* remark.

"'*Ra'su'l-ḥimár*,'" I answered, without reflection.

Murshid did not fail to detect a sequence in my thought of which I myself was quite unaware.

"Yes," said he, somewhat grimly, "a very curious expression; generally used in its Persian form, '*sar-i-khar*.' From whom did you hear it?"

"Oh," I replied in some confusion, "I am not sure—I have almost forgotten—That is, a friend of mine——"

"—was kind enough to apply it to me when I so inopportunely broke in upon your little private conference."

I attempted to stammer a disavowal, feeling extremely annoyed with myself for the folly of which I had been guilty, and yet half amused at the readiness with which a cap that fitted so remarkably well had been snatched up. *Murshid* paid no heed to my explanations.

"As you are so fond of metaphysics," he remarked severely, gazing straight before him the while, "you have no doubt studied the *Masnaví* of Mawláná Jalálu'd-Dín Rúmí, and may perhaps remember these lines, which I would in any case strongly commend to your attention—

'Chún basí iblís-i-ádam-rúy hast,
Pas bi-har dastí na-sháyad dád dast.'

'Since there are many devils in the guise of men,
One should not give one's hand into every hand.'"

"I am sure I hope there are not many such human devils in Shíráz," I exclaimed.

"On the contrary," he answered shortly, "in Shíráz they are particularly abundant."

The subject dropped, but it took some time to smooth the ruffled feelings of my companion. Indeed, I am not sure that I ever regained his goodwill, or succeeded in obliterating the remembrance of my unhappy remark.

Except for this incident the excursion was a very pleasant one, though we halted so long in two gardens belonging to the Princes (who were much more bent on a good ride, and a quiet tea and smoke under the trees of their heritages, than on antiquarian research) that we had very little time left to examine the *Ḳaṣr-i-Abú-Naṣr.* It is quite a small enclosure surrounded by stones, carved with a few bas-reliefs like those at Persepolis, but devoid of inscriptions. Whether these undoubtedly ancient stones were originally placed in their present position I do not know; but one does not see what object can have induced anyone to bring them there from Persepolis or Dárábjird. Of the four doorways which the building possessed, only one is standing, the other three having fallen, in consequence of "excavations" undertaken at the command of Ferhád Mírzá. The faces of the beautiful great figures cut in bas-relief on the stones of the gateway have, like some of those at Persepolis, been wilfully destroyed. On one of the fallen stones, however, is a bas-relief representing a procession of captives or slaves laden with presents, which is almost uninjured.

Small as the extent of this interesting spot was, I had not time to examine it satisfactorily. The sun was close to the horizon when we reached the ruins, and had now completely disappeared from view. It was high time to direct our steps towards the city with all haste, if we did not desire to be benighted in the open plain. As it was, we nearly lost our way several times, and only regained the city after blundering through marshes and streams innumerable towards the twinkling lights which marked its situation.

The badness of the road prevented us all riding together, and I found myself, during the greater part of the way, next one of the princes. After he had exhaustively questioned me concerning the amount of my income, the sources whence it was derived, my occupation, my object in visiting Persia, and the like, he expressed a great desire to travel in Europe.

"Do you think I could find any employment in England?" he asked.

"It would not be easy," I answered, "for our country is already over-full, and many are compelled to emigrate. Besides, you do not know our language. If you did come, I doubt if you would like it after the novelty was gone. Why should you desire to leave Shíráz? Your lot seems to me very enviable: you have a beautiful house, numerous horses and servants, gardens and villages such as we have visited to-day, and all this in one of the fairest spots I have ever seen. What motive can you possibly have for desiring to leave all this?"

"I am tired of the useless and aimless life we are compelled to lead here," he replied; "every day it is the same thing:—in the morning we read or practise calligraphy till lunch; afterwards we sleep for an hour or two; then we have tea and smoke *ḳalyáns*; then—unless we have visitors—we go for a ride or walk; then supper and bed. It is wearisome."

"Could you not obtain some definite employment from the Government here?" I demanded.

"The Government would not employ us," he answered, "just because we are of royal descent. Is it so in your country? Is high birth there an impediment to promotion? But they are distrustful of us because we are of kingly race. They prefer to employ persons of lowly origin, whom they can chastise for any fault. But suppose it were us, suppose we were to neglect our work or help ourselves to the public money, they could not punish us because we are so distinguished (*mutashakhkhiṣ*). So they decline to employ us at all."

This was the longest excursion which I made while resident in Shíráz. Indeed the objects of interest in the immediate vicinity of the city are so numerous that it is not necessary to go far afield. Of some of these it is time to speak briefly.

Of course the tombs of Ḥáfiẓ and Sa'dí first attracted my footsteps; indeed I would have visited them the first day after my arrival had it been possible, and was unable to rest till I had done so. Before speaking of them in detail it will be well to give the reader some idea of the relative situations of the various places which I shall notice.

Most of these lie to the north of the city. Let the reader, therefore, suppose himself to have followed the Iṣfahán road (already partially described at the end of the preceding chapter) for about a mile and a half, and to have ascended the rise leading to the *Tang-i-Alláhu Akbar*. Spanning this at its narrowest point is the arch on which rests the *ḳur'án-i-hafdah mani* already mentioned. Close to this, on the western side of the road, is a raised platform called *Mashriḳeyn*, on which is a little pleasure-garden and coffee-house commanding a fine view. On the opposite side of the valley, a little above the bottom, along which flows the stream of *Ruḳnábád*, is another building standing on a platform. This is called *Takht-i-Niẓám*, and is a celebrated resort of gamblers and dice-players. On the summit of the hill above this (*i.e.* the hill to the east of the *Tang*) is a curious little brick building called *Kehváré-i-Dív* ("the Demon's Cradle"), probably by reason of two horn-like projections from the roof.

Here we pause, and, looking southward towards the city, enjoy a magnificent view, bisected, as it were, by the broad white line formed by the road along which we came from the town to the *Tang-i-Alláhu Akbar*. Let us first consider the objects of interest which lie to the east of this. The chief of these, beginning with the remotest, are as follows:—

The *Sa'diyyé* (Tomb of Sa'dí) standing somewhat apart from the gardens scattered in such rich profusion in the plain below us. It lies at the foot of the hills, half concealed in a little valley which runs into them at this place, and is not conspicuous from most points of view.

The *Ḥáfiẓiyyé* (Tomb of Ḥáfiẓ), far more popular and better cared for, rendered conspicuous by its tall dark cypresses and white walls.

Chahil-tan ("Forty bodies"), and *Haft-tan* ("Seven bodies"), pleasant shady groves interspersed with commodious buildings, which afford a quiet retreat to those who, wearied of worldly cares, adopt the calm life of the dervish.

Then come the gardens, amongst which two are conspicuous—

Bágh-i-Dilgushá, the favourite haunt of the Ṣáḥib-Díván; and—

Bágh-i-Ján-numá, situated close to the road.

This completes what we may call the "eastern hemisphere" of our panorama, with the exception of the *Cháh-i-Murtaẓá 'Alí* ("'Alí's well"), situated on another summit of the hills behind and to the east of our place of outlook, the *Kehváré-i-Dív*. Of this I shall speak presently.

Let us now turn to the "western hemisphere." Crossing the road from the *Bágh-i-Ján-numá* just mentioned, we come to another very fine garden, the *Bágh-i-Naw*[1].

Some distance to the north-west of this, farther from the road and on the slopes of the hills, is the splendid but neglected *Bágh-i-Takht* ("Garden of the Throne"), conspicuous for the white terraces and buildings which stand at its farther end, looking towards the city over avenues of judas-trees (*erghaván*).

1 See footnote on p. 297, *supra*.

Beyond and above this, perched half-way up the mountain side, stands a small white edifice surrounded by a few cypresses. This is called *Bábá Kúhí*.

The whole plain is dotted with gardens, but on the slopes of the hills which bound it towards the west, overlooked by the dazzling summit of the *Kúh-i-Barf* ("Snow Mountain"), there is a compact mass of them extending for several miles. This is *Masjid-Bardí*.

Amongst the gardens west of the city are two belonging to my host the Nawwáb. The nearer of these is called *Bágh-i-Sheykh*, and the pleasant dwellings situated therein are occupied by the English members of the telegraph staff, the Superintendent, and the Doctor, while their Armenian colleagues dwell in the town. The farther one, distant perhaps two or three miles from the city, is situated close to the river-bed, on its northern side. It is called *Rashk-i-Bihisht* ("the Envy of Paradise"). Two pleasant picnics in this charming spot (of which the second was brought to an untimely end, so far as I was concerned, by an event which cut short my stay at Shíráz and altered all my plans) will be spoken of presently.

Having now given a general, and, I hope, a sufficiently clear account of the topography of Shíráz, I shall proceed to notice some of the places above-mentioned in greater detail, beginning with the tombs of Ḥáfiẓ and Sa'dí.

Both of these, together with the *Bágh-i-Dilgushá*, I visited on the same day, in company with one of the Nawwáb's servants. Though they are within an easy walk of the town, one of the Nawwáb's horses was placed at my disposal. It was a most beautiful animal, and the play of the muscles under its glossy skin gave token of great power, which, accompanied as it was by a display of freshness and spirit ("play," as the Persians admiringly call it), was to me a source rather of anxiety than of gratification. I would greatly have preferred to walk, but it is hard to persuade a Persian that one prefers walking to riding, and I was constrained to accept an offer which was kindly intended.

The tomb of Ḥáfiẓ occupies the centre of an enclosed garden beautifully planted with cypresses and orange-trees. It is marked by a simple oblong block of stone, engraved with inscriptions consisting for the most part of quotations from the poet's works. At the top is the following sentence in Arabic:—

"HUWA'L-BÁḲÍ WA KULLU SHEY'in HÁLIK."

"HE (*i.e.* GOD) IS THE ENDURING, AND ALL ELSE PASSETH AWAY."

Beneath this is the ode beginning—

"*Muzhdé-i-waṣl-i-tú kú? K'az sar-i-ján bar khízam;*
Ṭá'ir-i-ḳuds-am, va az dám-i-jihán bar khízam."

"Where is the good tidings of union with Thee? for I will rise up with my whole heart;
I am a bird of Paradise, and I will soar upwards from the snare of the world."

Round the edge of the stone is inscribed the ode beginning—

"*Ey dil, ghulám-i-sháh-i-jihán básh, ú sháh básh!*
Peyvasté dar ḥimáyat-i-luṭf-i-Iláh básh!"

"O heart, be the slave of the King of the World, and be a king!
Abide continually under the protection of God's favour!"

Written diagonally across the two triangular spaces formed by the upper corners of the tombstone is the couplet—

"*Bar sar-i-turbat-i-má chún guzarí himmat khwáh,*
Ki ziyárat-gah-i-rindán-i-jihán khwáhad shud."

"When thou passest by the head of our tomb, invoke a blessing,
For it will be the place of pilgrimage of (all) the libertines of the world."

The corresponding spaces at the lower end of the tablet bear the well-known lines composed to commemorate the date of the poet's death:—

"*Chirágh-i-ahl-i-ma'ná Kh'ájé Ḥáfiẓ,*
[*Ki sham'í búd az núr-i-tajallí,*
Chú dar khák-i-Muṣallá sákht manzil]
Bi-jú táríkh-ash az 'KHÁK-I-MUṢALLÁ.'"

"That Lamp of the mystics, Master Ḥáfiẓ,
[Who was a candle of light from the Divine Effulgence,
Since he made his abode in the Earth of Muṣallá]
Seek his date from 'the Earth of Muṣallá.'"[1]

The unequalled popularity still enjoyed by Ḥáfiẓ is attested by the multitude of graves which surround his tomb. What Persian, indeed, would not desire that his ashes should mingle with those of the illustrious bard from whom contemporary fanaticism would fain have withheld the very rites of sepulture?

More remote from the city, and marked by a much humbler edifice, lies the grave of Sa'dí. Popular—and deservedly popular—as his *Gulistán* and *Bústán* are, alike for the purity of style, richness of diction, variety of matter, and sententious wisdom which characterise them, in Persia itself his *Díván* is probably more widely read and more highly esteemed. Indeed it may be questioned whether in his own country his odes are not as much admired, as ardently studied, and as often quoted as those of Ḥáfiẓ. But over his memory lies a shadow sufficient to account for the fact that few, if any, of his countrymen have cared to share his last resting-place, and that his grave stands alone in the little enclosure. Sa'dí, it is generally believed, was a Sunní; and whether it be true, as some of his admirers assert, that in professing this form of belief he merely practised the concealment of his real convictions (*ketmán*) authorised by Shí'ite ethics whenever considerations of personal safety appear to require it, the suspicion that he was really an adherent of this sect, so odious to every Shí'ite Persian, was sufficiently strong to impel a fanatical *Mujtahid* of Shíráz to destroy the tombstone originally erected over the poet's grave. The present stone was set up at the expense, and by the orders, of the Ḳiwám—the father of the

1 Only the first and last of these four lines are given on the tombstone, the intermediate ones having probably been omitted for lack of space. Each letter of the Arabic alphabet has a numerical value (these values ranging through the units, tens, and hundreds to one thousand), and the words "*Khák-i-Muṣallá*" ("Earth of Muṣallá") are numerically equivalent to [A.H.] 791 (= A.D. 1389).

Ṣáḥib-Díván. It bears the same Arabic inscription, testifying to the transitoriness of all things but God, as that which is engraved on the tomb of Ḥáfiẓ. Below this are engraved the opening lines of that canto of the *Búsṭán* written in praise of the Prophet.

At the *Ḥáfiẓiyyé* I had been unable to see the copy of the poet's works kept there for purposes of divination and augury, as the guardian of the shrine (*mutawallí*) was engaged in performing his devotions. At the *Sa'diyyé* I was more fortunate; the *mutawallí* was disengaged, and readily produced the manuscript of the complete works (*kulliyyát*) of the poet. It is very well written, and beautifully ornamented, but not old, for it dates only from the reign of Karím Khán the Zend (*c.* A.D. 1770). Twelve pages, which had been destroyed or lost, have been replaced by the skilful hand of Mírzá Farhang, the poet.

The Garden of Dilgushá, whither I proceeded on leaving the *Sa'diyyé*, is very beautiful, with its tanks of clear water, avenues of orange-trees, and variety of flowers. The gardener brought me a present of wall-flowers (*kheyrí*), and I entered into conversation with him. He said that the Ṣáḥib-Díván, to whom it had belonged, had been passionately attached to it, and that the thought of abandoning it to strangers, who might neglect it or injure its beauty, had added the sharpest sting to the humiliation of his dismissal. That the Ṣáḥib-Díván was a bad administrator I have no doubt, but he was not cruel, and this love for his garden appears to me a pleasing trait in his character. Indeed, one cannot help pitying the old man, dismissed from the office he had so long held, and recalled from his beloved Shíráz to the capital, to meet the doubtful mood of a despot, while the name he left behind served as the butt whereon the poetaster and the satirist might exercise their wit till such time as a new object of scorn and derision should present itself. For it is not only the graceful and melodious lays of Ḥáfiẓ, Sa'dí, or Ḳá'ání, which, accompanied by the soft strains of the *si-tár* and the monotonous beat of the *dunbak*, delight the joyous revellers who drink the wine of Khullar under the roses bordering some murmuring streamlet; interspersed with these are rhymes which, if less lofty, seldom fail to awaken the applause of the listeners. We are apt to think of the Persians as an entirely sedate, grave, and almost melancholy people; philosophers, often pessimist, seldom mirthful. Such a type does indeed exist, and exists in plenty. Yet amongst all Orientals the Persians are perhaps those whose idea of humour most nearly approaches our own, those in whom the sense of the ludicrous is most highly developed. One is amazed at the ready repartees, brilliant sallies of wit, bon-mots, and "chaff" which fly about on all sides in a convivial gathering of Persian literary men.

"'Chaff,'" the reader may exclaim, "is it possible that the compatriots of 'Omar Khayyám can condescend to 'chaff'?"

Not only is it possible, but very far from unusual; more than this, there is a very rich vocabulary of slang, of which the existence would hardly be suspected by the student of Persian literature. This is not all. The Persians have a multitude of songs—ephemeral, of course, and not to be bought in the book-shops—which, if they are not comic, are most decidedly topical. These compositions are called *taṣníf*, and their authors, for the most part, modestly—perhaps wisely—prefer to remain anonymous.

In such lampoons, in words devoid of ambiguity, and with a frankness bordering on brutality, were the faults and failings of the Ṣáḥib-Díván held up to ridicule and obloquy. I only remember a few lines of one of the most popular of these songs. They ran as follows:—

"*Dilgushá-rá sákht zír-i-sursurak,*
Dilgushá-rá sákht bá chúb ú falak,
Ḥeyf-i-Dilgushá!
Ḥeyf-i-Dilgushá!"

"He made Dilgushá under the 'Slide,'[1]
He made Dilgushá with the sticks and pole[2],
Alas for Dilgushá!
Alas for Dilgushá!"

From all that I have said it will be sufficiently evident that the Ṣáḥib-Díván was extremely unpopular with the Shírázís. Perhaps his own misdeeds were not the sole cause of this unpopularity. The memory of the black treachery of his ancestor, Ḥájí Ibráhím Khán, may be answerable to some extent for the detestation in which he was held. The story of this treachery is briefly as follows:—

On the death of Karím Khán, the noble and chivalrous prince of the Zend dynasty, and the succession of the no less noble, no less chivalrous, but far more unfortunate Luṭf 'Alí Khán, Ḥájí Ibráhím Khán was retained by the latter in the influential position which he had previously occupied. So far from suspecting that one attached to him and his family by every bond of gratitude could meditate his betrayal, Luṭf 'Alí Khán reposed the fullest confidence in his unworthy minister, and entrusted to him those powers which rendered possible an act of infamy as hateful as the tyrant in whose service it was done. The fortune of the Zend was already on the decline: already the tide of battle had turned against him, and Shíráz had awakened from a dream of happiness to find the Ḳájár bloodhounds baying beneath her walls. Then Ḥájí Ibráhím Khán conceived the diabolical idea of securing his own safety and wealth by selling his kind master to a foe as implacable as he was cruel, as mean in spirit as he was hideous in aspect. Áḳá Muḥammad Khán readily accepted

1 The "Slide" (*sursurak*) is a smooth incline on the hillside to the east of the *Tang-i-Alláhu Akbar* above the garden of *Dilgushá*.

2 "The sticks and pole," *i.e.* the bastinado. The pole in question is employed to retain the ankles of the culprit during the infliction of the punishment. It is simple in construction, consisting merely of a straight piece of wood pierced towards the middle by two holes a short distance apart, through which is passed a loop of rope. This loop, thrown round the ankles of the victim, and made taut by a few turns, renders flinching impossible.

the traitor's services, promising in return for these that so long as he lived Ibráhím Khán should be honoured and protected. So one night the gates of Shíráz were opened to the usurper; and it was only by heroic efforts that Luṭf 'Alí Khán succeeded in escaping for the time from his cruel enemy, and, cutting his way through all who sought to bar his progress, fled eastwards towards Kirmán.

Áḳá Muḥammad Khán kept his word to the letter. So long as he lived, Ḥájí Ibráhím Khán was loaded with favours. But when the tyrant felt his last hour approaching, he called to his side his successor, Fatḥ 'Alí Sháh, and addressed him in words to this effect:—

"As soon as I am dead, and you are established on the throne which I have won, let your first act be to extirpate, root and branch, the family of Ḥájí Ibráhím Khán. I swore to him that, as a reward for his treachery, I would protect and honour him *as long as I lived.* This oath I have faithfully kept; but when I am dead it will be no longer binding. Therefore I counsel you to be rid of the traitor and all his brood, for one who did not scruple to betray a master who had shown him nothing but kindness will certainly not hesitate to do the same again should opportunity offer. Let not one of that accursed family remain, for truly has the poet said—

'*'Áḳibat gurg-zádé gurg shavad,*
Garché bá ádamí buzurg shavad.'

'At length the wolf-cub will become a wolf,
Even though it grow up amongst men.'

Let no compunction stay your hand; let no false clemency tempt you to disobey my dying injunctions."

Fatḥ 'Alí Sháh had no sooner mounted the throne than he proceeded to execute the last behest of his predecessor. From all parts of the empire the descendants of the traitor to whom the new king owed his undisputed supremacy were sought out. Perhaps, when he had in some measure slaked his thirst for blood, Fatḥ 'Alí Sháh remembered that the black sin which he was now visiting on the innocent progeny of the criminal had after all been perpetrated in his interests and for the consolidation of his power. At any rate, he so far mitigated the rigour of his instructions as to spare some few of the doomed family after they had been deprived of their eyesight and otherwise mutilated. Only one, whose tender years moved the compassion of the executioners, escaped unharmed. That one was the father of the Ṣáḥib-Díván. Can we wonder if, when such punishment was meted out to the offspring of the traitor by the tyrant whom he served, hatred should be the portion of his descendants from the city which he betrayed? So much for the Ṣáḥib-Díván. We must now return to Shíráz and its environs.

The garden of *Haft-tan* I visited with my Armenian friend. It is a pleasant secluded spot, well fitted to calm the spirits and elevate the thoughts of the dervishes who dwell within its shady precincts. The presence of a large and savage-looking dog, which rushed at us with loud barkings as soon as we entered the gate, somewhat marred this impression of quietude at first: it was, however, soon secured by one of the dervishes. We sat for a while by the seven graves from which the place takes its name, and drank tea, which was brought to us by the kindly inmates. A venerable old dervish entered into conversation with us, and even walked with us as far as the gate of the city. He was one of those dervishes who inspire one with respect for a name which serves but too often to shelter idleness, sloth, and even vice. Too often is it the case that the traveller, judging only by the opium-eating, *ḥashísh*-smoking mendicant, who, with matted hair, glassy eyes, and harsh, raucous voice, importunes the passers-by for alms, condemns all dervishes as a blemish and a bane to their country. Yet in truth this is far from being a correct view. Nowhere are men to be met with so enlightened, so intelligent, so tolerant, so well-informed, and so simple-minded as amongst the ranks of the dervishes.

The only other object of interest outside the city which demands any detailed notice is the *Cháh-i-Murtazá 'Alí*; for the gardens not described above, beautiful as they are, possess no features so distinctive as to render description necessary. The *Cháh-i-Murtazá 'Alí* ("Alí's well") is situated about half a mile to the north-east of the *Kehváré-i-Dív*, on the summit of the hills east of the *Tang-i-Alláhu Akbar*. A building of considerable size, inhabited by the custodian of the shrine and his family, surmounts the "well," which is reached by descending a very slippery stone staircase of nineteen steps. This staircase opens out of a large room, where visitors can rest and smoke a *kalyán*. Above the archway which surmounts it are inscriptions in Arabic and Persian of no very ancient date. Half-way down the rocky stair is a wider space, which forms a sort of landing. At the bottom is a small cave or grotto, wherein is a little well, such as one often sees by English roadsides, into the basin of which water continually drips from the rock above. Opposite this a tablet shaped like the tombstones seen in old churchyards is carved on the wall. In the centre of this is a rude design, which appears to be intended for a flower growing in a flower-pot. On either side of this are two lines in Arabic, but these are so effaced by time and the touches of visitors to the shrine that they are almost illegible. In front of this tablet is a place for votive candles, which are brought hither by the devout. We were not allowed much time for examining the place, the guardian of the shrine continually calling out to us from above that the air was bad and would do us an injury, which, indeed, was possibly true, for it seemed to me to be loaded with carbonic acid or other stifling gases. Having ascended again to the room above, we stayed a while to smoke a *kalyán* and talk to the custodian. He knew little about the age or history of the place, only asserting that in ancient days it had been a fire-temple, but that in the days of Muḥammad the fire had been for ever quenched by a miraculous bursting forth of the water from the well.

I have now described all the more interesting places which I visited outside the city. It remains to say something of those situated within its walls. There are several fine mosques, the most celebrated of which is Sháh Chirágh, but to these I was not able to gain access, and of them I cannot therefore speak. The narrow, tortuous streets differ in no wise from those of other Persian towns, but the bazaar demands a few words of notice. It was built by Karím Khán the Zend, and, though not very extensive, is wide, lofty, and well constructed. As regards the wares exposed for sale in its shops, the long muzzle-loading guns manufactured in the city (which, primitive as they may appear to a European, are capable of doing wonders in the hands of the Persian marksmen) chiefly attract the notice of the stranger. The book-shops are few in number, and the books which they contain are brought for the most part from Ṭeherán, there being no printing-press in Shíráz. Indeed, so far as I know, the only presses in Persia are at Ṭeherán, Iṣfahán, and Tabríz.

All, or nearly all, the European wares sold in Shíráz are, as one would expect, of English manufacture. The sale of these is chiefly in the hands of the Armenian and Zoroastrian merchants who inhabit the *Karaván-saráy-i-Rawghaní* and the *Karaván-saráy-i-Mushír*. In the shop of one of the Armenian traders I observed English guns, ammunition, tennis-shoes, tobacco, preserves, potted meats, writing materials, note-books, an Indian sun-helmet, and a musical box; articles which would be vainly sought for in Ṭeherán, where nearly all, if not all, the European goods come from Russia.

The number of Zoroastrians in Shíráz does not exceed a dozen. They are all merchants, and all natives of Yezd or Kirmán. To one of them, named Mihrabán, a Yezdí, I paid one or two visits. On the occasion of my first visit he informed me with delight that he was expecting a Parsee from Bombay in a few days, and expressed a hope that I would come and see him. A fortnight later, as I was passing near the caravansaray, I heard that the expected guest had arrived, and turned aside to Mihrabán's shop to see him. At first sight I took him for a European, for he wore English clothes, and on his head a cloth cap of the kind known as "deer-stalkers." Our conversation was conducted in English, which he spoke well—much better than Persian, in which, at any rate colloquially, he was far from proficient, having learned to pronounce it after the fashion prevalent in India. I found that he was on his way to Europe, which he had already visited on a previous occasion, and that he had chosen the overland route through Persia, because he desired to behold the ancient home of his ancestors. I asked him how he liked it.

"Not at all," he replied; "I think it is a horrible country: no railways, no hotels, no places of amusement—nothing. I have only been in Shíráz a couple of days, and I am tired of it already, and mean to leave it in a day or two more."

"I think it is a beautiful place," I answered, "and though I have been here more than a fortnight, I am in no wise wearied of its charms, and have not begun to think of quitting it yet."

"Beautiful!" he exclaimed; "you cannot surely mean that you admire it? What can you find to like in it—you, who have seen London and Paris—who have been accustomed to civilised countries?"

"Perhaps that is just the reason why I *do* like it," I answered, "for one just gets the least bit tired of 'civilised countries' after a while: they are all so much alike. Here everything is delightfully novel and refreshing. Of course, you will go to Yezd to see your co-religionists there?"

"Not I!" he replied; "I shall go straight to Ṭeherán as fast as I can, only stopping a day or two in Iṣfahán on the way. My sole desire is to get out of this country as soon as I can into one where there are railways and other appliances of civilisation. As for my co-religionists, I have no particular wish to see more of them than I have done at present. I suppose they are like this man" (pointing to his host, who stood by smiling, unconscious of the purport of his guest's remarks)—"little better than savages."

"Well," I said, mentally contrasting the ingratitude of this admirer of civilisation with the humble but cordial hospitality of the host whom he affected to despise, "I am not a Zoroastrian, yet I intend to visit Yezd before I leave Persia, expressly to see your co-religionists there, and I wonder that you too do not wish to acquaint yourself with their condition."

I then bade farewell to my Parsee friend and his host, but I fell in with the former again on his journey northwards, as will be set forth in its proper place.

The Ṣáḥib-Díván had quitted Shíráz before the Feast of the Nawrúz. The new governor, Prince Iḥtishámu'd-Dawla (the son of Ferhád Mírzá), whom I had already seen at Ṭeherán, did not enter the city till the thirteenth day after it. This circumstance was for me very fortunate, since it enabled me not only to witness the ceremonies attendant on his entry, but also to visit the citadel (*Arg*) during his absence.

The entry of the new governor into the city was a very fine sight. He had been in the neighbourhood for several days, but the astrologers had fixed on the thirteenth day after the Nawrúz as most auspicious for his inauguration. From a Persian point of view it was so, for, as it is a universal holiday, all the people were enabled to take part in the rejoicings. From a European standpoint the selection seemed scarcely so happy, for the day chosen was the first of April.

Having been misinformed as to the time when the Prince would arrive, I was too late to see more than the entry of the procession into the great square in front of the citadel (*Meydán-i-Arg*). From the lofty roof of the majestic building which now contains the telegraph-offices I obtained a good view of the whole pageant. The Prince, mounted on a handsome gray horse, was surrounded by all the nobles of Shíráz and the neighbourhood, and preceded by a number of soldiers and couriers, and a band mounted on camels, while a vast crowd followed and filled the square. A roar of artillery greeted his arrival, causing the building on which we stood to tremble. From what I heard I should fancy that the sight outside the city was even finer. Both sides of the road as far as the *Tang-i-Alláhu Akbar* were lined with spectators, while numerous deputations came out to meet and welcome the new governor.

The citadel (*Arg*) is a large and handsome pile containing a fine garden, in the centre of which is a building called, from the shape of its roof, *Kuláh-i-Firangí* ("the European's Hat"). The interior of this is cruciform, four elongated rooms opening out of the central hall, in the middle of which is a fountain. The lower part of the walls is composed of the beautiful marble of Yezd. The building is entered on either side by three steps, each of which is made of a single block of stone. It was in this building, I believe, that the Bábí captives taken at Níríz were exhibited to Fírúz Mírzá, then governor of Shíráz. These captives, consisting entirely of women and little children (for the men had all been slain on the spot), were subsequently confined in an old caravansaray just outside the Iṣfahán gate, where they suffered great hardships, besides being exposed, as the Bábí historian asserts, to the brutality of the soldiers.

On the outer wall of the principal block of buildings is a series of bas-reliefs representing the exploits of the old heroes of ancient Persia. These have been gaudily coloured by order of the young Prince Jalálu'd-Dawla. Some of the rooms in this block are very beautiful, but several have been converted into bakehouses, and the paintings on their walls blackened with smoke and dirt. One very pretty room contained a portrait of Náṣiru'd-Dín Sháh, painted at the beginning of his reign, while the ceiling was adorned with representations of female figures. On the side of the room opposite to the windows and entrance were three doors leading to apartments beyond. Over each of these was inscribed a verse of poetry.

The first ran thus:—

> "*Sar-i-dushman ú dúst bar ín dar-ast,*
> *Bar ín ástán pásbán ḳayṣar-ast.*
> *Yakí khwást k'afsar nihad—sar nihád:*
> *Yakí sar nihád—ángah afsar nihád.*"

> "At this door are laid the heads of enemies and friends,
> On this threshold kings stand sentinel.
> One desired to wear a crown—he lost his head:
> Another laid down his head—and then wore a crown." [1]

The second was as follows:—

> "*Báshad dar-i-raḥmat ki Khudá kardé firáz!*
> *Mardum sú-yi ú chu Ka'ba árand namáz!*
> *Chún Ka'ba bi-khwánamash? Ki áyad bi-niyáz*
> *Ínjá Mugh ú Hindú ú Musulmán bi-namáz.*"

> "May it be the door of mercy which God has opened!
> May men pray towards it as towards the *Ka'ba*!
> How shall I call it '*Ka'ba*'? For hither come in supplication
> Magian and Hindú and Musulmán to pray."

The third ran thus:—

> "*Ín dar (ki bád tá bi-abad sijda-gáh-i-khalḳ!)*
> *Díd ásmán, ú guft, 'Bar-ú pásbán man-am!'*
> *Dawlat bar ástáné-i-ú bar nihád sar*
> *Ya'ní, 'Kaminé chákar-i-ín ástán man-am!'*"

> "This door (may it be till eternity the place of the people's reverence!)
> Heaven saw, and said, 'Over it I am the sentinel!'
> Fortune laid down her head on its threshold,
> As though to say, 'I am the humble servant of this threshold.'"

Several of the fireplaces in the different rooms bore appropriate verses inscribed on them. Two of these may serve as examples. The first runs thus:—

> "*Az bukhárí má ṭaríḳ-i-dústí ámúkhtím,*
> *Khwíshtan-rá az baráyi hamnishínán súkhtím.*"

> "We have learned the way of friendship from the grate,
> We have consumed ourselves for the sake of our neighbours."

1 That is, one revolts and is beheaded, while another submits and is rewarded with a crown.

The second is as follows:—

> "*Bi-ghayr az bukhárí na-dídím kas*
> *Ki bá dushman ú dúst garmí dihad.*"
>
> "Except the grate, we have seen no one
> Who is warm alike towards friend and foe."

Having now attempted to depict the city of Shíráz—its palaces, gardens, shrines, pleasure-grounds, and places of resort—I must return once more to the life within its walls. As I have said, there was no lack of society, and I enjoyed opportunities of witnessing a variety of Persian entertainments. As I have already described the general features of these in speaking of Ṭeherán, I shall endeavour to be as concise as possible in this place, merely noticing such points as were novel to me.

Two days after my arrival at Shíráz I was invited with the Nawwáb to an entertainment given by an Armenian gentleman connected with the telegraph. On reaching the house soon after sunset I was cordially received by the host, who introduced me to his wife and another lady relative, and to his cousin, whom I have already had occasion to mention more than once as the companion of my excursions. The latter was about twenty-one years of age, had resided for a long time in Bombay, where he had been connected with the press, and spoke English perfectly, as did my host. The ladies preferred to talk Persian, in which language one of them was remarkably proficient, reading with ease the most difficult poetry. After a short while the other guests arrived. These were three in number: the *Begler-begi*, a young and somewhat arrogant nobleman; a friend of his, less arrogant but more boisterous; and a turbaned and bearded philosopher. To the latter I was introduced as a student of Metaphysics, and he at once proceeded to question me on the books I had read, the teachers with whom I had studied, and, finally, on some of those knotty problems which, long buried in oblivion in Europe, still agitate the minds and exercise the ingenuity of the Persian schoolmen. From a trying cross-examination as to my views on the primordial atom (*juz' alladhí lá yatajazzá*) I was fortunately relieved by the entrance of two Jewish minstrels and a dancing-boy, who had been engaged for our entertainment. The attention of the philosopher began to wander; his eyes were fixed on the evolutions of the dancer; his hands and feet beat time to the music. Wine was offered to him and not refused; metaphysics was exorcised by melody; and ere the hour of departure arrived, the disciple of Aristotle and Avicenna lay helpless on the floor, incapable of utterance, insensible to reproof, and oblivious alike of dignity and decorum. It is but just to say that this was the only occasion on which I witnessed so disgraceful a sight in Shíráz.

The Jewish minstrels of whom I have spoken appeared to be the favourite artists in their profession, for they were present at almost every entertainment of which music formed a part. One of the two men was noted for the hideous contortions into which he could twist his face. He was also, as I learned, an admirable mimic, and excelled especially in personating the Firangí Ṣáḥib and the Muḥammadan Mullá. These representations I did not witness, the former being withheld out of respect for my feelings, and the latter reserved for very select audiences who could be trusted to observe a discreet silence; for a poor Jew would not willingly run the risk of incurring the resentment of the powerful and fanatical priests. The dancing-boy cannot have been more than ten or eleven years old. When performing, he wore such raiment as is usual with acrobats, with the addition of a small close-fitting cap, from beneath which his black hair streamed in long locks, a tunic reaching half-way to the knees, and a mass of trinkets which jingled at every movement. His evolutions were characterised by agility and suppleness rather than grace, and appeared to me somewhat monotonous, and at times even inelegant. I saw him for the second time at the house of Ḥájí Naṣru'lláh Khán, the Ílkhání. On this occasion he super-added to his ordinary duties the function of cup-bearer, which he performed in a somewhat novel and curious manner. Having filled the wine-glass, he took the edge of the circular foot on which it stands firmly in his teeth, and, approaching each guest in turn, leaned slowly down so as to bring the wine within reach of the drinker, continually bending his body more and more forwards as the level of the liquid sank lower. One or two of the guests appeared particularly delighted with this manœuvre, and strove to imprint a kiss on the boy's cheek as he quickly withdrew the empty glass.

Amongst the guests was one who had just arrived from the North with the new governor. He was very conversational, and his talk was almost entirely about philosophy. What his views were I could not ascertain; at first I was inclined to suspect he might be a Bábí, for he greeted me with the remark that he had been looking forward to seeing me ever since he left Iṣfahán, where he had heard a good deal about me. This remark he accompanied with a look full of meaning, and followed it up by asking me if I had met a young Frenchman, M. R——, who had lately passed through Persia. This strengthened my suspicions, for I had heard much of the gentleman in question: how he had been for some while amongst the Bábís in Syria, how he had received from their chiefs letters of introduction and recommendation, and how, by reason of these, he had been greeted with a perfect ovation by the Bábís in every Persian town which he had visited. I began to be afraid that some indiscretion on the part of my loquacious friend would betray my dealings with the Bábís, which, for many reasons, I was anxious to keep secret. I therefore answered guardedly that I had not met the French traveller, and enquired what manner of man he was.

"I met him several times and liked him very much," he replied.

One or two of those present who had been listening to our conversation began to manifest signs of curiosity, observing which I hastened to change the subject. It was not long, however, before religious topics again came up, and I began to think that I had mistaken my friend's opinions, for now he spoke in the strangest manner, alternately putting forward views quite incompatible, and delighting, apparently, in the perplexity which his paradoxes caused me. At last I asked him point-blank what his real opinions were.

"You know very well," he replied.

I assured him that he was mistaken, and pressed him for a clearer answer.

"Well, they are the same as yours," he said; and with this unsatisfactory reply I was forced to be content.

I have already alluded to the pleasant picnics in the garden of *Rashk-i-Bihisht*, to which, on two occasions, I accompanied the Nawwáb. The number of guests at each of these was about a dozen, while at least as many servants were in attendance to cook the food, lay the cloth, and prepare tea and *kalyáns*. On the first occasion I was awakened at half-past seven in the morning by Ḥájí Ṣafar, who informed me that the Nawwáb was already preparing to start. I dressed as quickly as I could, but on descending into the courtyard found that he had already gone on to receive his guests, leaving his uncle, Ḥájí Dá'í, to wait, not in the best of tempers, for my appearance. I apologised meekly for my unpunctuality, excusing myself by saying that I did not know we were to start so early.

"Of course we were to start early," he retorted, "before the sun should be high and the day grow hot."

"Yes, if it were summer that would be necessary," I answered, "but it is hardly spring yet. I don't think it will be very hot today," I added, gazing at the cloudy sky.

"Well, the guests were asked for this time, the Nawwáb has already gone on to receive them, and the horses have been waiting for a long while. Come! Let us start at once."

On reaching the garden, which was situated at a distance of about two miles from the town, we found the chief guests already assembled. Amongst them were two princes, Siyávush Mírzá and Jalálu'd-Dín Mírzá, cousins to one another, and descendants of Fatḥ-'Alí Sháh's eldest son, the *Farmán-farmá*. The latter was accompanied by his son, a handsome boy of about fourteen. Of the remaining guests, three were brothers belonging to a family of some consideration in Shíráz. One of them, Abú'l-Ḳásim Khán, I had already met at the Nawwáb's; another, Hidáyatu'lláh Khán, attracted my attention by his firm refusal to drink wine, which he appeared to regard with unqualified disapproval. I had a good deal of conversation with him subsequently, and found him both agreeable and intelligent. The eldest brother was named Khán-Bábá-Khán. A previous acquaintance of mine, remarkable not less for his great business capacities and intimate knowledge of the country round Shíráz than for his extremely ugly countenance, which had gained for him the sobriquet of "Ḥájí Ghúl" ("the ogre," as one may translate it), joined us somewhat later. One of the Jewish minstrels of whom I have spoken, Arzaní by name, was also present, and continued during the morning to entertain us with music and song, assisted therein by Shukru'lláh, the blind minstrel, and occasionally by such of the guests as possessed musical talent.

The rain, which had been threatening all the morning, presently descended in a steady downpour. As we watched the dripping trees from the shelter of the summer-house where we were seated, I expressed regret that the weather should be so bad.

"Bad!" was the answer I received, "why, it is beautiful weather! Just the day one would wish; a real spring day."

I found it difficult at first to understand this view, which was evidently shared by all present except myself. The fact is, that in Persia, where during the summer hardly a drop of rain descends to moisten the parched earth, the welcome showers of spring, on which the abundance of the crops, and consequently the welfare of all classes, so entirely depends, are regarded with a genuine delight and admiration which we can scarcely comprehend. There is nothing which a Persian enjoys more than to sit sipping his wine under the shelter of a summer-house, while he gazes on the falling rain-drops, and sniffs up the moist, soft air, laden with the grateful scent of the reviving flowers.

After lunch, which was served about mid-day, the room was darkened by lowering a great curtain suspended outside the windows, and most of the guests composed themselves to sleep. About 3 p.m. they began to rouse themselves; tea and pipes were brought, and conversation and music recommenced till about sunset. The rain having ceased, we mounted our horses and wended our way back to the city.

It will be seen that I had plenty of amusement during my stay at Shíráz, and that of a varied character. To have described all the social gatherings wherein I took a part would have been wearisome to the reader, and I have therefore selected as specimens only those which were typical of a class, or marked by special features of interest. Neither was I limited to Persian society. The chief of the telegraph, as well as the medical officer attached to that department, had left Shíráz on a visit of inspection the day after my arrival, so that I had only met them once on the morning of their departure. But with the rest of the telegraph staff, several of whom were married, I spent many pleasant hours, and often enjoyed a game of tennis with them in the garden where they dwelt.

Hitherto I have spoken only of the lighter aspect of Persian life in Shíráz; of social gatherings where wine and music, dance and song, beguiled away the soft spring days, or the moonlit nights. It is time that I should turn to other memories—gatherings where no wine flowed and no music sounded; where grave faces, illumined with the light of inward conviction, and eyes gleaming with unquenchable faith, surrounded me; where the strains of the rebeck were replaced by low, earnest tones speaking of God, of the New Light, of pains resolutely endured, and of triumph confidently expected.

The memory of those assemblies can never fade from my mind; the recollection of those faces and those tones no time can efface. I have gazed with awe on the workings of a mighty Spirit, and I marvel whereunto it tends. O people of the Báb! sorely persecuted, compelled to silence, but steadfast now as at Sheykh Ṭabarsí and Zanján, what destiny is concealed for you behind the veil of the Future?

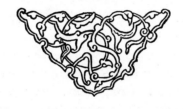

CHAPTER XI

SHÍRÁZ (*continued*)

"*Shíráz pur ḳawghá shavad, shakkar-labí peydá shavad;*
Tarsam k'az áshúb-i-lab-ash bar ham zanad Baghdád-rá."

"Shíráz shall be full of tumult; one shall appear with lips sweet as sugar;
I fear lest through the riot of his lips he may cast Baghdád into confusion."

"*Ey ki mí-pursí zi ráh-i-Ka'ba-i-waṣl-am nishán,*
Z'ustakhwán-i-kushtagán ráhíst sar tá sar safíd!"

"O thou who askest a sign of the road to the Sanctuary of my Presence,
It is a road white from beginning to end with the bones of the slain!"

IN attempting to convey a correct impression of past events, it is often difficult to decide how far their true sequence may be disregarded for the sake of grouping together things naturally related. To set down all occurrences day by day, as they actually took place, is undoubtedly the easiest, and, in some ways, the most natural plan. On the other hand, it often necessitates the separation of matters intimately connected with one another, while the mind is distracted rather than refreshed by the continual succession of topics presented to it. For this reason I have thought it best to include in a separate chapter all that I have to say concerning my intercourse with the Bábís in Shíráz. Had this intercourse been more closely interwoven with the social life which I have endeavoured to portray in the preceding chapter, such dissociation might have been inadvisable, and even impossible. As it was, it was a thing apart; a separate life in a different sphere; a drama, complete in itself, with its own scenes and its own actors.

Those who have followed me thus far on my journey will remember how, after long and fruitless search, a fortunate chance at length brought me into contact with the Bábís at Iṣfahán. They will remember also that the Bábí apostle to whom I was introduced promised to notify my desire for fuller instruction to his fellow-believers at Shíráz, and that he further communicated to me the name of one whose house formed one of their principal resorts. I had no sooner reached Shíráz than I began to consider how I should, without attracting attention or arousing comment, put myself in communication with the person so designated, who occupied a post of some importance in the public service which I will not more clearly specify. His name, too, I suppress for obvious reasons. Whenever I have occasion to allude to him, I shall speak of him as Mírzá Muḥammad.

Whilst I was still undecided as to the course I should pursue, another unlooked-for event suddenly removed all difficulties. I have already mentioned Mírzá 'Alí, a young Persian with whom I had previously been intimately acquainted in Europe. Three days after my arrival he came to pay me a visit. I hardly recognised him at first, in the tall lambskin cap and long cloak which he wore, and was equally surprised and delighted at this unexpected meeting. He did not stay long, but before leaving invited me to come and see him on the following day.

I had scarcely entered the room where he was waiting to receive me, when the cursory glance which I cast round was riveted by an Arabic text which hung on the wall. Yet it was not so much the Arabic characters which attracted my attention (though these too seemed in some way strangely familiar), as a line of writing beneath them. There was no mistaking the parallel oblique strokes and the delicate curves and spirals which sprang from them. Only once before had I seen that character in the hands of the Bábí *dallál* at Iṣfahán.

I withdrew my eyes from the tablet and turned them on Mírzá 'Alí, who had been attentively watching my scrutiny. Our glances met, and I knew at once that my conjecture was right.

"Do you know Mírzá Muḥammad?" I asked presently.

"I know him well," he replied; "it was he who informed me that you were coming. You have not seen him yet? Then I will take you there one day soon, and you shall meet other friends. I must find out when he will be disengaged, and arrange a time."

"I did not know," said I, "that you....Tell me what you really think...."

"I confess I am puzzled," he answered. "Such eloquence, such conviction, such lofty, soul-stirring words, such devotion and enthusiasm! If I could believe any religion it would be that."

Before I left he had shown me some of the books which he possessed. One of these was a small work called *Madaniyyat* ("Civilisation"), lithographed in Bombay, one of the few secular writings of the Bábís. Another was the *Kitáb-i-Aḳdas* ("Most Holy Book"), which contains the codified prescriptions of the sect in a brief compass. The latter my friend particularly commended to my attention.

"You must study this carefully if you desire to understand the matter," he said; "I will get a copy made for you by our scribe, whom you will also see at Mírzá Muḥammad's. You should read it while you are here, so that any difficulties which arise may be explained. I am acquainted with a young Seyyid well versed in philosophy, who would perhaps come regularly to you while you are here. This would excite no suspicion, for it is known that you have come here to study."

Rejoiced as I was at the unexpected facilities which appeared to be opening out to me, there was one thing which somewhat distressed me. It was the Báb whom I had learned to regard as a hero, and whose works I desired to obtain and peruse, yet of him no account appeared to be taken. I questioned my friend about this, and learned (what I had already begun to suspect at Iṣfahán) that much had taken place amongst the Bábís since those events of which Gobineau's vivid and sympathetic record had so strangely moved me. That record was written while Mírzá

Yaḥyá, *Ṣubḥ-i-Ezel* ("the Morning of Eternity") was undisputed vicegerent of the Báb, and before the great schism occurred which convulsed the Bábí community. Now, I found, the Báb's writings were but little read even amongst his followers, for Behá had arisen as "He whom God shall manifest" (the promised deliverer foretold by the Báb), and it was with his commands, his writings, and his precepts that the Bábí messengers went forth from Acre to the faithful in Persia. Of Mírzá Yaḥyá, whom I had expected to find in the place of authority, I could learn little. He lived, he was in Cyprus, he wrote nothing, he had hardly any followers; that was all I was told, and I was forced to try to reconcile myself to the new, and at present, ill-comprehended, position of affairs. At any rate I had found the Bábís, and I should be able to talk with those who bore the name and revered the memory of one whom I had hitherto admired in silence—one whose name had been, since I entered Persia, a word almost forbidden. For the rest, I should soon learn about Behá, and understand the reasons which had led to his recognition as the inaugurator of a new dispensation.

A day or two after the events narrated above I received another visit from Mírzá 'Alí, who was on this occasion accompanied by the young Bábí Seyyid of whom he had spoken. They remained with me more than an hour, and the Seyyid talked much, asking me numberless questions about anatomy, physiology, chemistry, and other sciences, but speaking little about his own views. Before they left it was arranged that on the following afternoon I should accompany them to the house of Mírzá Muḥammad.

On the following afternoon I sallied forth to the house of Mírzá 'Alí, accompanied by my servant, Ḥájí Ṣafar, whom I would rather have left behind had I been able to find the way by myself. I met Mírzá 'Alí at the door of his house, and we proceeded at once to the abode of Mírzá Muḥammad. He was not in when we arrived, but appeared shortly, and welcomed me very cordially. After a brief interval we were joined by another guest, whose open countenance and frank greeting greatly predisposed me in his favour. This was the scribe and missionary, Ḥájí Mírzá Ḥasan, to whose inopportune meeting with *Murshid* in my room I have already alluded. He was shortly followed by the young Seyyid who had visited me on the previous day, and another much older Seyyid of very quiet, gentle appearance, who, as I afterwards learned, was related to the Báb, and was therefore one of the *Afnán* ("Branches")—a title given by the Bábís to all related, within certain degrees of affinity, to the founder of their faith. One or two of my host's colleagues completed the assembly.

I was at first somewhat at a loss to know how to begin, especially as several servants were standing about outside, watching and listening. I enquired of Mírzá 'Alí if I might speak freely before these, whereupon he signified to Mírzá Muḥammad that they should be dismissed.

"Now," he said, when this order had been given and obeyed, "speak freely, for there is no 'ass's head' (*ra'su'l-ḥimár*[1]) here."

I then proceeded to set forth what I had heard of the Báb, his gentleness and patience, the cruel fate which had overtaken him, and the unflinching courage wherewith he and his followers, from the greatest to the least, had endured the merciless torments inflicted on them by their enemies.

"It is this," I concluded, "which has made me so desirous to know what you believe; for a faith which can inspire a fortitude so admirable must surely contain some noble principle."

Then began a discussion between myself on the one hand, and the young Seyyid and Ḥájí Mírzá Ḥasan on the other, of which I can only attempt to give a general outline. Disregarding those details of persons, past events, and literary history about which I was so desirous to learn, they proceeded to set forth the fundamental assumptions on which their faith is based in

1 See p. 300, *supra*.

a manner which subsequent experience rendered familiar to me.

"The object for which man exists," they said, "is that he should know God. Now this is impossible by means of his unassisted reason. It is therefore necessary that prophets should be sent to instruct him concerning spiritual truth, and to lay down ordinances for his guidance. From time to time, therefore, a prophet appears in the world with tokens of his divine mission sufficient to convince all who are not blinded by prejudice and wilful ignorance. When such a prophet appears, it is incumbent on all to submit themselves to him without question, even though he command what has formerly been forbidden, or prohibit what has formerly been ordained."

"Stay," I interposed; "surely one must be convinced that such prohibition or command is sanctioned by reason. If the doctrine or ordinance be true, it must be agreeable to the idea of Absolute Good which exists in our own minds."

"We must be convinced by evidence approved by reason that he who claims to be a prophet actually is so," they replied; "but when once we are assured of this, we must obey him in everything, for he knows better than we do what is right and wrong. If it were not so, there would be no necessity for revelation at all. As for the fact that what is sanctioned in one 'manifestation' is forbidden in another, and *vice versâ*, that presents no difficulty. A new prophet is not sent until the development of the human race renders this necessary. A revelation is not abrogated till it no longer suffices for the needs of mankind. There is no disagreement between the prophets: all teach the same truth, but in such measure as men can receive it. One spirit, indeed, speaks through all the prophets; consider it as the instructor (*murabbí*) of mankind. As mankind advance and progress, they need fuller instruction. The child cannot be taught in the same way as the youth, nor the youth as the full-grown man. So it is with the human race. The instruction given by Abraham was suitable and sufficient for the people of his day, but not for those to whom Moses was sent, while this in turn had ceased to meet the needs of those to whom Christ was sent. Yet we must not say that their religions were opposed to one another, but rather that each 'manifestation' is more complete and more perfect than the last."

"What you say is agreeable to reason," I assented; "but tell me, in what way is the prophet to be recognised when he comes? By miracles, or otherwise?"

"By miracles (if by miracles you mean prodigies contrary to nature)—No!" they answered; "it is for such that the ignorant have always clamoured. The prophet is sent to distinguish the good from the bad, the believer from the unbeliever. He is the touchstone whereby false and true metal are separated. But if he came with evident supernatural power, who could help believing? who would dare oppose him? The most rebellious and unbelieving man, if he found himself face to face with one who could raise the dead, cleave the moon, or stay the course of the sun, would involuntarily submit. The persecutions to which all the prophets have been exposed, the mockery to which they have been compelled to submit, the obloquy they have borne, all testify to the fact that their enemies neither feared them nor believed that God would support them; for no one, however foolish, however froward, would knowingly and voluntarily fight against the power of the Omnipotent. No, the signs whereby the prophet is known are these:—Though untaught in the learning esteemed of men, he is wise in true wisdom; he speaks a word which is creative and constructive; his word so deeply affects the hearts of men that for it they are willing to forgo wealth and comfort, fame and family, even life itself. What the prophet says comes to pass. Consider Muḥammad. He was surrounded by enemies, he was scoffed at and opposed by the most powerful and wealthy of his people, he was derided as a madman, treated as an impostor. But his enemies have passed away, and his word remains. He said, 'You shall fast in the month of Ramaẓán,' and behold, thousands and thousands obey that word to this day. He said, 'You shall make a pilgrimage to Mecca if you are able,' and every year brings thither countless pilgrims from all quarters of the globe. This is the special character of the prophetic word; it fulfils itself; it creates; it triumphs. Kings and rulers strove to extinguish the word of Christ, but they could not; and now kings and rulers make it their pride that they are Christ's servants. Against all opposition, against all persecution, unsupported by human might, what the prophet says comes to pass. This is the true miracle, the greatest possible miracle, and indeed the only miracle which is a proof to future ages and distant peoples. Those who are privileged to meet the prophet may indeed be convinced in other ways, but for those who have not seen him his word is the evidence on which conviction must rest. If Christ raised the dead, you were not a witness of it; if Muḥammad cleft the moon asunder, I was not there to see. No one can really believe a religion merely because miracles are ascribed to its founder, for are they not ascribed to the founder of every religion by its votaries? But when a man arises amongst a people, untaught and unsupported, yet speaking a word which causes empires to change, hierarchies to fall, and thousands to die willingly in obedience to it, that is a proof absolute and positive that the word spoken is from God. This is the proof to which we point in support of our religion. What you have already learned concerning its origin will suffice to convince you that in no previous 'manifestation' was it clearer and more complete."

"I understand your argument," I replied, "and it seems to me a weighty one. But I wish to make two observations. Firstly, it appears to me that you must include amongst the number of the prophets many who are ordinarily excluded, as, for example, Zoroaster; for all the proofs which you have enumerated were, so far as we can learn, presented by him. Secondly, though

I admit that your religion possesses these proofs in a remarkable degree (at least so far as regards the rapidity with which it spread in spite of all opposition), I cannot altogether agree that the triumph of Islám was an instance of the influence of the prophetic word only. The influence of the sword was certainly a factor in its wide diffusion. If the Arabs had not invaded Persia, slaying, plundering, and compelling, do you think that the religion of Muḥammad would have displaced the religion of Zoroaster? To us the great proof of the truth of Christ's teaching is that it steadily advanced in spite of the sword, not by the sword: the great reproach on Islám, that its diffusion was in so large a measure due to the force of arms rather than the force of argument. I sympathise with your religion, and desire to know more of it, chiefly because the history of its origin, the cruel fate of its founder, the tortures joyfully endured with heroic fortitude by its votaries, all remind me of the triumph of Christ, rather than the triumph of Muḥammad."

"As to your first observation," rejoined the Bábí spokesman, "it is true, and we do recognise Zoroaster, and others whom the Musulmáns reject, as prophets. For though falsehood may appear to flourish for a while, it cannot do so for long. God will not permit an utterly false religion to be the sole guide of thousands. But with Zoroaster and other ancient prophets you and I have nothing to do. The question for you is whether another prophet has come since Christ: for us, whether another has come since Muḥammad."

"Well," I interrupted, "what about the propagation of Islám by the sword? For you cannot deny that in many countries it was so propagated. What right had Muḥammad—what right has any prophet—to slay where he cannot convince? Can such a thing be acceptable to God, who is Absolute Good?"

"A prophet has the right to slay if he knows that it is necessary," answered the young Seyyid, "for he knows what is hidden from us; and if he sees that the slaughter of a few will prevent many from going astray, he is justified in commanding such slaughter. The prophet is the spiritual physician, and as no one would blame a physician for sacrificing a limb to save the body, so no one can question the right of a prophet to destroy the bodies of a few, that the souls of many may live. As to what you say, that God is Absolute Good, it is undeniably true; yet God has not only Attributes of Grace but also Attributes of Wrath—He is *Al-Ḳahhár* (the Compeller) as well as *Al-Laṭíf* (the Kind); *Al-Muntaḳim* (the Avenger) as well as *Al-Ghafúr* (the Pardoner). And these Attributes as well as those must be manifested in the prophet, who is the God-revealing mirror."

"I do not agree with you there," I answered. "I know very well that men have often attributed, and do attribute, such qualities as these to God, and it appears to me that in so doing they have been led into all manner of evil and cruelty, whereby they have brought shame on the name of their religion. I believe what one of your own poets has said:

'*Az Khayr-i-Maḥz juz nikú'í náyad,*'
'Naught but good comes from Absolute Good,'

and we cannot falsify the meaning of words in such wise as to say that qualities which we universally condemn in man are good in God. To say that revenge in man is bad, while revenge in God is good, is to confound reason, stultify speech, and juggle with paradoxes. But, passing by this question altogether, you can hardly imagine that a prophet in whom the 'Attributes of Wrath' were manifested could attract to himself such as have believed in a prophet in whom were reflected the 'Attributes of Grace.' Admitting even that a prophet sent to a very rude, ignorant, or froward people may be justified in using coercion to prepare the way for a better state of things, and admitting that Muḥammad was so justified by the circumstances under which he was placed, still you cannot expect those who have learned the gentle teaching of Christ to revert to the harsher doctrines of Muḥammad, for though the latter was subsequent as regards time, his religion was certainly not a higher development of the religion of Christ. I do not say that Muḥammad was not a prophet; I do not even assert that he could or should have dealt otherwise with his people; but, granting all this, it is still impossible for anyone who has understood the teaching of Christ to prefer the teaching of Muḥammad. You have said that the God-given message is addressed to the people of each epoch of time in such language as they can comprehend, in such measure as they can receive. Should we consider *time* only, and not *place*? May it not be that since the stages of development at which different peoples living at the same time have arrived are diverse, they may require different prophets and different religions? The child, as you have said, must be taught differently as he grows older, and the teacher accordingly employs different methods of instruction as his pupil waxes in years and understanding, though the knowledge he strives to impart remains always the same. But in the same school are to be found at one time pupils of many different ages and capacities. What is suitable to one class is not suitable to another. May it not be the same in the spiritual world?"

At this point there was some dissension in the assembly; the young Seyyid shook his head, and relapsed into silence; Mírzá 'Alí signified approval of what I had said; Ḥájí Mírzá Ḥasan strove to avoid the point at issue, and proceeded thus:

"I have already said that what is incumbent on every man is that he should believe in the 'manifestation' of his own age. It is not required of him that he should discuss and compare all previous 'manifestations.' You have been brought up a follower of Christ. We have believed in this 'manifestation' which has taken place in these days. Let us not waste time in disputing about intermediate 'manifestations.' We do not desire to make you believe in Muḥammad but in Behá. If you should be convinced of the truth of Behá's teaching you have passed over the stage of Islám altogether. The last 'manifestation' includes and sums up all preceding ones. You say that you could not accept Islám because its laws and ordinances are harsher, and, in your eyes, less perfect than those laid down by Christ. Very well, we do not ask you to accept Islám; we ask you to consider whether you should not accept Behá. To do so you need not go back from a gentle to a severe dispensation. Behá has come for the perfecting of the law of Christ, and his injunctions are in all respects similar; for instance, we are commanded to *prefer rather that we should be killed than that we should kill.* It is the same throughout, and, indeed, could not be otherwise, for Behá *is* Christ returned again, even as He promised, to perfect that which He had begun. Your own books tell you that Christ shall come '*like a thief in the night*,' at a time when you are not expecting Him."

"True," I replied, "but those same books tell us also that His coming shall be '*as the lightning, that lighteneth out of the one part under heaven and shineth unto the other part under heaven.*'"

"There can be no contradiction between these two similes," answered the Bábí; "and since the phrase '*like a thief in the night*' evidently signifies that when Christ returns it will be in a place where you do not expect Him, and at a time when you do not expect Him—that is, suddenly and secretly—it is clear that the comparison in the other passage which you quoted is to the suddenness and swiftness of the lightning, not to its universal vividness. If, as the Christians for the most part expect, Christ should come riding upon the clouds surrounded by angels, how could He be said in any sense to come '*like a thief in the night*'? Everyone would see him, and, seeing, would be compelled to believe. It has always been through such considerations as these that men have rejected the prophet whose advent they professed to be expecting, because He did not come in some unnatural and impossible manner which they had vainly imagined. Christ was indeed the promised Messiah, yet the Jews, who had waited, and prayed, and longed for the coming of the

Messiah, rejected Him when He did come for just such reasons. Ask a Jew now why he does not believe in Christ, and he will tell you that the signs whereby the Messiah was to be known were not manifest at His coming. Yet, had he understood what was intended by those signs, instead of being led away by vain traditions, he would know that the promised Messiah had come and gone and come again. So with the Christians. On a mountain[1] close by Acre is a monastery peopled by Christian priests and monks, assembled there to await the arrival of Christ on that spot as foretold. And they continue to gaze upwards into heaven, whence they suppose that He will descend, while only a few miles off in Acre He *has* returned, and is dwelling amongst men as before. O be not blinded by those very misapprehensions which you condemn so strongly in the Jews! The Jews would not believe in Christ because He was not accompanied by a host of angels; you blame the Jews for their obstinacy and frowardness, and you do rightly. But beware lest you condemn yourselves by alleging the very same reason as an excuse for rejecting this 'manifestation.' Christ came to the Jews accompanied by angels—angels none the less because they were in the guise of fishermen. Christ returns to you as Behá with angels, with clouds, with the sound of trumpets. His angels are His messengers; the clouds are the doubts which prevent you from recognising Him; the sound of trumpets is the sound of the proclamation which you now hear, announcing that He has come once more from heaven, even as He came before, not as a human form descending visibly from the sky, but as the Spirit of God entering into a man, and abiding there."

"Well," I replied, "your arguments are strong, and certainly deserve consideration. But, even supposing that you are right in principle, it does not follow that they hold good in this particular case. If I grant that the return of Christ may be in such wise as you indicate, nevertheless mere assertion will not

1 Mount Carmel.

prove that Behá is Christ. Indeed, we are told by Christ Himself that many will arise in His name, saying, 'See here,' or 'See there,' and are warned not to follow them."

"Many have arisen falsely claiming to be Christ," he answered, "but the injunction laid on you to beware of these does not mean that you are to refuse to accept Christ when He does return. The very fact that there are pretenders is a proof that there is a reality. You demand proofs, and you are right to do so. What proofs would suffice for you?"

"The chief proofs which occur to me at this moment," I replied, "are as follows:—You admit, so far as I understand, that in each 'manifestation' a promise has been given of a succeeding 'manifestation,' and that certain signs have always been laid down whereby that 'manifestation' may be recognised. It is therefore incumbent on you to show that the signs foretold by Christ as heralding His return have been accomplished in the coming of Behá. Furthermore, since each 'manifestation' must be fuller, completer, and more perfect than the last, you must prove that the doctrines taught by Behá are superior to the teaching of Christ—a thing which I confess seems to me almost impossible, for I cannot imagine a doctrine purer or more elevated than that of Christ. Lastly, quite apart from miracles in the ordinary sense, there is one sign which we regard as the especial characteristic of a prophet, to wit, that he should have knowledge of events which have not yet come to pass. No sign can be more appropriate or more convincing than this. For a prophet claims to be inspired by God, and to speak of the mysteries of the Unseen. If he has knowledge of the Unseen he may well be expected to have knowledge of the Future. That we may know that what he tells us about other matters beyond our ken is true, we must be convinced that he has knowledge surpassing ours in some matter which we can verify. This is afforded most readily by the foretelling of events which have not yet happened, and which we cannot foresee. These three signs appear to me both sufficient and requisite to establish such a claim as that which you advance for Behá."

"As regards knowledge of the future," replied Ḥájí Mírzá Ḥasan, "I could tell you of many occasions on which Behá has given proof of such. Not only I myself, but almost all who have been at Acre, and stood in his presence, have received warnings of impending dangers, or information concerning forthcoming events. Some of these I will, if it please God, relate to you at some future time. As regards the superiority of Behá's doctrines to those of Christ, you can judge for yourself if you will read his words. As regards the news of this 'manifestation' given to you by Christ, is it not the case that He promised to return? Did He not declare that one should come to comfort His followers, and perfect what He had begun? Did He not signify that after the Son should come the Father?"

"Do you mean," I demanded in astonishment, "that you regard Behá as the Father? What do you intend by this expression? You cannot surely mean that you consider Behá to be God Himself?"

"What do you mean by the expression 'Son of God'?" returned the Bábí.

"Our learned men explain it in different ways," I answered; "but let us take the explanation which Christ Himself gave in answer to the same question—'As many as do the will of God are the sons of God.' Christ perfectly fulfilled the will of God; He had—as I understand it—reached the stage which your Ṣúfís call 'annihilation in God' (*fená fi'lláh*); He had become merged in God in thought, in will, in being, and could say truly, 'I am God.' Higher than this can no one pass; how then can you call Behá 'the Father,' since 'the Father' is Infinite, Invisible, Omnipresent, Omnipotent?"

"Suppose that in this assembly," replied the other, "there were one wiser than all the rest, and containing in himself all, and more than all, the knowledge which the others possessed collectively. That one would be, in knowledge, the Father of all the others. So may Behá be called 'the Father' of Christ and of all preceding prophets."

"Well," I answered, by no means satisfied with this explanation, "apart from this, which I will pass by for the present, it appears to me that you confuse and confound different things. The coming of the Comforter is not the same thing, as we understand it, as the return of Christ, yet both of these you declare to be fulfilled in the coming of Behá. And whereas you spoke of Behá a little while ago as Christ returned, you now call him 'the Father.' As regards the Comforter, we believe that he entered as the Holy Spirit into the hearts of the disciples soon after the Jews had put Christ to death. I know that the Muḥammadans assert that the prophecies which we apply to this descent of the Holy Spirit were intended to refer to Muḥammad; that for the word *παράκλητος* they would substitute *περικλυτός*, which is in meaning nearly equivalent to Aḥmad or Muḥammad, signifying one 'praised,' or 'illustrious.' But if you, as I suppose, follow the Muḥammadans in this, you cannot apply the same prophecy to Behá. If the promise concerning the advent of the Comforter was fulfilled in the coming of Muḥammad, then it clearly cannot apply to the coming of Behá. And, indeed, I still fail to understand in what light you regard Islám, and must return once more to the question concerning its relation to Christianity and to your religion which I put some time ago, and which I do not think you answered clearly. If news of the succeeding 'manifestation' is given by every messenger of God, surely it is confined to the 'manifestation' immediately succeeding that wherein it is given, and does not extend to others which lie beyond it. Assuming that you are right in regarding Islám as the completion and fulfilment of Christianity, your religion must be regarded as the completion and fulfilment of Islám, and the prophecies concerning it must then be sought in the Ḳur'án and Traditions rather than in the Gospel. It is therefore incumbent on you, if you desire to convince me, first of all to prove that Muḥammad was the promised Comforter, and that his religion was the fulfilment of Christianity; then to prove that the coming of the Báb was foretold and signified by Muḥammad; and only after this has been done, to prove that Behá is he whom the Báb foretold. For it is possible to believe in Muḥammad and not to believe in the Báb, or to believe in the Báb and not to believe in Behá, while the converse is impossible. If a Jew becomes a Muḥammadan he must necessarily accept Christ; so if a Muḥammadan becomes a believer in Behá he must necessarily believe in the Báb."

"To explain the relations of Islám to Christianity on the one hand, and to this manifestation on the other, would require a longer time than we have at our disposal at present," replied the Bábí apologist; "but, in brief, know that the signs laid down by each prophet as characteristic of the next manifestation apply also to all future manifestations. In the books of each prophet whose followers still exist are recorded signs sufficient to convince them of the truth of the manifestation of their own age. There is no necessity for them to follow the chain link by link. Each prophet is complete in himself, and his evidence is conclusive unto all men. God does not suffer His proof to be incomplete, or make it dependent on knowledge and erudition, for it has been seen in all manifestations that those who have believed were men whom the world accounted ignorant, while those who were held learned in religion were the most violent and bitter opponents and persecutors. Thus it was in the time of Christ, when fishermen believed in Him and became His disciples, while the Jewish doctors mocked Him, persecuted Him, and slew Him. Thus it was also in the time of Muḥammad, when the mighty and learned among his people did most furiously revile and reproach him. And although in this manifestation—the last and the most complete—many learned men have believed, because the proofs were such as no fair-minded man could resist, still, as you know, the Muḥammadan doctors have ever shown themselves our most irreconcilable enemies, and our most strenuous opposers and persecutors. But those who are pure in heart and free from prejudice will not fail to recognise the manifestation of God, whenever and wherever it appears, even as Mawláná Jalálu'd-Dín Rúmí says in the *Masnaví*—

> '*Díde'í báyad ki báshad shah-shinás*
> *Tá shinásad Sháh-rá dar har libás.*'
>
> 'One needs an eye which is king-recognising
> To recognise the King under every disguise.'"

As it was growing late, and I desired to make use of the present occasion to learn further particulars about the literature of the Bábís, I allowed the discussion to stand at this point, and proceeded to make enquiries about the books which they prized most highly. In reply to these enquiries they informed me that Mírzá 'Alí Muḥammad the Báb had composed in all about a hundred separate treatises of different sizes; that the name *Beyán* was applied generally to all of them; and that the book which I described as having been translated into French by Gobineau must be that specially designated as the *Kitábu'l-Aḥkám* ("Book of Precepts"). Behá, they added, had composed about the same number of separate books and letters. I asked if all these works existed in Shíráz, to which they replied, "No, they are scattered about the country in the hands of believers—some at Yezd, some at Iṣfahán, some in other places. In Shíráz the total number of separate works is altogether about a dozen."

"If that be so," I remarked, "I suppose that some few works of greater value than the others are to be found in every community of believers; and I should be glad to know which these are, so that I may endeavour to obtain them."

"All that emanates from the Source (*maṣdar*) is equal in importance," they answered, "but some books are more systematic, more easily understood, and therefore more widely read than others. Of these the chief are:—(1) The *Kitáb-i-Aḳdas* ('Most

Holy Book'), which sums up all the commands and ordinances enjoined on us; (2) The *Íḳán* ('Assurance'), which sets forth the proofs of our religion; (3) Dissertations on Science—astronomy, metaphysics, and the like—which we call *Ṣuwar-i-'Ilmiyyé*; (4) Prayers (*Munáját*) and Exhortations (*Khuṭab*). Besides these there is a history of the early events of this 'manifestation,' written by one who desired to keep his name secret."

"Can you get me these?" I enquired, "especially the *Kitáb-i-Aḳdas* and the History (for I already possess the *Íḳán*)? And was the writer of the History one of yourselves?"

"I will get a transcript of the *Kitáb-i-Aḳdas* made for you if I can," replied Mírzá 'Alí, "and meanwhile I will borrow a copy for you to read. I daresay some of us can lend you the History also. It is not altogether good. The author devotes too large a portion of his work to abuse of the Muḥammadan doctors and reflections on the Persian Government, while, on the other hand, he omits many events of real importance. Besides that, I do not like his pretence of being a French traveller; for we all know, and indeed anyone who reads his book can see, that he was not a European. I do not know his name, but I expect Ḥájí Mírzá Ḥasan does."

"I know it," answered the person appealed to, "but it is a secret which I am not entitled to divulge, though, as the writer is dead now, it could make very little matter even were it generally known. I may tell you this much, that he was one of the secretaries of Mánakjí[1] Ṣáḥib at Ṭeherán. When he began to write he was quite impartial, but as he went on he became convinced by his investigations of the truth of the matter, and this change in his opinions is manifest in the later portion of the

1 Mánakjí, the son of Limjí Húshang Hátaryárí, was for many years maintained by the Parsees of Bombay at Ṭeherán to watch over the interests of the Persian Zoroastrians. He died about the year 1890. Full particulars of the circumstances under which the *New History* here alluded to was composed will be found in the Introduction to my translation of that work.

work. The book was sent to the Supreme Horizon[1] when it was finished, but was not altogether approved there, and I believe that another and more accurate history is to be written[2]. However, you will learn a good deal from this one."

"Have you got any of the poems of Ḳurratu'l-'Ayn?" I demanded; "I have heard that she wrote poems, and should like very much to see some of them, and obtain copies."

"Yes," they answered, "she wrote poems, and some of them are still extant; but we have none of them here in Shíráz. You would most likely find them, if anywhere, at Ḳazvín, her native place, at Hamadán, which she visited after her conversion, or at Ṭeherán, where she suffered martyrdom. In Khurásán and Mázandarán, also, they might be found, but here in the South it is difficult."

It was now past sunset, and dusk was drawing on, so I was reluctantly compelled to depart homewards. On the whole, I was well satisfied with my first meeting with the Bábís of Shíráz, and looked forward to many similar conferences during my stay in Persia. They had talked freely and without restraint, had received me with every kindness, and appeared desirous of affording me every facility for comprehending their doctrines; and although some of my enquiries had not met with answers as clear as I could have desired, I was agreeably impressed with the fairness, courtesy, and freedom from prejudice of my new acquaintances. Especially it struck me that their knowledge of Christ's teaching and the gospels was much greater than that commonly possessed by the Musulmáns, and I observed with pleasure that they regarded the Christians with a friendliness very gratifying to behold.

Concerning the books, they were as good as their word. I received on the following day manuscripts of the History and of

1 *I.e.* Acre, the residence of Behá'u'lláh, "the Sun of Truth."

2 The *Traveller's Narrative*, composed by Behá'u'lláh's son, 'Abbás Efendí, about the year 1886, was the outcome of this intention. It was published by me with a translation in 1891.

the *Kitáb-i-Akdas*, and was told that I might keep them as long as I liked, but that a fresh copy of the latter would be made for me by Ḥájí Mírzá Ḥasan, the scribe. Both books were finally, ere I left Persia, made over to me as a free gift, and are now in my possession.

Four days after the conference described above, I received a note from Mírzá 'Alí informing me that Ḥájí Mírzá Ḥasan had come to see him, and that I might join them if I wished. Of course I hastened thither at once, taking with me the *Kitáb-i-Akdas* (which I had meanwhile read through) to ask the explanation of certain passages which I had been unable fully to understand. Most of these Ḥájí Mírzá Ḥasan explained to me, but the very complicated law of inheritance he could not altogether elucidate. In answer to my question whether polygamy was sanctioned by their religion, he replied that two wives are *allowed*, but believers are recommended to limit themselves to one. I then enquired whether it was true, as asserted by Gobineau, that circumcision had been abolished. He answered that it was ignored, being a thing altogether indifferent. Sundry other points wherein the ordinances of the new religion differed from those of Islám, such as the prohibition of shaving the head or wearing long locks (*zulf*) like the Persians, and the regulations for prayer, were then discussed.

Two days later Mírzá 'Alí again paid me a visit, and remained for about two hours. From him I learned sundry particulars about the Bábís of which his European education had enabled him to appreciate the interest, but which would probably never have been mentioned to me by Ḥájí Mírzá Ḥasan or my other friends, who, as is so often the case in the East, could not understand a mere desire for information as such, and who therefore would speak of little else but the essential doctrines of their religion. Amongst other things he told me that, besides the new writing (known only to a few), many of the Bábís had cornelian seals on which was cut a curious device. These seals were all engraved by a certain dervish belonging to the sect, who spent his life in travelling from town to town. The device in question, which I subsequently saw, is shaped thus:—

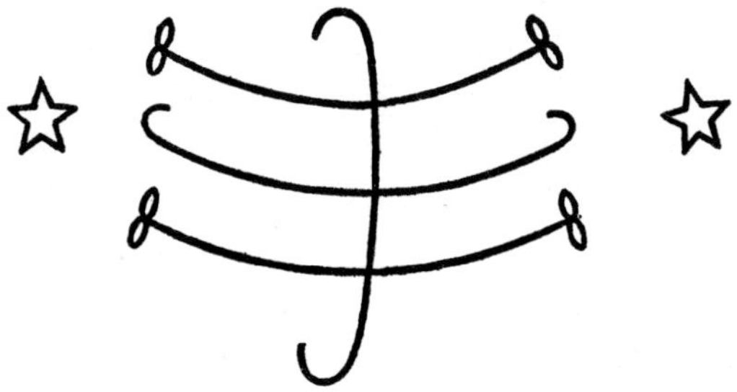

As to its significance[1] Mírzá 'Alí professed himself ignorant. I questioned him about the prophecies of Behá alluded to at the house of Mírzá Muḥammad, and he replied that I had better ask Ḥájí Mírzá Ḥasan, who had been much at Acre, and knew far more about them than he did. One of the best known instances, he added, was connected with the history of the martyrs of Iṣfahán. Soon after their death, Sheykh Báḳir, who had been chiefly instrumental in bringing it about, received a terrible letter of denunciation from Acre, wherein it was announced that he would shortly die in disgrace and ignominy, which actually occurred a little while afterwards. "Sheykh Báḳir's miserable end is a matter of notoriety in Persia," concluded my friend, "but I will try to get Ḥájí Mírzá Ḥasan or one of the others to show you the epistle in which it is foretold, and to relate to you all the details of the matter, for I quite understand the importance which you attach to prophecy in the sense in which you commonly understand it in Europe." About sunset Mírzá 'Alí rose to depart, but before leaving invited me to spend the next day in a garden near Masjid-Bardí which belonged to him. "I shall ask Ḥájí Mírzá Ḥasan and some other friends," he added, "and we can discuss matters undisturbed and

1 I have since learned that it is a monogram of Behá's name. Cf. p. 522 *infra*.

uninterrupted, for I shall take care not to have any prating inquisitive servants about; only my faithful black, and one or two others on whom I can rely." I gladly accepted the invitation and we parted.

Early next morning I met my friend and Ḥájí Mírzá Ḥasan at the gate of the city. As soon as I perceived them I gave Ḥájí Ṣafar permission to withdraw, telling him that I should not need him again before evening. When he was gone, Mírzá 'Alí informed me that the other guests would proceed independently to the garden, as it was perhaps inadvisable for all of us to be seen together. After a pleasant walk of about forty minutes (for I had entreated my friend to dispense with horses) we reached the garden, and betook ourselves to an upper chamber in a little summer-house standing in its midst. Though the day was cloudy, no rain fell till 10.30 a.m., by which time all the other guests had arrived. These were three in number, all men past middle age, grave and venerable in appearance. Two of them, both Seyyids, and both of the number of the *Afnán*[1], I had met already. The third wore a white turban, and brought with him, concealed beneath his cloak, two books.

After the usual interchange of greetings, Mírzá 'Alí suggested to the possessor of the books that he should read a portion aloud; and the Epistle addressed to Napoleon III, exhorting him to believe and warning him of his approaching humiliation, was accordingly chosen as containing one of the most remarkable prophecies of Behá. The prophecy in question I have published elsewhere[2] in an account given to the Royal Asiatic Society of the Literature and Doctrines of the Bábís, but two verses of it may be repeated here. They run as follows:—

"*Because of what thou hast done, affairs shall be changed in thy kingdom, and empire shall depart from thine hands, as a punishment for thine action....*

"*Thy glory hath made thee proud. By my life! It shall not endure, but shall pass away, unless thou takest hold of this firm rope. We have seen humiliation hastening after thee, while thou art of those that sleep.*"

1 See above, p. 330.

2 *Journal of the Royal Asiatic Society*, October 1889, p. 968.

When the reader ceased, I asked for permission to examine the books, which was readily accorded. The one from which the Epistle to Napoleon had been read, contained, besides this, the whole of the *Kitáb-i-Aḳdas*, and the other Epistles addressed to the rulers of the principal countries in Europe and Asia. These comprised letters to the Queen of England, the Emperor of Russia, the Sháh of Persia, and the Pope of Rome, as well as one addressed to a Turkish minister who had oppressed the Bábís. I asked when these were written, but no one present seemed to know the exact date, though they thought that it was about twenty years before, when Behá was in Adrianople. Besides these "Epistles to the Kings" (*Alwáḥ-i-Saláṭín*) were one or two other letters addressed to believers, amongst which was one written to the Bábí missionary whom I had met at Iṣfahán while he was in exile at Khartoum with Ḥájí Mírzá Ḥasan. These epistles were, as I learned, known collectively as the *Súra-i-Heyḳal*[1].

The other book was a larger volume, containing many *súras* without name or title, some of considerable length, some quite short. This collection was termed by my companions "The Perspicuous Book" (*Kitáb-i-Mubín*). While I was engaged in examining it breakfast was announced, and we repaired to an adjoining room, where a sumptuous repast of savoury *piláws* and *chiláws*, prawns, melons, and other delicacies was laid out. I wished to take my place on the floor with the other guests, but this Mírzá 'Alí would not permit, saying that he knew I should be more comfortable if I would sit at the table which he had provided expressly for me.

After the meal one or two of the guests lay down to sleep for a while, and in the narrower circle conversation seemed to flow more freely. I succeeded at length in inducing my Bábí

1 Abstracts of these letters were published by me in English in the *Journal of the Royal Asiatic Society* for October 1889, and the full text of the *Súra-i-Heykal* has been edited by Baron Rosen in vol. vi of the *Collections Scientifiques de l'Institut des Langues Orientales* (St Petersburg, 1891). Of this edition I published a notice in the *J.R.A.S.* for April 1892.

friends to give me some further account of the Báb, and of the history of their faith. The sum of what they told me was as follows:—

Each of the prophets is the "manifestation" of one of the Names (or Attributes) of God. The name manifested in the Báb was the highest of all—*Wáḥid*, the One. Hence it is that 19 is amongst the Bábís the sacred number according to which all things are arranged—the months of the year, the days of the month, the chapters in the *Beyán*, the fines imposed for certain offences, and many other things. For 19 is the numerical value of the word *Wáḥid* according to the *abjad* notation, in which each letter has a numerical equivalent, and each word a corresponding number, formed by the addition of its component letters. This sacred number was manifested even at the first appearance of the Báb, for eighteen of his fellow-students at once believed in him. These eighteen are called "the Letters of the Living" (*Ḥurúfát-i-Ḥayy*), because they were the creative agents employed by the Báb for bestowing new life upon the world, and because the numerical value of the word *Ḥayy* is 18. All of them were inspired and pervaded by the Báb, the One (*Wáḥid*), and with him constitute the manifested Unity (*Wáḥid*) of 19. Thus the visible church on earth was a type of the one God, one in Essence, but revealed through the Names, whereby the Essence can alone be comprehended. But this is not all. Each of the nineteen members of the "Unity" gained nineteen converts, so that the primitive church comprised 361 persons in all. This is called "The Number of All Things" (*'adad-i-kulli shey*), for 361 is the square of 19 and the further expansion thereof, and it is also the numerical equivalent of the words *kulli shey*, which mean "All Things." This is why the Bábí year, like the *Beyán*, is arranged according to this number in nineteen months of nineteen days each. But the Bábí year is a solar year containing 366 days. These five additional days are added at the beginning of the last month, which is the month of fasting, and are commanded to be spent in entertaining one's friends and the poor, as it is written in the *Kitáb-i-Akdas*—

"*Place the days which are in excess over the months before the month of fasting. Verily we have made them the manifestations of the* [*letter*] *Há* [= 5] *amongst the nights and days. Therefore are they not comprised within the limits of the months. It is incumbent on such as are in Behá to feed therein themselves, and their relatives; then the poor and distressed.... And when the days of giving* [*which are*] *before the days of withholding are finished, let them enter upon the fast.*"

Immediately after the month of fasting comes the great festival of the *Nawrúz*, which inaugurates a new year. That the old national festival, which marks the period when the sun again resumes his sway after the dark cold winter is past and the earth again clothes herself with verdure, should be thus consecrated again by the Bábís is one sign amongst many of the Persian genius by which the new faith was inspired.

Sheykh Aḥmad Aḥsá'í, who taught at Kerbelá about the beginning of the nineteenth century, first began to hint darkly that the days wherein the promised Imám should appear were at hand. When he died (A.D. 1826) his pupil, Ḥájí Seyyid Káẓim of Resht, succeeded him, and spoke more clearly on the same theme, especially towards the end of his life. Amongst the number of those who attended his lectures were Mírzá 'Alí Muḥammad the Báb, and Ḥájí Muḥammad Karím Khán of Kirmán. Now when the former arose and declared himself to be the promised Imám, foretold by the lately deceased teacher, the latter strenuously opposed him, and claimed the supremacy for himself. And some followed Karím Khán, whilst others (and these were the majority) recognised the claim of Mírzá 'Alí Muḥammad the Báb. These latter were henceforth called Bábís, while the former retained the title of Sheykhís, thereby implying that they were the true exponents of the doctrine of Sheykh Aḥmad, and that the Bábís had departed therefrom; for before that time all alike who accepted the Sheykh's teaching were called by this name. Thus it is that, although the Báb and the majority of his disciples had previously to the "manifestation" been called Sheykhís, the Sheykhís of to-day (*i.e.* the followers of Karím Khán of Kirmán) are the bitterest and fiercest enemies of the Bábís.

Behá, whose proper name is Mírzá Ḥuseyn 'Alí, of Núr, in Mázandarán, was one of those who believed in the Báb. He was arrested at Ámul on his way to join the Bábís, who, under the leadership of Mullá Ḥuseyn of Bushraweyh, were entrenched at Sheykh Ṭabarsí. In 1852 he narrowly escaped death in the great persecution wherein the intrepid Suleymán Khán, the brilliant and beautiful Ḳurratu'l-'Ayn, and a host of others, suffered martyrdom. It was proved, however, that he had but just arrived at Ṭeherán, and could not have had any share in the plot against the Sháh wherein the others were accused of being involved, so his life was spared, and, after an imprisonment of about four months, he was allowed to leave Persia and take up his residence at Baghdád. Mírzá Yaḥyá, "*Ṣubḥ-i-Ezel*" ("the Morning of Eternity"), Behá's half-brother (then only about twenty-two years of age), was at that time recognised as the Báb's successor, having been designated as such by the Báb himself, shortly before he suffered martyrdom at Tabríz. His supremacy was recognised, at least nominally, by all the Bábís during the eleven years' sojourn of their chiefs at Baghdád, but even then Behá took the most prominent part in the organisation of affairs, the carrying on of correspondence, and the interviewing of visitors. In 1863 the Ottoman Government, acceding to the urgent requests of the Persian authorities, removed all the Bábís, including Behá and Mírzá Yaḥyá, "*Ṣubḥ-i-Ezel*," from Baghdád to Constantinople, and thence to Adrianople, where they arrived about the end of the year. Here at length Behá cast aside the veil, proclaimed himself as "He whom God shall manifest," whose coming the Báb had foretold, and called on all the Bábís, including Mírzá Yaḥyá, "*Ṣubḥ-i-Ezel*," to acknowledge his claim and submit to his authority. Many of the Bábís did so at once, and their number increased as time went on, so that now the great majority of them are followers of Behá, though a few still adhere to Mírzá Yaḥyá, and these are called Ezelís. But at first the disproportion between the Behá'ís and the Ezelís was but slight, and the rivalry between them was great, resulting, indeed, in some bloodshed. So the Turkish Government decided to separate them, and accordingly sent Behá and his followers to Acre in Syria, and Mírzá Yaḥyá and his family to Famagusta in Cyprus. Now the reason why Behá was sent to Acre was, as his followers assert, that its climate is exceedingly unhealthy, and that it was hoped that he might die there. For the Persian ambassador, the French minister, and 'Álí Páshá, the Turk, had consulted together as to the means whereby the new faith might be crushed. The Persian suggested that Behá should be killed, but the Turk refused to do this openly, saying that it would be a much better plan to send him and his followers to a place where they would soon die. But Behá divined their wicked intention, and rebuked it in the "Epistles to the Kings," declaring that 'Álí Páshá should die in exile, and the power of France fail before the foe, while he remained unharmed in the place whither they had sent him. And these things were fulfilled; for two years later France began to recoil before the German arms, while 'Álí Páshá died far from his native land. But Behá continued to live and prosper, and even dreary Acre smiled with fresh gardens and seemed to gain a purer air[1].

And now, the afternoon being far advanced, it was time to retrace our steps to the city. The rain had ceased and the evening was soft and balmy, but the roads were terribly muddy. In spite of this we had a pleasant walk back to the town, where we arrived a little before dusk, after a most delightful day.

On the morrow, as I was sitting in my room after breakfast

1 I give this account as it was given to me by the Bábís of Shíráz, but I do not think that it is altogether correct. For instance, I think that not 'Álí Páshá, but Fu'ád Páshá, who actually died at Nice in 1869, was the Turkish statesman concerned.

wondering what to do, a note came from Mírzá 'Alí asking me to be ready at 3 p.m. to accompany him to the house of one of the *Afnán* (*i.e.* a member of the Báb's family), and meanwhile to prepare any questions which I might desire to ask, as I should meet there one of the most learned Bábís in Shíráz, whose manifold and undisputed talents had caused his co-religionists to bestow on him the title of *Kámil*[1] ("Perfect"). Joyfully signifying my acceptance of the invitation, I sat down to glance hastily through the *Kitáb-i-Aḳdas* and make notes of such passages as presented any difficulty. At the appointed time Mírzá 'Alí's black servant came to conduct me to the place of meeting, where, besides some of those whom I had met in the garden on the previous day, the illustrious Kámil himself was present. After the customary greetings were over, I was invited to lay my difficulties before him, an invitation with which I hastened to comply.

My first question related to the laws of inheritance and the partition of property, but here I was not more fortunate than on a previous occasion, even Kámil being compelled to admit that he could not altogether comprehend them. I therefore passed on to the passage in the *Kitáb-i-Aḳdas* wherein the "Pilgrimage to the House" (*Ḥajju'l-Beyt*) is enjoined on all male believers who are able to perform it, and enquired what was meant by "the House" in question. To this Kámil replied that the house in Shíráz wherein the Báb formerly dwelt was intended. I asked eagerly if I might not be permitted to visit it while in Shíráz, whereat they looked doubtfully at one another, and said that they would try to manage it, but that it was difficult —firstly, because the present inmates of the house were all women; secondly, because the house was well-known to the Musulmáns, who would not fail to remark so unusual an event as the visit of a Firangí to a Bábí shrine.

1 His actual title was similar to, but not identical with, this. Considerations of expediency have led me to alter it as above.

My third question related to the following verse:—

"*It is not meet for any one to demand pardon before another; repent unto God in presence of yourselves; verily He is Forgiving, Bounteous, Mighty,* (*and*) *Swift to repent.*"

"What does this prohibition refer to?" I demanded of Kámil.

"To the power which your priests claim of absolving men of sin," he replied.

"But surely," I urged, "since this claim is in the first place confined to Christendom, and in the second place is limited to the priests of one sect amongst the Christians, it seems hardly necessary to prohibit it here."

"It is not confined to Christians," he replied, "for the *mullás* here claim very similar powers, though perhaps they formulate them in a less definite manner. When a man has embezzled or extorted money, and his conscience pricks him, he goes before one of our clergy and states the case to him, whereupon the latter takes a small sum from him in the name of religion, and declares the remainder purified thereby. All such tricks of priests and *mullás* are forbidden in this verse."

The fourth question which I put forward provoked a more fruitful discussion. It related to the verse wherein the Ṣúfís and others who lay claim to inward knowledge are condemned in the following terms:—

"*And there are amongst them such as lay claim to the inner and the inmost* (*mystery*). *Say, 'O liar! By God, what thou hast is but husks which we have abandoned to you as bones are abandoned to the dogs.'*"

"Surely," I demanded, "not only is the doctrine of the Ṣúfís in many ways near akin to your own, but it is also purer and more spiritual by far than the theology of the *mullás*. Do you condemn Manṣúr-i-Ḥalláj for saying, 'I am the Truth' (*Aná'l-Ḥakḳ*), when Behá makes use of the same expression? Do you regard Jalálu'd-Dín Rúmí as a liar when you continually make use of the *Maṣnaví* to illustrate your ideas?"

"No," answered Kámil, "assuredly Manṣúr and Jalálu'd-Dín

spoke with a true inspiration. This verse in no wise applies to them, nor to any of the Ṣúfís of past days; these were illumined with a true light in such wise that many of them clearly hinted at this 'manifestation,' as, for example, Ḥáfiẓ does, where he says—

'Ey ṣabá, gar bigzarí bar sáḥil-i-rúd-i-Aras
Búsé zan bar khák-i-án wádí, va mushkín kun nafas.'

'O zephyr, if thou passest by the banks of the river Araxes,
Implant a kiss on the earth of that valley, and make fragrant thy breath.'

For it was in the fortress of Mákú, by the Araxes, that His Highness the Point of Revelation (*i.e.* the Báb) spent the last three years of his life. Those intended by the verse in question are such as would oppose a pretended inward illumination to the full light of the present 'manifestation.'"

"So far as I understand you, then," I replied, "you admit the Ṣúfí doctrine, that a man may, by self-renunciation and intense abstraction, attain to the degree of 'Annihilation in God,' and that in this condition he may truly say, 'I am God,' inasmuch as he has forgone self, escaped from the illusions of plurality, and realised the unity of True Being. If this be so, I do not clearly understand in what way you regard the prophet as his superior, for surely no degree can be higher than this. As your proverb says, 'There is no colour beyond black' (*bálá-tar az siyáh rangí níst*). Still less do I see how you can speak of one prophet as superior to another, unless you place all but the highest in a lower rank than the Ṣúfí who has attained to absorption into the Divine Essence."

"When we speak of one prophet as superior to another," answered Kámil, "we speak in a manner purely relative, for the Universal Spirit (*Rúḥ-i-Kullí*) speaks through all of them alike. But inasmuch as they speak in divers manners, according to the capacity of their hearers, and according to the requirements of time and place, to us they appear in different degrees of perfection. The sun, for example, is the same to-day as it was yesterday, yet we say, 'To-day it is hotter than it was yesterday,' because we enjoy a fuller measure of its heat. But we do not by this expression mean to imply that there is any alteration in the sun itself. In the World of Ideas, regard the Universal Spirit as the sun which rises in each 'manifestation' from a different horizon. Or regard it as the Instructor of mankind, speaking always to those whom it addresses in a manner suitable to their comprehension, just as a teacher instructs children in the alphabet, boys in grammar, youths of riper age in logic, rhetoric, and other sciences, and full-grown men in philosophy. The teacher is always one and the same, but he manifests himself more or less perfectly according to the aptitude of those whom he addresses. So it is with the Universal Spirit, which speaks through all the prophets: only its outward vestment changes, and the phraseology of which it makes use; its essence and the message which it utters are ever the same. And since this Universal Spirit is Absolute Good, we must believe that it always has a manifestation in the world; for it is better that a tree should continually bear fruit than that it should only bear fruit at long intervals, and we are bound to attribute all that is best to the Spirit. Hence it follows that during the long intervals which separate one prophetic dispensation from the next, there must be in the world silent manifestations of the Spirit intrinsically not less perfect than the speaking manifestations whom we call prophets. The only difference is that a 'claim' (*iddi'á*) is advanced in the one case and not in the other. And it is only to this claim that the verse about which you enquire refers, as likewise does the verse, '*Whosoever claimeth a dispensation before the completion of a full thousand years is indeed a lying impostor.*'"

I now put to Kámil the following question, which I had already propounded in my first meeting with the Bábís of Shíráz:—"If the references to Christ's coming which occur in the Gospel refer to this manifestation, then they cannot be applied, as they are by the Muslims, to Muḥammad; in which case

Muḥammad's coming was not foretold by Christ, and Islám loses a proof which, as I understand, you regard as essential to every dispensation, viz. that it shall have been foreshadowed by the bearer of the last dispensation." To this he replied that in each dispensation announcement was made of future manifestations in general, and that what Christ said concerning His return applied equally to the advent of Muḥammad, and of the Báb, and of Behá. Muḥammad's title, *Khátamu'l-Anbiyá* ("Seal of the Prophets"), did not, he explained, signify, as the Muḥammadans generally suppose, "the last of the Prophets," as is proved by a passage occurring in one of the prayers used by pilgrims to Kerbelá and Nejef, wherein Muḥammad is called "the Seal of the prophets who have gone before, and the Key of those who are to come."

"Do you," I asked, "regard Zoroaster as a true prophet?"

"Assuredly," he replied, "inasmuch as every religion which has become current in the world, and has endured the test of time, must have contained at least some measure of truth, however much it may have been subsequently corrupted. Only a Divine Word can strongly affect and continuously control men's hearts: spurious coin will not pass, and the uninterrupted currency of a coin is the proof of its genuineness. The architect is proved to be an architect by his ability to construct a house; the physician is shown to be a physician by healing sickness; and the prophet vindicates his claim to the prophetic office by establishing a religion. These two things are his sufficient proof, and these only: that he has wisdom immediate and God-given, not acquired from men; and that his word so penetrates and controls men that for its sake they are willing to give up all that they most prize, and even to lay down their lives."

So completely was Kámil dominated by this conception of the nature of the proof required to establish a claim to prophethood, that I could not make him see the importance of any other evidence. "Had the Báb," I enquired, "explicitly or by implication signified the attributes, qualities, or personal peculiarities of his successor?" "No," he answered, "he merely spoke of him as '*Man yudh-hiruhu'lláh*' ('He whom God shall manifest'), without further describing him." "Could not dates of publication be proved for some of the prophecies wherein, as I had heard, Behá had foretold the downfall of Napoleon the Third, the assassination of the late Emperor of Russia, and other events of general notoriety?" Kámil thought that very possibly they could, but he evidently attached no importance to the question, and did not consider that the power of foretelling future events was any proof of a divine mission. As to the right of a prophet to inflict death, openly or secretly, on those who stubbornly opposed him, he took exactly the same view as the young Bábí Seyyid whom I had previously questioned on this matter. A prophet was no more to be blamed for removing an obdurate opponent than a surgeon for amputating a gangrenous limb.

Before I left I was shown several books and epistles which I had not previously seen. Amongst the latter was one addressed to a Christian, and another containing consolations addressed to one of Mírzá 'Alí's uncles on the occasion of his father's death and his own bankruptcy, on account of which (for he had failed to the extent of 60,000 *túmáns*) he was then in sanctuary at the Masjid-i-Naw. I was also shown a specimen of the *Khaṭṭ-i-tanzílí*, or "revelation-writing"; *i.e.* the almost illegible draft of Behá's utterances made by his amanuensis, Áḳá Mírzá Áḳá Ján, called *Khádimu'llláh* ("the Servant of God"), who, as I was informed, wrote with such speed that he could take down 1500 verses in an hour, this being, as it appears, the maximum of rapidity attained by Behá's revelations. Very few, however, save the amanuensis himself, could read this "revelation-writing."

A seal, on which was inscribed the name Ḥuseyn, both in the Arabic character and in the *Khaṭṭ-i-badí'*, or new writing invented by the Bábís, was also shown to me by one of those present. This new writing bears some superficial resemblance to the Armenian character. Each letter consists of a thick oblique stroke descending from right to left, to which are appended various fine curves and flourishes, all the thick lines being parallel and equidistant. I finally left at about eight o'clock, one of my Bábí friends remarking on the quick flight of the time, which, he added, was due, in their belief, to the fact that in spiritual converse such as we had held the soul soars above the limitations of Time and Space, and ceases to take cognisance of them.

A few days after this I again called on my friend Mírzá 'Alí. Shortly after my arrival, Ḥájí Mírzá Ḥasan joined us, and for nearly three hours we talked without intermission about the Bábí religion, save for a short time, when we were interrupted by an "ass's head."[1] The conversation ran, for the most part, on announcements of coming events by Behá, of which Ḥájí Mírzá Ḥasan related the following instances from his own personal experience:—

"You have heard of the 'Martyrs of Iṣfahán,'"[2] said he. "Well, shortly before their death I was at Acre with Ḥájí Mírzá Ḥasan 'Alí, whom you met at Iṣfahán, and Áḳá Seyyid Hádí. A day or two before the time fixed for our return to Persia we were with Behá, in a garden whither he sometimes repairs. He was seated, and we, according to our custom, were standing before him. Presently he bade us sit down, and ordered an attendant to give us tea. While we were drinking it he said, 'A great event will shortly take place in Persia.' In the evening Áḳá Seyyid Hádí privately enquired of him where this event would happen, and was informed that it would be in the 'Land of Ṣád' (Iṣfahán). Seyyid Hádí wrote to some of his friends in Persia, and in his letter mentioned this prophecy. When we reached Persia, Ḥájí Mírzá Ḥasan 'Alí remained at Ṭeherán, while I continued my journey towards Iṣfahán. At Káshán I was met by the news of the martyrs' arrest. As they were very rich I

1 See p. 300, *supra*. 2 See pp. 232–4, *supra*.

confidently anticipated that they would be able to regain their liberty by means of a heavy bribe to the authorities; neither did I connect this news with Behá's prophecy, for I rather understood that as pointing to some general catastrophe, such as a plague, famine, or earthquake. Four or five days later, however, came the news of their martyrdom, and I, instead of proceeding to Iṣfahán, turned back to Ṭeherán, knowing now that this was the event foreshadowed by Behá[1]. At the execution the *Imám-Jum'a*, seeing the headsman waver, had put his hand to his throat, and said, 'If there be any sin in this, let it be upon my neck!' Shortly afterwards he fell into disgrace, and retired to Mashhad, where he was attacked with abscesses in the throat (*khanázír*), of which he died. About a month after the death of the martyrs, Sheykh Báḳir received a letter from Acre containing the most terrible denunciations and prophecies of misfortune[2]. He subsequently went to Kerbelá. On returning thence to Iṣfahán he discovered that both his wife and his daughter (who was extremely beautiful) had been seduced by the prince-governor. His complaints and demands for redress resulted only in the production of a letter from his wife to her paramour, proving that she had made the first advances. Other troubles and misfortunes succeeded this, and Sheykh Báḳir presently died, as Behá had foretold, without having been able to enjoy his ill-gotten gains.

"This is one instance of Behá's prescience, about which you enquired. I will give you another, in which I myself was more closely concerned; but indeed such experiences are common to most of us who have been privileged to hold intercourse with our Master. I and Ḥájí Mírzá Ḥasan 'Alí, whom you saw at Iṣfahán, had been to visit Behá at Adrianople before he was

1 Ḥájí Mírzá Ḥasan here added an account of the events which had led to the death of the two Seyyids. This I have already given at pp. 232–3, *supra*, so I will not repeat it here.

2 Mírzá 'Alí told me that he had himself seen and copied this letter when a boy, before the calamities which it foreshadowed had befallen Sheykh Báḳir.

transferred to Acre. We received instructions to proceed thence to Egypt to encourage the Bábís resident there, and to avert a threatened schism. On the steamer in which we took our passage was a merchant of Tabríz, named Ḥájí Muḥammad Ja'far, who was also a believer. Just before we started we were ordered to avoid all conversation with him during the voyage. Although we were completely at a loss to understand the object of this prohibition, we obeyed it implicitly. In due course we safely reached Egypt, and there set ourselves diligently to confirm and encourage the believers, to check the schism which seemed impending, and to spread the faith amongst our compatriots in Egypt, so far as occasion served. The Persian Consul, unable to prevent our compatriots from visiting us, sent word to us that he was desirous of hearing about our religion, as he had been long absent from Persia, and had been unable to satisfy himself as to the truth of the matter. We, suspecting no evil (for we thought that in Egypt we ran no risk of arrest or imprisonment), accepted his invitation, and, on an evening which he appointed, visited him at the consulate. We sat talking with him till five or six hours after sunset, speaking freely and unreservedly about religious questions. When, however, we rose to take our leave, we were seized by the consul's servants and detained in his house, while messengers were sent to search our lodgings and seize our books and papers. Next day the consul accused us to Ismá'íl Páshá of heresy and sedition, representing us as confessedly belonging to a mischievous and dangerous sect, imbued with revolutionary ideas, which was hostile to all authority, and had already attempted the life of the Sháh of Persia. Of our heresy, he added, the five or six books found in our lodgings (books which we regarded as abrogating the Ḳur'án) would afford ample evidence. The case was laid before the Council of Enquiry (*Majlis-i-istinṭáḳ*). We were declared infidels and apostates, and, without a hearing, condemned to transportation for life to Khartoum in the Soudan. Thither we were sent, together with six or seven of our brethren. Ḥájí Muḥammad Ja'far of Tabríz, our fellow-traveller from Adrianople, was amongst the accused, but he was acquitted, as it was proved that we had not spoken to him on board the ship, and this was taken as presumptive evidence that he had no acquaintance with us. Then we understood why Behá had forbidden us to speak with him on the voyage, for had we done so he would have been involved in our misfortune."

"How long were you imprisoned at Khartoum?" I enquired; "and how did you effect your escape?"

"We remained there for seven years," replied Ḥájí Mírzá Ḥasan, "and for some time we were unable to communicate with our Master, or even to ascertain whither he had been removed (for vague rumours of his removal from Adrianople reached us). At length we foregathered with some Christian missionaries, whose goodwill we won by manifesting an interest in their doctrines. By means of these we were able to send a letter to Behá, informing him of our condition. On receiving our letter, Behá at once indited an answer, consoling us in our misfortune and announcing that our oppressor, Ismá'íl Páshá, would shortly fall from power, and that we should in a little while again stand in the presence of our Master. This letter was entrusted to an Arab called Jásim[1], who started at once for Khartoum, where he arrived six months later. When we received it there seemed to be no likelihood that the promises of deliverance which it contained would be fulfilled; but we were at least no longer wholly cut off from our friends, for the Arab not only took back with him our answer, but made arrangements

1 In the *Journal of the Royal Asiatic Society* for April 1892, pp. 311, 312, I have attempted to prove that one of the epistles now included in what is called by the Bábís the *Súra-i-Heykal* (the text of which has been published in full by Baron Rosen in vol. vi of the *Collections Scientifiques de l'Institut des Langues Orientales de St Pétersbourg*, pp. 149–192) is this very letter. Jásim, as I was informed at Acre, is merely a vulgar and local pronunciation of the name Ḳásim.

with believers at Suez to forward our letters in the future. Soon after this your English general came to Khartoum; I forget his name, but you will probably remember it."

"General Gordon," I answered.

"Yes," rejoined Ḥájí Mírzá Ḥasan, "that was it. Well, soon after his arrival he enquired about the prisoners whom he found in Khartoum, and especially about us and the other Persians. As he could find no crime recorded against us, he interrogated us as to the reason of our confinement. We told him that we were innocent of any crime, and that we had been condemned unheard, without a chance of defending ourselves. Our statement was confirmed by the prison officials, and General Gordon accordingly telegraphed to Ismá'íl Páshá demanding the reason of our detention. The replies which he received were vague and unsatisfactory, and he accordingly released us, telling us that we were free to stay or go as we pleased. Ḥájí Mírzá Ḥasan 'Alí and myself at once availed ourselves of this permission, and set out for Acre, but our companions, having wives and families at Khartoum, chose to remain there. Soon after this, as you know, Ismá'íl Páshá was deposed, and the prophecy contained in the epistle was fulfilled.

"You see that in all these cases when the prophecy was uttered there seemed to be no likelihood of its fulfilment; indeed, when we received instructions to act in a certain way, we seldom understood the reason till afterwards. For instance, on one occasion Ḥájí Mírzá Ḥasan 'Alí and myself were about to return to Persia from Acre by way of Diyár Bekr, Mosul, and Rawándíz. We were to take with us certain books destined for a believer at Tabríz; but, though we intended to proceed thither ourselves, we were instructed to convey them no farther beyond the Persian frontier than we could help, but to hand them over to some trustworthy person as soon as possible after entering Persia. Accordingly, when, on reaching Soúch Bulák, we heard that a certain believing merchant was staying in the caravansaray, we sent a message to him, informing him that we wished to see him at once on a matter of importance. He understood the nature of our business and what was toward, and, though with no small trepidation, came out to us at once. We walked away from the town, he following us, till we came to a streamlet, where we sat down and signed to him to do likewise. We explained to him our object in seeking him, and handed over to him the books, which he took with some reluctance, promising to convey them to Tabríz on the first opportunity. Next day we started for Tabríz, but we had not gone one parasang when we were attacked by Kurdish robbers and stripped of everything save our shirts and drawers. Had the books been with us, they too would have been lost. As it was, we had to return in this plight to Soúch Bulák. We laid a complaint before the Governor of Tabríz, Ḥuseyn Khán, son of the Ṣáḥib-Díván, and he promised us a hundred *túmáns*[1] as compensation, but this we never received."

"These are certainly very strange experiences," I said; "but of course the evidential value of prophecies referring to events of public notoriety, and existing in written form before those events came to pass, would be greater."

"Well, is there not the epistle to 'Álí Páshá,"[2] answered Ḥájí Mírzá Ḥasan, "in which his death in a foreign land, as well as the assassination of the Turkish ministers whom Cherkez Ḥasan slew, is clearly foreshadowed? And is there not also the epistle to Sheykh Báḳir, by whom the martyrs of Iṣfahán were done to death, of which you have already heard? These epistles are well known, and the events to which they refer are notorious. But let me tell you how Ḥájí Muḥammad Ja'far, who escaped exile to Khartoum, showed his devotion to Behá. When it was

1 £30 sterling.

2 I think, for reasons stated at pp. 271–2 of the *Journal of the Royal Asiatic Society* for 1892, that Fu'ád Páshá, not 'Álí Páshá, is really intended. I have not, however, thought myself justified in altering the notes of these conversations recorded in my diary. Cf. n. 1 on p. 353, *supra*.

decided by the Turkish Government to remove our Master and his family and relatives, as well as Mírzá Yaḥyá [1], from Adrianople, they at first determined to dismiss his followers with their passports and a sum of money for their journey to Persia. Ḥájí Muḥammad Ja'far refused to agree to this, declaring that he would not be separated from his master. He was told that he must obey the Sulṭán's orders. Thereupon he drew his knife, and, before they could prevent him, inflicted a severe wound on his throat; neither would he allow the surgeon who was immediately summoned to sew it up until he had received an assurance that he should be allowed to accompany Behá to Acre. The Turkish authorities were therefore obliged to telegraph to Constantinople that Behá's followers could not be separated from him, as they would rather kill themselves than leave him. However, the Turks tried to send some of them with Mírzá Yaḥyá to Cyprus; but these, on discovering whither their ship was bound, cast themselves into the sea to swim to the ship in which Behá was a passenger. They were finally allowed to accompany him to Acre, and only Mírzá Yaḥyá and his family [2] were conveyed to Cyprus, where they still remain."

"Why," I asked, "do you speak of Mírzá Yaḥyá as though he were of no account? In the books about your religion which I read in Europe he is described as the Báb's chosen successor, and, after him, as the chief of your sect?"

"Yes," replied Ḥájí Mírzá Ḥasan, "it is true that he was one of the early believers, and that at first he was accounted the successor and vicegerent of the Báb. But he was repeatedly

1 *I.e. Ṣubḥ-i-Ezel.* This title, however, is seldom given by the followers of Behá to Mírzá Yaḥyá. At most they call him "*án shakhṣ-i-Ezel,*" "that person Ezel."

2 This, as I subsequently discovered, is not strictly accurate. Four of Behá's followers (*Sheykh 'Alí Sayyáḥ*, *Muḥammad Báḳir*, *'Abdu'l Ghaffár*, and *Mushkin-ḳalam*) were sent with *Ṣubḥ-i-Ezel* to Cyprus. The first and second died in the island in 1871 and 1872 respectively; the third escaped in 1870; and the last left for Acre (where I saw him in the spring of 1890) in 1886.

warned not to withhold his allegiance from 'Him whom God shall manifest,' and threatened that if he did so he would fall from the faith, and become as one rejected. In spite of these clear warnings of his Master, he refused to acknowledge the new manifestation when it came; wherefore he is now regarded by us as of no account."

"Has he any followers in Cyprus?" I asked.

"Hardly any," answered Ḥájí Mírzá Ḥasan; "he writes absurd and meaningless letters to his partisans and to such as he hopes to persuade; but he is afraid to come to Persia (though the Turks have given him permission to do so [1]), fearing lest we should kill him."

"And would you kill him?" I enquired.

"I ask pardon of God! We are not authorised to kill anyone," replied the Bábí missionary.

Next day I again met Ḥájí Mírzá Ḥasan at the house of my friend Mírzá 'Alí. He had with him a commentary on the *Kitáb-i-Aḳdas*, with the aid of which we attempted, with but partial success, to unravel the complicated law of inheritance laid down by Behá. I was able, however, to learn from it something more about the arrangement of the Bábí year. This consists of nineteen months of nineteen days each, the same names serving alike for the months of the year and the days of the month. These names are as follows:—(1) *Behá*, (2) *Jalál*, (3) *Jemál*, (4) *'Aẓímat*, (5) *Núr*, (6) *Raḥmat*, (7) *Kalimát*, (8) *Kamál*, (9) *Asmá*, (10) *'Izzat*, (11) *Mashiyyat*, (12) *'Ilm*, (13) *Ḳudrat*, (14) *Ḳawl*, (15) *Masá'il*, (16) *Sharaf*, (17) *Sulṭán*, (18) *Mulḳ*, (19) *'Ulá*. According to this arrangement, the week is completely abolished; the third day of the eighth month, for example, is called *Yawmu'l-Jemál min shahri'l-Kamál*, "the day of Beauty (*Jemál*) in the month of Perfection (*Kamál*)." But, pending the retention of the week,

1 This also is a mistake. It was only after the English occupation of Cyprus that the Bábís interned at Famagusta were given permission to leave the island, on condition of forfeiting the pensions which they enjoyed.

new names have been given to the days composing it, as follows:—

Sunday,	*Yawmu'l-Jemál.*	Wednesday,	*Yawmu'l-'Iddál.*
Monday,	„ *Kamál.*	Thursday,	„ *Istijlál.*
Tuesday,	„ *Fiẓál.*	Friday,	„ *Istiḳlál.*

Saturday, *Yawmu'l-Jalál*[1].

I learned a few more new facts about the Bábís on this occasion. The relations of the Báb (of whom I saw several at Shíráz) are called "*Afnán*," and the sons of Behá "*Aghṣán*," both of these words meaning "branches." Behá's eldest son, 'Abbás Efendí[2], is called *Ghuṣn-i-Akbar* ("the Most Great Branch"), and also *Ákáyi Sirru'lláh* ("the Master, God's Mystery"), while another of his sons, named Mírzá Muḥammad 'Alí, is entitled *Ghuṣn-i-A'ẓam* ("the Most Mighty Branch")[3]. I was also shown the epistle from Behá to Sheykh Báḳir of which I had heard so much, and copied from it the passage which, as the Bábís declared, foreshadowed the recent disgrace of the Ẓillu's-Sulṭán. The translation of this passage is as follows:—"*Verily we heard that the provinces of Persia were adorned with the ornament of justice; but when we made enquiry we found them well-springs of injustice and sources of violence. Verily we see justice under the claws of oppression: We asḳ God to free it by an exercise of power and an act*

1 For a fuller account of the arrangement of the Bábí calendar, and of the system of intercalation employed to keep it in correspondence with the solar year (for the *Nawrúz*, which corresponds with the entry of the sun into the sign of the Ram and the vernal equinox, marks the beginning of the Bábí, as of the old Persian, year), see vol. ii of my *Traveller's Narrative written to illustrate the Episode of the Báb*, pp. 412–425. See also pp. 350–1, *supra*.

2 I have described the impression produced upon me by this remarkable man at pp. xxxv-xxxvi of vol. ii of my *Traveller's Narrative.*

3 Him I did not see at Acre; he was probably living in seclusion. Afterwards he became the Pontiff of the Behá'í Bábís, agreeably to Behá's testamentary depositions published in the original by Baron Rosen in vol. ii of the *Zapisski*, pp. 194–6. Behá died on 29th May (16th, old style) 1892. In my diary, as well as in my first article on the Bábís in the *Journal of the Royal Asiatic Society* for July 1888, I have wrongly transposed the titles of these two sons of Behá.

of authority on His part. Verily He is a Protector over whomsoever is in the earth and in the heavens."

One of the older Bábís whom I had previously met was present for a while; and I urgently repeated a request, which I had already made, that I might be taken to see the house (called "*Beyt*"—"the House" *par excellence*) formerly inhabited by the Báb. There had been some difficulty about this—firstly, because its inmates at that time were without exception women; and secondly, because it was feared that my visiting it would excite the suspicion of the Muḥammadans, to whom also the house was well-known; but these difficulties appeared to have been surmounted, and I received a promise that on the next day but one my wish should be gratified. It was therefore in the highest spirits that I took leave of my Bábí friends and turned homewards; but alas for my hopes, destined to disappointment; for, had I known it, there was already awaiting me there that which was to cut short my pleasant days in Shíráz, and debar me from the accomplishment of the "visitation" which I so ardently desired to perform.

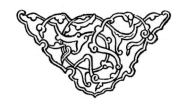

CHAPTER XII

FROM SHÍRÁZ TO YEZD

"*Mará dar manzil-i-Jánán ché já-yi-'aysh, chún har dam*
Jaras faryád mí-dárad, ki bar bandíd maḥmil-há?"

"Shall my Beloved one's house delight me,
When issues ever and anon
From the relentless bell the mandate,
''Tis time to bind thy litters on'?"

(ḤÁFIẒ, translated by Herman Bicknell.)

IT was, as I have said, in the best of spirits that I returned on the evening of this Friday, the 12th of April, to the house of my kind host the Nawwáb. I was well pleased with my environment at Shíráz, and more especially with the progress which I had made in cultivating the acquaintance and winning the confidence of the Bábís, from whom I had already obtained several precious manuscripts and much valuable information. On the morrow there was to be another picnic in the garden of *Rashk-i-Bihisht* ("the Envy of Paradise"), and on the following day I was to be allowed to visit the Báb's house. My mind was therefore filled with pleasant anticipations as I entered the Nawwáb's house.

"Ṣáḥib, you are late," exclaimed the servant who met me in the doorway; "where have you been? A telegram has come for you, and we would have sent it to you at once, but we knew not where you were."

I rushed upstairs to my room and tore open the telegram. It was a very long one, and the substance of it was this: that a European lady, travelling northwards to Ṭeherán with her husband, had been taken ill at Dihbíd, five stages from Shíráz; that her husband had been obliged to continue his journey; that she had been treated for some time by Dr S—— (then absent on a tour of inspection along the Bushire road), with whom communications had been maintained by means of the telegraph; that she was now much worse, being, indeed, in a very critical condition; and that Dr S——, unable to go to Dihbíd himself, had suggested that I, having a medical qualification, might go instead of him. The symptoms of the patient were fully described, and I was asked, in case I could come, to bring with me certain drugs which were not contained in the medicine-chest at Dihbíd. These, it was added, I could obtain from the acting head of the telegraph-office at Shíráz.

I sat down with the telegram in my hand to consider what I ought to do. A few moments' reflection showed me that, however unwilling I might be to quit Shíráz, and however diffident I might be as to my fitness to deal with what I clearly perceived was a difficult and critical case, I could not with a clear conscience refuse to go. It was a sore disappointment to me to tear myself away from Shíráz, and to forgo the visit to the Báb's house, to which I had so eagerly looked forward; to ride post for nearly 120 miles to confront a medical crisis, such as my inexperience ill fitted me to cope with, and which, as I anticipated, was but too likely to terminate fatally even before my arrival, was, moreover, a prospect that daunted me not a little. My duty, however, was perfectly clear; and when I joined the Nawwáb and Ḥájí Dá'í at supper, I told them that in all likelihood it was the last meal we should eat together for some time. As soon as it was over, I made the best of my way through the dark lanes leading to the *Bágh-i-Sheykh*, to consult with the acting head of the telegraph, and to obtain such medicines and instruments as I might require. The medical stores, which we ransacked, left very much to be desired, both as regards extent and quality, and it was with a miserably insufficient outfit that I returned about 1 a.m. to my abode. Even then, tired though I was, it was some while ere my anxiety suffered me to sleep.

Next day it seemed at first as though after all I might escape the dreaded ordeal; for in the morning a message came from Dihbíd giving a somewhat more favourable account of the patient, and bidding me not to start till further notice. I therefore decided to accompany the Nawwáb to the picnic at *Rashk-i-Bihisht*; but before doing so I made all my arrangements for quitting Shíráz. I had decided during the night that, should I be compelled to go to Dihbíd, I would not return directly to Shíráz, but would proceed to Yezd (a city that I greatly desired to visit, both because of its remote situation and essentially Persian character, and because it is the chief stronghold of Zoroastrianism in Persia), and thence make my way perhaps to Kirmán, and so back by Níríz and Dáráb. I therefore drew thirty *túmáns* (nearly £10) in cash for my travelling expenses, and obtained a cheque on Ardashír Mihrbán, the leading Zoroastrian merchant at Yezd, for the balance still remaining to my credit (147½ *túmáns*, or about £45). I also obtained a letter of introduction to this same Ardashír from one of the Zoroastrians at Shíráz, named Khusraw, and received from my kind friend Mírzá 'Alí a promise of letters to certain highly-considered Seyyids of Yezd to whom he was related. Having furthermore purchased a pair of saddle-bags (*khurjín*) and sundry other necessaries for my journey, I had transacted all my business, and was able to follow the Nawwáb to the garden of *Rashk-i-Bihisht*.

I found there the same company as on the previous occasion, but, as the weather was fine, they were sitting out in the garden on a stone platform overshadowed by trees, instead of in the summer-house. The time passed pleasantly in the usual fashion; and as sunset approached, and still no summons came from the telegraph-office, I began to hope that my time at Shíráz was, after all, not destined to be cut short. As I was returning from a solitary ramble round the garden, however, I suddenly caught sight of the *farrásh* of the telegraph-office, and knew, before I had heard the message which he brought, that my hope was disappointed. Hastily bidding farewell to the Nawwáb and his guests, I set off at once with the *farrásh* to the *Bágh-i-Sheykh*.

"Haste is of the devil, and tardiness from the All-Merciful," says a very Oriental proverb, and it is indeed an ill thing to be in a hurry in an Eastern land. It was well enough to have an order for three post-horses; but these, notwithstanding all my importunity, were not forthcoming till the following afternoon, and then, that no element of delay might be lacking, I discovered that my servant Ḥájí Ṣafar had gone off to the bazaars to buy a saddle. Even when we did ultimately start at about 3.15 p.m., I had to submit to several further delays for the purchase of sundry forgotten articles which were declared necessary; and it was already late in the afternoon when, from the summit of the *Tang-i-Alláhu Akbar*, I turned in my saddle to take what proved to be my last look at beautiful Shíráz. It was the very day, even the very time, when I was to have made my eagerly-desired visit to the Báb's house; and instead of this, here I was with my back to Shíráz, and the rain beating in my face, with a hundred miles and more to ride, to what I much feared would prove to be a death-bed. Remembering that life hung in the balance I urged on my horse, and presently found myself in the great plain of Marv-Dasht. Ḥájí Ṣafar and the *shágird-chápár* (post-boy) were far behind me, but, thinking that I remembered the way, I heeded this but little, and pushed on as fast as I could towards a group of poplar-trees beneath the eastern hills, which, as I thought, marked the position of Zargán. I was mistaken, however, for when I drew near them I found nothing but gardens; and it was in almost complete darkness and pouring rain that, drenched to the skin, and in the worst of tempers, I finally entered the narrow streets of Zargán, and alighted at the post-house, where (as it appeared impossible to proceed farther), I spent a miserable night, which wet clothes and prowling cats rendered almost sleepless.

Next morning I was off before 7 a.m. My first stage was to Púzé ("the Snout"), hard by Persepolis and Iṣṭakhr, of Achæmenian and Sásánian splendour. I had promised the *shágird-chápár* a present of two *ḳráns* if he brought me there by 9.30, and our pace at first was consequently good. But when the little solitary post-house of Púzé was already in sight, the miserable, jaded horse which I rode, after relapsing from a spasmodic and laboured trot into a walk of ever-increasing slowness, came to a dead stop, and I was forced to dismount and walk the last few hundred yards. Just before this took place, there met us three post-horses which a *shágird-chápár* was leading back from Púzé to Zargán. I stopped him, and demanded whether I should find horses at Púzé, as I wished to continue my journey without delay; intending, in case of need, to impṛess into my service the horses of which he had charge. He assured me that there were three fresh horses in the post-house, ready to start at once, and I left him, wondering whether he was speaking the truth. I wronged him by my suspicions; what he had told me was exactly and literally true, for, a few minutes later, these "three fresh horses, ready to start at once," issued from the post-house (now only a hundred yards distant) with another traveller, and set off northwards!

On reaching the post-house I found, of course, that there were no horses to be had; and there was nothing for it but to sit on a carpet on the roof and try to dispel my annoyance with tea and tobacco. I found that the traveller who had taken off the horses, as it were under my very nose, was none other than the Bombay Parsee whom I had met at Shíráz, and who was so anxious to get back to a land of railroads and hotels. He was so disgusted with caravan-travelling, and especially with the extortions of the servant whom he had engaged at Bushire, that he had decided to continue his journey alone by the post, although he was a very indifferent rider, and had only accomplished two stages during the whole of the previous day. It appeared that he had slept at Púzé that night, and was loitering about, without much intention of starting, when he saw me approaching; whereupon he hastened to secure his horses and set off before I arrived to contest their possession.

It was not till after mid-day that horses were forthcoming and I was able to proceed on my journey. At the very last moment, a woman brought her son to me, saying that she had heard I was a doctor, and begging me to examine an injury in his arm and prescribe for him. I was in no mood to tarry there any longer, and, telling her that if she had chosen to come to me any time during the last three hours I could have given her my undivided attention, but that now it was too late, I rode rapidly away. The *shágird-chápár* who accompanied us, stimulated by the promise of a present, exerted himself to accomplish his two *parasangs* an hour, and, by leaving the post-road and fording the river (which here runs to the west of it), effected so great a saving of distance that I caught up the Parsee just as he was leaving the post-house of Ḳiwám-ábád. I was obliged, however, to wait there for an hour and a half before I could obtain horses to take me on to Murgháb; though I was more than ever desirous of reaching Dihbíd that night if possible, as I had met my friend Muḥammad Ḥasan Khán Ḳáshḳá'í on his way to Shíráz, and he had told me that my presence was urgently required there.

The ride to Murgháb was delightful, the horses being good and the night superb. I passed the Parsee hard by the Tomb of Cyrus, and traversed the ruins of that classic plain by the light of a crescent moon, which hung suspended like a silver lamp in the clear, dark-blue sky. Once some great beast—a hyæna, probably—slunk, silent and shadow-like, across the path and disappeared in the bushes. It was 10 p.m. when I reached the post-house of Murgháb, where, much against my will, I was obliged to remain for the night. The Parsee arrived soon after me, and we established ourselves in the *bálá-ḳháné* or upper chamber. I could not help pitying him, for he was travelling in a manner at once costly and uncomfortable; and while he had, as he informed me, paid the servant who accompanied him from Bushire to Shíráz the exorbitant sum of 8½ *túmáns* for eleven days' bad service, he became involved in a lengthy, violent, and unprofitable altercation with the boy who had brought him from Ḳiwám-ábád about a trifling present of a *ḳrán*. The consequence of this was that all the post-house people were against him, and my *shágird-chápár*, well pleased with his reward, assured me that I should have the best and the Parsee the worst of their horses on the morrow.

Next morning, after a cold and uncomfortable night, I was off before 6 a.m., but, for all the fair words of the *shágird-chápár*, there fell to my lot the most miserable and ill-conditioned beast that ever it was my lot to bestride. So bad were all its paces, and so rough and steep the road, that it was past mid-day when I finally alighted at the telegraph-office of Dihbíd. Needless to say how anxious I was to learn news of my patient, or with what heartfelt thankfulness I heard from Mr and Mrs Blake, who welcomed me at the door, that she had taken a turn for the better, and was now practically out of danger. When I had eaten and rested a while, I visited her, and found that it was even as they had said: the crisis was past, and all that was left for me to do was to watch over the period of convalescence, which, fortunately, was short. Day by day I had the satisfaction of seeing a marked improvement in her condition, and it was only as a matter of precaution, and at the request of my host and hostess, that I remained for twelve days at Dihbíd, at the end of which time she was already able to walk out in the garden.

Dihbíd is one of the loneliest and bleakest spots that I saw in Persia. The village, so far as I recollect, consists of not more than fifteen or twenty hovels, a dilapidated caravansaray, the post-house, and the telegraph-office. This last is a spacious and comfortable dwelling, with a fair-sized garden attached to it; but its remote and solitary situation, and the severe cold of the winter season, must render it a very undesirable station to inhabit for a period of any length. The time which I spent there, however, passed pleasantly enough, for my host and hostess were kindness itself, and the surrounding country, though desolate, was not altogether devoid of interest. The worst feature of the place, indeed, in my estimation, was the complete lack of educated Persian society, the villagers being, without exception, poor peasants and quite illiterate. Such as they were, however, I saw a good deal of them; for of course it very soon became known that I was a "*ḥakím*"; and not from the village of Dihbíd only, but from the neighbouring hamlets of Ḳaṣr-i-Ya'ḳúb, Kushk, and Khurramí, the lame, the halt, and the blind flocked to consult me. Indeed, though I had no wish to practise the healing art, I soon found myself in the position of "le médecin malgré lui," for it would have been cruel and churlish to refuse these poor folk such service as the paucity of drugs and appliances at my disposal, and my own lack of practical experience, permitted me to render them. So every day, after I had attended to my own special patient, and sat for some time conversing with her, playing with her pet mongoose (a charming little animal), and hearing how the Persian wise women who had been called in before my arrival had treated her with what one can only describe as "tincture of Al-coran" (made by writing a text from the sacred volume on the inside of a cup or saucer, and then dissolving it in water), I used to hold a sort of reception for my Persian *clientèle*. The cases about which I was consulted were of the most miscellaneous character, varying in gravity from corneal opacities to cardiac disease, and from soft corns to epilepsy; but I do not propose to inflict on my readers any account of their symptoms, diagnosis, or treatment. Two of them, however, from a certain element of pathos which they seem to me to possess, are perhaps deserving of a brief mention.

The first of them was a little boy, aged twelve, named Khán Mírzá, who was suffering from paralysis and wasting of the arms and legs. When I had completed my examination of him and heard the history of his sickness, I knew that I could do nothing for him, and, as gently as possible, told his father and mother, who had brought him to me, that I was powerless to help them, adding that I was doubtful whether the best physicians in Firangistán, with the best appliances at their disposal, could restore him to health.

"Ṣáḥib," they wailed, "we know that you can cure him if you like. We are only poor peasants, and we cannot reward you as you have a right to expect, but tell us what sum of money will satisfy you, and if possible we will obtain it."

I told them that to cure their child it was not money I wanted, but the power of working miracles.

"Can you not believe me," I concluded, "when I tell you that I would rejoice to help you if I could, but that it is beyond my skill, and not mine only, but that of the greatest physicians of our country? I neither desire nor would consent to accept your money, but I have no right to deceive you with false hopes. Surely you must understand that there are diseases which no physician can heal, and that, for instance, when the *ejel*[1] comes, Jálínús and Buḳráṭ[2] themselves have no resource but to cry, '*there is no strength and no power save in God the Supreme, the Mighty!*'"[3]

"You speak truly," answered the father; "but that only holds good of death."

"How, then," said I, "does it come to pass that even amongst the rich there are blind and deaf and halt and dumb persons, who would give any price to be restored to health if they could find one to cure them, but who go down to their graves unhealed?"

1 *I.e.* the appointed time to die.

2 *I.e.* Galen and Hippocrates, who still to the Persian typify the perfection of medical skill.

3 "*Lá ḥawla wa lá ḳuvvata illá bi'lláhi'l-'Aliyyi'l-'Aẓím*," a form of words used by the Muḥammadans when all hope is gone, and only a miracle can avert disaster.

"It is because they cannot get hold of a physician like you,"[1] replied the man. In the face of such faith what could one do but make up a prescription which, if it were not likely to do much good, could at least do no harm?

The other case to which I have alluded was a poor old man, called Mashhadí Khudá-Raḥm, who lived at some distance from Dihbíd. The first time he came was late one afternoon, when I had seen all my other patients, and was resting after my labours. My servant (whether out of consideration for me, or to emphasise his own importance) refused to let him see me or to inform me of his arrival. The poor old man thought that he had been turned away because he had not brought a present, and when he returned and was finally admitted to me, he had in his hands a couple of fowls as a propitiatory offering. These he begged me to accept, promising that in the morning he would bring me a lamb; and it was with great difficulty that I succeeded in making him understand that I had no wish to deprive him of any portion of his scanty possessions. I found that his son had gone down to the turbulent and lawless town of Abarḳúh some two months previously, and had there been stabbed in a quarrel about a girl to whom he was attached. Since then the old father's eyesight had been gradually failing "through much weeping," as he said; and it was for this that he had sought me. I did the best I could for him (which, I fear, was not much), and he went on his way and was no more seen by me.

Of the country round about Dihbíd I need say but little. Hard by the village stands a ruined tower, with enormously thick walls built of dried clay, which the country-folk believe to have been one of the seven hunting-palaces of Bahrám Gúr[2]. I was

1 "*Bi-jihat-i-ánki misl-i-shumá ḥakímí gír-ashán namí-áyad.*" The expression *gír ámadan* (to be got hold of), though not, I think, found in classical, is common in colloquial, Persian.

2 "The *haft gunbudh*" of Bahrám (or Varahrán) V, surnamed "*Gúr*" (the "wild ass"), from his fondness for chasing that animal, are familiar to every student of Persian literature. The king in question reigned from A.D. 420

informed by one of the inhabitants that coins and ornaments had been dug up in its vicinity. Round about the tower are some curious rocks, looking like dried masses of mud. Many of these are hollowed out into caves, in which the wandering tribesmen take up their abode in summer. The stream which flows past Dihbíd, crossing the main road a few yards south of the telegraph-office, runs in a south-westerly direction to Ḳaṣr-i-Ya'ḳúb ("Jacob's Castle"), where, as I was told, it forms a lake, in which are fish of considerable size. Some distance to the east of the stream, and about two and a half or three miles south-west of Dihbíd, stands a solitary withered tree hard by a ruined and deserted village and graveyard known as Mazra'i-Sabz. This tree, as I was informed by Mr Blake, is said to be haunted by a white-robed woman. I could learn no particulars about the legend connected with this ghost, and only mention it because it is the sole instance of this type of apparition which came to my knowledge in Persia. To the north and north-west of Dihbíd lie the hamlets of Kushk, Ḥuseyn-ábád, and Khurramí, which I did not visit, and which are, I believe, places of but little importance. The whole plateau is, as I have said, of considerable elevation, and owing, I suppose, to the rarefaction of the air, one is liable when walking to experience a certain curious and unpleasant shortness of breath.

It was 29th April when, my patient being convalescent and able to take the air in the garden adjoining the telegraph-office, I finally quitted Dihbíd and turned my face eastwards towards Yezd. After the somewhat monotonous though pleasant fortnight which I had spent at Dihbíd, I looked forward eagerly to the excitement of a journey through country far wilder and less known than any which I had hitherto traversed. I had some

to 438. At Shíráz I was told by Ḥájí Naṣru'lláh Khán, the *Íl-Khání*, that the sites of all these seven-hued palaces were known to him. He gave me a list of them, but I did not write it down at the time, and only remember that he identified the *Ḳaṣr-i-zard* or "yellow tower" with Kushki-zard, on the *sar-ḥadd* (or high-level) road to Shíráz.

difficulty in obtaining animals for the march, but at length succeeded in hiring a mare for myself, and two donkeys for my servant and baggage, for which I was to pay the moderate sum of seven *túmáns* (rather more than £2), it being understood that the journey to Yezd was to be accomplished in six or seven days. A fine handsome young man named Bábá Khán was to act as guide, and to take charge of the animals. This arrangement, satisfactory enough to myself, was very distasteful to Ḥájí Ṣafar, who was greatly incensed at being expected to ride a donkey, and was only pacified with some difficulty.

We left Dihbíd about 7.30 in the morning, as our intention was to push past the caves of Hanishk (where two or three musket-men are stationed as a guard, and where it is possible to halt for the night) and reach one of the flourishing villages which lie like islands of verdure in the sandy desert of Abarḳúh. The Yezd road quits the main road from Shíráz to Iṣfahán close to the Dihbíd caravansaray, and runs in a north-easterly direction towards the tail of the mountains above Hanishk. These we reached about 10.30 a.m., and then began the long descent towards the plain. The sides of the narrow ravines through which our path wound were abundantly decked with flowers, concerning which I questioned Bábá Khán, who turned out to be a very intelligent and agreeable companion. There were tall, hyacinth-like spikes, with white blossoms and very thick succulent stems, called *Kurroghlú*; fine large mountain chrysanthemums, called *Dá'údí*; abundance of wild rhubarb (*Riwás*); and a little ill-smelling plant with orange-brown flowers, named *Már-giyáh* (snake-grass). After passing a beautifully green grassy spot called Gúshtí, well watered by a stream which ran down the ravine, where some peasants were pasturing their cows and donkeys, we came, at 11.15 a.m., to a point where the valley opened out somewhat and allowed us to see for the first time the great sandy plain (*ḳaffé*) of Abarḳúh spread out at our feet. This plain, which at its narrowest point (where we proposed to cross it) is about fifteen parasangs (fifty-two miles) in width, runs, roughly speaking, from north-west to south-east, and is bounded on both sides by mountains, the highest of which, behind which lies Yezd, were streaked with snow. The plain itself is a dreary, sandy waste, encrusted here and there with patches of salt; yet notwithstanding this (or perhaps partly because of this), the villages which lie on its western border—Ismin-ábád, Mihr-ábád, Sháráz, and the larger town of Abarḳúh—present a singularly fresh and verdant appearance. Near to the town of Abarḳúh, and to the east of it, is a line of black jagged hills, rising abruptly from the plain, and crowned with ruins of some size, amongst which a dome called Gunbudh-i-'Álí is particularly conspicuous.

At 11.30 we reached Hanishk, and halted for lunch. There are no buildings here, but only a few caves in the rock, which serve the *tufankchís* (musket-men) there stationed for a dwelling; a couple of fine mulberry-trees, under which we rested; a stream; and a spring of clear, cool water. Leaving Hanishk again at 12.45, we continued our descent, and finally, at about 2.15 p.m. emerged from the narrow jaws of the ravine into the plain, which from this point slopes but very slightly downwards towards Abarḳúh. At 3.30 we passed a ruined cistern (*ab-anbar*) covered by a dome, and about 6.30, just as the sun was setting, reached the beautiful green oasis formed by the gardens of Mihr-ábád, where we were to halt for the night. Round about these, enclosed within a high outer wall to keep off the drifting sand, lay fields of corn and of the white poppy (for opium is largely produced in all this district); and I was amazed to see what the skilful irrigation of the Persians could do for even so unpromising a soil. It is more irrigation, not railways and factories, that Persia needs to increase her prosperity; and were the means for this forthcoming, many a dreary desert might yet blossom with the rose and the poppy.

There is, of course, no post-house at Mihr-ábád, nor, so far as I know, a caravansaray; but I was far from regretting this, as

I obtained a much more delightful resting-place in a beautiful rose-garden near the gate of the village. I was, it is true, obliged to sleep in the open air; but, apart from the lack of privacy which it involved, this was a luxury rather than a hardship, the temperature in this low hill-girt plain being so much higher than at Dihbíd that I seemed to have passed in one day from early spring to midsummer. In a sort of alcove in the high mud wall a carpet was spread for me, and here I esconced myself, Ḥájí Ṣafar taking up his position under the opposite wall. Tea was soon prepared, and while I was drinking it the gardener brought me two great handfuls of loose rose-leaves—a pretty custom, common in this more eastern part of Persia.

Needless to say, visitors soon began to arrive; and, as none of them thought of moving till midnight, I had plenty of opportunity of observing their characteristics. In several ways they appeared to me to differ very widely from any type of Persian which I had hitherto seen, notably in this, that they manifested not the least curiosity about my business, nationality, or religion. Sullen, independent, quarrelsome, and totally devoid of that polished manner which characterises most of their countrymen, they talked for the most part with one another, and appeared to take little interest in anything except sport, horses, fire-arms, spirits, and opium. The only occasion on which Dáráb Khán, the son of a local magnate, addressed me with any appearance of interest was when he demanded whether I had with me any strong drink. I told him I had not. "You lie," replied he; "all Firangís drink." I then recollected that I had a little pocket-flask half-filled with whisky. "Well, I have this small quantity," I said, "in case of emergencies." "Let me see it," said he. I handed it to him, whereupon he unscrewed the top, sniffed at the whisky, and finally put the flask to his mouth, drained it at one gulp, and threw it back to me with a grimace. I asked him what he thought of it. "Poor stuff," he said—"no better than our *'araḳ*, if as good. You are certain you have no more?"

I told him I had not another drop, and thereat he ceased to pay any further heed to me.

Dáráb Khán had with him a very handsome page; another most savage-looking attendant named Ḥuseyn, with enormously long drooping moustaches, which gave him somewhat the appearance of a Chinaman; one or two younger brothers; and several friends. They all sat together, servants and masters, without distinction of rank; they were nearly all armed to the teeth; and they nearly all smoked opium and drank as much spirits as they could get.

As we had made a long stage on the first day, and as the heat was now considerable, Bábá Khán decided to await the approach of evening before starting to cross the desert. In consequence of this I saw plenty of Dáráb Khán and his dissolute companions, who kept coming and going from 8 a.m. onwards. One, Ja'far Khán, also came to consult me with symptoms of indigestion and disordered liver. Having received a blue pill, he became communicative, and entertained me with a panegyric on a certain Mullá Ghulám Riẓá of Taft (near Yezd), who was highly reputed for his medical skill, and a dissertation on Persian pharmacology. Drugs, he explained, were primarily divisible into two classes: "hot" (used for combating "cold" diseases), amongst which the most efficacious were *bábúné*, *afsantín-i-Rúmí*, and *gul-i-gáv-zabán*; and "cold" (useful for the treatment of "hot" maladies), of which *ríshé-i-khaṭmí* (hollyhock root), *ríshé-i-kásní*, and *ríshé-i-kadú* enjoyed the highest reputation. This interesting dissertation was unfortunately interrupted by the arrival of two or three of Dáráb Khán's younger brothers (so, at least, I judged them to be from their likeness to him), who forthwith began to pull about my effects and examine my clothes and bedding. One of them, seeing Ḥájí Ṣafar smoking a cigarette, plucked it out of his mouth and began to smoke it himself, whereupon he was, to my great delight, seized with so violent a fit of coughing that he had to retire. The relief afforded by his absence was, however, of short duration, for he soon came back, accompanied by a man who complained of that most usual of Persian ailments "pain in the loins" (*dard-i-ḳamar*). This latter I declined to treat, whereupon he said, "Since you will not give me any medicine, I will have a cigarette." I accordingly made him one, which he smoked rapidly, but without much apparent enjoyment, for he suddenly threw it away and departed hastily without a word. It was evident that cigarettes were a novelty in the plain of Abarḳúh.

I was now left for a while in comparative peace; for my host, after amusing himself for a while by firing bullets with his long Shírází gun at the birds on the garden wall, turned Dáráb Khán's troublesome young brothers out of the garden and shut the door. At 3.30 p.m. the animals were laden and ready to start. Ḥájí Ṣafar gave the owner of the garden five *ḳráns* (about three-and-sixpence), with which he was evidently well satisfied, for he came and showed me the money, remarking, "This was not necessary, nor so much." He then gave me a large bunch of roses as I was about to mount, and walked beside me to the outskirts of the village, where he bade us farewell. As soon as he had gone, Ḥájí Ṣafar began to abuse the people of the village roundly for their churlishness, adding that one of the boys had stolen a pair of goloshes and other articles out of my baggage, but that he had recovered them. "I should like to have given him a good thrashing," he concluded, "but I thought you would not like it." Prudence, I imagine, had something to do with his self-restraint, for the Abarḳúhís are not the kind of people one would care to anger.

Our course at first lay nearly due north, towards the fantastic, jagged hills which rise abruptly from the sandy plain close by the city of Abarḳúh. As we passed between two ridges of these, I could plainly see the ruined domes, minarets, and walls which crown their summits. The largest dome stands at the northern end of the northern ridge, and is called *Gunbudh-i-'Alí*. I should greatly have liked to explore these ruins, and to see something of the city of Abarḳúh, which Ja'far Khán declared to be "the oldest city in Persia, except Salkh" (by which, I suppose, he meant Iṣṭakhr), and to be full of ancient monuments; but unfortunately this was impossible. Emerging from between these rocky ridges, we found ourselves once more in the open sandy plain, and could discern at a short distance several small villages. In a little while we passed one of them, called Sháráz, just beyond which the road bifurcated, the left-hand or more northerly branch (for we had now again turned nearly due east) leading to Shams-ábád; the right or more southerly one to Ḥakím. We followed the latter, and reached Ḥakím about 6.45 p.m. as it was getting dusk. Here we found a small caravan of donkeys, laden with wheat for Yezd; and, learning that this was not to start till the moon rose, we halted in the plain for rest and refreshment.

After supper I lay gazing at the starry sky till sleep overcame me. About midnight Ḥájí Ṣafar awoke me, and soon afterwards we started at a good pace (for these caravans of donkeys travel faster than ordinary caravans) on the long desert stage which was to bring us to Cháh-Begí, the first habitable spot on the Yezd side of the desolate plain. Bare and hideous as this desert is by day, seen in the silver moonlight it had a strange weird beauty, which produced on me a deep impression. The salt-pools and salt-patches gleamed like snow on every side; the clear desert air was laden with a pungent briny smell like a sea-breeze; and over the sharply-defined hills of Yezd, towards which we were now directly advancing, hung the great silvery moon to the right, and the "Seven Brothers" (*haft birádarán*), or Great Bear, to the left. I kept in advance of the caravan, and watched with a keen pleasure the stars "beginning to faint on a bed of daffodil sky," till first the "caravan-killer" (*ḳáraván-* or *chárvádár-ḳush*) and then the morning star dissolved in the rosy flush which crept upwards from behind the eastern mountains, and suddenly, like a ball of fire, the sun leaped up over their serrated summits, scattering the illusions of the night, and bringing into view chains and ridges of low hills which had hitherto seemed to form part of the main mass.

As it grew light, a man carrying a large wallet over his shoulders, and walking rapidly, came up with me. I saluted him, and entered into conversation. He was, as I gathered, a *ḳáṣid*, or courier, with letters from Ábádé for Yezd. He told me that he had been a soldier in one of the Ẓillu's-Sulṭán's regiments till these were disbanded. He did not like a soldier's life, and had once deserted, walking from Iṣfahán to Ábádé (about 130 miles) in two days. He had also walked from Yezd to Mashhad by the desert road in twenty days, and from Ṭeherán to Mashhad in the same time. He asked me many questions about England and its government, and complained bitterly of the heavy taxation to which the Persian peasantry were subjected. The tax on a donkey was, he said, two *túmáns* (about 13*s.*) a year, and on a sheep three *túmáns* (nearly £1). He further informed me that bread was dear at Yezd, costing three *panábáts* (one and a half *ḳráns*, or about 11*d.*) the *man*; and that during the great famine about sixteen years earlier it had risen to sixteen *ḳráns* (about 10*s.*) the *man*, and that the people were in some cases driven to eat human flesh to appease their hunger. As we approached Cháh-Begí we passed numerous tamarisk-bushes (*gaz*), which, as my companion told me, had formerly been much more abundant, till they were cut down by order of the Government, because they afforded a harbour to highway robbers of the Bakhtiyárí and other nomad tribes. He gave the people of Abarḳúh a very bad character, declaring that fatal quarrels were of constant occurrence there.

We reached Cháh-Begí, a miserable walled village, containing a few sordid and quarrelsome inhabitants, a little before 7 a.m., and alighted at the dilapidated caravansaray, in front of which stood several sickly trees. I spent the whole day in the large, dusty, ruinous chamber allotted to me; sleeping, eating, washing to the very limited extent permitted by the surroundings, and writing up my diary, being the only resources available for passing the long, hot day. A certain excitement, which can hardly be described as pleasurable, was produced from time to time by the appearance of sundry large and offensive insects; first a tarantula (*roteyl*, or *khâyé-gaz*), which was killed on the wall where it sat by a kick from Bábá Khán, who informed me in an encouraging manner that they had just killed another one outside, and that, as these were probably a pair, there was nothing to apprehend. I failed to see the conclusiveness of this reasoning, and (as I had left my bedstead at Shíráz, and was therefore obliged to spread my bedding on the floor) continued to keep a good look-out, for which I was presently rewarded by seeing a large black creature, shaped something like a gigantic wood-louse, emerge deliberately from a cranny in the wall. I threw half a brick at it, and it vanished with a horrid splash. After this I felt little inclination for sleep, but after supper fatigue overcame me and I fell into a deep slumber, from which I was aroused about an hour after midnight by Ḥájí Ṣafar.

It was with sincere delight that I quitted this detestable spot about 1.30 a.m., and found myself once more on the road in the cool, clear moonlight. Having nothing else to do, I watched and timed the changes in the sky which heralded the dawn. At 3.30 a.m. the "False Dawn" (*Ṣubḥ-i-Kádhib*) appeared, a little to the north of the point whence the sun subsequently arose. At 3.45 a rosy tinge was perceptible in the sky. At 4.0 the morning star began to shine over the hills. At 4.30 it was quite light, and at 4.55 the sun rose; but it was not till 6 a.m. that the day began to grow warm. An hour later we entered the village of Bághistán, where the road bifurcated. Taking the right-hand branch, we presently passed the castellated village of Írdún, situated on a small hill, and, at about 8 a.m., reached a beautiful village named Gōd-i-Shírdán or Sharíf-ábád, which, with its shady lanes, rippling streams, and verdant trees, reminded me more of my native land than anything I had seen for many a long day. Here we halted; and in one of the well-kept gardens which gave to the village so flourishing an appearance I spread my bed under a yellow rose-tree, and slept for a while till tea was ready. I then found that the little streamlet beside me had been diverted into another channel for the irrigation of another part of the garden, and, as it now threatened to inundate my resting-place, I was obliged to alter my position. Just as I had effected this, and was preparing to go to sleep again, a deputation of the principal inhabitants of the village and the neighbouring hamlet of Dih-i-Pá'ín was announced. Of course they wanted medical advice; but, needless to say, they did not touch on the business which had brought them till they had exhausted all other topics of conversation. Amongst other things they informed me that two men had lately been put to death by the new Governor of Yezd for drinking wine. I expressed surprise, adding that if the Governor of Shíráz were to take it into his head to deal thus harshly with wine-drinkers, he would soon have no subjects left to govern. "Yes," replied my informant, "but, thank God, this is not Shíráz."

Other persons gradually joined the group which had gathered round me, amongst these being a respectable-looking, though poorly-clad, man, who had joined our caravan at Ḥakím. Presently one of those present asked me if I knew Russian. "No," I said, "why should I? A great distance separates the English from the Russians." "One man only intervenes between them," remarked my fellow-traveller. I looked at him in wonder. "You are not a Russian," I exclaimed. "I am a Russian subject, at any rate," he replied, "though a Musulmán; my native place is Eriván."

At length my visitors began to approach the object which had brought them. "Was it true," they asked, "that I had some knowledge of medicine?" I answered in the affirmative. "Would I visit a woman in their village who was stricken with a grievous sickness?" they continued. I asked whether she could not come and see me, but they told me that she was too ill, adding that their village was quite close at hand. It proved to be about two miles off, and on my arrival there the whole population (some twenty or thirty souls) turned out to stare at me, and followed me into the sick-room. The patient, a middle-aged woman, was lying on the floor in the middle of the room, and was evidently very ill; though, owing to the impossibility of making a careful examination, and the distracting effect of the eager crowd of onlookers, who kept up a continual buzz of conversation, I was unable to satisfy myself as to the nature of her complaint. When I had prescribed such medicines as appeared to me most likely to afford her some relief, I was called upon to examine several other sick persons, and it was only with much difficulty that I was able to get away. As I was leaving, one of the principal inhabitants of the village presented me, as a reward for my trouble, with a saddle-cover, which I bestowed on Bábá Khán, who had come with me to carry my box of drugs and instruments. Ḥájí Ṣafar was greatly annoyed at what he called the meanness of the people, declaring that I might have gained a hundred *túmáns* in fees since I left Dihbíd but for my lamentable weakness in giving advice gratis.

We left Gōd-i-Shírdán about 4.30 next morning, it being then quite light; but though it was mid-day before we reached Sunij, our next halting-place, we did not suffer any inconvenience from the heat, as we were again ascending into a cool and mountainous region. The wheat-laden donkeys had started at an earlier hour, but the Erivání, whose acquaintance I had made on the previous day, had preferred to wait for us, and I had a good deal of conversation with him. I found him a pleasant and intelligent companion, for he had travelled widely, and spoke, besides his own Caucasian Turkish, Ottoman Turkish, Russian, Persian, and Arabic. He told me that it was now three years since he had left Eriván, whence he had journeyed to Tabríz, Ṭeherán, Iṣfahán, Kirmánsháh, Baghdád, Bushire, and Shíráz. He was now proceeding to Yezd, having come with a caravan northward bound as far as Dihbíd, where he had been detained for ten days ere he could find means of continuing his journey. He had heard at Dihbíd that I was going to Yezd, but had hesitated to join me, not knowing what manner of man I might be. "Yesterday, however," he concluded, "I watched you with those people in the garden, and saw that you were not wanting in 'crop,'[1] for you never once showed any irritation at their absurd and impertinent questions, but continued to answer them with a smile and a jest." I asked him whither he was bound, and when he expected to return to his home. He replied that from Yezd he intended to go to Mashhad, and thence through Afghanistan to India; and that it would be two years at least ere he again reached Eriván. I asked him if he did not fear to trust himself amongst the treacherous and cruel Afghans, but he answered, "No, with patience and courage a man can go wheresoever he will on God's earth."

The road which we traversed this day was singularly beautiful, and the country looked prosperous and well cared for. We passed two villages, however, one on the right and another on the left, named Ḥaydar-ábád and 'Abbás-ábád respectively, which had been deserted owing to the failure of their water supply. The trees in their gardens were still for the most part green and luxuriant, but already the fragile mud walls were falling into ruin; and, meditating on this process of rapid decay, I ceased to wonder at the many Persian towns and villages mentioned by early geographers and historians of which no trace remains, and which it seems impossible to identify. At a considerable distance to

1 *Ḥawṣala*, properly the crop of a bird, or the stomach of an animal, is commonly used in Persian in the sense of patience, evenness of temper, or capacity for stomaching insults or annoyances. So a short-tempered or impatient man is described as *tang-ḥawṣala*. Thus Náṣiru'd-Dín Sháh says in one of his poetical compositions—

"*Dúst na-báyad zi dúst dar gilah báshad; Mard na-báyad ki tang-ḥawṣala báshad.*"

"Friend should not complain of friend; a man should not be short-tempered."

the right (north), on a low conical hill, the Castle of Bunáft, with the village of the same name below it, was clearly visible; and, farther east, the precipitous black crag called Ḳal'at-i-Zard ("the Yellow Castle"), which, as Bábá Khán informed me, is only accessible by one path, and at the foot of which lies the village of Balkh-ú-Guríz. Farther on we passed the village of Kattú (also on the right), by which runs the direct road from Yezd to Bawánát, and soon afterwards turned the northern end of the vast pile of cliffs which forms this western face of the Shír-Kúh, and, following a ravine to the left, down which rushed a clear, cool mountain stream, presently reached the beautiful Alpine village of Sunij, a mass of gardens and groves situated amidst the grandest rock-scenery. A more charming spot for a summer residence could hardly be conceived, and the people of Yezd are fortunate in being able to retreat so easily from their baking, sandy plains to this and other equally delightful highland resorts.

I succeeded in obtaining a very comfortable lodging, past the door of which ran a stream of beautiful clear water. In the afternoon I was visited by a number of the inhabitants, who were of the true Yezdí type, fair-skinned and gray-eyed, with loosely-coiled bluish turbans, and the curious sing-song drawl which always characterises the speech of Yezd. This accent reminded me strongly of the south Northumbrian in English, the modulation of the voice in both cases being very similar; it is generally much laughed at in Persia, but to me it always seemed soothing, and at times rather pretty. My visitors, of course, were very inquisitive, and asked me more than the usual number of questions, chiefly about my religion and the business that had brought me into a region so seldom traversed by Europeans. "Was it true," they asked, "that Europeans accounted the flesh of the pig a lawful food?" "Had we fixed ablutions and prayers?" "How were marriages celebrated in Europe, and what were the regulations as to dowry?" Presently a comical-looking old man broke in, declaring that as for my business, he had no doubt that

I had come "to effect disruptions in Church and State" (*rakhné dar dín ú mamlakat kardan*), else how did I come to know the geography of the country, and to be so anxious for information as to the names of all the villages, mountain-peaks, and streams in the neighbourhood? Here the Eriváni interposed, saying that all the Europeans, even the children, learned geography by means of maps such as I possessed. Thereupon my map was at once called for and exhibited to an admiring crowd, some of whom, however, expressed great disappointment that I had not also a microscope (*khurdé-bín*), so that they might by its aid see what was going on in the streets of Yezd!

Next day we were off about 5.30 a.m., many people assembling to witness our departure. Amongst these was the old man who had regarded me with such suspicion on the previous evening, but he seemed to have changed his opinion of me for the better, for, in bidding me farewell, he begged me, should I again pass that way, by no means to omit a visit to the ancient castle of Shawwáz, situated ten parasangs away, in the direction of 'Alí-ábád. Our host accompanied us till we were clear of the village and on the road to Taft, his little son following us somewhat farther, plaintively calling out to Ḥájí Ṣafar in his childish Yezdí drawl, "*Ye' tá mácham na-kardí!*" ("Thou hast not given me one kiss")—a remark to which Ḥájí Ṣafar only replied with an outburst of mirth and mimicry, which caused the boy to turn petulantly away.

The road which we followed was again singularly picturesque, for it led us almost immediately below the rugged and precipitous cliffs of the Shír-Kúh, rent and shattered on every ridge into fantastic towers and needles. We were now again descending towards the plain of Yezd, and in a valley to the left could discern amongst several others the village of 'Alí-ábád, through which passes another road from Yezd to Abarḳúh. The conversation of my Eriváni friend did much to dispel the monotony inseparable from even the most picturesque march. Amongst other things, he told me a rather clever variation of the well-known, though probably fictitious, anecdote concerning the interview between the poet Ḥáfiẓ and Tímúr-i-lang, the Tartar conqueror, better known as Tamerlane, who, as the story runs, angrily demanded of Ḥáfiẓ how he had dared, in one of his poems, to say that he would give Samarḳand and Bukhárá for the black mole on his beloved's cheek. According to the usual version of the tale, Ḥáfiẓ replied, "Yes, sire, and it is by such acts of generosity that I have been reduced to the poverty in which you see me"; whereupon Tímúr laughed, and ordered a sum of money to be given him. According to my companion's account, however, the poet effected his deliverance by an ingenious emendation in the obnoxious line. "'*Bakhsham Samarḳand ú Bukhárá-rá!*'" ('I would give Samarḳand and Bukhárá') he exclaimed; "those are not my words! What I wrote was, '*bakhsham si man ḳand ú du khurmá-rá*' ('I would give three stone of sugar and a couple of dates'), and some ignorant scribe has altered it into this!"

We reached the large and flourishing village of Taft about mid-day, two hours and a half after passing another prosperous and pretty village called Khuráshé. Taft was looking its best on that fine May morning, the luxuriant green of its gardens being pleasantly varied by the bright red flowers of the pomegranates in which they abound. A wide, sandy river-bed, at this season devoid of water, divides it into two parts, whereof the northern is inhabited by the Zoroastrians and the southern by the Muḥammadans. We followed this river-bed, which appeared to serve also as a road, for some distance, till we came to a point where the houses were more abundant and the gardens fewer. Here we halted, and began to look for a lodging, which I finally obtained in a sort of pavilion in the middle of a large square. Four rooms, raised somewhat above the level of the ground, opened out of the central hall of this pavilion, which was surrounded by a few trees, and appeared to offer desirable and comfortable quarters. Unfortunately, these rooms were lighted by iron-barred windows opening on to the square, and I soon found myself an object of interest to a crowd of blue-turbaned, bearded men, and fair-faced, gray-eyed boys, who watched me using a knife and fork to eat my lunch with uncontrolled delight and amusement. They were perfectly well-behaved, and evidently had no desire to annoy me; but I never before realised what the lions in the Zoological Gardens have to put up with!

Later in the afternoon I went for a short walk down the road-river with my Erivání friend, after extricating myself with some difficulty from a crowd of people with sore eyes and other ailments for which they desired treatment. In the course of our walk we were accosted, to my great delight, by two of the yellow-robed Zoroastrians, whom I now saw for the first time in the raiment which in Yezd and Kirmán serves to distinguish them, even at a distance, from their Muḥammadan fellow-citizens, but which in other parts of Persia they are permitted to lay aside. The Erivání asked them what was their religion, to which they proudly replied, "*Zardushtí, Kiyání*" ("Zoroastrian, Achæmenian"), whereat he laughed not a little. On returning to my lodging, I found a handsome clever-looking man waiting to see me. From his talk I had little doubt that he was a Bábí, for he enquired very minutely into the Christian belief as to the advent of the Messiah, adding, "Perhaps He *has* come, and you have not recognised Him," and presently, "Have you heard news of the Manifestation?" But when I asked him point-blank whether he was "of that sect" (*az án ṭá'ifa*), he only replied "*Khudá dáná*" ("God knows"), and soon after left me.

Next morning (Saturday, 5th May) we started about 5 a.m., so as to reach Yezd before the day grew hot. Our road sloped continuously, but gently, downwards towards the city, which was in view almost from the beginning of the march. As we were leaving Taft, a little boy came up and presented me with a rose, and farther on an old man who was working in a field near the road offered me the like attention, neither of them expecting or receiving any reward for what, in these parts of Persia, which have not yet been spoiled by Europeans, is an act of pure kindliness and courtesy towards strangers. We passed successively the large and flourishing villages of Mubáraké and Chamr on the right, and Zeyn-ábád on the left, while on a low spur of the mountains to the south of the road the white *dakhmé* or "tower of silence" of the Zoroastrians was plainly visible. Leaving these behind us, we presently entered the sandy plain wherein lies the ancient city of Yezd, towards which we wound our way through gardens and cornfields. As we approached it, I was much puzzled as to the nature and function of numerous tall chimney-like structures, the like of which I had not hitherto seen. Knowing that Yezd gloried in the title "*Dáru'l-'Ibádat*" ("the Abode of Devotion"), I was for a moment disposed to regard them as a new variety of minaret; but I soon learned that they were really *bád-gírs* or wind-chimneys, designed to collect and convey into the interiors of the better class of houses such breaths of fresh breeze as might be stirring in the upper regions of the air which lay so hot and heavy over that sun-parched plain. It was still comparatively early in the day when we passed through the city gates, and, after some enquiry, alighted at the caravansaray of Ḥájí Ḳambar, where we secured two rooms, or rather cells, at a little distance from one another. My first business was to despatch my letters of introduction to the Seyyids and to Ardashír Mihrabán the Zoroastrian, requesting them to appoint a time at which I might call and see them; having done which, I occupied the interval which must elapse before the return of my messenger in making such toilette as the circumstances admitted of.

CHAPTER XIII

YEZD

> "*Ey ṣabá! bá sákinán-i-shahr-i-Yezd az má bi-gú,*
> *'K'ey sar-i-ḥaḳḳ-ná-shinásán gúy-i-chawgán-i-shumá!*
> *Garché dúr-ím az bisáṭ-i-ḳurb, himmat dúr níst;*
> *Bandé-i-Sháh-i-shumá'ím, ú ṣaná-khwán-i-shumá!'*"

> "East-wind, when to Yezd thou wingest, say thou to its sons from me,
> 'May the head of every ingrate ball-like 'neath your mall-bat be.
> What though from your daïs distant, near it by my wish I seem,
> Homage to your King I render, and I make your praise my theme.'"
>
> (Ḥáfiẓ, translated by Herman Bicknell.)

SCARCELY had I cleansed myself from the dust of travel, when I was informed that one had come who would have speech with me; and on my signifying my readiness to receive him, a portly old man, clad in the dull yellow raiment of the guebres, was ushered in. Briefly saluting me, he introduced himself as the Dastúr Tír-andáz, high-priest of the Zoroastrians of Yezd, and proceeded to inform me that the Governor of the city, His Highness Prince 'Imádu'd-Dawla, having learned that a European had just arrived in the town, had instructed him to interview the said European and ascertain his nationality, the business which had brought him to Yezd, and his rank and status, so that, if he should prove to be "distinguished" (*muta-shakhkhiṣ*), due honour might be shown him.

"As for my nationality," I replied, "I am English. As for my business, I am travelling for my own instruction and amusement, and to perfect myself in the Persian language. And as for my rank, kindly assure the Governor that I have no official status, and am not 'distinguished' at all, so that he need not show me any honour, or put himself out of the way in the least degree on my account."

"Very good," answered the fire-priest, "but what brings you to Yezd? If your only object were to learn Persian, you could have accomplished that at Ṭeherán, Iṣfahán, or Shíráz, without crossing these deserts, and undergoing all the fatigues involved in this journey."

"Well," I said, "I wished to see as well as to learn, and my travels would not be complete without a sight of your ancient and interesting city. Besides which, I desired to learn something of those who profess the faith of Zoroaster, of which, as I understand, you are the high-priest."

"You would hardly undergo all the fatigues of a journey across these deserts for no better reason than that," he retorted; "you must have had some other object, and I should be much obliged if you would communicate it to me."

I assured him that I had no other object, and that in undertaking the journey to Yezd I was actuated by no other motive than curiosity and a desire to improve my mind. Seeing, however, that he continued sceptical, I asked him point-blank whether he believed my word or not; to which he replied very frankly that he did not. At this juncture another visitor was announced, who proved to be Ardashír Mihrabán himself. He was a tall, slender, handsome man, of about forty-five or fifty years of age, light-complexioned, black-bearded, and clad in the yellow garments of the Zoroastrians; and he spoke English (which he had learned in Bombay, where he had spent some years of his life) fluently and well. After conversing with me for a short time, he departed with the Dastúr.

Hardly had these visitors left me when a servant came from the Seyyids to whom I had letters of introduction, to inform me that they would be glad to see me as soon as I could come. I therefore at once set out with the servant, and was conducted by him first to the house of Ḥájí Seyyid M——, who, surrounded by some ten or a dozen of his friends and relatives, was sitting out in the courtyard. I was very graciously received by them; and, while sherbet, tea, and the *ḳalyán*, or water-pipe, were successively offered to me, the letter of introduction given to me by Mírzá 'Alí was passed round and read by all present with expressions of approval, called forth, as I suppose, not so much by the very flattering terms in which it had pleased my friend to speak of me, as by what he had written concerning my eagerness to learn more of the Bábí religion, to which my new friends also belonged. Nothing was said, however, on this topic; and, after about an hour's general conversation, I left in company with Mírzá M—— to visit his father Ḥájí Mírzá M—— T——, to whom also I had a letter of introduction. There I remained conversing till after dusk, when I returned to the caravansaray, and, while waiting for my supper, fell into so profound a slumber that my servant was unable to wake me.

To go supperless to bed conduces above all things to early rising, and by 6.30 a.m. on the following morning I had finished my breakfast, and was eager to see something of the city of Yezd. My servant wished to go to the bath, but the Eriváni, who had attached himself to me since I first made his acquaintance, volunteered to accompany me. We wandered for a while through the bazaars, and he then suggested that we should enquire of some of the townsfolk whether there was any public garden where we could sit and rest for a time. I readily acquiesced in this plan, and we soon found ourselves in the garden of Dawlatábád, where we sat in a shady corner and conversed with an old gardener who had been for thirteen months a slave in the hands of the Turcomans. He had been taken prisoner by them near the Ḳal'at-i-Nádirí about the time that Ḥamzé Mírzá was besieging Mashhad (1848), and described very graphically his experiences in the Turcoman slave-market; how he and his companions in misfortune, stripped almost naked, were inspected and examined by intending purchasers, and finally knocked down by the broker to the highest bidder. He had finally effected his escape during a raid into Persian territory, in which he had accompanied the marauders as a guide, exactly after the manner of the immortal Ḥájí Bábá. He and the Eriváni joined cordially in abusing the Turcomans, whom they described as more like wild beasts than men. "They have no sense of fear," said the latter, "and will never submit, however great may be the odds against them; even their women and children will die fighting. That was why the Russians made so merciless a massacre of them, and why, after the massacre was over, they piled up the bodies of the slain into a gigantic heap, poured petroleum over it, and set it on fire, that perhaps this horrible spectacle might terrify the survivors into submission."

About mid-day we returned to the caravansaray, and I was again forced to consider my plans for the future, for Bábá Khán came to enquire whether he should wait to convey me back to Dihbíd, or whether I intended to proceed to Kirmán on leaving Yezd. I paid him the remainder of the money due to him, gave him a present of seven *ḳráns*, and told him that, unless he heard from me to the contrary before sunset, he might consider himself free to depart.

Later in the afternoon, two Zoroastrians came to inform me that Ardashír Mihrabán, in whose employment they were, was willing to place his garden and the little house in it at my disposal during my stay at Yezd. It had been occupied about a month before by another Englishman, Lieutenant H. B. Vaughan, who had undertaken a very adventurous and arduous journey across Persia, from Bandar-i-Lingé, on the Persian Gulf, to Dámghán or Sháhrúd, on the Mashhad-Ṭeherán road, and who had tarried for some while at Yezd to make preparations for crossing the western corner of the great Salt Desert. I of course gratefully accepted this offer, for the caravansaray was not a pleasant dwelling-place, and besides this, I was anxious to enjoy more opportunities of cultivating the acquaintance of the Zoroastrians, for which, as I rightly anticipated, this arrangement would give me exceptional facilities. I could not repress a feeling of exultation when I reflected that I had at length succeeded in so isolating myself, not only from my own countrymen, but from my co-religionists, that the most closely allied genus to which I could be assigned by the Yezdís was that of the guebres, for whom I already entertained a feeling of respect, which further knowledge of that much-suffering people has only served to increase.

Ḥájí Ṣafar was out when this message was brought to me, and, as I could not leave the caravansaray until I had instructed him as to the removal of my baggage, we were compelled to await his return. During this interval a message came from Ḥájí Seyyid M——, asking me to go to his house, whither, accordingly, on my servant's return, I proceeded in company with the two Zoroastrians, one of whom, named Bahman, spoke English well.

On arriving at Ḥájí Seyyid M——'s house, I was delighted to find a theological discussion in progress. An attempt was evidently being made to convert an old *mullá*, of singularly attractive and engaging countenance, to the Bábí faith. Only one of the Bábís was speaking, a man of about thirty-five years of age, whose eloquence filled me with admiration. It was not till later that I learned that he was *'Andalíb* ("the Nightingale"), one of the most distinguished of the poets who have consecrated their talents to the glory of the New Theophany. "And so in every dispensation," he resumed, as soon as I had received and returned the greetings of those present, "the very men who professed to be awaiting the new Manifestation most eagerly were the first to deny it, abandoning the 'Most Firm Hand-hold' of God's Truth to lay hold of the frail thread of their own imaginings. You talk of miracles; but of what evidential value are miracles to me, unless I have seen them? Has not every religion accounts of miracles, which, had they ever taken place, must, one would have thought, have compelled all men to believe; for who would dare, however hard of heart he might be, to fight with a Power which he could not ignore or misunderstand? No, it is the Divine Word which is the token and sign of a prophet, the convincing proof to all men and all ages, the everlasting miracle. Do not misunderstand the matter: when the Prophet of God called his verses "signs" (*áyát*), and declared the Ḳur'án to be his witness and proof, he did not intend to imply, as some vainly suppose, that the eloquence of the words was a proof. How, for instance, can you or I, who are Persians, judge whether the eloquence of a book written in Arabic be supernatural or not? No: the essential characteristic of the Divine Word is its penetrative power (*nufúdh*): it is not spoken in vain, it compels, it constrains, it creates, it rules, it works in men's hearts, it lives and dies not. The Apostle of God said, 'in the month of Ramaẓán men shall fast from sunrise to sunset.' See how hard a thing this is; and yet here in Yezd there are thousands who, if you bade them break the fast or die, would prefer death to disobedience. Wherever one arises speaking this Word, know him to be a Manifestation of the Divine Will, believe in him, and take his yoke upon you."

"But this claim," said the old *mullá*, "this claim! It is a hard word that He utters. What can we do or say?"

"For the rest, He hath said it," replied 'Andalíb, "and it is for us, who have seen that this Divine Word is His, to accept it." There was silence for a little while, and then the old *mullá* arose with a sigh, and repeating, "It is difficult, very difficult," departed from our midst.

Soon afterwards I too left, and, accompanied by my Zoroastrian friends, made my way to the garden of Ardashír Mihrabán, situated at the southern limit of the town, hard by the open plain. I found my host and the old fire-priest awaiting me, and received from both of them a most cordial welcome. The latter informed me with some elation that the Governor, Prince 'Imádu'd-Dawla, had, in spite of my representations (which he, like the Dastúr, no doubt regarded as the fabrications of an accomplished liar, whose readiness in falsehood afforded at least some presumptive evidence of a diplomatic vocation), decided to treat me as "distinguished," and would on the morrow send me a lamb and a tray of sweetmeats as signs of his goodwill. "His Highness wished to send them sooner," he concluded, "but I told him that you were not yet established in a suitable lodging, and he therefore consented to wait. When the presents come, you will have to call upon him and express your thanks." I was rather annoyed at this, for "distinction" in Persia means much useless trouble and expense, and I wished above all things to be free and unconstrained; but I did not then know Prince 'Imádu'd-Dawla for what he was, the most just, righteous, and cultured governor to be found in any town or province of Persia. Devotion to philosophical studies, and the most tolerant views of other religions, did not prevent him from strictly observing the duties laid upon him by his own creed; he was adored by the poor oppressed Zoroastrians, who found in him a true protector, and, I believe, by all well-disposed and law-abiding persons: and it was with a very sincere sorrow that I learned, soon after my return to England, that he had been dismissed from the office which he so nobly and conscientiously filled.

The change from the hot, dusty caravansaray to this beautiful garden was in itself a great pleasure, and my delight was enhanced by the fact that I was now in an environment essentially and thoroughly Zoroastrian. My servant and the Eriváni, indeed, still bore me company; but, except for them and occasional Musulmán and Bábí visitors, I was entirely thrown on the society of the yellow-robed worshippers of fire. The old priest, Dastúr Tír-andáz, who at first seemed to regard me with some suspicion, was quite won over by finding that I was acquainted with the spurious "heavenly books" known as the *Desátír*, about the genuineness of which neither he nor Ardashír appeared to entertain the slightest doubt. Ardashír sat conversing with me after the others had departed, for it had been stipulated by Ḥájí Seyyid M—— that my meals were to be provided by himself; and as his house was at some distance from the garden, it was nearly 10 p.m. before I got my supper. "*Khánéi-dú ḳed-bánú ná-rufté bihtar*" ("The house with two landladies is best unswept"), remarked my host, as the night advanced without any sign of supper appearing. However, the time was not wasted, for I managed to get Ardashír to talk of his religion and its ordinances, and especially of the *ḳushtí* or sacred cord which the Zoroastrians wear. This consists of seventy-two fibres woven into twelve strands of six fibres each, the twelve strands being further woven into three cords of four strands each. These three cords, which are plaited together to form the *ḳushtí*, represent the three fundamental principles of the Zoroastrian faith, good thoughts (*hu-manishní*), good words (*hu-go'ishní*), and good deeds (*hu-ḳunishní*), the other subdivisions having each in like manner a symbolical meaning. The investiture of the young Zoroastrian with the *ḳushtí* admits him formally to the church of "those of the Good Religion" (*Bih-dínán*); and he is then taught how to tie the peculiar knot wherewith it must be re-fastened at each of the *punj-gáh*, or five times of prayer. Ardashír also spoke of the duty incumbent on them of keeping pure the four elements, adding that they did not smoke tobacco out of respect for fire.

Although of the three weeks that I spent at Yezd there was not one day which passed unprofitably, or on which I did not see or hear some new thing, I think that I shall do better to disregard the actual sequence of events in recording what appears worthy of mention, so as to bring together kindred matters in one connection, and so avoid the repetitions and ruptures of sequence which too close an adherence to a diary must necessarily produce.

First, then, of the Zoroastrians. Of these there are said to be from 7000 to 10,000 in Yezd and its dependencies, nearly all of them being engaged either in mercantile business or agriculture. From what I saw of them, both at Yezd and Kirmán, I formed a very high idea of their honesty, integrity, and industry. Though less liable to molestation now than in former times, they often meet with ill-treatment and insult at the hands of the more fanatical Muḥammadans, by whom they are regarded as pagans, not equal even to Christians, Jews, and other "people of the book" (*ahlu'l-ḳitáb*). Thus they are compelled to wear the dull yellow raiment already alluded to as a distinguishing badge; they are not permitted to wear socks, or to wind their turbans tightly and neatly, or to ride a horse; and if, when riding even a donkey, they should chance to meet a Musulmán, they must dismount while he passes, and that without regard to his age or rank.

So much for the petty annoyances to which they are continually subject. These are humiliating and vexatious only; but occasionally, when there is a period of interregnum, or when a bad or priest-ridden governor holds office, and the "*lúṭís*," or roughs, of Yezd wax bold, worse befalls them. During the period of confusion which intervened between the death of Muḥammad Sháh and the accession of Náṣiru'd-Dín Sháh, many of them were robbed, beaten, and threatened with death, unless they would renounce their ancient faith and embrace Islám; not a few were actually done to death. There was one old Zoroastrian still living at Yezd when I was there who had been beaten, threatened, and finally wounded with pistol shots in several places by these fanatical Muslims, but he stood firm in his refusal to renounce the faith of his fathers, and, more fortunate than many of his brethren, escaped with his life.

So likewise, as I was informed by the Dastúr, about twelve years previously the Muḥammadans of Yezd threatened to sack the Zoroastrian quarter and kill all the guebres who would not consent to embrace Islám, alleging as a reason for this atrocious design that one of the Zoroastrians had killed a Musulmán. The governor of Yezd professed himself powerless to protect the guebres, and strove to induce them to sign a document exonerating him from all blame in whatever might take place; but fortunately they had the firmness to refuse compliance until one of the Musulmáns who had killed a Zoroastrian woman was put to death, after which quiet was restored.

On another occasion a Musulmán was murdered by another Musulmán who had disguised himself as a guebre. The Muḥammadans threatened to sack the Zoroastrian quarter and make a general massacre of its inmates unless the supposed murderer was given up. The person whom they suspected was one Námdár, a relative of the chief fire-priest. He, innocent as he was, refused to imperil his brethren by remaining amongst them. "I will go before the governor," he said, "for it is better that I should lose my life than that our whole community should be endangered." So he went forth, prepared to die; but fortunately at the last moment the real murderer was discovered and put to death. Ardashír's own brother Rashíd was murdered by fanatical Musulmáns as he was walking through the bazaars, and I saw the tablet put up to his memory in one of the fire-temples of Yezd.

Under the enlightened administration of Prince 'Imádu'd-Dawla, the Zoroastrians, as I have already said, enjoyed comparative peace and security, but even he was not always able to keep in check the ferocious intolerance of bigots and the savage brutality of *lúṭís*. While I was in Yezd a Zoroastrian was bastinadoed for accidentally touching with his garment some fruit exposed for sale in the bazaar, and thereby, in the eyes of the Musulmáns, rendering it unclean and unfit for consumption by true believers. On another occasion I heard that the wife of a poor Zoroastrian, a woman of singular beauty, was washing clothes near the town, when she was noticed with admiration by two Musulmáns who were passing by. Said one to the other, "She would do well for your embraces." "Just what I was thinking," replied the other wretch, who thereupon approached her, clasped her in his arms, and tried to kiss her. She resisted and cried for help, whereupon the Musulmáns got angry and threw her into the stream. Next day the Zoroastrians complained to the Prince-Governor, and the two cowardly scoundrels were arrested and brought before him. Great hopes were entertained by the Zoroastrians that condign and summary punishment would be inflicted on them; but some of the *mullás*, acting in concert with the *Maliku't-tujjár* or chief merchant of Yezd (a man of low origin, having, as was currently reported, *kolí* or gipsy blood in his veins), interfered with bribes and threats, and so intimidated an old Zoroastrian, who was the chief witness for the prosecution, that he finally refused to say more than that he had heard the girl cry out for help, and on looking round had seen her in the water. I know not how the matter ended, but I greatly fear that justice was defeated.

On another occasion, however, the Prince-Governor intervened successfully to check the following unjust and evil practice. When a Zoroastrian renounces his faith and embraces Islám, it is considered by the Musulmáns that he has a right to the property and money of his unregenerate kinsmen. A case of this sort had arisen, and a sum of ninety *túmáns* (nearly £28) had been taken by the renegade from his relatives. The latter appealed to the Prince, who insisted on its restoration, to the mortification of the pervert and his new friends, and the delight of the Zoroastrians, especially old Dastúr Tír-andáz, who, when he related the incident to me, was almost incoherent with exultation, and continually interrupted his narrative to pray for the long life and prosperity of Prince 'Imádu'd-Dawla. Nor was this the only expression of gratitude which the Prince's justice and toleration called forth from the poor oppressed guebres. One day, as he himself informed me, on the occasion of my farewell visit to his palace, he was riding abroad accompanied by three servants only (for he loved not ostentation) when he met a party of Zoroastrian women. Reining in his horse, he enquired how things went with them, and whether they enjoyed comfort and safety. They, not knowing who he was, and supposing him to be an ordinary Persian gentleman, replied that, though formerly they had suffered much, now, by the blessing of God and the justice of the new governor, they enjoyed perfect safety and security, and feared molestation from none. Then they asked him to what part of the country he belonged; and he, when he had fenced with them for a while, told them, to their astonishment and confusion, who he was!

I was naturally anxious to see some of the fire-temples, and finally, after repeated requests, a day was fixed for visiting them. I was taken first to the oldest temple, which was in a very ruinous condition (the Muḥammadans not suffering it to be repaired), and presented little of interest save two tablets bearing Persian inscriptions, one of which bore the date A.Y. 1009 as that of the completion of the tablet or the temple, I know not which. Leaving this, we proceeded to a newer, larger, and much more flourishing edifice, on entering which I saw, to my great delight, in a room to the left of the passage of entry, the sacred fire burning bright on its tripod, while around it two or three *múbads* or fire-priests, with veils covering their mouths and the lower part of their faces, droned their Zend liturgies. These veils, as Ardashír informed me, are intended to obviate the danger of the fire being polluted by the officiating priest coughing or spitting upon it. I was not, however, allowed to gaze upon this interesting spectacle for more than a few moments, but was hurried on to a large and well-carpeted room in the interior of the building, looking out on a little courtyard planted with pomegranate trees. Here I was received by several of the fire-priests, who regaled us with a delicious sherbet. The buildings surrounding the other three sides of the courtyard were, as I was informed, devoted to educational purposes, and serve as a school for the Zoroastrian children. This temple was built comparatively recently by some of Ardashír's relatives, and on one of its walls was the memorial tablet to his murdered brother Rashíd.

Leaving this, we visited a third temple, a portion of which serves as a theological college for the training of youths destined for the priesthood, who, to some extent at least, study Zend and Pahlaví; though I do not fancy that any high standard of proficiency in the sacred languages is often attained by them. The space allotted to these young theologians was not very ample, being, indeed, only a sort of gallery at one end of the chief room. At the opposite end was spread a carpet, on which a few chairs were set; and in a niche in the wall stood a little vase containing sprigs of a plant not unlike privet which the *dastúr* called by a name I could not rightly catch, though it sounded to me like "*náwá*." This plant, I was further informed, was used in certain of their religious ceremonies, and "turned round the sun"; but concerning it, as well as sundry other matters whereof I would fain have learned more, my guides showed a certain reserve which I felt constrained to respect. Here also I was allowed a glimpse of the sacred fire burning in a little chamber apart (whence came the odour of ignited sandalwood and the droning of Zend chants), and of the white-veiled *múbad* who tended it. A picture of Zoroaster (taken, as Ardashír told me, from an old sculpture at Balkh), and several inscriptions on the walls of the large central room, were the only other points of interest presented by the building.

On leaving this temple, which is situated in the very centre of the "*Gabr-Maḥalla*," or Zoroastrian quarter, I was conducted to the house of Ardashír's brother, Gúdarz, between rows of Zoroastrian men and boys who had come out to gaze on the Firangí stranger. To me the sight of these yellow-robed votaries of an old-world faith, which twelve centuries of persecution and insult have not succeeded in uprooting from its native soil, was at least as interesting as the sight of me can have been to them, and I was much struck both by their decorous conduct and by the high average of their good looks. Their religion has prevented them from intermarrying with Turks, Arabs, and other non-Aryans, and they consequently represent the purest Persian type, which in physical beauty can hardly be surpassed.

At the house of Ardashír's brother, Gúdarz, I met the chief-priest of the Zoroastrians, who was suffering from gout, and a number of my host's male relatives, with whom I stayed conversing till 8.30 p.m., hospitably entertained with tea, wine, brandy, and *ḳebábs*. Wine-drinking plays a great part in the daily life of the guebre; but, though I suppose not one total abstainer could be found amongst them, I never but once saw a Zoroastrian the worse for drink. With the Musulmáns the contrary holds good; when they drink, it is too often with the deliberate intention of getting drunk, on the principle, I suppose, that "when the water has gone over the head, what matters it whether it be a fathom or a hundred fathoms?" To a Zoroastrian it is lawful to drink wine and spirits, but not to exceed; to a Muḥammadan the use and the abuse of alcohol are equally unlawful. The Zoroastrian drinks because he likes the taste of the wine and the glow of good fellowship which it produces; the Muḥammadan, on the contrary, commonly detests the taste of wine and spirits, and will, after each draught, make a grimace expressive of disgust, rinse out his mouth, and eat a lump of sugar; what he enjoys is not *drinḳing*, but *being drunḳ*, even as the great mystical poet Jalálu'd-Dín Rúmí says—

"*Nang-i-bang ú khamr bar khud mí-nihí*
Tá damí aẓ khwíshtan tú vá-rahí."

"Thou takest on thyself the shame of hemp and wine
In order that thou may'st for one moment escape from thyself."

The drinking-cup (*jám*) used at Yezd and Kirmán is not a glass but a little brass bowl. On the inside of this the Zoroastrians often have engraved the names of dead friends and relatives, to whose memory they drink as the wine goes round with such formulæ as "*Khudá pidarat biyámurzad*" ("May God pardon thy father!"), "*Khudá mádarat biyámurzad*" ("May God pardon thy mother!"), "*Khudá biyámurzad hama-i-raftagán-rá*" ("May God pardon all the departed!"). The following inscription from Ardashír's drinking-cup may suffice as a specimen:—

"*Ṣáḥiba-i-marḥúm Mihrabán ibn Rustam-i-Bahrám. Har kas kár farmáyad* 'Khudá biyámurzí' *bi-Mihrabán-i-Rustam, va Sarvar-i-Ardashír, va Gulchihr-i-Mihrabán bi-dihad: haftád pusht-i-íshán amurzídé bád!* 1286 *hijrí*."

"The wife of the beatified Mihrabán, the son of Rustam, [the son] of Bahrám. Let every one who may make use [of this cup] give a '*God pardon!*' to Mihrabán [the son] of Rustam, and Sarvar [the son] of Ardashír, and Gulchihr [the daughter] of Mihrabán: may they be pardoned unto seventy generations! A.H. 1286."

In drinking to the health of companions the formula (used also by Muḥammadans when they drink) is "*Bi-salámatí-i-shumá!*" ("To your health!"), the answer to which is "*Núsh-i-ján-bád!*" ("May it be sweet to your soul!"). I had ample opportunity of learning how to drink wine "according to the rite of Zoroaster," for almost every afternoon Ardashír, accompanied either by Dastúr Tír-andáz, or by his brother Gúdarz, or by his manager Bahman, or by other Zoroastrians, used to come to the garden and sit by the little stream, which for a few hours only (for water is bought for a price in Yezd) refreshed the drooping flowers. Then, unless Muḥammadan or Bábí visitors chanced to be present, wine and '*araḳ* were brought forth by old Jamshíd, the gardener, or his little son Khusraw; fresh young cucumbers, and other relishes, such as the Persian wine-drinker loves, were produced; and the brass drinking-cups were drained again and again to the memories of the dead and the healths of the living.

It was on these occasions that conversation flowed most freely, and that I learned most about the Zoroastrian religion and its votaries. This is not the place to deal with the subject systematically, and I shall confine myself to noticing a few matters which actually came under discussion.

The Zoroastrian year is solar, not lunar like the Muḥammadan, and consists of twelve months of thirty days each, and five additional days called *gátá* (corresponding to the Muḥammadan "*ḳhamsa-i-mustaraḳa*") to bring the total up to 365. The year begins at the vernal equinox, when the sun enters the sign of Aries (about 21st March), and is inaugurated by the ancient national festival of the *Nawrúz*, or New Year's Day, which, as has been already mentioned, is observed no less by the Muḥammadans than by the Zoroastrians of Persia. Each day of the month is presided over by an angel or archangel (of whom there are seven, called *Amshaspands*, to each of which a day of the first week is allotted), save that three days, the 8th, 15th, and 23rd of the month, are, like the first, sacred to Ormuzd. These are holy days, and are collectively known as the *Si-dey*. The following is a list of the days of the month, each of which is called by the name of the angel presiding over it:—(1) *Ormuzd*; (2) *Bahman*, the angel of flocks and herds; (3) *Urdí-bihisht*, the angel of light; (4) *Shahrívar*, the angel of jewels, gold, and minerals; (5) *Sipandarmaz*, the angel of the earth; (6) *Khurdád*, the angel of water and streams; (7) *Amurdád*, the angel of trees and plants; (8) *Dey-bi-Ádhar*, the first of the *Si-dey*, sacred to Ormuzd; (9) *Ádhar*; (10) *Ábán*; (11) *Khír*; (12) *Máh*; (13) *Tír*; (14) *Gúsh*; (15) *Dey-bi-Mihr*, the second of the *Si-dey*; (16) *Mihr*; (17) *Surúsh*; (18) *Rashn*; (19) *Farvardín*; (20) *Bahrám*; (21) *Rám*; (22) *Dád*; (23) *Dey-bi-Dín*, the third of the *Si-dey*; (24) *Dín*; (25) *Ard*; (26) *Ashtád*; (27) *Ásmán*; (28) *Zámyád*; (29) *Muntra-sipand*; (30) *Anárám*. Of these thirty names twelve belong also to the months, as follows:—

SPRING (*Bahár*).	1. *Farvardín.* 2. *Urdí-bihisht.* 3. *Khurdád.*	AUTUMN (*Pá'íz*).	7. *Mihr.* 8. *Ábán.* 9. *Ádhar.*
SUMMER (*Tábistán*).	4. *Tír.* 5. *Amurdád.* 6. *Shahrívar.*	WINTER (*Zamistán*).	10. *Dey.* 11. *Bahman.* 12. *Sipandarmaz.*

The week has no place in the Zoroastrian calendar, with which, as I have elsewhere pointed out (*Traveller's Narrative*, vol. ii, p. 414, n. 1; and *J.R.A.S.* for 1889, p. 929), the arrangement of the solar year instituted by the Bábís presents many points of similarity which can hardly be regarded as accidental[1]. As an example of the very simple manner in which dates are expressed according to the Zoroastrian calendar, I may quote the following lines from a Persian poem occurring in a Zend-Pahlaví MS. of the Vendídád of which I shall have something more to say shortly:—

"*Bi-rúz-i-Gúsh, u dar máh-i-Amurdád*
Sene nuh-sad, digar bud haft u haftád,
Zi fawt-i-Yazdijird-i-shahriyárán
Kujá bigzashté búd az ruzgárán,
Navishtam nisf-i-Vendídád-i-avval
Rasanidam, bi-lutf-i-Ḥakk, bi-manzil."

"On the day of Gúsh (the 14th day), and in the month of Amurdád (the 5th month),
When nine hundred years, and beyond that seven and seventy,
From the death of Yazdijird the king
Had passed of time,
I wrote the first half of the Vendídád,
And brought it, by God's grace, to conclusion."

A little consideration will show the reader that one day in each month will bear the same name as the month, and will be under the protection of the same angel. Thus the nineteenth day of the first month will be "the day of Farvardín in the month of Farvardín," the third day of the second month "the day of Urdí-bihisht in the month of Urdí-bihisht," and so on. Such days are kept as festivals by the Zoroastrians.

The angel Rashn, who presides over the eighteenth day of each month, corresponds, in some degree, to the angels Munkar and Nakír in the Muḥammadan system. On the fourth day after a Zoroastrian dies this angel comes to him, and weighs in a balance his good and his bad deeds. If the former are in excess, the departed is admitted into paradise; if the latter, he is punished—so my Zoroastrian friends informed me—by being

1 Cf. pp. 367–8, *supra*.

re-incarnated in this world for another period of probation, which re-incarnation is what is signified by the term "hell" (*dúzakh*)[1]. Paradise, in like manner, was understood by my friends of Yezd in a spiritual sense as indicating a *state* rather than a *place*. I shall not readily forget an altercation on this subject which arose between the Dastúr Tír-andáz and my Muḥammadan servant Ḥájí Ṣafar. The latter had, I think, provoked the dispute by applying the term *átash-parast* ("fire-worshipper") to the followers of Zoroaster, or it had been otherwise introduced. The Dastúr at once flashed out in anger. "What ails you if we prostrate ourselves before the pure element of fire," said he, "when you Muḥammadans grovel before a dirty black stone, and the Christians bow down before the symbol of the cross? Our fire is, I should think, at least as honourable and appropriate a *ḳibla* as these, and as for worshipping it, we no more worship it than do you your symbols. And you Muḥammadans" (turning to Ḥájí Ṣafar) "have of all men least right to charge us with holding a gross or material creed; you, whose conception of paradise is as a garden flowing with streams of milk and wine and honey, and inhabited by fair boys and languishing black-eyed maidens. Your idea of paradise, in short, is a place where you will be able to indulge in those sensual pleasures which constitute your highest happiness. I spit on such a paradise!" Ḥájí Ṣafar cried out upon him for a blasphemer, and seemed disposed to go further, but I bade him leave the room and learn to respect the religion of others if he wished them to respect his. Later on, when the Zoroastrians had gone, he renewed the subject with me, remarking that the Dastúr deserved to die for having spoken such blasphemy; to which I replied that, though I had no desire to interfere with his conscience, or, in general, to hinder him in the discharge of the duties imposed upon him by his religion, I must request him to put a check

1 I suspect, however, that this is a modern doctrine, derived from the apocryphal *Desátír* alluded to at p. 403, *supra*.

upon his zeal in this matter, at least so long as he remained in my service.

In general, however, I found my Zoroastrian friends very tolerant and liberal in their views. Ardashír was never tired of repeating that in one of their prayers they invoked the help of "the good men of the seven regions" (*ḳhúbán-i-haft ḳishvar*), *i.e.* of the whole world; and that they did not regard faith in their religion as essential to salvation. Against the Arabs, indeed, I could see that they cherished a very bitter hatred, which the Dastúr at least was at little pains to conceal; Ḳádisiyya and Nahávand were not forgotten; and, with but little exaggeration, the words of warning addressed to the Arabs settled in Persia in the second century of the *hijra* by Naṣr ibn Seyyár, the Arab Governor of Khurásán, might be applied to them:—

"*Fa-man yakun sá'ilí 'an aṣli dínihimu,*
Fa'inna dínahumu an yuḳtala'l-'Arabu."

"And should one question me as to the essence of their religion,
Verily their religion is that the Arabs should be slain."

From these poor guebres, however, I received more than one lesson in meekness and toleration. "Injustice and harshness," said Bahman to me one day, "are best met with submission and patience, for thereby the hearts of enemies are softened, and they are often converted into friends. An instance of this came within my own experience. One day, as I was passing through the *meydán*, a young Muḥammadan purposely jostled me and then struck me, crying, 'Out of the way, guebre!' Though angered at this uncalled-for attack, I swallowed down my anger, and replied with a smile, 'Very well, just as you like.' An old Seyyid who was near at hand, seeing the wanton insolence of my tormentor, and my submission and patience, rebuked him sharply, saying, 'What harm had this poor man done to you that you should strike and insult him?' A quarrel arose between the two, and finally both were taken before the Governor, who, on learning the truth of the matter, caused the youth to be beaten. Now, had I in the first instance given vent to my anger, the Seyyid would certainly not have taken my part, every Musulmán present would have sided with his co-religionist against me, and I should probably have been beaten instead of my adversary."

On another occasion I had been telling another of Ardashír's assistants named Írán about the Englishman at Shíráz who had turned Muḥammadan. "I think he is sorry for it now," I concluded, "for he has cut himself off from his own people, and is regarded with suspicion or contempt by many of the Musulmáns, who keep a sharp watch over him to see that he punctually discharges all the duties laid upon him by the religion of Islám. I wish him well out of it, and hope that he may succeed in his plan of returning to his home and his aged mother; but I misdoubt it. I think he wished to join himself to me and come here, that he might proceed homewards by way of Mashhad; but I was not very desirous of his company."

"It is quite true," replied Írán, "that a bad companion is worse than none, for, as Sa'dí says, it is better to go barefoot than with tight shoes. Yet, if you will not take it amiss, would you not do well, if you return to Shíráz, to take this man with you, and to bring him, and if possible his Muḥammadan wife also, to England? This would assuredly be a good action: he would return to the faith he has renounced, and his wife also might become a Christian; they and their children after them would be gained to your religion, and yours would be the merit. Often it happens that one of us Zoroastrians, either through mere ignorance and heedlessness, or because he is in love with a Muḥammadan girl whom he cannot otherwise win, renounces the faith of his fathers and embraces Islám. Such not unfrequently repent of their action, and in this case we supply them with money to take them to Bombay, where they can return, without the danger which they would incur here, to their former faith. Often their Muḥammadan wives also adopt the Zoroastrian religion, and thus a whole family is won over to our creed."

"I was not aware," I remarked, "that it was possible under any circumstances for one not born a Zoroastrian to become one. Do you consent to receive back a renegade after any lapse of time?"

"No," answered Írán, "not after six months or so; for if they remain Musulmáns for longer than this, their hearts are turned black and incurably infected by the law of Islám, and we cannot then receive them back amongst us."

Of the English, towards whom they look as their natural protectors, the Persian Zoroastrians have a very high opinion, though several of them, and especially Dastúr Tír-andáz, deplored the supineness of the English Government, and the apathy with which it regards the hands stretched out to it for help. "You do not realise," said they, "what a shield and protection the English name is, else you would surely not grudge it to poor unfortunates for whom no one cares, and who in any time of disturbance are liable to be killed or plundered without redress." After my return to England I, and I think Lieutenant Vaughan also, made certain representations to the Foreign Office, which I believe were not ineffectual; for, as I subsequently learned, a Zoroastrian had been appointed British Agent in Yezd. This was what the Zoroastrians so earnestly desired, for they believed that the British flag would protect their community even in times of the gravest danger.

Although the Zoroastrian women do not veil their faces, and are not subjected to the restrictions imposed on their Muḥammadan sisters, I naturally saw but little of them. Twice, however, parties of guebre girls came to the garden to gaze in amused wonder at the Firangí stranger. Those composing the first party were, I believe, related to Ardashír, and were accompanied by two men. The second party (introduced by old Jamshíd the gardener, who did the honours, and metaphorically stirred me up with a long pole to exhibit me to better advantage) consisted of young girls, one or two of whom were extremely pretty. These conducted themselves less sedately, and, to judge by their rippling laughter, found no little amusement in the spectacle.

Old Dastúr Tír-andáz was to me one of the most interesting, because one of the most thoroughgoing and least sophisticated, of the Zoroastrians. He appeared to be in high favour with the governor, Prince 'Imádu'd-Dawla, from whom he was continually bringing messages of goodwill to me. In three of the four visits which I paid to the Prince, he bore me company, standing outside in the courtyard while I sat within. My first visit was paid the morning after I had received the lamb and the tray of sweetmeats wherewith the Prince, on the representations of the Dastúr, already described, was graciously pleased to mark his sense of my "distinction." Accompanied by the Prince's *píshkhidmat*, or page-in-waiting (an intolerably conceited youth), and several *farráshes*, who had been sent to form my escort, we walked to the Government House, which was situated at the other end of the town, by the *Arg* or citadel. The Dastúr, who walked by my side, was greatly troubled that I had not a horse or attendants of my own, and seemed to think that my apparel (which, indeed, was somewhat the worse for wear) was hardly equal to the occasion. As I preferred walking to riding, and as I had not come to Yezd to see princes or to indulge in ostentatious parade, these considerations did not affect me in the least, except that I was rather annoyed by the persistence with which the Dastúr repeated to the Prince-Governor that I had come *chápár* (by post-horses) from Shíráz with only such effects as were absolutely necessary, and that a telegram must be sent to Shíráz to have my baggage forwarded with all speed to Yezd. The Prince, however, was very good-natured, and treated me with the greatest kindness, enquiring especially as to the books on philosophy and mysticism which I had read and bought. I mentioned several, and he expressed high approval of the selection which I had made, especially commending the *Lawá'iḥ* of Jámí, Láhijí's Commentary on the *Gulshan-i-Ráz*, and Jámí's

Ashi'atu'l-Lama'át, or Commentary on the *Lama'át* of 'Iráḳí. Of Ḥájí Mullá Hádí's *Asráru'l-Ḥiḳam*, on the other hand, he did not appear to have a very high opinion. He further questioned me as to my plans for the future, and, on learning that I proposed to proceed to Kirmán, promised to give me a letter of recommendation to Prince Náṣiru'd-Dawla, the governor of that place, and also, to my consternation, expressed his intention of sending an escort with me. I was accompanied back to the garden by the *farráshes*, to whom I had to give a present of two *túmáns* (about 13*s*.).

The Prince's attentions, though kindly meant, were in truth somewhat irksome. Two days after the visit above described, he sent his conceited *píshkhidmat* to enquire after my health, and to ask me whether I had need of anything, and when I intended to visit a certain waterfall near the Shír-Kúh, which he declared I must certainly see before quitting his territories. For the moment I escaped in polite ambiguities; but two days later the *píshkhidmat* again came with a request that, as Ramaẓán was close at hand, I would at once return with him to the Government House, as the Prince wished to see me ere the fast, with the derangement of ordinary business consequent on it, began. I had no resource but to comply, and after giving the *píshkhidmat* tea, which he drank critically, I again set out with him, the Dastúr, and the inevitable *farráshes*, for the Prince's residence. On leaving the palace shortly before sunset, the Dastúr mysteriously asked me whether, if I were in no particular hurry to get home, he might instruct the *farráshes* to take a more devious route through the bazaars. I consented, without at first being able to divine his object, which was no doubt to show the Musulmáns of Yezd that I, the Firangí, was held in honour by the Prince, and that he, the fire-priest, was on the most friendly and intimate terms with me.

After this visit I enjoyed a period of repose, for which, as I imagine, I was indebted to the fast of Ramaẓán. The Zoroastrians, of course, like myself, were unaffected by this, and so was my servant Ḥájí Ṣafar, who came to me on the eve of the fast to know what his duty in the matter might be. He explained that travellers were exempt from the obligation of fasting, provided they made good the omission at some future date; but that if I could promise to remain at Yezd for ten clear days of Ramaẓán, he could fast for those ten days, postponing the remainder of his fast till some more convenient time. It was of no use, he added, to begin fasting unless he could reckon on ten consecutive days, a shorter period than this not entering into computation. I declined to bind myself by any such promise (feeling pretty sure that Ḥájí Ṣafar would not be sorry for an excuse to postpone the period of privation till the season of short days), and so, though it was not till Ramaẓán 13th that I actually quitted Yezd, he continued to pursue the ordinary tenor of his life.

Amongst the minor annoyances which served to remind me that even Yezd was not without its drawbacks, were the periodical appearances in my room of scorpions and tarantulas, both of which abound in the dry, sandy soil of this part of Persia. Of these noxious animals, the latter were to me the more repulsive, from the horrible nimbleness of their movements, the hideous half-transparent grayness of their bodies, and the hairiness of their legs and venomous mandibles. I had seen one or two in the caravansaray where I first alighted, but, on removing to the clean and tidy little house in Ardashír's garden, hoped that I had done with them. I was soon undeceived, for as I sat at supper the day after my arrival, I saw to my disgust a very large one of singularly aggressive appearance sitting on the wall about three feet above the floor. I approached it with a slipper, intending to slay it, but it appeared to divine my intentions, rushed up the wall and half across the ceiling with incredible speed, dropped at my feet, and made straight for the window, crossing in its course the pyramid of sweetmeats sent to me by the Prince, over which its horny legs rattled with a loathsome clearness which almost turned me sick. This habit of dropping from the ceiling is one of the tarantula's many unpleasant characteristics, and the Persians (who call it *roteyl* or *khâyé-gaz*) believe that it can only bite while descending. Its bite is generally said to be hardly less serious than that of the scorpion, but Ardashír assured me that people were seldom bitten by it, and that he had never known its wound prove fatal. The Yezdís, at all events, regarded its presence with much more equanimity than I did, and the *Kalántar*, or mayor, of the Zoroastrians displayed no alarm when a large specimen was observed sitting on the ceiling almost exactly over his head. The Prince-Governor manifested somewhat more disgust when a tarantula made its appearance in his reception-room one evening when I had gone to visit him; but then he was not a Yezdí.

As regards scorpions, I killed a small whitish one in my room shortly after I had missed my first tarantula. A day or two afterwards old Jamshíd the gardener brought me up another which he had just killed in the garden, and seized the occasion to give me a sort of lecture on noxious insects. The black wood-louse-like animal which I had slain at Cháh-Begí he declared to have been a "*súsmár*" (though this word is generally supposed to mean a lizard). Having discussed this, he touched briefly on the *tír-már* (earwig?), *ṣad-pá* (centipede), and *hazár-pá* (millipede), concluding with the interesting statement that in every ant-hill of the large black ants two large black scorpions live. I suggested that we should dig up an ant-hill and see if it were so, but he declined to be a party to any such undertaking, seeming to consider that such a procedure would be in very indifferent taste. "As long as the scorpions stay inside," said he, "we have no right to molest them, and to do so is to incur ill-luck." So my curiosity remained unsatisfied.

Old Jamshíd was very particular in the observance of his religious duties, and I constantly heard him muttering his prayers under my window in that peculiar droning tone which so impressed the Arabs that they invented a special word for it. Ardashír, who had seen the world and imbibed latitudinarian ideas, affected to regard this performance with a good-natured contempt, which he extended to many of the Dastúr's cherished convictions. One day, for instance, mention was made of *ghúls* and other supernatural beings. "Tush," said Ardashír, "there are no such things." "No such things!" exclaimed the Dastúr, "why I have seen one myself." "No, no," rejoined Ardashír, "you saw a man or a mule or some other animal in the gloaming, and, deceived by the half-light, the solitude, or your own fears, supposed it to be a *ghúl*." Here I interposed, begging the Dastúr to narrate his experience, which he readily consented to do.

"I was riding back from Taft to the city one evening," said he, "when, nearly opposite our *dakhmé*, I lost my way. As I was casting about to discover the path, I suddenly saw a light before me on the right. I thought it must come from the village of Ḳásim-ábád, and was preparing to make for it, when it suddenly shifted to my left hand and began to approach me. It drew quite near; and then I saw a creature like a wild pig, in front of which flitted a light like a large lantern. I was horribly frightened, but I repeated a prayer out of the *Desátír*, whereupon the thing vanished. It soon reappeared, however, this time in the form of a mule, preceded by a man bearing a lantern, and thus addressed me: '*Ey ádamí-zád! Ínjá ché mí-kuní?*' ('O son of man! What dost thou here?') I replied that I had lost my way. Thereupon it pointed out a path, which, as it assured me, would lead me to the city. I followed this path for some distance, but it only led me farther out of my way, until at last I reached a village where I found some of our own people. These set me in the right road, and would have borne me company to the city, but I would not suffer them to do so, believing that I should have no further difficulty. On reaching a bridge hard by the city, I again saw the creature waiting for me by the roadside: it again strove to mislead me, but this time I paid no heed to it, and, pushing past it, reached my house in safety. Its object was to lead me into some desolate spot and there destroy me, after the manner of *ghúls*. After this experience you will understand that I am firmly convinced of the existence of these creatures."

I was not so much troubled at Yezd by applications for medical advice and treatment as I had feared, partly because, after my experiences at Dihbíd and Gōd-i-Shírdán, I had forbidden Ḥájí Ṣafar and Bábá Khán to say a word about my having any medical knowledge, and partly because Ardashír would not suffer strangers of whom he knew nothing to come to his garden to see me. Once, however, when I was sitting talking to Bahman and Írán in Ardashír's office (situated on the ground floor of one of the chief caravansarays in the city), a crowd of people assembled outside to stare at me, from which a Seyyid presently disengaged himself, and asked me whether I would cure him of an enlarged spleen. I asked him how he knew that it was his spleen that was affected. He replied that the Persian doctors had told him so. "What the Persian doctors can diagnose, can they not treat?" I enquired. "Yes," he replied, "they can; but they prescribe only two remedies, *sharáb* and *zahráb*[1], of which one is unlawful and the other disgusting." I finally told him that I could not undertake to treat him without first examining him, and that if he wished this he must come and see me in Ardashír's garden. He never came, however; or, if he did, he was not admitted.

The Zoroastrians are, as a rule, good gardeners, and have some skill in the use of simples. From Ardashír and his gardener, Jamshíd, I learned the names and supposed properties of many plants which grew in the garden. Unfortunately the little botanical knowledge I ever possessed had grown so rusty by long disuse that often I was unable to supply the English

1 Wine and urine.

name, or even to refer the plant to its proper order. However, I give the following list as a contribution towards a better knowledge of the Persian nomenclature. *Púdana* or *púdanak*; *kásní*, accounted "cool" and good for the liver; from it is prepared a spirit called *'arak-i-kásní*; *turb* (radish); *gáv-gúsh* (fighting-cock); *áftáb-gardán*, or *gul-i-khurshíd* (sunflower); *bíd-anjír*, or *bíd-angír* (castor-oil plant); *rázdáné* (fennel), said to be an analgesic; *yúnjé* (clover); *taré*, a small plant resembling garlic and with a similar smell, said to be good for hæmorrhoids; *sháh-taré*, accounted "hot and moist"; a decoction of it, taken in the morning on an empty stomach, is said to be good for indigestion and disorders of the stomach; *shavíj*, a "hot" umbelliferous plant with a yellow blossom; *gashníj*, a "cold" umbelliferous plant with a white flower; *chughandar* (beetroot); *gul-i-khatmí* (hollyhock); *kalam* (cabbage), called by the guebres in their dialect *kumní*; *isfináj* (spinach?); *káhú* (lettuce); *kadújé* (ragged-robin or campion); *karanfil* (passion-flower).

I have alluded to the dialect spoken amongst themselves by the Zoroastrians of Persia, and by them called "*Darí*." This term has been objected to by M. Clément Huart, who has published in the *Journal Asiatique* several valuable papers on certain Persian dialects, which he classes together under the name of "Pehlevi-Musulmán," and regards as the descendants of the ancient Median language preserved to us in the Avesta. The chief ground of his objection is that the description of the Darí dialect given in the prolegomena of certain standard Persian dictionaries does not at all agree with the so-called Darí spoken by the guebres of Yezd and Kirmán. Personally, I confess that I attach but little importance to the evidence of the Persian lexicographers in this matter, seeing that it is the rarest thing for an educated Persian to take any interest in local dialects, or even to recognise their philological importance; and I shall therefore continue provisionally to call the dialect in question by the name given to it by those who speak it. That it is closely allied to the

Ḳohrúdí, Káshání, Sívandí, Lurí, and other dialects spoken in remote and isolated districts of Persia, and generically termed by the Persians "*Furs-i-ḳadím*" ("Old Persian"), is, however, not to be doubted.

This Darí dialect is only used by the guebres amongst themselves, and all of them, so far as I know, speak Persian as well. When they speak their own dialect, even a Yezdí Musulmán cannot understand what they are saying, or can only understand it very imperfectly. It is for this reason that the Zoroastrians cherish their Darí, and are somewhat unwilling to teach it to a stranger. I once remarked to Ardashír what a pity it was that they did not commit it to writing. He replied that there had at one time been some talk of translating the *Gulistán* into Darí, but that they had decided that it was inexpedient to facilitate the acquisition of their idiom to non-Zoroastrians. To me they were as a rule ready enough to impart information about it; though when I tried to get old Jamshíd the gardener to tell me more about it, he excused himself, saying that a knowledge of it could be of no possible use to me.

The following is a list of the Darí words and phrases which I collected at Yezd:—

Hamushtudwun, to arise (shortened in speaking to *hamushtun*); imperative, *hamusht*; present tense (1 sing.) *hamushtude'* or *hamushtudem*; (2 sing.) *hamushtudí*, (3 sing.) *hamushtud*, (1 plur.) *hamushtudím*, (2 plur.) *hamushtudíd*, (3 plur.) *hamushtu-dand*.

Wotwun, to say; imperative, *ve-va*; past tense, *ám-vut*, *ud-vut* or *t'ad-vut*, *osh-vut* or *inoshvut*, (plur.) *má-vut* or *má-má-vut*, *do-vut*, *sho-vut*. Don't talk = *vuj khé ma-ku'* (*khe* = *khud*, self; *ma-ku'* = *makun*, do not do or make).

Gráftun, to take; *ashnuftan*, to hear; *dídwun*, to see; *kushtwun*, to strike.

Venodwun, to throw. "Turn (lit. throw) the water into that channel," "*Wōw de ō jú ve-ven*" (*wow* = water; *de* = to, into; *ō* = that).

Náshte' or *náshtem*, I sat; (2 sing.) *náshtí*; (3 sing.) *násht*; (1 plur.) *má-náshtun*. Imperative (2 sing.) *únik*; (2 plur.) *únigít*.

Ve-shu, go; *ko'íshí*, whither goest thou? *Hamashtún va-shím*, let us arise and go; *má ve-shím*, let us go. *Ve-shu gau*, go down; *shumá gav-shít*, do you go down. *Me-wú ve-she*, I want to go.

Bi-yú, come; *múné ú*, come here; *mè byú'í*, may I come?

Omúda ve-bú, be ready.

Wōw, water. *Dumined*, 'araḳ, spirit (so called, they say, because it distils "from the end of the pipe," *dum-i-ney*). *Kilowel*, wine (said to be onomatopœic, from the noise it makes as it is poured out of the bottle). *Waḳt-i-kilowel davarta*, the time for wine has passed.

Gaff, talk; *gaff zadan*, to talk. *Bawz*, a bee. *Rúzhgárat nyák*, good day.

Those who desire fuller information about this interesting dialect, which well deserves a more careful and systematic study than it has yet received, may consult General Houtum-Schindler's admirable paper on the Zoroastrians of Persia (*Die Parsen in Persien, ihre Sprache, etc.*) in vol. xxxvi of the *Zeitschrift der Deutschen Morgenländischen Gesellschaft* (pp. 54–88); Ferdinand Justi's article in vol. xxxv of the same periodical (pp. 327–414); Berésine's *Dialectes Persanes* (Kazan, 1853); and the articles of M. Huart in series viii of the *Journal Asiatique* (vol. vi, p. 502; vol. xi, p. 298; vol. xiv, p. 534).

In this connection I may also cite a verse written in the Káshání dialect by a Káshí who wished to "take off" [1] the speech of his fellow-townsmen.

"'*Pas-khún u písh-khún ki pur bafr bíd*
Shubbe na-dárad ki zameystún risíd.
Kísé-i-sabbún bi-tih-i-salt nih;
Bígh zadand; nawbat-i-ḥammún risíd.'"

"Now that the front-yard and back-yard are full of snow,
There is no doubt that winter has come.
Put the soap-bag in the bottom of the basket (?);
They are blowing the horn; the time for the bath has come."

While I am on the subject of these linguistic curiosities, I may as well mention a method of secret communication sometimes employed in Persia, the nature and applications of which were explained to me by my Eriváni friend a few days before his departure for Mashhad. Such of my readers as have studied Arabic, Persian, Turkish, or Hindustání will know that besides

1 The slang expression for "to take a person off" (in the sense of to make fun of or mimic him) is "*tú-yi kúk-i-kasí raftan.*" *Kúk kardan* means to wind up a watch; applied to a person it means to rile, put in a passion. "I riled him and he got in a wax" is in Persian slang, "*kúk-ash kardam u bi-ásmán raft,*" "I wound him up, and he went up to the sky."

the ordinary arrangement of the letters of the Arabic alphabet there is another arrangement called the "*abjad*" (from the four letters *alif*, *bá*, *jím*, *dál* which begin it) representing a much older order. The order of the letters in the *abjad* is expressed by the following series of meaningless words, consisting of groups of three or four letters each supplied with vowel-points to render them pronounceable:—*abjad*, *hawaz*, *hoṭí*, *kalaman*, *sa'faṣ*, *karashat*, *thakhadh* (*ṣakhadh*) *ḍadhagha* (*zazagha*). In this order each has a numerical value; *alif* = 1, *bá* = 2, *jím* = 3, *dál* = 4, and so on up to *yá* = 10; then come the other tens, *káf* = 20, *lám* = 30, and so on up to *káf* = 100; then the other hundreds up to *gheyn* = 1000. The manner in which, by means of this *abjad*, words and sentences may be made to express dates is familiar to all students of these languages, and I will therefore only give as a specimen, for the benefit of the general reader, the rather ingenious chronogram for the death of the poet Jámí, premising that he was a native of the province of Khurásán; that "smoke" or "smoke of the heart" is a poetical term for sighs; and that to "come up from" in the case of a number means to be subtracted from.

This, then, is the chronogram: "*Dúd az Khurásán bar ámad*," "Smoke (sighs) arose from Khurásán," or "*dúd* (*dál* = 4, *váv* = 6, *dál* = 4; total 14) came up (*i.e.* was subtracted) from Khurásán" (*khá* = 600, *rá* = 200, *alif* = 1, *sín* = 60, *alif* = 1, *nún* = 50; total 912). Taking 14 from 912 we get the date of Jámí's death, A.H. 898 (= A.D. 1492).

The method of secret communication above alluded to consists in indicating first the word of the *abjad* in which the letter to be spelt out occurs, then its position in that word. In communicating by raps, a double rap knocks off each word of the *abjad*, while on reaching the word in which the desired letter occurs its position in that word is indicated by the requisite number of single raps. An instance will make this clearer. It is desired to ask, "*Nám-i-tú chíst?*" ("What is thy name?"): the letters which spell out this message are—*nún*, *alif*, *mím*, *tá*, *váv*, *jím* (for *chím*), *yá*, *sín*, *tá*. *Nún* is in the fourth word of the *abjad*, and is the fourth letter in that word (*ḳalaman*). It is therefore indicated by three double raps (removing or knocking off the three first words, *abjad*, *hawaz̤*, *ḥoṭí*, and thus bringing us to the next word, *ḳalaman*), followed by four single raps (showing that it is the fourth letter in this word). The remaining letters are expressed in similar fashion, so that if we represent double raps by dashes and single raps by dots, the whole message will run as follows: — — — . . . . (*nún*); . (*alif*); — — — . . . (*mím*); — — — — — . . . . (*tá*) — . . (*váv*); . . . (*chím* or *jím*); — — . . . (*yá*); — — — — . (*sín*); — — — — — — . . . . (*tá*).

Messages can be similarly communicated by a person smoking the *ḳalyán* or water-pipe to his accomplice or partner, without the knowledge of the uninitiated. In this case a long pull at the pipe is substituted for the double rap, and a short pull for the single rap. Pulling the moustache, or stroking the neck, face, or collar (right side for words, left side for letters), is also resorted to to convert the system from an auditory into a visual one. It is expressed in writing in a similar fashion, each letter being represented by an upright stroke, with ascending branches on the right for the words and on the left for the letters. This writing is called, from the appearance of the letters, *ḳhaṭṭ-i-sarví* ("cypress-writing") or *ḳhaṭṭ-i-shajarí* ("tree-writing"). In this character (written, in the usual way, from right to left) the sentence which we took above ("*nám-i-tú chíst?*") will stand as follows:—

The mention of enigmatical writings reminds me of a matter which I omitted to speak of in its proper place—I mean the Pahlaví and Zend manuscripts preserved in the fire-temples of Yezd. Although I knew that Yezd had long since been ransacked for such treasures, and that, even should any old manuscripts remain, it would be impossible to do more than examine them (a task which I, who knew no Pahlaví and only the merest rudiments of Zend, was but little qualified to undertake), I naturally did not omit to make enquiries on the subject of the Dastúr and Ardashír. As I expected, most of the manuscripts (especially the older and more valuable ones) had been sent to the Parsees of Bombay, so as to be safe from the outbursts of Muḥammadan fanaticism to which the Zoroastrians of Yezd are always liable; but in one of the fire-temples I was shown two manuscripts of the sacred books, the older of which was, by the kindness of the Dastúr, lent to me during the remainder of my stay at Yezd, so that I was enabled to examine it thoroughly.

This manuscript, a large volume of 294 leaves, contained, so far as I could make out, the whole of the Vendídád, with interspersed Pahlaví translation and commentary written in red, the headings of the chapters being also in red, and the Avesta text in black. On f. 158 was inscribed a Persian poem of fifty-nine couplets, wherein the transcriber, Bahrám, the son of Marzabán, the son of Ferídún, the son of Bahrám, details the circumstances of his life and the considerations which led him to undertake the transcription of the sacred volume. From this it appeared that when the aforesaid Bahrám was thirteen years of age, his father, Marzabán-i-Ferídún, left his country (presumably Yezd), and, at the command of the reigning king, settled in Ḳazvín. After a while he went to Khurásán, and thence to Kirmán, where he died at the age of fifty-seven. The death of his father turned Bahrám's thoughts to his religion, which he began to study diligently with all such as could teach him anything about it. At the age of sixteen he seems to have transcribed the Yashts; and at the age of twenty he commenced the transcription of the Vendídád, of which he completed the first half (as stated in the verses cited on p. 413, *supra*), on the 14th day of the month of Amurdád, A.Y. 977. On the page facing that whereon this poem is written are inscribed the dates of the deaths of a number of Zoroastrians (belonging, probably, to the family of the transcriber), beginning with Bahrám's father Marzabán-i-Ferídún, who died on the day of Varahrám (Bahrám), in the month of Farvardín, A.Y. 970. The last date is A.Y. 1069. The writing of the manuscript is large, clear, and legible, and it bears throughout the signs of careful work. One side of f. 29 is occupied by a diagram indicating, I believe, the successive positions in which the officiating priest or *múbad* must stand in relation to the fire-altar while performing some of the ceremonies connected with the hôma-sacrifice. This sacred plant (the *hôma*, or *húm*, as it is now called) is found in the mountains about Yezd, but I could not succeed in obtaining or even in seeing a specimen while I was there. After my return to Cambridge, however, the Dastúr kindly sent me some of the seeds and stalks of it packed in a tin box. I gave some of the former to the Cambridge Botanical Gardens. Unfortunately they did not grow up, but they were identified by Mr Lynch, the curator, as a species of *Ephedra*.

Near the end of the volume I found the following short prayer in Persian: "*Shikast u zad bád Ahríman-i-durvand-i-kaj, avá hamá díván u druján u jáduván*," "Defeated and smitten be Ahriman the outcast, the froward, with all the demons and fiends and warlocks." Some of the original leaves of the manuscript had been lost, and replaced by new ones written in a bad hand on common white paper.

It is time, however, to leave the Zoroastrians, and to say something of the Bábís of Yezd, with whom also I passed many pleasant and profitable hours. But this chapter has already grown so long that what I have to say on this and some other matters had better form the substance of another.

CHAPTER XIV

YEZD (*continued*)

"*Chand, chand az ḥikmat-i-Yúnániyán*
Ḥikmat-i-Ímániyán-rá ham bi-khwán!"

"How long, how long of the wisdom of the Greeks?
Study also the wisdom of the people of faith!"

"*Án Gheyb-i-mumtani'*, *ki hamí-guft* '*Lan tará!*'
Ínak, tarání-gú bi-jihán áshikár shud.
Kashf-i-ḥijáb kard: khudá-há, bishárati!
Ínak, ẓuhúr-i-a'ẓam-i-Parvardigár shud!"

"That unapproachable Unseen, which was wont to say, 'Thou shalt not see Me,'
Lo, melodious with song, hath appeared in the world!
It hath lifted the veil: good tidings, O gods!
Lo, the Supreme Theophany hath come!"

IN the last chapter I have spoken chiefly of the Zoroastrians; in this I propose to say something concerning my dealings with the Bábís of Yezd, of whom also I saw a good deal. And first of all a few words are necessary as to the relations subsisting between the votaries of these two religions, the oldest and the newest which Persia has produced. Their relations to one another are of a much more friendly character than are the relations of either of them towards the Muḥammadans, and this for several reasons. Both of them are liable to persecution at the hands of the Muḥammadans, and so have a certain fellow-feeling and sympathy. Both of them are more tolerant towards such as are not of their own faith than the Muḥammadans, the Zoroastrians, as already said, regarding "the virtuous of the seven climes" as their friends, and the Bábís being commanded by Behá to "associate with men of all religions with spirituality and sweet savour," and to regard no man as unclean by reason of his faith. Moreover the Bábís recognise Zoroaster as a prophet, though without much enthusiasm, and are at some pains to conciliate and win over his followers to their way of thinking, as instanced by the epistles addressed by Behá from Acre to certain of their number; while some few at least of the Zoroastrians are not indisposed to recognise in Behá their expected deliverer, Sháh Bahrám, who, as Dastúr Tír-andáz informed me, must appear soon if they were to be rescued from their abasement, and "the Good Religion" re-established. The Dastúr himself, indeed, would not admit that Behá could be this promised saviour, who, he said, must come before the next *Nawrúz* if he were to come at all; but others of his co-religionists were less confident on this point, and in Kirmán I met at least one who was, so far as I could ascertain, actually a Bábí. The marked predilection towards the Bábís displayed by Mánakjí, the late Zoroastrian agent at Ṭeherán, at whose instigation the *Táríkh-i-Jadíd*, or "New History" of the Báb's "Manifestation," was written, must also have re-acted powerfully on his Zoroastrian brethren[1].

I may here mention a very absurd fiction, which I have more than once heard the Zoroastrians maintain in the presence of Musulmáns or Bábís, namely, that Zoroaster was identical with Abraham. The chief argument whereby they seek to establish this thesis is as follows: "You recognise five '*nabí-i-mursal*'" (prophets sent with new revealed scriptures, as opposed to prophets merely sent to warn and preach repentance, who are called "*nabí-i-mundhir*"), say they, "to wit, Abraham with the

1 I have already remarked on the hatred with which the Zoroastrians regard the Arabs, and the fact that the Bábí movement was entirely Persian in origin no doubt inclines them to look favourably on it. One of them said as much to me; the Semitic peoples, he added, were comparable to ravening beasts of prey, and the Aryan races to the peaceful and productive animals. An unmodified Semitic religion, he maintained, could never be really acceptable to Aryans.

Ṣuḥuf ('Leaves,' 'Tracts,' or 'Epistles'), Moses with the *Tawrát* (Pentateuch), David with the *Mazámír* (Psalms), Jesus with the *Injíl* (Gospel), and Muḥammad with the *Ḳur'án*; and you believe that the book of each of these five, and a remnant of his people, shall continue in the world so long as it lasts. Now of each of the last four the book and the people exist to our day, but where is the *Ṣuḥuf* of Abraham, and where his followers? Does it not seem probable to you that the *Ṣuḥuf* is our Avesta, that Abraham is but another name for Zoroaster, and that we are his people?" As further proof of this contention, Ardashír declared that mention was made of Baráhím, who was evidently the same as Ibráhím (Abraham), in the *Sháh-námé*; and I think he strove to connect this word with Brahman and Bahrám, for he was capable of much in the way of etymology and comparative philology. I do not suppose that in their hearts many of the Zoroastrians really believe this nonsense, but it has always been a great object with them to get themselves included amongst the *ahlu'l-ḳitáb*, or people to whom a revealed book recognised by the Muḥammadans has been vouchsafed, inasmuch as these enjoy many privileges denied to the pagan and idolater.

My first introduction to the Bábís of Yezd I have already described. The morning after I had taken up my quarters in Ardashír's garden I received a message from Ḥájí Seyyid M—— about 6 a.m., inviting me to take my early tea in a garden of his situated close at hand. Thither I at once repaired, and, after a while, found myself alone with the Bábí poet 'Andalíb.

"How was it," he began, "that the Jews, although in expectation of their Messiah, failed to recognise him in the Lord Jesus?"

"Because," I answered, "they looked only at the letter and not the spirit of their books, and had formed a false conception of the Messiah and his advent."

"May not you Christians have done the same," he continued, "with regard to Him whose advent you expect, the promised

'Comforter'? May He not have come, while you continue heedless? Within a few miles of Acre is a monastery of Carmelite monks, who have taken up their abode there to await the return of Christ, because their books tell them that He will return there. He *has* returned there, almost at their very door, yet they recognise Him not, but continue gazing up to heaven, whence, as they vainly suppose, He will descend."

"Consider the parable of the Lord of the vineyard," he resumed after a while, "which is contained in your gospel. First, He sent servants to demand his rights from those wicked men to whom the vineyard was let; these were the prophets before Christ. Then He sent His own Son, whom they killed; this was Christ Himself, as you yourselves admit. And after that what shall the Lord of the vineyard do? '*He will come* and destroy the husbandmen, and will give the vineyard unto others.'"[1]

"Do you then regard Behá as the Lord of the vineyard, that is to say, as God Himself?" I enquired in astonishment.

"What say your own books?" he replied. "Who is He who shall come after the Son?"

"Well, but what then say you of Muḥammad?" I demanded, "for if you accept this parable and interpret it thus there is no place left for him, since he comes after the Son and before the Lord of the vineyard."

"He was a messenger sent to announce the advent of the Lord of the vineyard," replied 'Andalíb.

"Then," said I, "he was less than the Son."

"Yes," answered 'Andalíb, "he was." He then spoke of other matters; of the devotion of the youth Badí', who came on foot from Acre to Ṭeherán, there to meet a cruel death, with Behá's letter to Náṣiru'd-Dín Sháh; of the martyrs of Iṣfahán, and the miserable end of their persecutors, Sheykh Báḳir and the Imám-Jum'a; of the downfall of Napoleon III, foretold by Behá in the epistle addressed to the French Emperor

1 Mark xii, 9.

when he was at the zenith of his power, and read by himself four years before the accomplishment of the prediction. Concerning Badí' he remarked, "Even Christ prayed that, if possible, this cup might pass from Him, while this lad joyfully hastened with unhalting and unswerving feet over many a weary mile of desert and mountain, bearing his own death-warrant in his hand, to quaff the draught of martyrdom." As we were leaving the garden he took me by the hand and besought me to go to Acre and see Behá for myself. "How noble a work might be yours," he said, "if you could become assured of the truth of his claim, in spreading the good news through your country!"

Next day I received a visit from a *sarhang*, or colonel, who filled at that time a rather responsible post at Yezd, whence he has since been transferred to another important town in the south of Persia. He too proved to be a Bábí, and conversed very freely about the new Manifestation. "In accordance with the injunction '*address men according to the measure of their understanding*,'" said he, "it behoves every divine messenger to impart to his people only so much spiritual knowledge as they are capable of receiving; wherefore, as mankind advances in education, the old creeds necessarily lose their significance, and the old formulæ become obsolete. So, if a child were to ask what we meant by saying that knowledge was sweet, we might give it a sugar-plum and say, 'It resembles this,' so that the child, liking the sugar-plum, might desire knowledge; though, as a matter of fact, the two have nothing in common. To rough uncultivated men, such as the Arabs with whom Muḥammad had to deal, the pleasures of Divine Love cannot be more clearly symbolised than as a material paradise of beautiful gardens and rivers of milk and wine and honey, where they shall be waited on by black-eyed maidens and fair boys. Now we have outgrown this coarse symbolism, and are fitted to receive a fuller measure of spiritual truth and wisdom from him who is the Fountain-head of wisdom and the wisest of all living men, Behá."

Two days later I was invited by Ḥájí Seyyid M—— to spend the day with him and his friends in one of his gardens situated outside the town, on the road to Taft. He kindly sent his servant with a horse to convey me thither, and I had lunch and tea there, returning home about sunset. There were a good many guests (all, so far as I could make out, being Bábís), including 'Andalíb and a very vivacious little merchant on whom, in consideration of the very humorous manner in which he impersonated, for our amusement, the venal conduct of a certain eminent *mullá* of Yezd on the judgment-seat, the title of "Sheykh" was bestowed. The garden, with its roses, mulberry-trees, pomegranates in full blossom, syringas (*nastarjan*), cool marble tanks, and tiny streams, was like a dream of delight, and I have seldom spent a pleasanter day anywhere. I conversed chiefly with 'Andalíb, who read me some of his own poems, and also wrote down for me one of the beautiful odes attributed to the Bábí heroine and martyr Ḳurratu'l-'Ayn[1]. He talked a good deal about the identity of all the prophets, whom he regarded as successive Manifestations or Incarnations of the Divine Will or Universal Reason.

"If that is so," I urged, "how can you speak of one Manifestation as more perfect than another, or one prophet as superior to another?"

"From our human point of view," he replied, "we are entitled to speak thus, although from the standpoint of the Absolute it is incorrect. It is the same sun which rises every day to warm and light us, and no one for a moment doubts this; yet we say that the sun is hotter in summer than in winter, or warmer to-day than yesterday, or in a different sign of the zodiac now from that which it occupied a month ago. Speaking relatively to ourselves this is perfectly true, but when we consider the sun apart from accidents of time, place, environment, and the like, we

1 The text of this, with a translation into English verse, will be found at pp. 314–16 of vol. ii of my *Traveller's Narrative*.

perceive it to be ever one and the same, unchanged and unchangeable. So is it with the Sun of Truth, which rises from the horizon of the heart, and illuminates the Spiritual Firmament."

"Is it not strange, then," I asked, "that different prophets should advance different claims, one announcing himself as the 'Friend of God,' another as the 'Interlocutor of God,' another as the 'Apostle of God,' another as the 'Son of God,' and another as God Himself?"

"No," he answered, "and I will strive to make it clearer by means of a parable. A certain king holding sway over a vast empire desired to discover with his own eyes the causes of disorders which prevailed in one of his provinces, so that he might take effectual measures to remedy them. He determined, therefore, to go thither himself, and, laying aside his kingly state, to mix with the people on terms of intimacy. So he wrote a letter, declaring the bearer of it to be an officer of the king's household, sealed it with the royal seal, and, thus provided, went in disguise to the province in question, where he announced that he was an officer sent by the king to enquire into the disorders prevailing amongst the people, in proof of which he produced the royal warrant which he had himself written. After a while, when order had been in some degree restored, and men were more loyally disposed, he announced himself to be the king's own minister, producing another royal warrant in proof of this. Last of all he threw off all disguise and said, 'I am the king himself.' Now, all the time he was really the king, though men knew him not; yet was his state and majesty at first not as it was at last. So is it with the Divine Will or Universal Reason, which, becoming manifest from time to time for our guidance, declares Itself now as the Apostle of God, now as the Son of God, and at last as God Himself. We are not asked to acknowledge a higher status than It sees fit to claim at any particular time, but the royal signet is the sufficient proof of any claim which It may advance, including that of the Supreme Majesty itself. But, as Mawláná Jalálu'd-Dín Rúmí says:—

> *'Didé'i báyad ki báshad shah-shinás,*
> *Tá shinásad Sháh-rá dar har libás.'*
>
> 'It needs an eye which is king-discerning
> To recognise the King in whatever garb.'"

Later on I asked Ḥájí Seyyid M—— what he considered to be the difference between the Ṣúfí saint who had attained to the "Station of Annihilation in God," wherein, like Manṣúr-i-Ḥalláj, he could cry, "I am the truth," and the prophet. "What, in short," I concluded, "is the difference between the '*I am God*' of Manṣúr, and the '*I am God*' of Behá? For, as your own proverb has it, 'There is no colour beyond black.'"

"The difference," said he, "is as the difference between our sitting here and saying, 'See, this is a rose-garden,' and one saying, 'I am such-and-such a rose in that garden.' The one reaches a point where, losing sight and cognisance of self, he wanders at will through the World of Divinity (*'Álam-i-Láhút*); the other is the throne on which God sits, as He Himself saith, 'He set Himself upon the Throne' (*istawá 'ala'l-'arsh*)[1]. One is a perfect reflection of the sun cast in a pure clear mirror; the other is the sun itself."

A few days later, after the month of Ramaẓán had begun, I paid another visit to Ḥájí Seyyid M——'s house, where three of my Zoroastrian friends presently joined me. 'Andalíb, as usual, was the chief spokesman, and, amongst other things, laid down the dogma that faith and unbelief were the root or essence of the whole matter, and good or bad actions only branches or subsidiaries. This position I attacked with some warmth.

"Suppose a Jew and a Christian," said he, "the former merciful, charitable, benevolent, humane, pious, but rejecting and denying Christ; the latter cruel, selfish, vindictive, but accepting and reverencing Him. Of these two, which do you regard as the better man?"

1 Ḳur'án vii, 52; x, 3 etc.

"Without doubt the Jew," I answered.

"God forbid!" replied he. "Without doubt the Christian. God is merciful and forgiving, and can pardon sin."

"Can He not then pardon unbelief?" I demanded.

"No," he answered, "from those who do not believe is taken the spirit which once they had, to which the present wretchedness and abasement of the Jews bears witness."

As it did not appear to me that the nations professing the Christian religion had suffered much abasement on account of their rejection of Muḥammad, I said, thinking to get the better of the argument, "Do you consider that every people which rejects a new Manifestation must be similarly abased?"

He did not fall into my trap, however. "No," he answered, "not unless they have been guilty of some special act of hostility or cruelty towards the bearer of the new gospel."

"What, then," I demanded, "of the Muḥammadans? Can one conceive of greater hostility or cruelty than they showed towards the Báb and those who followed him? Shall they too be abased?"

"Yea, verily," he answered, "and grievous shall be their abasement! Look at these poor guebres" (pointing to my Zoroastrian friends), "how miserable is their condition! And why? Because of the sin of Khusraw Parvíz, who tore up the letter which the Apostle of God sent to him, inviting him to embrace Islám. Yet had he some excuse; for he was a great king, belonging to a mighty dynasty which had ruled for many generations; while the letter was from an unknown member of a despised and subject race, and was, moreover, curt and unceremonious in the extreme, beginning, '*This is a letter from Muḥammad, the Apostle of God, to Khusraw Parvíz.*' What shall we say of the king who not only tore up the letter, but slew with the most cruel torments the messenger of one greater than Muḥammad, the letter being, moreover, written in the most courteous and conciliatory tone? But the Christians never acted thus towards Muḥammad, and some, such as the Abyssinian Najáshí, did all in their power to succour and protect those who, for their belief in him, had become wanderers and exiles."

I tried to ascertain 'Andalíb's beliefs as to the future life, a subject on which I have always found the Bábís singularly reticent, and he told me that, according to their belief, the body, the vegetable soul, and the animal soul—all the lower principles, in fact—underwent disintegration and redistribution, while the "luminous spirit" (*rúḥ-i-núrání*) survived to receive rewards or punishments, whereof the nature was unrevealed and unknown. He then turned upon the Zoroastrians and upbraided them for their indifference in matters of religion. "For all these years," he concluded, "you have been seeing and hearing of Jews, Christians, and Muḥammadans: have you ever taken the trouble to ascertain the nature of their beliefs, or of the proofs and arguments by which they support them? If for a single week you had given half the attention which you devote to your worldly business to a consideration of these matters, you would, in all probability, have attained to certainty. What fault can be greater than this indifference and neglect?"

A few days after this I returned the *Sarhang's* visit. He received me very kindly in his house, situated near the mosque of Mír Chakmákh, and, though it was Ramaẓán, gave me tea, and himself drank a little hot water. The conversation at once turned on religion. He began by discussing the martyrdom of Imám Ḥuseyn, "the Chief of Martyrs," and of 'Abbás, 'Alí Akbar, and the rest of his relatives and companions, at Kerbelá, declaring that had it not been for the wrongs suffered by these, Islám would never have gained one-tenth of the strength it actually possesses. From this topic he passed to the Bábí insurrection, headed by Áḳá Seyyid Yaḥyá of Dáráb, which was put down with great severity in the summer of 1850.

"Two of my relatives were in the army of the malignants,"

he began, "so I know a good deal about what took place, and more especially how God punished them for their wickedness. When orders came from Ṭeherán to Shíráz to put down the insurrection, my maternal grandfather, the *Shujá'u'l-Mulk*, received instructions to march against the Bábís of Níríz. He was somewhat unwilling to go, and consulted two of the clergy, who reassured him, telling him that it was a *jihád*, or holy war, and that to take part in it would ensure him a great reward in the future life. So he went, and what was done was done. The malignants, after they had slain 750 men of the Bábís, took the women and children, stripped them nearly naked, mounted them on camels, mules, and asses, and led them forth through an avenue of heads severed from those who had been their husbands, brothers, fathers, and sons, towards Shíráz. When they arrived there they were lodged in a ruined caravansaray just outside the Iṣfahán gate, opposite to an *imámzádé*, near to which the soldiers encamped under some trees. There, exposed to all manner of hardships, insults, and persecutions, they were kept for a long while, during which many of them died. And now hear how God took vengeance on some of those who were prominent as persecutors of his saints.

"My grandfather, the *Shujá'u'l-Mulk*, when stricken down by his last illness, was dumb till the day of his death. Just at the end, those who stood round him saw his lips move, and, stooping down to hear what he was whispering, heard him repeat the word 'Bábí' three times. Immediately afterwards he fell back dead.

"My great-uncle, Mírzá Na'ím, who also took part in the suppression of the Níríz rising, fell into disgrace with the Government, and was twice heavily mulcted—10,000 *túmáns* the first time, 15,000 *túmáns* the second. His punishment did not stop here: he was made to stand bareheaded in the sun, with syrup smeared over his face to attract the flies; his feet were crushed in the Ḳájár boot; and his hands submitted to the *el-chek*, that is to say, pieces of wood were inserted between his fingers, round which whip-cord was tightly bound, and on the whip-cord cold water was poured to make it contract. Nor were these the worst or most degrading torments to which he was subjected[1].

"I will tell you another instance of Divine Vengeance. There was in Shíráz a certain Sheykh Ḥuseyn, who bore the honorific title of *Náẓimu'l-'Ulamá*, but who was generally known, by reason of his injustice, as '*Ẓálim*' ('Tyrant'). He was not only concerned in the events I have described, but manifested a specially malignant hatred towards the Báb. So far did this hatred carry him, that when the Báb was before Ḥuseyn Khán, the Governor of Fárs, he drew his penknife from his pen-case, and cried, 'If you will not order his execution, I will kill him with this.' Later on, when the Báb had gone to Iṣfahán, he followed him thither, declaring that he would not cease to dog his footsteps till he had enjoyed the satisfaction of carrying out the death sentence on him; till at last the Governor of Iṣfahán sent him back to Shíráz, telling him that whenever that time came the *mír-ghaẓab*, or executioner, would be ready to do his duty. Well, after his return to Shíráz, he became affected with a scrotal swelling, which attained so enormous a size that he could hardly sit his horse, and had to be lifted into the saddle. Later on, before he died, his face turned black, save that one side was flecked with white spots; and thus he lay in his bed, loathsome alike to sight and smell, smearing his countenance with filth, and crying upon God to whiten his face on the Last Day, when the faces of others should be black. So he died."

A few days after this I again paid a visit to Ḥájí Seyyid M——'s house. 'Andalíb, of course, was there, and took tea with me, explaining that as his throat was sore he was not fasting that day. He had found the passages, occurring in Behá's epistle to one of the Turkish ministers who had oppressed him, wherein the

1 *Tukhm-i-murgh-há-yi garm dar maḳ'ad-ash firú kardand.*

catastrophes impending over the Ottoman Empire were foretold. The first (which was in Arabic) ran as follows:—

"*And if He please, He will assuredly make you as scattered dust, and will overtake you with vengeance on His part: trouble shall appear in your midst, and your realms shall be divided: then shall ye lament and humble yourselves, and shall not find for yourselves any ally or helper.*"

The second (in Persian) ran thus:—

"*But wait, for God's wrath is made ready, and ye shall shortly behold that which hath descended from the Pen of Command.*"

It was a pretty sight to see Ḥájí Seyyid M—— with his little child, to which he appeared devotedly attached, and which he would seldom suffer to be long out of his sight. When I had read the passage above translated, he took the book from me and held it out to the little one, saying "*Kitáb-rá mách kun*" ("Kiss the book"), which, after some coaxing, it was prevailed upon to do. A baby Bábí!

On the following afternoon I again visited the *Sarhang*. Another man, to whom he did not introduce me, was with him when I arrived, but soon left. The *Sarhang* upbraided me for wishing to leave Yezd so soon, saying that he had not seen nearly as much of me as he would have liked, and then asked me whether I had attained any greater certainty in the matter of the Bábí religion. I stated certain difficulties and objections, which he discussed with me. He also showed me some Bábí poems, including one by "*Jenáb-i-Maryam*" (the sister of Mullá Ḥuseyn of Bushraweyh, the Báb's first convert and missionary), written in imitation of a rather celebrated ode of Shams-i-Tabríz. While we were examining these, a servant entered and announced the arrival of "*Khudá*" ("God"), and close on his heels followed the person so designated—a handsome, but rather wild-looking man—whose real name I ascertained to be Ḥájí Mírzá Muḥammad, commonly called "*Díváné*" ("the Madman"). The *Sarhang* introduced him as one controlled by Divine Attraction ("*majdhúb*"), whose excessive love for God was proof against every trial, and who was deeply attached to the words of Christ (especially as recorded in the Gospel of St Matthew), which would move him to tears. The "Madman," meanwhile, had taken up one of the volumes of Bábí *Alwáḥ* (Epistles) which the *Sarhang* had brought out, and began to read from it in a very melodious voice. "If you could understand all the beauties of these words," he said, as he concluded his reading and laid down the book, "you would at once be firmly convinced of the truth of the New Manifestation."

I tried to put some questions on religious matters to them, but at first they would hardly listen to me, pouring forth torrents of rhapsody. At length, however, I succeeded in stating some of the matters on which I wished to hear their views, viz. the position accorded by them to Islám in the series of Theophanies, and the reasons for its lower standard of ethics and morality, lower ideal of future bliss, and greater harshness of rule and practice, as compared with Christianity. The answers which they returned made me realise once again how widely separated from each other were our respective points of view. They seemed to have no conception of Absolute Good or Absolute Truth: to them Good was merely what God chose to ordain, and Truth what He chose to reveal, so that they could not understand how anyone could attempt to test the truth of a religion by an abstract ethical or moral standard. God's Attributes, according to their belief, were twofold—"Attributes of Grace" (*Ṣifát-i-Jemál* or *Luṭf*), and "Attributes of Wrath" (*Ṣifát-i-Jalál* or *Ḳahr*): both were equally divine, and in some dispensations (as the Christian and Bábí) the former, in some (as the Mosaic and the Muḥammadan) the latter predominated. A divine messenger or prophet, having once established the validity of his claim by suitable evidence, was to be obeyed in all things without criticism or questioning; and he had as much right to kill or compel, as a surgeon has to resort to amputation or the actual cautery, in cases where milder methods of treatment would be likely to prove inefficacious. As for the Muḥammadan paradise, with its jewelled thrones, its rivers of milk and wine and honey, its delicious fruits, and its beautiful attendants, it fulfilled its purpose; for every people must be addressed in words suited to the measure of their intellectual capacity, and the people to whom the Prophet Muḥammad was sent could not have apprehended a higher ideal of future bliss. They could see nothing immoral or unsatisfactory in a man's renouncing pleasures forbidden in this life so as to enjoy them everlastingly in a future state.

Wishing to ascertain the views of the *Sarhang* and his friend "*Díváné*" on Ṣúfíism and its saints, I briefly described to them certain phases of thought through which I myself had passed, and certain conclusions as to the relation and significance of different religions which its teachings had suggested to me. "In a well-known aphorism," I concluded, "it is said that '*the ways unto God are as the number of the souls of the children of men.*' Every religion is surely an expression, more or less clear and complete, of some aspect of a great central Truth which itself transcends expression, even as Niẓámí says:—

> '*Sitánad zabán az raḳíbán-i-ráz,*
> *Ki tá ráz-i-Sulṭán na-gúyand báz.*'

> 'He taketh the tongue from such as share the mystery,
> So that they may not repeat the King's secret.'

Thus in Islám the Absolute Unity of God is above all insisted upon; in the Dualism of the Zoroastrians the eternal conflict between Good and Evil, Light and Darkness, Being and Not-being, the One and the Many, is symbolised; while the Christian Trinity, as I understand it, is the Trinity of the Sun, the Sun-beams which proceed from the Sun, and the Mirror, cleansed from every stain, wherein these falling produce (neither by Absorption of the Mirror into the Sun, nor by Incarnation of the Sun in the Mirror, but by Annihilation of the Mirror-hood of the Mirror in the Sun's effulgence) a perfect image of the Sun.

Even Idolatry subsists only by virtue of a truth which it embodies, as Sheykh Maḥmúd Shabistarí says:—

> '*Musulmán gar bi-dánistí ki but chíst,*
> *Bi-dánistí ki dín dar but-parastíst.*'
>
> 'Did the Musulmán understand what the Idol is,
> He would know that there is religion even in idolatry.'

So in every religion there is Truth for those who faithfully and earnestly seek it; and hence we find amongst the followers of religions apparently most divergent, living in lands and times so widely separated as to preclude all possibility of intercommunication, men who, led by that Inner Light which lighteth every one who cometh into the world, have arrived at doctrines practically identical. Is not this identity a sign of their truth? Is it not, moreover, far more consistent with God's universal mercy to reveal Himself thus inwardly to every pure soul than by a written scripture confided only to a comparatively small section of the human race? If salvation is only for the people of the Ḳur'án, then how hard is the lot of my people, to most of whom no more than its name, if so much, is known! If, on the other hand, only the people of the Gospel are to be saved, what possible chance of eternal happiness has been given to the great bulk of your fellow-countrymen?"

From a Ṣúfí I should have confidently expected a cordial endorsement of these views, but not from a Bábí; and I was therefore surprised by the acclamations with which both of my companions received them, and still more so by the outburst of wild enthusiasm which they evoked in "*Díváné*," who sprang from his seat, waving his arms and clapping his hands, with cries of "You have understood it! You have got it! God bless you! God bless you!"

"Well, then," I continued, "what do you consider to be the difference between a prophet and a saint who by purification of the heart and renunciation of self has reached the degree of

'Annihilation in God'? For, as your own proverb says, 'There is no colour beyond black.'"

"The difference," they replied, "is this. The saint who has reached this degree, and can, like Manṣúr the wool-carder, say, '*I am the Truth*,' has no charge laid on him to guide and direct others, and is therefore not bound to be cautious and guarded in his utterances, since the possible consequences of these concern himself alone, and he has passed beyond himself; while the prophet is bound to have regard to the dictates of expediency and the requirements of the time. Hence it is that, as a matter of fact, most of the great Ṣúfí saints were put to death, or subjected to grievous persecutions."

I did not see "the Madman" again, but the *Sarhang* paid me a farewell visit on the morrow, and brought with him another officer, who, as I was informed, belonged to the 'Alí-Iláhí sect, and was, like many of that sect, very favourably disposed towards Bábíism, concerning which the *Sarhang* spoke freely before him.

Meanwhile the time of my departure was drawing near, and it was in some degree hastened by the kindly-meant but somewhat irksome attentions of the Prince-Governor. He, as I have already mentioned, had set his heart on my visiting a certain waterfall in the mountains, without which, he declared, my journey to Yezd would be incomplete. As I had no particular desire to see this waterfall, and was anxious to avoid the trouble and expense in which the mounted escort which he wished to send with me would certainly have involved me, I determined to parry his proposals with those expressions of vague gratitude which I had already learned to regard as the most effectual means of defence in such cases, and meanwhile to complete my preparations for departure, and quietly slip away to Kirmán with a farewell letter of thanks and apologies, to be despatched at the last moment.

There was no particular difficulty about obtaining mules

for the journey, but it appeared to be impossible to hire a horse for myself to ride. Personally, I was quite indifferent as to whether I rode on a horse or a mule, but my friends, both Bábís and Zoroastrians, were horrified at the idea of my entering Kirmán on the humbler quadruped: "it would be so undignified," they said, "so derogatory to my state, so incompatible with the idea of distinction!" At first I was disposed to deride these notions, pointing out that the well-known Arabic proverb, "*Sharafu'l-makán bi'l-makín*" ("the dignity of the dwelling is in the dweller") might fairly be paralleled by another, "*Sharafu'l-markab bi'r-rákib*" ("the dignity of the mount is in the rider"); but they evidently felt so strongly on the subject that, seeing that I had received much kindness at their hands, and was the bearer of letters of recommendation to their friends at Kirmán, I finally gave way, and asked them what they advised.

"I advise you to give up the idea of going to Kirmán altogether," said 'Andalíb; "you will get no good by it, and you see the difficulties that it involves. Go to Acre instead; that will be easily done on your homeward journey, and therefrom far greater blessings and advantages are likely to result."

"But," said I, "I am in some sort pledged to go to Kirmán, as I have written to Shíráz and also to my friends in England stating this to be my intention."

"You are quite right," said Ardashír, "and I for my part advise you to adhere to your plan, for to change one's plans without strong reason is to lay one's self open to a charge of indecision and lack of firm purpose."

"Well," I rejoined, "if I am not to go there on a mule, and cannot hire a horse, what am I to do? Shall I, for instance, walk, or would it be more 'dignified' to go on a camel?"

"Post," said one.

"Buy a horse," said another.

"As for posting," I said, "I have had enough of that. I never understood the force of the proverb, '*Es-safar sakar*'

('Travel is travail'[1]) till I posted from Shíráz to Dihbíd. But as for buying a horse, that is a more practicable idea, supposing that a suitable animal is forthcoming at a moderate price. A friend of mine at Ṭeherán told me that he kept a horse so as to be able to enjoy the luxury of going on foot; because, so long as he had no horse, it was supposed that the cause of his walking was either parsimony or poverty; but when it was known that he had one, his pedestrian progress was ascribed to eccentricity. Now I do not wish to be regarded as poor, still less as parsimonious; but I have no objection to being credited with eccentricity, and I should greatly enjoy the liberty of being able to walk as much and as often as I please."

After my guests had gone I talked the matter over with Ḥájí Ṣafar, who was strongly in favour of my buying a horse. Although he continued to recur with some bitterness to the fact that he had entered Yezd riding on a donkey, he was good enough to make no difficulties about riding a mule to Kirmán.

Next day Bahman came bringing with him the muleteer who was to supply me with the two mules I needed for my journey. He also brought a horse belonging to a Zoroastrian miller, who was willing to sell it for eighteen *túmáns* (nearly £6). It was by no means an ill-looking animal, and both Ḥájí Ṣafar and myself, having mounted it and tried its paces, liked it well. However, with a view to forming a better idea of its capacities, I had it saddled again in the evening and went for a short ride outside the town, from which I returned delighted, with a full determination to buy it. Shortly after my return the owner came to the garden, and the bargain was soon concluded to the satisfaction of all concerned. Ḥájí Ṣafar was especially delighted.

1 Literally, "travel is hell-fire." Between *Safar* and *Saḳar* there exists that species of word-play technically termed *tajnís-i-khaṭṭí*, or "linear pun"; that is to say, the two words, as written in the Arabic character, are identical in outline, and differ only in diacritical points. This play is ingeniously preserved in Sir Richard Burton's translation or paraphrase of the proverb, which is here given in the text.

"You will have to give me three or four *túmáns* a month more now," he said, "to look after your horse."

"Or else engage another servant," I suggested. His face fell.

"Don't be afraid," I continued: "I have enough trouble with you already. You shall have the groom's wages in addition to your own, and you can either look after the horse yourself or engage someone else to do so; only, in the latter case, please to understand clearly that the selection, appointment, payment, and dismissal of the groom is to be entirely in your hands, and that in no case will I listen to any complaints on either side, or mix myself up in any way in the quarrels you are sure to have."

Ḥájí Ṣafar was so elated by this arrangement that he launched out into a series of anecdotes about one of his former masters, named Ḥájí Ḳambar, who had held some position of authority (that of chief constable or governor, I believe) in Ṭeherán, some fifteen years previously. Although his own morals do not seem to have been beyond reproach, he punished the offences of others with great severity. He ordered a dervish who had got drunk on *'araḳ* to be bastinadoed for three hours; and even Seyyids were not protected from castigation by their holy lineage, for which, nevertheless, he would profess the greatest respect, causing the dark-blue turbans and sashes which were the outward sign thereof to be transferred to a tree or bush, to which he would then do obeisance ere he bade his *farráshes* beat the unlucky owner of the sacred tokens within an inch of his life. "One evening," continued Ḥájí Ṣafar, "I and three others of his *píshḳhidmats* (pages) were taking a stroll in the town when we noticed in a coffee-house a man accompanied by what we at first took to be a very handsome youth, round whose *ḳuláh* a handkerchief was tied in Kurdish fashion, so as to conceal the hair. On looking more attentively, however, we were convinced that this seeming youth was really a woman in disguise, so we arrested the two, and brought them to Ḥájí Ḳambar's house. Then I went to him, and said, 'Master, we have brought something to show you.' 'And what may that be?' he asked. 'Come with me,' I said, 'and I will show you.' So he followed me into the room where our prisoners were waiting. 'A nice-looking boy, is he not?' said I, pointing to the younger of the two. 'Well, what have you brought him here for?' demanded my master. 'And nicely dressed too,' I continued, disregarding his question; 'look at the pretty Kurdish handkerchief he has wound round his *kuláh*,' and as I spoke I plucked it off, and the girl's hair, escaping from constraint, fell down over her shoulders. When the Ḥájí discovered that our prisoner was a girl dressed in man's clothes he was very angry, reviled her in unmeasured terms, and ordered her to be locked up in a cupboard, on which he set his seal, till the morning. In the morning she was taken out, placed in a sack, and beaten all over by the *farráshes*, after which her head was shaved, and she was released."

I had not yet bought my horse or completed my preparations for departure, when I was again sent for by the Prince-Governor. This time I had not to go on foot, for one of my Bábí friends insisted on lending me a very beautiful white horse which belonged to him. I tried to refuse his kind offer, saying that the Dastúr was to accompany me to the Government House, and that as he could not ride I would rather go on foot also.

"In our country," I said, "we are taught to respect age and learning, and the Dastúr is old and learned, for which reason it appears to me most unseemly that I should ride and he walk beside me. He is a Zoroastrian, I am a Christian; both of us are regarded by the Musulmáns as infidels and unclean, and, if they could, they would subject me to the same disabilities which are imposed on him. Let me, therefore, walk beside him to show my contempt for those disabilities, and my respect for the Dastúr and his co-religionists."

"If you desire to better the Zoroastrians," replied my friend, "it is advisable for you to go to the Prince with as much state and circumstance as possible. The more honour paid to you, the better for them." The Dastúr himself took exactly the same view, so there was nothing for it but to acquiesce.

Half an hour before sunset the horse and servant of my friend came to the garden, and immediately after them the usual band of Government *farráshes* with a large lantern. I had arrayed myself in a new suit of clothes, made by a Yezdí tailor, of white shawl-stuff, on the pattern of an English suit. These were cool, comfortable, and neat; and though they would probably have been regarded as somewhat eccentric in England, I reflected that no one at Yezd or Kirmán would doubt that they were the ordinary summer attire of an English gentleman. Ḥájí Ṣafar, indeed, laughingly remarked that people would say I had turned Bábí (I suppose because the early Bábís were wont to wear white raiment), but otherwise expressed the fullest approval.

The first question addressed to me by the Prince on my entering his presence was, "When are you going?" On hearing that I proposed to start on the next day but one, he turned to the Dastúr and enquired whether he intended to accompany me. The Dastúr replied that he could not do so, as one of the Zoroastrian festivals, which necessitated his presence in Yezd, was close at hand, and that as it lasted a week I could not postpone my departure till it was over. Hearing this, the Prince wished to rearrange my plans entirely. I must go on the morrow, he said, to visit the waterfall and the mountains, remain there five days, then return to the city to see the Zoroastrian festival, and after that accompany the Zoroastrians to some of their shrines and holy places. Protestations were vain, and I was soon reduced to a sulky silence, which was relieved by the otherwise unwelcome intrusion of a large tarantula, and its pursuit and slaughter. After conversing for a while on general topics, and receiving for translation into English the rough draft of a letter which the Prince wished to send to Bombay to order photographic apparatus for his son, Minúchihr Mírzá, I was suffered to depart.

I now determined to carry into effect my plan of taking French leave of the Prince; and accordingly, my preparations being completed, on the very morning of the day fixed for my departure I wrote him a polite letter, thanking him very heartily for the many attentions he had shown me; expressing regrets that the limited time at my disposal would not suffer me either to follow out the programme he had so kindly arranged for me or to pay him a farewell visit; and concluding with a prayer for the continuance of his kindly feeling towards myself, and of his just rule over the people of Yezd. This letter I confided to the Dastúr, who happened to be going to the Government House, together with the English translation of the order which the Prince wished to send to the Bombay photographer.

I now flattered myself that I was well out of the difficulty, and returned with relief to my packing; but I had reckoned altogether without my host, for in less than an hour I was interrupted by the Prince's self-sufficient *píshkhidmat*, who brought back the letter to the Bombay photographer with a request that I would write a literal translation of it in Persian. This involved unpacking my writing materials, and while I was engaged in this and the translation of the letter, one of the servants of my Bábí friends came with a horse to take me to their house. Towards this man the *píshkhidmat* behaved with great insolence, asking him many impertinent and irrelevant questions, and finally turning him out of the room. At length I finished the translation, and, to my great relief, got rid of the *píshkhidmat*, as I hoped, for good. I then proceeded to the house of my Bábí friends, bade them a most affectionate farewell, received from them the promised letters of recommendation for Kirmán, and the names of the principal Bábís at Núk, Bahrám-ábád, and Níríz, and returned about sunset to the garden. Here I found the Dastúr, Ardashír, and Bahman awaiting me, and also, to my consternation, the irrepressible *píshkhidmat*, who brought a written message from the Prince, expressing great regret at my departure, and requesting me, if possible, to come and see him at once. As the hour of departure was now near at hand, and I was weary and eager for a little rest before setting out on the long night-march to Sar-i-Yezd, I would fain have excused myself; but, seeing that my Zoroastrian friends wished me to go, I ordered my horse to be saddled, and set out with the *píshkhidmat*. We rode rapidly through the dark and narrow streets, but in crossing the waste ground in front of the Government House my horse stumbled in a hole and fell with me, luckily without doing much harm to himself or me. The Prince was greatly concerned on hearing of my fall, and would hardly be persuaded that it was of no consequence; indeed, I was rather afraid that he would declare it of evil augury for my journey, and insist on my post-poning my departure. However, this, my farewell interview, passed off as smoothly as could be wished, and I sat for about an hour smoking, drinking sherbet, and conversing. He paid me many undeserved compliments, declaring that the letter I had written to him was better than he could have believed it possible for a European to write, and that he intended to send it to the prime minister, the *Amínu's-Sulṭán*. I, in return, expressed the genuine admiration with which I regarded his just, liberal, and enlightened rule; prayed that God might prolong his shadow so long as the months repeated themselves and the days re-curred; and finished up by putting in a good word for the Zoro-astrians. So we parted, with mutual expressions of affection and esteem; but not till he had made me promise to accept the escort of a mounted *tufankchí* or musket-man, and further placed in my hands a letter of recommendation to the Prince-Governor of Kirmán. Of this, which was given to me open and unsealed, I preserved a copy, which, as it may be of interest to the curious, I here translate, premising only that the terms in which Prince 'Imádu'd-Dawla was kind enough to describe me, exaggerated as they appear in English, are but the commonplaces of polite Persian.

"*In the Abode of Security of* KIRMÁN. *May it be honoured by the august service of the desirable, most honourable, most illustrious, nobly-born lord, the most mighty, most puissant prince, His Highness Náṣiru'd-Dawla (may his glory endure!), governor and ruler of the spacious domain of Kirmán.*

"*On the fourteenth of Ramazán was it despatched. 2468*[1].

"May I be thy sacrifice!

"Please God [our] religious devotions are accepted, and the care of God's servants, which is the best of service, on the part of the desirable, most honourable, most illustrious, most mighty and eminent prince (may his glory endure!) is approved in the divine audience-hall of God; for they have said—

> 'By service and succour of men we win to the grace of the Lord:
> By this, not by rosary, gown, or prayer-mat, we earn our reward.'

"At all events, the bearer of this letter of longing and service is my respected and honoured friend, of high degree, companion of glory and dignity, Idúárd Barúm Ṣáḥib, the Englishman, who, having come to visit this country, and being now homeward bound, hath set his heart on Kirmán and the rapture of waiting upon the servants of the nobly-born prince. Of the characteristics of this illustrious personage it is needless for me to make any representation. After meeting him you will be able to appreciate his good qualities, and the degree of his culture, and how truly sensible and well informed he is, for all his youth and fewness of years. The laudable traits which he possesses, indeed, are beyond what one can represent. Since he has mentioned that he is setting out for Kirmán, my very singular devotion impelled me to write these few words to the Blessed Presence. I trust that the sacred person of Your desirable, most illustrious, most mighty, and eminent Highness may be conjoined with health and good fortune. More were redundant."

(*Sealed*) 'IMÁDU'D-DAWLA.

It was two hours after sunset when I returned to the garden, and finally got rid of the Prince's *píshkhidmat* with a present of two or three *túmáns*. Ḥájí Ṣafar said that he should have had a watch or some other gift of the kind rather than money, which, he feared, might be refused or taken amiss. However, I had no watch to spare; and I am bound to confess that he was condescending enough to accept the monetary equivalent with grace if not gratitude. The *farráshes* having likewise been dismissed

1 This mystic number, corresponding to the word *Badúḥ*, is generally written under the address on a letter to ensure its safe arrival. Redhouse says it is the name of an angel who is supposed to watch over letters, but I never succeeded in obtaining a satisfactory explanation of it.

with presents of money, I was left in peace with my Zoroastrian friends, who, after drinking a farewell cup with me, departed, with the exception of Bahman, Ardashír's confidential clerk, who remained behind to give me a statement of my finances, and to pay over to me the balance still to my credit. The amount for which I had brought a cheque from Shíráz was 147½ *túmáns* (nearly £45), of which I found that I had drawn 45 *túmáns* during my stay at Yezd. The balance of 102½ *túmáns* I elected to receive in cash to the amount of 32½ *túmáns* and a cheque on a Zoroastrian merchant of Kirmán for the remaining 70 *túmáns*, both of which Bahman, who was as business-like, careful, and courteous as any English banker could have been, at once handed over to me, receiving in return a receipt for the whole sum with which I had been credited at Yezd.

Little now remained to be done but to eat my supper, put a few finishing touches to my packing, and distribute small presents of money to some of those who had rendered me service. They came up in turn, called by Ḥájí Ṣafar; old Jamshíd the gardener received 12 *ḳráns*, his little son Khusraw 6 *ḳráns*, another gardener named Khudá-dád 12 *ḳráns*, and Ḥájí Seyyid M——'s servant, 20 *ḳráns*. The farewells were not yet finished, for just as I was about to drink a last cup of tea, two of my Bábí friends came, in spite of the lateness of the hour, to wish me God-speed. Then they too left me, and only Bahman was present to watch the final departure of our little caravan as it passed silently forth into the desert and the darkness.

CHAPTER XV

FROM YEZD TO KIRMÁN

"*Raftam u burdam dágh-i-Tú dar dil*
Wádí bi-wádí, manzil bi-manzil."

"I journeyed on, bearing the brand of Thy grief in my heart,
From valley to valley, from stage to stage."

FIVE men and five beasts constituted the little company in which I quitted Yezd. Besides myself and my horse, there was Amír Khán, one of the "Arab" tribesmen of Ardistán, whom the prince had sent as a mounted escort to see me safely to the marches of his territory; the muleteer with his three mules, two of which only were hired by me; my servant Ḥájí Ṣafar; and a young Tabrízí named Mírzá Yúsuf, who had formerly been his fellow-servant, and to whom, at his request, and on the recommendation of my friend the *Sarhang*, I had given permission to accompany me to Kirmán (where he hoped to obtain employment from Prince Náṣiru'd-Dawla) and to ride on one of the lightly-laden mules. Mírzá Yúsuf, a conceited and worthless youth, had, as I subsequently discovered, and as will be more fully set forth in its proper place, been passing himself off at Yezd as a Bábí, so as to obtain help and money from rich and charitable members of that sect; and it was by this means, no doubt, that he had induced the *Sarhang* to bespeak my favour for him. Were all his fellow-townsmen like him, no exaggeration would be chargeable against the satirist who wrote—

"*Zi Tabrízí bi-juz ḥízí na-biní:*
Hamán bihtar, ki Tabrízí na-biní."

"From a Tabrízí thou wilt see naught but rascality:
Even this is best that thou should'st not see any Tabrízí."

Outwardly, however, Mírzá Yúsuf was sufficiently well-favoured and civil-spoken, and it was only after my arrival in Kirmán that I detected in him any worse quality than complacent self-satisfaction and incurable idleness.

Amír Khán, being well mounted, soon wearied of the slow march of the caravan, and urged me to push on with him at a brisker pace. I did so, thinking, of course, that he knew the way; but this proved to be a rash assumption, for, after traversing the considerable village of Muḥammad-ábád, he lost the road and struck off into the open desert, where the soft sand proved very arduous to my horse, which began to lag behind. A halt which Amír Khán made (not to allow me to come up with him, but to say his prayers) brought us once more together, but the subsequent appearance of two gazelles at some distance to our left was too much for his self-control, and he set off after them at full gallop. I soon abandoned all idea of following him, and, having now realised his complete uselessness, both as a guide and a guard, continued to make my solitary way in the direction which I supposed to be correct. After some time, Amír Khán, having got a shot at the gazelles and missed them, returned in a more subdued frame of mind, and, after again losing the way several times, we finally reached the post-house of Sar-i-Yezd about sunrise. The remainder of the caravan being far behind, I had nothing to do, after seeing to the stabling of my horse, but to lie down on the mud floor with my head on the rolled-up great-coat which I had strapped to the saddle at starting, and go to sleep.

I was awakened about three hours later by Ḥájí Ṣafar for my morning tea, and passed the day in the post-house writing and making up my accounts. About sunset I received a visit from a Zoroastrian who was coming up to Yezd from Kirmán. He remained with me for about an hour, chatting and drinking tea, and informed me, amongst other things, that he had spent several years in Bombay and Calcutta; that the Governor of Kirmán, Prince Náṣiru'd-Dawla, was a most enlightened and popular ruler; that Kirmán was much cooler than Yezd, as proved by the fact that the mulberries were not yet ripe there, and that cucumbers were still scarcely to be obtained; that the poverty of the inhabitants, always great, had been increased by the depreciation in shawls, which fetched less than a third of their former price; but that, as against this, the crops, and especially the opium crop, had been remarkably good in the last year.

We left Sar-i-Yezd between three and four hours after sunset by the light of a nearly full moon, my Zoroastrian friend coming to bid me farewell and wish me God-speed. Amír Khán, who kept dozing off in his saddle, again led us astray; and, while we were wandering about amongst the sandhills, there reached our ears a faint cry, which, in that solitary and ghostly desert, caused us to start with surprise. Amír Khán, however, followed by myself, made for the spot whence it appeared to come, and there, huddled together between two sandhills, we presently discerned a group of about half a dozen persons (three men, three women, and, I think, one child at least) gathered round a diminutive donkey. As we approached, they again addressed us in tones of entreaty, but in a dialect which was to me quite unintelligible. Amír Khán, however, understood them. They were from the "City of Barbar" (*Shahr-i-Barbar*, which he explained, was near Sístán, on the eastern frontier of Persia), and were bound for Kerbelá, drawn thither by a longing desire to visit the place of martyrdom of the Imám Ḥuseyn. They had lost their way in the desert and were sorely distressed by thirst, and the boon they craved was a draught of water. My heart was filled with pity for these poor people, and admiration for their faith and piety; and as I bade Ḥájí Ṣafar give them to drink from the leather bottle he carried, there ran in my mind the words of Ḥáfiẓ—

"*Ánche ján-i-'áshiḳán az dast-i-hajrat mí-kashad*
Kas na-dídé dar jihán, juz tishnagán-i-Kerbelá."

"What the souls of thy lovers suffer at the hands of thy separation
None hath experienced in the world, save the thirsty ones of Kerbelá."

Thereat, and by the blessings and thanks which they poured forth as they gulped down the water, was my compassion still further moved, and I felt constrained to give them also a small piece of money. For this Amír Khán warmly applauded me, as we rode off, telling the pilgrims that they were within a short distance of the village of Sar-i-Yezd. "Those who give," said he, "of that which God hath given them will never want, and those who will not give are not profited, even in this life, by their avarice. Only yesterday a beggar asked me for money. I replied that I had none, though I had three *ḳráns* and a half in my pocket at that moment. But when I looked for these a little later, I found that they were gone, no doubt to punish me for my niggardly conduct."

After this incident the march continued in sleepy silence; but towards dawn Amír Khán, who was riding beside me, suddenly woke up from his doze, and remarked, with complete irrelevance to anything that had gone before, "No sect are worse than the Bábís."

"Why?" I enquired, wondering what had caused him to introduce spontaneously a subject generally avoided with the most scrupulous care by Persian Musulmáns.

"They worship as God," he replied, "a man called Mírzá Ḥuseyn 'Alí, who lives at Adrianople. A friend of mine at Yezd once told me that he was going there. I asked why. 'To visit God' (*bi-ẓiyárat-i-Ḥaḳḳ*), he answered. When he got there he was asked what work his hands could do. 'None,' said he, 'save writing; for I am a scrivener by profession.' 'Then,' said they, 'there is no place for you here, and we do not want you.' He was not allowed to see Mírzá Ḥuseyn 'Alí at all, but was given a handkerchief which he had used, and invited to make an offering of three *túmáns*. So he returned thoroughly disgusted, 'for,' said he, 'God does not take presents.'"

While I was considering how I should meet this sally, and whether Amír Khán, knowing that I had had dealings with the

Bábís at Yezd, was anxious to warn me against them, he solved the difficulty by again dozing off into a fitful slumber, from which he awoke "between the wolf and the sheep" (*meyán-i-gurg ú mísh*), as the Persians say—that is, at early dawn. As soon as he had collected his scattered wits, he cast his eyes round the horizon in hopes of being able to discern our next halting-place, Zeynu'd-Dín, and, after some scrutiny, declared that we had passed it during his sleep, and that it was "over there" (pointing to a dark line on the plain behind us, some distance off the track which we were following). Luckily, warned by previous experience, I paid no heed to his opinion, and, supported by Ḥájí Ṣafar, insisted on continuing our advance, for which we were rewarded by finding ourselves in less than half an hour at Zeynu'd-Dín, where there is nothing but a caravansaray and a very good post-house. I alighted at the latter, and, after a cup of tea, slept for about six hours.

Zeynu'd-Dín is the last halting-place within the territories of Yezd, and consequently Amír Khán had been instructed to accompany me only thus far on my journey, and to obtain for me another mounted guard belonging to the jurisdiction of the Governor of Kirmán. I had, however, no desire to avail myself of this unnecessary luxury, and hinted as much to Amír Khán as I placed in his hand ten *ḳráns*. He took the hint and the money with equal readiness, and we parted with mutual expressions of esteem. The evening was cloudy, with occasional gusts of wind, and every now and then a great pillar of sand or dust would sweep across the plain, after the fashion of the *jinnís* in the *Arabian Nights*. The road presented little of interest, being ever the same wide ill-defined track, through a sandy plain enclosed between two parallel mountain chains, running from the north-west to the south-east. At one place I noticed a number of large caterpillars (larvæ of *Deilephila euphorbiæ*, I think), feeding on a kind of spurge which grew by the roadside. No trace of cultivation was visible till we came within a *farsaḳh* of

Kirmánsháhán, when we passed two or three villages at about the same distance to the east of the road. We reached Kirmánsháhán half an hour before sunset, and alighted at the post-house, which was the best I had seen in Persia. There are also two caravansarays, one old and one new. As no meat was obtainable, I made my supper off eggs fried in oil, and then went to sleep.

I woke about two hours before dawn to find the people of the post-house eating their morning meal preparatory to entering on the day's fast. Ḥájí Ṣafar and the muleteer, however, were sleeping so peacefully that it seemed a shame to wake them, so I lay down again and slept for another two hours, when I was awakened by Ḥájí Ṣafar. It was quite light when we started, but this was of little advantage, as the scenery was precisely the same in character as on the previous day. The road, however, hugged the western range of mountains more closely, and indeed at one point we passed inside a few outlying hills. Kirmánsháhán was in sight for two hours and a quarter after we had left it, and we had no sooner crossed a slight rise which finally hid it from our view than we caught sight of the caravansaray of Shemsh, which, however, it took us nearly three hours more to reach.

A more dismal spot than Shemsh it would be hard to imagine. There is nothing but the aforesaid caravansaray and a post-house (singularly good, like all the post-houses between Yezd and Kirmán) standing side by side in the sandy, salt-strewn plain. As I rode up to the latter edifice, I saw a little stream, very clear and sparkling, carefully banked up between mud walls which conducted it into a small pond. Being overcome with thirst, I flung myself from my horse and dipped my face into it to get a long draught of what I supposed to be pure fresh water. To my disappointment it proved to be almost as salt as the sea. There was no other water to be had, and Ḥájí Ṣafar had thrown away what was left from Kirmánsháhán; nor did my hope that boiling might improve it, and that a decent cup of tea might at least be obtainable, prove well-founded. No one who has not tried it can imagine how nasty a beverage is tea made in a copper teapot with brackish water. Luckily my kind Zoroastrian friends had forced me to accept two bottles of beer from them as I was leaving Yezd, and these, in that thirsty wilderness, were as the very elixir of life. Even so the day was a horrible one, and seemed almost interminable. Swarms of flies, distant thunder, and a violent gusty wind increased my despondency; and the only discovery in which a visit to a neighbouring mud-ruin resulted was a large and very venomous-looking serpent. Altogether I was heartily glad to leave this detestable place about four and a half hours after sunset, by the light of a radiant moon.

The monotony of the march to the next stage, Anár, was only twice broken, first by meeting a string of twenty-five camels going up to Yezd, whose drivers greeted us with the usual "*Furṣat báshad!*" ("May it be opportune!"); and secondly by the appearance of some wild beast which was prowling about by the road, but which, on our approach, slunk off into the desert. About dawn we arrived at Anár, a flourishing village containing a good many gardens, and surrounded by fields in which men were busy reaping the corn. Here we alighted at the post-house to rest and refresh ourselves before continuing our march to the next stage, Beyáz, which we reached without incident a little before sundown.

Beyáz is a small hamlet containing a few trees, and not devoid of signs of cultivation. Three or four camels were resting and taking their food in a field opposite the post-house, where I alighted in preference to the large but dilapidated caravansaray. Soon after our arrival, a party of mounted *ghuláms* rode up, and bivouacked outside under the trees. One of these, as Ḥájí Ṣafar informed me, was anxious to "challenge" my horse. This practice (called *muwází bastan*) I was surprised to find amongst the Persians, as I had hitherto only met with it in the pages of

Mr Sponge's Sporting Tour. For those not familiar with that entertaining work, I may explain how the transaction would have been conducted if I had given my consent (which, needless to say, I did not do). The *ghulám* who had "challenged" my horse suggested that the postmaster (*ná'ib-chápár*) should act as umpire between the two animals, and to this Ḥájí Ṣafar (acting, as he chose to consider, as my representative) agreed. Ḥájí Ṣafar then informed the *ná'ib-chápár* that I had bought my horse for thirty *túmáns* (as a matter of fact it had only cost me sixteen *túmáns*), but the latter valued it still higher, at thirty-five *túmáns*. However, he valued the *ghulám's* horse at forty *túmáns* (it was probably worth twelve at the outside), so that the "award" was that my horse should "give" the *ghulám's* horse five *túmáns*, or, in other words, that I should give the *ghulám* my horse and five *túmáns* in money for his horse.

We left Beyáz about four hours before sunset, and continued our south-easterly march along a track so ill-defined that I felt impelled to make a wide detour towards the telegraph-posts, which lay some distance to the east, in the expectation of finding something more like a high road. As dusk drew on the whole character of the country began to change: rivulets and streams intersected it in every direction; the air grew moist and damp, like that of a fen; and the night re-echoed with the shrill chirping of grasshoppers and the hoarse croaking of frogs. Once we lost our way amongst the ditches and cornfields, and floundered about for some time in the dark ere, rather by good luck than good management, we again struck the road. Flickering lights in the distance, probably will-o'-the-wisps, kept our hopes of speedy arrival alive; but it was only after repeated disappointments that the welcome outline of the post-house of Kushkúh loomed out, like some "moated grange," through the darkness. We had to wake the postmaster ere we could gain admission, and no sooner was my bed spread in the porch of the *bálá-kháné*, or upper chamber, than I fell sound asleep, lulled by a chorus of frogs and grasshoppers, till supper-time, after which I again composed myself for slumber.

When Ḥájí Ṣafar brought me my tea next morning, he informed me that the muleteer, Zeynu'l-'Ábidín, had decided to remain at Kushkúh, to rest his beasts after their forced marches of the last day or two, till sundown, so as to accomplish the seven long parasangs which separated us from the considerable town of Bahrám-ábád (the capital of the district known as Rafsinján) during the night. I was not sorry for the rest, and, though much pestered by flies, passed a tolerably comfortable day in the little post-house. We started by starlight about three hours after sunset, but in about an hour the moon rose up to light us on our way. The night was quite chilly and the march very tedious, and even when soon after dawn we sighted Bahrám-ábád, a weary length of wilfully sinuous and serpentine road remained to be traversed ere we finally alighted at the post-house.

At Bahrám-ábád I had a letter of introduction from Ḥájí Seyyid M—— to the chief of the posts in that district, which, after lunch, I caused to be conveyed to him. He came to visit me without delay, and after sitting for a short time carried me off to his office in the caravansaray. While I was there several persons came to see him, amongst them a fine-looking young Khán of Rafsinján, who had just returned from Sírján by way of Páríz and Gōd-i-Aḥmar. He had with him the body of an enormous lizard (*buz-majjé*) which he had shot on the road. About three hours before sunset my host took me to his house and gave me tea, after which I was waited upon successively by deputations of Zoroastrians and Hindoos, both of which classes regard an Englishman as their natural friend and ally. The Zoroastrians were only three in number: one of them was Ardashír Mihrabán's agent, and of the other two one was an old man called Mihrabán, and the other a young man named Ardashír. They told me that there were in all about twenty or twenty-five Zoroastrians in

Bahrám-ábád; that their co-religionists in Kirmán were much less subject to insult and annoyance, and in all ways better off, than those in Yezd; and that the chief products of Rafsinján were, besides cereals, almonds and pistachio-nuts, which were exported to India.

After the departure of the Zoroastrians, the whole Hindoo community (save one, who was ill) waited upon me. There were fourteen of them, men and youths, all natives of Shikárpúr, and they brought me as a present an enormous block of sugar-candy. One of them had recently been robbed of a large sum of money, and, as the Persian Governor could not succeed in capturing the thief, and would not make good the loss, he begged me to make a representation of the facts to the English Embassy at Ṭeherán. I promised to come and inspect the scene of the outrage, if I had time, without further committing myself; and shortly afterwards the deputation withdrew. I remained to supper with the postmaster, who made me eat to repletion of his excellent *piláw*, washed down with a delicious sherbet, and strove to persuade me to stay the night with him; but I excused myself on the ground that the muleteer would probably wish to start. However, on arriving at the *chápár-khané*, whither he insisted on accompanying me, I found that, as the morrow, 21st Ramaẓán, was the anniversary of the Imám 'Alí's death, and consequently an unlucky day, neither Ḥájí Ṣafar nor the muleteer wished to continue the march till the following evening.

I did not go out next day till about three hours before sunset, when the postmaster sent his servant to bring me to his house. I conversed with him for about two hours, and he enquired very particularly about the signs which should herald Christ's coming, but did not make any further allusion to the beliefs of the Bábís, which, I believe, were his own. Our conversation was interrupted by the arrival of one of the Hindoos, who wished me to inspect the scene of the recent robbery, which I agreed to do. We found all the other Hindoos assembled in the caravan-saray where they lodged, and I was at once shown the inner room whence the safe (containing, as they declared, 400 *túmáns* in cash, and 14,000 *túmáns* in cheques and letters of credit) had been abstracted by the thieves, who, as it was supposed, had entered by the chimney. Ten or fifteen men had been arrested on suspicion by the Governor, Mírzá Hidáyatu'lláh, but, as there was no sufficient evidence against any of them, they had been released. I took notes of these matters, and promised to bring them to the notice of some of my friends in the English Embassy if I got the chance; and we then conversed for a time, while I smoked a *ḳalyán* which they brought me. They questioned me closely as to the objects of my journey, and refused to credit my assertion that I was travelling for my own instruction and amusement, declaring that I must be an agent of the English Government.

"Why don't you take Persia?" said one of them at length: "you could easily if you liked."

"I suppose the thief who took your money put the same question to himself with regard to it," I replied, "and yet you feel that you have a just ground of complaint against him. People have no right to take their neighbours' property, even if they think they can do so with impunity, and states are no more entitled to steal than individuals." The Hindoos appeared to be still unconvinced, and my sympathy for their loss was considerably abated.

I returned to the postmaster's house for supper, after which he caused soft pillows and bolsters to be brought, and insisted on my resting for a couple of hours before starting. At the end of this time Ḥájí Ṣafar awoke me to tell me that the caravan was ready to start, and, after a final cup of tea and a hasty farewell to my kind host, I was once more on the road. We lost our way at the very start, and wandered about for some time in the star-light, until we came to one or two small houses. The *ná'ib-chápár* of Bahrám-ábád, who had joined our party, hammered at the door of one of these till an old peasant, aroused from his sleep, came out, and directed us on our way. But this did not satisfy the *ná'ib-chápár*, who compelled the poor old man to accompany us for a mile or so, which he rather unwillingly did; though two *ḳráns* which I gave him as he was leaving us more than satisfied him for the trouble he had incurred.

About dawn, while still distant some two parasangs from our halting-place, Kabútar Khán, we passed a company of men, with a young girl enveloped in a white *chádar*, who were going down to Kirmán, and exchanged a few words with them. We reached the post-house of Kabútar Khán (which seemed to be entirely in the charge of a very quaint old woman) about an hour after sunrise, and remained there till about three hours after sunset, when we again set out for Bághín. The man who had been our companion on the previous stage again joined us, being now mounted on a very small donkey which he had hired for thirty *sháhís* (about twopence) to take him to Bághín. A little boy named 'Abbás accompanied the donkey, and several times the man dismounted to allow him to ride for a while, on which occasions he would break out into snatches of song in his sweet, childish voice.

Before we reached Bághín, the great broad plain running towards the south-east, which we had followed since leaving Yezd, began to close in, and mountains appeared in front of us, as well as on either hand. Soon after dawn we reached Bághín (which is a small village surrounded by a considerable extent of cultivated ground), and, as usual, put up at the post-house. Here we remained till four hours after sunset, when the mules were loaded up for the last time, for that night's march was to bring us to our journey's end. Our course now lay nearly due east, along a good level road; and when the dawn began to brighten over the hills before us, Kirmán, nestling, as it seemed, at the very foot of their black cliffs, and wrapped like one of her own daughters in a thin white mantle of mist and smoke, gladdened our straining eyes.

My original intention had been to alight in the first instance at the post-house, but as this proved to be situated at some distance outside the city walls, and as I was eager to be in the very centre of the town without further delay, I decided to take up my quarters instead at one of the caravansarays. It was fortunate that I did so; for events so shaped themselves that my sojourn at Kirmán, instead of lasting only ten days or a fortnight, as I then intended, was prolonged for more than two months; and, for reasons soon to be mentioned, it would probably have been difficult for me to have quitted the post-house if I had once taken up my abode there without offending my good friend the postmaster of Kirmán.

On entering the city we first made our way through the bazaars to the caravansaray of the Vakíl, which we were told was the best; but here there was no room to be had, so, after some delay, during which I was surrounded by a little crowd of sightseers, we proceeded to the caravansaray of Ḥájí 'Alí Áḳá, where I obtained a lodging. While the beasts were being unloaded I was accosted by two Zoroastrians, one of whom proved to be Ardashír Mihrabán's agent, Mullá Gushtásp. (All the Zoroastrians in Kirmán are entitled "Mullá," even by the Muḥammadans.) They came into my room and sat down for a while, and Gushtásp told me that he had found a place for me to stay in during my sojourn at Kirmán in a garden outside the town. They soon left me, and, after a wash and a shave, I slept till nearly noon, when I was awakened by a *farrásh* from the telegraph-office, who was the bearer of a telegram from Cambridge, which had been sent on from Shíráz. The original, which, of course, was in English, arrived by post the same evening, and ran—"Please authorise name candidate for Persian readership, Neil." The Persian translation (made, I believe, at Káshán, where the wires from Shíráz and Kirmán to the capital join) was as follows:—"*Khwáhish dáram idhn bi-dihíd shumá-rá baráyi mu'allimí-i-fársí taklíf kunam. Níl.*" I was rather overwhelmed by the reflection that even here at Kirmán I was not beyond the reach of that irrepressible nuisance of this age of ours, electricity.

Ḥájí Ṣafar had already succeeded in discovering a relative in Kirmán (a cousin on his mother's side, as I understood)—a sleek, wily-looking man of about fifty, generally known as "Ná'ib Ḥasan"—whom he brought to see me. While he was with me, a Greek of Constantinople, who had turned Musulmán and settled in Kirmán, joined the party, and conversed with me a little in Turkish. Then came servants from the telegraph-office to enquire on the part of their master (a prince as well as a telegraphist, but then, as I have already remarked, princes are not rare in Persia) how I did, and when I would come and visit him (for I had an introduction to him from my friends at Yezd, who had also written to him about me); and hard on the heels of these came the son of the postmaster of Kirmán (to whom also I had letters of recommendation), so that I had hardly a moment's leisure. This last visitor carried me off to see his father at the Central Post Office in the town. The postmaster, a kindly-looking man, past middle age, with a gray moustache and the rank of colonel (*sartíp*), gave me a most friendly welcome, but reproached me for being a day later than he had been led to expect by the postmaster of Bahrám-ábád, who appeared to have sent him a message concerning me. "Although I am in poor health," said he, "and am, as you see, lame in one foot, I rode out nearly three parasangs to meet you yesterday, for I wished to be the first to welcome you to Kirmán; and I also wanted to tell you that the *chápár-kháné*, which is well built and comfortable, and is intended for a residence, is entirely at your disposal, and that I hope you will stay in it while you are here."

I next proceeded to the telegraph-office to visit the prince, whom I found sitting at the instrument with his pretty little son opposite him. He in turn insisted that I should take up my abode at a new telegraph-office which had just been completed for him, and it was with great difficulty that I got him to acquiesce in the plan which I had formed of inspecting the three residences chosen for me in advance by my kind friends of Kirmán. Indeed I was somewhat embarrassed by their hospitality, for I was afraid that, whichever place I selected, I could hardly hope to avoid giving offence to the owners of the other two. As, however, it was clear that I could not live in all of them, I decided in my own mind that I would just choose the one I liked best; and accordingly, after I had conversed for a short while with the prince, I set off with the postmaster's son to visit the *chápár-khúné* to the north, and the Zoroastrian garden to the south, of the town.

The *chápár-khúné* proved fully worthy of the praises bestowed on it by the postmaster, for the rooms in it were spacious, clean, and comfortable, and looked out on to a pleasant garden. We smoked a cigarette there, while horses were saddled to take us to the garden of the Zoroastrians. Thither we rode through the town, which we entered by the north gate (called *Derwázé-i-Sulṭání*) and quitted by the south gate (*Derwázé-i-Náṣiriyyé*). In the garden, which was just outside the latter, we found the two Zoroastrians who had first accosted me in the caravansaray, Ardashír's agent, Gushtásp, and Ferídún, a man of about twenty-five years of age, with both of whom I afterwards became very intimate. After sitting for a while in the *chár-faṣl* or summer-house, which stood in the middle of the garden, and partaking of the wine, *'araḳ*, and young cucumbers which the Zoroastrians, according to their usual custom, had brought with them, we returned together to the caravansaray. Ná'ib Ḥasan presently joined us, and outstayed all my other visitors. As he seemed inclined to take the part of confidential adviser, I informed him of the difficulty in which I was placed as to the selection of a lodging from the three proposed. After reflecting a moment, he said, "*Ṣáḥib*, you must of necessity run the risk of offending two out of three persons, and therefore, as you cannot avoid this, you need only consult your own inclination in the matter. If you accept the prince's offer and take up your abode in the telegraph-office, you will be continually subjected to some degree of constraint, and will be always surrounded by inquisitive and meddlesome servants. If you go to the *chápár-khání*, you will be outside the city, and will only see the friends of the *sartíp* of the post-office. In the guebres' garden, on the other hand, you will be your own master, and will be free and unconstrained. My advice, therefore, is, that you should select the last, and make polite excuses to the prince and the *sartíp*." As this counsel seemed good to me, I determined to act on it without delay; and it was arranged, at Ná'ib Ḥasan's suggestion, that I should transfer myself and my possessions to the garden on the following morning, so that ere my apologies should reach the prince and the *sartíp* the transfer might be an accomplished fact, admitting of no further discussion. Soon after this Ná'ib Ḥasan departed, and I was left at leisure to enjoy the welcome letters which that day's post had brought me from home.

The move to the garden was duly effected on the following morning (Wednesday, 5th June, 25th Ramaẓán) with the help of Ná'ib Ḥasan, Ferídún, and a Zoroastrian lad named Rustam, who was brother to my friend Bahman of Yezd. Of this garden, which was my residence for the next two months, I may as well give a brief description in this place. Its extent was several acres. It was entirely surrounded by a high but rather dilapidated mud wall. It was divided transversely (*i.e.* in a direction parallel to the main road leading to the *Derwázé-i-Náṣiriyyé*, or southern gate of the city, which bounded it to the west) by another mud wall (in which was a gap which served the purpose of a gate), and longitudinally by a stream—not one of the niggardly, three-hours-a-day streams of Yezd, but a deep, clear brook, in which I was often able to enjoy the luxury of a bathe. Besides the summer-house, or *chár-faṣl*, of which I have already spoken, and which stood in the middle of the northern half of the garden, about half-way between the stream and the northern wall, there was a larger building, consisting of two rooms and a small courtyard, standing on the very edge of the stream. It was in this more spacious building that I established myself on my arrival, using the larger of the two rooms (which had windows to the east and south, the former looking out into the courtyard, the latter on to the stream) for myself, and leaving the smaller chamber at the back to Ḥájí Ṣafar and Mírzá Yúsuf; but afterwards, when the heat waxed greater (though it was at no time severe), I lived for the most part in the little summer-house, which, being open to the air on all four sides, was cooler and pleasanter. From the larger building another wall ran westwards towards the main road leading to the *Derwázé-i-Náṣiriyyé*, partially cutting off the south-west portion of the garden from that which I occupied. This south-west or outer part of the garden appeared to be in some measure public property, for often, as I passed through it to reach the gate, I saw groups of women washing their linen in the stream which traversed it. The garden had been originally planned and laid out by a former vizier of Kirmán (whose son, Mírzá Jawád, a man of about fifty years of age, occupied a house in another garden not far distant from this), but he, ere his death (so, at least, I gathered), having fallen into disgrace and comparative poverty, it had been neglected and suffered to run wild, and was now let to some of the Zoroastrians, who used it chiefly for the cultivation of plants useful either as food or medicine. In truth it was rather a wilderness than a garden—albeit a fair and fragrant wilderness; and never a calm, clear summer night, sweet with the scent of the rose and melodious with the song of the nightingale, but I am again transported in the spirit to that enchanted ground. Is there one who dares to maintain that the East has lost its wonder, its charm, or its terror? Then he knows it not; or only knows that outer crust of commonplace which, under the chill influence of Western utilitarianism and practical sense, has skimmed its surface.

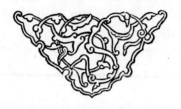

CHAPTER XVI

KIRMÁN SOCIETY

"Har chand ki az rúyi karímán khajilím,
Gham níst, ki parvardé-i-ín áb u gilím:
Dar rúyi zamín níst chú Kirmán já'í;
Kirmán dil-i-'álam-ast, ú má ahl-i-dilím!"

"Although we stand abashed in the presence of the noble,
It matters not, since we have drawn nourishment from this earth and water:
On the face of the earth there is no place like Kirmán;
Kirmán is the heart of the world, and we are men of heart."

IN no town which I visited in Persia did I make so many friends and acquaintances of every grade of society, and every shade of piety and impiety, as at Kirmán. When I left I made a list of all the persons who had visited me, or whom I had visited, and found that the number of those whom I could remember fell but little short of a hundred. Amongst these almost every rank, from the Prince-Governor down to the mendicant dervish, was represented, as well as a respectable variety of creeds and nationalities—Belúchís, Hindoos, Zoroastrians, Shí'ites and Sunnís, Sheykhís, Ṣúfís, Bábís, both Behá'í and Ezelí, dervishes, and *ḳalandars* belonging to no order, fettered by no dogma, and trammelled by but few principles. Hitherto I had always been more or less dependent on the hospitality of friends, whose feelings I was obliged to consult in choosing my acquaintances; here in Kirmán the garden where I dwelt was open to all comers, and I was able without let or hindrance to pursue that object which, since my arrival in Persia, had been ever before me, namely, to familiarise myself with all, even the most eccentric and antinomian, developments of the protean Persian genius. I succeeded beyond my most sanguine expectations, and, as will presently be set forth, found myself ere long in a world whereof I had never dreamed, and wherein my spirit was subjected to such alternations of admiration, disgust, and wonder, as I had never before in my life experienced.

All this, however, did not come to me at once, and would not, perhaps, have come at all but for a fortunate misfortune which entirely altered all my plans, and prolonged the period of my stay at Kirmán from the fortnight or three weeks which I had originally intended to a couple of months. For just as I was about to depart thence (having, indeed, actually engaged a muleteer for the journey to Shíráz by way of Sírján, Khír, and Níríz), I fell a victim to a sharp attack of ophthalmia, which for some weeks compelled me to abandon all idea of resuming my travels. And this ophthalmia, from which I suffered no little pain, had another result tending to throw me more than would otherwise have been the case into the society of dervishes, dreamers, and mystics. Judge me not harshly, O thou who hast never known sickness—ay, and for a while partial blindness—in a strange land, if in my pain and my wakefulness I at length yielded to the voice of the tempter, and fled for refuge to that most potent, most sovereign, most seductive, and most enthralling of masters, opium. Unwisely I may have acted in this matter, though not, as I feel, altogether culpably; yet to this unwisdom I owe an experience which I would not willingly have forfeited, though I am thankful enough that the chain of my servitude was snapped ere the last flicker of resolution and strenuousness finally expired in the Nirvana of the opium-smoker. I often wonder if any of those who have returned to tell the tale in the outer world have wandered farther than myself into the flowery labyrinths of the poppy-land, for of him who enters its fairy realms too true, as a rule, is the Persian opium-smoker's epigram—

"*Ḥaẓrat-i-afyún-i-má har maraẓí-rá rewást,*
Lík chú 'ádí shudí, khud maraẓ-i-bí-dewást."

"Sir Opium of ours for every ill is a remedy swift and sure,
But he, if you bear for a while his yoke, is an ill which knows no cure."

Although it was some while after my arrival in Kirmán that I became numbered amongst the intimates of the aforesaid Sir Opium, he lost no time in introducing himself to my notice in the person of one of his faithful votaries, Mírzá Ḥuseyn-Ḳulí of Bam (a pleasant, gentle, dreamy soul, of that type which most readily succumbs to the charm of the poppy), who came to visit me in Ná'ib Ḥasan's company on the very day of my entry into the garden. Soon after this, too, I came into daily relations with another bondsman of the all-potent drug, one 'Abdu'l Ḥuseyn, whom Ḥájí Ṣafar, in accordance with the agreement made between himself and myself at Yezd, had hired to look after my horse. He was far advanced on the downward path, and often, when sent to buy bread or other provisions in the shops hard by the city-gate, would he remain away for hours at a time, and return at last without having accomplished his commission, and unable to give any account of how the time had passed. This used to cause me some annoyance till such time as I too fell under the spell of the poppy-wizard, when I ceased to care any longer (because the opium-smoker cares not greatly for food, or indeed for aught else in the material world save his elixir); nay, I even found a certain tranquil satisfaction in his vagaries. But I must leave for a while these delicious reminiscences and return to the comparatively uneventful fortnight with which my residence at Kirmán began. Of this I shall perhaps succeed in giving the truest picture by following in the main the daily entries which I made in my diary.

On the day of my instalment in the garden (*Wednesday, 5th June, 25th Ramaẓán*) I received several visitors besides the opium-smoker of Bam. Chief amongst these was a certain notable Sheykh of Ḳum, whose doubtful orthodoxy had made it expedient for him to leave the sacred precincts of his native town for happy, heedless Kirmán. Here he had succeeded in gaining the confidence and esteem of Prince Náṣiru'd-Dawla, the Governor, in whose society most of his time was passed, either in consultation on affairs of state, or in games of chance, for which he cared the less because he was almost invariably the loser. He was a burly, genial, kind-hearted gentleman, with but little of the odour of sanctity so much sought after in his native town, and a fund of wit and information. I afterwards saw much of him, and learned that he was an Ezelí Bábí, so far as he was anything at all (for by many he was accounted a free-thinker, "*lá-madhhab*"); but in this first interview he gave no further indication of his proclivities than to enquire whether I had not a copy of Mánakjí's *New History* of the Bábí Theophany. With him came two brothers, merchants of Yezd, whom I will call Áḳá Muḥsin and Áḳá Muḥammad Ṣádiḳ. Of the former, who was an orthodox Shí'ite, I saw but little subsequently; but with the younger brother, a man of singular probity and most amiable disposition, I became rather intimate, and from him I met with a disinterested kindness which I shall not omit to record in its proper place. He too was a Bábí, but a follower of Behá, not of Ezel; as also was a third brother, who, being but a lad of fifteen or sixteen, was suddenly so overcome by a desire to behold the face of Behá that he ran away from Kirmán with only five *túmáns* in his pocket, with the set purpose of making his way to Acre, on the Syrian coast, in which project, thanks to the help of kindly Zoroastrians at Bandar-i-'Abbás, and the Bábís of Bombay and Beyrout, he was successful. I subsequently made the acquaintance of another lad whose imagination was so stirred by this exploit that he was determined to imitate it at the first opportunity, though whether or no his plan was realised I cannot say.

Thursday, 6th June, 26th Ramaẓán.—Soon after I was up I received a visit from Ná'ib Ḥasan (who, indeed, lost no time in establishing himself in the position of my guide, philosopher, and friend, and who seldom allowed a day to pass without giving me the pleasure of his society for a good many hours, including at least one meal). With him came Rustam, the young Zoroastrian of whom I have already spoken, who, on this occasion, outstayed the Ná'ib. This Rustam was a well-mannered and intelligent lad, whose only fault was an unduly deferential manner, which at times I found rather irksome. He asked me many questions about my country and about America ("*Yangí-dunyá*," "the New World"), in which, like several other Persians whom I met, he appeared to take an extraordinary interest; for what reason I know not, since he had not the excuse of supposing, like some Muḥammadans, that thence, by some underground channel, Antichrist (*Dajjál*) shall reach the well in Iṣfahán from which, at the end of time, he is to appear.

In the afternoon I went into the town, accompanied by Ḥájí Ṣafar and Mírzá Yúsuf, notwithstanding a message which I received from the Sardár of Sístán informing me of his intention of paying me a visit. We passed the walls, not by the adjacent *Derwázé-i-Náṣiriyya*, but by another gate called *Derwázé-i-Masjid* ("the Mosque Gate"), lying more to the west, from which a busy thoroughfare (thronged, especially on "Friday eve," with hosts of beggars) leads directly to the bazaars, and paid a visit to my Zoroastrian friends in the caravansaray of Ganj 'Alí Khán (where, for the most part, their offices are situated) and to the post-office. In the bazaars I met a quaint-looking old Hindoo, who persisted in addressing me in his own uncouth Hindí, which he seemed to consider that I as an Englishman was bound to understand. We returned about sunset by the way we had come, and met crowds of people, who had been to pay their respects to a deceased saint interred in a mausoleum just outside the Mosque Gate, re-entering the city.

On reaching the garden I found another visitor awaiting me—an inquisitive, meddlesome, self-conceited scion of some once influential but now decayed family, who, in place of the abundant wealth which he had formerly possessed, subsisted on a pension of 150 *túmáns* allowed him by the Prince-Governor in consideration of his former greatness. For this person, whose name was Ḥájí Muḥammad Khán, I conceived a very particular aversion. He manifested a great curiosity as to my rank, my income, and the object of my journey, and presently assured me that he detected in me a remarkable likeness to the Prince of Wales, with whom, he declared, he had struck up an acquaintance one evening at the Crystal Palace. "Don't attempt to deceive me," he added, with many sly nods and winks: "I understand how one of noble birth may for a time be under a cloud, and may find it expedient to travel in disguise and to forgo that state and circumstance to which he is justly entitled. I am in somewhat the same position myself, but I am not going to continue thus for long. I have had a hint from the *Amínu's-Sulṭán*, and am wanted at Ṭeherán. There are those who would like to prevent my reaching the capital," he continued mysteriously, "but never fear, I will outwit them. When you leave Kirmán for Shíráz, I leave it in your company, and with me you shall visit Shahr-i-Bábak and many other interesting places on our way thither." Ná'ib Ḥasan fooled him to the top of his bent, unfolding vast and shadowy pictures of my power and affluence, and declaring that I had unlimited credit with the Zoroastrian merchants of Kirmán; which falsehoods Ḥájí Muḥammad Khán (whom copious libations of beer were rendering every moment more credulous and more mysterious) greedily imbibed. When he had gone I remonstrated vigorously with the Ná'ib for his mendacity. "I suppose it is no use for me to remind you that it is wicked to tell lies," I remarked, "but at least you must see how silly and how futile it is to make assertions whereof the falsity cannot remain hidden for more than a few days, and which are likely to land me in difficulties." But the Ná'ib only shook his head and laughed, as though to say that lying was in itself an artistic and pleasurable exercise of the imagination, in which, when there was no reason to the contrary, he might fairly allow himself to indulge. So, finding remonstrance vain, I presently retired to rest in some disgust.

Friday, 7th June, 27th Ramazán.—In the morning I was visited by an old Zoroastrian woman, who was anxious to learn whether I had heard in Ṭeherán any talk of Afláṭún ("Plato") having turned Musulmán. It took me some little while to discover that the said Afláṭún was not the Greek philosopher but a young Zoroastrian in whom she was interested, though why a follower of "the good Mazdayasnian religion" should take to himself a name like this baffles my comprehension. In the afternoon I was invaded by visitors. First of all came a Belúch chief named Afẓal Khán, a picturesque old man with long black hair, a ragged moustache, very thin on the upper lip and very long at the ends, and a singularly gorgeous coat. He was accompanied by two lean and hungry-looking retainers, all skin and sword-blade; but though he talked much I had some difficulty in understanding him at times, since he spoke Persian after the corrupt and vicious fashion prevalent in India. He enquired much of England and the English, whom he evidently regarded with mingled respect and dislike. "Ḳal'at-i-Náṣirí is my city," he replied, in answer to a question which I put to him; "three months' journey from here, or two months if your horse be sound, swift, and strong. Khán Khudádád Khán is the Amír, if he be not dead, as I have heard men say lately." He further informed me that his language was not Belúchí but Bráhú'í, which is spoken in a great part of Belúchistán.

The next visitors to arrive were the postmaster, Áḳá Muḥammad Ṣádiḳ (the young Yezdí merchant of whom I have already spoken), and the eldest son of the Prince-Telegraphist. The last upbraided me for taking up my abode in the garden instead of in the new telegraph-office, which his father had placed at my disposal; but his recriminations were cut short by the arrival of a Tabrízí merchant, two Zoroastrians, an Ezelí Bábí (whom I will call Mullá Yúsuf, to distinguish him from my Tabrízí satellite Mírzá Yúsuf), who appeared on this occasion as a zealous Musulmán, and undertook to convince me on some future occasion of the superiority of Islám to Christianity; and a middle-aged man of very subdued demeanour (how deceptive may appearances be!), dressed in a long *jubbé*, fez, and small white turban, after the manner of Asiatic Turks, to whom, under the pseudonym of Sheykh Ibráhím of Sulṭán-ábád, I shall have frequent occasion to refer in this and the succeeding chapter. These, in turn, were followed by four more Zoroastrians, including Gushtásp, Ferídún, and Rustam, who outstayed the other visitors, and did not depart till they had pledged me in wine after the rite of the Magians, after which I had supper with Ná'ib Ḥasan, and sat talking with him till nearly midnight.

Saturday, 8th June, 28th Ramazán.—In the morning I visited one of the shawl-manufactories of Kirmán in company with Rustam, Ná'ib Ḥasan, and Mírzá Yúsuf of Tabríz. Our way lay through the street leading to the Mosque Gate, which, by reason of the Saturday market (*Báżár-i-Shanba*), was thronged with people. The shawl-manufactory consisted of one large vaulted room containing eleven looms, two or three of which were standing idle. At each loom sat three workers, one skilled workman in the middle, and on either side of him a *shágird* or apprentice, whom he was expected to instruct and supervise. There were in all twenty-five apprentices, ranging in years from children of six and seven to men of mature age. Their wages, as I learned, begin at ten *túmáns* (about £3) a year, and increase gradually to twenty-four or twenty-five *túmáns* (about £7. 10*s*.). In summer they work from sunrise to sunset, and in winter they continue their work by candle-light till three hours after sunset. They have a half-holiday on Friday (from mid-day onwards), thirteen days' holiday at the *Nawrúz*, and one or two days more on the great annual festivals, while for food they get nothing as a rule but dry bread. Poor little Kirmánís! They must toil thus, deprived of good air and sunlight, and debarred from the recreations and amusements which should brighten their childhood, that some grandee may bedeck himself with those sumptuous shawls, which, beautiful as they are, will evermore seem to me to be dyed with the blood of the innocents! The shawls manufactured are of very different qualities. The finest, of three or three and a half ells in length, require twelve or fifteen months for their completion, and are sold at forty or fifty *túmáns* apiece; others, destined for the Constantinople market, and of much coarser texture, can be finished in a month or six weeks, and are sold for ten or fifteen *ḳráns*. Of late, however, the shawl trade had been on the decline; and the proprietor of this establishment told me that he was thinking of closing his workshops for a year, and making a pilgrimage to Kerbelá, hoping, I suppose, to win by this act of piety the Divine favour, which he would have better merited by some attempt to ameliorate the condition of the poor little drudges who toiled at his looms.

I next visited the one fire-temple which suffices for the spiritual needs of the Kirmán Zoroastrians, and was there received by the courteous and intelligent old Dastúr and my friend Ferídún. I could not see the sacred fire, because the *múbad* whose business it was to tend it had locked it up and taken the key away with him. In general appearance this fire-temple resembled those which I had seen at Yezd. I enquired as to the manuscripts of the sacred books preserved in the temple, and was shown two: a copy of the Avesta of 210 leaves, transcribed in the year A.H. 1086 (A.D. 1675–6), and completed on "the day of Ábán, in the month of Bahman, in the year 1044 of Yezdigird," by the hand of Dastúr Marzabán, the son of Dastúr Bahrám, the son of Marzabán, the son of Ferídún; and a copy of the Yashts, completed by the hand of Dastúr Isfandiyár, the son of Dastúr Núshírván, the son of Dastúr Isfandiyár, the son of Dastúr Ardashír, the son of Dastúr Ádhar of Sístán, on "the day of Bahman, in the month of Isfandarmad, in the year 1108 of Yezdigird," corresponding to A.H. 1226 (A.D. 1811). I found that the Dastúr was much interested in the occult science of geomancy (*'ilm-i-ramal*), which, he informed me, required the assiduous study of a lifetime ere one could hope to attain proficiency. He was also very full of a rare old book called the *Jámásp-náma*, of which he said only one copy, stolen by a Musulmán named Ḥuseyn from the house of a Zoroastrian in Yezd, existed in Kirmán, though he had information of another copy in the library of the Mosque at Mashhad. This book he described as containing a continuous series of prophecies, amongst which was included the announcement of the return of Sháh Bahrám, the Zoroastrian Messiah, to re-establish "the Good Religion." This Sháh Bahrám, to whose expected advent I have already alluded at p. 432 *supra*, is believed to be a descendant of Hurmuz the son of Yezdigird (the last Sásánian king), who fled from before the Arab invaders, with Peshútan and other fire-priests, to China; whence he will return to Fárs by way of India in the fullness of time. Amongst the signs heralding his coming will be a great famine, and the destruction of the city of Shushtar.

In the evening I went for a ride outside the city with Ferídún, Rustam, and the son of the postmaster. We first visited a neighbouring garden to see the working of one of the *dúlábs* generally employed in Kirmán for raising water to the surface. The *dúláb* consisted of two large wooden wheels, one set horizontally and the other vertically in the jaws of the well, cogged together. A blindfolded cow harnessed to a shaft inserted in the axle of the former communicated a rotatory motion to the latter, over which a belt of rope passed downwards into the well, to a depth of about five ells. To this rope earthenware pitchers were attached, and each pitcher as it came uppermost on the belt emptied its contents into a channel communicating with a small reservoir. The whole arrangement was primitive, picturesque, and inefficient.

From the *dúláb* we proceeded to the "old town" (*shahr-i-ḳadím*), situated on the craggy heights lying (if I remember rightly) to the west of the present city, and said to date from the time of Ardashír-i-Bábakán, the founder of the Sásánian dynasty. There are a number of ruined buildings on these heights, including one known as the *Ḳadam-gáh*, where vows and offerings are made by the Kirmánís. From this place we proceeded to another valley, closed to the south by beetling cliffs studded with cavernous openings which are said to extend far into the rock. High up on the left of this valley is a little building known as Daryá-Ḳulí Beg, whither, leaving our horses below, we ascended, and there sat for a while drinking wine by the light of the setting sun. My companions informed me that formerly the mouth of the valley below had been closed by a *band* or dyke, and all the upper part of it converted into a gigantic lake whereon boat races, watched by the king and his court from the spot where we sat, took place on certain festal occasions.

As we rode homewards in the gathering twilight the post-master's son craved a boon of me, which I think worth mentioning as illustrative of that strange yearning after martyrdom which is not uncommon amongst the Bábís. Bringing his horse alongside of mine at a moment when the two Zoroastrians were engaged in private conversation, he thus addressed me:—"Ṣáḥib, you intend, as you have told me, to visit Acre. If this great happiness be allotted to you, and if you look upon the Blessed Beauty (*Jemál-i-Mubáraḳ*, *i.e.* Behá'u'lláh), do not forget me, nor the request which I now prefer. Say, if opportunity be granted you, 'There is such an one in Kirmán, so-and-so by name, whose chief desire is that his name may be mentioned once in the Holy Presence, that he may once (if it be not too much to ask) be honoured by an Epistle, and that he may then quaff the draught of martyrdom in the way of the Beloved.'"

Sunday, 9th June, 29th Ramaẓán.—To-day I received a demonstration in geomancy (*'ilm-i-ramal*) from a young Zoroastrian,

Bahrám-i-Bihrúz, whom I met in Mullá Gushtásp's room in the caravansaray of Ganj-'Alí Khán. The information about myself with which his science supplied him was almost entirely incorrect, and was in substance as follows:—"A month ago you received bad news, and suffered much through some absent person.... Fifteen days ago some physical injury befell you....By the next post you will receive good news....In another month you will receive very good news....You are at present in good health, but your caloric is in excess and the bilious humour predominates....Your appetite is bad, and you should take some laxative medicine." This is a fair specimen of the kind of answer which he who consults the *rammál* (geomancer) is likely to get; but it is fair to say that Bahrám laid claim to no great proficiency in the science. However, he promised to introduce me to a Musulmán who was reputed an adept in the occult sciences, including the *taskhír-i-jinn*, or command of familiar spirits, and this promise, as will presently be set forth, he faithfully kept.

While Bahrám was busy with his geomancy, a dervish boy, who afterwards proved to be a Bábí, entered the room where we were sitting (for the dervish is free to enter any assembly and to go wherever it seemeth good to him), and presented me with a white flower. I gave him a *ḳrán*, whereupon, at the suggestion of one of those present, he sung a *ghazal*, or ode, in a very sweet voice, with a good deal of taste and feeling.

Later on in the day I visited Mírzá Raḥím Khán, the *Farrásh-báshí*, and Sheykh Ibráhím of Sulṭán-ábád, whom I have already had occasion to mention. The latter, as I discovered, had, after the manner of *ḳalandars* of his type, taken up his abode in the house of the former, till such time as he should be tired of his host, or his host of him. Thence I went to the house of the Sheykh of Ḳum, where I met two young artillery officers, brothers, one of whom subsequently proved to be an Ezelí Bábí. I was more than ever impressed with the Sheykh's genial, kindly manner, and wide knowledge. I enquired of him particularly as to the most authentic and esteemed collections of Shí'ite traditions, and he mentioned two, the *Mi'ráju's-Sa'ádat* ("Ascent of Happiness"), and a very large and detailed work in fifteen or sixteen volumes, by Jemálu'd-Dín Ḥasan ibn Yúsuf ibn 'Alí of Ḥilla entitled *'Allláma* ("the Great Doctor"), called *Biḥáru'l-Anwár* ("Oceans of Light"). We then talked for a while about metaphysics, and he expressed astonishment at the lack of interest in the subject generally prevalent in Europe; after which we passed by a natural transition to the doctrines of the Sheykhís and Bábís, about which he gave me not a little information. It had been intended that I should visit the Prince-Governor in company with the Sheykh, but the visit was postponed, as the Prince sent word that he was indisposed, and wished to sleep.

In the evening I received another visit from the garrulous Ḥájí Muḥammad Khán, who seemed to me rather less disagreeable than on the occasion of his first call. After his departure a temporary excitement was caused by the discovery of a theft which had been committed in the garden. A Shírází muleteer, who intended shortly to return home by way of Sírján and Níríz, had greatly importuned me to hire his mules for the journey, and this I had very foolishly half consented to do. These mules were accordingly tied up in the garden near my horse, and it was their coverings which, as the muleteer excitedly informed us, had been removed by the thief. The curious thing was that my horse's coverings, which were of considerably more value, had not been touched, and I am inclined to believe that the muleteer himself was the thief. He caused me trouble enough afterwards; for when, owing to the ophthalmia with which I was attacked, I was obliged to rescind the bargain, he lodged a complaint against the poor gardener, whom he charged with the theft. A *farrásh* was sent by the *vazír* to arrest him; whereupon the said gardener and his wife, accompanied by the myrmidon of the law, came before me wringing their hands, uttering loud lamentations, and beseeching me to intercede in their favour. So, though my eyes ached most painfully, I was obliged to write a long letter to the *vazír* in Persian, declaring the gardener to be, to the best of my belief, an honest and worthy fellow, and requesting, as a personal favour, that he might be subjected to no further annoyance. I furthermore took the precaution of promising a present of money to the *farrásh* when he returned with the gardener, in case the latter had suffered no ill-treatment; and, thanks to these measures, I succeeded in delivering him from the trouble in which the malice of the muleteer threatened to involve him; but the effect of the exertion of my eyes in writing the letter was to cause a recrudescence of the inflammation, which had previously been on the decline. So the muleteer had his revenge, which, I suppose, was what he desired and intended.

Monday, 10th June, 30th Ramazán.—In the morning I visited several persons in the town, including two of my Zoroastrian friends, Shahriyár and Bahman. The shop of the former was crowded with soldiers just home from Jásk and Bandar-i-'Abbás, so that conversation was impossible, and I left almost immediately. Bahman, on the other hand, had only one visitor, an old seyyid named Áḳá Seyyid Ḥuseyn of Jandaḳ, of whom I afterwards saw a good deal—in fact rather more than I wished. He conversed with me in a very affable manner, chiefly, of course, on religious topics, and, amongst other things, narrated to me the following curious legend about Christ:—

"Once upon a time," said the Seyyid, "the Lord Jesus (upon whom be peace) entered into a certain city. Now, the king of that city had forbidden any one of his subjects, on pain of death, to shelter Him or supply Him with food; nevertheless, seeing a young man of very sorrowful countenance, He craved his hospitality, which was at once accorded. After the Lord Jesus had supped and rested, He enquired of His host wherefore he was so sorrowful, and eventually ascertained that he had fallen in love with the king's daughter. Then said the Lord Jesus, 'Be of good cheer, thou shalt win her. Go to the king's palace to-morrow, and demand her in marriage, and your proposal will not be rejected.' So the young man, marvelling the while at his own audacity, repaired on the morrow to the palace, and demanded to see the king, into whose presence he was presently ushered. On hearing his proposal the king said, 'My daughter shall be yours if you can give her a suitable dowry.' So the young man returned sadly to his home (for he knew that such a dowry was far beyond his means) and told the Lord Jesus what had passed. Then said the Lord Jesus, 'If you will go to such-and-such a spot and search there you will find all that you need.' He did so, and found much gold and silver, and many precious stones of great worth—diamonds, pearls, rubies, emeralds, and the like, beyond all that even the daughter of a king could expect or desire. So the king bestowed on him his daughter's hand. But after a time the Lord Jesus bade him leave all this and follow Him, and he, knowing now that the Great Treasure, compared to which all that he had given as the princess's dowry was as mere worthless dross, was with Christ alone, abandoned all for his Master's sake. And indeed, as this legend shows, amongst all the prophets there was none who taught the 'Path' (*Ṭaríḳat*) like the Lord Jesus, and this remains amongst you Christians in some measure even now, though the 'Law' (*Sharí'at*) which he brought has little by little disappeared before Islám, so that no vestige of it is left."

In the evening I received a visit from some of the leading members of the Hindoo community, thirteen or fourteen in number, who begged me to let them know if, at any time, they could be of service to me in any way. "We owe you this," said they, "for it is through the protection of your government that we are able to live and carry on our business here in safety and security." Later in the evening I partook of supper with several of the Zoroastrians at the *dúláb* of the elder Gushtásp.

Tuesday, 11*th June*, 1*st Shawwál*.—In the morning I had a visit from Rustam, the young Zoroastrian. He told me, amongst other things, of the persecutions to which his co-religionists were occasionally exposed. "Formerly," said he, "it would often happen that they carried off one of our boys or girls, and strove to compel them by threats and torments to become Musulmáns. Thus on one occasion they seized upon a Zoroastrian boy twelve years of age, carried him to the public bath, and forced him to utter the Muḥammadan profession of faith, and to submit to the operation of circumcision. On another occasion they abducted two Zoroastrian girls, aged fifteen and twenty respectively, and, by every means in their power, strove to compel them to embrace the religion of Islám. One of them held out against their importunities for a long while, until at last they turned her out almost naked into the snow, and she was ultimately compelled to submit."

In the afternoon I again went into the town to pay some visits. I entered it by the *Derwázé-i-Gabr*, to the east of the *Derwázé-i-Náṣiriyyé*, and visited an old mosque situated near to that gate. This mosque had, as I was informed, been wilfully destroyed by a former governor of the city, but it still showed traces of its ancient splendour. After visiting the Hindoos and some of my Zoroastrian friends, I proceeded to the house of the Sheykh of Ḳum, with whom, as it had been arranged, I was to pay my respects to the Prince-Governor. After drinking tea we accordingly repaired to the *Bágh-i-Naṣiriyyé*, which is situated near to the gate of the same name. On the arrival of Prince Náṣiru'd-Dawla we were conducted to an upper chamber, where he received me in the kindliest and most friendly manner. He talked to me chiefly about the condition of Belúchistán (which, as well as Kirmán, was under his government), and declared that a very notable improvement had taken place during the last few years. I then presented my letter of recommendation from Prince 'Imádu'd-Dawla of Yezd, and took occasion to mention the forlorn condition of Mírzá Yúsuf of Tabríz, and his hope that the shadow of the Royal Protection might not be withheld from him, and that he might aspire to be numbered amongst the Prince's servants.

In the evening I was again entertained at supper by one of my Zoroastrian friends named Shahriyár. All the other guests were of "the good religion" save myself, Ná'ib Ḥasan (who still continued to accompany me everywhere, and to consider himself as invited to every feast whereunto I was bidden), and a singer named Faraju'lláh, who had been summoned for our entertainment.

Wednesday, 12*th June*, 2*nd Shawwál*.—Towards evening I was visited by the Belúch chief, Afẓal Khán, and his son; Seyyid Ḥuseyn of Jandaḳ; the Sheykh of Ḳum, and his friend the young Bábí gunner; and Mullá Yúsuf the Ezelí. Between the last and Seyyid Ḥuseyn a violent dispute arose touching the merits and demerits of the first three caliphs (so called), 'Omar, Abú Bekr, and 'Othmán, whereby the other visitors were so wearied that they shortly departed, and finally the Seyyid was left in undisputed possession of the field, which he did not abandon till he had prayed the prayers of sundown (*maghrib*) and nightfall (*'ashá*), and explained to me at length the significance of their various component parts, adding that if I would remain in Kirmán for one month he would put me in possession of all the essentials of Islám. Ná'ib Ḥasan and Ferídún had supper with me in the *chár-faṣl*, or summer-house, on the roof of which I sat late with the latter, and finally fell asleep, with the song of a nightingale, sweet-voiced as Isráfíl, ringing in my ears.

Thursday, 13*th June*, 3*rd Shawwál*.—In the morning, while walking in the bazaars, I met Afẓal Khán, the Belúch, with his ragged and hungry-looking retainers. He invited me to return with him to his lodging, situated near the *Derwáẓé-i-Ríg-ábád*, and I, having nothing else to do, and not wishing to offend him, accepted his invitation. On our arrival there he insisted, notwithstanding my earnest protests, on sending out for sherbets and sweetmeats wherewith to do me honour, and he put me to further shame by continued apologies for the unfurnished condition of his abode and the humble character of his entertainment, repeating again and again that he was "only a poor Belúch." Presently he got on the subject of his wrongs. The English Government, so he declared, had taken into their service one of his relatives, who had forthwith made use of his new privileges to dispossess him of all his property, and, generally speaking, to make his life a burden to him. He had therefore come to Kirmán to seek employment from Prince Náṣiru'd-Dawla. "If he will not help me," concluded Afẓal Khán, "I intend to go to Mashhad and seek assistance from the English officials residing there; and if they will do nothing for me, I will place my services at the disposal of the Russians." Shortly afterwards I rose to go, alleging, when Afẓal Khán pressed me to stay, that I had letters to write. "What letters?" he enquired suspiciously. "Oh," I answered carelessly, "letters of all sorts, to Yezd, to Shíráz, and" (this, though true, was not said altogether without mischievous intent) "to Mashhad." Then Afẓal Khán, as I had anticipated, became very perturbed, and anxiously inquired what acquaintances I had at Mashhad, evidently supposing that I intended to inform the English representatives there of his intentions, so that they might intercept him in case he should attempt to reach Russian territory. But, indeed, the poor fellow's services, on which he evidently set a high value, were not likely to be accounted as of much value by anyone else —Persian, English, or Russian.

In the afternoon I visited Mullá Yúsuf the Ezelí, who, though he talked about nothing else than religion, confined himself, much to my disappointment, to the Muḥammadan dispensation. He admitted my contention that by many paths men may attain to a knowledge of God, and that salvation was not for the votaries of one religion only, but maintained that, though all roads led to the same goal, some were safe, short, and sure, and others circuitous and perilous, "wherefore," said he, "it behoves us to seek the shortest and safest way, whereby we may most speedily, and with least danger, attain the desired haven." We had a good deal of discussion, too, about the code of laws established by Muḥammad, some of which (as, for example, the punishment of theft by amputation of the hand) I condemned as barbarous and irrational. To this he replied by arguing that the *lex talionis* was intended merely to fix the extreme limit of punishment which could be inflicted on an offender, and that forgiveness was as highly extolled by the Muḥammadan as by the Christian religion. This discussion lasted so long that on reaching the gate on my homeward way I found it shut, and was obliged to creep through a hole in the city wall known to the cunning Ná'ib Ḥasan.

Friday, 14th June, 4th Shawwál.—This afternoon Mullá Yúsuf the Ezelí and one of his friends came to visit me and continue the discussion of yesterday. They talked much about Reason, and the Universal Intelligence, which, according to the words "*Awwalu má k͟halak͟a'lláhu'l-'Ak͟l,*" was the first Creation or Emanation of God, and which, at diverse times and in diverse manners, has spoken to mankind through the mouth of the prophets. Reason, said they, is of four kinds; *'ak͟l bi'l-k͟uwwa* ("Potential Reason," such as exists in an untaught child); *'ak͟l bi'l-fi'l* ("Actual" or "Effective Reason," such as belongs to those of cultivated intelligence); *'ak͟l bi'l-malak͟a* ("Habitual Reason," such as the angels enjoy); and *'ak͟l-i-mustakfí* ("All-sufficing Reason"). This last is identical with the "First Intelligence" (*'ak͟l-i-awwal*), or "Universal Reason" (*'ak͟l-i-k͟ullí*), which inspires the prophets, and, indeed, becomes incarnate in them, so that by it they have knowledge of all things—that is, of their essences, not of the technical terms which in the eyes of men constitute an integral part of science. Whosoever is endowed with this "All-sufficing Reason," and claims to be a prophet, must be accepted as such; but unless he chooses to advance this claim, men are not obliged to accord him this rank. Next in rank to the prophet (*nabí*) is the saint (*valí*), whose essential characteristic is a love for God which makes him ready to lay down his life willingly and joyfully for His sake. The love of the *valí* is such that by it he often becomes insensible to pain. Thus it is related of 'Alí b. Abí Ṭálib, the first Imám, that he was once wounded in the foot by an arrow. Attempts made to extract it only resulted in detaching the shaft from the barb, which remained in the wound, and caused so much pain that it seemed impossible for 'Alí to endure any further operation. Then said one of his sons, "Wait till the time for prayer comes round, for when my father is engaged in prayer he becomes unconscious of all earthly things, being wholly absorbed in communion with God, and you can then extract the arrow-head without his so much as feeling it." And this they did with complete success.

Mullá Yúsuf told me another anecdote about 'Alí, which, though it is well-known to students of Arabic history[1], will bear repetition. He had overthrown an infidel foe, and, kneeling on his prostrate body, was about to despatch him with his sword, when the fallen unbeliever spat in his face. Thereupon 'Alí at once relinquished his hold on his adversary, rose to his feet, and sheathed his sword. On being asked the reason of this, he replied, "When he spat in my face I was filled with anger against him, and I feared that, should I kill him, personal indignation would partially actuate me; wherefore I let him go, since I would not kill him otherwise than from a sincere and unmixed desire to serve God."

At this point our conversation was interrupted by the arrival of Mírzá Yúsuf of Tabríz accompanied by one of the Prince's servants, who in turn were followed by Ferídún and Ná'ib Ḥasan. The two last and Mírzá Yúsuf remained to drink wine after the others had gone; and Mírzá Yúsuf, who was in a boastful humour, began to say, "If you wish to know anything about

1 See, for instance, *el-Fakhrí* (ed. Ahlwardt), p. 54.

the Bábís, I am the man to tell you, for I knew all their chief men at Yezd, and, indeed, professed myself a convert to their doctrines so as to gain their confidence. They gave me some of their books to read, including one[1] wherein the reader was addressed in such words as 'O child of Earth,' 'O child of my handmaid,' and the like." And in fact Mírzá Yúsuf had succeeded in finding out a good deal about the Bábís, though his information was in some matters erroneous. He declared, for instance, that Ḳurratu'l-'Ayn was put to death by being cast from the summit of the Citadel (*Arg*) at Tabríz, but that the first time she was launched into the air she was so buoyed up by her clothes that she escaped all hurt[2]. My last visitor was Seyyid Ḥasan of Jandaḳ, whose arrival caused the other guests to conceal the wine, and, at the earliest possible opportunity, to depart. He was in a captious frame of mind, finding fault with the newspaper *Akhtar* (of which the Sheykh of Ḳum had sent me a recent issue) for talking about the Ẓillu's-Sulṭán's "resignation" (*isti'fá*), instead of calling it, in plain Persian, his dismissal (*'azl*), and taking exception to sundry idioms and expressions in a letter from the Prince-Governor of Yezd, which, at his request, I allowed him to read.

Saturday, 15*th June*, 5*th Shawwál*.—To-day, while I was sitting in the shop of a merchant of my acquaintance, Ḥájí 'Abdu'lláh of Shíráz, Bahrám-i-Bihrúz hurried up to inform me that his friend the magician, Ḥájí Mírzá Muḥsin, the controller of spirits and genies, was at that moment in his shop, and that if I would come thither he would present me to him. I wished to go at

1 The book entitled *Kalimát-i-maknúna-i-Fáṭima* ("Hidden Words of Fáṭima") is intended. See for a description of this book my *Catalogue of Twenty-seven Bábí MSS.* in the *Journal of the Royal Asiatic Society* for 1892, pp. 671–5.

2 Mírzá Yúsuf had evidently mixed together a real fact—the Báb's martyrdom in the square of the citadel at Tabríz—and a story referring to the miraculous escape of a woman cast from its summit, which story has been already referred to at p. 64, *supra*.

once, but Ḥájí 'Abdu'lláh and Ná'ib Ḥasan strove to detain me, and while we were engaged in discussion the magician passed by the shop in person. Ḥájí 'Abdu'lláh invited him to enter, which he at first declined to do, and made as though he would pass on; but suddenly changing his mind he turned back, entered the shop, and seated himself amongst us.

"This Ṣáḥib," said Ná'ib Ḥasan, as soon as the customary greetings had been interchanged, "has heard of your skill in the occult sciences, and desires to witness a specimen of the powers with which you are credited."

"What would it profit him?" replied the magician; and then, turning to me, "Is your motive in desiring to witness an exhibition of my powers a mere idle curiosity? Or is it that you seek to understand the science by means of which I can produce effects beyond the power or comprehension of your learned men?"

"Sir," I answered, "my object in making this request is, in the first instance, to obtain ocular evidence of the existence of powers generally denied by our men of learning, but which I, in the absence of any sufficient evidence, presume neither to deny nor to affirm. If, having given me such evidence of their existence as I desire, you will further condescend to acquaint me with some of the principles of your science, I need not say that my gratitude will be increased. But even to be convinced that such powers exist would be a great gain."

"You have spoken well," said the magician with approval, "and I am willing to prove to you the reality of that science concerning which you doubt. But first of all let me tell you that all that I can accomplish I do by virtue of powers centred in myself, not, as men affirm, by the instrumentality of the *jinn*, which, indeed, are mere creatures of the imagination, and have no real existence. Has any one of you a comb?"

Ḥájí 'Abdu'lláh at once produced a comb from the recesses of his pocket, and handed it to Ḥájí Muḥsin, who threw it on the ground at a distance of about three feet from him to the left. Then he again turned to me, and said—

"Are your men of learning acquainted with any force inherent in the human body whereby motion may be communicated, without touch, to a distant object?"

"No," I replied, "apart from the power of attraction latent in amber, the magnet, and some other substances, we know of no such force; certainly not in the human body."

"Very well," said he, "then if I can make this comb come to me from the spot where it lies, you will have to admit that I possess a power whereof your learned men do not even know the existence. That the distance is in this case small, and the object light and easily movable, is nothing, and does not in the least degree weaken the force of the proof. I could equally transport you from the garden where you live to any place which I chose. Now look."

Then he moistened the tip of his finger with his tongue, leaned over to the left, and touched the comb once, after which he resumed his former position, beckoned to the comb with the fingers of his left hand, and called "*Bi-yá, bi-yá*" ("Come! come!"). Thereat, to my surprise, the comb spun rapidly round once or twice, and then began to advance towards him in little leaps, he continuing the while to beckon it onwards with the fingers of his left hand, which he did not otherwise move. So far one might have supposed that when he touched the comb with his moistened finger-tip he had attached to it a fine hair or strand of silk, by which, while appearing but to beckon with his fingers, he dexterously managed to draw the comb towards him. But now, as the comb approached within eighteen inches or so of his body, he extended his left hand beyond it, continuing to call and beckon as before; so that for the remainder of its course it was receding from the hand, always with the same jerky, spasmodic motion.

Ḥájí Muḥsin now returned the comb to its owner, and

requested me for the loan of my watch. I handed to him the clumsy, china-backed watch which I had bought at Ṭeherán to replace the one which I had lost between Erzeroum and Tabríz, and he did with it as he had done with the comb, save that, when he began to call and beckon to it, it made one rapid gyration and a short leap towards him, and then stopped. He picked it up, looked closely at it, and returned it to me, saying, "There is something amiss with this watch of yours; it seems to me that it is stolen property."

"Well," I replied rather tartly, "I did not steal it at any rate; I bought it in Ṭeherán for three *túmáns* to replace my own watch, which I lost in Turkey. How it came into the hands of him from whom I bought it I cannot, of course, say."

After this the magician became very friendly with me, promising to visit me in my lodging and show me feats far more marvellous than what I had just witnessed. "You shall select any object you choose," said he, "and bury it wherever you please in your garden, so that none but yourself shall know where it is hidden. I will then come and pronounce certain incantations over a brass cup, which will then lead me direct to the place where the object is buried." Hearing that I was to visit the *vazír* of Kirmán, he insisted on accompanying me.

The *vazír* was a courteous old man of very kindly countenance and gentle manners, and I stayed conversing with him for more than half an hour. A number of persons were present, including the *kalántar*, or mayor, whose servant had that morning received a severe application of the bastinado for having struck the *ked-khudá*, or chief man, of a village to which he had been sent to collect taxes or rents. Ḥájí Mírzá Muḥsin, who lacked nothing so little as assurance, gave the *vazír* a sort of lecture on me (as though I were a curious specimen), which he concluded, somewhat to my consternation, by declaring that he intended to accompany me back to my own country, and to enlighten the ignorance of its learned men as to the occult sciences, of which he was a master.

On leaving the *vazír's* presence, I accompanied the magician to his lodging, and was introduced to his brother, a fine-looking man of middle age, dressed after the fashion of the Baghdádís in *jubbé*, fez, and white turban, who spoke both Arabic and Ottoman Turkish with fluency. There were also present a number of children, belonging, as I gathered, to Ḥájí Mírzá Muḥsin, who was still mourning a domestic tragedy which had recently led to the death of his eldest son, a lad of sixteen. "Ah, you should have seen him," he said, "such a handsome boy, and so quick and clever. None of my other children can compare with him." He did not acquaint me with the details of his son's untimely death, which, according to Ná'ib Ḥasan, were as follows:—One of Mírzá Muḥsin's servants, or disciples, had a very beautiful wife, with whom his son fell madly in love. Mírzá Muḥsin, on being informed by the boy of his passion, promised to induce the girl's husband to free her by divorce. In this he succeeded, but, instead of bestowing her hand on his son, he married her himself. The lad remonstrated vehemently with his father, who only replied, "It was for my sake, not yours, that her former husband divorced her." Thereupon the boy, in an access of passionate disappointment, shot himself through the head two stages out from Kirmán, whither they were then journeying from Sírján.

Sunday, 16*th June*, 6*th Shawwál*.—To-day I was invited to take my mid-day meal (*nahár*) with the postmaster. On my way thither I encountered, near the *Derwázé-i-Masjid*, one of my Zoroastrian friends, Key-Khosraw, who informed me with some excitement that two "Firangís" had just arrived in Kirmán. "Come and talk to them," he added, "for they are now in the street a little farther on." I accordingly followed him, though with no great alacrity, for I enjoyed the feeling of being the only European in Kirmán, and had no wish to spoil the unmixedly

Persian character of my environment by forming an acquaintance with two promiscuous Europeans, who might very likely, I thought, be mere adventurers, and whose presence I was inclined to resent. We soon found one of the newcomers, a little gray-bearded Frenchman, who was very reticent as to his object in visiting Kirmán, and told me no more than that his companion (also French) spoke English much better than himself (which I could readily believe, for his pronunciation was vile, and his vocabulary most meagre), and that they had come from Turkistán (Bukhárá and Samarḳand) by way of Mashhad, and thence through the deserts, by way of Tún and Ṭabas, to Kirmán. He then went on to enquire with some eagerness whether there were in the town any *cafés* or wine-shops (wine-shops in Kirmán!), and seemed much disconcerted when he heard that there were not. I soon left him, and proceeded to the postmaster's house.

There I found one Mírzá Muḥammad Khán, of the Sháh Niʿmatu'lláhí order of dervishes; Sheykh Ibráhím of Sulṭán-ábád; and another, a parcher of peas (*noḳhúd-biríz*) by profession, whom, as I shall have to say a good deal about him before I bid farewell to Kirmán, and as I do not wish to mention his real name, I will call Ustá Akbar. Till lunch-time we sat in the *tanbal-ḳháné* ("idler's room" or drawing-room), smoking *ḳalyáns* and conversing on general topics, including, of course, religion. The postmaster told me that he had a book wherein the truth of each dispensation, down to the present one (or Bábí "Manifestation"), was proved by that which preceded it; and this book he promised to lend me so soon as it was returned to him by a Zoroastrian in whose hands it then was. I asked him about the signs which should herald the "Manifestation" of the "End of Time," and he said that amongst them were the following:—That men should ride on iron horses; that they should talk with one another from great distances; that they should talk on their fingers; and that men should wear women's clothes and women

men's; "of which signs," he added, "you will observe that the first clearly indicates the railroad, the second the telephone, and the third the telegraph; so that nothing is wanting to apprise men of the advent of the Most Great Theophany." I enquired of him, as I had previously enquired of the Sheykh of Ḳum, as to the best and most authentic collections of Shí'ite traditions, and he mentioned with especial commendation the *Uṣúl-i-Káfí*, the *Rawẓa-i-Káfí*, and the *Man lá yaḥẓurí* of Faḳíh.

After lunch most of the guests indulged in a nap, but the parcher of peas came and talked to me for a while in a very wild strain, with which I subsequently became only too familiar. "If you would see Adam," he said, "I am Adam; if Noah, I am Noah; if Abraham, I am Abraham; if Moses, I am Moses; if Christ, lo, I am Christ." "Why do you not say at once 'I am God'?" I retorted. "Yes," he replied, "there is naught but He." I tried to ascertain his views as to the future of the human soul, but could extract from him no very satisfactory answer. "As one candle is lit from another," he said, "so is life kindled from life. If the second candle should say, 'I am the first candle,' it speaks truly, for, in essence, it is indeed that first candle which has thrust forth its head from another garment."

Presently we were interrupted by the arrival of visitors, the officious and meddlesome Ḥájí Muḥammad Khán, and the Mullá-báshí. As soon as the customary forms of politeness had been gone through, the latter turned to me, saying—

"Ṣáḥib, what is all this that we hear about you and Ḥájí Mírzá Muḥsin the magician? Is it true?"

"If you would kindly tell me what you have heard," I replied, "I should be better able to answer your question."

"Well," he answered, "Ḥájí Mírzá Muḥsin is telling everyone that you, being skilled in the Magic of the West, had challenged him to a contest; that you gave what proofs you could of your power, and he of his; but that he wrought marvels beyond your power, and, amongst other things, wrote a few lines on a piece of paper, burned it before your eyes, and then drew it out from your pocket. That thereupon you had said that if he could summon the spirit of your father and cause it to converse with you in the French language, you would embrace the religion of Islám; and that he had done what you demanded. Is this true? and are you really going to become a Musulmán?"

"Really," I replied, "I am not; and, were I disposed to do so, Ḥájí Muḥsin (whom, after what you have told me, I must regard as a liar of quite exceptional attainments) is not exactly the sort of person who would effect my conversion. As for his story, every word of it is false; all that actually happened was this" (here I described our meeting in Ḥájí Shírází's shop). "Furthermore, my father, by the grace of God, is alive and in good health; neither do I see why, in any case, he should address me in French, since my language and his is English."

On returning to the garden I found Afẓal Khán the Belúch and his retainers, Mullá Gushtásp, and Áḳá Seyyid Ḥuseyn of Jandaḳ, awaiting my arrival. The first, somewhat overpowered by the Seyyid's theology, probably, left very soon; but the Seyyid, as usual, stayed a long while and talked a great deal. He first of all produced a small treatise on physiognomy (*'ilm-i ḳiyáfa*), of which he declared himself to be the author, and proceeded to apply the principles therein laid down to me. "You have a long arm and long fingers," said he, "which shows that you are determined to wield authority and to exercise supremacy over your fellows, also that you take care that whatever work you do shall be sound and thorough." He next produced a collection of aphorisms which he had written out for me, of which the only one I remember is, "Eat the bread of no man, and withhold thine own bread from none." He then dictated to me four questions connected with religion, which he wished me to copy out on four separate pieces of paper, and send to the Prince-Governor, with a letter requesting him to submit them to four learned theologians (whom he named), and to require them to give an immediate answer, without consulting together or taking time to reflect. "You will see," the Seyyid remarked, with an anticipatory chuckle, "that they will all give different answers, and all wrong, so that the Prince will recognise the inadequacy of their learning." I only remember one of these questions, which ran as follows: "Which of the four gospels now in the hands of the Christians is the *Injíl* mentioned in the Ḳur'án?"

While we were engaged in this conversation, the proprietor of the garden, Mírzá Jawád, son of Áḳá Seyyid Raḥím, the late *vazír* of Kirmán, was announced. He was a portly, pleasant-looking man of about forty-five or fifty, and was accompanied by his son, a very beautiful boy of unusually fair complexion, with dark-blue eyes, and long eyebrows and eyelashes, rendered even more conspicuous than they would naturally have been by a liberal application of *surma* (antimony). The Seyyid, however, did not allow their presence long to interrupt the unceasing stream of his eloquence, and began to catechise me about the gospels, asserting that the very fact of there being four proved that they were spurious, and that the true gospel had disappeared from the earth. He then enquired whether wine was lawful according to our law. I replied that it was, inasmuch as we knew that Christ Himself tasted wine on several occasions. "I take refuge with God!" cried the Seyyid; "it is a calumny: this alone is sufficient to prove that your gospels are spurious, for none of the prophets have ever drunk wine." "Well," I said, "I do not quite see your object in trying to disprove the genuineness of our gospels. I imagine that you wish to convince me of the truth of Islám, but please to remember that if you could succeed in convincing me that the gospels now in our hands are forgeries, you having no other and genuine gospel to put in their place, you would be no nearer converting me to Islám, but rather further from it than at present. You would either make me disbelieve in revealed religion altogether, or you would drive me back on the Pentateuch and make me a Jew." "There is something in that," replied the Seyyid, "and I am now disposed to understand the matter in a different way. The word *sharáb* originally means any kind of drink, since the verb *shariba*, from which it is derived, is employed in a perfectly general sense. Your priests have not understood this, and have wrongly explained it as wine. The very miracle which you adduce as evidence proves my point, for you say that the attendants at the wedding feast were bidden to fill the jars with *water*. It is quite clear that what Christ wished to show was, that water was the best and most exhilarating of drinks, and that it was lawful, not unlawful, like wine." The little boy seemed to take the liveliest interest in this discussion, and kept whispering suggestions to the Seyyid, for he, like his father, was imbued with the ideas of the Sheykhís, and was evidently not unwilling to make a display of his knowledge.

The Seyyid outstayed the other visitors, and, squatting down by the little stream, proceeded to give me much advice (a thing whereof he was ever prodigal), mingled with hints and warnings which I was for some time unable to comprehend.

"Don't cultivate the acquaintance of so-and-so" (mentioning one of my Bábí friends) "too much," he began, "and don't visit his house more than you can help. The Prince doesn't like him."

"Why doesn't he like him?" I enquired.

"The Prince had a very beautiful wife called *Panba* ('Cotton')," rejoined the Seyyid, "and one day in a fit of temper he said to her, 'Go to your father's house,' but without explicitly divorcing her. Your friend Mírzá —— lived next door to her father, saw her, was smitten with her charms, and took her in marriage; and when the Prince (who soon repented of his hasty conduct) desired to take her back, he found that she was the wife of another. Naturally he was greatly incensed with Mírzá ——."

"Naturally," I said, "but he would hardly be incensed with me for visiting him."

"You don't understand my point," said the Seyyid. "The

people of Kirmán are the greatest gossips and scandal-mongers under the sun; and the people of Kirmán will say that you go there to see Panba, who is the most beautiful woman in the city."

"What nonsense!" I exclaimed, "why, I never even heard of Panba till this moment, and when I go to see Mírzá —— I am naturally not introduced to his wives."

"Never you mind that," said he; "take my advice and keep away from his house. You can't be too careful here. You don't know what the Kirmánís are like. It was a most fortunate thing that Mírzá Jawád found me here when he came to see you."

"It was very nice for him," I replied, "no doubt. But why so specially fortunate?"

"Because," answered he, "seeing that I am your friend and associate, and hearing our improving conversation, he will think the better of you, and will be the slower to credit any slanders against you which he may hear."

"I am not aware," said I, "that I have given any occasion for slander."

"Perhaps you do not know what people say about your servant Ḥájí Ṣafar's *ṣígha*?" returned he.

"What do you mean?" I demanded sharply; "I was not aware that he had a *ṣígha*."

The Seyyid laughed—a little, unpleasant, incredulous laugh. "Really?" said he; "that is very curious. I should have supposed that he would have consulted you first. Anyhow, there is no doubt about the matter, for I drew up the contract myself. And men say that the *ṣígha*, though taken in his name, was really intended for you."

Here I must explain what a *ṣígha* is[1]. A Shí'ite may, according to his law, contract a temporary marriage with a woman of his

1 For fuller details see Querry's *Droit Musulman* (Paris, 1871), vol. i, pp. 689–695, from which admirable compendium of Shí'ite law I have drawn several of the particulars given in the text.

own, or of the Jewish, Christian, or (though some contest this) Magian faith, for a fixed period of time, which may vary from a fraction of a day to a year or several years. Properly speaking, it is the contract drawn up by the officiating *mullá* (in which both the period of duration of the marriage, and the amount of the dowry—though this last may be no more than a handful of barley—must be specified), which is called the *ṣígha*, but the term is commonly applied to the woman with whom such marriage is contracted. This species of marriage (if it can be dignified by this name), though held in very proper detestation by Sunnite Muḥammadans, is regarded by the Shí'ites as perfectly legal, and children resulting from it are held to be lawful offspring. Though prevalent to some extent throughout Persia, it flourishes with especial vigour in Kirmán, where, owing to the great poverty of the people, the small dowry bestowed on the *ṣígha* induces many parents to seek for their daughters such engagement. Bad as this institution is at the best, the *mullás*, by one of those unrighteous legal quibbles of which they are so fond, have succeeded in making it yet more abominable. According to the law, a *ṣígha*, on completing the contracted period, must, before going to another husband, wait for forty-five days or two months to ascertain whether or no she is with child by the former husband. This, however, only applies to cases where the marriage has been actually consummated. So, as many of these women are practically *ṣíghas* by trade, and do not wish to be subjected to this period of probation, the *mullás* have devised the following means of evading the law. When the contracted period of marriage has come to an end, the man makes a fresh contract with the woman for another very short period; this second (purely nominal) marriage, being with the same man as the first, is legal without any intervening period of probation, and is not consummated; so that, on its expiration, the woman is free to marry another man as soon as she pleases.

The Seyyid's hints, whether intended maliciously or prompted by a friendly feeling, caused me a good deal of disquietude; for, absurd and false as the slander was, I clearly saw that if it gained the credence of the vulgar it might become a source of actual peril. Ḥájí Ṣafar, who made no attempt to exculpate himself, was of the same opinion, and entreated me to leave Kirmán as soon as possible. "Ṣáḥib," he concluded, "you do not know the malice and mischief of which these accursed Kirmánís are capable; if we stay here much longer they will find some pretext for killing us both."

"Nonsense," I said, "they are a quiet, peaceable, down-trodden folk, these same Kirmánís, though over-fond of idle tattle. Besides you know what Sheykh Sa'dí says—'*án-rá ḳi ḥisáb páḳ-ast aẓ muḥásabé ché báḳ-ast?*' ('To him whose account is clean what fear is there of the reckoning?') But in future I hope that you will be careful to avoid doing anything which may compromise my good name. I have no wish to interfere either with your religion, or with such indulgences as are accorded to you by it, but I have a right to expect that you will avoid anything which is liable to discredit my character." And so the matter dropped, the quotation from Sa'dí being more effective (as quotations from Sa'dí or Ḥáfiẓ always are with a Persian) than any quantity of argument.

I have had occasion to allude to the unrighteous quibbles whereby the *mullás*, while keeping the letter, contravene the spirit of the law; and I may here add an instance (which was related to me to-day by one of my Bábí friends) of the gross ignorance which sometimes characterises their decisions. A certain man in Kirmán, wishing to expose this ignorance, addressed the following question to a distinguished member of the local clergy. "I agreed with a labourer," said he, "to dig in my garden a hole one yard square for eight *ḳráns*: he has dug a hole half a yard square. How much should I pay him?" "Half the sum agreed upon, of course," said the *mullá*, "that is to say four *ḳráns*." After thinking for a while, however, he corrected himself: "two *ḳráns* is the sum which you legally owe him," he declared; and this decision he committed to writing and sealed with his seal. Then the enquirer demonstrated to him that the labour required to excavate a hole measuring half a yard in each direction was only an eighth part of that needed for the excavation of one measuring a yard in each direction. This conclusion the cleric resisted as long as he could, but, being at length compelled to admit its justice, he got out of the difficulty by declaring that, though *mathematically* the labourer could only claim one *ḳrán*, his *legal* due was two *ḳráns*.

Monday, 17th June, 7th Shawwál.—This afternoon I visited a young secretary of the Prince's with whom I had become acquainted, and found him with the son of the Prince-Telegraphist, Mullá Yúsuf, and other congenial friends (all, or nearly all, Ezelí Bábís) sitting round a little tank which occupied the centre of the room, and smoking opium. The discussion, as usual, turned on religion, and Mullá Yúsuf gave me some further instances of the quibbles whereby the Shí'ite clergy and their followers have made the law of no effect. "There are," said he, "six obligations incumbent on every Musulmán, to wit, Prayer (*ṣalát*), Fasting (*ṣiyám*), Pilgrimage (*ḥajj*), Tithes (*khums*), Alms (*zakát*), and, under certain circumstances, Religious Warfare (*jihád*). Of these six, the last three have practically become null and void. Of Religious War they are afraid, because the infidels have waxed strong, and because they remember the disastrous results which attended their more recent enterprises of this sort[1]. As for the Tithes (*khums*, literally 'fifths'), they should be paid to poor Seyyids or descendants of the Prophet. And how do you suppose they manage to save their money and salve their consciences at the same time? Why, they place the amount of the money which they ought to give in a jar and pour treacle (*shíré*) over it; then they offer this jar to a poor Seyyid (without,

1 See my *Traveller's Narrative*, vol. ii, pp. 118–119, and n. 3, on the former.

of course, letting him know about the money which it contains), and, when he has accepted it, buy it back from him for two or three *ḳráns*! Or else they offer him one *túmán* on condition that he signs a receipt for fifty." I turned these admissions against Mullá Yúsuf when he began to argue for the superiority of Islám over Christianity. "You yourself," I said, "declare that the essential characteristic of the prophetic word is that it has power to control men's hearts; and as you have just told me that out of six things which Muḥammad made binding on his followers, three have become of none effect, you cannot wonder if I question the proof of Islám by your own criterion. God knows that the mass of professing Christians are very far from putting into constant practice all the commands laid upon them by Him whom they profess to follow; but I should be sorry to think that His precepts and example had as little effect on my countrymen as those of Muḥammad, on your own showing, seem to have on yours."

On returning to the garden I found a note from the officious Ḥájí Muḥammad Khán, enquiring whether I had learned anything more about the two Frenchmen who had arrived in Kirmán. He had also left with Ḥájí Ṣafar a verbal message asking for some brandy, which message, by reason of Seyyid Ḥuseyn's presence, Ḥájí Ṣafar communicated to me in Turkish. "Don't attempt to conceal anything from me," exclaimed the Seyyid, "by talking a foreign language, for I perfectly understand what you are talking about." This, however, was, as I believe, a mere idle boast.

From Mullá Yúsuf I to-day obtained a more circumstantial account than I had yet heard of an event which some time ago created a good deal of excitement in Kirmán, especially amongst the Bábís. A lad of fifteen, the son of an architect in the city, who had been brought up in the doctrines of the Sheykhís, turned Bábí, and, inspired by that reckless zeal which is the especial characteristic of the "people of the Beyán," repaired to

Langar, the headquarters of the Sheykhís and the residence of the sons of Ḥájí Muḥammad Karím Khán, and there publicly addressed the assembled Sheykhís on the signs of the Manifestation of the Imám Mahdí and the general theory of Theophanies. The Sheykhís, believing him to be one of themselves, at first listened complacently enough as he developed his doctrine, and were even pleased with his eloquence and fervour. But when, after declaring that in each dispensation there must needs be a "Point of Darkness" opposed to the "Point of Light," a Nimrod against an Abraham, a Pharaoh against a Moses, an Abú Jahl against a Muḥammad, an Antichrist (*Dajjál*) against a Mahdí, he so described the "Point of Light" and "Point of Darkness" of this cycle as to make it clear that by the former he meant Mírzá 'Alí Muḥammad the Báb, and by the latter Ḥájí Muḥammad Karím Khán, the fury of his audience burst forth; they seized him, dragged him from the mosque, reviled him, cursed him, pelted him with stones, bound him to a tree, and scourged him most cruelly. In spite of all they could do, however, he continued to laugh and exult, so that at last they were obliged to release him.

Tuesday, 18th June, 8th Shawwál.—This afternoon, I received another visit from Afẓal Khán the Belúch, who wished me to give him a letter of introduction to my friend the Nawwáb Mírzá Ḥasan 'Alí Khán at Mashhad, whither he proposed to proceed shortly. Then he began to persuade me to accompany him thither, and thence onwards to Ḳandahár and Ḳal'at-i-Náṣirí, his home in Belúchistán. "You say you are a traveller," concluded he, "desirous of seeing as much as you can of the world: well, Belúchistán is part of the world, and a very fine part too; not Persian Belúchistán, of course, which is a poor, miserable place, but our own land." I declined his seductive offer, and thereupon he taunted me with being afraid. At this juncture the Sheykh of Ḳum and the postmaster's son arrived.

"Well," said the Sheykh, when the usual greetings had been

exchanged, "what do you make of these two Firangís who have come to Kirmán?"

"Hitherto," I replied, "I have hardly seen them, and consequently am not in a position to form an opinion."

"They declare themselves to be Frenchmen," continued the Sheykh, "but if so it is a very astonishing thing that they should be so wanting in good manners as they appear to be, for we always suppose the French to be remarkable amongst European nations for their courtesy and politeness."

"Your supposition is correct, as a rule," I answered, "even though there be exceptions; but you know the aphorism '*en-nádiru k'al-ma'dúm*' ('the exceptional is as the non-existent'). In what way have they shown a lack of courtesy?"

"Why," said the Sheykh, "his Royal Highness the Prince (may God perpetuate his rule!) naturally wished to see them and ascertain the business which had brought them here, so he sent a message inviting them to visit him. They refused to come. He was naturally very angry; but, seeing that they were Firangís, and so (saving your presence) not to be judged by our standards of good behaviour, he swallowed down his annoyance, and sent another message saying, 'Since you do not wish to visit me, I must needs visit you.' In answer to this second message they sent back word that their lodging was not suitable for receiving so august a personage. His Royal Highness hesitated to punish their churlishness as it deserved; but, finding that they had with them a Persian attendant lent to them by the Governor of Mashhad (with whom Prince Náṣiru'd-Dawla is not on the best of terms), he ordered him to come to the palace for interrogation on the following day; 'for,' thought he, 'him at least I can oblige to speak.' When the Firangís found that their fists were going to be opened[1] in spite of them, they decided to accompany their man before the Prince, and, without giving any notice of their visit, in they marched with their great dirty boots (which

1 *I.e.* that their secrets were going to be disclosed.

they never even offered to remove); neither would they give any satisfactory account of themselves or their business. We think it probable that they are come after walnut-trees, which, as men say, they cut and polish in some manner known to themselves, in such a way that pictures or reflections of any scene which may have taken place in the neighbourhood of the tree appear in the polished surface of the wood; but of this you probably know more than we do. The question is, are they really Frenchmen, as they assert?"

"I don't know," said I; "all I can say is that they talk French, so far as I can judge, as though it were their native language."

"Don't you believe a word of it," broke in the Belúch; "they are no more French than I am. Who are the French that they should dare to act towards his Royal Highness as these men have done? No; they are either Russians or English; of that you may be sure."

We laughed at the Belúch's ideas on the balance of power in Europe, while he continued with increasing excitement—

"If his Royal Highness will but give me a hint, I will seek out these Firangís in their lodging—I and my companions here—and will kill them, and cut off their heads, and lay them at the Prince's feet."

"And how would you do that?" asked the Sheykh, with difficulty suppressing his mirth.

"Do it?" rejoined Afẓal Khán; "easily enough. I would find out where they lodged, walk in one fine day with an '*es-selámu 'aleykum*' ('peace be upon you'), and cut them down with this sword of mine before they had time to speak, or flee, or offer the slightest resistance."

"Oh," said the Sheykh, "but that wouldn't be at all right; you shouldn't say 'peace be upon you' to a man you are just going to kill."

"Why not?" retorted the Belúch, "they are infidels, *káfirs*, and such it is lawful to slay in any manner."

"But he is a *káfir* too," slyly remarked the Sheykh, pointing towards myself.

"Yes, I know he is," exclaimed the Belúch, "and if only——" Here he was interrupted by a general roar of laughter.

"O most excellent Khán," I cried, as soon as the general merriment had somewhat subsided, "now your fist is opened! Now I see why you were so eager for me to accompany you to your interesting, hospitable country. A long journey, in sooth, would it have been, and one, as I think, on which I might have set out singing—

> '*Dam-i-raftan-ast, 'Urfí; bi-rukhash nazáré'í kun,*
> *Ki umíd-i-báz-gashtan kas az ín safar na-dárad.*'
>
> "'Tis the moment of departure, O 'Urfí; take a last look at his face,
> For from this journey none may hope to return.'"

The Belúch hung his head in some confusion, and then began to laugh gently. "You are quite right, Ṣáḥib," he said, "but I know very well that you are an agent of your government, engaged in heaven knows what mischief here."

"Why, look at me," I replied; "I live, as you see, like a dervish, without any of the circumstance or having which befits an envoy of such a government as ours."

"Ay," he retorted, "but you English are cunning enough to avoid ostentation when it suits your own ends to do so. I know you to my cost, and that is the way it always begins."

And so the matter dropped, and that was the last I saw of my friend Afẓal Khán.

Later on several other visitors came; the Seyyid, of course; Ḥájí Shírází, who was immensely convivial, having, as he informed me, drunk half a bottle of brandy "for his stomach's sake"; and the parcher of peas. The last drew me aside out of the hearing of the Seyyid (between whom and himself subsisted a most violent antipathy), and said he had come to ask me to have supper one night with him, the postmaster, and some other congenial friends, so that we could converse quietly and without fear of intrusion.

"Thank you," I said, "I shall be very pleased to come any evening that suits you, and I am no less anxious than yourself for an opportunity for some quiet conversation; for hitherto, though I know that many of my friends here are Bábís, we have only talked on side-issues, and have never come to the main point. And it is about the Báb especially, and Ḳurratu'l-'Ayn, and the others, not about Behá, that I want to hear. It was he whom I heard about and learned to admire and love before I left my native country: and since my arrival in Persia, though I have conversed with many Bábís, it is always of Behá that they speak. Behá may be very well, and may be superior to the Báb, but it is about the Báb that I want to hear."

"Yes," he replied, "you shall hear about him, for he is worth hearing about—the Lord Jesus come back to earth in another form. He was but a child of nineteen when his mission began, and was only twenty-six when they killed him—killed him because he was a charmer of hearts, and for no crime but this—

> '*Dar kudám millat-ast ín, dar kudám madhhab-ast ín?*
> *Ki kushand dilbarí-rá, ki, "Tú dil-rubá chirá'í?"*'
>
> 'In what church, in what religion, is this lawful,
> That they should kill a charmer of hearts, saying, "Why dost thou steal hearts?"'"

"Whose is that verse?" I enquired.

"Oh," he replied, "the original verse is 'Iráḳí's, and runs thus—

> '*Dar kudám millat-ast ín, dar kudám madhhab-ast ín?*
> *Ki kushand 'áshiḳí-rá, ki, "Tú 'áshiḳam chirá'í?"*'
>
> 'In what church, in what religion, is this lawful,
> That they should kill a lover, saying, "Why art thou my lover?"'

But we have altered the verse to suit our purpose."

At this point the Seyyid was seen approaching us, and the parcher of peas fled as from the Angel of Death. But Ḥájí Shírází outstayed even the Seyyid, and after supper consumed as much brandy as he could get, observing repeatedly in a rather unsteady voice that no amount of it produced any effect upon him, because moisture so greatly predominated in his natural temperament.

Wednesday, 19th June, 9th Shawwál.—This morning I received a visit from a very melancholy person, who, I think, held the office of treasurer to the Prince-Governor. He told me that he did not like Europeans, and would not have come to see me if he had not heard that I, unlike most of them, took an interest in religious questions, into which he forthwith plunged, arguing against the possibility of the use of wine being sanctioned by any true prophet, and defending the seclusion of women and the use of the veil. Against these last I argued very earnestly, pointing out the evils which, as it appeared to me, resulted from them. He was silent for a while after I had finished speaking, and then said:—

"It is true; I admit the force of your arguments, and I cannot at this moment give a sufficient and satisfactory answer to them, though I believe there must be one. But I will not attempt to give an insufficient answer, for my sole desire is to be just and fair."

Before he left he told me that he suffered much from indigestion, brought on by excessive meditation, adding, "I fear, I fear greatly." I asked him what he feared, and he replied, "God."

In the afternoon Ferídún came to me while I was sitting in Ḥájí Shírází's shop, to arrange for a visit to the *dakhmé*, or "tower of silence" of the Zoroastrians. Ḥájí Shírází was most insolent to him, calling him a son of a dog ("*pidar-sag*"), a *gabr*, and the like. I saw poor Ferídún flush up with an anger which it cost him an effort to control, and would fain have given the drunken old Ḥájí a piece of my mind, had I been certain that he did not intend his rudeness for playful banter, and had I not further feared that in any case my remonstrances would only increase his spite against Ferídún, which I could only hope to suppress so long as I remained at Kirmán. I told Ferídún this afterwards, and he not only approved my action, but begged me not to interfere in any similar case. "It would do no permanent good," he said, "and would only embitter them against us. But do not forget what we poor Zoroastrians have to suffer at the hands of these Musulmáns when you return to your native land, and try, if you can, to do something for us."

Towards evening I rode out with Gushtásp and Ferídún to the lonely *dakhmé* situated on a jagged mountain-spur at some little distance from the town. Gushtásp rode his donkey; but Ferídún, who was a bold and skilful rider, had borrowed a horse, for the Zoroastrians at Kirmán are not subjected to restrictions quite so irksome as those which prevail at Yezd. We stopped twice on the way to drink wine, at a place called *Sar-i-pul* ("Bridge-end"), and at a sort of half-way house, where funerals halt on their way to the *dakhmé*, or rather *dakhmés*, for there are two of them, one disused, and one built by Mánakjí, the late Zoroastrian agent at Ṭeherán, a little higher up the ridge. At the foot of this we dismounted, Mullá Gushtásp remaining below to look after the animals, while I ascended with Ferídún by a steep path leading to the upper *dakhmé*. Here Ferídún, whose brother had recently been conveyed to his last resting-place, proceeded to mutter some prayers, untying and rebinding his girdle or *kushtí* as he did so; after which he produced a bottle of wine and poured three libations to the dead, exclaiming as he did so, "*Khudá bi-yámurzad hama-i-raftagán-rá*" ("May God forgive all those who are gone!"), and then helped himself and passed the wine to me. Observing an inscribed tablet on the side of the *dakhmé* (which was still some twenty yards above us) I called my companion's attention to it, and made as though I would have advanced towards it; but he checked me. "None," said he, "may pass beyond this spot where we stand, save only those whose duty it is to convey the dead to their last resting-place, and a curse falls on him who persists in so doing." As he spoke he pointed to a Persian inscription cut on the rock beside us, which I had not previously observed, wherein a curse was invoked on anyone whom curiosity, or a desire "to molest the dead," should impel to enter the *dakhmé*. Near this was inscribed the well-known verse—

> "*Ey dúst! bar jenázé-i-dushman chú bigzarí,*
> *Shádí ma-kun, ki bar tú hamín má-jará buvad.*"

> "O friend! when thou passest by the corpse of thine enemy
> Rejoice not, for on thee will the same fate fall."

Below this was recorded the date of the *dakhmé's* completion —Dhí'l-Ḥijjé 20th, A.H. 1283 (25th April, A.D. 1867), corresponding to the year 1236 of Yezdigird.

On returning to the garden I found the inevitable Seyyid Ḥuseyn, who had arrived soon after I had gone out, and, in my absence, had been inflicting his theological dissertations on Ná'ib Ḥasan. It had been arranged that I should visit a certain Mírzá Muḥammad Ja'far Khán (a nephew of the great leader of the Sheykhís and antagonist of the Bábís, Ḥájí Muḥammad Karím Khán), who had called upon me a few days previously: and the Seyyid, hearing this, insisted on accompanying me. On reaching his house, which stood alone at some distance from the town, we were received by him and a stout pallid youth named Yúsuf Khán (who, I believe, was his cousin or nephew) in the *tanbal-kháné*, or lounging-room, the walls of which were profusely decorated with a strange medley of cheap European prints and photographs representing scripture incidents, scenes from *Uncle Tom's Cabin*, scantily clothed women, and other incongruous subjects, arranged in the worst possible taste. The low opinion of my host's character with which this exhibition inspired me was not bettered by his conversation, which was, so far as I remember, singularly pointless. He evidently felt ill at ease in the presence of the Seyyid, who enquired very searchingly as to the reception which the eldest of Ḥájí Muḥammad Karím Khán's sons, the chief of the Sheykhís, had met with at the holy shrines of Kerbelá and Nejef, whither he had recently gone. So far as we could learn, he had been anything but cordially received, and at Káẓimeyn the people had not suffered him to preach in the mosque. On my return to the garden I had supper with Ná'ib Ḥasan, who aspersed the character of my new acquaintance in a way which I cannot bring myself to repeat.

Thursday, 20th June, 10th Shawwál.—This morning I paid a visit to one of the most eminent members of the clergy of Kirmán, the *mujtahid* Mullá Muḥammad Ṣáliḥ-i-Kirmání. He was a fine-looking man, with a long black beard and deeply furrowed brow, and received me with a somewhat haughty courtesy. He conversed on religious topics only, pointing out the beauties of the law of Islám, and taking great exception to the carelessness of Europeans in certain matters of purification. On leaving his house I was taken to see an iron foundry, where I was shown two excellent-looking Enfield rifles manufactured by a Kirmání gunsmith, in imitation of one of European workmanship lent to him by the Prince-Governor.

In the afternoon I received a visit from the two Frenchmen of whose arrival in Kirmán I have already spoken. Ḥájí Muḥammad Khán, Mullá Yúsuf, and Seyyid Ḥuseyn happened to come while they were with me; but the last, on a hint from Ná'ib Ḥasan that wine was likely to be produced, fled precipitately, to the satisfaction of everyone. The Frenchmen appeared, from their account, to have had a very rough journey from Mashhad to Kirmán, and not to enjoy much comfort even here; they were delighted with the wine, cognac, and tea which I placed before them (for they had not been able to obtain any sort of alcohol here, not knowing whither to go for it), and conversed freely on everything save the objects of their journey, of which they seemed unwilling to speak, though Ḥájí Muḥammad Khán, who really did speak French with some approach to fluency, endeavoured again and again to extract some information from them. He was so disgusted at his ill success that he afterwards announced to me his conviction that they were persons of no rank or breeding, and that he had no wish to see anything more of them.

In the evening I supped with the Prince-Governor, the party being completed by the Sheykh of Ḳum and the Prince-Telegraphist. The meal was served in European fashion in a room in the *Bágh-i-Náṣiriyya* palace, which was brilliantly illuminated. A great number of European dishes was set before us, no doubt in my honour, though, as a matter of fact, I should have greatly preferred Persian cookery. Wine, too, was provided, and not merely for show either. The Prince, acting, I suppose, on the aphorism, "Address men according to the measure of their understandings," conversed chiefly on European politics, in which I felt myself thoroughly out of my depth. He was, however, extremely kind; and when I left, insisted on lending me a horse and a man to conduct me home.

Friday, 21st June, 11th Shawwál.—In the afternoon I returned Mírzá Jawád's call, and found with him his son and his son's tutor, Mullá Ghulám Ḥuseyn, a Sheykhí, from whom I extracted the following account of the essential doctrines of his school:—

"The Bálásarís, or ordinary Shí'ites," said he, "assert that the essentials of religion are five, to wit, belief in the Unity of God (*tawḥíd*), the Justice of God (*'adl*), the Prophetic Function (*nubuwvat*), the Imámate (*imámat*), and the Resurrection (*ma'ád*). Now we say that two of these cannot be reckoned as primary doctrines at all; for belief in the Prophet involves belief in his book and the teachings which it embodies, amongst which is the Resurrection; and there is no more reason for regarding a belief in God's justice as a principal canon of faith than belief in God's Mercy, or God's Omnipotence, or any other of His Attributes. Of their five principles or essentials (*uṣúl*), therefore, we accept only three; but to these we add another, namely, that there must always exist amongst the Musulmáns a 'Perfect Shí'ite' (*Shí'a-i-ḳámil*) who enjoys the special guidance of the

Imáms, and acts as a Channel of Grace (*Wásiṭa-i-feyẓ*) between them and their Church. This tenet we call 'the Fourth Support' (*Rukn-i-rábi'*), or fourth essential principle of religion."

In the evening I was the guest of Ustá Akbar, the parcher of peas, at supper, and stayed the night at his house. Amongst the guests were Áḳá Fatḥu'lláh, a young Ezelí minstrel and poet, who sung verses in praise of the Báb, composed by himself; Sheykh Ibráhím of Sulṭán-ábád; one of his intimates and admirers, a servant of the Farrásh-báshí, named 'Abdu'lláh; a post-office official, whom I will call Ḥaydaru'lláh; and the pea-parcher's brother. As the evening wore on, these began to talk very wildly, in a fashion with which I was soon to become but too familiar, declaring themselves to be one with the Divine Essence, and calling upon me by such titles as "*Jenáb-i-Ṣáḥib*" and "*Ḥaẓrat-i-Firangí*" to acknowledge that there was "no one but the Lord Jesus" present. Wearied and somewhat disgusted as I was, it was late before they would suffer me to retire to rest on the roof.

Saturday, 22*nd June*, 12*th Shawwál*.—The party at Ustá Akbar's did not break up till about an hour and a half before sunset, when I returned to the garden accompanied by Sheykh Ibráhím, who from this time forth until I left Kirmán became my constant companion, though more than once, disgusted at his blasphemous conversation and drunkenness, I endeavoured to discourage his visits. But he was not one to be easily shaken off; and on these occasions, when my indignation had been specially kindled against him, he would make so fair a show of regret for his conduct that I was constrained to forget his unseemly behaviour. Moreover, he was a man well worth talking to, so long as he was sober or not more than half drunk, having travelled widely through Persia, Turkey, and Egypt; seen many strange things and stranger people; and mixed with almost every class and sect, as it is the privilege of his order to do. He was, indeed, one of the most extraordinary men whom I ever met, and presented a combination of qualities impossible in any but a Persian. Anarchist, antinomian, heretic, and libertine to the very core, he gloried in drunkenness, and expressed the profoundest contempt for every ordinance of Islám, boasting of how he had first eaten pork in the company of a European traveller with whom he foregathered in Egypt, and quoting in excuse for his orgies of *ḥashísh* and spirits this couplet from the *Masṇaví*—

"*Nang-i-bang u khamr bar khud mí-nihí*
Tá damí az khwíshtan tú vá-rahí."

"Thou disgracest thyself with *bang* and wine
In order that for a moment thou mayest escape from thyself."

I have seen him, on an occasion when by the laws of Islám the minor ablution was incumbent on him, take up an empty ewer (*áftábé*), and, when warned by his friends that it contained no water, reply, "Bah! What do I care? I only carry it to blind these accursed dogs of orthodoxy, who, if they had but proof of one-tenth of the contempt which I entertain for them and their observances, would tear me in pieces." He professed to be a Bábí, and (as will be related in its proper place) had all but suffered death for his beliefs. When a youth he had visited Behá at Acre and Ṣubḥ-i-Ezel in Cyprus, and declared himself to be a follower of the former, though in point of fact he paid no more attention to the commands and prohibitions of the *Kitáb-i-Aḳdas* than to those of the Ḳur'án, accounting all laws, human and divine, as made by the wise for fools to observe. In short, he was just a free-thinking, free-living, antinomian dervish or *ḳalandar*, a sort of mixture of 'Omar-i-Khayyám and 'Iráḳí, with only a fraction of their talent and culture, and ten times their disregard for orthodox opinion and conventional morality. Yet was he lacking neither in originality, power of observation and deduction, nor humour; and his intelligence, now sadly undermined by narcotics and alcohol, must have originally been sufficiently acute.

Such was the man in whose society it was my lot to pass

a considerable portion of my remaining days at Kirmán. Again and again, as I have said, I would have cast him off and been quit of him, but ever the interest of his extraordinary character and the charm of his conversation made me condone his faults and bear with him a little longer. He was a perfect repository of information concerning the roads, halting-places, towns, and peoples of Western Asia; you had but to ask him how to reach any town from a given starting-place, and he would in a few minutes sketch you out two or three alternative routes, with the stages, advantages, disadvantages, and points of interest of each. To give an instance, I had at this time some idea of quitting Persia by Hamadán, and making my way thence to the Mediterranean, and I enquired of Sheykh Ibráhím whether this project were feasible.

"Oh yes," he replied, "nothing can be easier. From Hamadán you will go to Sanandij, a march of four days; thence in four days to Suleymániyyé; thence in four days more to Mosul, where you must certainly pay a visit to Zeynu'l-Muḳarrabín."

"And who," enquired I, "is Zeynu'l-Muḳarrabín?"

"He is one of the most notable of 'the Friends'" (*Aḥbáb*, *i.e.* the Bábís), replied he, "and to him is entrusted the revision and correction of all copies of the sacred books sent out for circulation, of which, indeed, the most trustworthy are those transcribed by his hand. His real name is Mullá Zeynu'l-'Ábidín of Najaf-ábád. You may also see at Mosul Mírzá 'Abdu'l-Wahháb of Shíráz, the seal-engraver, who will cut for you a seal bearing an inscription in the New Writing (*Khaṭṭ-i-badí'*), and Mírzá 'Abdu'lláh '*Aláḳa-band*, both of whom are worth visiting."

"Are these the only Bábís at Mosul?" I enquired.

"Oh, no," he answered, "you will find plenty of them there and elsewhere on your route. You can tell them by their dress; they wear the Turkish fez with a small white turban, and a *jubbé*; they do not shave their heads, but on the other hand they never allow the *zulf* to grow below the level of the lobe of the ear. Well, to continue. From Mosul you will go in four days to Jezíré, thence in three days to Márdín, thence in four days to Diyár Bekr, thence in four days to 'Urfa, thence in two days to Suwárak, thence in three days to 'Awrá, thence in three days to Birejik, and thence in six days to Iskanderún (Alexandretta), where you can take ship for Constantinople, or Alexandria, or your own country, as you please. But you should by all means go to Acre, and visit Behá, so that your experience may be complete."

"You have visited Acre, have you not?" I enquired; "tell me what sort of place it is, and what you saw there."

"Yes," he replied, "I was there for seventy days, during which period I was honoured (*musharraf*) by admission to the Holy Presence twelve times. The first time I was accompanied by two of Behá's sons, by his amanuensis and constant attendant Áḳá Mírzá Áḳá Ján of Káshán, whom they call '*Jenáb-i-Khádimu'lláh*' ('His Excellence the Servant of God'), and by my fellow-traveller. All these, so soon as we entered the presence-chamber, prostrated themselves on the ground; but while I, ignorant of the etiquette generally observed, was hesitating what to do, Behá called out to me 'It is not necessary' ('*Lázim níst*'). Then said he twice in a loud voice, '*Báraka'lláhu 'aleykum*' ('God bless you!'), and then, 'Most blessed are ye, in that ye have been honoured by beholding Me, which thing saints and prophets have desired most earnestly.' Then he bade us be seated, and gave orders for tea to be set before us. My companion hesitated to drink it, lest he should appear wanting in reverence, seeing which Behá said, 'The meaning of offering a person tea is that he should drink it.' Then we drank our tea, and *Khádimu'lláh* read aloud one of the Epistles (*Alwáḥ*); after which we were dismissed. During my stay at Acre I was taken ill, but Behá sent me a portion of the *piláw* which had been set before him, and this I had no sooner eaten than I was restored to health. You should have seen how the other believers envied me, and how they begged for a few grains from my share! And this happened on two subsequent occasions. When I left Acre, Behá commended me, but bade me preach the doctrine no more, because I had already suffered enough in God's way."

Later on Mírzá Yúsuf of Tabríz joined us, and, thinking to please Sheykh Ibráhím, pretended that he too was a Bábí. But when Sheykh Ibráhím feigned ignorance of the whole matter, expressing surprise, and, in some cases, mild disapproval, at what Mírzá Yúsuf told him of the doctrines and practices of the sect, the latter, thinking that he had made a mistake, changed his ground, and told us that he had only pretended to be a convert to the new religion so as to get money from the rich and charitable Bábís at Yezd. I could hardly contain my laughter as I watched Mírzá Yúsuf thus entangling himself in the snare set for him by the Sheykh, who, meanwhile, never so much as smiled at the success of his stratagem. I expected, of course, that the whole story would become known to all the Bábís in Kirmán, but I think the Sheykh kept his own counsel, being less concerned with the exposure of hypocrisy, than with his own amusement.

After Mírzá Yúsuf's withdrawal, the Sheykh, having communicated to me a great deal of very scandalous gossip about the postmaster (whom he was by way of considering as one of his best friends), began to discuss with high approval the character of the free-thinking poet Náṣir-i-Khusraw, whose poems and apocryphal autobiography he had been recently reading. The episode in the autobiography which had especially delighted him, and which he repeated to me with infinite relish, runs as follows[1]:—

"After much trouble we reached the city of Níshápúr, there being with us a pupil of mine, an expert and learned metaphysician. Now in the whole city of Níshápúr there was no one who knew us, so we came and took up our abode in a mosque. As we walked through the city, at the door of every

1 I translate from the Tabríz edition of Náṣir-i-Khusraw's works, lithographed in A.H. 1280 (A.D. 1864), pp. 6, 7.

mosque by which we passed men were cursing me, and accusing me of heresy and atheism; but the disciple knew nothing of their opinion concerning me. One day, as I was passing through the bazaar, a man from Egypt saw and recognised me, and approached me, saying, 'Art thou not Náṣir-i-Khusraw, and is not this thy brother Abú Sa'íd?' In terror I seized his hand, and, engaging him in conversation, led him to my lodging. Then I said, 'Take thirty thousand *miṣḳáls* of gold, and refrain from divulging the secret.' When he had consented, I at once bade my familiar spirit produce that sum, gave it to him, and thrust him out from my lodging. Then I went with Abú Sa'íd to the bazaar, halted at the shop of a cobbler, and gave him my shoes to repair, that we might go forth from the city, when suddenly a clamour made itself heard near at hand, and the cobbler hastened in the direction whence the sounds proceeded. After a while he returned with a piece of flesh on the end of his bradawl. 'What,' enquired I, 'was the disturbance, and what is this piece of flesh?' 'Why,' replied the cobbler, 'it appears that one of Náṣir-i-Khusraw's disciples appeared in the city and began to dispute with the doctors thereof. These repudiated his assertions, each adducing some respectable authority, while he continued to quote in support of his views verses of Náṣir-i-Khusraw. So the clergy tore him in pieces as a meritorious action, and I too, to merit a reward, cut off a portion of his flesh.' When I learned what had befallen my disciple, I could no longer control myself, and said to the cobbler, 'Give me my shoes, for one should not tarry in a city where the verses of Náṣir-i-Khusraw are recited.' So I took my shoes, and came forth with my brother from Níshápúr."

The Sheykh then recited to me the two following fragments of Náṣir-i-Khusraw's verse, which, it will be allowed, are sufficient to account for the lack of favour wherewith he was regarded by the clergy of Níshápúr:—

" Iláhí, rást gúyam; fitné az tust,
Valí az tars na-t'vánam chakídan.
Agar rígí bi-kafsh-i-khud na-dárí
Chirá báyast Sheyṭán áfarídan?
Lab ú dindán-i-khúbán-i-Khaṭá-rá
Badín khúbí na-báyast áfarídan.
Bi-áhú mí-zaní 'Hey! Hey!' ki bigríz;
Bi-tází mí-zaní 'Hey!' bar davídan."

"O God, although through fear I hardly dare
To hint it, all our trouble springs from Thee.
Had'st Thou no sand or gravel in Thy shoes
What prompted Thee to bid the Devil be?
'Twere well an Thou had'st made the lips and teeth
Of Tartar beauties not so fair to see.
With cries of 'On!' Thou bid'st the hound pursue;
With cries of 'On!' Thou bid'st the quarry flee!"

"*Náṣir-i-Khusraw bi-dashtí mí-guzasht,*
Mast-i-lá-ya'ḳil, na chún mey-khwáragán.
Mabrazí díd u mazárí rú-bi-rú;
Báng bar zad; guft, 'k'ey nazzáragán!
Ni'mat-i-dunyá, va ni'mat-khwár bín;
insh ni'mat! insh ni'mat-khwáragán!'"

"Dead drunk (not like a common sot) one day
Náṣir-i-Khusraw went to take the air.
Hard by a dung-heap he espied a grave,
And straightway cried, 'O ye who stand and stare,
Behold the world! Behold its luxuries!
Its dainties, here—the fools who ate them, there!'"

Ere evening was past, the Sheykh, like Náṣir-i-Khusraw, was "dead drunk, not like a common sot," and finally, to my great relief, went to sleep, wrapped in his cloak, in a formless heap on the floor, where we left him till morning. He awoke very late, and was sipping his morning tea with a woe-begone air which contrasted strangely with his vivacity of the previous day, when visitors were announced, and my disagreeable acquaintance, Ḥájí Muḥammad Khán, accompanied by a pleasant, well-informed *mullá* named Ḥájí Sheykh Ja'far of Kerbelá, entered the room. He was more than usually impertinent and inquisitive; enquired when Sheykh Ibráhím had come to the garden, and, on learning from me that he had been there since the previous night, lifted his eyebrows in surprise, remarking that the Sheykh had said he came that morning early; and then proceeded to enquire pointedly how the postmaster was, and whether I had any fresh news from Adrianople or Acre, meaning, of course, to imply his belief that I was a Bábí. Finally, however, Ná'ib Ḥasan came to the rescue, reminding me in a loud voice that I had accepted an invitation to visit Hurmuzyár, one of my Zoroastrian friends, at his garden. He omitted to mention that the engagement was for the evening, but the intimation had the desired effect of causing Ḥájí Muḥammad Khán to retire, taking the divine with him.

I now wished to go out, but to this Sheykh Ibráhím objected, declaring that it was too hot; so we had lunch, and then adjourned to the summer-house, where he fell asleep over my Bábí history. On awakening from his nap he was more like his usual self, and began to entertain me with his conversation.

"So you met Sheykh S——, the Bábí courier, at Shíráz, did you?" he began; "a fine old fellow he is, too, and has had some strange experiences. Did he tell you how he ate the letters?"

"No," I replied; "tell me about it."

"Ah," he continued, "he is not given to talking much. Well, you must know that he goes to Acre once every year to convey letters from 'the Friends' in Persia and elsewhere, and to bring back replies. He takes Iṣfahán, Shíráz, Yezd, and the south, while Dervish Khávar takes Mázandarán, Gílán, and the northern part of 'Iráḳ, riding about on a donkey, selling drugs, and passing himself off as an oculist. The Sheykh, however, goes everywhere on foot, save when he has to cross the sea; and this, I fancy, he only does when he cannot well avoid it, at least since a ship in which he was a passenger was wrecked between Bushire and Baṣra, and everyone on board drowned save himself and another dervish, who managed to keep themselves above water by means of floating wreckage, until, after fourteen or fifteen hours' exposure, they were drifted ashore. As a rule, he so times his return from the interior as to reach Bushire early in the month of *Dhi'l-Ḥijjé*, whereby he is enabled to join the pilgrims bound for Jedda and Mecca. After the conclusion of the pilgrimage he makes his way to Acre, where he generally stays about two months, while the letters which he has brought are being answered. Though he is not, perhaps, honoured by admission to Behá's presence more than once or twice during this period, he is in many ways a privileged person, being allowed to go into the *andarún* (women's apartments) when he pleases, and to sit with outstretched feet and uncovered head even in the presence of the Masters (*Áḳáyán*, *i.e.* Behá's sons). When the letters are all answered, he packs them into his wallet, takes his staff, and sets off by way of Beyrout for Mosul, where he stays for about a month with Zeynu'l-Muḳarrabín, of whom I told you a few days ago. Thence he makes his way down the Tigris to Baghdád, and so across the frontier into Persia. He walks always off the beaten track to avoid recognition, and, for the same reason, seldom enters a town or village save to buy sufficient bread and onions (he is passionately fond of onions) to last him several days. These he packs away in his wallet on the top of the letters. At night he generally sleeps in a graveyard, or in some other unfrequented spot where he is not likely to be disturbed, unless there be some of 'the Friends' in the place where he halts, in which case they are always glad to give him a night's lodging. Well, it was about his eating his letters that I was going to tell you. Once in the course of his travels he was recognised in a village near Yezd, arrested, and locked up in an empty room to await examination by the *ked-khudá*, or head-man. The *ked-khudá* chanced to be engaged when word was brought to him that the Bábí courier had been caught. 'Leave him locked up where he is,' said he, 'till I can come.' Now the Sheykh is a man of resource, and, finding that the *ked-khudá* did not immediately come to examine him, he began to cast about for some means of destroying the compromising letters in his wallet; for he knew that if these should fall into the hands of the enemy the writers would get into trouble. Unluckily there was no fire, nor any means of making one; and the earth which formed the floor of the room was too hard to dig a hole in, even if it would have been safe to bury the letters in a place whence they could not afterwards be removed. There was only one thing left to do, namely, to eat them; and this the Sheykh proceeded to do. It was a tough meal, for their total weight amounted to several pounds, and some of them were written on thick, strong paper. In particular there was one great packet from Rafsinján which cost the Sheykh a world of trouble, and on the senders of which, as I have myself heard him say, he lavished a wealth of curses and expletives ere he finally succeeded in chewing it up and swallowing it. At length, however, the whole mass of correspondence was disposed of, and, when his persecutors arrived, there was the old Sheykh (with a very dry mouth, I expect, and, likely enough, somewhat uneasy within) sitting there as innocent-looking as could be. The *ked-khudá* and his man didn't pay much heed to that, though, nor to his protestations; but when they had turned his wallet inside out, and searched all his pockets, and found not so much as the vestige of a letter to reward them for their pains, they were rather taken aback, and began to think they had made a mistake. They gave him the bastinado to make all sure, but, as he continued to protest that he was no Bábí, and no courier, and knew nothing about any letters at all, they eventually had to let him go."

We were interrupted by the unwelcome arrival of Seyyid Ḥuseyn of Jandaḳ, and, quickly as I pushed the Bábí history under a cushion, he noticed the movement, and forthwith proceeded to make himself disagreeable (an accomplishment in which he excelled) to Sheykh Ibráhím, persistently and pointedly asking him about wine, where the best qualities were manufactured, how and when it was usually drunk, and the like, on all of which points the Sheykh professed himself perfectly ignorant. The Seyyid, however, continued to discourse in this uncomfortable strain, concluding severely with the aphorism, "*Man dána bi-dínin, lazimahu aḥkámuhu*" ("Whosoever professeth a faith, its laws are binding on him").

Presently the *Farrásh-báshí's* servant, 'Abdu'lláh, who was one of the Sheykh's intimates, joined us, and we had tea; but the Seyyid continued to act in the same aggressive and offensive manner, enquiring very particularly whether the cup placed before him had been properly purified since last it touched my infidel lips. Mírzá Yúsuf of Tabríz, who had brought it, answered pertly enough, and put the old man in a still worse temper, so that I was very glad when Ná'ib Ḥasan reminded me in a loud voice that it was time to set out for the garden of Hurmuzyár, whose guest I was to be that evening, and the Seyyid departed, grumbling as he went, "You have already forgotten the advice

I gave you the other day, 'Eat no man's bread, and grudge not thine own bread to any one.'"

Sheykh Ibráhím, though uninvited, insisted on accompanying me and Ná'ib Ḥasan to Hurmuzyár's entertainment. We found about twenty guests there assembled, all, with the exception of ourselves and Fatḥu'lláh, the minstrel, Zoroastrians; Rustams and Rashíds; Shahriyárs, Dínyárs, and Ormuzdyárs; Key-Khusraws and Khudá-murádṣ; Bahmans, Bahráms, Isfandiyárs and Mihrabáns. The entertainment was on a magnificent scale, the minstrel sang well, and the pleasure of the evening was only marred by the conduct of Sheykh Ibráhím, who got disgustingly drunk, and behaved in the most indecorous manner. "But that he came under your ægis," said Hurmuzyár to me afterwards, when I apologised for his behaviour, and explained how he had forced his company upon me, "we would have tied his feet to the poles and given him the sticks; for if sticks be not for such drunken brutes as him, I know not for what they were created." I was constrained to admit that he was right; but for all that I was unable to shake off my disreputable companion, who accompanied us back to the garden when we said good-night to our host, and slept heavily on the ground wrapped in his cloak.

The next day, Monday, 14th Shawwál, 24th June, will ever be to me most memorable, for thereon did I come under the glamour of the Poppy-wizard, and forge the first link of a chain which it afterwards cost me so great an effort to break. Thereon, also, was first disclosed to me that vision of antinomian pantheism which is the World of the Ḳalandar, and the source of all that is wildest and strangest in the poetry of the Persians. With this eventful day, then, let me open a new chapter.

CHAPTER XVII

AMONGST THE ḲALANDARS

"How sweet it were, hearing the downward stream,
With half-shut eyes ever to seem
Falling asleep in a half-dream!
To dream and dream, like yonder amber light,
Which will not leave the myrrh-bush on the height;
To hear each other's whisper'd speech;
Eating the Lotos day by day,
. . . . . .
To lend our hearts and spirits wholly
To the influence of mild-minded melancholy."
(TENNYSON.)

"*Tu va mulk u jáh-i-Sikandarí, man u rasm u ráh-i-Ḳalandarí;*
Agar án khush-ast, tu dar khurí; va gar ín bad-ast, mará sazá."

"Sikandar's pomp and display be thine, the Ḳalandar's habit and way be mine;
That, if it please thee, I resign, while this, though bad, is enough for me."
(*Ḳurratu'l-'Ayn.*)

THIS was how it came about.

On the afternoon of this notable day, about four hours before sunset, I went into the town to pay some visits, leaving Sheykh Ibráhím asleep in the garden. I first went to see the Frenchmen, about whose health I had heard disquieting reports, which, fortunately, turned out to be exaggerated. Having remained with them for rather more than half an hour, I proceeded to the house of the young artillery officer whose acquaintance I had made through the Sheykh of Ḳum. While I was sitting there conversing with him, and watching the grotesque antics of a large tame monkey (*'antar*) which he kept as a pet, I first became conscious of an uneasy sensation in my eye. My host, too, noticed that it appeared inflamed, and bade one of his servants bring a bowl of iced water that I might bathe it. So far from deriving any benefit from this treatment, however, it rapidly grew worse, so that, on my return to the garden, I was in considerable pain.

Now Ustá Akbar, the pea-parcher, whenever I urged him to tell me more about the Báb and his religion, used to declare that he could not talk freely on this topic save in some place where there was no fear of his being overheard; and it had therefore been arranged a day or two previously that on this evening he and a select company of his Bábí friends—to wit, Sheykh Ibráhím of 'Iráḳ, the *Farrásh-báshí's* man, 'Abdu'lláh, and the Ezelí minstrel, Fatḥu'lláh—should sup with me in the garden and spend the night there. Just as I was going out in the afternoon, Ustá Akbar had come to the garden bringing with him a Bábí merchant (whom I will call Áḳá Muḥammad Ḥasan of Yezd), just arrived on business in Kirmán from the little village in Rafsinján where he dwelt. He, having heard from Ustá Akbar an account of myself, was so curious to see me that he insisted on at once paying me a visit; and no sooner were they seated than the pea-parcher began to introduce him in his usual wild language.

"Here is Áḳá Muḥammad Ḥasan," said he, "come to do penance before you and entreat your forgiveness for his shortcomings, in that when you passed through Rafsinján he neither came out to meet you, nor brought you into his house, nor set you on your journey. I have scolded him well, saying, 'Áḳá Muḥammad Ḥasan, the Holy Spirit (*Rúḥu'l-Ḳuds*) passed through Rafsinján, and you had not so much as a word of welcome, nor advanced one foot from the other. Are you not ashamed of yourself?' He is now duly ashamed of himself, and will not be content till he receives from your lips the assurance of his pardon."

I was in a hurry to get rid of my visitors, as I had to go into the town; so, half assenting to Áḳá Muḥammad Ḥasan's proposal that I should spend a few days with him at his village before leaving the province of Kirmán, and inviting him to join us at supper that evening, when we should be able to talk to our hearts' content, I bade them farewell for the present.

On my return to the garden, about an hour after sunset, I found these two and Sheykh Ibráhím awaiting me. My eye was now so painful that I determined to cover it with a bandage, which at once called the attention of my guests to its condition. They all expressed the greatest concern, and Ustá Akbar begged me to allow him to try a remedy which he had never known to fail. In this request he was so importunate that at last I most foolishly consented. Thereupon he went out into the garden and gathered some leaves from the hollyhock or other similar plant, with which he soon returned. Then he called for an egg, broke it into a cup, removed the yolk, leaving only the white, and bade me lie down on the floor on my back, and, if possible, keep the inflamed eye open. Then he poured the white of the egg over the eye, covered it up with the leaves, and entreated me to remain still as long as I could, that the treatment might work. It did work: in two or three minutes the pain became so acute that I could bear it no longer, and called for warm water to wash away the horrid mess which half-blinded me. Ustá Akbar remonstrated, but I told him that the remedy was worse than the disease.

"Ah," said he, "it is clear that I have made a mistake. When you told me that you had been bathing your eye in iced water, I assumed that this cold was the cause of the affection, and so applied a hot remedy. Now it is evident that it is due not to cold but to heat, so that a cold remedy should be applied. And I know one which will not disappoint you."

"Thank you," I rejoined, "if it is anything like the last I should prefer to have nothing to do with it."

"It is nothing like the last," he answered. "What I would suggest is that you should smoke a pipe of opium. That is a cold drug most potent in the treatment of hot maladies, and of its efficacy you cannot but have heard."

Opium! There was something fascinating about the idea. The action on the mental functions exercised by narcotic drugs had always possessed for me a special interest, and though the extremely unpleasant results of an experiment on the subjective effects of *Cannabis Indica* (Indian hemp) which I had tried while a student at St Bartholomew's Hospital had somewhat cooled my enthusiasm for this sort of research, the remembrance of that dreadful evening when Time and Space seemed merging in confused chaos, and my very personality appeared to be undergoing disintegration, had now sufficiently lost its vividness to make me not unwilling to court some fresh experience of this kind. So, after a few moments' reflection, I signified my willingness to try Ustá Akbar's new cure; and ten minutes later my whole being was permeated with that glow of tranquil beatitude, conscious of itself, nay, almost exultant in its own peaceful serenity, which constitutes the fatal charm of what the Persians call *par excellence* "the Antidote" (*tiryáḳ*).

At this juncture the young Ezelí minstrel, and, soon afterwards, 'Abdu'lláh arrived, and we adjourned to the summer-house, where Ḥájí Ṣafar had spread a cloth on which were disposed dishes of fruit, sweets, and *ájíl* (pistachio-nuts, melon-seeds, and the like, strongly salted to whet the appetite), and bottles of wine and '*araḳ*.

The conversation, though it did not flag, was at first quiet enough. My guests spoke in the usual strain of the succession of prophetic cycles, of the progressive character of Revelation, and of the increasing strength of the Theophanic Sun in each appearance. "The Lord Jesus," said they, "was as a sun shining in the Fourth Heaven, which is the 'Station of the Spirit' (*Maḳám-i-Rúḥ*). Muḥammad was in the Fifth Heaven, which is the 'Station of Reason' (*Maḳám-i-'Aḳl*). The *Nuḳté-i-Beyán*, 'His Holiness our Lord the Supreme' (*i.e.* the Báb) appeared yet higher, in the Sixth Heaven or 'Station of Love' (*Maḳám-i-'Ishḳ*); and Behá, in whom all previous Manifestations find their fulfilment and consummation, occupies the Seventh or highest Heaven, and is a perfect Manifestation of the Unseen and Incomprehensible Essence of the Divinity."

Then suddenly some one bade the minstrel sing; and he, in high-pitched, plaintive voice, every modulation of which seemed to stir the soul to its very depths, burst forth with an ode of the Bábí heroine *Ḳurratu'l-'Ayn*, whereof the translation which I here give can but dimly reflect the passion and the fire.

"The thralls of yearning love constrain in the bonds of pain and calamity
These broken-hearted lovers of thine to yield their lives in their zeal for Thee.
2 Though with sword in hand my Darling stand with intent to slay, though I sinless be,
If it pleases Him, this tyrant's whim, I am well content with His tyranny.
As in sleep I lay at the dawn of day that cruel Charmer came to me,
And in the grace of His form and face the dawn of the morn I seemed to see.
4 The musk of Cathay might perfume gain from the scent those fragrant tresses rain,
While His eyes demolish a faith in vain attacked by the pagans of Tartary.
With you, who contemn both love and wine for the hermit's cell and the zealot's shrine,
What can I do? For our faith divine you hold as a thing of infamy.
6 The tangled curls of thy darling's hair, and thy saddle and steed are thine only care;
In thy heart the Infinite hath no share, nor the thought of the poor man's poverty.
Sikandar's pomp and display be thine, the *Ḳalandar's* habit and way be mine;
That, if it please thee, I resign, while this, though bad, is enough for me.
8 The country of 'I' and 'We' forsake; thy home in Annihilation make,
Since fearing not this step to take thou shalt gain the highest felicity."[1]

1 This translation, together with the original text, I first published in the *Journal of the Royal Asiatic Society* for 1889, the former at pp. 936–7, the latter

When he had finished this ode, and the cries of "*Ey ján!*" ("O my life!") and "*Ḳurbán-at gardam!*" ("May I be thy sacrifice!"), which, interjected more than once even in the course of the song, burst forth with uncontrollable enthusiasm at its conclusion, had ceased, the minstrel once more began to sing. I cannot recall the actual words of this song, save in a few places, but the general tenor of it was not far from the paraphrase which I here offer—

"As you gaze on the heaving Ocean's foam
A myriad bubbles meet your eye;
The rain-drops fall from their heavenly home
To ascend no more, it would seem, on high;
But all shall return when their race is run,
For their source is one, their source is one!

"Through glasses of every tint and hue
Fair and bright shine the rays of light;
Some may be violet, and some be blue,
Some be orange, and some be white;
But in essence and origin all are one,
For the source of all is the radiant Sun!

"Beaker and flagon and bowl and jar,
Of earth or crystal, coarse or fine,
However the Potter may make or mar,
Still may serve to contain the Wine;
Should we this one seek, or that one shun,
When the Wine which lends them their worth is one?"

Again the minstrel was silent, and Sheykh Ibráhím, with flushed face and glittering eyes, began to speak. "Yes," said he, "we are all one. What matter if the vessels differ in honour and degree one from another, when in truth their honour is but from

at p. 991. For the benefit of those not accustomed to this style of mystical verse, in which the Persians so greatly delight, I may remark that by such terms as "the Beloved," "the Darling," "the Friend," and the like, God (or in this case the Báb) is intended; that the "cruelty" and "tyranny" attributed to Him are not regarded as reproaches, but rather as praise of His "independence" (*istighná*); that Islám is the faith "demolished by His eyes" though "in vain attacked by the pagans of Tartary"; and that couplets 5 and 6 are addressed respectively to the dry votaries of orthodox piety, and to such as care only for the world and its pleasures.

the wine they hold, which perisheth not though they be broken in pieces? And what is this Wine which perisheth not, which pervadeth all things? God, you will answer. Then, what, I say again, is God? An imaginary abstraction? A projection of your own personality and conceptions thrown on the sky above?

'Hích ism-i-bí-musammá dídé'í?
Yá zi GÁF *ú* LÁM*-i-'gul' gul chídé'í?*
Ism justí; raw, musammá-rá bi-jú:
Mah bi-bálá dán, na andar áb i-jú.'

'Did'st ere a Name without an Object see,
Or cull a rose from R, O, S, and E?
Thou seek'st the Name; to find the Object try:
The Moon's not in the stream, but in the sky.'

What, then, means the 'meeting with God' spoken of in the Ḳur'án? Who are 'those who shall meet their Lord'? Can you meet an Abstraction? Nay, is not this Abstraction, after all, but the creation of your own mind, and as such dependent on you and inferior to you? No, God is something real, visible, tangible, definite. Go to Acre and see God!"

"Now God forbid," I exclaimed in utter horror of the frightful anthropomorphism thus suddenly laid bare before me, "God forbid that it should be so! Why, the very verse which you cited from the *Masnaví* bears witness against you—'The Moon's not in the stream but in the sky'—that is to say, as I understand it, 'Look for the Reality outside and beyond this phenomenal world, not in these transient reflections whereby, clearly or dimly, it is mirrored amongst mankind.' The mirror wholly depends on the original, and owes all to it; the original stands in no need of the mirror. '*Exalted is God above that which they allege!*'"

Then Fatḥu'lláh, the minstrel, broke in. "O *Ḥazrat-i-Firangí!*" he exclaimed, "all these ideas and thoughts about God which you have, yea, your very doubts and wonderings, are your creatures, and you are their creator, and therefore above them, even according to the verse you quote, '*Exalted is God above that which they allege!'* Jesus, who is the Spirit of God (*Ruḥu'lláh*), passed into His Church and is manifested in them; therefore was it that when His Holiness, the Point of Revelation (*i.e.* the Báb) was asked 'What are the Firangís?' he replied, 'They are Spirit.' You are to-day the Manifestation of Jesus, you are the Incarnation of the Holy Spirit, nay, did you but realise it, you are God!"

"God forbid!" I exclaimed again, "speak not after this impious fashion, and know that I regard myself as the least of God's servants and the most inconsistent and unworthy of those who profess to take the Lord Jesus as their pattern and exemplar!"

"'*Verily, I am a man like unto you!*'" shouted Sheykh Ibráhím; "thus said the Prophet, whose object, like all the prophets who preceded and followed him, was to make us *men*. So said Behá to me in Acre, 'I desire that all men should become even as I am!' If any one says that Behá has attained to anything whereunto we also may not attain, he lies and is an ignorant fool!" Here he glared fiercely round the assembly to see if anyone would venture to contradict him, and, as no one did so, continued: "On the forehead of every man is written, in that writing whereof you wot, either '*Hádhá Mu'min*' ('This is a Believer'), or '*Hádhá Káfir*' ('This is an Infidel'). On that side of your forehead uncovered by the bandage which you have bound over your eye I read '*Hádhá Mu'*...,' and I know that were the bandage removed I should see '*-min*' written on the other side. O *Jenáb-i-Ṣáḥib!* O *Ḥaẓrat-i-Firangí!* when you go back to Firangistán you must stir up trouble and mischief (*fitné ú fasád*); you must make them all Bábís."

They talked much after this fashion, while I listened in consternation, half-frightened at their vehemence, half-disgusted at their doctrines, yet withal held spell-bound by their eloquence. "Was this, then," I thought to myself, "the root of the matter, the heart of that doctrine which promised so fairly, whereof the votaries whom I have hitherto met seemed so conspicuous for their probity, piety, sobriety, and devoutness? Have I mistaken for a gleam of heaven-sent light a will-o'-the-wisp, born of the dead, disintegrated creeds of Mazdak and el-Moḳanna', and the terrible 'Old Man of the Mountain,' before the daggers of whose emissaries the chivalry of East and West fell like the grass before the scythe of the mower? And have I tracked it onwards, step by step, only to find at last that its home is in this quagmire of antinomian anthropomorphism? Or are these indeed no more Bábís than they are Muḥammadans, but men who, in true Persian fashion, disguise atheism in the garb of religion, and bedeck it with the trinkets of a mystical terminology?"

At length, long after midnight, we adjourned for supper to the other buildings, and, ere the conclusion of the meal, Sheykh Ibráhím's conversation grew so blasphemous and disgusting that on the first opportunity I arose and returned, distressed and angry, to the summer-house, followed by my guests. The merchant from Rafsinján, whose conversation had throughout been more moderate and reasonable than that of the others, and Fatḥu'lláh, the minstrel, whose vehemence was the outcome of an emotional and excitable nature—not of wine, which he eschewed—noticed my disgust, and approached me to enquire its cause.

"What is it that has offended me?" I replied: "What should it be but Sheykh Ibráhím's disgusting behaviour? The all-controlling influence exerted by the Prophetic Word over the hearts of men is one of the chief proofs to which you appeal in support of your religion. Is not wine forbidden in your religion as rigorously as in Islám? What is the use of your professing all this devotion to him whom you regard as the Mouthpiece of God, and kissing the *Kitáb-i-Aḳdas*, which you regard as the Word of God, if you condone so gross a violation of the laws which it contains, and of all laws, whether of religion, ethics, or good taste?"

Sheykh Ibráhím at this moment staggered up to us with cries

of drunken defiance, and, laying his hand on my arm, demanded what we were talking about. I shook him from me with a gesture of uncontrollable loathing, and, followed by the other two, retired to a little distance from the summer-house.

"You are right," they rejoined, as soon as we were out of Sheykh Ibráhím's sight and hearing, "and the Sheykh's conduct is to be deplored. But then old habits will force themselves to the surface at times, and, after all, to know and recognise the Truth is the great thing."

"But action is better than assent," said I, "and to do is greater than to know. What think you of this parable which we find in our Gospels?" And I repeated to them the parable of the two sons bidden by their father to go and do his work, of whom the one said, "I go," and went not, and the other said, "I will not go," but afterwards went.

"Ay," said they, "but for all that, both were sons. Knowledge is like a telescope, wherewith we view the distant Land of Promise. We may be standing in the mud, chilled by snow and sleet, or drenched with rain, yet with this telescope we may see and correctly describe the orange and myrtle-groves of the Promised Land. And this knowledge the Sheykh has none the less, because at times he wallows, as now, in the mud of sin."

"But this vision of the Promised Land," I replied, "is of no use unless you set out to reach it. Better is he who, without seeing it or knowing where it lies, faithfully follows one who will lead him thither, though he be compelled to walk blindly, than he who supinely gazes at it through this telescope."

They were silent for a while, distressed, as it seemed, at my distress, and somewhat ashamed of the Sheykh's conduct. Then said the merchant of Rafsinján:—

"*Ṣáḥib*, we will now bid you farewell and depart, for see, the dawn grows bright in the sky, and we had best return."

"Nay," I answered, fearing lest I had offended them, "tarry

at least till the city-gates are open, and sleep for a while, and then depart in peace."

But they would not be persuaded, and departed with sorrowful and downcast faces, all save Sheykh Ibráhím (who was in no condition to move) and 'Abdu'lláh, who would not forsake his friend. So I left these two in the summer-house, and went back to the room where we had eaten supper, and bathed my eye, which had again become very painful, and, after a time, fell asleep.

It was the afternoon of the next day when I awoke, and learned with some relief that 'Abdu'lláh had departed soon after the other guests, and the Sheykh about noon. My eye was so painful that it was impossible to think of going out, and there was nothing to distract my attention from the pain which I suffered (for to read was, of course, impossible) till, about three hours before sunset, a telegram from my friend, the Chief of the Telegraph at Yezd, was brought to me, informing me that he had just received my letter and had answered it by that day's post, and enquiring after my health. The telegram must have travelled very slowly, or the letter very fast, for hardly had I finished writing the answer to the former when the latter was brought by the postmaster of Kirmán, who was accompanied by the young Bábí merchant, Áḳá Muḥammad Ṣádiḳ. In the letter, which was most kindly worded, were enclosed copies of two poems for which I had asked—the one by Ḳurratu'l-'Ayn [1], the other by Jenáb-i-Maryam, the sister of the Báb's first apostle, Mullá Ḥuseyn of Bushraweyh. These I showed to my visitors, who read them with manifest delight, and, the subject being thus introduced, the conversation turned on the Bábís, and especially on Ḳurratu'l-'Ayn, of whose death the postmaster gave me the following account, which he professed to have had from the lips of her gaoler, Maḥmúd Khán the Kalántar:—

1 Of this poem, which is written in the same rhyme and metre as that translated at p. 535, *supra*, the text and translation will be found at pp. 314–16 of vol. ii of my *Traveller's Narrative*.

"The day before she suffered martyrdom," said the postmaster, "she told those about her that her death was to take place, saying, 'To-morrow evening the Sháh will send after me, and his messenger will come riding, and will desire me to mount behind him. This I do not wish to do, wherefore I pray you to lend me one of your horses, and to send one of your servants to escort me.' Next day all this came to pass. When she was brought in before the Sháh in the palace of the Nigáristán, and bidden to renounce the Báb, she refused, and persisted in her refusal. So she was cast into a well which is in the garden, and four large stones were thrown down upon her, and the well was then filled up with earth. As for Maḥmúd Khán, he was, as you know, strangled by order of the father of Prince Náṣiru'd-Dawla, our governor, during the bread-riots in Ṭeherán, and his body dragged by the feet through the streets and bazaars."[1]

The postmaster also talked a little about the Ezelís, saying that they were more numerous in Kirmán than anywhere else, and that even in Kirmán they were but few in number. Amongst them he mentioned Fatḥu'lláh, the minstrel, and a certain *mullá* whom I will call Mullá Hádí, but the Sheykh of Ḳum he would not include in his enumeration, "for," said he, "though he sympathises with the Ezelís and courts their society, he is in point of fact a free-thinker and a materialist." After the departure of these guests I was visited by my Zoroastrian friends, Gushtásp and Ferídún, who came to condole with me, and to enquire after the ophthalmia, repeating over and over again, "*Bad na-báshad!*" ("May it not end ill!"), till I was depressed not a little.

Monday, 8*th July*, 28*th Shawwál*.—This morning I received a visit from one Murtaẓá-ḳuli Khán Afshár, who, soon after his arrival, produced a great roll of verse in manuscript, from

1 The accounts of Ḳurratu'l-'Ayn's death are very various, but this one, at least, I do not regard as having any claims to authenticity. Cf. Gobineau's *Religions et Philosophies dans l'Asie Centrale*, pp. 292–95; Polak's *Persien*, vol. i, p. 353; and my *Traveller's Narrative*, vol. ii, pp. 313, 314.

which he proceeded to read me selections. This verse was, I fancy, his own composition, but about the writer I could learn no more than that his poetical pseudonym (*taḵhalluṣ*) was *Bí-nawá*, and that he was still living. My visitor was very anxious to give me the manuscript, so that I might take it back with me to Europe and get it printed, but I excused myself, assuring him that it could be better and more conveniently published in Persia. In point of fact it was not worth publishing anywhere, being remarkable only for its monotonous harping on the topics of death, corruption, and the torments of hell, and for its badness of taste and poverty of style. Over and over again was this idea repeated in substance: "How many moon-faced beauties, whose stature was as that of the cypress tree, have gone down into the grave with only scorpions, snakes, worms, and ants for their companions in their narrow bed!" Only one poem, in praise of the reigning king, offered the least variety. This began with an account of the Sháh's travels in Europe, which was followed by a description of the Bábí rising and its suppression, a long passage being devoted to Ḳurratu'l-'Ayn. My visitor remained with me for some time after I had succeeded in checking this recitation of doggerel, but his conversation was not much more lively than his verse, for he talked of nothing else but the horrors of hell and the delights of paradise, both of which he depicted in the crudest and most grossly material colours.

Tuesday, 9th July, 29th Shawwál.—This evening I was again the guest of the Zoroastrians at the garden of Mullá Serúsh, and sat down to supper with some twenty-five followers of "the Good Religion." The evening passed much as usual, with wine, song, and minstrelsy, save that one Fírúz by name, having taken rather more to drink than was good for him (a rare thing amongst the Zoroastrians), favoured the company with a rather vulgar imitation of the performances of dancing-boys. There was some talk of Zoroaster and the miracles ascribed to him, and of the descent to earth of ten flames (*ádhar*), distinguished from fire (*átash*) by being devoid of all property of scorching or burning. Three of these, so my hosts informed me, had returned to heaven, and one had in recent times migrated from Khurásán, where it suffered neglect, to Yezd. It was not till after midnight that I was suffered to depart, and then only on giving a promise that I would return first thing the next morning.

It was on this night that a jerk of the chain which I had suffered Sir Opium to wind round me, first made me conscious of the fact that I had dallied over-long with him. Eight days had now elapsed since this dalliance began, and, though I had smoked what may well be termed "the Pipe of Peace" pretty regularly during this period, the fact that once or twice I had abstained from smoking it at the usual time, without suffering inconvenience, had lulled me into a false sense of security. "After all," I had said to myself, "a great deal of exaggeration is current about these things; for how few of those in England who talk so glibly about the evils of opium-smoking, and waste their time and other people's money in trying to put a stop to it, have any practical acquaintance at all with it; and, on the other hand, how many of my friends here, when they feel depressed and worried, or want to pass a quiet evening with a few congenial friends in discussing metaphysics and ontology, indulge in an occasional pipe. However, this resolution I make, that on the day when I shall be well enough to go out of this garden I lay aside my pretty opium-pipe (*váfúr*), with its *síḳh* (cleaning rod) and its *anbur* (charcoal tongs), which shall be to me thenceforth but as curiosities to hang up in my college rooms when I get back to Cambridge."

Well, to-night, as I reluctantly admitted to myself, the time had come to put my resolution into practice. And how did I do it? I kept it, after a fashion, just for that one night—and what a night it was! In vain I longed for sleep, in vain I tossed to and fro on my couch till the stars grew pale in the sky, for an indefinable craving, to which was presently superadded a general sense of uneasiness pervading all the facial nerves, warred with the weariness which possessed me. I was ashamed to wake my servant and bid him kindle a fire, else had my resolution not held even for one night; indeed, as it was, it can hardly be said to have held, since at last in desperation I drenched some tobacco in laudanum, taken from the little medicine-chest I had with me, rolled it into a cigarette, and tried, though with but little satisfaction, to smoke it.

And this is the way of opium. You may smoke it occasionally at long intervals, and feel no after-craving. You may smoke it for two or three days consecutively, and abandon it without difficulty; then you may, after an interval of one or two days, do the like once more, and again forsake it; and then, having smoked it once or twice again, you will try to put it from you as before, and you will find you cannot—that the fetters are forged which, likely enough, you will wear for ever. So next day I relapsed into bondage, and, when a few days later I told my plight to a friend of mine (the Prince's secretary and an Ezelí Bábí), who was a confirmed "*váfúrí*" (opium-smoker), he clapped his hand on his thigh and exclaimed, "*Ḥálá dígar guẓasht! Váfúrí shudé-íd!*" ("Now, at any rate, it is all over! You have become an opium-smoker!"). Neither did he say this without a certain air of contentment, if not of exultation; for it is a curious fact that, although the opium-smoker will, as a rule, never tire of abusing his tyrant, he will almost always rejoice to see another led into the same bondage, and will take the new captive by the hand as a brother.

Thursday, 11*th July*, 2*nd Dhi'l-ḳa'da.*—Last night I received a telegram from Shíráz informing me that a telegram addressed to me there had arrived from England, in which I was requested to signify my acceptance of the post of Persian Lecturer, to which I had been appointed at Cambridge. Accordingly, I went into the city an hour or two after sunrise to despatch an answer. Near the Mosque Gate I met Ustá Akbar, the pea-parcher, who invited me to lunch with him when I had completed my business. I readily accepted his invitation, and walked with him to his shop, where I stayed talking with him for a few minutes. A young Tabrízí named Raḥmán Beg was there, and Ustá Akbar, pointing at him, asked me jestingly, "whether I could make this Turk a Bábí?"

My business at the telegraph-office did not take long. The telegram, though destined for England, had, of course, to be written in Persian, and I managed to condense it, including the address, into seven words, for which I paid twenty *ḳráns* and thirteen *sháhís* (about 16*s.* 6*d.*), the tariff having luckily been reduced within the last few days. I then returned to Ustá Akbar's house and had lunch with him, after which I wrote some letters, including one to Prince Náṣiru'd-Dawla, the governor. In this I ventured to say a few words in favour of Mírzá Yúsuf of Tabríz (at whose urgent request, supported by Seyyid Ḥuseyn of Jandaḳ, I had been induced to take what certainly was rather a liberty), asking the Prince, in case he could not find him employment, whether he would give him the means of reaching his native town of Tabríz, where he had friends and relatives.

I stayed to supper with Ustá Akbar, Fatḥu'lláh, the Ezelí minstrel, being the only other guest. We ate our meal on the roof (for it was a beautiful moonlight night), and sat so late talking, drinking tea, and smoking opium, that, as the time for shutting the city-gates had long passed, I agreed to my host's proposal that I should spend the night there. Bolsters, pillows, and quilts were accordingly brought up on to the roof, but, though our host soon composed himself to sleep, I sat late talking to the Ezelí. I asked him to tell me how he had become a Bábí, and he related as follows:—

"A year or two ago," he began, "I fell desperately in love; so that, on the rare occasions when my good fortune suffered me to pass a few moments in the presence of my beloved, I was for the most part as one annihilated and overcome with bewilder-

ment, submerged in the ocean of adoration, and repeating in the
language appropriate to my condition Sheykh Saʻdí's lines—

> "*Ajab-ast bá vujúdat ki vujúd-i-man bi-mánad;*
> *Tu bi-guftan andar á'í, ú mará sukhan bi-mánad!*"

'The wonder is that I survive the while I gaze on thee;
That thou should'st speak, and power of speech should still be left to me!'

Or, as another has said—

> '*Agar khwáham gham-i-dil bá tu gúyam, já namí-yábam;*
> *Agar já'í kunam peydá, turá tanhá namí-yábam;*
> *Agar tanhá turá yábam, va já'í ham kunam peydá,*
> *Zi shádí dast u pá gum mí-kunam, khud-rá namí-yábam!*'

'I find no place where I to thee my passion may declare,
Or, if I find the place, with thee I find my rival there,
Or, if at length I find a place, and find thee there alone,
In vain I seek myself, for self has melted into air!'

But more often it happened that I was compelled to bear with
separation, and then I would console myself as best I might by
reading and singing the odes of Saʻdí, which seemed to me
specially applicable to my condition.

"Now one day a friend of mine begged me to lend him my
Diván of Saʻdí, promising to give me instead another and a
better book. With some reluctance I consented to the exchange,
and received from him the mystical *Maṣnaví* of Jalálu'd-Dín
Rúmí. When I began to read this, I at first bitterly repented the
bargain. 'What is all this,' I asked myself, 'about the flute
making lamentation because of its separation from the reed-bed—
and what has it to do with me?' But gradually the inner meaning
began to dawn upon me; the love of the True and Eternal
Beloved displaced from my heart the earthly passion which had
filled it; and I realised the meaning of what the mystics say, '*El-
Mejáẓu kanṭaratu'l-Ḥaḳíḳat*' ('the Phenomenal is the Bridge to
the Real'). Yes,

> '*Imrúẓ Sháh-i-anjuman-i-dilbarán yakíst,*
> *Dilbar agar haẓár buvad, dilbar án yakíst.*
> *Man behr-i-án yakí du jihán dáda-am bi-bád;*
> '*Aybam ma-kun, ki ḥáṣil-i har du jihán yakíst.*'

'To-day, at the Feast of Fair ones, to One is assigned the Throne,
For though of the fair there are thousands there, in beauty He stands alone.
For Him I forsake this world and that, and am counted in both undone;
Withhold your blame, nor think it shame, for the sum of the worlds is One.'

"One day, passing by the city-gate, I heard a man reading from a book which he held in his hand. The sweetness of the words and their dignity charmed me, and I stopped to ask him what book it was. At first he appeared unwilling to tell me, but at length, yielding to my persuasion, he told me that it was the *Beyán* of Mírzá 'Alí Muḥammad, the Báb. He consented to lend me the book for a while; and as I read it my assurance increased that this indeed was the Word of God."

"What, then, think you of Behá?" I demanded, "for these would make him greater than the Báb."

"I know not," he replied; "for me the Báb sufficeth, neither can I comprehend a station higher than His."

Friday, 12th July, 3rd Dhi'l-ḳa'da.—I woke late, and found that Fatḥu'lláh and Ustá Akbar had both gone out, the latter leaving word that he would return soon. An old man named Mírzá Ja'far, a dervish of the Dhahabí order, presently arrived. He told me that he was at present engaged in fasting and other religious exercises, and that he had an "Inner Light." Presently Ustá Akbar returned with a shoemaker of his acquaintance, named Ustá Ghulám Riẓá, who brought with him a book of verses composed in praise of Behá by the Bábí poet Nabíl. These, which in their eulogies were fulsome beyond belief, he proceeded to read, the pea-parcher encouraging him with occasional exclamations of "*Zíbá mí-ḳhwánad!*" ("He does read nicely!"). During a momentary pause the Dhahabí dervish ventured to make some remarks containing an allusion to his "Inner Light," whereupon the shoemaker turned savagely upon him, crying—

"Who cares for your 'Inner Light,' owl and bat that you are? The Sun of Truth shines radiant in the mid-heaven of the Theophany, and do you dare obtrude your foolish fancies and vain imaginings, or seek to distract us thereby from that which will truly advantage us?"

At this arrogant and insolent speech anger overcame me, and I said to the shoemaker—

"Silence! How dare you speak in so unseemly a manner to this old man, who, according to his belief, is seeking to draw near to God? After all, age is revered and courtesy of demeanour approved in every religion, and you do but ill commend to others the creed which you profess by conduct such as this." Then the shoemaker hung his head and was silent.

On my way home I called on Áḳá Muḥammad Ṣádiḳ, the young Bábí merchant, at the caravansaray where he dwelt, and he, on learning that I had taken to smoking opium, entreated me to abandon it ere it was too late. He also begged me to lend him the manuscript of the *Kitáb-i-Aḳdas* ("Most Holy Book") which had been given to me at Shíráz, that he might transcribe it for himself, and this request, at least, I was ready to grant, though the other, as I began to fear, came too late.

When I returned to my garden about sundown I found that Seyyid Ḥuseyn of Jandaḳ had been several times to see me, and had enquired most persistently as to my whereabouts; and that Sheykh Ibráhím, his friend 'Abdu'lláh, and a dervish who had brought me a present of apples, were still patiently awaiting my arrival. I found them sitting by one of the streamlets near the summer-house, and half a glance sufficed to show me that that Sheykh, at least, was a good deal the worse for drink. As I approached he greeted me with a loud screech of welcome, and strove to stagger to his feet, but quickly subsided into the expectant arms of 'Abdu'lláh, crooning out a couplet from the *Maṣnaví*, which, when he was in this state, he never tired of repeating—

"*Bádé ney dar har sarí shar mí-kunad;*
Ánchunán-rá ánchunán-tar mí-kunad."

"'Tis not in every head that wine works ill;
That which is *so*, it maketh *more so still*."

After informing me with some incoherence that he was charged with a message to me from one of the principal physicians of Kirmán inviting me to lunch with him on the following day, he continued, chuckling to himself at the reminiscence—

"Your friend the Seyyid of Azghand" (so he chose to call him, confounding this place with Jandaḳ, which was in reality his birthplace) "has been here, but I, your most humble servant and sincere friend Sheykh Ibráhím (now, as you perceive, not quite himself), have put him to flight, together with another rascally Seyyid whom he brought with him."

"I wish you would not insult my guests," said I. "Who was this other Seyyid?"

"How do I know?" he shouted defiantly; "all I know is this, that just outside the garden-gate he was attacked by a singularly intelligent dog, and came in here shaking with fright. When he had somewhat recovered, he and the Azghandí Seyyid began talking about you. 'What like is this Firangí?' enquired he. 'Not a bit like other Firangís,' replied the Azghandí, 'inasmuch as, instead of going after old tiles and other rubbish such as they mostly love, he goes after religions, and consorts with Musulmáns, Sheykhís and Bálásarís, Ṣúfís, and even Zoroastrians.' 'How about Bábís?' asked the other. 'How should I know?' says the Azghandí. 'My brother when on a journey once occupied the opposite litter (*ḳajávé*) to the chief of their gang,' continued he. Then I felt it was high time to put him to rights a bit, so I said, 'You ugly, wizened old fox (for, in the World of Similitudes I behold you as such, and so did that most sagacious dog who wished to tear you in pieces at the door, in which wish I hope he may be more successful when you depart), what do you know about Bábís, and how dare you speak of one whose greatness and glory far transcend your mean comprehension in such disrespectful terms?' I saw him change colour, and soon after he left, without waiting for the tea which your excellent servant Ḥájí Ṣafar was preparing for him. Ḥájí Ṣafar! Ḥájí Ṣafar! Where is Ḥájí Ṣafar?"

Ḥájí Ṣafar approached. He was sulky and morose, offended, as it appeared, at my having remained so long away without telling him where I had gone, and grumbled accordingly. I bade him be silent, and Sheykh Ibráhím continued in a loud and aggressive tone—

"I have heard from the postmaster how he surprised you in close confabulation with those foul and benighted Ezelís at the house of the Sheykh of Ḳum. Mullá Hádí, a noted Ezelí, was there, and you were talking glibly enough when the postmaster entered, but, on seeing him, you at once changed the conversation."

Presently, to my great relief, Sheykh Ibráhím and 'Abdu'lláh rose to depart. As they were leaving, Ḥájí Ṣafar met us, and again complained of my want of consideration for him in leaving him ignorant of my whereabouts. Sheykh Ibráhím loudly applauded his solicitude, which I, on the other hand, was inclined to resent as impertinence. In consequence, we had words, and he threatened to leave me on the morrow and return to Ṭeherán; but later on, when he brought my supper, he had repented of his decision, and offered an apology for his conduct, explaining it by saying that he had just had news that his mother was seriously ill, and that this had greatly disturbed his mind, and caused him to forget himself.

Saturday, 13th July, 4th Dhi'l-ḳa'da.—According to my promise, I lunched to-day with the physician of whom I have already spoken. On my arrival I found Sheykh Ibráhím (already much disguised in liquor) and 'Abdu'lláh, together with my host and his little boy, a pretty child of eight or nine years of age, who amused us by repeating 'Obeyd-i-Zákání's celebrated poem of "the Cat and the Mouse" (*Músh-u-gurbé*). In the evening I was the guest of my host's rival, a physician of the old Galenic school, with a splendid contempt for the new-fangled doctrines of pathology and treatment which are beginning to make way amongst the medical men of Ṭeherán. His son was a determined Bábí, and confided to me his intention of running away from Kirmán and setting out alone and on foot for Acre. Ustá Akbar joined us presently, and after supper we sat late, talking, drinking tea, and smoking opium.

Sunday, 14th July, 5th Dhi'l-ḳa'da.—Soon after we had drunk our morning tea I left, and paid a visit to one of my Ezelí friends, the Prince's secretary, who invited me to stay to lunch. In the intervals of conversation he amused himself by making the tea-glasses float in the little tank which occupied the middle of the room, pushing them from one side to the other, and objurgating them with shouts of "*Gúr-i-pidar-ash la'nat!*" ("Curses on the grave of its father!"), when, receiving too violent a push, they filled with water and sank to the bottom. On returning to the garden about sunset I found that a number of visitors, including the postmaster and two of his men, the Prince-Telegraphist, the insufferable Ḥájí Muḥammad Khán, and Mullá Yúsuf and Fatḥu'lláh, the Ezelís, had been to see me, while the Sheykh of Ḳum and one of his friends were still awaiting my arrival. The Sheykh brought me a photograph of Prince Náṣiru'd-Dawla bearing an inscription in his own hand, together with a very kind answer to the letter which I had addressed to him some days previously concerning Mírzá Yúsuf of Tabríz. This letter, even after making a large deduction for Persian politeness, was so gratifying that I cannot forbear translating it—

"My dear and respected Friend,

"From the receipt of your letter, and the perusal of the pleasing contents of your script, I derived the utmost gratification. My delight at the handwriting and coherent diction of that honoured friend was chiefly owing to the fact that it is in Europe that you have thus perfectly acquired the Persian language, and have obtained so thorough a mastery of composition and style. May God, if it so please Him, bring this dear friend of mine safely back to his native country, and gladden him with the sight of his honourable father and mother and kindred! I regret having met that dear friend so seldom, nor has your sojourn in Kirmán been of any length; yet such is the regard which I have conceived for you during this short period that it will never quit my heart.

'Hamíshé dar barábar-i-chashmam muṣavvarí.'
'Thy face will stand depicted for ever in my sight.'

I shall ever supplicate God for your safety and advancement, and I shall be much pleased if now and then a letter from you should reach me from Firangistán. As for Mírzá Yúsuf, the request of that honoured friend is of course most gladly granted by me, and I have ordered that he shall receive money for the expenses of his journey....I send a portrait of myself as a keepsake for that dear friend."

When I had read this letter, the Sheykh of Ḳum informed Mírzá Yúsuf of Tabríz that fifteen *túmáns* (about £5) was the sum assigned to him by the Prince. Mírzá Yúsuf was, of course, overjoyed, and Seyyid Ḥuseyn of Jandaḳ, who had interested himself a good deal in the matter, was also very pleased, "but," said he to me, "don't suppose that these fifteen *túmáns* were given to Mírzá Yúsuf; they were given to you, and the obligation lies on your neck, for so much money was not raised in Kirmán save at the price of blood." This, of course, was a mere figure of speech, yet it somewhat damped my joy, and would have done so more had I known how worthless Mírzá Yúsuf would prove himself.

Monday, 15th July, 6th Dhi'l-ḳa'da.—To-day I lunched with the Sheykh of Ḳum, where I met the young Ezelí artillery officer of whom I have already spoken. After lunch the Prince's head-cook dropped in. He was an amusing fellow, and had seen something of the world, having been for some time a servant at the Persian Embassy in London, in the remembrance of which he gloried. It was he, I found, who had prepared the elaborate meal of which I had partaken with the Prince-Governor, for he had learned the art of European cookery while in London, though, as he told me, the ambassador, unless he had company, generally preferred to have Persian dishes set before him. I asked him whether the materials for these were generally forthcoming in London. "Oh yes," he replied, "I found them without much difficulty in the shops, but of course I made the ambassador pay well for them. I would buy egg-plants (*bádinján*), for instance, at a few pence each, and when I returned I would tell him with a long face that things were terribly dear here, and that I had paid a shilling apiece for them. Yes, those were fine times, and I wish I were back in London again."

The cook presently departed, and the Sheykh began to speak more freely about Behá than he had hitherto done. He produced a copy of the lithographed Bombay edition of the *Íḳán*, which he told me had been sent him by the Behá'ís, and pointed out with great disapproval a passage where the Shí'ites are called "that foul and erring sect." He also showed me some letters addressed to him and other Ezelís by Behá, and took great exception to several passages in them, especially to one where Behá said, "A child who has been blessed by beholding me is greater than all the people of the Beyán." Then he gave me an account of the attempt on the Sháh's life by the Bábís in 1852, which I will not repeat here, as I have already published it in the second volume of my *Traveller's Narrative* (pp. 323–4). The young artillery officer told me that for four years he had in vain sought to enter into relations with the Bábís, and had only succeeded at last by acquainting himself with a part of their terminology, and so leading some of his acquaintances whom he believed to be adherents of the sect to make open confession of their doctrines in his presence.

Tuesday, 16*th July*, 7*th Dhi'l-ḳa'da*.—This afternoon I paid a visit to Mírzá Jawád's house. He himself was away, but I found his son and one or two other boys reading with their tutor, Mullá Ghulám Ḥuseyn, who, on my arrival, at once dismissed the class. I made some further enquiries of him concerning the Sheykhí literature, and he gave me the following supplementary list of books:—By Sheykh Aḥmad Aḥsá'í, "The Commentary on the 'Visitation'" (*Sharḥ-i-Ziyárat*) and the *Favá'id* (text and commentary) in Arabic, and the "Aphorisms" (*Jawámi'u'l-ḳalám*) in Persian; by Ḥájí Seyyid Káẓim of Resht, the Commentary on 'Alí's sermon called the '*Khuṭba-i-Ṭuṭunjiyya*,' and the "Commentary on the Ḳaṣída"; by Ḥájí Muḥammad Karím Khán, the *Faṣlu'l-ḳhiṭáb* (on Tradition), the *Irshádu'l-'Awámm* ("Direction of the Common People"), the *Ṭaríḳu'n-naját* ("Way of Salvation"), the *Izháḳu'l-Báṭil* ("Crushing of Falsehood"), and the *Tír-i-Shiháb* ("Meteor-bolt"), both directed against the Bábís, the *Fiṭratu's-salíma* ("Sound disposition"), the *Nuṣratu'd-Dín* ("Help of Religion"), and the *Sulṭániyya*, an Apology for Islám, written in Persian.

Wednesday, 17*th July*, 8*th Dhi'l-ḳa'da*.—This morning, before I was dressed, Seyyid Ḥuseyn of Jandaḳ came to see me. While he was with me, an old man named Mashhadí 'Alí, who kept a shop just outside the city-gate, came to lodge a complaint against Ná'ib Ḥasan's brother, a muleteer whom I had some thoughts of engaging for the journey to Shíráz. He was accompanied by a *farrásh* sent by the *vazír* (who, in the absence of the Prince-Governor, was administering justice), and his complaint was that he had been subjected to a violent and unprovoked attack on the part of Ná'ib Ḥasan's brother, for which he demanded redress. He had been before the *vazír*, who said that, as the defendant was in some sort under my protection, he would prefer to leave his punishment to me; but that he hoped I would inflict the bastinado upon him, if the complainant could prove his case to my satisfaction. Now, I have no doubt that the *vazír* meant kindly, but I could not help wishing he would execute whatever he conceived to be justice according to his own lights, without making me a judge and arbiter over his subjects—a position which I was very far from coveting. The Seyyid, however, who saw only an unhoped-for opportunity of displaying his Solomon-like wisdom and delivering some epoch-making decision, was delighted, and bade Ḥájí Ṣafar bring the complainant, the defendant, the *farrásh*, and any witnesses who might be forthcoming, before us. The defendant was luckily away in the country, and as the only "witness" (if such he could be called, for it did not appear that he knew anything more about the case than that the defendant was his cousin, and therefore, in his view, to be exculpated) was Ḥájí Ṣafar, our little tribunal was of very modest dimensions. The "case," however, lasted some time, the complainant, the "witness," and the *farrásh* all talking at once, and the first two swearing to everything and at everybody, so that even the loquacious Seyyid could hardly make himself heard. At last, however, silence was obtained, and the Seyyid, with great gravity, gave it as his decision that Ná'ib Ḥasan's brother should give the defendant a new shirt as a token of regret for his alleged violence, on condition that the charge should be suffered to drop; and that the *farrásh* should receive a present in money from me for his trouble. And as this seemed the easiest way out of the difficulty, it was unanimously agreed to. I hope the old man got his shirt, but I cannot be sure of it, as the *farrásh*, having received his money, naturally lost all further interest in the case. I wished to give the old man the price of his shirt, but this the Seyyid would not permit, declaring that the *farrásh* would certainly take it from him.

I had lunch when the Seyyid left, and then began to write in Persian an account of my travels for the Prince-Governor, who had requested me to furnish him with a brief narrative of my journey. About two hours before sunset, however, the Seyyid came back, bringing with him two books, one a book of his own composition, called *Víráníyyé*, and the other one of Ḥájí Muḥammad Karím Khán's refutations of Bábí doctrine, from both of which he read to me aloud. I was laughing in my sleeve at the garbled account given by the Sheykhí leader of his rival's life and pretensions, when suddenly the Seyyid stopped reading, pricked up his ears, and began to gaze intently in the direction of the gate, whence arose mirthful peals of laughter, mingled with the notes of a flute.

"What is this unseemly noise?" he enquired angrily.

The question was answered a moment later by the appearance

of Mírzá Yúsuf of Tabríz, mounted on a white ass, fully caparisoned and laden with saddle-bags and other properties. He advanced towards the summer-house at a rapid amble, and, after displaying himself before us to his satisfaction, dismounted, seated himself before us with a conceited smirk, and awaited our congratulations. At this juncture, almost before the Seyyid had recovered power of speech, Sheykh Ibráhím joined us.

"'*Listen to the flute when it tells its tale!*'" cried the Seyyid, as soon as he could speak; "what does all this mean, Mírzá Yúsuf? Where did you get that donkey?"

"I bought it," replied Mírzá Yúsuf, "with the money His Royal Highness the Prince (may God prolong his life!) bestowed upon me."

"Bought it!" exclaimed the Seyyid, "why, you were a pauper, and this money, only granted you at the urgent request of the Ṣáḥib (on whose neck lies the burden of obligation to the Prince), was intended to convey you to Tabríz. And the saddle, the saddle-bags, your smart *ḳamar-band*, and your other gear, how did you get them?"

"I bought them too," answered Mírzá Yúsuf, pertly enough; "how else should I come by them? You don't suppose I stole them?"

"You bought them too!" repeated the Seyyid. "And may I ask how much money you have left out of the fifteen *túmáns* the Prince gave you?"

Mírzá Yúsuf pulled out three or four *ḳráns* from his pocket. "So much," he replied.

"And how are you going to get to Tabríz, may I ask, with three *ḳráns*?" demanded the Seyyid.

"On my donkey," retorted Mírzá Yúsuf with a laugh; "what else did I get it for?" No doubt he cherished hopes of extracting further sums of money from the charitable Bábís of Yezd, according to the plan which he had exposed with such refreshing simplicity to Sheykh Ibráhím and myself. But he could hardly allude to this in the Seyyid's presence.

"You impertinent little fool!" cried the Seyyid angrily; "is it for this that I have interested myself in your case—you who two days ago were so humble—'a poor orphan whom none would pity!'—you who would make me believe that you were so careful about your religious duties that Ḥájí Ṣafar's occasional neglect of his prayers pained your tender conscience, and who now come prancing into my presence on your precious ass deafening me with your unrighteous flute-playing?"

"You don't understand these things, Master Seyyid," rejoined Mírzá Yúsuf; "you are not a man of the world, but a recluse, a man of the pen and the pulpit, a votary of the rosary and the reading-desk." And he made a grimace aside to Sheykh Ibráhím, whom he expected to enlist on his side against the common enemy.

For once, however, the Sheykh was at one with the Seyyid. "It is related," said he, sententiously, "that once the ass complained to God, saying, 'Why hast Thou created me, seeing that Thou hast already created the Turk?' Answer came, 'Verily We have created the Turk in order that the excellence of thine understanding might be apparent.' Mírzá Yúsuf is a Turk, a Tabrízí. What would you have?"

So Mírzá Yúsuf, somewhat abashed, withdrew; and thereupon, as I anticipated, the Sheykh and the Seyyid began to quarrel about the manner in which the former had seen fit to treat the friend of the latter on the previous Friday. The Seyyid for his part was politely sarcastic.

"I said to my friend," quoth he, "'You have had the misfortune to displease the worthy Sheykh, no doubt inadvertently, by talking of one whom he affects to revere with unbecoming levity, and applying to him an appellation generally used of robber captains and the like. It would be best for you to propitiate him by presenting to him one of those inlaid and enamelled pen-cases in the manufacture of which you are so skilful.' He promised to follow my advice, and you may expect to receive his gift shortly."

"You are too considerate," rejoined the Sheykh, "but really I am unworthy of so great an honour." Then, suddenly losing control of his tongue, "And who, I should like to know, is this rascally brother of his who enjoyed the unmerited and unappreciated honour of travelling in the company of one whose greatness and holiness are as much beyond his comprehension as the splendour of the sun is beyond the comprehension of the bat or the mole? I will tell you who he is: he is now at Ṭeherán, and makes his living by buffoonery of the lowest kind, and the Sháh, who loves buffoonery, especially in a Seyyid, has given him the title of *Ḳiwámu's-Sádát*. There is another younger brother, who is in high favour with certain of the nobles about the court, and whose influence has conduced in no small degree to the exaltation of his family."

"And do you mean to say," enquired the Seyyid, aghast at the scandalous details of Persian Court life furnished by the Sheykh, "that this is the state of things prevailing in Ṭeherán, 'the abode of the Caliphate' (*Dáru'l-Khiláfat*), at the court of him whom we account the Defender of the Faith and Protector of Religion?"

"Assuredly I do," replied the Sheykh, "and I can tell you more surprising things than this if you care to hear them, from which you will be better able to judge of the claims which Náṣiru'd-Dín Sháh has to these titles." And thereupon he launched out into a variety of scandalous anecdotes, which it is to be hoped had no foundation in fact, and which in any case are best unrecorded. Neither could he be diverted from this topic till the Seyyid departed in consternation, an object at which, in all probability, he had from the first aimed.

"And now, Sheykh," I said, when we were alone, "will you tell me more fully about the murder of the seven Ezelís who were sent with Behá and his followers to Acre? You mentioned the fact a few days ago, and added that you had seen the assassins yourself during your stay there, and that they still received their prison allowance, though at large, and wore gyves on their ankles."

"Yes," replied the Sheykh, who had drunk enough *'araḳ* to render him communicative, and not enough to make him incoherent, "they were twelve in number who slew the Ezelís, and nine of them were still living when I was at Acre. This was the way of it. When Behá advanced his claim at Adrianople, and his half-brother, Ṣubḥ-i-Ezel, refused to admit it, the Bábís were divided into two factions, some going with the former, and some holding fast to the latter. So high did the feeling run that the matter ended in open strife, and two Ezelís and one Behá'í were killed. So the Turkish Government determined to separate the two, and arranged to banish Mírzá Yaḥyá (*Ṣubḥ-i-Ezel*) and his followers to a town in Cyprus near the sea-shore, of which I cannot now remember the name, and Mírzá Ḥuseyn 'Alí (*Behá'u'lláh*), with his family and adherents, to Acre. But, knowing the two factions to be on the worst possible terms, it occurred to them that it would be advantageous to themselves to keep a few of each in the stronghold of the other, so that, should any Persian or other traveller come to Acre or Cyprus with the intention of visiting Behá or Ezel, these adherents of the rival claimant to supreme power might co-operate with the government in throwing obstacles in his way. So they sent three of Behá's followers (one of whom, Mushkín-Ḳalam, so-called from his extraordinary skill in calligraphy, is still [1892] alive) to Cyprus with Ezel, and seven Ezelís with Behá to Acre.

"Now as far as concerned Ezel this plan worked well enough, for Mushkín-Ḳalam set up a little coffee-house at the port where travellers must needs arrive, and whenever he saw a Persian land, he would invite him in, give him tea or coffee and a pipe, and gradually worm out of him the business which had brought him thither. And if his object were to see Ṣubḥ-i-Ezel, off went Mushkín-Ḳalam to the authorities, and the pilgrim soon found himself packed out of the island. But at Acre it was different. The seven Ezelís—Áḳá Ján, called '*Kaj-Kuláh*' ('Skew-Cap'), who had served with distinction in the Turkish artillery; Ḥájí Seyyid Muḥammad of Iṣfahán, one of the original companions of the Báb; Mírzá Riẓá, nephew of the last, and a scion of the same royal race of the Ṣafavís (for both were descended from Sháh 'Abbás the Great); Mírzá Ḥaydar 'Alí of Ardistán, a wonderful fire-brand (*átashí gharíb*), beside whom our mutual friend Mírzá Muḥammad Báḳir of Bawánát was no more than a spark; Ḥájí Seyyid Ḥuseyn of Káshán; and two others, whose names I forget—lived all together in a house situated near the gate of the city. Well, one night, about a month after their arrival at Acre, the twelve Behá'ís of whom I have spoken determined (but without having received instructions from Behá) to kill them, and so prevent them from doing any mischief. So they went at night, armed with swords and daggers, to the house where the Ezelís lodged, and knocked at the door. Áḳá Ján came down to open to them, and was stabbed before he could cry out or offer the least resistance. He was a young man, but very strong, so that once in the Russian war he had without aid picked up a cannon-ball and thrown it into the mouth of the gun. Then they entered the house and killed the other six.

"When the Turks heard what had been done, they imprisoned Behá and all his family and followers in the caravansaray, but the twelve assassins came forward and surrendered themselves, saying, 'We killed them without the knowledge of our Master or any of our brethren; punish us, then, not them.' So they were imprisoned for a while; but afterwards, at the intercession of 'Abbás Efendí, Behá's eldest son, were suffered to be at large, on condition only of remaining in Acre, and wearing steel fetters on their ankles for a time."

"It was a horrible deed," I remarked.

"Nay," said the Sheykh, "it was soon over for them; I have seen worse than that myself. Love cannot exist without strife, and, as has been said, '*affliction is the portion of affection.*'"

"What do you allude to," enquired I, "when you say that you have seen worse than this yourself?"

"To an experience which befell me when I was a mere lad,"[1] answered the Sheykh, "and had but recently entered into this circle. I was in Sulṭán-ábád then—my native place—and the Friends used to meet regularly at night-time, the men in one room and the women in an adjoining apartment, to read the Holy Books and hold spiritual converse. All went well for a while; our conventicles escaped the notice of the authorities, and might have continued to do so, had it not been for a traitor, Mullá 'Alí, now *píshnamáz* of one of the mosques of Sulṭán-ábád (as his father Mullá Ḥuseyn was then) who, to insinuate himself amongst us and compass our destruction, feigned belief in our doctrines, and for five or six months continued to frequent our assemblies until he knew us all, and discovered where our books were concealed.

"Now this wretch used to be a constant visitor at the house of one of the chief adherents of our faith, a theologian named Mullá Muḥammad 'Alí, with whom he used to read the sacred books. One day he requested permission to borrow a copy of the *Beyán*, which was at once granted him. Having thus secured possession of the book, he forthwith proceeded to the house of Ḥájí Áḳá Muḥsin, the philosopher (*ḥaḳamí*), and laid it before him. Áḳá Muḥsin (whom a study of philosophy had rendered comparatively tolerant) invited Mullá Muḥammad 'Alí to his house to discuss the matter with him, intending, should he not succeed in convincing him and inducing him to renounce his opinions, to do no more than expel him and his associates from the city. He further summoned another leading Bábí, Mullá

1 The date of this occurrence, so far as the Sheykh could recollect it, was about A.H. 1278 (A.D. 1861–2).

Ibráhím, the author of commentaries on the *Kubrá*, *Shamsiyya*, and other treatises on Logic, and at that time tutor to Prince Náṣiru'd-Dawla, Governor of this city, whose father, Prince Nuṣratu'd-Dawla, was then Governor of Sulṭán-ábád. He was the first to arrive, and while these two were engaged in discussion, Ḥájí Seyyid Muḥammad Báḳir, *Mujtahid*, suddenly entered the room with a knife concealed under his cloak, and, seeing Mullá Ibráhím, cried out, 'Do you hold converse or engage in controversy with this viper?' Even as he spoke he drew forth his dagger, and smote the Bábí thrice—on the side of the head, the back of the neck, and the back of the chest—so that he fell dead to the ground. A moment later the other Bábí, Mullá Muḥammad 'Alí, ignorant of what had passed, entered the room, and was in turn stabbed by the *Mujtahid*, as was also a third, named Kerbelá'í Raḥmatu'lláh, who followed him.

"When news of these doings was brought to Prince Nuṣratu'd-Dawla, the Governor, he sent a message to the *Mujtahids*, saying, 'Leave this matter alone, for I will see to it.' Then he sent and arrested all the Bábís whose names were known to Mullá 'Alí the traitor, and furthermore caused a number of those whose opinions were suspected to pass before him, so that he might identify those whom he had seen at the Bábí conventicles. Some twenty or thirty of us in all, including myself, were denounced, and forthwith cast into a loathsome underground dungeon, where we lay, chained together in a row, hardly able to move, and in dire suspense, for that night and the whole of the next day.

"It was on the second night of our captivity that we heard a tramp of feet without; then the key grated in the lock, the door opened, and the executioner, accompanied by several of his assistants, bearing lanterns and the implements of his ghastly craft, entered. 'I am come to kill the Bábís,' said he, as the *farráshes* set down the lanterns on the floor; and we, of course, supposed that one and all we were doomed to die.

"I was seventh in the row. Passing the first and second,

the man of blood halted before Ustá Maḥmúd, the pea-parcher (*noḳhúd-biríz*), of Káshán. They forced open his mouth, crammed a wet handkerchief rolled into a ball into his gullet, and drove it down his throat with a wooden peg and a mallet. For a minute or two, with gaping mouth, blackening face, and eyes starting from his head, he continued to struggle; then he fell back on the floor, and one of the executioner's assistants sat on his face till the last quiver died away.

"They next came to Kerbelá'í Ḥaydar, the furrier (*pústíndúz*), of Kábul, whom they slew in like manner; and we, seeing this (for he was fourth in the row, next to Ustá Maḥmúd), made sure that all of us were to die. We were mistaken, however, for they passed by the fifth and sixth in the row, and myself (the seventh), and did not halt again till they came opposite to Mírzá Ḥasan of Sulṭán-ábád, the surgeon, who was next beyond me. And when they had made an end of him, and of Mírzá Aḥmad of Tafrísh, who sat next beyond him, they gathered up their instruments of death, together with the lanterns, and, without saying another word, left us there in the darkness, the living and the dead chained together.

"It was an awful night, as you may imagine, for us who lay beside our murdered companions, expecting to share their fate, or one yet worse, on the morrow. But amongst us was one poor hunchbacked cobbler, who, during the horrible scenes which had just been enacted, had not once changed colour, and he continued to console us, reciting poems suitable to our situation, chanting verses from the sacred books, and crying, 'A strange paradise is this! Yet, if we are to die to-morrow, it is at most that we shall eat so many pounds less of bread and meat ere our bodies return to the dust and our souls to the source whence they came.' He grew more excited as he talked, and at last, 'Let us kill one another now,' he said; 'I will show you how it may be done—I will press and press so gently that you shall hardly know it, on the veins of the neck, and life will ebb quietly away. How much better to die thus, in all love and affection, by the hands of our friends than as these did by the hands of the headsman!' It was only with the greatest difficulty that we could restrain him from carrying out his purpose, and so continue anxiously awaiting the morning.

"No more of us, however, were doomed to suffer death on this occasion, save one old woman, nearly seventy years of age, the wife of Ḥájí Áḳá Muḥsin's paternal uncle. Her they sent to Ṭeherán; and when they asked the Sháh what should be done with her, he said, 'It is not good for a woman to be imprisoned,' wherefore they strangled her in the women's apartments of the palace, and cast her body into a well. The rest of us were released about a fortnight later, after the governor had extorted from us as much money as he could—in my case three hundred *túmáns*."

I was not a little moved by this horrible story, and regarded the Sheykh with increased interest and respect, for after all a man who has looked death in the face (and such a death!) for conscience sake is worthy of respect, though he be a drunkard and a libertine. I could not help thinking what a strange combination of good and evil he must be—such a combination as would be almost impossible save amongst the Persians—but I only said:—

"You have suffered much for your faith, it would seem."

"Ay," he said, "nor was that the only time, though it was the most terrible. I was imprisoned in the jail (*anbár*) at Ṭeherán for three months and seventeen days, along with five other Bábís, Áḳá Jemál of Burújird, son of Mullá 'Alí, who was entitled 'the Proof of Islám' (*Ḥujjatu'l-Islám*); Mírzá Abu'l-Faẓl of Gulpáyagán, the secretary of Mánakjí, the Zoroastrian agent at the Persian Court, and the compiler, under his directions and instructions, of the *New History* of this Most Great Theophany[1];

1 This is a mistake. Mírzá Ḥuseyn of Hamadán was Mánakjí's secretary, and he it was who, with the help of Mírzá Abu'l-Faẓl, compiled the *New History*. See the Introduction to my translation of that work, pp. xxxiv–xlii.

Ustá Áhangar, Mullá 'Alí Akbar of Shimrán, and Ḥájí Mullá Ismá'íl *Dhabíḥ*. For the first three days and nights our captivity was very grievous, for, in the hopes of extorting money from us or our friends, they subjected us by day to various torments, and by night put our necks in the 'collar' (*ṭawḳ*), and our feet in the stocks (*ḳhalíl*), but we determined to bear our sufferings rather than appeal for money to our friends, knowing that to produce money would be only to increase the zeal of our tormentors. And after thus enduring for three days we were rewarded by an abatement of our torments."

Sheykh Ibráhím next related to me what had once passed between himself and the Sháh's eldest son, the Ẓillu's-Sulṭán, and the account given to him by the prince of the death of the martyrs of Iṣfahán, which, as I have already published it in the notes to the second volume of my *Traveller's Narrative* (pp. 401–3), I will not here repeat, especially as I have already referred to this episode more than once in the course of these pages. I then again attempted to ascertain his views on the future life and on the nature of the divinity ascribed to Behá, but the '*araḳ* which he had drunk was beginning to take effect, and he was growing gradually incoherent. Concerning the soul, he said that it was imperishable, and that when the body died it looked calmly and unconcernedly on at the preparations for interment. Pure and impure souls, he added, were like clean and dirty water—the pure poured back into the brook, the impure cast forth upon the ground to become mingled with it. As for Behá, the Sheykh said: "I have heard him say in my presence, 'I do not desire lordship over others; I desire all men to become even as I am.'" When I remarked that many of his followers declared him to be divine in quite another sense than those who, according to the Ṣúfí doctrine, had escaped from self and become merged in God, the Sheykh simply remarked, "Then they are in error." He added that Behá had forbidden him from preaching, or making any attempts at proselytising, saying that he had already suffered enough for his faith. And after this, the last rational remark to which he gave utterance, he relapsed into ribaldry and incoherence, and presently fell asleep.

Thursday, 18*th July,* 9*th Dhi'l-ḳa'da.*—Towards evening I went into the town and called at the post-office, where the postmaster lent me a poem in praise of Behá, composed by one Na'ím of Ábádé, a poor man of no education, whose power of verse-writing is regarded by his co-religionists as a divine gift, and little short of miraculous. His verses are partly in Persian, partly in Arabic, and of the latter, at any rate, it may truly be said that they are of the most miraculous character. Ustá Akbar, the pea-parcher, was also there. He was, after his wont, very mysterious, and informed me that a relation of the postmaster's, who was a "Mullá," and who possessed some of Ḳurratu'l-'Ayn's poems, was anxious to see me, but that I must not mention this to the postmaster, as he might be displeased. I was somewhat surprised at what appeared to me so unnecessary a stipulation, but attributed it to Ustá Akbar's love of mystery. It was only afterwards (for the pronouns in Persian do not distinguish gender) that I discovered that the "Mullá" in question was a lady, who regarded herself as a "manifestation" (*maẓhar*), or re-incarnation, of Ḳurratu'l-'Ayn. It was accordingly arranged that I should meet this "Mullá" on the next day but one, at the house of one of the officials of the post-office. As I did not know where he lived, I enquired as to how I should find my way thither. Ustá Akbar naturally selected the most cumbrous and mysterious method he could think of. I was to walk slowly past his shop at a certain hour on the Saturday in question, and he would tell his apprentice to be on the look-out for me, and, as soon as he saw me, to run out, pass me, and precede me at a distance of twenty or thirty yards to the rendezvous.

This plan was duly carried out, and on the afternoon of the appointed day I found myself in a room in the house of Ḥaydaru'lláh Beg, the postman, where, besides my host, were seated the "Manifestation of Ḳurratu'l-'Ayn" and a Bábí dervish, the former engaged in smoking a *ḳalyán*, the latter an opium-pipe. I was filled with astonishment at seeing a lady in the room, and my astonishment was increased when I heard the others address her as "Mullá," and ascertained that she was the learned Bábí who had expressed a wish to make my acquaintance. She greeted me very politely, bowing repeatedly as she exclaimed, "*Musharraf! Muzayvan! Chashm-i-má rawshan!*" ("[You have made the house] honoured [and] adorned! Our eyes are brightened!") and then asking me how long it was since I had believed. I was somewhat embarrassed by this question, and tried to explain that I was an enquirer only, whereupon she began to give a long and rather garbled version of Christ's prayer in the Garden of Gethsemane, which she concluded by bidding me not be like that disciple who denied his Master.

By this time eight or nine other persons had joined us, including Sheykh Ibráhím and his friend 'Abdu'lláh, in consequence of which the recitation of Ḳurratu'l-'Ayn's poems, which I had been so eager to hear, was postponed. Several Bábí books, however, were shown to me, including one containing the *Kalimát-i-Maknúna*, or "Hidden Words of Fáṭima,"[1] of which the surpassing eloquence was greatly praised by all present.

"Will you not smoke a *ḳalyán*?" enquired Sheykh Ibráhím, turning suddenly to me. I signified assent, and he called for one to be brought. "A good one, mind, for the Ṣáḥib," he cried, as the servant left the room.

In a minute or two the *ḳalyán* was brought, and as I took it, and, according to the customary etiquette, offered it in turn to all present before putting my lips to it, I fancied that I was watched with a certain attention and subdued amusement for which I could not account. The first whiff of smoke, however,

1 See vol. ii of my *Traveller's Narrative*, pp. 123–6, and n. 2 at foot of p. 123 and *Catalogue and Description of* 27 *Bábí MSS*. (*J.R.A.S.* for 1892), pp. 671–4

explained the cause of this. My experience with *Cannabis Indica* while I was a student at St Bartholomew's Hospital had not been altogether fruitless, since it had indelibly impressed on my memory the taste of this hateful drug, which now again, for the third time in my life, struck on my palate. "Oh," thought I to myself, "so this is the trick you thought to play on me, is it?" But I continued to smoke on slowly and deliberately till the Sheykh, unable any longer to control his curiosity, asked me how I found the *ḳalyán*.

"Nice enough," I answered, "but I fear it somewhat, for, unless I am much mistaken, you have put 'Master Seyyid'[1] into it."

I do not think that during the whole time I was in Persia I ever scored so great a success as by this simple remark. That I —a mere European—should be able to recognise the taste of *ḥashísh* was much, but that I should know it, so to speak, by its pet name, was indeed to prove myself well matured (*puḳhté*) by travel and the society of persons of experience.

"How ever did you know that?" enquired the Sheykh amidst the laughter and applause of the others.

"Because I am a Firangí must I needs be an ass?" I demanded, with a show of indignation.

Sheykh Ibráhím was delighted, and proceeded to unfold to me many mysteries connected with the use of narcotics in Persia. He told me of an oil called *Rawghan-i-Ḥashísh* ("Oil of Indian Hemp"), prepared from a plant named *Tátúré* (? Datura), of which half a *noḳhúd* would render a man insensible for twenty-four or thirty-six hours. This, he said, was often employed by

1 *Ḥashísh* is thought so badly of in Persia that it is usually spoken of, even by those who use it, by some nickname, such as *Áḳá-yi-Seyyid* ("Master Seyyid"), *Ṭúṭí-i-asrár* ("The Parrot of mysteries"), or simply *Asrár* ("Mysteries"), the first two alluding to its green colour. One of the odes of Ḥáfiẓ, beginning "*Aláyá ṭúṭí-yi gúyá-yi asrár, Mabádá khálíyat shakkar ẓi minḳár*" ("O Parrot, who discoursest of mysteries, may thy beak never want sugar!"), is addressed to the drug.

Persian adventurers in Turkey and Arabia (especially at Mosul and Mecca) to stupefy persons whom they wished to rob. Mixed with the food intended for the victim's consumption its flavour is imperceptible, and the protracted insensibility to which it gives rise allows the thief ample time to decamp. These revelations were, however, interrupted by the arrival of a *murshid*, or spiritual director, of the Sháh-Ni'matu'lláhí order of dervishes, who asked me point-blank what my religion was, and was much annoyed when I answered him with the well-known tradition, "*Ustur dhahabaka, wa dhahábaka, wa madhhabak*" ("Conceal thy gold, thy destination, and thy creed").

Monday, 22nd July, 13th Dhi'l-ḳa'da.—To-day another threatened collision between Seyyid Ḥuseyn of Jandaḳ and Sheykh Ibráhím was with difficulty averted. The former had dropped in during the afternoon to read me selected extracts from Ḥájí Muḥammad Karím Khán's attack on the Bábí doctrines, when the latter most inopportunely joined us. The two glared at one another for a while, and then the Seyyid, who had a really remarkable faculty for making things disagreeable, began to ask the Sheykh whether he had been to Acre lately, and other similar questions. I interposed, and, to my great relief, succeeded in changing the conversation, and getting the Sheykh to talk about his travels. He told us about the Yezídís (the so-called "Devil-worshippers") of Mosul and its environs. "They extend for a distance of three stages west of Mosul," said he, "and strange folk they are—uglier than you can imagine, with immense heads and long unkempt beards, and dressed in white or crimson clothes. They refuse to regard any sect or any person, even the Devil (whom they call '*Malaḳ-i-Ṭá'ús*,' the 'Peacock Angel'), as bad; and if any unwary traveller curses him, or 'Omar, or Shimr, or anyone else whom most men are wont to curse, or if he spits on the ground, they consider it incumbent on themselves to kill him, though every man of them should suffer death in retaliation. They have a sort of temple whither they repair for their devotions, and there, as I have heard (for none save themselves may enter), they from time to time spread a banquet, and then let loose a cock. If the cock eats the food, they consider their offering as accepted, but if not, as rejected."

Tuesday, 23rd July, 14th Dhi'l-ḳa'da.—In the afternoon I rode into town and visited the Sheykh of Ḳum. He called to his little daughter (a child six or seven years of age), who was on the roof, to come down and speak to me, but she, with precocious modesty, hid her face with a corner of her shawl and refused.

"Why wilt thou not come down and speak to the Firangí Ṣáḥib?" enquired her father.

"Because I am shy," cried the little one from the roof, peeping out from behind her extemporised veil.

"Thou art not wont to be so shy before others," he continued; "why then before this one?"

"I do not reckon them as men," she replied, with a toss of her head, and ran away to hide, while we both burst out laughing, and I remarked that such a compliment from the lips of a child was indeed gratifying.

The Sheykh talked rather freely about Bábíism. "The allegations made by the Musulmáns about the Bábís," said he, "though untrue, are in most cases founded to some extent upon fact. They say, for instance, that the Báb wrote Arabic which violated all the rules of grammar. This is not true; but it is true that he made use of grammatical forms which, though theoretically possible, are not sanctioned by usage, such as '*Waḥḥád*,' from *Waḥíd*; '*Farrád*,' from *Faríd*, and the like. So, too, they accuse Ḳurratu'l-'Ayn of unchastity. That is a lie—she was the Essence of Purity; but after His Holiness the Point [*i.e.* the Báb] had declared the Law of Islám abrogated, and ere he had promulgated new ordinances, there ensued a period of transition which we call '*Fatrat*' ('the Interval'), during which all things were lawful. So long as this continued she may very possibly have consorted, for example, with Mullá Muḥammad 'Alí of Bárfurúsh as though he had been her husband, though afterwards, when the New Law was revealed, she and all the others were most rigorous in its observance."

At this point we were joined by a certain Mullá whom I knew to be the chief Ezelí in Kirmán, and to have an enormous collection of Bábí books. I was extremely anxious to draw him into conversation on this topic, when, to my great chagrin, the postmaster (who was, as will be remembered, a determined Behá'í) was announced. He looked at us suspiciously, evidently guessing the subject which occupied our thoughts, and forthwith there fell upon us a sense of constraint which soon brought about the dispersion of the assembly.

On leaving the Sheykh's house I was making for the telegraph-office to condole with the Prince-Telegraphist on the death of his eldest son, the poor lad whom I had last seen smoking opium at the house of my friend, the secretary of the governor, when I was met by Mírzá 'Alí Naḳí Khán, the brother of the chief of the *Farráshes*, and by him detained in conversation. While we were talking, a murmur suddenly arose that the Prince-Governor was coming, and everyone began to bow down, with arms folded across their breasts, in humble obeisance. When the Prince saw me he called me to him, brought me with him into his garden, and bade his servants bring tea, *ḳalyáns* and cigarettes. He did not talk much, being busy reading a packet of letters which had just been placed in his hands, and examining a fine gold repeater which had arrived by the same post; so, when I had sat for a short time, I asked permission to retire—which was accorded me. I then proceeded to the telegraph-office, where I found the Prince-Telegraphist looking very sad and dejected, and surrounded by five or six Bábís of note, who, like myself, had come to offer condolence.

On returning to my garden about two hours after sunset, I found the pea-parcher and a rather notable dervish of the

Sháh-Ni'matu'lláhí order, named Sháhrukh, awaiting me. They had supper with me, and stayed all night. The dervish smoked a great quantity of opium and recited a vast amount of mystical poetry, of which his memory appeared to contain an inexhaustible store. The pea-parcher retired for a while, leaving us alone, and presently returned in a state of boastful intoxication. "I am Adam!" he cried, again and again; "I am Moses! I am Jesus! I am Muḥammad! What say you to that?" I was so disgusted that at last I could not refrain from answering, "Since you ask my opinion, I should say that you have had too much to drink, and are now talking blasphemous nonsense."

Wednesday, 24th July, 15th Dhi'l-ḳa'da.—My guests departed early, soon after sunrise, Ustá Akbar awakening me to communicate the message which had brought him to the garden on the previous evening. "There is a poor opium-kneader (*tiryáḳ-mál*) of my acquaintance," said he, "one of 'the Friends,' who is most anxious to entertain you at his house, and has so importuned me to bring you, that for the sake of peace I had to promise that I would do so. He wanted you to sup with him and stay the night at his house, but, having regard to its meanness, I told him that this would not be convenient to you, so it has been arranged that we shall lunch there to-morrow and spend the day. Come, therefore, in two hours' time to the caravansaray of Ganj 'Alí Khán, and there one shall meet you who will conduct you to the opium-kneader's house."

I fell asleep again when Ustá Akbar had gone, and did not awake for several hours. Just as I was going out with 'Abdu'l-Ḥuseyn I met the opium-kneader, who, poor man, had already come once to the garden that morning to guide me to his house, whither we at once proceeded. Ḥaydaru'lláh Beg, and Naṣru'lláh Beg of the post-office, a dervish named Ḥabíbu'lláh, and the pea-parcher, were the other guests, and later we were joined by the Prince-Telegraphist's secretary and Sheykh Ibráhím, who, though uninvited, had by some occult means discovered that an entertainment was in progress, which I suppose he considered would not be complete without his presence. Soon after my arrival the dervish-boy, whose sweet singing had so delighted me one day in the caravansaray of Ganj 'Alí Khán, entered the room with a *ḳalyán*, which he presented to me with the Bábí salutation, "*Alláhu Abhá.*" All those present, indeed, were Bábís; and after lunch, as we sat sipping our tea and taking an occasional whiff of opium, quantities of Bábí poems by Ḳurratu'l-'Ayn, Suleymán Khán, Nabíl, Rawḥá (a woman of Ábádé), and others, were produced and handed round or recited, together with the Báb's *Seven Proofs* (*Dalá'il-i-Sab'a*), Behá's *Lawḥ-i-Naṣír*, and other tracts and epistles. Before my departure I succeeded in arranging with the Prince-Telegraphist's secretary that he should copy out for me a selection of these treasures, which the owners kindly consented to place at his disposal.

Thursday, 25th July, 16th Dhi'l-ḳa'da.—In the afternoon I went into the city by the Mosque Gate, through which crowds of people were pouring forth to visit the cemetery, the "Eve of Friday" (*Shab-i-Jum'a*) being the favourite time for the performance of this pious act. The Bábí dervish-boy was amongst the crowd, and, dervish-fashion, placed a sprig of mint in my hand as he passed, but without asking or waiting for the small sum of money which is generally expected in return for this compliment. In the square of the caravansaray of Ganj 'Alí Khán, I saw Ustá Akbar standing, and approached him to speak with him. While we were conversing, there came up to me a certain dervish, who had once visited me in my garden, and craved an alms "for the sake of Behá." Now in general I made it a rule to respond, as far as possible, to such calls; but against this particular dervish I cherished some resentment, for this reason. On the day when he visited me in the garden, Sheykh Ibráhím chanced to be with me; and him, either from previous knowledge, or from some chance remark which he let drop, the dervish recognised as a Bábí. So when he had sat with us for a while, drunk several cups of tea, and pocketed a *ḳrán* and half a stick of opium, he went out, found Seyyid Ḥuseyn of Jandaḳ performing his ablutions at the stream by the gate, and told him that I was certainly a Bábí, or in a fair way to become one, since I was continually in the society of notorious Bábís. All this, of course, was repeated to me; and as I had treated this not very agreeable or intelligent dervish thus courteously rather on Sa'dí's principle that "the dog's mouth is best stopped with a morsel," I was naturally incensed at his indiscretion. So when he asked me "for the sake of Behá" to give him money, I bade him begone with scant ceremony; and when he continued to importune me, declaring that he had no bread for that night's supper, I turned angrily upon him, saying, "No opium, I suppose you mean!"

"Ay," said he, "no opium: neither bread nor opium. For the sake of Behá give me some money!"

"You ingrate (*namaḳ-ḥarám*)!" I exclaimed, exasperated at his pertinacity and indiscreetness (for already a little crowd was gathering round us to listen to our dialogue, and to stare at "the Firangí Bábí," from whom alms were demanded "for the sake of Behá"), "how dare you come to me again for money after what you have done?"

"I am no ingrate," he answered, "and whoever says so wrongs me. What have I done that you should be thus angry with me?"

"What have you done?" I retorted; "when you came to the garden, did I not give you money and tea and opium, and speak you fair? And did you not, with the money and the opium in your pocket, and the taste of the tea in your mouth, go out and make mischief against me, spreading idle and damaging reports?"

Then at last he slunk away with some appearance of shame.

Friday, 26th July, 17th Dhi'l-ḳa'da.—During the greater part of the day I was occupied in writing for the Prince-Governor the brief account of my journey which he had requested me to compose for him. Towards evening, Sheykh Ibráhím, 'Abdu'lláh, and the self-sufficient and conceited cobbler, whose rudeness to the old Dhahabí dervish had so displeased me, arrived simultaneously. 'Abdu'lláh soon went off, thinking that he might be wanted by his master, and I was left with the other two. Both talked, and Sheykh Ibráhím drank a great deal; but as regards the talking, the cobbler had at first the best of it, and presently he demanded my copy of the *Íḳán*, and said he would read aloud to us—an accomplishment on which he greatly prided himself.

Sheykh Ibráhím bore with this reading, or rather chanting, as long as he could, gulping down his rage and his '*araḳ* together, till finally one or both of these proved too much for him, and he suddenly turned ferociously on the unsuspecting cobbler.

"Beast and idiot!" he cried, "cannot you be silent when there are men present, and let them talk without interrupting them with your abominable gabbling? Your silly head is so turned by Ustá Akbar and others, who listen to your reading, and applaud it with cries of '*Zíbá mí-ḳhwánad!*' ('How nicely he reads!') that you are inflated with conceit, and do not see that this Firangí here, who knows ten times as much Arabic as you do, is laughing at you under his lip, because in every word of Arabic which you read you violate a rule of grammar. Silence then, beast, and be no more intoxicated with Ustá Akbar's '*Zíbá mí-ḳhwánad!*'"

The poor cobbler was utterly taken aback by this unexpected sally. "Forgive me, O Sheykh!" he began; "I am only a poor ignorant man——"

"Man!" cried the Sheykh, waxing more and more wroth; "I spit on the pates of the father and mother of the dog-mamma![1] Man, forsooth! You are like those maggots (*ḳharáṭín*) which thrust forth their heads from rotten fruit and wave them in the air under the impression that they are men. I count you not as belonging to the world of humanity!"

1 A slightly refined translation of the Persian "*Rídam bi-kellé-i-pidar u mádar-i-nené-sag*," a form of abuse which was a great favourite with the Sheykh, who was not given to mincing words.

"O Sheykh!" exclaimed the poor cobbler, "Whatever you may please to say is right. I have eaten dirt! I have committed a fault! I am the least of your servants!"

"But I will not accept you as my servant," shouted the Sheykh; "you are not in my world at all. I take no cognisance of your existence." And so he stormed on, till the wretched cobbler, now reduced to tears, grovelled at his feet, begging for enlightenment and instruction, and saying, "You are a great and a wise man; your knowledge is far beyond ours; you have travelled and seen the world, and looked on the Blessed Beauty (*Jemál-i-Mubáraḳ*, *i.e.* Behá'u'lláh, the Bábí hierarch at Acre). Tell me what to think, and what to believe, and what to do, and I will accept it." Finally the Sheykh was appeased, and they embraced and made up their quarrel.

Saturday, 27*th July*, 18*th Dhi'l-ḳa'da*.—This day was chiefly notable to me because, for the first time for several weeks, I succeeded in resisting the growing craving for opium which possessed me. This had now begun to cause me some anxiety, for I felt that the experiment had gone quite far enough. "It is all very well," I thought to myself, "to enter into the world of the opium-smoker—and the experience was needed to complete my view of dervish life—but if I do not take care I shall become a dervish in reality, living from hand to mouth, engrossed with smoking opium and 'weaving metaphysic' (*'irfán-báfí*), and content if I can but postpone the business or trouble of to-day till to-morrow—a to-morrow which never comes. It is high time I took measures to put an end to this state of things." The plan which I devised for putting an end to my servitude was based upon the observation that it is not so much the smoking of opium as the regular smoking of opium at a fixed time, that is dangerous. I believe that, speaking generally, anyone may indulge in an occasional pipe with impunity; but I had accustomed myself to smoke opium regularly after supper, and so soon as this time came round, an indescribable craving came upon me, which only the drug could assuage. It therefore seemed to me that the first step towards emancipation must be to alter, and gradually to increase, the interval, which, so far as I remember, I effected somewhat in the following way:—One day, instead of waiting till after supper, I smoked a small amount of the drug at the time of afternoon tea. Next day I waited till supper-time, thus extending the interval of abstinence from twenty-four to thirty hours. On the third day I sat up very late and smoked a very little opium just before retiring to rest. And on the fourth day I went to bed in reasonable time, and succeeded in falling asleep before the craving came upon me, not returning to the drug till the afternoon of the fifth day, thus farther extending the interval from thirty to forty hours. Thus gradually did I free myself from a thraldom which, as I believe, can hardly be broken in any other way.

Sunday, 28th July, 19th Dhi'l-ḳa'da.—To-day I lunched with Ustá Akbar to meet the postmaster of Kirmán; the chief of the telegraph at Rafsinján, who was on a visit to Kirmán; and several other Bábís of the Behá'í faction. On my entrance they greeted me with an outburst of raillery, induced, as it appeared, by their belief that I was disposed to prefer the claims of Ṣubḥ-i-Ezel to those of Behá, and that I had been influenced in this by the Sheykh of Ḳum and his friends. I was at first utterly taken aback and somewhat alarmed at their vehemence, but anger at the unjust and intolerant attitude towards the Ezelís which they took up presently came to my aid, and I reminded them that such violence and unfairness, so far from proving their case, could only make it appear the weaker. "From the statement of Sheykh Ibráhím," I concluded, "who is one of your own party, it appears that your friends at Acre, who complain so much of the bigotry, intolerance, and ferocious antagonism of the Muḥammadans, and who are always talking about 'consorting with men of every faith with spirituality and fragrance,' could find no better argument than the dagger of the assassin wherewith to convince the unfortunate Ezelís who were their companions in exile, and I assure you that this fact has done more to incline me from Behá to Ezel than anything which the Sheykh of Ḳum or his friends have said to me. It would be more to the point if, instead of talking in this violent and unreasonable manner, you would produce the *Beyán* (of which, ever since I came to Kirmán, and, indeed, to Persia, I have been vainly endeavouring to obtain a copy), and show me what the Báb has said about his successor." The postmaster and Ustá Akbar eventually admitted that I was right, and promised to try to obtain for me a copy of the *Beyán*. After this, amicable relations were restored, and the atmosphere seemed clearer for the past storm.

On returning to the garden I found Seyyid Ḥuseyn and one Mírzá Ghulám Ḥuseyn awaiting my arrival. They stayed for some time, and, as usual, talked about religion. With Mírzá Ghulám Ḥuseyn I was much pleased, though I could not satisfy myself as to his real opinions. He told me that he had read the gospels attentively, and was convinced of their genuineness by the deep effect which the words of Christ recorded in them had produced on his heart. He added that he could interpret many of the prophecies contained in the Book of Revelation as applying to Muhammad, and would do so for my benefit if I would visit him in the *Káravánsaráy-i-Gulshan*, where he lodged.

Monday, 29th July, 20th Dhi'l-ḳa'da.—This evening there was another stormy scene in the summer-house, of which, as usual, Sheykh Ibráhím was the cause. He and the parcher of peas came to visit me about sundown, bringing with them a poor scrivener named Mírzá Aḥmad, who had made for himself copies of certain writings of the Bábís, with which, as being a dangerous possession, he was, I was informed, willing to part for a small consideration. Now to guard himself from suspicion, in case the book should fall into the hands of an enemy, he had placed at the end of the *Kitáb-i-Aḳdas*, which stood first in the volume, a colophon, wherein he had described it as "the book of the accursed, misguided, misleading sect of the Bábís." This colophon, which had not been seen by either of his companions, caught my eye as I turned over the pages; but I made no remark, and, fearing trouble if it should meet other eyes, quickly closed the book and laid it aside. Shortly afterwards, Ustá Akbar, wishing to speak with me privately, drew me apart. When we returned, it was to find that the explosion which I dreaded had taken place, and that Sheykh Ibráhím, having taken up the book and seen the objectionable words, was pouring forth the vials of his wrath on the poor scrivener, who, overcome with shame and terror, was shaking like an aspen, and on the verge of tears. It was only with the greatest difficulty that I could stem the torrent of threatening and abusive language which the Sheykh continued to pour forth, and lead Mírzá Aḥmád out into the garden, where he sat down by the stream and began to weep. Finally, I succeeded in comforting him a little with fair words and a larger sum of money than he had expected, but the evening was not a harmonious one, and the acquisition of a new manuscript was the only feature in it which caused me any satisfaction.

Wednesday, 31*st July*, 22*nd Dhi'l-ḳa'da.*—In the morning Seyyid Ḥuseyn came, bringing with him a kindly and courteous old divine of the Sheykhí sect, named Mullá Muḥammad of Júpár. When lunch-time came I invited them to eat with me, "although," I added with a smile, "I am in your eyes but an unclean infidel." "Now God forbid that it should be so!" exclaimed the old *mullá*; "in His Name (exalted is He!) will we partake of your food." So Ḥájí Ṣafar set before them delicate and strange meats, whereof they ate with great contentment, and presently departed, well pleased with their entertainment. Thereupon I again set to work on the account of my journey which I was writing for the Prince-Governor, intending later to go into the city; but word came from Mírzá Jawád's son that he would visit me with his tutor, and about three hours before sunset they arrived. I was greatly displeased at the conduct of the aforesaid tutor, Mullá Ghulám Ḥuseyn, on this occasion; for soon after his arrival there was placed in my hands a letter from one of my Bábí friends at Yezd, which he, with gross impertinence, requested me to show him. This I naturally declined to do, but he, unabashed, picked up the envelope from the ground where it lay, and began to criticise the superscription, which ran as follows:—

> "*Wuṣúluhu bi'l-khayr! Dar Kirmán bi-muláḥaẓa-i-'álí-jenáb-i-faẓá'il-niṣáb-i-jemílu's-sajáyá va'l-ma'áb Ḥakím-i-labíb Edwárd Ṣáḥib (ẓída faẓluhu va ẓáda tawfíḳuhu) musharraf shavad.*"

Which being interpreted is—

> "May its arrival be with good! In Kirmán by the perusal of Edward Ṣáḥib of lofty dignity, endowed with virtues, excellent of qualities and of resort, the discerning philosopher (may his excellence be augmented and his guidance be increased!) may it be honoured."

"'Discerning philosopher,' 'excellent of resort,'" read Mullá Ghulám Ḥuseyn. "What right have you, a Firangí, to such titles as these? Either be this thing or that—a Firangí or a Persian."

An end was put to this unpleasant conversation by the return of Seyyid Ḥuseyn and the old *mullá* of Júpár, who were soon followed by Ustá Akbar and several other persons, mostly Bábís. In this ill-assorted and incongruous assembly, which threatened momentarily to terminate in an explosion, I was oppressed as by a thunderstorm, and I was almost thankful when the rudeness of Ustá Akbar finally put the Sheykhís to rout, leaving the Bábís in possession of the field. These also departed a little later, leaving me at last in peace. They wished me to go with them on the morrow or the following day to Máhán, to visit the shrine of the great Ṣúfí saint, Sháh Ni'matu'lláh. I told them that I had already promised to go with some of my Zoroastrian friends; whereupon they urged me to break with these "*gabr-há-yi najis*" ("unclean pagans"), as they called them, and would hardly take

"No" for an answer. But at last, when, after listening in silence to their efforts to persuade me, I replied, "It is no use talking more about it; I have given my word to the Zoroastrians, and will not go back on it, for my word is one"—they turned away impatiently, exclaiming, "Go with the guebres, and God pardon thy father!"

Next day I had a telegram from Shíráz enquiring when I proposed to return thither, and urging me to leave Kirmán without further delay. This caused me some annoyance, as I had no wish to leave it yet, and hoped to obtain permission from Cambridge to postpone my return to England till January, so that I might go by Bandar-i-'Abbás and the Persian Gulf to Baghdád, and thence to Damascus and Acre, which would be impossible till the cooler weather came. I therefore had recourse to the opium-pipe, and deferred answering the message till the following day, when I visited the telegraph-office and despatched an answer to the effect that I had no intention of quitting Kirmán at present. I found my friend the Prince-Telegraphist still much cast down at the loss of his eldest son. His mind was evidently running much on the fate of the soul after its separation from the body, and he asked me repeatedly, "What think you of the matter? what have you understood?" He also talked more openly than he had hitherto done about the Bábí religion, saying that as between the rival claimants to the pontificate, Behá and Ezel, he found it hard to decide, but that as to the divine mission of Mírzá 'Alí Muḥammad, the Báb, there could, he thought, be no doubt. Then his secretary, who was an ardent believer in Behá, read extracts from the epistles and treatises which he was copying for me, and asked if these were like the words of a mere man; but the poor prince only shook his head, sorrowfully, saying, "It is a hard matter; God knows best!"

Next day a term was put to my uncertainty (though not in the way I wished) by the arrival of a telegram from England, which had been translated into Persian and sent on from Shíráz, bidding me be in Cambridge by the beginning of October. There was no help for it then; I must leave Kirmán, and that without much delay, and, abandoning all idea of Baghdád, Acre, and a camel-ride across the Syrian Desert, post to Ṭeherán, and return home by the Caspian Sea and Russia. It was a bitter disappointment at the time, and on the top of it came, as is so often the case, another, which, though small in comparison, gave me that sense of things going generally wrong which almost everyone must at some time have experienced. My Zoroastrian friend, who was to have taken me to Máhán, sent word that a misfortune had befallen him (the death of his brother in Ṭeherán, as I afterwards discovered), which rendered this impossible; and my Bábí friends, who had previously so greatly importuned me to accompany them, had now made other arrangements, so that it seemed likely that I should have to leave Kirmán without visiting the tomb of the celebrated Saint Sháh Ni'matu'lláh.

I had now no excuse for prolonging my stay at Kirmán; yet still I could not summon up resolution to leave it. It seemed as though my whole mental horizon had been altered by the atmosphere of mysticism and opium smoke which surrounded me. I had almost ceased to think in English, and nothing seemed so good in my eyes as to continue the dreamy speculative existence which I was leading, with opium for my solace and dervishes for my friends. Peremptory telegrams came from Shíráz, sometimes two or three together, but I heeded them not, and banished all thought of them with these two potent antidotes to action of which I have spoken above. Their influence must have been at its height at this time, for once or twice I neglected for a day or two even to write my diary—a daily task which I had hitherto allowed nothing to keep me from accomplishing. The record of the incidents which marked the day preceding the first break of this sort shows the elements of external disturbance and internal quietism in full conflict—on the one hand, a tripartite telegram from the English Superintendent of the Telegraph at Shíráz, the chief of the Persian office at the same place (the same whom I had known at Yezd, whence he had recently been transferred), and my former host, the Nawwáb, strongly urging me to start at once; on the other, two wildly mystical poems given to me by a dervish *murshid*, or spiritual director, whom I had left in a state of unconsciousness produced by some narcotic compound which I had refused to taste, and of which he had offered to prove the innocuousness by eating it.

Some decision, however, was imperatively called for, and could not much longer be deferred; for, amongst other things, my money had nearly come to an end, and I could only obtain a fresh supply in Ṭeherán, Iṣfahán, or Bushire. In this strait my friends came to my assistance with a delicacy and a generosity which I shall not readily forget. I was making arrangements for borrowing, at 5 per cent. interest, a sufficient sum to take me at least as far as Iṣfahán or Ṭeherán, when, almost simultaneously, by a Bábí and a Zoroastrian merchant, I was offered any advance that I might need. I was at first unwilling to borrow from either of them, remembering the Arabic proverb, "*el-ḳarḍu miḳráḍu'l-mawaddat*" ("Borrowing is the scissors of friendship"), but they would take no denial, especially the Bábí, who said that he should feel deeply hurt if I refused to accept his offer. Finally, I consented to avail myself of his kindness, and borrowed from him a sum of sixty or seventy *túmáns* (about £20), for which he declined to accept any interest, and could only be prevailed upon with difficulty to take a receipt. This sum I duly remitted to his agent at Ṭeherán on my arrival there.

And now Ḥájí Ṣafar, who, in spite of occasional fits of perversity and sulkiness, had always shown himself a faithful and loyal servant, came to the rescue. He had been much troubled (and not without reason) at the state of indecision and inactivity into which I had lapsed, which state he ascribed to some spell cast over me by the Bábís, to whom he had even addressed threats and remonstrances. So one night, while waiting on me at supper, he unfolded to me a plan which he had formed, as follows:—

"*Ṣáḥib*," he began, "you cannot stay on here for ever, and you know that you are wanted in England at the beginning of the month of Ṣafar next (7th October 1888). Now I have been thinking how you can stay at Kirmán as long as possible, see as much new country as possible, and still be back in your own country in time. If you return to Shíráz and go thence to Bushire, and there take ship, you will not arrive in time, even if we could start at once, which we cannot do, as it will not be easy to find mules for the journey. It is much better, then, that we should go to Ṭeherán, and that you should return thence through Russia. The advantages of this plan are that you can have a week or ten days more here; visit your friends at Rafsinján on the way; see your friends at Yezd, Káshán, Ḳum, and Ṭeherán again; be in the capital for the Muḥarram passion-plays, which you will nowhere see so well performed; and traverse Mázandarán or Gílán, both of which, as I can assure you, are very remarkable countries, which you ought to see before leaving Persia. I will undertake to sell your horse for not less than you gave for it, and before it is sold I will arrange for you to visit Máhán, as you wished to do. You can write to Shíráz for your things to be sent to meet you at Ṭeherán, where also you will be able to buy any more books of which you have need. What do you think of my plan? Have I not spoken well?"

That he had spoken well there was no doubt; his plan was the best that remained possible, and he had baited it cunningly. With a sudden sense of shame at my own lethargy, and gratitude to Ḥájí Ṣafar for his wise admonition, I determined once and for all to shake off this fatal quietism which had been so long growing on me, and at once to take the steps necessary for the execution of his plan.

Two days later, on 9th August, everything was in proper train. The expedition to Máhán had presented some difficulties, but they were overcome by Ḥájí Ṣafar's energy. He came to me about sundown on that day with a smile of triumph and satisfaction. "*Ṣáḥib*," said he, "it is all arranged: you will go to Máhán and perform your visitation to the shrine, and that without bearing the burden of obligation to anyone. I have found an old man, an uncle of the gardener's, and a regular 'desert-walker' (*biyábán-gasht*), who will bear you company and show you the way; for I must remain here to complete our preparations for the journey. I will bring you your supper directly, and then you had better go to sleep for a while; for if you start four hours after sunset, you will still be at Máhán by daybreak. You will remain there all to-morrow, travel back in the same way to-morrow night, and be here at daybreak on Sunday morning."

The silent march to Máhán (for the old guide stalked on before me with swift untiring gait, only looking round now and again to see that I was following him) was pleasant in spite of its monotony. Never had my horse carried me so well as on this our last journey together. Once again my spirit was refreshed and rejoiced by the soft night air and the shimmer of the moonlight on the sand-hills, until the sky grew pale with the dawn, and the trees and buildings of Máhán stood clear before us.

We went straight to the shrine of the great Saint Sháh Ni'matu'lláh, and were admitted without difficulty in company with other pilgrims. One of the dervishes attached to the shrine read the *ziyárat*, or form of visitation. Then he said to me, as the other pilgrims were kissing the tombstone, "*Ṣáḥib*, Sháh Ni'matu'lláh was a great man." I acquiesced. "In the world of the gnostics there is no difference of sects," he continued. Again I agreed. "Then," said he, "seeing that this is so, it were not amiss for you to kiss his tombstone." I did as he desired, and then, having visited the various buildings connected with the shrine, returned with the dervishes to their *ḳahvé-ḳháné* ("coffee-house" or guest-chamber), where I had tea and slept till noon.

In the afternoon the dervishes took me to see some of the gardens which surround Máhán. In one of these, called the *Gardan-i-Shutur* ("Camel's Neck"), a charming spot, I met my friend Serúsh, the Zoroastrian, who was still mourning the death of his brother, and had come to Máhán for a day's solitude and quiet before starting for Ṭeherán to wind up his affairs.

About two hours before sunset, after another cup of tea, I bade farewell to the kindly dervishes, mounted my horse, and started homewards with my guide, well pleased with Máhán and its people, and disposed to regard as a gratuitous slander that cynical verse:—

"*Bihisht-i-rúyi zamín-ast ḳiṭ'a-i-Máhán,*
Bi-sharṭ-i-ánki takán-ash dihand dar dúzakh."

"The district of Máhán would be an earthly paradise,
On condition that it should be well shaken over hell." [1]

To our left lay the village of Langar, the headquarters of the Sheykhís, where live the sons of the Báb's great rival and antagonist, the late Ḥájí Muḥammad Karím Khán of Kirmán. I asked my guide whether we could not visit it on our way. To this he consented, and in a short while we found ourselves in the quiet lane where dwell the "*Áḳá-zádas*" ("Sons of the Master"). Here we met a Sheykhí divine, whom my guide accosted, telling him that I wished to pay my respects to the *Áḳá-zádas*; and before I had time to consider whether I should do well to thrust myself upon the leaders of a sect for which I had but little kindliness, I found myself in the courtyard of their house. At the farther end of this courtyard mats and carpets were spread, and on these sat in rows some dozen sour-looking, heavy-turbaned Sheykhí students, to whom two of Karím Khán's sons, seated in the place of honour, were

1 *I.e.* That all its inhabitants should be shaken from it into hell.

expounding the text of a work of their father's called the *Faṣlu'l-Khiṭáb*. Ashamed to retreat, I advanced and sat down on my heels like the others in the lowest place. Of those nearest to me, some glared indignantly at me and others edged away, but no other notice was taken of my arrival till the lecture was over, when one of the *Áḳá-zádas* addressed me, remarking that he had heard I was "going after religions" (*'aḳib-i-madhhab mí-gardíd*). I replied that he had been correctly informed.

"Well," said he, "and have you found a religion better than that in which you were brought up?"

"No," I replied.

"What of Islám?" continued he.

"It is a good religion," I answered.

"Which is best," said he: "the Law of Islám or your Law?"

"Why do you ask me this question?" I replied; "my apparel answers for me. If I thought Islám the better, I should not come here clad in this raiment, but rather in turban and '*abá*."

Thereat the younger students laughed, and the *Áḳá-zádas*, remarking that it was the time for the evening prayer, went off to the mosque, leaving a cousin of theirs, who wore the dress of a layman, to entertain me till their return. He gave me tea, and would have had me stay to supper, so as to converse with the *Áḳá-zádas*, but I excused myself, and soon after their return from the mosque took my departure. One of Karím Khán's sons accompanied me to the gate. I thanked him for his hospitality.

"Our Prophet hath bidden us '*honour the guest*,'" said he.

"'*Even though he be an infidel*,'" I replied, completing the quotation; whereat we parted with laughter.

Another silent ride through the moonlit desert, and, as the sun rose above the horizon, I alighted for the last time from my honest old horse at the gate of my garden in Kirmán. The arrangements for his sale had been already concluded, and that very day the servant of his new master brought me a cheque for eighteen *túmáns* (about £6, two *túmáns* more than I had paid for him), and led him away. And as I gave him a final caress (for I had come to love the beast after a fashion), I felt that now indeed I had finally broken with the pleasant Persian life of the last three months.

CHAPTER XVIII

FROM KIRMÁN TO ENGLAND

"*Yaḳúlúna inna'l-mawta ṣa'b*^{un}*, wa innamá*
Mufáraḳatu'l-aḥbábi wa'lláhi aṣ'abu!"

"They say that Death is hard, but by the Name of God I swear
That separation from one's friends is harder still to bear!"

"*Shab-i-shanba ẓi Kirmán bár kardam;*
Ghalaṭ kardam, ki pusht bar yár kardam."

"On Friday night I loaded up from Kirmán;
I did ill, for I turned my back on my friend."

IT was on Sunday morning that I parted with my horse, and my departure was arranged for the following Tuesday. On that day, while paying a farewell visit to the young Bábí merchant who had so kindly advanced me the money which I needed for my journey back to Ṭeherán, I met the postmaster's son. He appeared to be sulky with me for some reason—probably because of my friendliness with the Ezelís and apologies for their attitude—and coldly observed that the sooner I left Kirmán the better, and that if I could leave that very night it would be best of all. I answered that this was impossible, but that I would perhaps start on the morrow. "Then you must go early in the morning," said he, "so as to avoid collision with the post."

When I told this to Sheykh Ibráhím, on whom I next called, he was greatly incensed.

"Nonsense," said he, "the rascally burnt-father only wants to get your money as soon as may be, so that he may get drunk, eat sweetmeats, and play the libertine. You must stop here to-night and sup with me and some others of your friends. I will ask the postmaster and his scoundrel of a son too, and you shall see how small they will sing after I have had a talk with them. I'll warrant they will be humble enough then, and will let you have your horses whenever it may please you."

Somewhat comforted by the Sheykh's confidence in his own powers, I went off with Ustá Akbar to pay a visit to some of my Bábí friends who were employed in the post-office in a subordinate capacity, after which we returned to Sheykh Ibráhím's abode. He had been as good as his word: the postmaster and his son were there, both, to use the Sheykh's expression, "the very essence of submission" (*maḥẓ-i-taslím*), ready to let me have horses for my journey whenever it might please me. The evening passed off harmoniously after this, the Sheykh cooking the supper himself, only stopping occasionally to address a remark to one of us.

"O thou who art buried in this land of *K* and *R*,"[1] he cried out to me in one of these pauses, "why should you leave this place, since you like it so well?"

"Because," I replied, "I must be back at the University of Cambridge early in the autumn. My leave of absence is nearly at an end, and they have summoned me to return."

"I spit on the University of Gímbrij" (so he pronounced it), answered the Sheykh; and to such revilings he continued at intervals to give vent throughout the evening.

When one begins to procrastinate there is no end to it. I wished to start on Thursday, 16th August, but at the last moment, when I was actually ready for the journey, word came from the post-office that the post (which was due out on that day) was so heavy that there were no horses to spare; and from one cause and another my actual departure was deferred till the evening of Sunday, 19th August. All day I was busy with farewells, to which there seemed to be no end, for several of my friends were loth to bid me a final good-bye, and I too shrank from the

1 *I.e.* Kirmán, which is so called by the Bábís, and in the *Kitáb-i-Aḳdas*.

parting, for I knew how unlikely it was that I should ever see them again. To this thought the postmaster, who had recovered his wonted kindliness of manner, gave expression. "In this world we shall see one another no more, as I think," said he, "but in another world we shall without doubt meet again, and that world is the better, for there all things will be made clear, and there will be no more parting."

My last visit was to the Prince-Telegraphist. On my way thither I was stopped in the street by the Bábí cobbler who had been so roughly rebuked by Sheykh Ibráhím for his chanting of the sacred books. He was in a great state of agitation, and cried out to me with tears in his eyes—

"Ṣáḥib, you will go to Acre, if not now, then at some future time, and you will see the Supreme Beauty [1]. Do not forget me then; mention me there, and let my name be remembered in the Holy Presence!"

The post-horses, ready laden for the journey, called for me at the telegraph-office. It was after sunset, but the Prince had caused the northern gate of the city to be kept open for me after the usual hour of closing, so that I was able to linger a little while longer in the city which had cast so strange a glamour over me. At last, however, I rose regretfully and bade him farewell; and, as the great gate closed behind me with a dull clang, and I found myself in the open plain under the star-spangled sky, I thought that I had seen the last of all my Kirmán friends. But when we halted at the post-house (which, as before said, stands some distance outside the city to the north), there were Sheykh Ibráhím and Ustá Akbar the pea-parcher come out to see the last of me, and I had to dismount and smoke a last pipe with them; while the Sheykh, who was subdued and sorrowful, told me how his friend 'Abdu'lláh had fled, none knew whither, with such raiment only as he wore, leaving word that he was bound for Acre, and would not return till his eyes had gazed on the

1 *I.e.* Behá'u'lláh.

"Supreme Beauty." "You may very likely come up with him on the road," he concluded, "in which case I pray you to stop him, reason with him, and if necessary send him back in the custody of some trustworthy person, else will he certainly perish ere his mad quest be accomplished."

It was three hours past sunset when I at length mounted and turned my face northwards. At midnight I was at Bághín, the first stage out from Kirmán, and there I rested for a while in a garden belonging to Ná'ib Ḥasan, whom we had overtaken on the way, and who set before me melons and other delicious fruits. Soon after daybreak I was at Kabútar Khán, where I slept till noon was passed, and then, after lunch and tea, set out for Rafsinján, where I was to stay for the night with the telegraphist, a Bábí whose acquaintance I had made at Kirmán. On the way thither I passed two of my dervish friends, who, with banners, alms-gourds, and all the paraphernalia of professional mendicants, were returning from Rafsinján; and, somewhat later, Ná'ib Ḥasan's brother, who presented me with a melon. A little after this I met one of the officials of the Kirmán post-office (also a Bábí, with whom I was well acquainted) returning from the limit of the Kirmán district, to which it was his duty to escort the post. After a brief conversation we exchanged horses, I taking the ugly black beast which had brought him from Rafsinján. In spite of its ill looks, it got over the ground at an amazing pace, and, guided by another Bábí in the postal service (all the post-office officials about Kirmán seemed to be Bábís), I arrived at my friend's house in Kamál-ábád, hard by Bahrám-ábád, in good time for supper, at which I met my old friend the postmaster of the latter place.

I had arranged before leaving Kirmán to spend two days with another of my Bábí friends, Áḳá Muḥammad Ḥasan of Yezd (my guest on the occasion of that wild banquet described at p. 534 *supra*), who lived at a little village distant only about five miles from Bahrám-ábád, somewhat off the main road. I had not altogether wished to consent to this fresh delay, but Áḳá Muḥammad Ḥasan was determined that it should be so, and had secured my compliance by a rather cunning device. Hearing that I was very desirous of obtaining a manuscript of the Persian *Beyán*, and that Ustá Akbar had found one which the owner was willing to part with, he bought it himself, sent it off by post the same day to his home, lest I should induce him to change his mind, and then, when he bade me farewell, promised to give me the book I so greatly longed to possess if I would visit him on my way north. Only after his departure did I learn the trick that had been played upon me, for not till Ustá Akbar explained that this was the manuscript about which he had spoken to me did I realise with mixed indignation and amusement how I had been duped. Now, if I wanted my *Beyán*, it was clear that I should have to go to Áḳá Muḥammad Ḥasan's village for it, and I was not going to lose the only chance that I had yet had of obtaining this precious volume for the sake of gaining two paltry days.

As there was no question, therefore, of getting beyond this village for the present, and no object in arriving there before evening, I stayed with my friends at Bahram-abad till half an hour before sundown, when I again mounted the ugly black horse which had carried me so well on the previous day, and set off at a tearing gallop. As I drew near the village I descried a little group assembled on a small conical hill just outside it. Their figures stood out clear against the setting sun, and I could see that they were watching for my arrival. Even as I espied them, one of them, my host's son, a handsome lad of eighteen or nineteen, disengaged himself from their midst, and, mounting a large white ass which stood ready, advanced at a rapid amble to meet me. I should have stopped to greet him, but the black horse would hardly consent to be checked in his headlong career, and in about a minute more I was in the middle of the group. Having dismounted, I had to exchange embraces with my host and his Bábí friends (some ten or a dozen in number), a proceeding which, in spite of its patriarchal character, was rather tedious. Then, taking me by the hand, my host led me through the village street, which was lined with curious onlookers, to his house.

I remained here for two days—days which passed pleasantly but uneventfully. There was the usual tea-drinking, smoking of opium and tobacco, and long debates—in shaded rooms by day and in the moon-lit garden by night—on religious and philosophical questions. There were several guests besides myself, some of whom had come from Kirmán to meet me. Amongst these was one, a dyer by trade, whose good sense and moderation especially impressed me. To him I expressed my dissatisfaction at the exaggerated language employed by Nabíl, the poet, and other Bábís in speaking of Behá. He agreed with me, but said that allowance must be made for them if their affection for their Master prompted them at times to use language which calmer reason could not approve.

My host had a large collection of Bábí manuscripts, together with some photographs, which he showed us with much pride and yet more caution, never suffering more than one book at a time to leave the box in which he kept his treasures. For liberal as the Bábís are in all else, they hoard their books as a miser does his gold; and if a Bábí were to commit a theft, it would be some rare and much-prized manuscript which would vanquish his honesty. And so it was that, when the moment of my departure arrived, I came near to losing the manuscript of the Persian *Beyán* which had served as the bait to lead me to this remote hamlet of Rafsinján. My host begged me to leave it with him for a month, for a week, even for five days; in five days, he said, he could get it copied, and it should then be sent after me to Yezd, or Ṭeherán, or any other place I might designate. I was obdurate, however, for I yearned to possess the book, and felt that I was entitled to have it; neither dared I leave it behind me, fearing lest the temptation to keep it should prove too strong for my Bábí friends. So at last, when the discussion had grown protracted, I said—

"I have eaten your bread and salt, and am your guest. If you will have the book, take it; but I would almost as lief give you my head."

"Then," said he, after a moment's pause, "take it; if such be your feeling, we cannot ask you to give it up."

So I put the precious volume in my pocket with a sense of profound thankfulness, and, accompanied by my friends, walked out a little distance from the village before mounting. Once more we embraced; and then, tightening the wide leather belt in which I carried my money, and buttoning the hardly-won *Beyán* into my breast-pocket, I hoisted myself into the saddle, and, amidst a shower of good wishes for the journey, again set my face towards Yezd.

It was about an hour before sunset on Thursday, 23rd August, when I resumed my northward journey. Three hours after sunset I was at Kushkúh, where I stopped only to change horses. At about 3 a.m. on the Friday I was at Beyáz, and soon after sunrise at Anár. Here I rested and had luncheon, not starting again till the afternoon. About sundown I was at Shemsh, where such bad horses were provided that I did not reach Kirmánsháhán till 9 or 10 p.m. There I had supper, tea, and—I regret to add—a pipe of opium, which greatly comforted me; and then I slept till daybreak.

Next day (Saturday, 25th August) I reached Zeynu'd-Dín two hours after sunrise, and ate a melon while the fresh horses were being saddled. Soon after leaving this place the *shágird-chápár* (post-boy) who accompanied us raised an alarm of thieves, and indeed we saw three horsemen wheeling round us in the distance. I fancy, however, that they were waiting there in the hopes of rescuing some of their comrades who had recently been captured at Kirmán and were being sent in chains to

Ṭeherán to undergo judgment. At any rate they did not molest us.

About noon we arrived at Sar-i-Yezd, where I halted for lunch for an hour or two. As I was preparing to start, a Kirmání woman who was standing by called out to me, "We pray God to bring you back to Kirmán." I suppose she was a Bábí, and regarded me as a co-religionist; though how she knew anything about me I was at a loss to imagine.

Rather more than an hour before sunset I reached Muḥammad-ábád, a sort of suburb of Yezd. Here I visited the brother of the young Bábí merchant who had befriended me at Kirmán, meaning only to stay for a short time; but nothing would serve him save that I should be his guest that night, and go on to Yezd on the following morning. I was not loth to accept his hospitality; and a right pleasant evening we passed on a roof overlooking beautiful gardens redolent with the perfume of flowers and resonant with the song of the nightingale. Here it was, I think, that I smoked my last opium-pipe in Persia, amidst surroundings the most perfect that could be imagined.

Next evening (Sunday, 26th August) I supped with the Bábí Seyyids at Yezd, where I remained till the following Friday, lodging at the post-house, which is situated at the northern extremity of the town. I saw most of my old friends, except the Prince-Governor, during these five days, and received from all of them a very cordial welcome, but the Bábí Seyyids were not a little vexed to find that I had foregathered with the Ezelís at Kirmán. "I told you," remarked the poet 'Andalíb, "that no good would come of your going there, and I was, it seems, perfectly right."

I left Yezd at sunrise on Friday, 31st August, and entered the great sand-desert which bounds it on the north. It and the long post-ride to Káshán were equally monotonous, and need little more description than a list of the stages, times, and distances, which were as follows:—

Yezd to Meybút or Meybud, where I arrived about 2 p.m., after a two hours' halt at 'Izz-ábád to visit an acquaintance, ten parasangs. Thence to Chifté, which we reached about 5 p.m., six parasangs. Thence to Aghdá, where we arrived about half an hour after dusk, four parasangs. Here we were delayed by the post, which always has the first right to horses, till late in the night, when, after supper and a short sleep, we started by bright moonlight, and reached the desolate post-house of Naw-Gunbudh (whence a road leads to Iṣfahán) half an hour before sunrise on 1st September (nine parasangs).

1st September.—Slept till noon at Naw-Gunbudh. Thence a dreary stage of six parasangs brought us about 4 p.m. to the queer old rambling town of Ná'in. Half an hour after sunset we reached Neyistának (six parasangs), where the son-in-law of one of the postal officials of Yezd, with whom I had made acquaintance, hospitably entertained me to supper.

2nd September.—Left Neyistának a little before daybreak, accompanied by an intelligent and handsome little *shágird-chápár*, and arrived (eight parasangs) during the forenoon at Jauḳand, a pretty place, abounding in trees and streams, where I would fain have lingered a while to converse with the singularly amiable and courteous postmaster. While I was waiting for fresh horses to be saddled, two or three villagers came in, well-favoured, genial fellows, who told me that an old dialect nearly akin to that of Ḳohrúd was spoken in this and the neighbouring villages. After a short halt the fresh horses were led out, and I bade farewell to the kindly postmaster, who exhorted me to deal gently with them, as they had just been watered. The *shágird-chápár*, a bright handsome lad named Ḥaydar, saw to this; for he was proud of his horses (and rightly, for they actually had to be held in), and prattled incessantly about them, till, after a ride of five parasangs, we reached the little town of Ardistán.

Here I had an introduction to a Bábí, who took me to his house, gave me fruit, tea, and pipes, and showed me a manuscript of the works of a mystical poet of Ardistán named Pír-i-Jemál, in whose verses, as he declared, the "manifestation" of the Báb had been foreshadowed. I left Ardistán about two hours and a half before sunset, the boy Ḥaydar again bearing us company. The horses supplied to us were so bad that when we had gone a short distance we had to send back two of them and take on two of the horses we had brought from Jauḳand, to the delight of Ḥaydar and the disgust of the poor old postmaster of Ardistán, who had to refund part of the money which he had received.

After a stage of six parasangs we reached Mughár, where I had supper and slept for a while by the side of a stream which ran past the post-house, starting again soon after midnight. Five parasangs more brought us to Khálid-ábád about sunrise; six more parasangs to Abú Zeyd-ábád about noon on 3rd September. The horses which brought us thither had been very bad, but those now supplied to us were even worse; so, as it was impossible to urge them out of a walk, I resigned myself to the inevitable, bought some melons, and thus eating the fruit and crawling along in true caravan fashion, entered Káshán soon after sunset, and was again hospitably received at the telegraph-office by Mr Aganor. Here I remained that night and all next day to make some purchases and see one or two of my old friends.

I left Káshán about sunset on 4th September, and reached Sinsin at 10 p.m., and Pasangán about sunrise the next morning. I was very tired and would fain have rested a while, but the post from the south was behind us, and there was nothing for it but to push on, unless I wished to run the risk of being stranded for a day at this desolate spot. At 10 a.m. on 5th September I was at Ḳum, where I was most hospitably received at the telegraph-office, and enjoyed a welcome rest of twenty-four hours, for I was by this time half-dead with weariness, not being used to such severe riding.

6th September.—Left Ḳum at 9 a.m.; reached Raḥmat-ábád

(four parasangs) at 11 a.m.; Kushk-i-Bahrám (seven parasangs) at sunset; and Pík (four parasangs) about midnight. Here I had supper and slept till daybreak.

7th September.—Started at 6 a.m., and, after a hot and dusty ride of six parasangs, reached Ribáṭ Karím, a populous and rather pretty village, during the forenoon. Here I stopped for lunch, after which I set off, about three and a half hours before sunset, to accomplish the last stage (seven parasangs) of this wearisome journey. We had good horses, and shortly before sunset found ourselves at a little roadside tea-house, distant one parasang from Ṭeherán. Here we halted to drink tea, when Ḥájí Ṣafar suddenly observed that if we didn't make haste the southern gates of the city would be shut, and we should have to make a long detour to obtain admission. We at once set off and galloped in as hard as we could go, but all to no purpose, for the nearest gate was already shut, nor could the gatekeeper be induced by threats or promises to re-open it. He only did his duty, poor man; but I was so angry and disappointed that I gave him the benefit of the whole vocabulary of powerful abuse and invective which I had learned from Sheykh Ibráhím, and it was perhaps as well that the solid gate stood between us. I was ashamed of my outburst of temper afterwards, but those who have ever made a journey of 600 miles on Persian post-horses will be ready to make some allowances for me. Luckily we found the Sháh 'Abdu'l-'Aẓím gate still open, and, threading our way through the bazaars, we alighted about 8.30 p.m. at Prevost's hotel, where Ḥájí Ṣafar left me to go and visit his relatives.

The return to what must, I suppose, be called civilisation was anything but grateful to me; I loathed the European dishes set before me, the fixed hours for meals, the constraint and absence of freedom, and above all the commonplace and conventional character of my surroundings. Seven months had elapsed since I quitted Ṭeherán for the south, and during this time I had been growing steadily more and more Persian in thought and speech alike. The sudden plunge back into European life came upon me as a shock which was not mitigated even by the charm of novelty, and it took several days to reconcile me at all to my surroundings, my whole wish being at first to get away from the degenerate capital at the earliest possible date. Many of my friends, too, had left Ṭeherán, or gone into the surrounding villages for the hot weather, so that life was much duller than it had been during my previous stay.

In spite of my desire to get away from Ṭeherán, it took me thirteen days to transact all my business. First of all I had to find out about the steamers from Mashhad-i-Sar, the port whence I intended to sail for Russia (for I would not take the well-known Resht and Enzelí route); then there were books to be bought, packed up, and sent off by way of Bushire to Cambridge; Bábís, to whom I had letters of introduction, to be visited; money arrangements to be made; and last though not least, *ta'ẓiyas* to be seen, for it was the beginning of the month of Muḥarram, and the national mournings for Ḥasan, Ḥuseyn, and the other saints of the Shí'ite Church were in full swing.

To the chief Bábís of Ṭeherán I was introduced by a merchant of Shírván (a Russian subject), to whom I carried a letter of recommendation. They entertained me at lunch in a house near the Dúláb Gate, and I was much impressed by their piety and gravity of demeanour, so unlike the anarchic freedom of the Kirmán Bábís. As a psychological study, however, they were less interesting, neither did I see enough of them to become intimate with them.

As I intended to spend all my available money on books, I was at some pains to ascertain what was to be had, and where it could be had cheapest. I therefore visited several booksellers and asked them to furnish me with a list of books and prices, telling them that, as I hated haggling, I should make no remarks on the prices quoted, but simply buy what I needed from him who would sell cheapest. This plan had the best effect, since they did not know what other shops I had visited, and could, therefore, make no coalition against me; and I soon filled a large tin-lined box with a good selection of useful works of reference which seldom find their way to Europe, where bad Indian editions are, as a rule, the only things readily obtainable. I also bought a few curiosities, and a complete suit of Persian clothes, which was made for me under Ḥájí Ṣafar's supervision. Amongst the booksellers I made the acquaintance of a delightful old man, a real scholar, who, when he could collect two or three manuscripts of some rare book which took his fancy (generally a philosophical or mystical work), would, at his own risk, and with no one to assist him, lithograph as correct and good a text as he could. Of course he got no encouragement or help from the great, who in earlier and better days might have recognised his worth, and supplied him with the means of carrying on his labour of love on a larger scale. His name, so far as I remember, was Sheykh Muḥammad Ḥuseyn of Káshán. Whether he still lives I know not; but I shall ever remember him as one of the best types of the unobtrusive, kindly, disinterested, enthusiastic scholar and bibliophile of the East that it has been my lot to meet.

On Wednesday, 6th Muḥarram (12th September), I dined with my kind friend Mr Fahie at the telegraph-office. The Sháh's Prime Minister, the *Amínu's-Sulṭán*, was giving a *rawẓa-khwán*, or religious recitation, on a splendid scale in the adjoining house, and after dinner we adjourned to the roof to watch it. On this occasion a whole regiment of soldiers, as well as a number of other guests, were being entertained by the generous *vazír*. Supper was provided for all of them, and I counted over a hundred trays of food as they were brought in by the servants.

Next evening I accompanied several members of the English Embassy to the Royal *tekyé*, a theatre specially constructed and set apart for the dramatised representations of Muḥarram (*ta'ziyas*), which are to the Shí'ite Muḥammadan what the

Miracle-plays of Ober-Ammergau are to Christians of the Romish Church. The theatre is a large circular building—roofless, but covered during Muḥarram with an awning. There are boxes (*táḳchés*) all round, which are assigned to the more patrician spectators, one, specially large and highly decorated, being reserved for the Sháh. The humbler spectators sit round the central space or arena in serried ranks, the women and children in front. A circular stone platform in the centre constitutes the stage. There is no curtain and no exit for the actors, who, when not wanted, simply stand back. The acting is powerful, though somewhat crude, and it is impossible not to be influenced by the deep feeling evinced by both actors and audience. The *ta'ziyas* comprise at least some thirty or forty episodes, the representation of any one of which requires two or three hours. Some of them are drawn from the histories of the Jewish prophets, and these are the less interesting because the spectators are less profoundly moved by them; the majority, however, illustrate the misfortunes of the Shí'ite Imáms. Those connected with the fatal field of Kerbelá, culminating in the death of the "Prince of Martyrs" (*Seyyidu'sh-shuhadá*), the Imám Ḥuseyn, are the most moving; but I fancy that the Persians are, as a rule, not very willing to admit Europeans or Sunnite Muḥammadans, so greatly are the religious feelings of the spectators stirred by the representation of the supreme catastrophe of the *'Áshúrá*, or tenth of Muḥarram. On that day bands of men (especially soldiers of Ádharbáyján) parade the streets in white garments, which are soon dyed with gore; for each man carries a knife or sword, and, as their excitement increases with cries of "*Yá Ḥasan! Yá Ḥuseyn!*" and beating of breasts, they inflict deep gashes on their heads till the blood pours forth and streams over their faces and apparel. It is an impressive sight, though somewhat suggestive of Baal-worship.

The *ta'ziya* which I was privileged to see represented the bereaved women of the Holy Family before the impious Shimr,

Yezíd's general. Shimr was clad in a complete suit of chain-armour, and the captive women were brought in before him mounted on barebacked camels. Them he entreats with the greatest brutality, driving them with a whip from the corpse of Ḥuseyn, round which they gather to weep and lament. The *mise-en-scène* and costumes were good; but the effect was spoiled in some measure by the introduction of a number of the Sháh's carriages, with postilions barbarously dressed in a half-European uniform, in the middle of the piece. This absurd piece of ostentation seemed to me typical of Ḳájár taste[1].

I had been much exercised in mind as to the safe conveyance of my precious Bábí manuscripts to England. The box of books which I was sending home by Bushire would, I knew, be months on the road, and I wished to begin to work at my manuscripts immediately on my return. On the other hand, I had heard such dreadful accounts of the Russian Custom-house that I was afraid to take them with me. Finally I decided to sew them up carefully in thick linen, direct the parcel to my home address, and send it, if I could obtain permission, in the Embassy bag, which is conveyed monthly to Constantinople by a special bearer, and there handed over to the Queen's messenger for transport to London. It cost me an effort to part with my beloved and hardly-won manuscripts, even for so short a time, but I felt that this was the safest plan; and, accordingly, having packed and directed them with the greatest care, I rode out to Ḳulahak, the summer quarters of the English Embassy, situated about six miles to the north of Ṭeherán, and, to my great relief, saw the precious packet sealed up in the bag.

I had been delayed in starting from Ṭeherán, and so reached

1 An English translation of some twenty or thirty of the more important *ta'ziyas* has been published in two handsome volumes by Sir Lewis Pelly, formerly Resident on the Persian Gulf. One of them ("*Les Noces de Kassem*") is given in French by Gobineau in his *Religions et Philosophies dans l'Asie Centrale* (pp. 405–437), which also contains a general account of the Muḥarram Passion-plays (pp. 381–403 and 439–459).

the Embassy too late for lunch; I stayed at Ḳulahak till about 5.30 p.m. visiting some of my Persian friends, and did not get back to the city till nearly 7 p.m.; and that evening I had been invited by my servant Ḥájí Ṣafar to sup with him at his house and then to visit some of the smaller *ta'ziyas* and *rawza-khwáns* with him in disguise. As I had had nothing to eat all day but tea and biscuits, I was well-nigh famished before supper-time, and returned to the hotel about midnight almost dead-beat. So tired was I that it was some time before I could even summon up energy to undress.

Next day I woke at I know not what time, feeling faint, ill, and helplessly weak, as though every bone in my body were broken. No one came near me, and it was not till evening that I could make the effort to rise and obtain some food. After drinking a plate of soup and some tea, I again fell asleep, and woke next morning somewhat better, though still too weak to rise till evening. As two of my Persian friends had promised to take me into the town to see something more of the Muḥarram mournings and spectacles, I then made a fresh effort, got up, had dinner, and, as soon as they arrived, put on a Persian coat (*sardárí*) and lambskin hat (*kuláh*), and sallied forth in this disguise, well content to feel myself for the time a Persian amongst Persians. We spent a pleasant and interesting evening, visiting unmolested the *Masjid-i-Sháh* (Royal Mosque) and the houses of two notable divines, the Imám-Jum'a and Mullá 'Alí of Kand.

On Tuesday, 18th September, I concluded my purchase of books, on which I spent something over £10. For the benefit of Persian students, I append a list of the twenty-six volumes which I bought for this sum, together with their prices. The first fifteen I obtained from my good old friend Sheykh Muḥammad Ḥuseyn of Káshán, the last eleven from another bookseller.

1. The *Burhán-i-Jámi'*, a very excellent and compact dictionary of Persian words, composed in the reigns of Fatḥ-'Alí Sháh

and Muḥammad Sháh, by Muḥammad Karím ibn Mahdí-Ḳulí Mírzá, and chiefly based on the *Burhán-i-Ḳáṭi'* and the *Farhang-i-Rashídí*, lithographed in Tabríz in A.H. 1260 (A.D. 1844). Price 10 *ḳráns*.

2. The *Díván of Anvarí* (Tabríz edition of A.H. 1266). Price 12 *ḳráns*.

3. The *Ḳiṣaṣu'l-'Ulamá* ("Stories of Celebrated Divines"), by Muḥammad ibn Suleymán et-Tanakábuní, together with two other treatises, one called *Sabílu'n-naját* ("The Way of Salvation"), and the other, by Seyyid Murtaẓá *'Alamu'l-Hudá*, called *Irshádu'l-'Awámm* ("The Layman's Guide"). Second edition, lithographed in Ṭeherán in A.H. 1304. Price 10 *ḳráns*.

4. The *Sharḥ-i-Manẓúma*, or text and commentary of the philosophical poem (Arabic) of the great modern philosopher of Persia, Ḥájí Mullá Hádí of Sabzawár. Lithographed at Ṭeherán in A.H. 1298. Price 20 *ḳráns*.

5. The *Díván of Saná'í*, one of the most celebrated of the early mystical poets of Persia (died about A.D. 1150). Lithographed. Not dated. Price 8 *ḳráns*.

6. The *Ḥadíḳatu'sh-Shí'a* ("Garden of the Shí'ites"), an extensive work on Shí'ite doctrine and history. Second volume only, dealing with the Imáms. Lithographed at Ṭeherán in A.H. 1265. Price 12 *ḳráns*.

7. The mystical commentary on the Ḳur'án of Sheykh Muḥyi'd-Dín ibnu'l-'Arabí, a very notable Moorish mystic, who flourished during the latter part of the twelfth and earlier part of the thirteenth century of our era. Lithographed in India (? Bombay) in A.H. 1291 (A.D. 1874). Price 30 *ḳráns*.

8. Philosophical treatises of Mullá Ṣadrá, with marginal commentary by Hájí Mullá Ḥádí. Lithographed. No date. Price 10 *ḳráns*.

9. The *Tadhkiratu'l-Khaṭṭáṭín* ("Biographies of Calligraphists") and the Travels in Persia, Turkey, Arabia, and Egypt, of Mírzá Sanglákh, a large and extremely handsome volume, beautifully

lithographed in a fine *naskh* handwriting in A.H. 1291 at Tabríz. Price 25 *ḳráns*.

10. The poems of 'Unṣurí, a contemporary of Firdawsí, and——

11. The poems of Farrukhí, another poet of the same period, both lithographed at Ṭeherán, the latter in A.H. 1301. Price 3 *ḳráns* for the two volumes.

12. The complete works of Ḳá'ání and Furúghí, two poets of the nineteenth century, together with the *Ḥadá'iḳu's-siḥr*, a treatise on rhetoric by Rashídu'd-Dín Waṭwáṭ. Lithographed in A.H. 1302 (? Ṭeherán). Price 14 *ḳráns*.

13. The *Fuṣúṣu'l-Ḥiḳam* by the celebrated mystic, Sheykh Muḥyi'd-Dín ibnu'l-'Arabí, mentioned above. Lithographed at Bombay in A.H. 1300. Price 5 *ḳráns*. (There is another edition of the same work lithographed at Ṭeherán in A.H. 1299, which I bought on another occasion.)

14. *Su'ál ú Jawáb* ("Questions and Answers"), a sort of catechism on Shí'ite law and ritual, by the great divine Ḥájí Seyyid Muḥammad Báḳir. Printed at Iṣfahán in the reign of Fatḥ-'Alí Sháh (A.H. 1247) under the patronage of Minúchihr Khán *Mu'tamadu'd-Dawla*, the governor of that place, by 'Abdu'r-Razzáḳ of Iṣfahán, assisted and instructed by Mírzá Zeynu'l-'Ábidín of Tabríz, who is described as "the introducer of this art (*i.e.* printing) into Persia." A fine piece of work. Price 8 *ḳráns*.

15. The *Ḥadíḳatu'l Ḥaḳíḳat*, a well-known early mystical poem by Ḥakím Saná'í (flourished during the earlier part of the twelfth century of our era); the two first chapters only, with commentary by the Nawwáb Muḥammad 'Alá'u'd-Dín Khán, poetically surnamed 'Alá'í, edited by Muḥammad Ruknu'd-Dín Ḳádirí Ḥiṣárí. Lithographed at Lúhárú. No date. Price 2½ *ḳráns*.

16. The last volume of Sipihr's great history, entitled *Násikhu't-Tawáríkh* ("The Abrogator of Chronicles"), containing part of the reign of Náṣiru'd-Dín Sháh. Price 5 *ḳráns*.

17. A little volume containing the quatrains of 'Omar

Khayyám, of Bábá Ṭáhir the Lur of Hamadán (the most celebrated dialectical poet of Persia), of Abú Sa'íd ibn Abi'l-Khayr (a notable mystic who died about the middle of the eleventh century of our era), and of Khwájé 'Abdu'lláh Anṣárí, together with some *ḳasídas* by Salmán of Sávé. Lithographed at Bombay during the vice-regency of Lord Lytton in A.H. 1297. Price 2 *ḳráns*.

18. A work on the evidences of Muḥammadanism, written at the request of Náṣiru'd-Dín Sháh (and hence called *Sulṭániyya*) by the Báb's rival, Ḥájí Muḥammad Karím Khán of Kirmán, the leader of the modern Sheykhí school. Price 3 *ḳráns*.

19. The poems of Minúchihrí (a contemporary of Firdawsí). Lithographed at Ṭeherán. No date. Price 2 *ḳráns*.

20. The *Asrár-náma* ("Book of Mysteries") of the celebrated mystical poet, Sheykh Farídu'd-Dín 'Aṭṭár. Lithographed at Ṭeherán, A.H. 1298.

21. The *Ḳiránu's-Sa'deyn* ("Conjunction of the Two Lucky Planets") of Amír Khusraw of Dihlí. Lithographed (? at Ṭeherán) in the reign of Náṣiru'd-Dín Sháh.

22. The *Díván* of the philosopher Ḥájí Mullá Hádí of Sabzawár, poetically surnamed *Asrár*. (There are two editions of this work, both lithographed, the one in A.H. 1299, the other in A.H. 1300.) Price 2 *ḳráns*.

23. A manuscript (incomplete) of Sheykh Farídu'd-Dín 'Aṭṭár's *Tadhḳiratu'l-Awliyá* ("Biographies of Saints"). Transcribed in A.H. 1209. Price 40 *ḳráns*.

24. The poems of Náṣir-i-Khusraw. Lithographed at Tabríz in A.H. 1280. Price 14 *ḳráns*.

25. An old manuscript of a highly-esteemed collection of Shí'ite traditions called *Rawẓatu'l-Káfí*. Price 30 *ḳráns*.

26. Mírkhwánd's Universal History, called *Rawẓatu'ṣ-Ṣafá*, with the supplement of Riẓá-Ḳulí Khán *Lálá-báshí*, poetically surnamed *Hidáyat*, carrying the record of events down to the reign of Náṣiru'd-Dín Sháh. Ten volumes in two. Lithographed at Ṭeherán, A.H. 1271–74. Price 70 *ḳráns*.

On returning to the hotel with a sturdy porter who bore my purchases, I found my old teacher Mírzá Asadu'lláh of Sabzawár, who had kindly come to bring me a short biography of his master Ḥájí Mullá Hádí the philosopher, and also an autograph of the great thinker.

Next day (Wednesday, 19th September) Ḥájí Ṣafar secured the services of a tinsmith, with whose aid we packed up and hermetically sealed my books and other purchases in a large wooden chest lined with tin, which luckily proved just large enough to contain them all. When it was closed up, we got porters to carry it to Messrs Ziegler's office in the *Káravánsaráy-i-Amír*, where I left it in the care of their agent for transport to England by way of Bushire The total value of its contents, as estimated by myself for the Custom-House, came to almost exactly 79 *túmáns* (£24).

On the afternoon of the following day, having concluded all my business, and said farewell to such of my friends as still remained in Ṭeherán, I started on my last march in Persia, which was to convey me through the interesting province of Mázandarán to the Caspian. I had succeeded in obtaining through Messrs Ziegler's agent 228 roubles in Russian money (the equivalent of 752 *ḳráns*, eight *sháhís* Persian). The rest of my money, amounting to 747 *ḳráns*, twelve *sháhís*, I carried with me in Persian silver and copper.

Our first stage was, as usual, to be a short one, of two or three parasangs only, but the moon had risen ere we reached our halting-place, the solitary caravansaray of Surkh Ḥiṣár ("the Red Fortress"), where I obtained a very good clean room, opening on to a little courtyard, through which ran a stream of limpid water. Soon after quitting Ṭeherán by the Shimrán Gate we had been joined by an ex-artilleryman, who had just been flogged and dismissed the service for some misdemeanour. He expressed a desire to accompany me to "*Landan*" (London), declaring that Persia was no fit place for an honest man, and actually went with us as far as Ámul, where I was not altogether sorry to lose sight of him.

Friday, 21st September.—Left Surkh Ḥiṣár about 7.30 a.m., and, after a dull ride through a barren, stony plain, reached the solitary and rather dilapidated caravansaray of Asalak an hour before noon. Here I stopped for lunch, and was entertained by a quaint old Seyyid who was suffering from a bad foot. He told me with great glee how he had recently succeeded in defrauding the revenue officers sent to collect his taxes. Being apprised of their intended visit, he had, in spite of his lameness, gone on foot to Ṭeherán (a distance of six parasangs), carrying with him all his cash (some twelve or thirteen *túmáns*), mostly in copper coins, which he there entrusted to the keeping of a friend. When the revenue officers came, there was no money to be found on the premises, and they were obliged to depart empty-handed after a fruitless search. On my departure I gave the old man a *ḳrán*, with which he was highly pleased.

Soon after leaving Asalak we entered the mountains, and the scenery began to improve rapidly, gradually assuming an almost English character; for our way was between green hedgerows, beyond which lay real grass meadows watered by rippling mountain streams and dotted with grazing cattle. Towards sundown we reached the pretty straggling village of Ágh, which consists of three distinct groups of houses separated by considerable intervals of road. We stopped at the last group, just before the steepness of the ascent begins. Here I obtained a delightful lodging in an upper chamber looking out on the most charming landscape imaginable.

Saturday, 22nd September.—Started about 7.15 a.m., and at once began to ascend steeply towards the pass by which we were to enter Mázandarán. The first part of our march was delicious, for our road was bordered by moss-grown walls, overshadowed by leafy trees, and crossed by innumerable streams, while around us lay green grassy fields such as my eyes had not looked upon for many a long day. As we advanced, the ascent grew gradually more abrupt, and the path began to climb the mountain side in a series of apparently interminable zigzags which has given to it the name of *Hazár Cham* ("the thousand twists"). At the summit of the pass is a little building where we had lunch ere commencing the descent into Mázandarán. Our downward course lay at first by the side of a rushing river (the Lár, I think), which soon plunged into a deep gorge. Far down in this gorge, on a little plateau which broke the sheer face of the opposite cliff, we could see the village of Ask, of which the mother of the Sháh's eldest son, the *Zillu's-Sulṭán*, is a native. How it is approached I could not imagine, for I could discern no signs of a path down the beetling precipice. On our left arose the mighty snow-capped cone of Mount Demávend, which can be ascended from this side without much difficulty, although the inhabitants of the village of Demávend, and, indeed, the generality of Persians, believe it to be inaccessible. For on its summit, according to ancient legend, was chained the tyrant Ẓaḥḥák by Ferídún, the deliverer of his country, the avenger of his race, and the restorer of the ancient royal house; and the accursed spirit of the usurper is popularly supposed still to haunt the cloud-capped peak of the mountain. But the inhabitants of the little village of René, where we halted for the night, have no such superstitious dread of the mountain, and some of them are in the habit of ascending it frequently to collect the sulphur which is to be found in a cave near the summit.

We left the beautiful Alpine village of René next morning (Sunday, 23rd September) about 7.30 a.m. The pretty winding road by which we continued to descend was so steep that for the first hour or so of our march I preferred to walk. At the bottom of the valley we again came to the river. In some places this had undermined and washed away the path, so that we were obliged to enter the water; but, on the whole, the road was a triumph of engineering skill, for soon the valley narrowed into a mere cleft with steep rocky sides, out of which the passage had been cut. This, the new road, runs along the left (western) side of the gorge; on the opposite side were discernible the remains of the old road, which had been built out from the cliff instead of cut in it. At one point on the new road a bas-relief of Náṣiru'd-Dín Sháh, surrounded by his courtiers, has been carved on the rocks.

About 2 p.m. we passed a village. No lodging was to be found there, so we proceeded on our way, halted for lunch in a cornfield, and, about 4 p.m., reached a house by a bridge, where the muleteer wished to halt for the night. Here also no decent lodging was to be found, and consequently, in spite of the mutterings of the muleteer, "*Ákhir Mázandarán-ast: ché mí-khwáhíd?*" ("After all it is Mázandarán: what would you have?"), we again pushed on, until, about sunset, we came to a little group of hovels, half caves, half huts, called Kalovan, where we halted. It was a sweet night, and its sweetness was enhanced by the shimmer of the moonlight and the murmur of the river; but inside the cave-hut, which I shared with the owners, it was close and warm, and the gnats were plentiful and aggressive.

Monday, 24th September.—We started about 7.30 a.m., and travelled for some time in the company of a Mázandarání muleteer, who gave me information which I had been unable to obtain from my own south-country *chárvádár* as to the position of the castle of Sheykh Ṭabarsí, that once redoubtable stronghold of the Bábís, which, if possible, I desired to visit before embarking at Mashhad-i-Sar. I found that it lay beyond Bárfurúsh, between that town and Sárí, some distance off the main road near a village called Káraghíl, and that if I were to visit it, it must be from Bárfurúsh.

As we advanced, the valley began to widen out, and the rocky cliffs, which had hitherto formed its sides, gave place to wooded slopes. In front, too, low wooded hills appeared, while round our path the wild pomegranate and other trees grew ever thicker and thicker, so that we could no longer see far about us. Soon we were out of the hill-country altogether, and entered a vast forest, where ferns and mosses grew thickly. Ever and anon we traversed beautiful glades, on the green sward of which were pitched here and there the black tents of nomads, whose cattle grazed peaceably round about the encampment. Save for these black tents, and a certain luxuriance of vegetation, the whole scene was wonderfully English in appearance, and I could almost have believed myself to be already back in my native land. In one of these delicious glades we halted for lunch, which consisted of cold boiled rice and fowl, called in Mázandarání parlance "*ḳetté*."

Later in the day the road got terribly bad, being sometimes so deep in mud and slush that the beasts could hardly advance. Our muleteer had intended to make for a village called Fírúz-Kuláh, but we, being somewhat in advance, passed the point where the road thither diverged from the road to Âmul, and were already some way advanced on the latter when the muleteer overtook us. A violent altercation arose between him and Ḥájí Ṣafar, for he would have had us turn back; but, learning from an old peasant who happened to pass by that Âmul was distant but one parasang, we insisted on proceeding thither, and the muleteer was finally compelled to a sullen submission.

Again the character of the country underwent a sudden change; for, emerging from the dense forest, we entered on a flat fenny plain, covered with long sedge-like grasses and tall bulrushes, and dotted with marshy pools and grazing cattle. About 6 p.m. we passed a little village with thatched cottages (which seemed strangely out of place in Persia, that land of clay houses and flat roofs), interspersed amongst which were curious wooden erections, each composed of four stout poles set vertically in the ground and supporting a sloping thatch. Beneath this, at a distance of some feet, was a sort of platform on which carpets and pillows were spread. I supposed that the inhabitants slept on these platforms during the hot weather to escape the mosquitoes, but Ḥájí Ṣafar said that it was to avoid the low-lying fogs which at night-time spread themselves over the surface of the ground.

About half an hour after passing this village we reached Ámul, one of the chief cities of Mázandarán, a picturesque straggling town divided into two parts by a large river, which is spanned by a long narrow bridge built of bricks. Crossing this bridge, we found quarters for the night in the house of a respectable citizen, but though the room allotted to me was clean and comfortable enough, the close, moist air, mosquitoes, and vagrant cats combined to keep me awake for some time.

Tuesday, 25th September.—We started about 7.30 a.m., and all day our course lay through flat marshy fen-lands, covered with rushes, sedges, and scrubby bushes. Snakes, lizards (some large and green, others small and brown), tortoises, and frogs abounded in and about the numerous stagnant pools by which we passed. The road was in many places little better than the surrounding quagmire, sometimes hardly discernible; and this notwithstanding the fact that it is the main highway between two of the chief cities of Mázandarán. About 5 p.m. we crossed the river Bábul by a fine bridge, and, turning sharply to the left (north) along its eastern bank, traversed a great common, used as a grazing-ground for cattle, and in a few minutes entered Bárfurúsh. On our right, as we entered, was a large lake covered with water-lilies, in the centre of which was an island. This island was joined to the shore by a bridge, and on it stood a summer-palace (called *Bágh-i-Sháh*, "the King's Garden"), which serves the Sháh as a residence when he visits this part of his dominions. Farther on we passed, just outside the town, the caravansaray (now in ruins) where the Bábís under Mullá Ḥuseyn of Bushraweyh, "the First Letter of Affirmation," defended themselves against the townsfolk of Bárfurúsh in the conflict which preceded the fiercer struggle at Sheykh Ṭabarsí. Entering the town, the spacious square of the *Sabzé Meydán*, or Herb Market, turned my thoughts to the concluding catastrophe of the great struggle of 1848–9, for there, in the summer of the latter year, Mullá Muḥammad 'Alí of Bárfurúsh, called by the Bábís "*Jenáb-i-Ḳuddús*" ("His Excellence the Most Holy"), suffered death, together with the chief of his surviving lieutenants, at the hands of the *Sa'ídu'l-'Ulamá* and his myrmidons. As we entered the main street of the city we found one of the Muḥarram representations (*ta'ziyas*) in progress, and some of the people would have had us turn aside; but we continued on our way, while I wondered whether the Báb's prophecy would ever be fulfilled, that a day would come when in these spots, hallowed by the blood of his martyrs, representations of their sufferings and steadfastness should move the sympathetic lamentations and tears of the children of those who slew them, and obliterate the remembrance of the martyrs of Kerbelá.

The town of Bárfurúsh is much finer and larger than Ámul, but less picturesque and old-world. We alighted at a rather dilapidated caravansaray near the centre of the town. Here I was visited in the course of the evening by a native of Kábul, a British subject, who showed me his passport with evident pride, and by one or two other persons, who informed me that the Russian ambassador had on the previous day passed through the town on his way to Sárí, whence, as I understood, he proposed to return to his own country by ship from Astarábád. I enquired of my visitors concerning Sheykh Ṭabarsí, which I still eagerly desired to visit. They told me that it was two parasangs distant from Bárfurúsh, to the south-east; and that the Bábís, drawing an analogy from the early history of Islám, called it "Kerbelá," Bárfurúsh "Kúfa," and the lake surrounding the Bágh-i-Sháh "the Euphrates" (*Furát*), and were still in the habit of making pilgrimages thither.

In the evening, after supper, I summoned Ḥájí Ṣafar, told him of my wish to visit Sheykh Ṭabarsí, and asked him whether it would be possible to do so. After thinking for a little while, he replied that as we must necessarily be at the port of Mashhad-i-Sar by nightfall on the following day to be in time for the steamer, which was to leave early on Thursday morning, the only practicable plan was that he should, if possible, secure the services of a competent guide and two stout Mázandarání ponies to convey me to the shrine and back to Bárfurúsh, and thence on, after a short rest, to Mashhad-i-Sar, whither he himself would proceed direct with the baggage. "All depends," he concluded, "on my success in finding a guide. If I can find one, I will wake you betimes in the morning, for you must start early; if not, you must perforce relinquish the project."

Next morning (Wednesday, 26th September) Ḥájí Ṣafar awoke me about 7 with the welcome intelligence that he had found a shopkeeper of Bárfurúsh, who owned two ponies, and was well acquainted with the road to Sheykh Ṭabarsí, whither, for a consideration, he was willing to guide me. While I was drinking my morning tea the aforesaid guide, an honest-looking, burly fellow, appeared in person.

"Well," said he, "I hear you want to visit Ṭabarsí; what for is no concern of mine, though why a Firangi should desire to go there baffles my understanding. However, I am ready to take you, if you will give me a suitable present for my trouble. But we must start at once, for it is two good parasangs there over the worst of ground, and you must, as I understand, get to Mashhad-i-Sar this evening, so that you should be back here at least two or three hours before sunset. If you don't like fatigue and hard work you had better give up the idea. What do you say? Will you go or not?"

"Of course I will go," I replied; "for what else did I seek you out?"

"Well said!" replied my guide, patting me on the shoulder; "then let us be off without delay."

In a few minutes we were in the saddle, and moving rapidly

along the high-road to Sárí on our sturdy, wiry little Mázandaráni ponies. "Whither away?" cried some of my guide's acquaintance as we clattered out of the town. "Sheykh," he replied laconically; whereat expressions of surprise and curiosity, which we did not stop to answer, would burst from our interrogators. Soon we left the high-road, and, striking across a broad, grassy common, entered trackless swamps and forests, in which my guide, well as he knew the country, was sometimes at fault; for the water lay deep on the rice-fields, and only the peasants whom we occasionally met could tell us whether or no a particular passage was possible. After crossing the swampy rice-fields, we came to thickets and woods, intersected by the narrowest and muddiest of paths, and overgrown with branches, through which we forced our arduous way. Thence, after fording a river with steep mud banks, we entered on pleasant open downs, and, traversing several small coppices, arrived about 10.30 a.m. at the lonely shrine of Sheykh Aḥmad ibn Abí Ṭálib-i-Ṭabarsí (so stands the name of the buried saint on a tablet inscribed with the form of words used for his "visitation" which hangs suspended from the railings surrounding his tomb), rendered immortal by the gallantry of the Bábí insurgents, who for nine months (October 1848 to July 1849) held it against overwhelming numbers of regulars and volunteers.

Sheykh Ṭabarsí is a place of little natural strength; and of the elaborate fortifications, said by the Musulmán historians to have been constructed by the Bábís, no trace remains. It consists at present of a flat, grassy enclosure surrounded by a hedge, and containing, besides the buildings of the shrine and another building at the gateway (opposite to which, but outside the enclosure, stands the house of the *mutawallí*, or custodian of the shrine), nothing but two or three orange-trees and a few rude graves covered with flat stones, the last resting-places, perhaps, of some of the Bábí defenders. The building at the gateway is two storeys high, is traversed by the passage giving access to the enclosure, and is roofed with tiles. The buildings of the shrine, which stand at the farther end of the enclosure, are rather more elaborate. Their greatest length (about twenty paces) lies east and west; their breadth is about ten paces; and, besides the covered portico at the entrance, they contain two rooms scantily lighted by wooden gratings over the doors. The tomb of the Sheykh, from whom the place takes its name, stands surrounded by wooden railings in the centre of the inner room, to which access is obtained either by a door communicating with the outer chamber, or by a door opening externally into the enclosure.

My guide, believing, no doubt, that I was at heart a Bábí come to visit the graves of the martyrs of my religion, considerately withdrew to the *mutawallí's* house and left me to my own devices for about three-quarters of an hour. I was still engaged in making rough plans and sketches of the place[1], however, when he returned to remind me that we could not afford to delay much longer. So, not very willingly, yet greatly comforted at having successfully accomplished this final pilgrimage, I mounted, and we rode back by the way we had come to Bárfurúsh, where we arrived about 3 p.m. "You are a Ḥájí now," said my guide laughingly, as we drew near the town, "and you ought to reward me liberally for this day's work; for I tell you that there are hundreds of Bábís who come here to visit Sheykh Ṭabarsí and can find no one to guide them thither, and these would almost give their ears to go where you have gone and see what you have seen." So when we alighted at a caravansaray near his house I gave him a sum of money with which he appeared well content, and he, in return, set tea before me, and then came and sat with me a while, telling me, with some amusement, of the wonderings and speculations which my visit to Sheykh Ṭabarsí had provoked amongst the townsfolk. "Some

1 These will be found in my translation of the *New History*, published by the Cambridge University Press.

say you must be a Bábí," he concluded, "but most incline to the belief that you have been there to look for buried treasure, 'for,' say they, 'who ever heard of a Firangí who cared about religion, and in any case what has a Firangí to do with the Bábís?' I, for my part, have done my best to encourage them in this belief; what took you to Ṭabarsí is no business either of theirs or of mine."

When I had rested for a while, a horse, on which was set a *pálán*, or pack-saddle, instead of an ordinary saddle, was brought round. My guide apologised for not himself conducting me to Mashhad-i-Sar, adding that he had provided a guide who knew the way well. With this new guide, a barefooted stripling, I set off for my last ride in Persia. Our way lay at first through beautiful shady lanes, and thriving villages composed of thatched cottages, both singularly English in appearance; and we made good progress until, about two miles from Mashhad-i-Sar, we emerged on the bare links or downs which skirt the coast, and almost simultaneously darkness began to fall. Here we lost our way for a while, until set in the road by an old villager; and at length, about 7.30 p.m., after traversing more lanes overshadowed by trees and brilliant with glow-worms, we saw the welcome light of the caravansaray which stands hard by the seashore at some distance beyond the village.

That night was my last on Persian soil, but I had little time to indulge in sentimental reflections, for it was late when I had finished my supper, and I had to dispose my baggage for a different manner of travelling from that to which I had been so long accustomed, besides settling up with Ḥájí Ṣafar. I paid him 163 *ḳráns* in all (about £5), of which sixty *ḳráns* were for his wages during September, thirty *ḳráns* for the first half of October (for he would not reach Ṭeherán for ten days probably), forty *ḳráns* for the hire of the horse I had ridden, and thirty-three *ḳráns* for journey-money. I also made over to him my saddle, saddle-bags, and cooking utensils, as well as some well-worn clothes, and further entrusted to him my revolver, which he was to give to one of my friends in Ṭeherán as a keepsake, together with several letters. This done, I retired to rest and slept soundly.

Next morning (Thursday, 27th September) Ḥájí Ṣafar woke me early, telling me that the steamer was in sight. This proved to be a false alarm, and when I went to the Russian agents (who had an office in the caravansaray) they declined to give me my ticket until the steamer actually appeared. These two agents either were, or feigned to be, excessively stupid; they affected not to understand either Persian or French, and refused to take payment for the ticket in anything but Russian money, so that it was fortunate that I had in Ṭeherán provided myself with a certain quantity of rouble notes. Finally the steamer hove in sight, the ticket was bought for twenty-five roubles, and I hastened down to the shore of the estuary, where several large clumsy boats were preparing to put off to her.

It was with genuine regret that I turned for a moment before stepping into the boat to bid farewell to Persia (which, notwithstanding all her faults, I had come to love very dearly) and the faithful and efficient Ḥájí Ṣafar. He had served me well, and to his intelligence and enterprise I owed much. He was not perfect —what man is?—but if ever it be my lot to visit these lands again, I would wish no better than to secure the services of him, or one like him. I slipped into his hands a bag of money which I had reserved for a parting present, and with a few brief words of farewell, stepped into the boat, which at once cast off from the shore, and, hoisting a sail, stood out towards the Russian steamer. The sea grew rougher as we left the shelter of the estuary, but with the sail we advanced quickly, and about 8.15 a.m. I climbed on board the *Emperor Alexander*, and, for the first time for many months, felt myself, with a sudden sense of loneliness, a stranger in the midst of strangers.

The only passengers who embarked besides myself were two

or three Persians bound for Mashhad, and with these I conversed fitfully (knowing not when next I might find chance of speech in an intelligible tongue) till we entered the vessel, when they took up their station forward as deck passengers, and I descended to the cabin. At 9 the steamer had turned about (for Mashhad-i-Sar is the end of this line) and was running eastwards for Bandar-i-Gaz, the port of Astarábád.

About 10.30 a bell announced breakfast, and I again descended to the cabin. I was the only cabin passenger, and on entering the saloon I was surprised to see two tables laid. At one were seated the officers of the vessel (three or four in number), busily engaged in the consumption of sardines, caviare, cheese, roasted potatoes, and the like, which they were washing down with nips of *vodḳa*, a strong spirit, resembling the Persian *'araḳ*. The other table was laid with plates, but the places were vacant. Wondering whether the officers were too proud to sit down at the same table with the passengers, I stood hesitating, observing which, one of the officers called out to me in English, asking me whether I felt sick. I indignantly repudiated the imputation, whereupon he bade me join them at their "*Zaḳouṣḳi*." So I sat down with them; and, after doing justice to the caviare and cheese, we moved on to the other table and had a substantial *déjeuner*. At 6.30 in the evening we had another similar meal, also preceded by *Zaḳouṣḳi*.

At 4 p.m. we reached Bandar-i-Gaz, the port of Astarábád, and anchored close to the shore, by a wooden barge serving as a pier, in full view of the little island of Ashurada. This now belongs to the Russians (who first occupied it on the pretext of checking the Turcoman pirates who formerly infested this corner of the Caspian, and then declined to give it back to the Persians), and around it several Russian war-ships were anchored. Some of their officers came on board our steamer, and later in the evening rockets were sent up from them in honour, as I suppose, of the Russian Ambassador, who, so far as I could learn (for everyone was very reticent and uncompanionable), was in the neighbourhood.

I went to sleep that night with the sweet scent of the forests of Mázandarán in my nostrils (for the wind was off the shore); but when I went on deck next morning (Friday, 28th September) not a tree was in sight, but only a long line of yellow sand-dunes, which marked the inhospitable Turcoman coast, whence in bygone days, ere the Russians stepped in and put a stop to their marauding, the Turcoman pirates issued forth to harry the fertile Persian lands, and bear back with them, to hateful bondage, hosts of unfortunate captives destined for sale in the slave-markets of Samarḳand and Bukhárá. At about mid-day we anchored off Chekishlar, where a number of Russian officers, two ladies, and a child, came on board to breakfast on the steamer. Immediately after breakfast we again stood out to sea.

That evening an official of the Russian police (who, I suppose, had come on board at Chekishlar) came up to me with one of the officers of the boat and demanded my passport, which, he said, would be returned to me at the Custom-House at Baku. I was very loth to part with it, but there was no help for it; and, inwardly chafing, I surrendered to him the precious document.

Early next morning (Saturday, 29th September) I awoke to find the vessel steaming along between a double row of sand-dunes towards Üzün-Áda ("Long-Island"), the point whence the Russian railway to Bukhárá and Samarḳand takes its departure. Passing the narrows, we anchored alongside the quay about 8.30 a.m. Being without my passport (which had probably been taken from me expressly to prevent me from leaving the steamer) I could not, even if I would, have gone on shore. But indeed there was little to tempt me, for a more unattractive spot I have seldom seen. It seemed to consist almost entirely of railway-stations, barracks, police-stations, and custom-houses, set in wastes of sand, infinite and immeasurable, and the Turcoman seemed to bear but a small proportion to the Russian inhabitants.

A number of passengers came on board here, all of whom, save one lady and three children, were Russian officers. The deck, too, was crowded with soldiers, who, after dinner, at a sign from their officer, burst out into a song with a chorus like the howling of wolves, which, I supposed, was intended for a national anthem. On retiring to my cabin I found to my disgust that my berth had been appropriated by a Russian officer, who had ejected my possessions and now lay there snoring hideously. I was angered at his discourtesy, but deemed it wisest to make no remonstrance. From my short experience of Russian travelling I should suppose that their military men make a point of occupying places already taken in preference to such as are vacant—at any rate, when the occupant is a civilian and a foreigner.

I woke about 6.30 a.m. on the following morning (Sunday, 30th September) to find myself at Baku (or Bádkúbé, as it is called by the Persians). Somehow or other I escaped the ordeal of the Custom-House; for, intending at first to breakfast on board, I did not disembark with the other passengers, and when afterwards, changing my mind, I went on shore, about 9.30 a.m., the pier was free of excisemen, and I had nothing to do but step into a cab and drive to the station, stopping on the way at a Persian money-changer's to convert the remainder of my Persian money into rouble notes.

The train did not start till 2.37 p.m., so I had some time to wait at the station, where I had lunch. The porters were inefficient and uncivil, the train crowded, and the scenery monotonous in the extreme, so that my long railway journey began under rather depressing auspices. Still there was a certain novelty in finding myself once more in a train, and after a while I was cheered by the entrance into my compartment of two Musulmáns of the Caucasus. With these I entered into conversation in Turkish, for which I presently substituted Persian on finding that one of them was familiar with that language. But I had hardly spoken ten words when a Russian officer, who sat next me on the right, and with whom I had had a slight altercation in French about one of my portmanteaux, which he alleged to be insecurely balanced in the rack, leaned forward with an appearance of interest, and then addressed me in perfectly idiomatic Persian. I discovered that he had been born in Persia (near Burújird, I think), and had learned Persian almost as his native language. To both of us, I think, but to myself certainly, it was a pleasure to speak it, and we became quite friendly.

I had intended to stay a day at Tiflis, where we arrived at 8.15 next morning (Monday, 1st October), but the friendly officer told me that the steamers for Odessa left Batoum on Tuesdays and Thursdays, and that, after cities more truly Oriental in character, Tiflis would offer but little attraction to me, so I determined to continue my journey without halt, in order to catch the morrow's boat. I had some difficulty in getting my ticket and finding my train, as no one seemed to talk anything but Russian, but at last I succeeded, though only after a waste of time which prevented me from making more than the most unsubstantial and desultory breakfast. This, however, was of little consequence, for I never knew any railway on which there were such frequent and prolonged stoppages for refreshment, or any refreshment-rooms so well provided and so well managed. The fact that there is only one train a day each way no doubt makes it easier to have all these savoury dishes and steaming *samovars* (tea-urns) ready for passengers on their arrival, but at no railway station in Europe have I seen food at once so cheap, so good, and so well served as in the stations of the Trans-Caucasian line.

The scenery on leaving Tiflis was fine, and at one point we caught a glimpse of splendid snow-capped mountains to the north; but on the whole I was disappointed, for the line lies so much in narrow valleys which bar the outlook that little is to be seen of the great Caucasian range. What could be seen of the country from the train was pretty rather than grand, and I was not sorry to reach Batoum at about 11.15 p.m., where I put up at the Hôtel de France, and, for the first time since leaving Ṭeherán eleven days previously, enjoyed the luxury of sleeping between sheets.

As the steamer for Odessa was not to leave Batoum till 3.30 p.m. on the following day (Tuesday, 2nd October), I had all the morning to look about me, but the town presented few features of interest, and the only thing that aroused my wonder was the completely European character assumed by a place which had only ceased to be Turkish twelve years before. I was very glad to embark on the steamer, which actually started about 4 p.m. Dinner was at 6, and afterwards I stayed on deck till after 11, when we arrived at Sukhoum-Kala.

Next evening (Wednesday, 3rd October) we reached Novo-Rassayask about 5 p.m., and lay there till late at night. There were several war-vessels in the fine harbour, which continued throughout the evening to send up rockets and flash the electric light from point to point.

Early on the morning of Thursday, 4th October, we reached Kertch, where, amongst other passengers, a very loquacious American came on board. He had been spending some time amongst the Russians, whom he did not much like or admire, though, as he told me, he believed them to be the coming nation.

Friday, 5th October.—Reached Yalta about 5 a.m., and lay there till 8. It is a very beautiful place, and I was told that the drive thence to Sebastopol along the coast traverses scenery so fair that it has been called "the Earthly Paradise." At 1.30 p.m. we reached Sebastopol, where the American left the steamer. The harbour struck me as very fine, but I, ignorant of things military, should never have guessed that the place would be a position of such remarkable strength.

On the following morning (Saturday, 6th October) we reached Odessa before 7 a.m. There was no Customs' examination, as we came from a Russian port, and I drove straight to the Hôtel d'Europe, thinking that my troubles were over, and that from this point onwards all would be plain sailing. Here, however, I was greatly out of my reckoning, as will shortly appear; for while I was visiting an English ship-owner, to whom I had a letter of introduction, he enquired whether I had had my passport *visé* for departure from Russia. I replied that I had not, as I was unaware that it was necessary. "Then," said he, "you had best get it done at once if you wish to leave this evening; give it to me, and I will send a man with it to your hotel that your landlord may see to it." I did so, and sat chatting there for another quarter of an hour, when we were interrupted by a telephonic message informing me that my presence was necessary.

The landlord met me at the hotel door. "I am afraid you will not be able to get your visa to-day," said he, "for it is past noon, and if the police grant it, it will only be as an act of grace. Your only chance is to take a cab, drive direct to the police-station, and request the prefect as a favour to visa your passport, explaining to him that you have but just arrived and wish to start to-night."

Fruitless errand, to seek such grace from the Russian police! Whether I offended them by omitting to remove my hat on entering the office I know not, probably this had something to do with it, for a man cried out at me in anger through a pigeon-hole, and was only quieted when I uncovered my head. Then it was some time before I could find anyone who spoke anything but Russian; but at last I was shown into an inner room where two men sat at a table, one portly, irascible, and clad in uniform; the other thin, white-haired, smooth-shaven, and sinister of countenance. I presented my passport, and explained in French the reasons which had prevented me from coming sooner, adding that I should feel deeply obliged if they would grant me the visa. The wizen-faced man answered in a high peevish voice in very bad French that I must come to-morrow.

"I cannot come to-morrow," I replied, "for I must leave to-night."

"You cannot leave to-night," he retorted as his portly colleague threw the passport back to me across the table; "if you wished to leave to-night you should have come earlier."

"But I tell you that I only arrived this morning," I answered.

"Then you must stay till to-morrow," they answered; and when I would have remonstrated, "Go," shouted the man in the uniform, "you waste our time and yours." And so, gulping down my anger and pocketing my passport, I left the office.

Here was a pleasant state of things! I was in hot haste to get back to England; I had travelled as fast as I could from the Persian capital, not even stopping at Tiflis, where I would gladly have spent a day; and now there seemed every likelihood of my being detained in this detestable Odessa for the whim of a Russian prefect of police. I asked my friend the ship-owner what I should do.

"I am afraid," said he, "that you can do nothing now. You seem to have offended the susceptibilities of the police in some way, and they will certainly not do anything to accommodate you, for their will is absolute, and argument is useless. A judicious bribe might have smoothed matters over if you had known how to give it and to whom, but I fear that the time for that has passed."

"Are you sure the passport needs a visa at all?" I enquired, remembering that the words "*bon pour se rendre en Angleterre par voie de la Russie*" had been inscribed on it at the English Embassy after it had received the Russian visa at Ṭeherán. My friend was at first inclined to maintain that the visa was indispensable, but I asked why, as I was not stopping even a single night at Odessa, and as I was travelling straight through Russia as fast as possible, it should need a visa here more than at Baku or any other town through which I had passed. Then he called a clerk more experienced in the ways of Russia than himself and asked his opinion. The clerk finally gave it as his decision that the passport was good without the visa of the Odessa police, unless the latter, apprehending my departure, should telegraph to the frontier stations not to let me pass.

"Well," said I, "the practical point is this, would you advise me to take this evening's train or not?"

"I hardly like to advise you," replied my friend, "but if I were in your place I should go and risk it."

"In that case," I rejoined, after a moment's reflection, "I will go."

I had some difficulty with the hotel-keeper ere he would consent to my departure, but at length, to my great relief, I found myself, with a ticket for Berlin in my pocket, ensconced in a compartment of the 7.40 p.m. train for the West. A pleasant and kindly Austrian who was returning to Vienna, and who would therefore bear me company as far as Oswiecim, was my fellow-traveller. He spoke English well, and gave me much seasonable help both at the Russian and the Austrian frontiers.

It was an anxious moment for me when, about 9 a.m. on the following day (Sunday, 7th October), the train steamed into the Russian frontier station of Woloczyska, and we were bidden to alight for the inspection of passports. A peremptory official collected these and disappeared with them into an office, while we waited anxiously outside. Presently he appeared with a handful of them and began to call out the names of the possessors, each of whom, as his name was called, stepped forward and claimed his passport. I waited anxiously, for mine was not there. The official retired to his office and again emerged with another sheaf of papers, and still I waited in vain, till all but one or two of the passports had been returned to their owners. "Haven't you got your passport yet?" enquired the kindly Austrian. "The train is just going to start." "I don't know what has become of it," I answered despairingly, making sure that my detention had been resolved upon. Thereupon he stepped forward and addressed the official, who in reply produced two or three passports, amongst which I recognised my own. I was very near trying to snatch it out of his hand, but luckily I restrained myself. "That is mine," I exclaimed. The Austrian translated what I had said to the official, who, after staring at me for a moment, threw the precious document to me. "He was surprised," said the Austrian, "to see so vast a collection of strange visas and inscriptions on the papers of a young man like you."

So much time had been consumed thus that I had to forgo all hope of breakfast, and thought myself fortunate in finding a few moments to change my Russian into Austrian money. Then I re-entered the train, and indescribable was my satisfaction when we steamed out of the station and left Russia behind us. The people, I doubt not, are honest and kindly folk, but the system of police supervision and constant restraint which prevails is, to an Englishman unused to such interference, well-nigh intolerable. I had suffered more annoyance during the few days of my passage through Russian territory than during all the rest of my journey.

Not yet, however, were my troubles over. Five minutes after leaving Woloczyska the train pulls up at the Austrian frontier station of Podwoloczyska for the Austrian Customs' examination. As it began to slacken speed, my Austrian friend asked me whether I anticipated any trouble there. I answered in the negative.

"What, for instance," said he, "have you in that wooden box?"

The box in question contained a handsome silver coffee-service of Persian workmanship, which a Persian gentleman, to whom I was under great obligations, had asked me to convey for him to one of his friends in England. I told my Austrian fellow-traveller this, whereupon he exclaimed:—

"A silver coffee-service! You will have trouble enough with it, or I am much mistaken. Why, do you not know that the Custom-House regulations in Austria as to the importation of silver are most stringent? You will be lucky if they do not confiscate it and melt it down."

I was greatly disquieted at this information, for I felt myself bound in honour to convey the silver entrusted to me safely to its destination; and I asked my companion what I had best do.

"Well," he said, "you must declare it at once on your arrival, and demand to have it sealed up for transmission to the Prussian frontier station of Oswiecim. I will give you what help I can."

I had another bad time at Podwoloczyska, but at length, thanks to the good offices of my fellow-traveller, the box containing the silver was sealed up with leaden seals and registered through to Oswiecim. All my luggage was subjected to an exhaustive examination, and everything of which the use was not perfectly apparent (such as my medicine chest and the Wolseley valise), was placed in the contraband parcel, for which I had to pay a considerable additional sum for registration. All this took time, and here, too, I had to abandon all idea of breakfast. By the time we reached Lemberg, at about 2 p.m., I was extremely hungry, having had practically nothing to eat since leaving Odessa on the previous evening; and I was glad to secure a luncheon-basket, the contents of which I had plenty of time to consume ere we reached the next station, where it was removed.

My original intention was to stay the night at Cracow, as I found that I should gain nothing by pushing on to Oswiecim, but now, seeing that the bundle containing the silver entrusted to my care must go through to the frontier, and anticipating further troubles at the Prussian Custom-House, I changed my plan, and, on arriving at Cracow, alighted from the train, reclaimed that portion of my luggage registered from Odessa, and re-registered it to Oswiecim, the Prussian frontier station and the point where the Vienna and Berlin lines diverge. I had just time to effect this ere the train started again.

At 11.30 on the night of this miserable day the train stopped at Oswiecim, and I emerged into the black wet night, the cheerlessness of which was revealed rather than mitigated by a few feeble oil lamps. With some difficulty I found a porter (for the place seemed wrapped in slumber), who, making me leave all my luggage in a locked room to await the Customs' examination on the morrow, and suffering me to retain only my greatcoat, led me through a perfect sea of mud to the miserable hotel opposite the station. There was a light in one of the windows, but, though we knocked vigorously for some time, no one came. At last the door was opened, on a chain, by a most ill-looking fellow, clad in a night-shirt and trousers, with a beard of two days' growth on his ugly chin. So little did I like his looks that I did not press for admission, which he on his part showed no inclination to grant me. So I returned to the empty waiting-room of the station, with its dimly-lighted, beery, smoke-laden atmosphere, thinking that after all I should not be much worse off sleeping on the wooden bench which ran round the walls, than in some of the Turkish stables and Mázandaráni hovels to which I had become inured in the course of my travels.

I do not think that the porter who accompanied me spoke German very fluently, and, as I could hardly speak it at all, communication was difficult. Tired out, wet, and discouraged, I was anxious to throw myself on the bench and forget my troubles in sleep. Yet still the porter stood by me, striving, as I supposed, to express his regret at my being compelled to pass so uncomfortable a night. So I roused myself, and, as well as I could, told him that it was really of no consequence, since I had passed many a good night in quarters no more luxurious. "This will do very well till the morning," I concluded, as I again threw myself down on the bench, thinking of that favourite aphorism of the Persians under such circumstances as those in which I found myself, "*Ákhir yak shab-ast, na hazár*" ("After all, it is for one night, not a thousand").

"It might do very well," explained the porter, "if you could stop here, but you cannot. We are going to shut up the station."

I again sprang to my feet. "I can't spend the night walking

about in the rain," I remonstrated, "and you see that the hotel will not admit me. Where am I to go?"

"Ay, that's just the question," retorted he.

We again emerged on to the platform, and my porter took counsel with some other station officials; but from the way they shook their heads and shrugged their shoulders I inferred that my chances of being allowed to remain there were but small. Finally, a gendarme with a gun and bayonet appeared, and I was invited to follow him, which I did apathetically, without the least idea as to whither we were bound.

Tramping after my guide through dark muddy lanes, I presently found myself at the door of a house, where the gendarme bade me wait for a minute while he entered. Presently, after much wrangling in Polish, he again emerged, and beckoned to me to follow him. We passed through an outer bedroom where several persons were sleeping, and entered a smaller inner room containing two beds, occupied by the owner of the house and his son. Between the former and my guide a further altercation ensued, and it seemed as though here also I was to find no rest. At last the owner of the house got out of bed, led me to a sort of window looking into an adjacent room which I had not hitherto noticed, and, pointing to a mass of human beings (vagrants, I suppose) sleeping huddled together on the floor, remarked that it was "pretty full in there."

I stepped back in consternation. "Well," continued he, "will you stay?"

"I must stay somewhere," I replied; "I am not allowed to stop in the railway station, I can't get into the hotel, and you can hardly expect me to spend the night out of doors in the rain."

"Well, you can sleep on that bench," said he, pointing to one which stood by the wall. I signified assent, and, as the gendarme prepared to depart, I offered him a small silver coin which looked like a sixpence. The effect was most happy. It had never occurred to me that these people would suppose me to be absolutely impecunious, but I fancy that this was the case, and that I did not sufficiently realise how shabby my appearance was in the old travel-stained clothes which I wore. At all events, the production of this little piece of silver acted like magic. My host, after asking the gendarme to let him look at it, turned to me with a marked increase of courtesy, and asked me whether I would like a bolster laid on the bench and some blankets wherewith to cover myself. I replied that I should, and ventured to suggest that if he had any bread in the house I should be glad of some, as I was ravenously hungry. "Cheese?" he enquired. I eagerly assented, and further asked for water, instead of which he brought me milk. I made a hearty meal, while his little son, who had been awakened by the noise, sat up and began to question me in bad French, which, as it appeared, he was learning at school.

Altogether I fared much better than I had expected, and, had it not been that my socks and boots were wet through, I should have been sufficiently comfortable. In the morning they gave me breakfast, made me inscribe my name in a book kept for that purpose, were delighted to find that I had a passport, and thankfully received the few shillings I gave them. Then the porter of the previous night returned to conduct me to the railway station, and I bade farewell to my entertainers, not knowing to this day whether or no I had passed that night under the sheltering roof of a Polish casual-ward.

By reaching the station an hour before the departure of the train (which started from Cracow, where I had intended to spend the previous night), I hoped to get my luggage cleared at the Custom-House, and the silver plate sealed up again for transmission through Germany in good time. Here again I was foiled, however, for I found that the Custom-House officers did not put in appearance till the arrival of the train. When they did come they were intelligent and courteous enough, but very rigorous in their examination of my luggage. About my opium-pipe, the nature of which (greatly to their credit, I thought) they at once recognised, they were especially curious. Then they must see the silver coffee-service, at the beauty of which they uttered guttural ejaculations of admiration. But when it came to the question of sealing it up again for transmission to the Dutch frontier, they declared that there was not sufficient time before the departure of the train, and that I should have to wait till the next, which did not start till the afternoon or evening.

I was so heartily sick of Oswiecim, and so eager to get to the end of my journey, that I could not face the prospect of further delay, especially as I had every reason to expect that I should have another similar experience at the Dutch frontier; so I enquired whether it would not be possible to have the package forwarded after me to England. They replied that it would, and introduced to me an honest-looking man, named Arnold Haber, who, they said, was an agent for the transmission of goods. To him, therefore, I confided the care of my precious but troublesome little box, which duly reached me some days after my return to Cambridge, with a heavy charge for duty from the Dover Custom-House.

It was with unalloyed satisfaction that I took my seat in the train, and, about 10 a.m., left Oswiecim behind me. At 2 p.m. I reached Breslau, where I had just time for a hasty meal, and at 10 p.m. I was at Berlin, just in time to see the Flushing night-mail, which I had hoped to catch, steam out of the station. So here I had to spend the night at a homely comfortable hotel, called the Berliner Hof, the luxuries of which a remembrance of my last night's discomfort enabled me to appreciate to the full.

Next morning (Tuesday, 9th October) I left Berlin at 7.45 a.m. for Flushing, and twenty-four hours later, without further adventure, landed once more in England. By half-past nine on the morning of that day (Wednesday, 10th October) I was at King's Cross, debating in my mind whether I should go straight to the North, or whether I ought first to visit Cambridge (where term had just begun) to report my arrival, and request a week's leave to visit my home. This indecision, however, was of brief duration, for my eagerness to see my home again would brook no delay, and increased nearness did but beget greater impatience. There are, I suppose, few pleasures in this world comparable to the return to a home one loves after a long absence abroad; and the realisation of this pleasure I could not bring myself to postpone for a moment longer than necessary.

Thus ended a journey to which, though fraught with fatigues and discomforts, and not wholly free from occasional vexations, I look back with almost unmixed satisfaction. For such fatigues and discomforts (and they were far fewer than might reasonably have been expected) I was amply compensated by an enlarged knowledge and experience, and a rich store of pleasant memories, which would have been cheaply purchased even at a higher price. For without toil and fatigue can nothing be accomplished, even as an Arab poet has said:—

"*Wa man ṭalaba'l-'ulá min ghayri kadd^{in}*
Aḍá'a'l-'umra fí ṭalabi'l-muḥáli."

"And he who hopes to scale the heights without enduring pain,
And toil and strife, but wastes his life in idle quest and vain."

INDEX